# THE NEGRO
## FROM AFRICA TO AMERICA

W. D. WEATHERFORD, Ph.D.

# THE NEGRO FROM AFRICA TO AMERICA

BY

## W. D. WEATHERFORD, Ph.D.

PRESIDENT OF SOUTHERN COLLEGE OF YOUNG MEN'S CHRISTIAN ASSOCIATIONS

AUTHOR OF

WITH AN INTRODUCTION BY
### JAMES H. DILLARD
PRESIDENT OF THE JEANES BOARD AND
THE JOHN F. SLATER FUND

NEGRO UNIVERSITIES PRESS
NEW YORK

Originally published in 1924
by George H. Doran Company, New York

Reprinted 1969 by
Negro Universities Press
A Division of Greenwood Publishing Corp.
New York

SBN 8371-2399-2

PRINTED IN UNITED STATES OF AMERICA

# INTRODUCTION

This book had to be written, and I know of no one better fitted to do the work than Dr. Weatherford. The reader will soon realize the large amount of devoted labor that has been put into the task. Dr. Weatherford is one of a growing group of Southern white men who are intelligently active in showing white and colored people how many vital interests they have in common. He has been a pioneer in this group.

In this extensive study the author offers no final solution of the race problem, but he states "principles of procedure," based upon a careful survey of the life and progress of black men and women through years of struggle and handicap. He sets forth with clearness and force the philosophy of "doing the next thing," a philosophy which is so simple that impatient students of race relations have been unwilling to accept it. He presents well arranged excerpts from white and colored writers who have tried to create an intelligent public opinion in matters which relate to the Negro and his problems. He makes no attempt to gloss over the dark side of slavery, or the degrading influences of lynching, or the continued injustice which the Negro must frequently face.

This book is the presentation of the tremendously important human problem—the problem of racial adjustment, which calls for wisdom, temperance, and the application of Christian principles to the affairs of everyday life, not only in America, but wherever the dark skin peoples of the earth are brought face to face with other peoples. The author makes a plea for social justice for all men and women. He presents evidence to show that the injustice which is inflicted upon a disadvantaged group will naturally be transferred to another group. He also makes a wholesome plea for the protection of Negro women, recognizing the fundamental importance of building up the Negro race by developing a wholesome family life.

Thoughtful white men and women are asking today as never before: "What is our duty toward the Negro?" Dr. Weatherford's answer is worth remembering: "It is my duty to do the next thing as I see it, and trust those who come after me to have as much wisdom, as much Christian spirit, and as much sense of justice as I have. . . . I must do my duty now and trust the results to God and future humanity." Action follows conviction,

v

741365

but conviction which is based on ignorance or incomplete knowledge is dangerous. This study summarizes a vast amount of knowledge dealing with race relations. Its comprehensive and well ordered array of facts and opinions should give the "man on the street," as well as the student of race relations, a guide for conduct and study. It brings home the sense of responsibility and calls for greater coöperation and broader tolerance.

Dr. Weatherford, in addition to describing Negro achievement whenever and wherever right conditions prevail, shows the relation of environment to progress or lack of progress, the relation of illiteracy and poverty to crime, and the relation of religion and education to unselfish and intelligent service. His study is free from shibboleths or other forms of cant. It presents the story of the gradual emergence of a race from darkness toward light by way of the hard and profitable discipline of adversity. The story, while realistic in its pictures of man's inhumanity to man, is still hopeful and constructive. The open-minded reader will close the volume with the high thought, what a noble achievement it would be for America to show the world that there can be coöperation with differences, that there can be a fair application of the Golden Rule in contacts and relations among the races of mankind.

JAMES H. DILLARD.

*Charlottesville, Va.*

# CONTENTS

# THE NEGRO
# FROM AFRICA TO AMERICA

# THE NEGRO FROM AFRICA TO AMERICA

## CHAPTER I

## THE CENTRAL ISSUE

*Racial Antipathy.* "There exists," says Putnam Weale, writing in 1910, "a widespread racial antipathy founded on colour—an animal-like instinct, if you will, but an instinct which must remain in existence until the world becomes Utopia. It is this instinct which seems to forbid really frank intercourse and equal treatment." [1] It is just this failure to "have really frank intercourse," and hence a failure to understand each other, which constitutes the supreme barrier to peace and seems to preclude the reign of good will among men. If one were so pessimistic as to believe that the world must reach a complete Utopia before any understanding between races could be had, then this volume would not have been written. But Weale is undoubtedly right that, at present at least, there is a barrier fixed, a seemingly insurmountable obstacle set between racial groups which makes misunderstanding and friction inevitable. The real thing needed is to find out what are the reasons why these friction points are so multiplied, and why racial antipathies do keep peoples from frank intercourse.

*Increased Racial Friction—Economic.* It can hardly be doubted that racial friction and racial jealousies have grown in the world at large during the last half century. This conflict is primarily economic, at least in origin. For long centuries the white man with his more advanced civilization, his greater economic progress, and his superior implements of force, has forged his way into almost every country of the world in order that he might exploit the wealth of these countries, which so often have lain dormant at the feet of a less aggressive and less greedy people. Inch by inch the white man drove the red man back in America, and, it must be confessed, often with a red handed cruelty and a rank injustice which will ever remain a blot on

[1] Weale: "The Conflict of Colour," p. 110.

the pages of history. He has held sway for many decades over the three hundred million brown men of India, he almost completely controls the destinies of the one hundred and forty or more millions of Africa. Even the teeming millions of Eastern Asia are not free from his dominance. The white man is a world conquering and world dominating species, restless of all barriers, and eager for new conquests always. His early ancestors came out of central Asia [2] and soon overran and conquered all Europe; from thence he has gone out to subjugate the whole world. Although the white races are outnumbered two to one by the colored races, the white man controls a large part of the world's area.[3] Of this the colored races are increasingly impatient, and either a new era of understanding must come or else the white races will ultimately find themselves overwhelmed. This is the deliberate conclusion of numerous students of the question.

*Policy of Exclusion.* But not only has the white man assumed dominance of the lands of other races; he has now begun to draw a circle around his own possessions and exclude all aliens from the same. This again is largely economic in nature. The colored races have long lived in a much lower economic state than has he, and hence they are able to underbid him in the economic market of labor. As in the realm of money, a cheap coin runs out a good coin, so in the realm of labor a cheap man will underbid and run out the man who must have a larger wage to subsist. On this basis Australia excludes orientals from her northern borders, California excludes Japanese, the laborers of eastern America clamor for the exclusion of the cheap laborers of southern Europe, and Stoddard [4] thinks the opening up of white lands to colored races will be at the peril of exterminating the white race. "A struggle has begun," says Weale, "between the white man and all the other men of the world to decide whether non-white men—that is yellow men, or brown men, or black men—may or may not invade the white man's countries in order there to gain their livelihood." [5]

*The World War and Race Friction.* The world war brought a new element into the situation. Colored races saw two factions of the white races at each other's throats, and furthermore thousands of the colored races were taught the white man's tactics of war. Colored soldiers fought well and successfully against white troops, thus scattering the old fear of the white race which was half superstition. It is certain that much of the subservience of colored races is forever gone, and a more independent colored people surely means new sources of friction under present con-

[2] Cf. Osbourne: "Men of the Old Stone Age," Ch. VI.
[3] Cf. Weale: "The Conflict of Colour," p. 111.
[4] Cf. Stoddard: "The Rising Tide of Colour."
[5] Weale: "The Conflict of Colour," p. 98.

ditions. No real student of the problem can doubt that the war greatly increased the points of friction between races.

*Ancient Origin of Race Friction.* Race friction is as old as races. In primitive life each group warred with every other group. The In-group had no use for the Out-group. The conditions of primitive society demanded that all those belonging to a family or group should stand together, defending each other, right or wrong, and sharing together all blessings or all ills. "The insiders in a we-group are in a relation of peace, order, law, government, and industry to each other. Their relation to all outsiders, or other groups, is one of war and plunder, except so far as agreement has modified it." [6] "Virtue consists in killing, plundering and enslaving outsiders." [7] Tylor tells us that the Mbayas of South America believed that their deity the "Great Eagle, had bidden them live by making war on all other tribes, slaying the men, taking the women for wives, and carrying off the goods." [8] Out of this constant warfare on all outside tribes grew not only hatred of all such tribes, but also an over-exaggeration of the virtues of the in-group. The modern expression of this emphasis on the virtue of one's own nation or group is technically called ethnocentrism. It leads to emphasis on all those elements of life in one's own group which are distinctive or peculiar, and hence has a tendency to strengthen such peculiarities. Customs or folkways thus become the first barriers against racial understanding. The Jews despised all Gentiles, the Greeks and Romans called all outsiders barbarians, certain Indians said that they alone were "people," and Nathaniel, a Jew, was sure no good thing could come out of Nazareth? [9]

*Custom as Basis for Friction.* When children, all of us thought others who acted differently from the customs of our own homes were "funny." It never occurred to us that their customs might be better than ours. Where customs differ, even grown-ups are apt to mark down those following the other customs as inferior. If one listens to the talk of ultra southerners as they return from the North, he is apt to detect a note of criticism of the inferior custom of that section, and if one rides on the through Florida trains as they carry northern people home the same critical note is sure to be heard. Difference of custom means difference of standard, is the line of argument. All customs save our own must be a bit inferior. Americans laugh at Chinese because they write from right to left, and Chinese think occidentals queer for the reverse reason. A friend of mine asked a Chinese why he wore his finger-nails long—and the Chinese replied by asking my friend

[6] Sumner: "Folkways," p. 12.
[7] *Ibid.*, p. 13.
[8] Tylor: "Anthropology," p. 225.
[9] John 1:46.

why he wore that white board around his neck. Custom has the atmosphere of the right, the superior way. All who do otherwise are inferior. "No creed, no moral code, and no scientific demonstration can ever win the same hold upon men and women as habits of action, with associated sentiments and states of mind, drilled in from childhood." [10]

*Custom Blinds Us.* This attitude toward the customs of others makes us incapable of really knowing or understanding the plainest elements of life in an alien people. An interesting illustration of this inability to understand the customs of another people is found in Miss Kingsley's account of a form of farewell in Africa. On taking leave of an old lady, Miss Kingsley's hand was seized and so far as she could tell the woman spat in it.[11] But Dr. Nassau says, "in pronouncing a blessing there is a violent expulsion of breath, the hand or head of the one blessed being held so near the face of the one blessing that sometimes in the act spittle is actually expelled upon him." [12] Miss Kingsley herself later recognized this as a proper explanation. It is a clear case that most casual travellers fail completely to understand those whom they observe and misinterpret their actions. So much is this true that no scientific student of anthropology takes any account whatever of the opinions or observations of a passing traveller.

*Mental Background and Interpretation of Truth.* This failure to understand an alien people is all the more heightened by the way in which all of us interpret mental stimuli. It is a well known fact that a mental stimulus applied to ten different minds makes ten different impressions. No two of them will be alike,— not primarily because the mental characteristics of the ten are so different, but because the mass of past mental experience for each is so different. This mass of past mental experience is the product of early training and of the long continued accumulation of daily living. This traditional material of the mental life colors all new thoughts that are presented, so that each mind thinks in terms colored by its own background. If an American hears of a new malignant disease he immediately thinks of some new germ which is preying on man, and begins a search for it as has recently happened with influenza; but if an African discovers a new form of malignant sickness he thinks in terms of an evil spirit which is troubling that body, and begins to hunt for the enemy who is bewitching him. The difference of interpretation is not due to difference in mental capacity or difference in mental process, but to difference in traditional material.

[10] Sumner: "Folkways," p. 61.
[11] Kingsley: "Travels in West Africa," p. 227.
[12] Nassau: "Fetichism in West Africa," p. 213.

*Folk Lore as Interpreter of a People.* It will be readily seen, therefore, that to understand another people we must know their traditional background. Herein lies the great value of folk lore, for through it alone we can fully appreciate the mental content of primitive life. "In all our thoughts," says Boas, "we think in terms of our own social environment. But the activities of the human mind exhibit an infinite variety of forms among the peoples of the world. In order to understand these clearly, the student must endeavor to divest himself entirely of opinions and emotions based on the peculiar social environment into which he is born. He must adapt his own mind so far as possible to that of the people whom he is studying. The more successful he is in freeing himself from the bias from the group of ideas based on the civilization in which he lives, the more successful he will be in interpreting the beliefs and actions of men. He must follow lines of thought new to him. He must participate in new emotions, and understand how, under unwonted conditions, both lead to action." [13] It is just this freeing oneself of mental bias, just this stepping outside one's own social environment, so to speak, that most people find impossible of accomplishment, and, therefore, they are never capable of really understanding alien peoples.

*Knowledge of Emotional Responses Needed.* Benjamin Kidd, in his "Social Evolution," written thirty years ago, made perfectly clear that the difference in the response of primitive and civilized peoples was not primarily due to difference in intellectual capacity, but much more largely due to the development of the emotional life of the two groups.[14] In order, therefore to understand any other people we must sympathetically understand their emotional background, we must enter into their feeling responses. This is no easy process and few people ever take the pains to accomplish it. Every person knows how difficult it is to know another person. The barrier which individual personality puts between one and another can never be completely crossed. Still more difficult is it if difference of sex is added. What man would have the hardihood to claim that he ever completely understood a woman—and while some women think they completely understand men, we have our doubts. Add to this difference of social environment due to difference in national life, say between Americans and English, and the difficulty of understanding is still greater. If now one adds the difference of race with all the inherited emotional responses, and all the accumulated mental attitudes of two different groups, it will be seen that mutual understanding between races is far from easy.

[13] Boas: "The Mind of Primitive Man," pp. 97-98.
[14] Cf. Kidd: "Social Evolution," Ch. IX.

*Consciousness of Differences.*   Professor Giddings[15] has clearly shown that in the meeting of any two individuals or groups there is decided conflict due to the consciousness of differences. The impressions of unlikeness, he claims, are apt to be much more vivid than the impressions of likeness.   Each peculiarity of dress, feature, speech, or manner stands out in bold relief to the mind of the other party.   Hence it happens that we exaggerate the differences between ourselves and a foreign group, and we are apt almost to overlook all resemblances.   Not until these resemblances come into view, and the unlikenesses are either forgotten or resolved can there be any real association.   When the likenesses have through association begun to predominate, then we begin to be conscious of Kind, and association is possible. This process of understanding must take place between any two individuals of the same group, and the readjustments of mental attitude in the process often produces violent disturbance.   Perhaps the most painful struggles of life are just those which take place in the field of social adjustments.   If an individual is unable to make such adjustments we call him anti-social.   If this struggle is severe even among members of the same race, how much more difficult must it be when members of widely separated races face one another.

*Mental States Follow Action.*   Mental adjustment can come about only through adjustment of activities, which is to say our emotional reactions follow our actions.   When we act alike we begin to feel alike.   When two individuals live side by side for a long time, by the power of imitation they begin to act alike and then only do their differences begin to resolve themselves.   A woman from Maine and one from Mississippi, living in the same house, would likely find themselves in utter conflict at first, both as to methods of procedure and as to processes of thought.   But if they lived long enough together, provided both were genuine, there would ultimately result a common basis of procedure and consequently much more of harmony of thought.   In like manner two distinct races with divergent customs and activities will find it difficult to understand each other.   It will only be possible for each to understand the other when they deliberately set themselves to see the reason for and the peculiar nature of the two sets of activities.   Sympathetic understanding of customs will bring sympathetic understanding of mental responses.

*The Central Issue.*   This is the central issue of the future, if we are to have peace, harmony and good will.   We can never have these until all races understand each other.   It was just this attempt to take the place of the African that enabled Leonard to know so fully the people of the Niger Valley:

[15] Giddings: "Principles of Sociology."

"All through life I have possessed the power of living a life which was positively dual in existence, of having within my own entity the capacity of absolute detachment, from either internal or external surroundings, as the case might be. And it was this power that I utilized to its fullest extent when I was in contact with these sons of Nature, which enable me to meet them, not merely more than half way, but, in reality, on their own ground or dunghill. For as their condition had from the outset elicited my sympathy, I threw myself heart and soul into their cause; so much so that I became oblivious to outside matters, and came in time to look at their own customs from their own point of view. And in this way only is it possible for the European to understand the African; for if he thinks white and writes black; or *vice versa,* writes white and thinks black, the result attained is bound to be an abortion, or only a hybrid.

*Civilized Man Has Misunderstood the Uncivilized.* "The fact of the matter is, that the civilized European has never been able to detach himself from his own very different intellectualities when studying the barbaric environment. Therefore in constituting himself a critic of barbaric methods, he has not in the true spirit of criticism been at all justified in doing so. For he has looked at the barbarian, or savage, from his own European standpoint, and in doing so has taken him much too literally, at the same time that he has not given these sons of Nature credit for the intelligence, the morality, and the knowledge which they in reality possess, quite forgetful of the fact that where religion is concerned they are naturally silent, and disinclined to part with any information. Because, in fact, his picture of them, based as it is on erroneous data and deductions, is altogether a misconception, inasmuch as it is drawn from a conception that is his own, and in no sense that of the people whom he is attempting to portray. So, unconsciously though it may be, he lends himself to the perpetration of an act of moral injustice, and in this conflicting way defeats his own good purpose in bringing the savage nearer to civilization. Apart from all other moral considerations, this is a serious blunder, for it goes without saying that where misunderstanding prevails between two human units that are unknown to and dissimilar to each other, in their moods and modes of thought, advancement, that is civilization, is simply impossible." [16]

*Unwillingness to Understand.* Not only is there inability to understand, but there is all too frequently lack of desire to understand. Lack of sympathy is one of the greatest barriers to interracial understanding. The first law of human friendship, accord-

[16] Leonard: "The Lower Niger and Its Tribes," pp. 3-4.

ing to Dr. Henry Churchill King, is mutual self-revelation and answering trust.[17]  The two responses are reciprocal.  I cannot reveal myself to you unless you trust me.  No man has ever yet revealed his best self in the presence of criticism or suspicion. But on the other hand one cannot be trusted until he has so revealed himself as to prove worthy of trust.  The more I reveal myself to you the more can you trust me if I am true, and the more you trust me the more can I reveal my soul to you.  If this law holds for mutual understanding and good will between individuals, equally does it hold between races.  Here perhaps has been the greatest failure on the part of those who would understand another people.  We do not look down to those whom we trust.  We do not condescend to those whom we really desire to understand.  One reason why white men have so rarely understood colored men is that they have not trusted them sufficiently. They have expected other races to reveal themselves without self-manifestation on the part of the white man and without trust or real appreciation.  This is an impossibility.  Dr. Charles Cuthbert Hall, once Barrows lecturer to India, claimed that no Occidental had ever really understood the mind of an Oriental because of a false mental attitude toward these peoples.  "The passive form of intolerance (which white men have toward other races) is self-withdrawal—passing by on the other side; looking with more or less contempt, and leaving to their fate with more or less indifference, Eastern races and their faiths.  It is the form in which intolerance secretes itself in an age boastful of intellectual breadth, and poisons its thinking at the heart.

*Anglo-Saxon Pride Blinds Us.*  "The pride of Anglo-Saxon culture is profound. . . . We are willing to enter into commercial relations with the East, wherever the instinct of self-advantage prompts the alliance.  Yet, after a hundred years of modern intercourse, the thought of the West, the sympathies of the West, the affiliative instincts of the West, have been held in reserve with a caution blended of distrust, contempt, and self-satisfaction. . . . Mr. Meredith Townsend, in his brilliant paper on the 'Mental Seclusion of India,' bids us observe that Englishmen 'dwell among these people (i.e. the Indian races), they talk their tongues, they do all manner of business with them, they live by giving them advice and orders, and yet they know next to nothing about them.' He proceeds to say: 'In the whole century of intercourse no Anglo-Indian has ever written a book which in the least degree revealed the inner character and motives of any considerable section or any great single class, of this immensely numerous people. It is as certain as any fact can be, that any Anglo-Indian who wrote a book perceived to be a "revealing" book about Indians, or

17 King: "The Laws of Friendship," p. 55 f.

any section of them, would, as his reward, receive fortune, reputation among his contemporaries, fame with posterity and yet no Anglo-Indian has ever done it, or, so far as appears, ever will do it.'

*Why We Fail to Understand Indians.* "When Mr. Townsend asks 'What is the solution of this mystery?' he admits that he has 'no full answer to give,' but conceives the best available answer to be that 'the Indian himself deliberately secludes his mind from the European with a jealous, minute, and persistent care, of which probably no man not gifted with an insight like that of Thackeray could succeed in giving even a remote idea.' However accurate may be this charge of voluntary mental seclusion (and so candid and honorable an observer as Mr. Meredith Townsend is not likely to be inaccurate), the disposition which he deplores has a probable origin, not in Oriental secretiveness, but in the spirit of intolerance which in its passive form of haughty self-withdrawal, has set the Western mind in a non-sympathetic attitude, prohibitive of spiritual fellowship. Those who have broken away from the Western conventionality of looking down upon the East, and of passing it by on the other side; those who have sought, not in the spirit of criticism, but in the spirit of love and respect, to enter the inner circle of the Oriental consciousness, find that the secretiveness of which Mr. Townsend complains is the result, rather than the cause, of Anglo-Saxon contemptuousness." [18]   Instead of mutual trust we usually find mutual suspicion. "The Congos have a proverb that runs thus: In a court of fowls the cockroach never wins his case: i.e., the verdict of one race against another is to be received with caution." [19]

*Races in South Misunderstand Each Other.* This is not only a world condition, it is specifically the central issue here in the South. The claim has often been made that the southern white man knows the Negro; but if self-revelation comes only in response to trust, one would certainly have to speak cautiously about the real knowledge which either race has of the other at the present time. Before the Civil War there was a close association between white and black, and in many instances a mutual respect and confidence betwen slave and master which gave solid basis for self-revelation. Many a slave knew something of the inner motive of his master and hence came to know the true bent of the white race; not a few masters saw in the faithfulness of his slave the proof of a genuine character. In spite, therefore, of the barrier which slavery raised, by degrading one group in the eyes of the other, there was a basis for understanding which so far

[18] Hall: "Christ and the Human Race," passim, pp. 41-44.
[19] Weeks: "Congo Life," p. 33.

has not been attained since the era of freedom opened. That we should have better understanding now than then cannot be doubted, but so far it has not been attained. It was just here that reconstruction did its most deadly work. By setting the white man and the black man in the South in political opposition, there were antagonisms aroused which broke down all confidence and hence destroyed all mutual understanding. To restore this understanding and bring white men and black men to a real knowledge of each other is perhaps the most fundamental task of our day.

*Conditions Favorable for Understanding.* It can hardly be doubted that the two races in the South are in position to bring about a mutual understanding such as no other two races have yet attained. There is here a common language which makes communication easy. In most of the contacts between two races the complication of language is a great barrier. There is here a common religion, and that the one religion which puts most emphasis on the value of the individual, thus superinducing respect for all others. There is a common economic task of subsistence from the soil, for it is still true that the majority of the people, both white and black, live on the soil. Most of all there is a deep sympathy—one might almost use the strong word *love*— between individuals of the two races inherited from their forefathers. Most of the best literature of the South gathers round the old associations of the plantation, where white and black mingled in mutual dependence and mutual helpfulness. Indeed, the opportunity to make a demonstration to the world of two races living side by side in mutual self-respect and mutual helpfulness can be worked out here in the South if it can be worked out anywhere. By such a demonstration—which is already on the way compared with the relation in any other section of the world—the South would set the life of humanity forward by a greater advance than might otherwise be made in many hundreds of years.

*Basis of Advance.* This can be done only by helping each race to understand more fully the customs, the thoughts, and the aspirations of the other race. This mutual understanding can be secured ultimately by trust of each other, for the final desideratum of knowledge of persons is open-minded sympathy. The facts which are presented in this volume are an attempt to help white men know the background, the traditional material on which the Negro race acts. It is an attempt to connect present conditions with the near and the far past, because a people does not drop its customs nor its modes of thought in a day. We believe that much of the present response of the Negro to social environment is influenced by the social heritage, not only from slavery but

from the far African past.  This is in no way an intimation that
the Negro has not progressed far beyond that past.  Indeed no
one can read the story of his marvelous progress without great
amazement, and the amazement is all the more heightened when
one sees the humble beginnings of the race.  On the other hand
there can be little doubt that there are vestigial remains of a far
social heritage in the present social reactions of the American
Negro, which if not understood will vitiate all of our judgments
concerning him.  It is hoped that the facts herein presented will
be so fair-minded and so sympathetic that they will help white
and black alike to know each other better and to trust each other
more fully—thus leading to a larger life for both.

## CHAPTER II

## AFRICAN BACKGROUND OF THE NEGRO

*The Dark Continent.* Africa next to Asia is the largest of the continents, having an estimated surface of 12,000,000 square miles. This tremendous figure has little content for us, but one is immediately awakened to its meaning, when told that it is sixty times as large as the German Empire, and one hundred times as large as the United Kingdom of Great Britain. Africa has long been called the "Dark Continent," which designation is finely descriptive if it is taken to mean a continent about which almost nothing has been known. Next to Tibet perhaps no other great expanse of the world's surface has been so tardily explored and described. There are evident reasons for this slow progress of African exploration.

*Why Africa is Unknown.* First to be noted is that the African coast line is almost unbroken in its entire 15,000 miles. While the continent is three times as large as Europe, its coast line is 4,000 miles shorter than that of its sister continent. This is due to the great number of inlets, bays, peninsulars, and capes of Europe, and the severe regularity of the African coast. In this respect Africa is the most forbidding of all the continents, offering few sheltering bays in which a vessel may find haven. Still again Africa is poorly supplied with navigable rivers. Its great rivers are the Congo, the Zambesi, the Niger, the Nile. Its smaller rivers are the Senegal, the Ogowe, the Orange, and the Limpopo. All of these rivers rise in the elevated interior and flow down through cascade after cascade to the sea, thus making navigation well-nigh impossible.

*The Congo.* The Congo, which carries to the sea the largest quantity of water of any of the African rivers, rises in the lake region toward the eastern coast, makes a long curve toward the north and then plunges down from its highland to sea level, through 200 miles of rocky brawles and picturesque cascades which made Henry Stanley's journey up the river one of immense labor and danger. Ocean steamers can ascend the Congo only 110 miles to Matadi.

*The Niger.* The Niger system rises in the northern portion of the West African Highland of Futa-Jallon, describes a great curve to the north, and drops into the lowlands of the Bight of Benin, where it spreads out into a series of nineteen or twenty marshes and smaller rivers among which the Nun, the Forcados, Bonny, and Cross Rivers are alone navigable by boats of any considerable size.[1] Each river has its sandbar guarding the mouth, and between alluvial mud and rocky shoals the main bed of the streams are made almost useless for sea-going crafts. Most of the ivory and slave traffic of the upper Niger has been carried on across the desert rather than attempt to follow the river to the coast.

*The Zambesi and Others.* The Zambesi River takes its rise in the far western part of the continent in southern Angola, sweeps across the central tableland, swerves suddenly northward toward Lake Nyasa, and then plunges down to the sea. James Bryce calls the Victoria Falls on the Zambesi "the only very grand natural object which South Africa has to show." [2] These falls effectually cut off all navigation and consequently help to lock the interior to the outer world. The Nile, as is well known, serves navigation better, therefore from that direction exploration and travel extend far up toward the heart of Africa, even as far back as the reign of the Pharaohs.

On the whole the rivers of Africa have given little encouragement to the traveller to explore the interior sections of Africa. "All the great rivers," says Keane, "Nile, Congo, and Niger, are interrupted by cataracts and rapids which cut off from outward intercourse populous regions whose fluvial systems ramify over many hundred millions of acres." [3]

"East of the Nile and of the great lakes there is no space between the plateau and the coast for the development of large streams." [4]

North of the Zambesi for 2400 miles there is not a great river and between the Senegal and the mouth of the Nile, a distance of 4800 miles, no stream of importance empties into the sea.

*The Mountains and Deserts.* Another barrier to the outside world is the system of mountains and deserts. Sahara, like the ring of fire, guarding the sleeping maiden in the early Norse myths, encircles central Africa from the north, cutting off all penetration for centuries until at last the camel was introduced, giving some access for trade, but not inviting exploration. The city of Timbuktu, long known to fame through the coastal tribes, was first visited by a white man, Major Laing, in 1825. Mungo Park, having failed to reach it a few years before, being drowned just on the eve of his arrival at this long looked for goal. To the southwest of Sahara the high tablelands of Futa-Jallon, rising at its highest point to the altitude of 10,000 feet, gives precipitousness to the upper reaches of the rivers, and forms an

[1] Leonard: "The Lower Niger and Its Tribes," p. 12.
[2] Bryce: "Impressions of Southeast Africa," p. 233.
[3] Keane: "Africa," Vol. 1, p. 6.
[4] *Ibid.,* Vol. 3, p. 7.

effectual barrier against easy exploration. Sweeping on down
the coast to the head of the gulf of Guinea, one finds the Kamerun
Mountains, whose giant peaks, the "Three Sisters," attain an
altitude of 14,000 feet, which, because they are so formidable
and are usually covered with snow, are called by the natives
the "Mountain of the Gods." [5]  These mountains pile themselves
precipitously above the sea, and thus effectually bar a passage
to the interior, which otherwise might have been found through
the sheltering bays of the gulf. Still further south, not only do
the rivers give poor facilities for navigation, but the heat, the
rainfall, the heavy growth of vegetation, the terrible fevers, and
insect pests of the torrid zone, have held the white man at a
distance for long centuries. The eastern coast is guarded by
a long line of mountains and tablelands, culminating in Kiliman-
jaro and Kenia, both over 18,000 feet high, which form the roof
of the continent and through which mountain chains all the
eastern rivers must pierce to find vent into the sea. It is this
general contour of the continent that causes Keane to remark,
"The comparative absence of navigable waters, of islands and
great harbors, combined with the great extent of desert wastes,
has mainly contributed to exclude Africa from the general life
of the commercial world." [6]  Like the mountain peoples of Tennessee, Kentucky and North Carolina, who for two centuries or
more have been held in isolation by their mountain fastnesses and
hence have fallen two centuries behind the procession of civilization, so the African peoples, shut in by the natural barriers of
their own continent for thousands of years, have dropped many
centuries behind the progress of civilization, not altogether because of less capacity, but mainly, at least, because of less
contacts.

*Africa Long Unknown.* Although Egypt was one of the
cradles, if not the cradle, of civilization, and the northern coast
of Africa has been known during the whole period of which
history gives an account, still Africa as a continent was not at
all seriously considered until after the establishment of the English Society for the Exploration of Africa in 1788. A few more
daring spirits had made journeys down the west coast as early
as the fourteenth century. Marco Pizzigani plotted part of the
coast as early as 1367, and the people of Dieppe claim to have
made a settlement on the Guinea coast as early as 1364.[7]  The
Portuguese, under Prince Henry, deserve the credit of having
really opened west Africa to exploration. In 1415 John I of
Portugal and his five sons attacked and captured Ceuta, a fort

[5] Keane: "Africa," Vol. 3, p. 371.
[6] *Ibid.,* Vol. 1, p. 5.
[7] *Ibid.,* p. 28.

which faces Gibraltar. Henry, the youngest of the five sons, following this initial exploit, determined to know more about the African continent and to Christianize its people. By 1445 his followers had explored the coast as far south as Cape Verde, and in 1461 they reached the coast of Sierra Leone. The death of Henry in 1460 did not dampen the Portuguese ardor, for in 1470 we find them at the Equator. Cape Lopez, near the mouth of the Congo, and many other geographical points, bear the names of these early Portuguese explorers, such as Lopez Goncolvez. "It is also certain that the Portuguese formed permanent settlements at several points along the coast, and the remains have even been discovered of buildings and of rusty guns in the island of Coniquet toward the center of the Gaboon Estuary. But for over three hundred and fifty years after the first discoveries, European commercial relations were mainly confined to the slave trade, those engaged in this nefarious business maintaining a studied silence and screening from the eyes of the outerworld the scenes of their profitable operations." [8]

*Mungo Park.* In 1796 the Society for the Exploration of Africa sent Mungo Park to the west coast to make an entrance through the Gambia River. His motives, as he declares, were "a passionate desire to examine into the productions of a country so little known; and to become experimentally acquainted with the modes of life, and character of the natives." [9] His directions from the society were "to pass on to the river Niger, either by way of Bambouk, or by such other route as should be found most convenient. That I should ascertain the course and if possible the rise and termination of that river. That I should use my utmost exertions to visit the principal towns or cities of its neighborhood, particularly Timbuctu and Haussa; and that I should be afterward at liberty to return to Europe either by way of the Gambia or by such other route, as, under the then existing circumstances of my situation and prospects, should appear to me to be most advisable." [10] Park reached the Niger, and proved that it flowed eastward, but he did not reach Timbuctu either on this journey or his subsequent journey of 1805, nor was he able to follow this river to its mouth. He did, however, arouse a tremendous amount of enthusiasm for African exploration which led Laing, Caille and Lander, and later Barth, Vogel, Nachtigal, Livingston and a score of others to give their lives to the discovery of this great continent.

*Africa and America.* Unfortunately for Africa, dreams of fabulous wealth in America drew the attention away from Africa

[8] Keane: "Africa," Vol. 3, p. 384.
[9] "Park's Travels," Vol. 1, p. 2.
[10] *Ibid.,* Vol. 1, p. 4.

for two hundred years. Africa was only secondary in that it furnished slaves to carry forward the work of the new continent. "When the New World was discovered," says Thornton, "West Africa was sacrificed to America. . . . We would like, therefore, to point out some points of contrasts and connection between the two. Firstly, the celebrated papal Bull of 1493 marked off the eastern world for the Portuguese and the western world for the Spaniards, so that at first each nation ran a different course. Next, while the West Indian Islands have comparatively a healthy climate, the west Africa coast is notoriously unhealthy for white men, and even its native inhabitants suffer constantly from malaria. Hence, while the West Indies became a sphere of European settlement, and one of the very few tropical ports of the world where colonists from Great Britain have made a home, the west coast of Africa, from first to last, has hardly been suitable even for temporary residence. Again, West Indian colonies have always been colonies of produce. . . . West Africa, on the contrary, though producing gold, palm oil, and jungle products, has, as a whole, no definite system of cultivation, no regular agricultural settlements, and no mining centers. Further, slavery in the West Indies promoted cultivation within certain limits, and retarded it in West Africa. It was impossible to develop (that) part of the world which was perpetually being drained of its labor supply." [11] Thus it is again seen how fortune retarded the development of a continent.

*Climate of Africa.* More of Africa lies within the Torrid Zone than that of any other continent, though South America is a fairly close second. In addition to Africa's Torrid Zone, however, there are two great desert regions, Sahara in the north and Kalahari in the south. The trade winds, "blowing from the northeast in the northern, from the southeast in the southern hemisphere, divert to the equator most of the vapors crossing their path, leaving elsewhere clear skies and arid lands." [12] Were it not for the fact that great stretches of the continent rise to high plateaus, the heat of the continent would be unendurable. As it is the western coast from the mouth of the Gambia River, at 12 degrees north latitude, to the settlement of Benguela, at 14 degrees south latitude, is a section of very heavy rainfall, heavy forestation, and humid climate. The annual rainfall in this section varies from 100 inches along the ivory coast, the gold coast, the slave coast and the Kamerun section, to between twenty and forty inches at the latitude of Benguela. This is the section, as will be seen later, from which most of the American slaves were drawn, and the influence of these climatic conditions on the

[11] Thornton: "Africa Waiting," pp. 48-49.
[12] Keane: "Africa," Vol. 1, p. 10.

development of the ancestors of our slaves will have a very vital bearing on our studies. The east coast of Africa is high and more open and the rainfall much lower, hence the climate is far more pleasant, varying from 50° to 70° mean temperature. The great section known as the Southern Cattle Zone, including the territory south of a line drawn from Benguela to the mouth of the Zambesi is also high and has a rainfall not to exceed ten or twelve inches. The great central section, known as the Sudan, stretching across the continent from the Atlantic coast to the Nile basin, between the lines of 15° and 5° north latitude, has in its northern section a high and dry climate. The central section of the continent known as Uganda, Buganda and neighboring territory, north and west of Lake Victoria, is also high and therefore temperate in climate although located almost astride the equator. These four sections in Africa which are high and temperate—the northern half of the Sudan, the southern Cattle Zone, the central section, west of Victoria, and the northeast coast, are very different from the lower sections of the continent in development, organization, and capacity of the people.

*The Resources of Africa.* Africa is rich in vegetable oils, fibres, gums and hardwood. "First among the trees of Africa is the oil palm, first in beauty, first in utility, and first in fertility." [13] "Is the traveler athirst and weary?—her luxurious foliage gives him shelter, whilst from her tree trunk pours forth a draught of foaming wine. Is the traveler without meat?—then her nut oil and palm cabbage provide a meal fit for a sylvan prince. What will you—merchant, traveler, native?—a loin cloth, a tool, a mat, a roof, a wall, a house, a fortune, or a sylvan picture?—these and more are to be found in the oil palm of West Africa." [14]

The cocoanut palm which thrives only near the coast is also a very prolific tree and grows in great profusion. From the oil palm we get "pure olive oil, lubricating oil, the oil of soap, the base of margarine, and during the war one of the ingredients of high explosives. From the cocoanut palm, our cocoa-mats, materials for making sacks and rope, false horse hair for stuffing cushions and nut butter or margarine." [15] Ground nuts, from which the French manufacture salad oils, grow in profusion. Cocoa originally secured from South America is now largely drawn from Africa.

The gum which is chief of all the products of Africa is rubber, which has turned millions of dollars into European treasuries. Among the African fibres, cotton easily holds first place,

[13] Harris: "Africa, Slave or Free," pp. 25-26.
[14] *Idem.*
[15] See Harris: "Africa, Slave or Free," pp. 26 and passim.

and the annual value of this crop now runs into the millions of dollars.

*Precious Metals.* South Africa is the world's greatest diamond field. It is estimated that $1,000,000,000 would no more than cover the value of diamonds taken from this section in the last fifty years. Harris thinks that the immense sum of gold for Solomon's temple was secured in Eastern Rhodesia. "The traveler through Rhodesia looks on in wonder at kopjes whose bowlders are linked together and then rendered impregnable to assault by hewn granite walls in most cases several feet thick. In any single ruin there must be hundreds of thousands and in some cases millions of granite blocks shaped by some prodigious human agency and then built into the walls and structures covering extensive areas of the territory in the Zambesi valley. . . . It is clear—at least to most people—that these extensive structures were not the work of the indigenous African, but that of some immigrant race—an immigrant race bent not upon civilization, but the exploitation of the resources of the valley. . . . Their implements remain to this day—not single instruments in a given spot, but hundreds of them, scattered over the entire territory— the implements of the gold seeker, picks, crucibles, gold wiring presses and metal engravers. Nor is this all, for many of the old workings remain to-day just as they were hurriedly forsaken on one tragic day many centuries ago, while scattered around in the debris are tiny fragments of pure gold, beads, wire and countless little nails all of solid gold." [16] Whether Harris is right in his conjecture or not, it is certain that Africa now has three great gold fields, the Gold Coast with an output of seven to eight million dollars annually, Southern Rhodesia with an output of twelve or more millions of dollars annually, and the Randt, which is richer than either of the other fields. Africa thus proves to be one of the very richest of the continents, with gold, diamonds, cotton, rubber, ivory, and the great oil products as her chief contributions to the world's wealth.

*The Inhabitants of Africa.* Some anthropologists have attempted to classify humanity on the basis of color, others on the basis of bodily form, others on the basis of mental characteristics, and still others as to cultural characteristics. One does not have to follow many of these attempts to reach the conclusion that no classification can be made which is completely discriminatory and obviates all overlapping and duplication. However, there are certain outstanding features of various types that at least give basis for general groupings. In all classifications there is recognition of the Negro as that part of humanity which has been developed under tropical conditions. Humanity sprang from

[16] Harris: "Africa, Slave or Free," pp. 46-47.

a common anthropoid stock which in prehistoric times was separated into various groups, which groups lived for continuous
centuries under decidedly different environments.   The environment of each stamped itself upon the biological life of the group
and gradually brought about racial differentiation.   The Negro
is that group of people who, because of this long process of natural selection and response to environment, has come to be the
race best adapted to the heat and humidity of the tropics.   It
would normally be expected, therefore, that there would be wide
differences between groups of the Negroid type, due to great
differences of heat, rainfall, elevation and products of the different sections of Africa.   This difference which we would naturally
expect, we actually find.

   *Classifications of Africans.*   Harris divides the inhabitants of
Africa into seven groups: [17]

1. The Semitic family, along the north coast and in
   Abyssinia.
2. The Hamitic family, mainly in the Sahara, Egypt, Galla,
   and Somali Land.
3. The Fulah and Nuba groups, in western, central, and
   eastern Sudan.
4. The Negro systems, in western and central Sudan,
   Upper Guinea, and the Upper Nile regions.
5. The Bantu family, everywhere south of about 6° N.
   Lat., except in the Hottentot domain.
6. The Hottentot group, in the extreme southwestern
   corner from the Tropic of Capricorn to the cape.
7. The Malayo-Polynesian family, in Madagascar.

   Professor Dowd divides the Negroes into five groups or
types: [18]   "First, the Negritos, including the dwarf races of the
Equatorial regions, the Bushmen of the Kalahari desert, and the
Hottentots of the Southern Steppe.

   "Second, the Negritians, including all the natives of dark skin
and woolly hair, occupying the territory of the Sudan.

   "Third, the Fellatahs, a race supposed to have sprung from
crossing the Berbers of the desert with Negritians of Sudan,—
(occupying the northern portion of the Sudan).

   "Fourth, the Bantus, including a vast population of somewhat
lighter color and less Negroid features than the natives of the
Sudan, occupying almost all of West Africa below the Sudan.

   "Fifth, the Gallas, including all of the lighter colored people
of East Africa from the Galla county to the Zambesi river.'"

   The second and fourth groups, that is the Negritians of the

[17] Harris: "Africa, Slave or Free," p. 5.
[18] Dowd: "The Negro Races," Vol. 1, Introduction.

great western Sudan and the Bantus of the west coast stretching from the Niger River to the southern point of Angola, are the groups with which our study is concerned, for from these groups come most of our American slaves.  To be sure, some slaves were introduced into Brazil and other sections of the New World, from the east coast of Africa, the chief point of traffic being Mozambique.  "In 1645 the first slaves were exported from Mozambique to Brazil.  This action was brought about by the fact that the province of Angola had fallen for a time into the hands of the Dutch, and therefore their (Portuguese) supply of slaves to Brazil was temporarily stopped.  In consequence of this, Mozambique and Zambesi for some years replaced West Africa as a slave market." [19]

*Negro Characteristics.*  The Negroes of Africa are not all black as most people have supposed.  They vary in color from the brownish yellow of the Bushmen whom Johnson describes as a "light olive yellow—through which the mantling of the blood can be seen in the cheeks" [20] to the sooty black Negro of the Sudan and the neighboring lands.  Nassau remarks: "Many of the Bantus have Caucasian-like features." [21]  The Gallas of the east coast are almost all much lighter in color, due partly to difference in climate, and partly to intermixture with Semitic and Hamitic peoples.  The Negroes of Buganda and the region east of Victoria Nyanza are also tall, straight and of a lighter color, due perhaps to similar causes.  Most Negro types have hair which is coarse and tightly curled, due to the elliptical shape of the hair follicle and the oblique emergence of the hair from the skin.  But here again there is great divergence.  "Occasionally in the Pigmy or Forest races the hair is brownish or greenish grey, or may even have a tinge of red." [22]  The author has frequently noticed that where Negroes are of mixed blood, the blond or reddish hair of the Nordic races has given decided tinge to the mulatto's hair.

The Negro of Africa does not have so much beard or bodily hair growth as the men of European type.  The typical Negro head is long (dolichocephalic) and decidedly prognathous, the width across the brow is usually less than across the cheek bone, giving the face a hexagonal rather than an oval form as among Europeans.[23]  The nose is decidedly flat, because the nasal spine is poorly developed or often absent.  The lips are usually thicker and turned outward. Johnson thinks the Negro is broader across the chest than any other human species except the Caucasian.

[19] Johnson: "The Colonization of Africa," p. 104.
[20] *Ibid.,* p. 2.
[21] Nassau: "Fetichism in West Africa."
[22] *Ibid.,* p. 3.
[23] Johnson: "The Negro in the New World," p. 5, passim.

There is much evidence that certain African tribes such as the pigmies are among the most primitive living men. To all these descriptions there are decided exceptions. "The difference in color is due to the influence of climate. Near the coast the greater forests and greater numbers of cloudy days protect the complexion from the sun and give it a lighter tint, while the open country of the North and the predominance of clear days, cause the pigmentation of the skin to thicken and darken, thus giving the complexion a deeper and more glossy black." [24]

Certain tribes, such as the Waganda of central Africa, are not so dolichocephalic, nor so prognathous, nor do they have such flat noses. They are lighter in color and many of the women are said to be very beautiful. It will readily be seen that there is no uniformity of type, but great variety, due to climate, food supply, labor and various other modifying causes.

*Brain Capacity of Negroes.*   Painstaking investigations have been made to determine the comparative weight and also the comparative capacity of cranial cavity in various races. "There is sufficient data available to establish beyond a doubt the fact that the brain weight of the whites is larger than that of most other races, particularly larger than that of the Negroes. That of the white male is about 1360 grams. The investigations of cranial capacities are quite in accord with these results. According to Topinard, the capacity of the skull of males of the Neolithic period in Europe is 1560 c. c. (44 cases); that of modern Europeans is the same (347 cases); that of the Mongoloid race, 1510 c. c. (68 cases), of African Negroes 1405 c. c. (83 cases); and of Negroes of the Pacific Ocean, 1460 c. c. (46 cases). Here we have, therefore, a decided difference in favor of the white race." [25] Boas proceeds to show that the measurement of the heads of eminent men seems to point to a larger brain capacity (1665 c. c. as compared with 1560 c. c.) and that the cranial capacity of forty-five criminals measured 1580 c. c. or more than the average. On the contrary, the brains of many eminent men are under the average in size, and the brain of white women is on the average nearly 100 c. c. smaller than the brain of white men. Few men in our day would have the hardihood to assert that the brain of the white woman is inferior to that of the white man. They are evidently different in quality, but it would be foolish to assert superiority on either side. While, therefore, difference in size may indicate greater capacity for the larger brain, anthropologists are very slow to assert this superiority. Besides there is wide variety among the Negroes themselves as to brain capacity, making it impossible to mark down the whole race as mentally inferior.

[24] Dowd: "The Negro Races," Vol. 2, p. 86.
[25] Boas: "The Mind of Primitive Man," p. 25.

Dowd, quoting Shrubsall, gives the following table of skull capacity for various tribes:

| | |
|---|---|
| Kafirs | 1540 c. c. |
| West Africa Negro | 1420 c. c. |
| Central Lake Negro | 1430 c. c. |
| Koranna Negro | 1425 c. c. |
| True Hottentot Negro | 1365 c. c. |
| The Herero | 1640 c. c. |
| Ova Mpo | 1512 c. c.[26] |

*Bases of Difference in Brain.* In accounting for difference in brain capacity among different Negroes, Dowd remarks: "The superior brain of any Zone must be accounted for, not by assuming that increased functions enlarge the brain and that this enlarged brain is transmitted by inheritance, but by assuming that natural selection causes those types to survive that fit the more strenuous environment. According to Woodruff, in a tropical country, where existence is easy, a large brain could not evolve. The general trend of increase of brain is away from the tropics." [27] With reference to racial inferiority or superiority, based on size of brain, Boas, who is one of the most thorough scholars, remarks: "Notwithstanding the numerous attempts that have been made to find structural differences between the brains of different races of men that could be directly interpreted in psychological terms, no conclusive results of any kind have been attained. The status of our present knowledge has been well summed up by Franklin P. Mall, to whose investigations I referred before. He holds, that, on account of the great variability of the individuals constituting each race, racial differences are exceedingly difficult to discover, and that up to the present time, none have been found that will endure serious criticism.[28]

*Political Life of the African Negro.* "The political life of the African Negro varies greatly with the location and advancement of the group. On the west coast neither climate nor geographic conditions are conducive to political organization. The land is low and marshy, full of small streams and luxurious growth, so tangled and matted as to make travel and communication slow, if not impossible. Interchange of ideas is further retarded by the absence of horses, mules and cattle, which in other countries are beasts used by couriers. These animals are all absent from the west coast, due to the tsetse fly, the bite of which is deadly to such animals, though harmless to man. Furthermore, the climatic conditions are such that travel is decidedly wearisome,

[26] Dowd: "The Negro Races," Vol. 2, p. 268, passim.
[27] *Ibid.,* p. 70.
[28] Boas: "The Mind of Primitive Man," p. 29.

and communication over large areas is not known.  It is practically impossible under these conditions to build any centralized
form of government.  Political life, therefore, consists in the
small tribes over which a chief holds sway,—a number of such
tribes loosely confederated together into small kingdoms.  In spite
of these facts, Keane says, "Notwithstanding the assumed incapacity of the Negro peoples to develop extensive political systems, some large Bantu states have been founded within, as well
as beyond, the Congo basin." [29]

*Political Life in East Africa.*  The Negroes of the Eastern
Zones have a somewhat broader political organization, due to the
fact of a more open country, better means of communication and
the necessity of protection against other tribes.  But even here
communication is rather difficult because of the high grass which
is more like our reed than like grass, and which grows so rapidly
that no path or road will stay open if unused for only a few
days.  In this section every Negro carries an iron knife to cut
his way through the grass, which custom has been thought by
some to be the basis of the Negro's fondness for the razor.

*Sudan Conditions.*  In the Sudan conditions were somewhat
more favorable to permanent governmental forms.  Certain parts
of the country are more open, food is plentiful, thus enabling
the government to keep an army in the field, hence several rather
large and permanent kingdoms were built up.

Dahomey, a small kingdom on the slave coast, has sufficiently
open country to allow of co-operation and aggressive military
operations.  It is said that this state at one time had an army
of 50,000 men, and its terrible fighting amazons of 3,000 women
were no inconsiderable military force.

"They rivalled their male companions in arms in prowess, contempt of death, and cold blooded cruelty." [30]  These Dahomans,
"according to Brocas measurements, take a foremost place
amongst the races of mankind for cranial capacity."  This Dahomey kingdom flourished for centuries and was one of the
most powerful allies of the slave traders during the seventeenth
and eighteenth centuries.  It is supposed that this country alone,
at the height of the slave trade, delivered an annual quota of
fifteen thousand slaves, most of which were captured from neighboring tribes.

*North East Kingdoms.*  Northeast of Dahomey there are other
kingdoms which have shown cohesive power and capacity of self
government.  Here the Fulah Negroes have built a number of
kingdoms which have stood long tests of time.  On the upper
reaches of the Niger, the Mandingan Negroes formed the Wassula

[29] Keane: "The Earth and Its Inhabitants," Vol. III, p. 440.
[30] *Ibid.*, p. 261.

nation, which seemed to have much coherence and power.  Further east the Haussa kingdom was a loose confederacy lasting for many centuries.  "Sokoto, occupying a great part of the space between the Niger and Lake Tchad, is the modern representative of the Fulah kingdom.  The city of Sokoto (once having a population of 120,000, according to Keane) has since been replaced as a capital by Warnu, twenty miles higher up the river of Sokoto. . . . Kano, southeast of Sokoto, is the commercial capital of Central Sudan, being the terminus of one of the principal routes across the Sahara. . . . When the caravans arrive from distant parts, its streets are thronged with merchants and the population rises at least to 60,000." [31]  Keane says: "In the sixteenth century, and probably earlier, Katsena (another one of the Haussa kingdom towns) was a center of civilization frequented by strangers from all quarters, and at that time the kings, although nominally vassals of Bornu, were practically independent.[32]

Bornu is another Negro kingdom, located just west of Lake Tchad.  "It has been a united power ever since Islam was introduced, a thousand years ago. . . . The capital, Kuka, is a walled town of 60,000 inhabitants and is the terminus to the Bilma route across the Sahara." [33]  The Sultan of Bornu once had a standing army of 30,000 soldiers and it has carried on a flourishing trade for centuries in slaves, ivory, ostrich feathers, etc.  When one reads the stories of these kingdoms hid away in the heart of Africa, and follows the stories of their chiefs and warriors, he at once realizes that the Negro has much governmental and organizing ability, much to the contrary of common or popular opinion.  Wherever in Africa the conditions of communication have permitted, namely, in the high regions of Central Africa, Uganda, etc., in the more open territory of the Sudan, and in the great Southern Cattle Zone, there the Negro has builded large empires, which, while more primitive than European states, nevertheless compare quite favorably with many of the white man's governments.  Unfortunately, for the reputation of the Negro, the fullest information we have had has pertained to the coast tribes of the equatorial region, where all the conditions militated against the building of large empires.  It is true that a large portion of our slaves came from people who had not developed any large capacity in self-government, but the development of other Negro groups into well organized states is clear proof that the Negro as a race is not incapable of self-government when and where the conditions admit of such development.

[31] Thornton: "'Africa Waiting," p. 56.
[32] Keane: "The Earth and Its Inhabitants," Vol. III, pp. 313, 314.
[33] Thornton, "Africa Waiting," p. 56.

*Economic Life of the African Negroes.* In the economic life of the African Negroes, there is as wide variation as in the political life. The dwellers in the Southern Cattle Zone, the Zulus, the Kafirs, and groups known as the Matabeles, the Mastonas, and the Herero, are most vigorous and aggressive peoples. The high land in which they dwell gives a more open country, where cattle raising is the chief industry. The krall or cattle pen is the center of every village, the huts or houses of the people being grouped around this pen, partly, at least, to protect their property against thieves. The milk of the cattle forms a staple of diet, and from the skins are made clothing and articles of household use. Occasionally, an animal is slain and eaten, but this seems to be an exception rather than a regular rule. The openness of the country permits of some farming, and maize, rice, millet and vegetables are grown.

*Industrial Art.* They manufacture iron, and the cutlery of this section is said to compare favorably with that of European countries. They have a pottery which is decidedly advanced, and manufacture baskets, hoes, axes, lances and numerous other implements. Being cut off from outside contacts, they have necessarily developed little or no trade and each group is largely self-sufficient and self-supporting. Dowd quotes Kidd in saying that the "Zulus have a division of labor into armourer, brazier, tanner, shoemaker, pipemaker, etc." [34]

*Economic Conditions in the Manioc Zone.* In the great region to the north of the Cattle Zone, which is sometimes called the Manioc Zone, due to the prevalence of this plant from which tapioca is made, and which was introduced into Africa by the Portuguese in the sixteenth century, the life is quite different. The region includes most of the territory between 10° south latitude and 5° north latitude, and is a land of heavy, tangled growth, heavy rainfall, a great system of rivers and tributaries, abundant animal life and great variety of climate. Hunting was originally the chief occupation of the people, the elephant yielding the coveted prize of ivory which for the last centuries has been so much in demand by the white man. Cattle and horses cannot be raised in this region, due to the tsetse fly, and other domestic animals are not very numerous. In reading the accounts of missionaries and travelers, goats, pigs and chickens seem to be practically the only source of meat diet. Due to scarcity of meat and salt, and perhaps partly due to certain religious rites, cannibalism has long held sway among these people. The gradual introduction of agriculture has lessened the prevalence of this practice, but among some of the more savage tribes, such as the Fang, it is still widely followed. Stanley found meat

[34] Dowd: "The Negro Races," Vol. II, p. 238.

very hard to get and the plain vegetable diet hard to endure. Speaking of its hardship on the upper reaches of the Congo, he says: "I had had no meat of any kind, of bird or beast for nearly a month, subsisting entirely on bananas or plantains, which, however varied in their treatment by the cook, failed to satisfy the jaded stomach." [35]

*Discouragement of Labor.* The climate and humidity are such as to discourage all regular work and hence slavery has been long known, both as a means of employing war captives and as a method of escaping that which is decidedly loathsome to the more powerful of the natives. The women tend the small fields and do all the work of preparing the food. Each woman must provide sufficient food for her own children and furnish her proportion of the food for the men of the household. In order to lighten her labor, slavery is welcomed by the woman and the introduction of additional women workers into a man's home—polygamy—is highly desirable from the standpoint of the head wife. Nassau says of the Ogowe people: "Polygamy was the universal custom of the country. Every heathen man planned to become a polygamist as soon as he could acquire the funds to buy another wife. Some few women welcomed the added wife; because being servants and practically slaves, the new servant helped to divide their work." [36]  But Nassau thinks that the African women submit to polygamy only because they are helpless.

*Agricultural Products.* Yams, ground nuts, pumpkins are grown in quantities, melons and beans are not unknown. Plantain is rather abundant but the banana is more scarce. Nassau says of the plantain: "Even after the long interval to the present time, and tasting every variety of vegetable, I know of none that I enjoy more than boiled ripe plantain." [37]  Dried fish, dried rats and insects are common food, and the meat of the hippopotamus and elephant are eagerly devoured.

*Industrial Arts.* Handicrafts have had considerable development. Huts or houses are rather well built, bark cloth is manufactured, baskets, mats and woven vessels are in common use, and, as all over Africa, iron is used for the manufacture of many common utensils. The village smith, though working with very crude tools, nevertheless, turns out pots, hoes, knives, spears and cutlery which is favorably compared with the cutlery of Sheffield. No one can read with care the history of this group of African peoples without realizing that the environment of life has done much to rob the native of habits of industry and thrift which are more prevalent in other parts of the world. The process

[35] Stanley, "In Darkest Africa," Vol. I, p. 480.
[36] Nassau: "My Ogowe," p. 83.
[37] *Ibid.*, p. 44.

# AFRICAN BACKGROUND OF THE NEGRO 37

of natural selection has bred up a race who are not too strenuous —for the fittest to survive in this humid climate are not those who try to "hustle life," but those who run a very quiet and uneventful course.

*The Banana Zone.* Still further to the north and stretching across the continent from Cape Palmas to Lake Albert, is a strip of country, four or five degrees in width, known as the Banana Zone. It includes all the ivory, gold and slave coast on the north of the gulf of Guinea, and extends inland perhaps two hundred miles, and as it stretches toward the east it swerves southward so that the main section of the zone lies squarely astride the equator. This section of the continent has the alternating hot and rainy humid seasons. The rainfall along the coast is more than one hundred inches annually, and the growth is as luxuriant as is to be found anywhere in the world. "But it is not possible," writes Leonard of the Niger Valley, "for any picture, whether drawn by the hand or conjured by the mind, to portray this painful monotony of the mangrove which nature has smirched in her dullest green, the muddy dinginess of the grey-brown turgid waters, the fœtid evil-smelling swamps of slime and ooze, reeking with malaria and with a life that is repulsive, and strongly suggestive of its surroundings—the loathsome churchyard crabs, recalling hideous memories; the slimy mud fish, linking the prehistoric past with the ever-advancing present; the crafty crocodiles sunning themselves on snags and sandbars, the huge, ungainly hippos, the hideous iguanas, and the gorgeously painted pythons, lurking in the forests for unwary victims; . . . these, which are some of the realities of the Delta, are as a rule to be seen." [38]

*Peoples of the Banana Zone.* The tribes of this zone are the Efik, the Ibo, the Ibeno, the Bongala, the Nyombe, the Fang and others. They are almost exclusively vegetarians, living mainly off of bananas and plantains. These grow profusely and spontaneously and need only to be gathered the year round. The eating of human flesh among the Ibo, thinks Leonard, was not primarily for the sake of meat diet, but as a religious ceremony. The "Okuku" is a kind of memorial service, held six months to a year after the burial of the dead, and is celebrated with even more pomp and elaborateness than the real funeral, which itself is always elaborate among African people. "This Okuku is performed in the house in which the late chief has been buried,— its most important feature being the sacrifice and the eating of a male or female slave. This unfortunate creature is generally bought after the chief's death, and is fattened and well treated, and no one inside or outside the house is allowed to offend the

[38] Leonard; "The Lower Niger and Its Tribes," pp. 13 and 14.

victim in any way, for fear he might learn the secret of his fate, and either commit suicide or run away." [39]

*People Browbeaten by Nature.* Leonard speaks feelingly about this great group of people of the western Banana Zone as having "had the misfortune to be tyrannized over by the inevitable and inexorable in nature, and who have never had even an opportunity of emerging from the grip of an environment that has arrested development and kept them in the same backward conditions of their forefathers." [40] Whatever be the cause of their backwardness, the inhabitants of this region, particularly these of the Niger delta, are as backward as any people in Africa. Perhaps the very bounty of nature has been their greatest handicap.

*Oppressive Climate and Idleness.* The climate is so hot and humid that human beings cannot work hard. To do so would be to court death. The native, therefore, acquires the habit of sloth and delay: "If he has anything of consequence to perform, it is a matter of indifference to him whether he does it to-day or to-morrow, or a month or two hence; so long as he can spend the present moment with any degree of comfort, he gives himself very little concern about the future." [41] Nature is bountiful in fruit and vegetables. Work is scarcely necessary to secure food. Clothing is neither needed nor desirable from the native's standpoint. Food laid away will not keep in so hot a climate, so why save and be provident? "The industrial limitations of the Fang are due to the bounty of nature, on the one hand, which renders economic development unnecessary, and on the other hand, to the ease of moving from place to place, thanks to the absence of any insuperable geographical barriers. A territory without natural boundaries, says Semple, 'obviates the necessity of applying more work and more intelligence to the old area. Hence dispersion takes the place of intensification of industry.'" [42] However, certain primitive industry was developed. Mungo Park, in 1796, found natives of the upper Niger manufacturing household articles. "They make very good soap, by boiling ground nuts in water and then adding a little of wood ash. They likewise manufacture excellent iron." [43] What little work there is must be done by slaves and women, both of whom despise it and would shirk if possible. No wonder that those of our American slaves who came from this region—and they were many—should neither know how to work nor desire to learn how.

*Evils of Idleness.* Along with this lack of work a whole brood of evils came. Not to work means to become immoral. A people

[39] Leonard: "The Lower Niger and Its Tribes," p. 161.
[40] *Ibid.*, p. 1.
[41] "Park's Travels," Vol. 1, p. 487.
[42] Dowd: "The Negro Races," Vol. II, pp. 163-164.
[43] "Park's Travels," Vol. I, p. 518.

has not yet been found that could withstand the test of idleness. Nor has any people ever developed self control and self mastery without passing through the school of toil. No one should wonder, then, that these people are lacking in a keen moral sense, have little of self control, and even less of the rigid sense of obligation. Milligan says: "The idle life of the Fang, especially in the interior, and his freedom from responsibility, seem to the impatient white man to have obliterated from his mind the sense of time. A Fang cannot conceive that he has wronged you if he comes several days late to keep an engagement. This unreliableness in everything where time is a factor is one of the chief trials of the white man in Africa. But he ought to regard the native's viewpoint and consider how very irritating and really discouraging to the native must be the white man's incessant hurry. 'We are not in a hurry,' says the black man. 'Why should you come to Africa to set us all hurrying? Has it made your own people so very happy that you want to share with us the blessings of haste?' " [44]  Furthermore, since work was the lot of a slave, all free men considered it degrading. Hence, our early slaves, brought from Africa, needed to learn to work and our slavery system did not change for them or for us the valuation of labor. Dr. Washington says: "It has been necessary for the Negro to learn the difference between being worked and working—to learn that being worked meant degradation, while working meant civilization; that all forms of labor are honorable and all forms of idleness disgraceful." [45]  Even the white race with its hundreds of years of civilization has not learned any too well the lesson of the joy and blessedness of toil. We surely cannot expect that the Negro, into whose biological structure has been built the fibre of idleness for many thousands of years, will in one or two hundred years, learn, as a whole race, what the white man has not fully learned in a thousand years of necessary toil.

*Family Life in Africa.* Family life is at low ebb in Africa, because of the position of womanhood. The woman is among all tribes considered decidedly inferior to man. Her duty is to provide food for the husband, carry his burdens, give birth to and rear his children. She may not even walk by his side in the village, nor may she ever eat as he eats. The men eat together and the women and children eat afterwards and have what is left. Speaking of a funeral feast in the Congo, Weeks says the women and the girls, at some little distance away "ate in a half shamefaced, apologetic fashion, out of sight of their lords and masters." [46]  Wives are bought for a price. Among the Fang

[44] Milligan: "The Jungle Folk of Africa," p. 223.
[45] Washington: "The Negro Problem," p. 9.
[46] Weeks: "Congo Life and Folklore," p. 38.

the price of a wife is "Ten goats, five sheep, five guns, twenty trade boxes (plain wooden chests), one hundred heads of tobacco, ten hats, ten looking glasses, five blankets, five pairs of trousers, two dozen plates, fifty dollars' worth of calico, fifty dollars' worth of rum, one chair and one cat." [47]   This is the price of the high class women, and "less dowry is paid for a child than for 'a whole woman,' as the Fang would say." [48]   "I have known instances where a child was betrothed before it was born, the dowry (purchase price) to be kept intact and returned in case the child should not be a girl." [49]

If a man does not have money to buy a wife, he may sell his sister to secure the amount needed.   "I have heard Fang boys boasting that they were rich because they had several sisters." [50] "For a debt, a man may give away a daughter or wife, but he may not give away a son or a brother." [51]

"If a man dies, his brother may marry (that is he inherits) any or all of the widows, or if there is no brother, a son inherits, and may marry any or all of the wives except his own mother. It is preferred that widows shall be retained in the family circle because of the dowry money that was paid for them, which is considered as a permanent investment." [52]   A woman does not inherit, if she bears no children her husband may demand the return of the dowry, she may be put away from the village for stealing, adultery, quarreling, but "there is no escape from marriage for a woman during her life except by repayment of the money received for her." [53]   The position of a person in Africa can be judged by the rites accorded them at death.   "Slaves, the poor, and especially poor women, are cast into the river, a prey to fishes, or into the forest, a prey to wild beasts and the scavenger 'driver ants'." [54]

*Treatment of Woman.*   A man may do almost any violence to a woman and she will have no redress.   "One day while I was in a Fang town on the river, I heard a woman crying in the next town as if in great pain.   I went to the town, and found in the palaver house a withered old savage punishing his young wife by putting her hand in a large and heavy block.   He made a small hole in the block and was dragging her hand through it. The hand was about one-third through the block and was already badly bruised.   The sight of the woman and her crying were unbearable.   I ordered the old chief to withdraw her hand imme-

[47] Milligan: "The Jungle Folk of Africa," p. 227.
[48] *Ibid.,* p. 230.
[49] *Ibid.,* p. 230.
[50] *Ibid.,* p. 226.
[51] Nassau: "Fetichism in West Africa," p. 5.
[52] *Ibid.,* p. 6.
[53] *Ibid.,* p. 7.
[54] Nassau: "My Ogowe," p. 76.

diately. He began to argue, but a moment later my hand clutched his throat and he found himself pinioned against the opposite wall. It was typical of the extreme injustice often committed against the African woman; a young woman married against her will to a very old man, with the inevitable consequence that she despised him and cared too much for somebody else. I have only three times in more than twice so many years laid violent hands upon a native; and all three times the outrageous treatment of a woman was the occasion." [55]

With this conception of womanhood, of course, the marriage tie is very loose, and the "idea of marrying 'just for love' is laughable." [56] Polygamy is almost universal, if the man is able to produce the price to buy more than one wife. Illicit relations are common among both the married and the unmarried. A husband will often do no more than demand a fine from another man who has led his wife astray, and Mary Kingsley remarks that "in spite of the strict laws against adultery, the relationship to you of the children born of your wives is not so certain." [57] A man does not marry a woman of his own village, for "those of the same village are closely related, usually brothers or first cousins, and their wives and children." [58] Parental authority is not exclusive; the whole town has more or less to say in the control and discipline of each child. The result is that while a score of parents are adding zest to existence in a fine squabble as to whether the child shall sit here, or he shall do this or that, the child heedless of conflicting orders does as he likes and goes where he pleases." [59]

The girls of the family are under certain strict rules, but their morals are decidedly neglected. They bestow their attentions on men rather freely and indiscriminately.

It cannot be said that there is any real home life. Among most tribes each wife has her own hut, but there is little or no privacy. Roscoe, writing of the northern Bantus, says: "There is little or no thought given to comfort in the huts; they are merely a protection against rain or cold by night. Four and often five men inhabit a hut with sometimes one or two women." [60] However, the morals of the northern Bantus are said to be far above that of the coast tribes.

*House Furnishings.* The furnishings of a native hut are very simple and very crude. The bed is made of two poles or rods across which are fastened a series of round slats. On this frame sometimes a thin covering is thrown, though more frequently the

[55] Milligan: "The Jungle Folk of Africa," pp. 228, 230.
[56] *Ibid.*, p. 226.
[57] Kingsley: "Travels in West Africa," p. 336.
[58] Milligan: "The Jungle Folk of Africa," p. 220.
[59] *Idem.*
[60] Roscoe: "The Northern Bantu," p. 64.

occupant lies down with no covering over him and nothing but the bare slats under him. A fire is kept burning in the hut to insure warmth, and often calves or goats are brought into the hut to increase the warmth. The ever present iron pot for cooking, a few pottery vessels, implements of war and the hunt, and a host of fetich bags, complete the furnishing of the barren, inhospitable dwelling of the average African Negro. The early slaves, therefore, did not bring with them to America a very exalted idea of morals or of family life. There was no real home life, and the bond between husband and wife was very loose. Slavery did comparatively little to change this condition, though it did give a bit more privacy, and the relation of husband and wife, while still loose, had at least the example of the white people to strengthen it, and was not very frequently broken up. Polygamy was scarcely known in slavery, though of course, promiscuous relationships were not uncommon.

*The Fight for Morality.* In part, because they inherited a loose moral life, and in part because the early slave owners considered them incapable of morality, our early slaves lived a very crude life, and kept that lack of moral discrimination which was for many decades the most serious handicap of the less developed element of the race. The very high death rate in Africa doubtless gave rise to a high birth rate, and hence accentuated the sex passion of the African Negro. This death and birth rate was not checked during slavery, but, on the other hand, many of the slave owners encouraged large families by making liberal presents to all who became mothers. Slavery thus took a crude inheritance and not infrequently fostered it in new surroundings, thus helping to write more indelibly in the constitution of the Negro traits and tendencies which the present leadership of the race is struggling hard to eradicate.

The student of the American Negro today must therefore come to his task with a knowledge of the Negro's past if he is to really understand him at the present. He must be willing to judge him as to the distance he has traveled since he left his African home, rather than compared with the white man who had thousands of years the start. He must recognize that traits built into a race during long centuries cannot be bred out in a few years or even a few decades, and that the political and economic life of the present American Negro in the light of his background, is nothing less than amazing.

It is only when we study the race with such a background in view, that we are able to estimate his *true* capacity.

## CHAPTER III

# RELIGIOUS AND SOCIAL LIFE IN AFRICA

*Influence of Religion.* In every country religion is the background of life. "There are no races, however crude, which are destitute of all idea of religion." [1] "Being natural to man, religion is universal among men. Exceptions to its universality are sometimes claimed, but if they exist at all they are of such a nature as really to establish the rule. In the lowest races of men religion is rudimentary and crude, and so low in grade or so concealed that perhaps a stranger may scarcely recognize it. Nevertheless, even here the essential elements are present, and man as man is a religious being." [2] Speaking of the development of man, Dr. Tiele of Leiden University remarks, "religion being a part of his inmost life, necessarily develops along with him." [3] This religion is not only innate in man but is a dominating factor in his social and economic activities. Of no people is this more true than it is of the Negro peoples of Africa. "Religion is intimately mixed with every one of these sociological aspects of family, rights of property, authority, tribal organization, judicial trials, punishments, intertribal relations and commerce." [4] "To get a clear and thorough insight into the characteristics and temperament of a people, it is, I think, essential first to obtain a comprehensive grasp of their religion, even before attempting to master their laws and customs." [5] One does not know a single great authority on Africa who does not feel that the Negro can be fully understood only by those who know something of his religious nature and its expressions. A brief review of the constituent elements of African religion is therefore necessary to our further study.

*African Conception of God.* The first element in the African religion is that of God, called by various tribes Njambi, Nzambi, Anzam, Anyambie, Yemi, Nyssiva, meaning variously, maker, creator, supreme being, great one, and even "Great Friend" and Father. The God who is maker has created his people and then gone off and left them to the mercies of the spirits, good or bad. Hence the native feels that he is an absentee God, who knows

[1] Jevons: "Introduction to the History of Religion," p. 7.
[2] Clarke: "Outline of Christian Theology," p. 2.
[3] Tiele, "Elements of the Science of Religion," Vol. I, p. 33.
[4] Nassau: "Fetichism in West Africa," p. 25.
[5] Leonard: "The Lower Niger and Its Tribes," p. 79.

little and perhaps cares less about their daily lives. The fact that
the African native thinks his God has gone away and left him
has caused many travelers to think that their religion is one of
pure superstition and has no definite idea of God in it. Those
who know them best do not agree with this idea. Mary Kingsley
calls Dr. Nassau the most competent authority on Bantu religions,
because of his long residence among them, his thorough knowledge
of the languages and "his singularly clear, powerful and highly
educated intelligence." [6]  Dr. Nassau says of the Central Africans,
"after more than forty years' residence among these tribes, flu-
entiy using their language, conversant with their customs, dwelling
intimately in their huts, associating with them in the varied relations of teacher, pastor, friend, master, fellow-traveler and guest,
and in my special office as missionary, searching after their religious thought (and therefore being allowed a deeper entrance
into the arcana of their souls than would be accorded to a passing
explorer), I am able unhesitatingly to say that among all the
multitude of degraded ones with whom I have met, I have. seen
or heard none whose religious thought was only a superstition.

*All Africans Believe in God.* "Standing in the village street,
surrounded by a company whom their chief has courteously sum-
moned at my request, when I say to him, 'I have come to speak
to your people,' I do not need to begin by telling them that there
is a God. Looking on that motley assembly of villagers,—the
bold, gaunt cannibal with his armament of gun, spear and dagger;
the artisan with rude adze in hand, or hands soiled at the antique
bellows of the village smithy; women who have hasted from their
kitchen fire with hands white with the manioc dough or still grasp-
ing the partly scaled fish; and children checked in their play with
tiny bow and arrow or startled from their dusty street pursuit
of dog or goat,—I have yet to be asked, 'Who is God?' [7]  The
belief in one Supreme Being is universal. Nor is this idea held
imperfectly or obscurely developed in their minds. The impression is so deeply engraved upon their moral and mental nature,
that any system of atheism strikes them as too absurd and preposterous to require a denial." [8]  In the Niger delta ancestor
worship is more accentuated and it was through this conception
of religion, thinks Leonard, that the Negro "eventually arrived
at a worship of the supreme God, from whom the origin of all
life was traced." [9]  Among Northern Bantu tribes there is a well
developed system of polytheism. Thus Muhama is the creator,
Gasani is the giver of children, Bijungo is the god of plagues,
Semuganda is the god of death, Ingo is the god who attends to

[6] Kingsley: "Travels in West Africa," p. 299.
[7] Nassau: "Fetichism in West Africa," p. 36.
[8] Wilson: "Western Africa," p. 209.
[9] Leonard: "The Lower Niger and Its Tribes," Introduction, p. xi.

the ordinary wants of men.[10] But throughout Africa the creator is supposed to be absent and indifferent to his people, having left them to the spirits.

*Belief in Spirits.* It thus arises that the second constituent element in African religion is spirits. These are of three kinds. First, spirits conterminous with God, having always existed, but never considered quite equal to God. Second, spirits created by God, but seemingly playing a very small part in the thinking or religion of the African. And third, spirits which are the souls of departed men. Speaking of these spirits, Mary Kingsley says: "Their number is infinite and their powers varied as human imagination can make them." [11] "Individual spirits of the same class vary in power; some are strong of their sort, some weak." [12]

*Each Person Has Two Spirits.* Each human being has two spirits, one the soul spirit, the other the body spirit. The spirit which corresponds to our conception of the soul lives after death, but the body spirit dies with the body. Dr. Nassau thinks this false conception of a double spirit has caused not a few Africans to be buried before they are dead, for when the sick one becomes unconscious the natives think he is dead, and only the body spirit is there shaking and troubling the body. He tells of such supposedly dead persons coming to consciousness on the way to the grave, and others having roused themselves in their death struggle to sitting postures in their shallow graves where they have barely been covered by a thin layer of dirt.[13] There seems also to be a belief in a dream soul which can wander at will even while the person is alive.

*Placating the Spirits.* When a man dies his spirit adds itself to that innumerable company of spirits which fill the world about us. The spirit needs food and care just as it did in its human incarnation, save that it now only consumes the essence of the food, leaving the visible or material food, which is eaten by the natives. A hut is built for the spirit of the departed man and food is regularly taken and left by the relatives. "I have seen in these sacred huts a dish of boiled plantain or a plate of fish. This food is generally not removed until spoiled. Sometimes, where the gift is a very large one, a feast is made; people and spirit are supposed to join in the festival, and nothing is left to spoil. That it is of use to the spirit is fully believed." [14] "Among the Ivani it was formerly customary, and no doubt still is, on the death of a chief or big person, to pour a couple of casks of rum or palm wine on the ground or over his grave, the idea being to

[10] Roscoe: "The Northern Bantu," Ch. 23.
[11] Kingsley: "Travels in West Africa," p. 300.
[12] *Ibid.*, p. 301.
[13] Nassau: "Fetichism in West Africa," p. 54.
[14] *Ibid.*, p. 92.

provide the departed soul with a sufficient supply of spirits for the entertainment of his ghostly visitors." [15]   In Nigeria, "It is also customary to bury implements, weapons, insignia of office, ornaments, and other articles, such as cloth, wearing apparel, plates, furniture, powder, pottery, wooden or clay images, in addition to the sacrificial victims, human and animal.  The reason given in explanation of this custom is, as has already been pointed out, that while the former are for the use of the departed soul in spirit-land, the latter are his personal attendants." [16]   Among the Inaku of the Niger valley it is customary to bury the chiefs inside the village, to build a hut over the grave, "which is always swept and kept clean, and offerings of food and medicines are regularly placed in two holes which are made in front of the mound." [17]

*American Survivals.*  The writer has found a survival of this old custom in America.  Wandering through a country cemetery in Hale county, Alabama, he noticed a number of fresh graves in the Negro section of the cemetery, and stuck into the fresh dirt of each grave mound were the half emptied bottles of medicine which the deceased had evidently been using before death. On investigation it was found that every Negro grave in the cemetery had had some such remains left on it.  Doubtless this custom is a lineal descendant from the African custom, but of course has lost its significance and probably no Negro now following it has any definite idea why he does so.  Thus does a custom far outlive its original purpose.

*Classes of Spirits.*  Nassau, writing of the West Coast, divides the spirits of departed men into five classes according to their habitat and functions.

*Inina.*  First, the inina (plural anina) of the Mpongwe tribes, called Nissim among the great Fang tribes of the interior. This is a kind of shadow spirit, or dim manifestation of the human personality.  Indeed among the Fang one's nissim, or shadow may be stolen by an enemy or may be injured by some one through stealth, in which case the person is sure to sicken and die.

*Ibambo.*  Second, the ibambo (plural abambo) which are vague beings corresponding to our idea of ghosts.  They have the capacity to become visible and this "epiphany is dreaded, not reverenced." [18]   This class of spirits seems to be very numerous and many ceremonies are performed to deliver the natives from their power.  They inhabit cemeteries, and may appear "on lonely paths in the forest by night."  The highly wrought imagination of the West African can see these terrible apparitions at every turn of

[15] Leonard: "The Lower Niger and Its Tribes," p. 166.
[16] *Ibid.*, p. 177.
[17] *Ibid.*, p. 183.
[18] Nassau: "Fetishism in West Africa," p. 65.

the road, and he lives in mental terror of them. His descendants
in America, at least the more ignorant types, have not shaken
themselves free from this same fear. It is a rare Negro who will
willingly go through a cemetery at night, and the ignorant white
man has absorbed not a little of this same superstition.

*Ombwiri.* The third class of spirits is ombwiri (plural awiri)
which correspond to the ancient dryads, each one living in a "local
rock, tree, promontory, or point of land, trespass on which by
human beings they resent." [19]   "The traveller must go by silently
or with some cabalistic invocation, with bowed or bared head, and
with some offering,—anything even a pebble. Such votive collec-
tions may be seen on many spots along the forest paths, deposited
there by the natives as an invocation of a blessing on their
journey." [20]  "The awiri are generally favorably disposed, especially to their former human relatives." [21]

*Nkinda.* A fourth class of spirits is called nkinda (plural
sinkinda). These are the souls of the common or ordinary people
as contrasted with awiri which are the souls of prominent men.
"Almost all sinkinda are evilly disposed. They come to the villages on visits to warm themselves by the kitchen fires or out of
curiosity to see what is going on, and sometimes, temporarily, to
enter into the bodies of the living, especially of their own family.
The entrance of a nkinda into a human body always sickens the
person. It may enter any one, even a child. If many of them
enter a man's body, he becomes crazy." [22]  These spirits are never
visible and hence are all the more feared by the people. They are
the spirits of disease and sickness, and often bring word of an
approaching epidemic.

Fifth, there are the Mondi. They are also spirits of sickness
and of hindering human plans. It will readily be perceived that
there are good and bad spirits, or that a particular spirit may be
good or bad according to its disposition at any particular moment.

*Origin of Evil Spirits.* In Nigeria the distinction between
good and bad spirits is accounted for more carefully. "The Ibo"
(from whom we got many of our slaves) place great faith in
the due and proper observance of the funeral ceremony, for they
are of the opinion that it enables the soul to go to God, and
to find its destination, and that without this sacred right the soul
is prevented by the other spirits from eating, or in any way
associating with them, and, in this manner, from entering into
the Creator's presence. So in this way it becomes an outcast and
a wanderer on the face of the earth, haunting houses and frequently burial grounds, or is forced perhaps to return to this

[19] Nassau: "Fetichism in West Africa," p. 67.
[20] *Idem.*
[21] *Ibid.,* p. 68.
[22] *Ibid.,* p. 69.

world in the form or body of some animal." [23]    Among the Ibo
a ghost is always one of these wandering spirits.    Such spirits are
supposed to form a class of demons though it is believed that
other spirits may return to earth to do evil to human beings.
Since proper funeral ceremonies determine the destiny and hence
character of the spirit as benevolent or malevolent, much emphasis is placed on these ceremonies.    Many a family spends all
its earthly fortune on making these rites elaborate, and not infrequently a period of mourning leaves a crushing debt upon the
family.

*Spirits and Proper Burial.*    I have no particle of doubt that
this punctiliousness about proper burial, accounts to some extent
for the terrible dread of many an ignorant Negro in the South,
lest when he dies he may not have a proper and decent burial.
As I have remarked before, customs cling to us long after their
origin has been forgotten and when they really have no meaning
whatever save that of a vague fear lest the breaking of the custom
will in some way bring harm.    A complete record of the effort of
the poorer class of Negroes to carry burial insurance would make
both an interesting and a heart-rending story.    Almost every
Negro of the poorer class carries such insurance, and has a superstitious dread lest there may be some slip and he fail to have
proper burial.    Of course one must take account of the pride of
even the poorer Negroes in being able to provide their own burial.
Some of the shrewder and less scrupulous of the race have
made comfortable fortunes out of this haunting fear of their kind.

*Return of the Spirits.*    The spirits may return in the form of
animals to plague and harm their family or their enemies.    Nassau
tells us of a man whose banana grove was being destroyed by a
bull elephant.    When asked why he did not kill the intruder, the
African said he feared to because he believed the spirit of his
"grandfather had taken up his abode in that animal."    It is, therefore, highly desirable that the spirits of the departed shall go away
and leave the family unmolested.    Therefore, when a person dies,
horns are blown, bells are rung, pans are beaten, mourners shout
aloud, pleading that the spirits will go away and leave the relatives
unmolested.    Describing the death of a chief's brother, Weeks
says: "The men fired off guns to frighten away evil spirits, to
give expression to their sorrow, and to inform the spirits in the
great mysterious forest town, whither all the spirits of the dead
go, that a great man was coming to join them." [24]    Leonard says
that the Aboh people (a branch of the Ibo in the Niger delta) are
skeptical about the efficacy of noise in driving away spirits, but
this he thinks is "more or less a solitary exception," "for go where

[23] Leonard: "The Lower Niger and Its Tribes," p. 142.
[24] Weeks: "Congo Life and Folklore," p. 23.

we will all over the delta, the strongest evidence in favor of the existence of the contrary belief is to be seen in the very practical demonstration of it in almost every community." [25]  "Of one tribe in the upper course of the Ogowe, I was told, who, in their intense fear of ghosts, and their dread of the possible evil influence of the spirits of their own dead relatives, sometimes adopt a horrible plan for preventing their return. With a very material idea of a spirit, they seek to disable it by beating the corpse until every bone is broken. The mangled mass is hung in a bag at the foot of a tree in the forest. Thus mutilated, the spirit is supposed to be unable to return to the village, to entice into its fellowship of death any of the survivors." [26]

Living thus in the presence of multitudes of spirits, which are disembodied and therefore ubiquitous, and which seem to retain their consciousness and memories of past experiences, the Negro is in constant terror lest he may be harmed by some spirit, whom he may have injured while in embodied human form. This constant element of fear has wrought greatly upon the emotions of the Negro as we shall see later, thus explaining in part his highly emotional temperament.

*Fetich in Religion.* The third constituent element in African religion is fetich.

If one's God is an absentee God, having left one to the mercy of the spirits, and if one is surrounded by multitudes of such spirits, good or bad, which may do one good or work one great harm, it would be the natural bent of the human mind to find a way to establish friendly relations with the good spirits and to ward off the power of evil spirits. This the African does through his system of fetich. A fetich is any rag, string, stick, tooth, piece of wood, shell, hair or what not, in which a spirit has been coaxed to take up its abode. The material object may be entirely useless and worthless, for the spirit abiding there is the only item of importance, and indeed it is sometimes thought that the more insignificant the material object the greater will be the manifest power of the spirit. Every man, therefore, must provide himself with a fetich or fetiches, for he must have a separate spirit to help him in each particular undertaking. He must have a special fetich for hunting, usually made with some combination of the flesh and horns or hair of the animal which he desires to kill. He must have another fetich for journeying, which is made in the light of the possible dangers that await him in travel, and the securing of the appropriate charm to meet such dangers. There is a fetich for war also, for victory does not depend on courage alone, but on the power of one's fetich. In these charms the natives have

[25] Leonard: "The Lower Niger and Its Tribes," p. 148.
[26] Nassau: "Fetichism in West Africa," p. 234.

absolute confidence, but if in the beginning of the battle, many of their comrades are killed, they will retire at once, acknowledging that their medicine did not work.  There are fetiches for trading, for sickness, for loving, for fishing and for every other activity of life.  All of these fetiches have something of the element of sympathetic magic in them.  Like produces like is the fundamental principle.  If you want a fetich, which will harm another man, get a hair from his head, or a nail paring, or anything else that belongs to him, and you are sure to have power over him.  If a woman wants to make a man love her, she scrapes a bit of skin from the sole of her foot and together with certain other mixtures she puts it into the food she cooks for him and it is sure to have the desired effect. Sympathetic magic is practiced by almost all primitive peoples everywhere.

*Powerless Fetiches.*  If your project fails, it is because your fetich was not strong enough.  Some other stronger spirit has overcome yours.  If you failed in war, your enemy had the stronger fetich.  You may cast yours away and get another in the hope that this time you will be fortunate enough to get the stronger one.  If the spirit leaves the material object then the wood or stone is useless.  So long as the spirit remains there is power in the fetich.  The native, "addresses his prayer to it, and extols its virtues; but should his enterprise not prosper, he will cast his deity aside as useless, and cease to worship it.  He will address it with torrents of abuse, and will even beat it to make it serve him better.  It is a deity at his disposal, to serve in the accomplishment of his desires; the individual keeps gods of his own to help him in his undertakings." [27]

*White and Black Art.*  "So long as these fetiches are used simply for protection, the owner is a practicer of white art, but, when they are used to injure others or force others to do certain things pleasing to the owner of the fetich, their possessor is said to practice black art.  It is this latter that keeps the African native in constant fear.  At any hour his enemy may by witchcraft destroy his property, rob him of his friends or take his life. All that an enemy has to do is to get some of his victim's hair, his nails, or water in which he has bathed, and have a witch doctor make a concoction which, buried in front of the victim's door or secretly hung in his room, will bring sure death.  If the man dies, this black art has worked; if he fails to die, then he himself has a fetich stronger than the spirit that was trying to induce his death.  In this murderous superstition the natives have absolute confidence." [28]  To ward off evil, an African child, on

[27] Menzies: "History of Religion," p. 32.
[28] Weatherford: "Negro Life in the South," pp. 123-124.

the day of its birth, has a string tied around its body with a fetich attachment of bones, teeth, or some other appropriate object.

*Present Day Charms.*   The lineal descendant of this custom is the tooth, the asafedita bag or some other charm hung around the necks of thousands of Southern Negro children, and as I have observed more than once around the necks of many ignorant white children.   The rabbit foot and the buckeye, carried by men, look back to the fetich for their meaning.   The African rarely ever attributes death to natural causes.   Immediately when one is taken sick or dies, the family begins the hunt for the evil person who has bewitched the unfortunate one, and soon enough the culprit is located.   They are murdered or sometimes given the poison ordeal which is usually effective in proving their guilt, for they die, and is not that positive proof that they were guilty?   This puts a tremendous power of revenge into the hands of unscrupulous rulers, for they can easily get a charge against any person whom they fear or hate.   This murderous custom undoubtedly accounts for part of the retardation of African life and civilization.   As soon as any man showed any leadership or dared to go against any custom however foolish or harmful, he was put to the ordeal, and eliminated.   Thus, all possible leadership was systematically killed off and only those who were willing to tread the beaten path and follow the established customs could live. Follow this process of elimination of leadership for centuries and who could wonder at their belated civilization.

*A Case of Witch Trial.*   In his "Congo-Life and Folklore," Weeks gives one of the finest illustrations of the way in which this superstitious procedure eliminates the strong.   Satu, the chief had died and of course his followers wanted to know who had bewitched him.   A witch finder from a neighboring village was sent for and Mavakala, the brother of Satu, was declared guilty. "What had Mavakala done to draw such an accusation upon himself?   On his brother's death he had cried as long and as loudly as any of them; he had neglected his person, worn old clothes, dressed his hair in mourning fashion, gone unwashed, and had carefully observed all the usual ceremonies of 'crying' for a near relative, and yet they charged him with bewitching his brother to death.   Yes, all his neighbors recalled these facts, but they interpreted them now in the light of this serious charge.   Of course, he had observed all these rites simply to deceive them.   He must have thought them fools to be duped by his proofs and protestations.   No, he must take the ordeal, and that quickly, and the ordeal-giver must be sent for immediately.   The whole of Mavakala's family was alienated from him, for was he not accused of the most heinous crime of which a human being can be guilty— witchcraft?

"What had Mavakala done to render himself so fatally unpopular? That evening the declaration of the witch-finder was discussed round all the fires, and as Bakula went from group to group I picked up many items of the indictment.

*The Ambitious Are Eliminated.* "Mavakala was an energetic, successful trader, and from each trading journey he came back the richer for his enterprise. They were jealous of his wealth; but among themselves they whispered that his increased riches were really due to witchcraft and not to his ability; and were not their suspicions justified, for was he not now accused of selling his brother's corpse to the white traders.

"I heard, too, that Mavakala was a skilled blacksmith, and had made good knives out of odd pieces of hoop iron taken from old cases, and bought, by him, from traders on the river. and had even made hoes and axes out of old bale iron. Many other clever things he had done, all of which were now by these superstitious people accepted as proofs of his witchcraft. He had awakened their jealousy by his energy and smartness in business; his skill and ingenuity in smithing had aroused their suspicions, and his prosperity had provoked their hatred. In any other country his ability would have been admired and honored, but on the Congo it was a sign of witchcraft, and always ended in death by the ordeal.

*Witchcraft Retards Progress.* "It was then I understood the reason for the backwardness of these people. They destroy their leaders and their best men, and the only hope of the people is deliverance from the curse of the witch-doctors.

"The next day the ordeal-giver (or ngol'a nkasa) arrived, bringing with him the ordeal bark which he had procured from the nkasa tree in the following manner. This tree is supposed to have a spirit; hence, when they are about to cut some of its bark for ordeal purposes, they address it in these words: 'I come to take a piece of your bark, and if the man for whom it is intended is a witch, let my machet bend when I strike you; but if he is not a witch, let my machet enter into you, and let the wind stop blowing.' The machet had not bent under the blow, and the omen being against Mavakala the ordeal-giver made his preparations with smug satisfaction.

*The Ordeal of Poison.* "Mavakala, accompanied by many of the men and lads of the town, was led to the bare top of a neighboring hill, where a rough shanty of palm fronds was built. The accused was pushed into this, and told to stretch out his arms, and not to touch anything. The ordeal-giver pushed a stone towards the poor wretch, with twenty-seven pieces of nkasa bark on it; and then he ground each piece of bark and slowly fed Mavakala with the powders.

"During the process the accused man vomited three times, and should therefore have been set free and carried back to the town with shouts of honor; but was not the omen against him? and besides, was he not obnoxious to his jealous and superstitious neighbors?

"Consequently, when the ordeal-giver proposed that further tests should be applied, there were none to lift up their voices in protest against the injustice of continuing the cruelty.

"Mavakala was dazed with the narcotic effects of the drug that had been forced on him, and his wits were dulled and muddled. He was taken with rough hands from the temporary hut and made to stand by himself, a swaying, lonely, pathetic figure—a type of all those who have been persecuted or have laid down their lives for the sole crime of being in the vanguard of their generation.

"While Mavakala stood swaying there, six twigs in rapid succession were thrown at his feet, and he as quickly had to name the trees to which they belonged.  This he did successfully, and then he was told to name the birds and butterflies that were sailing by.  Again he unerringly gave each its proper name; but now, just when he wanted his eyes to be at their keenest, he could feel them becoming blurred with the drug he had been forced to take. His tormentors called on him to name the ants crawling at his feet.  He faltered, stammered confusedly, and in stooping, that his poor, hazy eyes might have a better chance to recognize them, he fell, with a moaning cry, to the ground.

"In an instant the heartless, superstitious crowd was on him; sticks and machets, knives and guns, soon did their work on the poor mangled body.  None was too poor or mean to kick his carcass and spit in his face, and his bruised, gory corpse was left unburied upon the bare hill-top—a feast for the beasts of the forests and the birds of the air." [29]

*The Witch Doctor.*  The fourth element in religion among the Africans is the witch doctor or medicine man, so called because he concocts the fetich which is used to cure sickness and drive away evil spirits which cause disease.  He is almost as powerful as the chief himself since he has the power of life or death over every member of the tribe—except only the chief.  Through their ceremonies they decide all questions of guilt, by their ordeal they may murder whom they will, they charge large fees for their services and woe to any one who fails to pay or in any way incurs their enmity.  Describing the witch finder referred to in the preceding paragraph, Weeks says: "I have noticed that he was a small, active man with keen piercing eyes that seemed to jump from face to face and read the very thoughts of those who stood around.  He was dressed in the soft skins of monkeys and bushcats; around his neck was a necklace of rats' teeth mixed with

[29] Weeks: "Congo Life and Folklore," pp. 53-57.

the teeth of crocodiles and leopards. His body was decorated with pigments of different colors; thick circles of white surrounded the eyes, a patch of red ran across the forehead, broad strips of yellow chased each other down the cheeks, bands of red and yellow went up the arms and across the chest, and spots of blue promiscuously filled in the vacant spaces. At the different points of his curious dress were bells that tinkled at every movement. The boys looked at him in deep awe, the girls and women cowered away from him, and the men, though they feared him, greeted him with a simulated friendliness that ill-accorded with their nervousness.

"On the appointed day a great crowd gathered. No member of the clan was absent, except those on trading expeditions. The assembled people formed a great circle, into the middle of which the witch-finder danced and chanted to the beat of the drums. It was a hot day and the sun poured down its scorching rays on the performer, making him perspire so profusely that the various colors on his face and body ran into each other, adding grotesqueness to his ugliness.

"As he pranced and danced up and down the circle he put question after question, and was answered by the people with ndungu, or otuama, as he guessed wrongly or rightly about the dead man's ways.

"Presently he elicited the fact that the deceased had had a very bad quarrel with some one, and then he discovered that it was with a man in the town. By crafty questions the witch-doctor narrowed the circle of examination, the people, all excitement, really helping him though quite unaware that they did so; and at last, in a fandango of whirling skins and rotating arms and legs, he brought himself to a standstill in front of one of the men, and accused him of being the person who had bewitched the late chief to death." [30]

*Power of the Witch Doctors.* These monsters thus hold the entire community in constant fear of them and according to their superstitious wisdom measure out life or death. They undoubtedly believe in their own work, or at least are self-deceived—though they do not scruple to use their office to their own advantage.

*Constituent Elements in African Religion.* These then are the constituent elements of African religion, an absentee God, who created men and then left them; innumerable spirits that must be placated; fetiches which are used to ward off evil and work harm to enemies; and the witch doctor, partly honest, partly selfish, who holds the destiny of human life in his keeping. Such a religion has little or no moral power. Lying seems to be very

[30] Weeks: "Congo Life and Folklore," pp. 49-50, 51-52.

common, petty stealing is constantly practiced, sex immorality is disgustingly common. Cruelty to man and animal is so brutal and unvarnished that it sickens one. Witchcraft murder is a daily occurrence. All these and more are the outgrowth of the terrible fetich system, which paralyzes all ideals, and releases in every man something of the wild beast which fights to preserve its life. An absentee God is not calculated to produce strenuous moral life. If God has gone away into the corner of the universe of what avail are moral standards? To outwit the spirits is the final goal of life and if one outwit a few of his neighbors in passing so much the greater his victory.

*Influence of Absentee God.* Absentee landlordism is no better in religion than in farming, and he who has an absentee god is sure to have a loose standard of morals and a religion without much moral content. It is from absenteeism that much of the Negro religion of today is suffering and one has seen more than one white man who prayed on his knees on Sunday and preyed on his neighbors on Monday, all because his religion had no present or immanent God in it.

*African Prayer.* Prayer is a small item of religion in Africa. "Ejaculatory prayer, however, is made constantly, in the uttering of cabalistic words, phrases, or sentences adopted by or assigned to almost every one by parent or doctor. They are uttered by all ages and both sexes at any time, as a defence from evil, on all sorts of occasions,—e.g., when one sneezes, stumbles, or is otherwise startled, etc." [31] A father whose son had been wounded and was bleeding to death, "ran out of the hut, wildly gesticulating towards the sky, saying 'Go away! go away! O ye spirits! why do you come to kill my son?' and he continued for some time in a strain of alternate pleading and protestation.

"In another case I saw a woman who rushed into the street adjuring the spirits, and in the next breath humbly supplicating them, who, she said, were vexing her child that was lying in convulsions.

"Observe that while these were distinctly prayers, appeals for mercy, pathetic, agonizing protestations, there was no praise, no love, no thanks, no confession of sin,—only a long, pitiful deprecation of evil." [32]

*Little Moral Power.* Religion, therefore, among the African tribes has little moral lifting power, has almost no power of inspiration or consolation, but rather plunges the native into a pit of fatalism and utter despair. It not only robs the individual of hope but it robs the tribe of leadership by eliminating all who show initiative and capacity to move out of the beaten paths.

[31] Nassau: "Fetichism in West Africa," p. 98.
[32] *Idem.*

Religion has thus been a power in favor of stagnation, retarding the development of the peoples of this dark continent.

*Fetich as Government.* But fetich is not only a religion—it is a form of government, or perhaps one would best say it is used as the central power in a form of government. In Africa control is maintained largely through fear (as indeed our prisons and electrocutions in America show we undertake to control by fear, but fail) and all punishment is retributory and not reformatory. "In the native African tribal forms of government, while it would not be true to say that there is no justice in the customs they recognize, it is true that the only sentiment appealed to, in the enforcement and even in the enactment of supposed needed measures, is that of fear. Their religion being one of fear, it is therefore appealed to to lend its sanction and aid.

"Fetiches are set up to punish offenders in certain cases where there is an intention to make a law specially binding; this refers more particularly to crimes which cannot always be detected. A fetich is inaugurated, for example, to detect and punish certain kinds of theft; persons who are cognizant of such crimes, and who do not give information, are also liable to be punished by the fetich. The fetich is supposed to be able not only to detect all such transgressions, but has power, likewise, to punish the transgressor. How it exercises this knowledge, or by what means it brings sickness and death upon the offender, cannot, of course, be explained; but, as it is believed in, it is the most effectual restraint that can possibly be imposed upon evil-disposed persons.

*Ukuku.* "Among the Negro tribes of the Bight of Benin and the Bantu of the region of Corisco Island and of the Ogowe River, in what is now the Kongo-Français, there was a power known variously as Egbo, Ukuku, and Yasi, which tribes, native chiefs, and headmen of villages invoked as a court of last appeal, for the passage of needed laws, or the adjudication of some quarrel which an ordinary family or village council was unable to settle.

"In those councils an offender could be proved guilty of a debt or theft, or other trespass, and when it was no longer possible for him by audacity or mendacity to persist in his assertion of innocence, he would yield to the decision of the great majority against him. But there was no central government to enforce that decision or exact from him restitution. The only authority the native chiefs possessed was based on respect due to age, parental position, or strength of personal character. If an offender chose to disregard all these considerations, an appeal was then made to his superstitious fear.

*Mystery of Ukuku.* "Egbo, Ukuku, Yasi, was a secret society composed only of men, boys being initiated into it about the age of puberty. Members were bound by a terrible oath and under pain of death to obey any law or command issued by the spirit under which the society professed to be organized. The actual, audible utterance of the command was by the voice of one of the members of the society chosen as priest for that purpose. This man, secreted in the forest, in a clump of bushes on the outskirts of the village, or in one of the rooms of the Council House, disguised his voice, speaking only gutturally. The whole proceeding was an immense fiction; they believed in spirits and in the power of fetich charms, and they made such charms part of the society's ceremonies; but, as to the decisions, all the members knew that the decision in any case was their own, not a spirit's. They knew that the voice speaking was that of their delegate, not of a spirit. Yet for any one of them, or for any woman, girl, or uninitiated boy, to assert as much would have been death. And those men who would not have submitted to the same decision if arrived at in open council of themselves as men, and known before the whole village to be speaking only as men, would instantly submit when once the case had been taken to Ukuku's Court. They carried out that fiction all their lives. Let a man order his wives and other slaves to clear the overgrown village paths, they might hesitate to obey by inventing some excuse that they were too much occupied with other work, or that they would do it only when other people who also used the same path should assist; or if under the sting of a kasa-nguvu (lash of hippopotamus hide or manatus skin) they started to do the work, they might do it only partly or very unsatisfactorily. But let the man call in the other men of the village and summon a meeting of the society, the recalcitrants would submit instantly, and in terror of Ukuku's voice; much as they might possibly have suspected it was a human voice, they would not dare whisper the suspicion. They helped to carry on a gigantic lie. They taught their little children, both girls and boys, that the voice belonged to a spirit which ate people who disobeyed him. When the society walked in procession to or from their appointed rendezvous a crier with kasa-nguvu in hand, warned all on the path of the coming of the spirit. Women and children hastened to get out of the way; or, if unable to hide in time, they averted their faces. The penalty when a woman even saw the procession was a severe beating." [33]

"Like all government intended for the benefit and protection of the governed, Ukuku, when it happened to throw its power on the side of right, was occasionally an apparent blessing. It could end tribal quarrels and proclaim and enforce peace where no individual chief or king would have been able to accomplish the same result." [34]

[33] Nassau: "Fetichism in West Africa," pp. 139-141.
[34] *Ibid.*, p. 145.

If some group or individual seemed to be acting out of harmony with the best interest of the community, Ukuku could proclaim a boycott and starve or force the recalcitrant member or members into harmony.  It thus by inspiring superstitious fear was able to exert a very powerful influence.

*Women's Njembe Societies.*  In like manner the women have a secret society called Njembe, the power of which rests in its threat to use fetich medicines to enforce its mandates.  Young girls are initiated into this society through the most exacting and trying rights.  No white person has ever witnessed the ceremonies, but observation of the young women who came back from the bush after this two weeks' debauch proves that the ordeal of initiation must be terrible.  No native man has ever been able so far as investigators can find out to learn the secrets of the society.  "The object of the institution originally, no doubt, was to protect the females from harsh treatment on the part of their husbands." [35]

*Fetich and Family Life.*  Fetich also controls all family life.  Solidarity of the family and responsibility of all members for the acts of each and every member is the fundamental of African life.  This plan of organization applies also to the tribe which is only an enlarged family in which every one is related to every other one.  Thus if a member of one tribe murders a person from another tribe, the injured tribe is not at all particular about murdering in return the identical criminal, any member of the offending tribe will do just as well, for a tribe or a family is a unity and injury to one member is injury to all.  This family solidarity is fostered by respect for the family fetich which is only a degraded form of ancestor worship.  In the Niger delta in particular adoration of ancestral spirits is the prevailing form of religion.  "Every freeman is attended by a guardian spirit, usually in such cases where the latter has been an influential chief or a man of substance." [36]  In the New Calibar section, this ancestral spirit is supposed to dwell in the Duen-Fubara, i.e., image representing the head and shoulders of the deceased.  "This, which is carved out of wood and painted with different dyes, in imitation of the face and head, surmounts a large wooden base or tray that, as a rule, is placed in a recess.  On this tray, and surrounding the heads are horns, glasses, pots, chairs, and as many articles of this description as can be crammed on to it, arranged for the evident use of the spirit hereafter.

*Fetich and Worship of the Dead.*  In front of each pedestal three rudely made altars of mud are erected, with a hole in the middle of each, for the purpose of throwing food and libations that are constantly offered to the presiding spirits, who, it is

[35] Nassau: "Fetichism in West Africa," p. 250.
[36] Leonard: "The Lower Niger and Its Tribes," p. 190.

believed, eat and drink of them." [37] The ceremony of bringing this "Duen-fubara" from the sacred village of its manufacture to the hut of the deceased is very elaborate, and shows the seriousness of the belief in the custom.

*Family Fetich as Ancestor Worship.* Lower down the west coast this ancestor worship becomes more crude and revolting. Here the fetich is made of portions of the body of the deceased tied up in a bag and hung in the hut. "In the Benga tribe, just north of the equator, in West Africa, this family fetich is known by the name of Yaka. It is a bundle of parts of the bodies of their dead. From time to time as their relatives die, the first joints of their fingers and toes, especially including their nails, a small clipping from a lobe of the ear, and perhaps snippings of hair are added to it. But the chief constituents are the finger ends. This form descends by inheritance with the family. This is distinctly an ancestor worship." [38]

"This belief, however much of superstition it involves, exerts a very powerful influence upon the social character of the people. It establishes a bond of affection between the parent and the child much stronger than could be expected among a people wholly given up to heathenism. It teaches the child to look up to the parents, not only as its earthly protector, but as a friend in the spirit land. It strengthens the bonds of the filial affection, and keeps up a lively impression of a future state of being. The living prize the aid of the dead, and it is not uncommon to send messages to them by some one who is on the point of dying; and so greatly is this aid prized by the living that I have known an aged mother, to avoid the presence of her sons, lest she should by some secret means be dispatched prematurely to the spirit world, for the double purpose of easing of the burden of taking care of her, and securing for themselves more effective aid than she could render them in this world." [39]

*Belief in Spirits Restricts African Life.* The belief in innumerable spirits hedges about the daily life of the African with a thousand fears and prohibitions. If he starts on a journey and stumps his toe he had best turn back for this is a warning of sure failure. If a rat runs across your road and away from you it is good luck, but if it runs toward you you had best return home for it is a sign of the certain failure of your journey. If you see the brown bird, Mvia, crying "via, via," which means witch-palaver, you will certainly come to a bad end and may be burned as a witch. If a Nkuku bird crosses your path you will surely have bad luck. If an owl cries Kulu (spirit of the departed) near your camp at night, surely one of your party will

[37] Leonard: "The Lower Niger and Its Tribes," pp. 162-163.
[38] Nassau: "Fetichism in West Africa," p. 159.
[39] Quoted by Nassau, p. 166, from Wilson's "Western Africa."

die. The life of the native is so hedged about that one wonders how they ever accomplish anything. The survivals of these crude superstitions are not uncommon in the South. The author once knew a very competent country physician who, if a rabbit crossed the road in front of him from right to left, would invariably get off his horse and make a cross mark to prevent ill luck. He knew well an intelligent woman of pure Scotch blood, who believed firmly that an owl hooting on the comb of your roof at night was a sure messenger of death, for had it not happened thus twice in her own family before the loss of two children? Thus does the superstition of primitive man affect the life of our own land.

*Spirits and Sacred Ceremonies.* Marriage, birth and funeral ceremonies are all controlled by the natives' attitude toward the spirits. Thus if twins were born among the Calabar natives, it was an evil omen and the children were immediately put to death. In some other sections of the country, twins were not considered monstrosities, nor were they put to death, but ceremonies preventive of bad luck were punctiliously performed. In the delta of the Niger "the advent of twins is looked on in every home, not only with horror and detestation, but as an evil and a curse that is bound to provoke the domestic gods to anger and to retribution." [40] The birth of twins is supposed to be unnatural and due to the influence of evil spirits.

*Fear of Twins.* "In most cases the mothers, who are looked upon as unclean, are driven out of the town and into the bush, and unless given protection by the people of another community, or surreptitiously fed by some old crony, they often fare as badly as their off-spring, whom they look upon as the work of evil spirits." [41] Among certain other tribes the mother was isolated for sixteen days and was taboo to all persons save a few old women set apart to provide them with food and drink. After the sixteen days they underwent a ceremony of purification after which they were received back into their families. [42] Among some tribes mothers of twins are perpetually taboo, and are sent to live in a special village set apart for the use of all who are thus unfortunate—the place being called "twin town." These unfortunate women can only be visited by members of their family after elaborate sacrifices have been offered. [43] If one of the twins dies, a wooden image is substituted in its place, among certain tribes, some say, that the remaining twin may not be lonely, but it seems quite evident that the custom is the outgrowth of some superstitious fear. It is thought by some that the image is there, so that

[40] Leonard: "The Lower Niger and Its Tribes," p. 458.
[41] *Ibid.*, p. 459.
[42] *Ibid.*, p. 459.
[43] *Ibid.*, p. 460.

the spirit of the dead child, should it return, may enter into the wooden substitute instead of injuring the living child.

*Taboo—Its Origin and Power.* Taboo is another outgrowth of primitive superstition. The word is Polynesian in origin and means anything that is "strongly marked." The institution of taboo seems to be practically universal. "Things are taboo which are thought to be dangerous to handle or to have to do with: things "holy" and things "unclean" are alike taboo; the dead body, the new born child; blood and the shedder of blood; the divine king as well as the criminal; the sick, outcasts, and foreigners; animals as well as men; women especially, the married women as well as the sacred virgin; food, clothes, vessels, property, house, bed, canoes, the threshing floor, the winnowing fan; a name, a word, a day; all are or may be taboo because dangerous."[44] Taboo objects may injure one not only by being handled, but simply by being seen. The name of Jehovah in the Old Testament was taboo because sacred and for like reason it was said no person could see Jehovah and live. Among certain African natives the king may not be seen by the common people. To see him is certain death. Sometimes his feet alone may be seen, which Leonard thinks may account in part for the adoration of the feet of the Papal Pontiff and kissing of the feet of the images of saints.[45] Among the Northern Bantus, in the vicinity of Lake Victoria, the king lives in complete seclusion. He is fed from the milk of a sacred herd, and the milkman of this herd must be in perfect physical condition and is dedicated to his task. The milkman's hands must not touch the vessel into which he milks, and each vessel from which the king drinks must be immediately broken, because taboo. When the sacred herd is driven to and from the pasture, the herdsman shouts aloud to all men and women to hide themselves in the grass, lest looking upon the herd—sacred to the king—would kill them.[46]

*Illustrations of Taboo.* Ellis tells us that on the slave coast persons who touch the sacred pithon are thereby rendered taboo and must serve this god the rest of their lives. He further tells us that to make an oath binding the one swearing is caused to eat something that pertains to the deity, leaves gathered from a sacred spot or berries which are sacred to the deity. This reminds one of the custom still prevalent in courts today of making the witness kiss the Bible to bind his oath, thus bringing sacredness and solemnity to the obligation. Anything which has been dedicated to the spirits or to a chief is sacred or taboo. Thus in the New Testament Christ told the scribes and Pharisees that they

---

[44] Jevons: "Introduction to the History of Religion," p. 59.
[45] Leonard: "The Lower Niger and Its Tribes," p. 372.
[46] Roscoe: "The Northern Bantu," p. 9 f., passim.

dedicated their goods to God in order to be freed from sharing it with their parents.[47]    Food prepared for a chief is taboo and no native African will touch it.    Jevons quotes from Frazier's Golden Bough, a case of a New Zealand slave eating the remains of a dinner left by his chief.    He was unaware that it was a part of his chief's food, but when told the facts was immediately seized with convulsions and died a few hours later.[48]

*Taboo and the Evil Eye.*    To be seen by one who is taboo may bring great harm, to the person seen.    African maidens who for one reason or another were taboo were forced to wear broad brimmed hats to keep them from seeing and thus polluting many objects.    Umbrellas were carried over kings to keep them from injuring by sight those whom they might otherwise see.    The evil eye is the lineal descendant of this idea of taboo.    "The evil eye," says Sumner,[49] "is a concrete dogma and a primary inference from demonism."    This doctrine of the evil eye is akin to the old Greek idea of Nemesis.    Those who were specially lucky or prosperous were envied by the demons, and hence afflicted with calamity. "In the Sudan food is usually covered by a conical straw cover to prevent the evil eye.    Customs of eating and drinking in private and of covering the mouth when eating or drinking, belong here."[50]    The author has personally known many Negroes who firmly believed their bad luck, sickness or other handicaps came directly from some one who had as they call it—'put an evil eye on them.'

Strangers are taboo, because they belong to a different group and bring with them different spiritual powers.    Hence, it is not wise or proper to eat with them.    Ethnocentrism, or accentuation of the customs of one's own group over against the customs of other groups, arises out of this attitude toward strangers, and has had much to do with the growth of racial antagonisms.    "Unless we are going to ascribe division into castes to primitive society, we have in them a clear case of the growth of taboo, and of its extension by analogy; the members of the inferior caste are treated by the superior castes as criminals were treated by primitive society; outcasts are, like outlaws, taboo—eating especially, must be avoided "with publicans and sinners."[51]

*Taboo and the Dead.*    A corpse is peculiarly taboo.    "Immediately after death any cloth which the deceased was wearing is taken away, the corpse is washed, the limbs are straightened and dressed in the best cloth.    The persons who perform this office are regarded as unclean, and obliged to purify themselves before

[47] Mark 7:11.
[48] Jevons: "Introduction to the History of Religion," p. 83.
[49] Sumner: "Folkways," p. 515.
[50] *Ibid.,* p. 516.
[51] Jevons: "Introduction to the History of Religion," p. 73.

they can become clean again.  For to touch a dead body, or to have anything to do with a grave, is considered a pollution, and it is unlucky for a man to come into a house with the dirt of the grave upon his person." [52]  A superstitious awe and dread in the presence of a corpse is seen all over Africa, indeed a certain amount of this feeling is to be found all over the world.  But in Africa this natural dread is greatly heightened by the belief that the spirit of the departed man is lingering near by and may do harm to those who are in attendance.  In connection with burial ceremonies, Dr. Nassau tells us: "The digging of the grave, the carrying of the coffin, and the closing of the grave are all done only by men.  When these have finished the work of burial, they are in great fear, and are to run rapidly to the village, or to the nearest body of water, river or lake or sea.  If in their running one should trip and fall, it is a sign that he will soon die.  They plunge into the water as a means of purification from possible defilement.  The object of this purification is not simply to cleanse the body, but to remove the presence or contact of the spirit of the dead man or any other spirit or possible evil influence, lest they should have ill luck in their fishing, hunting and other work." [53]

*Taboo a Form of Reverence.*  Taboo did not originate out of a reasoning process, but was an *a priori* judgment, based on reverence and fear, felt in the presence of spirits about which primitive men knew little.  This sense of fear and reverence became one of the mightiest social factors in moulding primitive society.  To begin with, taboo was probably the first form of criminal law.  Thus, the king may declare a certain piece of property taboo and no one would dare trespass upon it.

*Taboo and Impiety.*  "In the oldest type of society," says Robertson Smith, impious acts or breaches of taboo were the only offences treated as crimes, e.g., there is no such crime as theft, but a man can save his property from invasion by placing it under a taboo, when it becomes an act of impiety to touch it.  I believe that in early society we may safely affirm that every offence to which death or outlawry is attached was primarily viewed as a breach of holiness, e.g., murder within the kin, and incest are breaches of the holiness of the tribal blood, which would be supernaturally avenged if men overlooked them.  Among the Hebrews such taboos are created by means of a curse (Judg. 17:2) and by the same means a king can give validity to the most unreasonable decrees.  (1 Sam. 14:24 f.).  But unreasonable taboos, as we see in the case of Saul and Jonathan, are sure to be evaded in the long run, because public opinion goes against them, whereas

[52] Leonard: "The Lower Niger and Its Tribes," p. 174.
[53] Nassau: "Fetichism in West Africa," pp. 218-219.

taboos that make for the general good and check wrong-doing are supported and enforced by the community, and ultimately pass into laws with a civil sanction. But no ancient society deemed its good order to be sufficiently secured by civil sanctions alone; there was always a last recourse to the curse, the ordeal, the oath of probation at the sanctuary,—all of them a means to stamp an offender with the guilt of impiety and bring him under the direct judgment of the supernatural powers." [54] It took a very bold and reckless man therefore to break over these sanctions. They were self-vindicating. If a man did break over a taboo, the supernatural powers were not relied upon, but men immediately wreaked upon the head of the offender the necessary punishment, lest by winking at the crime, they themselves, might be included in the punishments of the higher powers. Thus, taboo becomes a species of criminal law, which was automatically executed among savage peoples. As such it must have been a great power making for law and order.

*Taboo as a Social Force.* Taboo was also a social force. Since it was transmissible or so to speak contagious, any member of the tribe who transgressed and hence became unclean, thereby laid the whole group liable to the contagion. A sense of social responsibility was thus early developed, which was a necessary prerequisite for the growth and progress of any people. Taboo also carried within itself a certain amount of moral power. Since the evil of breaking a taboo arose from the presence of a supernatural power, good or bad, which was avenging itself on the trespasser, there would of necessity arise certain ideas of the rightness or wrongness of certain acts, which would ultimately crystallize into rules of holiness or of morality. Thus again a superstition becomes a gateway to moral progress.

*Psychic Life of the African.* Closely related to the religious life of the African native is his psychic reactions. [55] Careful study reveals a great variety of mental and emotional responses, due to differences of climate, differences of occupation, differences of religious belief, density of population and numerous other factors. All Negroes are supposed to be highly emotional as compared with the self-restrained white man. They may well be so described, but there is great variety in the various tribes with respect to the expression of emotion. Again all Negroes are supposed to be musical, but there are tribes where there is little or no singing and almost no musical instruments.

*Idleness and Emotionalism.* First of all, psychological life is decidedly influenced by work. In a community where food can

---

[54] Smith: "The Religion of the Semites," p. 163.

[55] For a full study of the psychological life of the various tribes, the reader is referred to Jerome Dowd's "Negro Races," Vol. II, which is the fullest and most discriminating piece of work that has been done on this subject.

be had for the taking without any particular effort or foresight, as is the case in the Banana Zone, it would not be likely that mental capacity would develop much. There would be no process by which those who were mentally deficient would be eliminated and hence no working of the law of natural selection to weed out the unfit and incapable. We should expect then that those persons who lived in the hot climate of Africa where fruit and vegetables grew in abundance would normally be less developed mentally than those who lived in a climate where foresight and the struggle for existence favored those who had a higher degree of intelligence and eliminated all others. This is precisely what we find when we study Africa. The coast tribes of the equatorial region and the tribes of the humid river deltas have through long centuries of ease and sloth developed a race of low mentality. Not that mentality is transmissible, but that in these sections the weak have not been weeded out of the whole group has necessarily been affected. Dowd [56] quotes Woodruff to the effect that, "the general trend of increase of brain is away from the tropics." "The colder and more forbidding and unfriendly the country, the larger are the brains of the natives."

*Idleness and Mental Lethargy.* Not only did the climate and conditions unfavorable for work affect the general average of brain capacity by failure to eliminate those who could not have survived in a more unfriendly environment, it tended to leave undeveloped the brain of all those who were surviving. There can be no doubt that a man's mind develops acuteness of perception and power of analysis only under the stress of necessity. If there is no need of forethought or watchfulness of the laws of nature, the normal tendency will be toward listlessness. So that the equatorial coast developed a race of men who were not mentally alert.

*Monotony and Emotion.* Furthermore, this lack of mental stimulus had a very decided influence on emotional reactions. The lack of variety of occupation and meager mental stimulus gave rise to a monotony and mental stagnation which is conducive to high emotionalism. Where the mind has little variety of activity it develops a feeble power of self-control. The native emotions, therefore, have primary sway and are left uncontrolled by the higher and stabilizing reasoning faculties. Variety of mental life acts as a balance wheel to emotions, by the fact that it divides the control of the life. Where emotions alone hold sway it is almost certain that they will be boisterous. This law of self-control is clearly exhibited in the difference between

[56] Dowd: "The Negro Races," Vol. II, p. 70.

rural and urban peoples. In the city where there are many forces to be met and where the mind, therefore, has a great variety of subjects to which it responds, there is much less of explosive emotionalism than one usually finds in the country, where monotony of mental life has in the past at least been the rule. Sparse population and hence lack of mental contact has a similar influence on the emotional reactions. Therefore, the tribes living in the low and marshy sections of Africa, where the humidity and the heat cause dense growth and hence make communication difficult, tend to develop isolation and monotony which heighten emotional life.

*Ignorance and Monotony.* One finds this law of motonony and emotionalism illustrated again by comparison of educated and uneducated people. The educated man has learned to adjust himself to a great variety of stimuli. He has by long practice learned to face all the facts and then deliberately act in the light of reason. In other words, he has developed a variety of capacities, and consequently is the slave of no one. There is balance and poise in his life. On the contrary, the uneducated person is one who has not learned to adjust himself to a great variety of stimuli. He has not developed the mental side of his nature. His judgment is in abeyance and his native emotions are supreme. Hence an emotional appeal to an uneducated audience gets a far greater response than such an appeal to an audience of trained persons.

*Primitive Mental Traits.* Commenting on the mental traits of primitive man, Boas says, "apparently the thoughts and actions of civilized man, and those found in more primitive forms of society, prove, that in various groups of mankind, the mind responds quite differently when exposed to the same conditions. Lack of logical connections, lack of control of will, are apparently two of its fundamental characteristics in primitive society. In the formation of opinions belief takes the place of logical demonstration. The emotional value of opinions is great and consequently they quickly lead to actions." [57] Davenport [58] shows that where there is keen perception, as is the case among most primitive men, and where there is low power of logical interpretation of those perceptions, the imagination fills in the gaps between perceptions and conclusions, giving rise to fanciful images or ideas. These ideas soon harden into the most sacred beliefs. This gives basis for the wildest of superstitions which play upon the simple mind. Fear, therefore, becomes one of the dominating influences in the mental reactions of primitive peoples. Herbert Spencer made fear of the living the basis of all political control,

[57] Boas: "The Mind of Primitive Man," pp. 98-99.
[58] Davenport: "Primitive Traits in Religious Revivals," p. 14 f.

and fear of the dead the basis of all religious control. One would hesitate to accept this as final, but there can be no doubt that fear is one of the controlling factors in primitive society. "The progress from brute to man," says William James, "is character-ized by nothing so much as by the decrease in proper occasions for fear." [59] It is a commonplace of psychology that fear is one of the greatest stimulants of explosive emotions—or to be more exact, fear is itself an emotion which expresses itself in the most explosive manner.

*Causes of African Fears.* Seen from this angle, the high emotion of the West African is easily understood. What man in the world had had more to fear than has he? The wild beasts of the jungle have sprung upon him unawares, during all the centuries. The water is filled with crocodiles, the air is filled with insect pests. Malaria and disease, while unseen, lurk every-where about him and during all the centuries these have swooped down upon him unseen and robbed him of his family and friends. Besides his illogical imagination has peopled the whole earth with innumerable spirits, which compass him on every side. The witch doctor makes these evil spirits tenfold more diabolical, and even his human enemies may at any moment take his life by witch-craft. Man is completely helpless in the hands of nature, the spirits, the witch doctors and scheming enemies. His life is one long nightmare of fear, and hence his psychological reactions are characterized by the highest and most extravagant emotionalism. No people in the world could have lived under the conditions that surround the West African and developed anything else than a highly emotional life. Their emotional nature, therefore, does not indicate either inferiority or superiority. It indicates that, like all other living beings, they are capable of and have responded to the psychic environment in which they found themselves. What they are is neither to their discredit nor to their honor. It is a simple fact of human response.

*Fear and Revival Emotions.* In the light of this background one can view with a new understanding the emotional type of early revivals. Our ancestors in America were beset on every hand with dangers. The savage Indian, the beasts of the forest, the severity of a new country, the struggle for mere existence planted in their biological natures an element of fear which made them capable of turbulent emotions. The revivals of Kentucky and Tennessee in 1800 were illustrations of wild and boisterous emotionalism which would be utterly impossible now when the element of fear has been so largely removed from the life of the majority of people.

*Brain Cell Inheritance.* Nor does one wonder that the Negro

[59] James: "Psychology, Briefer Course," p. 408.

of the South has an emotional nature and an emotional religion in the light of this African background, for an ancestral experience which is grounded in a race is not easily thrown off or outgrown. William James clearly recognizes this fact when he quotes Schneider as saying: "It is a fact that men, especially in childhood, fear to go into a dark cavern or a gloomy wood. This feeling of fear arises, to be sure, partly from the fact that we easily suspect that dangerous beasts may lurk in these localities— a suspicion due to stories we have heard and read. But, on the other hand, it is quite sure that this fear at a certain perception is also directly inherited. Children who have been carefully guarded from all ghost stories are nevertheless terrified and cry if led into a dark place, especially if sounds are made there. Even an adult can easily observe that an uncomfortable timidity steals over him in a lonely wood at night, although he may have the fixed conviction that not the slightest danger is near. The fact of such instinctive fear is easily explicable when we consider that our savage ancestors through innumerable generations were accustomed to meet with dangerous beasts in caverns, and were for the most part attacked by such beasts during the night and in the woods, and thus an inseparable association between the perceptions of darkness, caverns, woods and fear took place and was inherited." [60] Davenport speaks of "superstitious fancies, impulses, dreams, that seem to belong to another personality, though they may be our very own, by brain-cell inheritance from a dim and distant animal and human past." [61]

*The Negro's Heritage From Africa.* The Southern Negro has just such a past from which he inherits those elements which make him emotional. Nor will he be able to overcome this tendency in a generation. It is a slow process to change the biology of a people. But we know well enough the process by which it will be changed. It must be the process by which the white man and all other men have changed, a process of broadening interests, a process of new intellectual outreach, a process of new mental and physical reactions, in short, a process of genuine education, which changes not only the philosophy of the primitive but his biological reactions as well. When one thinks of the African background of the Negro and then stands in the presence of a Washington or a Moton, one wonders not at the backwardness of the race, but at its marvellous power of readjustment.

*Need of Knowing This Background.* It has been said that we do not and cannot really know a man until we know that from which he has reacted. Surely, no one can hope to under-

[60] James: "Psychology, Briefer Series," pp. 410-411.
[61] Davenport: "Primitive Traits in Religious Revivals," p. 22.

stand the present Negro who does not have some insight into his religious and social customs of the past. In the light of these we must judge him, not alone in the light of what he is, but in that broader and fairer light of the direction in which he is moving.

CHAPTER IV

## SLAVERY AND THE SLAVE TRADE

*Slavery World Wide.* Slavery is well nigh a universal custom among primitive peoples. Indeed, it has existed at one time or another in every nation known to history. Slavery was thoroughly intrenched in the customs of the early Jews. In Exodus 21, we read that a man who buys a slave must free him at the end of the sixth year—that is at the year of jubilee. If the slave is married, then his wife goes free also with the husband. If he marries another slave of his master, the woman and her children do not go free at jubilee, and the man if he chose could remain, in which case he had his ear pierced as a sign of perpetual slavery. The Babylonians had a law that a man might pay his debts by giving his wife or children as slaves, but they were free at the end of three years. A female slave with children might not be sold. Among the Jews a man could not sell his slave concubine into a foreign nation. (Ex. 21:8). According to Isaiah 16:14 and Deuteronomy 15:18, three years seems to have been the regular length of time which a Hebrew might serve as a slave, for Deuteronomy speaks of one serving six years as being a "double hired servant" who should not receive grudgingly the gifts from the flocks, the threshing floor, and the wine press, which the law required to be given to all Hebrews who were set free.

*Slavery in Greece and Rome.* During the Heroic Age of Greece, Myers says: "Slavery existed but the slaves did not constitute as numerous a class as they became in historic times, nor do they seem in general to have been treated harshly. Manual labor was not yet thought to be degrading." [1] Of slavery in the later period, Myers says: "No exact estimate can be made of their number, but it is believed that they greatly outnumbered the free population. Almost every freeman was a slave owner. It was accounted a real hardship to have to get along with less than half a dozen slaves." [2] These slaves were recruited from war captives, criminals, debtors, and foundlings who were reared as slaves. The Greek philosophers, including Plato and Aristotle, held to the maxim "slaves were domestic animals possessed of intelligence." All free Greeks felt it was impossible to build a state without slaves.

[1] Myers: "History of Greece," p. 31.
[2] *Ibid.,* p. 552.

70

Rome was a great slave holding state. Her cities were flooded with servants and her farms were worked with slave labor. "Slave labor cost the planter less than free labor; his slave could not be called away for military service as a hired laborer could," [3] so all struggled to increase their slave holdings. Crassus owned five hundred slaves, and one Claudius in the time of Augustus is said to have owned more than four thousand. The slaves of the Romans were often cultured people, taken in war from the Greeks, Sicilians, Carthaginians and others.

The condition of Roman slaves seems to have been hard. "They were systematically worked as hard as it was possible to make them work, and were sold or exposed to perish when too old to work. Such was the policy taught by the older Cato. The number on the market was always great; the price low; it was more advantageous to work them so hard that they had no time or strength to plot revolts. This is the most cynical refusal to regard slaves as human beings which can be found in history." [4]

*Early African Slavery-Cannibalism.* The Negroes of Africa, like all other primitive peoples, had slaves. Their slavery arose primarily out of intertribal wars. At first all those taken captive were slain. Later many of those slain were eaten, both because meat diet in Africa was scarce, and second because the eating of one's enemies added the strength of the enemy to the consumer's own strength. When finally the time arrived, that captives could be put to work instead of being murdered, it was a step forward in human progress. Sumner thinks slavery arose out of four motives. "It is due to ill feeling toward members of the out groups (other tribes), to the desire to get something for nothing, to the love of dominion which belongs to vanity, and to hatred of labor." [5] It seems that the women of Africa, who did all the domestic work, including the crude gardening, had something to do with the saving of war captives from death. By saving them alive and making slaves of them, part of the burden was lifted from the shoulders of the women.

*Number of Slaves.* In 1799 Mungo Park wrote: "The slaves in Africa, I suppose, are nearly in the proportion of three to one to the freemen. They claim no reward for their services, except food and clothing; and are treated with kindness or severity according to the good or bad disposition of their master. Custom, however, has established certain rules with regard to the treatment of slaves which it is thought dishonorable to violate. Thus, the domestic slaves, or such as are born in a man's own house, are treated with more lenity than those which are purchased with

[3] Allen: "A Short History of the Roman People," p. 150.
[4] Sumner: "Folkways," p. 280.
[5] *Ibid.,* p. 261.

money. But these restrictions on the power of the master extend not to the case of prisoners taken in war, nor to that of slaves purchased with money. All these unfortunate beings are considered as strangers and foreigners, who have no right to the protection of the law." [6] Park thinks that most Africans born free and later becoming slaves, enter this state for four reasons. First, they are made captives in intertribal war, and hence made slaves. Second, being overtaken by famine, they sell themselves to a more fortunate tribe to obtain food. Third, having fallen into heavy debt, they may be enslaved by their creditors. Fourth, having committed crime, they are by the custom of the tribe put to work as slaves. [7]

"In a country, divided into a thousand petty states, mostly independent and jealous of each other, where every freeman is accustomed to arms, and fond of military achievements, where the youth who has practiced the bow and spear from infancy, longs for nothing so much as an opportunity to display his valor, it is natural to imagine that wars frequently originate from very frivolous provocation. When one nation is stronger than another, a pretext is seldom wanting for commencing hostilities." [8]

*Slavery and Labor Shortage.* In great sections of Africa where land is plentiful and nature supplies food without much labor, no man will hire himself to another, for a bare subsistence may be had by all. Therefore, if a man desires any extra work done, which demands a considerable concentration of labor, he must get it done through slaves. Scarcity of labor, therefore, is a motive for slavery and indeed slavery has first flourished in countries when population was sparse and there seemed to be a need to compel men to work in large units.

*Agriculture and Slavery.* Agriculture has been favorable to growth of slavery. The work is simple enough to be done by unskilled labor when rightly directed. The work is laborious enough to make free men want to shun it. It requires less machinery than many other pursuits, and hence is suited to slaves. Usually an agricultural country can support large numbers of people and will permit slaves. On the other hand, a cattle raising or grazing country has never demanded many slaves. The work is not heavy or irksome, hence free men do not shun it. Resourcefulness is needed, hence slaves are not good workers, and lastly, the land does not yield abundant food, so that slaves cannot be fed. Therefore in those parts of Africa where cattle are the chief source of wealth, the northern and southern cattle zones, and also where hunting is the main source of food, we find few slaves. Wherever

[6] Park: "Travels," Vol. I, pp. 436-438, passim.
[7] *Ibid.*, p. 441.
[8] *Ibid.*, pp. 441-442.

agriculture sprang up there was work for laborers to do and slavery flourished.

*West Coast Favored Slavery.* The west coast of Africa had all the conditions favorable to slavery. First, the people were divided into hundreds of petty tribes whose juxtaposition brought them into constant conflict and therefore, filled the country with war captives. Second, the soil and climate combined in producing an easy and abundant food supply, so that there might be developed an idle or slave owning class without jeopardizing the means of subsistence. Third, the humidity and heat rendered work both irksome and destructive, and lastly, as Dr. Dowd points out, the farming was on such a small scale, with no outlet for surplus production, that all the slaves could not well be kept busy—hence there was readiness to sell slaves abroad. These are the conditions primarily which made West Africa from the Senegal River at 17° north latitude to Benguella at 13° south latitude, the market place for the slaves of all the world.

*Early Export of Slaves.* Slaves were taken from the interior of Africa and from the East coast in the earliest historic periods, as is evidenced by the inscriptions and pictures on the monuments of early Egypt. The first slaves, taken from Africa, to the Western World, were the fruit of Portuguese exploration. The story of these early adventures is most fascinating. In the latter part of the fourteenth century, John of Gaunt, and John of Portugal were both enemies to John of Castile. A treaty between the first two was sealed with the marriage of Philippa, daughter of John of Gaunt, Duke of Lancaster, to John of Aviz, usurper of the Portuguese crown in 1386. Of this marriage was born a number of sons, the three eldest of which were practically men when a treaty of peace was signed with Castile, 1411. John, the King of Portugal, desired to celebrate the event with a great International Tournament, in which these three sons, Duarte, twenty-one; Peter, twenty, and Henry, eighteen, might win their spurs. "But these immediately answered that such a tournament as proposed would not be anything like so worthy an object as an expedition against some valorous foe, whereby they might gain some real chivalrous distinction infinitely greater than was possible by any mere formal ceremony." [9]

*War on the Moors.* Ceuta, the fortress of the Moors, across the straits, was suggested as the expedition which would give fullest glory, for it was a task worthy of the boldest, and besides it was one the fulfillment of which would be a sacred boon to the Western World, for it would turn back the Mohammedan horde from Europe. Besides, beyond lay the wonderful land of Africa, about which little was known, but about which legend

---

[9] Martin: "The Golden Age of Prince Henry, the Navigator," p 20.

had woven wonderful stories. For more than three years, herculean efforts were made in preparation for the attack, which took place in August, 1415. Fifty-nine galleys of war, sixty-three transports, and one hundred and twenty vessels bearing provisions, were manned by thirty thousand sailors and twenty thousand soldiers. Ceuta was promptly subdued. The three sons were immediately knighted and King John prepared to return home. But Prince Henry had tasted wild adventure and remained behind. The remainder of his life was largely given to African interests. He determined to know more of the natives of Africa, being led on by intellectual curiosity, by desire to Christianize the natives, and doubtless by a desire to secure rich treasures.

*Prince Henry the Navigator.* "There mingled in Prince Henry's mind an odd medley of greed, chivalry and proselytizing zeal. The early voyagers looked upon themselves, with a curious naive simplicity, not only as merchant adventurers, but also as harbingers of the cross of Christ, sent to bring light out of darkness. They were as eager to save the souls of the heathen from the dangers of eternal damnation, which they firmly believed would be otherwise their fate, as to seize upon their lands, their riches and their daughters." [10]    Prince Henry, who had in him the passion for adventure, was constantly dreaming two dreams. First, he wanted to conquer Northern Africa and make it a colony of Portugal. This dream came to a disastrous end in 1437 when he was overwhelmingly defeated by the Moors at Tangiers. He immediately turned all his energy to the realization of his other dream—that is the exploration of the coast of Africa and finding a passage around it to the East. Five reasons for pushing this plan are given by Martin: [11] "To know the unknown; to crush the power of the Moor, to propagate the Christian faith, to communicate with the Ethiopian Christians of Prestor John; to find allies among them." Ship after ship was sent out, discovering some of the islands off the coast, and from time to time touching the coast itself. In 1441 "Antao Goncalvez and Nuno Tristao, sailing as far as Porto do Cavalleiro, returned with the first captives." [12]    These first captives were Moors, who offered to ransom themselves by showing the Portuguese where they could secure plenty of slaves (Negroes). Prince Henry immediately sent an embassy to the Pope to ask for a grant to the Portuguese crown of all lands discovered. This was the beginning of negotiations which later gave all Africa to Portugal and the Western World to Spain.

*The First Slaves Brought to Europe.* Goncalvez soon made

---

[10] Martin: "The Golden Age of Prince Henry, the Navigator," p. 22.
[11] *Ibid.,* p. 206.
[12] *Ibid.,* p. 207.

another journey and brought back with him gold, ostrich eggs and a number of Negro slaves. Soon a guild of merchant adventurers was formed at Lagos in Portugal and "for the first time also in history (1444), these explorers of Lagos regularly practiced a traffic in slaves." Moving along the coast, the first group of armed vessels fell upon the Moors and the natives, as Azurara, the chronicler piously remarks: "At last our Lord God, who always rewards the upright, wishing that day to recompense them (the Portuguese) for all the labor they had given in His service, and to reward them and pay them for their expenses, suffered them to capture men, women, and youths to the number of 165, besides those that were slain." [13] These slaves were landed on the beach at Lagos, where Prince Henry on horseback presided over the division of the booty; and the terrible slave traffic with Africa had begun.

*Pious Attitude of Slave Dealers.* Of the forty-six slaves that fell to the lot of Prince Henry, the chronicler remarks: "We see what was the reward that the Prince deserved at the hands of our Lord, for having thus given them the chance of salvation; and not only them, but many others whom he afterward acquired." [14] "There was no hypocrisy," says Martin, "in this. It was the genuine spirit of the age. Proselytizing zeal burnt fiercely then, and both Portuguese, and, later, Spanish pioneers made an invariable rule of baptizing their prisoners and victims, firmly convinced that thereby they were saving them from eternal damnation." [15]

*Rapid Increase of Slaves.* The number of slaves increased rapidly so that within ten years of the bringing in of the first Negroes, there were probably a thousand Negro slaves in Portugal, and from that time forward slaves were imported in ever increasing numbers. From Portugal, slaves were sold into Spain, and soon the Spanish entered with full zest into the slave catching business, even if Portugal did claim exclusive right to the African coast. In 1494, by the treaty of Tordessillas, the boundary line of Portugal's territory was moved westward to 370 leagues from Cape Verde, and thus it was later discovered that the Portuguese had inherited a great new country, Brazil. All the Western World, save Brazil, belonged to the Spanish by right of discovery and by boldness of asserted claims. When Columbus made his second journey to Hispaniola (Hayti) with fifteen hundred colonizers, in 1493, he wrote back to his government and offered to send Indian slaves to pay for the implements and provisions needed to carry on his work. Indeed, on his return he took a

---

[13] Martin: "The Golden Age of Prince Henry, the Navigator," p. 212.
[14] *Ibid.*, p. 214.
[15] *Ibid.*, p. 214.

few Indian slaves with him, but Isabella stopped the sale and commanded them returned to Hayti.

*Indians Made Poor Slaves.* The Indians were enslaved by the colonists but did not prove successful workers. They were too haughty and proud and not robust of body. Seeing the dreadful mortality of the Indians, Las Cassas, Bishop of Chiapia in Hispaniola, went to Spain to plead in their behalf. Speaking before Charles V himself, Las Cassas said: "At my first arrival in Hispaniola, it contained a million of inhabitants; and now (viz. in the space of about twenty years) there remains scarce the hundredth part of them."[16] A new source of labor must be found and the Spaniards naturally turned to Africa. But Portugal controlled Africa, so to checkmate them Spain refused to allow any slaves or goods taken to her own colonies save in Spanish vessels. In order to obviate this difficulty a special assent from the Spanish sovereign must be secured.

*The "Assiento."* Thus, arose the famous "assiento," which ultimately came to be simply a contract of Spain with some other power, whereby her provinces might be supplied with a certain number of slaves. This Assiento or trade license was first held by Portugal, who landed their first cargo of slaves in Hispaniola in 1502 and in 1518 contracted to furnish 4,000 slaves annually to the West Indies. All the first slaves were carried by way of Europe where they might be "Christianized" before being sent out to the colonies. Thus did the early slavers salve their conscience. The introduction of sugar cane culture into the islands in 1512 brought a more urgent demand for slaves, which was only poorly answered by the Spanish authorities.

*England's Part in the Slave Trade.* The English entered the West Africa slave trade in 1562, through John Hawkins, afterward knighted. Prior to this, "Elizabeth had lent her influence and assistance to a series of voyages to the African coast. Not only did she permit the use of four royal voyagers for the first expedition, but she spent five hundred pounds in provisioning them for the voyage. The value of these goods, sent to Africa, in these vessels, was five thousand pounds. According to the arrangement Queen Elizabeth received one third of the profits, which amounted to one thousand pounds."[17] In these voyages to Guinea, the English trade had been for gold, elephants' teeth and pepper. Trading in slaves had hardly occurred to these early adventurers. Nevertheless, as early as 1562, John Hawkins sailed for Sierra Leone with three vessels, and there captured three hundred Negroes whom he sold to the Spanish in Hispaniola.

---

[16] Quoted from Benezet's "Historical Account of Guinea" (London, 1794), p. 43.
[17] "Journal of Negro History," Vol. IV, p. 138.

The success of this voyage was so great that in 1564 there was fitted out a second slave raiding expedition, in which one of the Queen's ships, the Jesus, was employed. As before, Hawkins sold his slaves in the West Indies, this time with some difficulties, because the Spanish officials, who were forbidden to have any trade with foreigners, regarded the Englishmen as pirates." [18] On a third journey in 1567 Hawkins met with great disaster, losing all his ships save one, and barely escaping with his life. This practically put an end to English slave trading for a full century.

*Revival of English Slave Trading.* A desultory trade in native products was carried on by various English companies, but not until 1660 was the African trade undertaken again in earnest. In that year the "company of Royal Adventurers into Africa" was organized, and all rights ceded for the territory from Cape Blanco to Cape of Good Hope. Slavery was not mentioned in the charter. In 1663 a new charter was taken out by the company and the name changed to "The Company of Royal Adventurers of England Trading into Africa." By this time, the adventurers had discovered that the Negro trade could be made very lucrative. In that charter, therefore, they obtained "the whole, entire and only trade for the buying and selling, bartering and exchanging of, for or with any Negroes, slaves, goods, wares, or merchandise, whatsoever to be vented or found at or within any of the cities on the West Coast of Africa." [19] Soon the English were in conflict with the Dutch, who were at this time most active in the slave trade, and misunderstanding finally led to the Anglo Dutch war of 1665-7. [20] In 1713 the Assiento passed to the English in accordance with the agreement of which the English promised in thirty years to furnish to the Spanish colonies 144,000 slaves. Spain was to receive 200,000 crowns and a duty of 33½ crowns for each slave imported. It is believed that in the first twenty years of the contract, England imported more than double the number required for the thirty years, part of which, however, went to America and not to the colonies.

*Dutch Slave Trading.* The Dutch entered the slave trade in 1595, and soon established trading posts on the west coast. Elmina on the Gold Coast was perhaps their most active slave market. It was through the Dutch that the great number of Koromantes, Ashantis and other Gold Coast Negroes were imported into the Southern States. In 1621 the first Dutch West Indies Company was established, the settled policy of which was to furnish to all Dutch colonies all the slaves that they could or

[18] "Journal of Negro History," Vol. IV, p. 148.
[19] *Idem.*
[20] For full account of negotiations, see "Journal of Negro History," Vol. IV, p. 163.

would use. Thus it is seen that the Dutch, the English, the Spanish and the Portuguese were all eager for a full share in the slave trade. To these should be added, as will be seen later, a considerable number of ships belonging to New England merchants.

*Source of American Slaves.* The principal tribes which contributed to the American slaves were the Senegalese, the Mandingoes, Ibos, Efik, Iboni, Ibani, Koromantis, Wydyahs, and others from the grain, slave, gold, and ivory coasts, and various groups of Bantus from Kameroon, Gaboon, Loango, and Angola. The slaves were captured in the interior and driven to the coast for sale with great cruelty and heavy losses. Livingstone found that wherever the slavers had been it was much more difficult to deal with the natives. In the heart of Africa, Livingstone came upon a scene of recent slave catching which he describes as follows: "Wherever we took a walk, human skeletons were seen in every direction, and it was painfully interesting to observe the different postures in which the poor wretches had breathed their last. A whole heap had been thrown down a slope behind a village, where the fugitives often crossed the river from the East, and in one hut of the same village no fewer than twenty, drums had been collected, probably the ferryman's fees. Many had ended their misery under shade trees, others under projecting crags in the hills, while others lay in their huts with closed doors, which when opened disclosed the mouldering corpse with the poor rags around the loins, the skull fallen off the pillow, the little skeleton of the child, that had perished first, rolled up in a mat between two large skeletons. The sight of this desert, but eighteen months ago a well peopled valley, now literally strewn with human bones, forced the conviction upon us that the destruction of life in the middle passage, however great, constitutes but a small part of the waste, and made us feel that unless the slave trade—that monster iniquity which has so long brooded over Africa—is put down, lawful commerce cannot be established." [21]

*Method of Capturing Slaves.* Francis Moore, an Englishman, wrote of the method of securing slaves in the early part of the eighteenth century as follows: "Whenever this king (a Negro) wants goods or brandy he sends a messenger to the English governor at Fort James to desire he would send a sloop there with a cargo, this news being not at all unwelcome, the governor sends accordingly. After the arrival the King goes and ransacks some of the enemies' towns, seizing the people and selling them for such commodities as he is in want of, which commonly are brandy, guns, powder, balls, pistols, cutlasses for his attendants and soldiers; and coral and silver for his wives and concubines. In

[21] Blackie: "Life of Livingstone," p. 329.

case he is not in war with any neighboring king he then falls upon one of his own towns, which are numerous, and uses them in the same manner." [22]   Of the suffering due to such raids let a hardened slave merchant from Liverpool tell.  "The next day was appointed (by the African chief) for receiving the slaves; we found about two hundred confined in one place.  But here how shall I relate the afflicting sight I then beheld!  How can I sufficiently describe the silent sorrow which appeared in the countenance of the affected father, and the painful anguish of the tender mother, expecting to be forever separated from their tender offspring; the distressed maid wringing her hands in presage of her future wretchedness, and the general cry of the innocent from a dreadful apprehension of the perpetual slavery to which they were doomed." [23]   In spite of his lament, he bought some of the slaves and returned to the coast, but one is forced to conclude that if the scenes of slavery could so affect the professional dealer, it must have been heartrending indeed.

*Destruction of Life by Slave Catchers.*  That the catching of slaves was terribly expensive in human lives is proven by statements of many African explorers and missionaries.  "Dr. Livingstone was informed by Col. Rigdy, late British Consul of Zanzibar, that 19,000 slaves from the Nyasa region alone passed annually through the custom house there.  This was besides those landed at Portuguese slave ports.  In addition to those captured, thousands were killed or died of their wounds or famine, or perished in other ways so that not one fifth of the victims became slaves,—in the Nyasa district, probably not one tenth." [24]

*Horrors of Slave Coffle.*  But if Africa lost four lives for every one made a slave in the interior—and sometimes nine for every one—the expense in life of transport to the coast and over the ocean was almost as heavy.  When a group of captives had been taken they were herded together and kept until ready to start this march.  Often they were held in heavy irons to prevent escape.  On the march they were chained together into a coffle and marched under the eye of the slavers.  Mungo Park, on his first journey to the upper waters of the Niger, 1796, lost his whole retinue by capture and was forced to put himself under the care of a slave driver to get back to the coast.  He gives a most graphic description of such a coffle on its way to the port of embarkation.

"A deeply rooted idea that the whites purchase Negroes for the purpose of devouring them, or of selling them to others, that they may be devoured hereafter, naturally makes the slaves contemplate a journey towards the Coast with great terror; insomuch

[22] Benezet: "Historical Account of Guinea" (1794), p. 90.
[23] *Ibid.*, p. 102.
[24] Blackie: "Life of Livingstone," p. 306.

that the Slatees are forced to keep them constantly in irons, and watch them very closely to prevent their escape. They are commonly secured by putting the right leg of one, and the left of another, into the same pair of fetters. By supporting the fetters with a string, they can walk, though very slowly. Every four slaves are likewise fastened together by the necks, with a strong rope of twisted thongs; and in the night an additional pair of fetters is put on their hands, and sometimes a light iron chain passed round their necks.

"Such of them as evince marks of discontent are secured in a different manner. A thick billet of wood is cut about three feet long, and a smooth notch being made upon one side of it, the ankle of the slave is bolted to the smooth part by means of a strong iron staple, one prong of which passes on each side of the ankle. All these fetters and bolts are made from native iron; in the present case they were put on by the blacksmith as soon as the slaves arrived from Kancaba, and were not taken off until the morning on which the coffle departed for Gambia.

*Treatment at Assembling Stations.* "In other respects, the treatment of the slaves during their stay at Kamalia (the point of collection), was far from being harsh or cruel. They were led out in their fetters every morning, to the shade of the tamarind tree, where they were encouraged to play at games of hazard, and sing diverting songs, to keep up their spirits; for though some of them sustained the hardships of their situation with amazing fortitude, the greater part were very much dejected, and would sit all day in a sort of sullen melancholy, with their eyes fixed upon the ground. In the evening, their irons were examined, and their hand fetters put on; after which they were conducted into two large huts, where they were guarded during the night by Karfa's domestic slaves. But notwithstanding all this, about a week after their arrival, one of the slaves had the address to procure a small knife, with which he opened the rings of his fetters, cut the rope, and made his escape; more of them would probably have got off, had they assisted each other; but the slave no sooner found himself at liberty, than he refused to stop and assist in breaking the chain which was fastened round the necks of his companions." [25]

*Forced Marches of the Coffle.* This coffle was a small one of only 73 persons, and marches were forced, making often twenty-five miles per day. With irons on their feet and with loads on their backs, this must have been a most trying and exhausting journey,—a man with a spear followed each group of four slaves and each driver carried a heavy whip to encourage any who might be inclined to lag. One day after particularly hard marching,—

[25] Park: "Travels," Vol. I, pp. 484-486.

the slave owner Karfa, fearing bands of robbers,—a female slave, Nealee, was found particularly exhausted. The next morning she would eat no breakfast. About eleven o'clock, Park says, they were attacked by a swarm of bees, and poor Nealee, too weak to run, was cruelly stung by scores of the vicious little insects.

"When the Slatees had picked out the stings as far as they could, she was washed with water, and then rubbed with bruised leaves; but the wretched woman obstinately refused to proceed any farther; declaring that she would rather die than walk another step. As entreaties and threats were used in vain, the whip was at length applied; and after bearing patiently a few strokes, she started up, and walked with tolerable expedition for four or five hours longer, when she made an attempt to run away from the coffle, but was so very weak that she fell down in the grass. Though she was unable to rise, the whip was a second time applied, but without effect; upon which Karfa desired two of the Slatees to place her upon the ass which carried our dry provisions; but she could not sit erect; and the ass being very refractory, it was found impossible to carry her forward in that manner. The Slatees, however, were unwilling to abandon her, the day's journey being nearly ended; they therefore made a sort of litter of bamboo canes, upon which she was placed, and tied on it with slips of bark: this litter was carried upon the heads of two slaves, one walking before the other, and they were followed by two others, who relieved them occasionally. In this manner the woman was carried forward until it was dark, when we reached a stream of water, at the foot of a high hill called Gankaran-Kooro; and here we stopped for the night, and set about preparing our supper. As we had eaten only one handful of meal since the preceding night, and traveled all day in a hot sun, many of the slaves, who had loads upon their heads, were very much fatigued; and some of them snapt their fingers, which among the Negroes is a sure sign of desperation. The Slatees immediately put them all in irons; and such of them as had evinced signs of great despondency, were kept apart from the rest, and had their hands tied. In the morning they were found greatly recovered.

*Disposing of an Exhausted Slave.* "At daybreak poor Nealee was awakened; but her limbs were now become so stiff and painful, that she could neither walk nor stand; she was therefore lifted, like a corpse, upon the back of the ass; and the Slatees endeavored to secure her in that situation, by fastening her hands together under the ass's neck and her feet under the belly, with long slips of bark; but the ass was so very unruly, that no sort of treatment could induce him to proceed with his load; and as

Nealee made no exertion to prevent herself from falling, she was quickly thrown off, and had one of her legs much bruised. Every attempt to carry her forward being thus found ineffectual, the general cry of the coffle was, kang-tegi, kang-tegi, 'cut her throat, cut her throat'; an operation I did not wish to see performed, and therefore marched onwards with the foremost of the coffle. I had not walked above a mile when one of Karfa's domestic slaves came up to me, with poor Nealee's garment upon the end of his bow, and exclaimed, 'Nealee affeeleeta.' (Nealee is lost.) I asked him whether the Slatees had given him the garment as a reward for cutting her throat; he replied that Karfa and the schoolmaster would not consent to that measure, but had left her on the road; where undoubtedly she soon perished, and was probably devoured by wild beasts." [26]

*Early Slave Centers.* The earliest slave markets were Timbuctu, Kuka, Kano, Katsena and other cities on the northern border of the Sudan between the upper bend of the Niger and Lake Tchad. From this section for centuries, slaves have been carried north to the border states across the desert of Sahara. Usually they were taken in great caravans, often as many as four thousand at a time being marched across these burning sands. For the first half of their journey they had to be kept in heavy irons, to prevent escape. The heat, the lack of water, the carrying of burdens (jungle products) and long marches, and above all the mental depression of being slaves meant the death of thousands and thousands of slaves in these lonely wastes of sand. It is said that the most commonly traveled routes are so thoroughly marked with the bleaching skeletons of slaves, that one who is a stranger to the desert might well find his way across.

*Drain on Africa's Population.* After the caravans reached the middle of the desert, travel was easier because the irons were removed from the slaves. No slave would dare try to escape, since the weeks of travel back over the desert was sure death by starvation and thirst. The North African states thus bought annually many hundreds of thousands of slaves. During the high tide of the slave trade it is not at all unlikely that a million slaves a year went out from Central Africa and if Livingstone was right in estimating that for every one taken alive, four others died in battle or of wounds or of starvation, the devastation during those long decades of slavery must have been terrific. It is partly due to this fact that Africa is the most sparsely populated continent of the globe, though the Negroes are one of the most prolific of all races.

*The Middle Passage.* But the loss of life was not alone in the capture nor in the march to the sea. The middle passage was

[26] Park: "Travels," Vol. I, pp. 504-507.

fully as terrible, though not quite so destructive of life. Benezet quotes from a collection of voyages during the eighteenth century, a record about one Captain Philips who came in a "ship of 450 tons, along the coast of Guinea for elephant's' teeth, gold, and Negro slaves intended for the Barbadoes. Philips took seven hundred slaves on board, the men being all put into irons two by two, shackled together to prevent their mutinying or swimming ashore. He says that the Negroes are so loath to leave their own country that they often leap out of the canoe, boat, or ship into the sea, and keep under the water until they are drowned, to avoid being taken up and saved by the boats which pursue them. They had about twelve Negroes who willingly drowned themselves; others starved themselves to death. Philips was advised to cut off the legs and arms of some to terrify the rest (as other captains had done), but this he refused to do. From the time of his taking the Negroes on board to his arrival at Barbadoes, no less than three hundred and twenty died of various diseases." [27]

Sir Harry Johnson, describing a slave transport, quoting from Walsh's "Notices of Brazil," London, 1830, says: [28] "She was a very broad-decked ship, with a mainmast, schooner-rigged, and behind her foremast was that large, formidable gun, which turned on a broad circle of iron on deck, and which enabled her to act as a pirate, if her slaving speculation had failed. She had taken in, on the coast of Africa, 336 males and 226 females, making in all 562, and had been out seventeen days, during which she had thrown overboard fifty-five. The slaves were all enclosed under grated hatchways, between-decks. The space was so low that they sat between each other's legs, and stowed so close together that there was no possibility of their lying down, or at all changing their position, by night or day. As they belonged to and were shipped on account of different individuals, they were all branded, like sheep, with the owners' marks of different forms. . . . These were impressed under their breasts, or on their arms, and, as the mate informed me, with perfect indifference, 'queimados pelo ferro quento'—burnt with a red-hot iron. Over the hatchway stood a ferocious-looking fellow, with a scourge of many twisted thongs in his hands, who was the slave-driver of the ship. Whenever he heard the slightest noise below, he shook the whip over them, and seemed eager to exercise it. I was quite pleased to take this hateful badge out of his hand, and I have kept it ever since, as a horrid memorial of reality, should I ever be disposed to forget the scene I witnessed.

"As soon as the poor creatures saw us looking down at them

[27] Benezet: "Historical Account of Guinea," p. 101.
[28] "The Negro in the New World," Johnson, pp. 85-87.

their dark and melancholy visages brightened up. They perceived something of sympathy and kindness in our looks, which they had not been accustomed to, and, feeling instinctively that we were friends, they immediately began to shout and clap their hands. One or two had picked up a few Portuguese words and cried out 'Viva! Viva!' The women were particularly excited. They all held up their arms, and when we bent down and shook hands with them they could not contain their delight; they endeavored to scramble upon their knees, stretching up to kiss our hands, and we understood that they knew we were come to liberate them. Some, however, hung down their heads in apparently hopeless dejection; some were greatly emaciated, and some, particularly children, seemed dying.

*Crowded Conditions on Slave Ships.* "But the circumstance which struck us most forcibly was, how it was possible for such a number of human beings to exist, packed up and wedged together as tight as they could cram, in low cells, 3 feet high, the greater part of which, except that immediately under the grated hatchways, was shut out from light or air, and this when the thermometer, exposed to the open sky, was standing in the shade, on our deck, at 89 degrees. The space between-decks was divided into two compartments 3 feet 3 inches high; the size of one was 16 by 18 feet, and of the other 40 by 21 feet; into the first were crammed the women and girls; into the second, the men and boys; 226 fellow-creatures were thus thrust into one space 288 feet square; and 336 into another space 800 feet square, giving to the whole an average of 23 inches, and to each of the women not more than 13 inches, though many of them were pregnant. We also found manacles and fetters of different kinds, but it appears that they had all been taken off before we boarded.

*Suffering on the Slave Ships.* "The heat of these horrid places was so great, and the odor so offensive, that it was quite impossible to enter them, even had there been room. They were measured as above when the slaves had left them. The officers insisted that the poor suffering creatures should be admitted on deck to get air and water. This was opposed by the mate of the slaver, who, from a feeling that they deserved it, declared they would murder them all. The officers, however, persisted, and the poor beings were all turned up together. It is impossible to conceive the effect of this eruption—517 fellow-creatures of all ages and sexes, some children, some adults, some old men and women, all in a state of total nudity, scrambling out together to taste the luxury of a little fresh air and water. They came swarming up, like bees from the aperture of a hive, till the whole deck was crowded to suffocation, from stem to stern; so that it was impossible to imagine where they could all have come from, or how they could

have been stowed away. On looking into the places where they
had been crammed, there were found some children next the sides
of the ship, in the places most remote from light and air; they
were lying nearly in a torpid state, after the rest had turned out.
The little creatures seemed indifferent as to life or death, and
when they were carried on deck, many of them could not stand.

"After enjoying for a short time the unusual luxury of air,
some water was brought; it was then that the extent of their
sufferings was exposed in a fearful manner. They all rushed
like maniacs toward it. No entreaties, or threats, or blows, could
restrain them; they shrieked, and struggled, and fought with one
another, for a drop of this precious liquid, as if they grew rabid
at the sight of it.

"Out of this slaving ship during the first seventeen days of
their voyage fifty-five slaves, dying or dead from dysentery, had
been thrown overboard. Though there was a large stock of
medicines displayed in the cabin with a manuscript book containing directions how they should be used, the so-called doctor
on board was a negro who was unable to read! On many of
these slave-ships the sense of misery and suffocation was so
terrible in the 'tween-decks—where the height sometimes was only
eighteen inches, so that the unfortunate slaves could not turn
round, were wedged immovably, in fact, and chained to the deck
by the neck and legs—that the slaves not infrequently would go
mad before dying of suffocation. In their frenzy some killed
others in the hope of procuring more room to breathe. Men
strangled those next to them, and women drove nails into each
other's brains." [29]

*Findings of Committee of the British Parliament.* That this
statement of conditions quoted by Johnson is no exaggeration
could be proven from many sources. In 1790 the British Parliament made an exhaustive investigation of the condition of slavery.
They called before them fifty-eight prominent Englishmen who
had been in Africa and the West Indies, and many of whom had
made the middle passage journey. Captain Parrey of the Royal
Navy had measured the ship capacity of all the slavers lying in
Liverpool in 1788 and his testimony as to crowding was submitted
to this committee of Parliament. The facts assembled by this
committee showed conditions even worse than those quoted by
Johnson:

"Mr. Falconbridge also states on this head, that when employed in stowing the slaves, he made the most of the room, and
*wedged them in.* They had not so much room as *a man in his
coffin,* either in length or breadth. It was impossible for them
to turn or shift with any degree of ease. He had often occasion

[29] Quoted from Frances Moore's "Travels in Africa."

to go from one side of their rooms to the other, in which case he always *took off his shoes,* but could not avoid pinching them; he has the marks on his feet where they bit and scratched him. In every voyage when the ship was full they complained of heat and want of air.  Confinement in this situation was so injurious, that he has known them *go down apparently in good health at night and found dead in the morning.*  On his last voyage he opened a stout man who so died.  He found the contents of the thorax and abdomen healthy, and therefore concludes *he died of suffocation in the night.*

"He was never among them for ten minutes below together, but his shirt was as wet as if dipped in water.

"One of his ships, the Alexander, coming out of Bonny, got aground on the bar, and was detained there six or seven days, with a great swell and heavy rain.  At this time the air ports were obliged to be shut, and part of the gratings on the weather side covered; almost all the men slaves were taken ill with the flux.  The last time he went down to see them it was so hot he took off his shirt.  *More than twenty of them had fainted, or were fainting.*  He got, however, several of them hauled on deck. Two or three of these died, and most of the rest before they reached the West Indies.  He was down only about fifteen minutes, and became so ill by it, that he could not get up without help, and was disabled (the dysentery seizing him also) from doing duty the rest of the passage.  On board the same ship he has known two or three instances of *a dead and living slave found in the morning shackled together.*

"The *crowded state* of the slaves, and the *pulling off the shoes* by the surgeons as described above, that they might not hurt them in traversing their rooms, are additionally mentioned by Surgeons Wilson and Claxton.  The slaves are said also by Hall and Wilson to *complain* on account *of heat.*  Both Hall, Town, and Morely, described them as often in *a violent perspiration* or *dew sweat.* Mr. Ellison has seen them *faint* through heat, and obliged to be brought on deck, the steam coming up through the gratings like a furnace.  In Wilson's and Town's ships some have *gone below well in an evening,* and in the *morning have been found dead,* and Mr. Newton has often seen a dead and living man chained together and to use his own words, *one of the pair dead."* [30]

*Extent of the Slave Trade.*  Of the number of slaves exported from Africa, some idea can be gathered by reviewing the number of ships engaged at different periods in the business.  Liverpool alone had "by 1753 eighty-seven ships, totaling about eight thousand tons burthen and rated to carry some twenty-five thousand

[30] Abstract of Evidence before a select committee of House of Commons, 1790; republished 1859; p. 47 f.

slaves. Eight of these vessels were trading on the Gambia, thirty-eight on the Gold and Slave Coasts, five at Benin, three at New Calabar, twenty at Bonny, eleven at Old Calabar, and ten in Angola." [31] "For the year 1771 the number of slavers bound from Liverpool was reported at one hundred and seven with a capacity of 29,250 Negroes, while fifty-eight went from London rated to carry 8136, twenty-five from Bristol to carry 8810 and five from Lancaster with room for 950. Of this total of 195 ships 43 traded in Senegambia, 29 on the Gold Coast, 56 on the Slave Coast, 63 in the Bights of Benin and Biafra, and 4 in Angola." [32]

By 1801, Philips tells us the Liverpool ships had increased to 150 and had a capacity of 52,557 slaves, about half of these traded in the ports of Angola.[33] Just before the closing of the legal slave trade to American ports in 1808, when England had forbidden the slave traffic, Rhode Island had 59 ships engaged in the traffic, Baltimore had 4, Charleston had 61, Boston had 1, Norfolk had 2 and Connecticut had 1. During the years 1804-1807, British and French vessels landed 21,027 slaves in the South, and American vessels landed 18,048.[34] Even after the slave traffic was prohibited it still went on. In the Congress of Verona it was charged that "in seven months of the year 1821, no less than 21,000 slaves were abducted and three hundred and fifty-two vessels entered African ports north of the equator." [35] In 1837 imports into South America were estimated as high as 200,000 annually, and one province of Brazil alone was said to have received 173,000 slaves in the years 1846-1849.[36] Thus did Africa through the centuries, lose her richest possessions, her people. But the end is not yet.

*Modern African Slavery.* Modern Africa suffers from nothing so much as from lack of sufficient labor supply, consequently, slavery still exists, not now in the form of African owning African, but of European nations exploiting the labor of these people. As late as 1914 a German paper in the Kameroons said: "What would become of this colony if the natives are not compelled to do any work? How shall export values be created, and how is it posible to increase the value of imports? For what purpose have we got the colonies? What service is the native to us if he does not want to work?" [37] A deputy of the Central party in Germany spoke out boldly in 1914, saying: "There had been

[31] Phillips: "American Negro Slavery," p. 32.
[32] *Ibid.*, p. 32.
[33] *Ibid.*, p. 33.
[34] DuBois: "The Suppression of the Slave Trade," pp. 90-91.
[35] *Ibid.*, p. 138.
[36] *Ibid.*, p. 142.
[37] Harris: "Africa," p. 74.

more loss of life on the plantations than in the slave hunts of former years." [38]    Harris says, "that in German East Africa alone there are today over 180,000 domestic slaves." [39]

*Modern Portuguese Slavery.*    The Portuguese have kept up their old slaving traditions.    In 1912 Mr. Harris quotes an authority on Angola as saying : "Including the very large number of natives, who, by purchase or birth, are the family slaves of the village chiefs and other fairly prosperous natives, we might probably reckon at least half the population as living under some form of slavery." [40]    Describing an Angola town and what he found there, Harris continues : "Behind the mountainous coast of Angola, the town of Novo Redondo hides itself in a hollow, as if ashamed of its history, or perhaps so that its traffic in human beings during past centuries might escape the attention of watchful cruisers.    There, amongst a group of slaves and freemen, I met a woman with a story more eloquent than others because it was also so recent, so vivid and so forceful.    She had not been long on the coast, for only a few months ago she had for the first time witnessed the Atlantic breakers tossing themselves with their impetuous fury on that strip of rocky shore.    The hour was that of the mid-day rest, and the woman was sitting sadly apart from the other laborers.    A glance at her attitude, coiffure and other characteristics rendered her a somewhat singular figure in that group of serviçaes, still there was a familiarity which surely could not be mistaken—somewhere in Central Africa those cicatrized arms, that braided head, had a tribal home.

" 'True, white man, I have come from far ; from the land of great rivers and dark forests !'

" 'How were you enslaved ?' I asked.

" 'They charged me with theft and then sold me to another tribe and they in turn to a black trader.    This man drove me for many "moons" along the great road until a white man at D—— bought me and sent me here.'

" 'Where am I going now?    Who can tell?    I suppose I shall be sold to a planter.'

"There was no need of the slave's reiterated assertion that she had been nearly ten months marching down to the coast ; the locality of her tribe was plainly set forth on the forearm by the indelible cicatrizing knife of her race.    The journey from Batetela tribe of the Congo to the shores of Novo Redondo cannot be much less than 1500 miles.    This was one of the most recent cases we discovered and shows that the slave trade in Portuguese territory is a question of the moment." [41]

[38] Harris: "Africa," p. 75.
[39] *Ibid.,* p. 67.
[40] Harris: "Dawn in Darkest Africa," p. 175.
[41] *Ibid.,* pp. 177-179.

In 1919 these words are quoted about the destruction of slavery on a modern trail through Angola into the interior regions: "The path is strewn with dead men's bones. You see the white thigh-bones lying in front of your feet, and at one side, among the undergrowth, you find the skull. These are the skeletons of slaves who have been unable to keep up with the march, and so were murdered or left to die." [42]

*Belgian Congo Atrocities.* Of the destruction of life in the Congo under Belgian rule one must be content with a single quotation from Richard Harding Davis, who went to the Congo to investigate the conditions. "Few schemes," says Mr. Davis, speaking of the plan of gathering rubber and ivory, "few schemes devised have been more cynical, more devilish, more cunningly designed to incite a man to cruelty and abuse. To dishonesty it was an invitation and a reward. It was this scheme of 'payment by results' evolved by Leopold, sooner than allow his agents a fixed and sufficient wage that led to the atrocities. One result of this system was that in seven years, the natives condemned to slavery in the rubber forests brought in rubber to the amount of fifty-five millions of dollars. But its chief results were the destruction of entire villages, the flight from their homes in the Congo of hundreds of thousands of natives, and for those that remained misery, death, the most brutal tortures and degradations, unprintable, unthinkable." [43]

Thus the tale of Africa's misfortune continues. She is a dark continent indeed. Browbeaten by the climate and by the terrors of animal and insect life; held in bondage by her own terrible and destructive superstitions, robbed of her leadership by the superstitions of the witch-doctors; despoiled of her laborers for foreign markets by the multiplied millions, and now robbed of her wealth and her few surviving millions by the greedy hands of European nations; who could wonder that the many native Africans are belated and uncivilized people. The cry of this people riseth to high heaven and none seem to take notice of her distress.

[42] Harris: "Africa," p. 91.
[43] Davis: "The Congo and Coasts of Africa," pp. 43-44.

CHAPTER V

## SLAVERY IN THE WEST INDIES

*Early Explorations.* When Don Cristobal Colon, better known as Christopher Columbus, set out on his first sea voyage he had not thought of finding a new world, but of finding a new and shorter way to an old world with great riches. He and those who sent him had one supreme purpose and that was to get rich. After sailing westward for ten weeks he landed with his three tiny vessels on the coast of Watling Island, which in gratitude for a safe journey he called San Salvador. He immediately wrote back to Ferdinand and Isabella that there were "no better people on earth" than those who had received him here. After a brief stay at Watling Island he sailed south touching Long Island, and Crooked Island, both belonging to the Bahama group, and sixteen days after he had first sighted land he disembarked on Cuban soil. He wrote a letter to his sovereign, which we presume he delivered in person, in which he describes Cuba as follows: "There is a river which discharges itself into the harbor which I have named Porto Santo, of sufficient depth to be navigable. I had the curiosity to sound it, and found it eight fathom; yet the water is so limpid, that I can easily discern the sand at the bottom. The banks of this river are embellished with lofty palm-trees, whose shades give a delicious freshness to the air; and the birds and the flowers are uncommon and beautiful. I was so delighted with the scene, that I had almost come to the resolution of staying here the remainder of my days; for, believe me, Sire, these countries far surpass all the rest of the world in beauty and conveniency; and I have frequently observed to my people, that, with all my endeavors to convey to your majesty an adequate idea of the charming objects which continually present themselves to our view, the description will fall greatly short of the reality." [1]

*Gold Seekers Disappointed.* But however enthusiastic Columbus was about the natural beauty of Cuba he was greatly disappointed that he did not find the fabulous wealth he was seeking. So he pushed on past Maisi,—the peninsula that still bears the name,—in search of Bahio which the natives told him lay to the east and where great riches could be found. On December 6th he arrived at the Island of Hayti, called by the natives Bahio, or

[1] Coke: "History of the West Indies," Vol. I, pp. 78-79 (published 1808).

"great country," and named by Columbus Espanola—Little Spain —known in English history as Hispaniola. Here one of the three ships, Santa Maria, ran aground and Guacanagari, the cacique (native chief or king) sent his bold swimmers who rescued the crew and cargo, getting all ashore on Christmas day. Using the timbers of his wrecked ship, Columbus built a fort and leaving forty-three men, he sailed back to Spain taking a few natives, a very small amount of gold, and most glowing accounts of his adventure to his grateful sovereign. Until his dying day Columbus was not aware of the fact that Cuba was an island and not the mainland he had gone to seek.

*Natives of the West Indies.* The natives of the Bahama Islands, of Cuba, and of the western portion of Hispaniola, afterward called Hayti, were Arawak Indians about whom Columbus wrote enthusiastically: "The natives love their neighbors as themselves. Their conversation is the sweetest imaginable; their faces always smiling; and so gentle and affectionate are they that I swear to your Highness there is not a better people in the world." Early historians describe them as "Hospitable, generous and unsuspicious. They engaged in no warfare, committed no depredations, and invaded no man's right. Satisfied with the productions which nature spontaneously yielded in this prolific region, they engaged her bounties without solicitude, and they extended their thoughts to no romantic speculations beyond the confines of their wants and supplies." [2] Legér remarks "On the whole they were kind, polite, merciful. Their good qualities caused their ruin." [3]

*Natives of Lesser Antilles More Savage.* On the other hand the inhabitants of the Lesser Antilles were Caribs, a warlike people, "fierce, aggressive, unyielding, pitiless to their enemies and their victims, but hospitable and generous to kinsman and friends." [4] These Caribs were cannibalistic, but had made some progress toward civilization. They worshipped one God, had some family life, did farming on a small scale, and lived in houses built of poles. Some of the more adventurous of this tribe had invaded the eastern and central section of Hispaniola and at the time of Columbus' landing were ruled over by a bold and heroic cacique—Caonabo. The native products of the islands found by Columbus, were cotton, tobacco, corn, plantain, and gold.

*Spanish Treatment of the Indians.* The kindness of the natives was repaid by the Spaniards with cruelty, robber, murder and slavery. Some were put to work gathering cotton and tobacco, others were put to mining for gold. At first the Indians were not enslaved outright but under the guise of being taught Chris-

[2] Coke: "History of the West Indies" (1808), Vol. I, p. 86.
[3] Leger: "Hayti," p. 21.
[4] Fiske: "The West Indies," p. 31.

tianity, each Spaniard had a number of Indians assigned to him and they were put at hard work. They were allowed to live in their own villages. But this did not produce wealth fast enough, so in 1506, pretending there was not enough time to teach them, and that going back to their native huts at night undid most of the work of the day, on grant of Ferdinand, the Spaniards were assigned a certain number of natives each, who lived about them in actual slavery. "It was observed in behalf of religion, that so long as the natives were tolerated in their idolatrous superstitions they would never embrace the doctrines of Christianity; but that as this distribution of them would deprive them of an opportunity of worshipping idols, so it would place them more immediately under the care of their masters, who would be enabled to give them that necessary instruction which their case required. In behalf of policy it was urged, that while these Indians continued to live in hordes, agreeably to customs of their ancestors, they would be meditating revolts from their tributary state; and they would keep the Spaniards in perpetual alarm, and create an increasing expense to government to establish soldiers to prevent their insurrection and to protect the Spaniards and their Indian slaves." [5] So severe were their tasks and so cruel was their treatment that twenty years of Spanish occupation sufficed to reduce the population from one million to a very few thousand in Hayti. The story of the stubborn resistance of Caonabo, and his beautiful Queen Anacaona, is one of the most thrilling accounts of early American history.[6] "Five shiploads of the subjugated natives were sent to Seville to be sold as slaves, of which Queen Isabella, greatly to her credit, did not approve." [7] A little later two shiploads of natives were sent to Spain as slaves, and the Queen set them all free.

*Demand for New Labor Supply.* The rapid destruction of the natives meant that a new labor supply must be found, for the Spaniards despised work, and would almost rather starve than be forced to it. Hence Columbus asked that Negroes should be sent out. Out of pity for the Arowak Indians who were not strong and hence unable to stand the strain of slavery, we saw in the last chapter that Las Cassas, plead to have the more robust Negroes take the place of the feeble natives. Thus in the name of religion and mercy was undertaken a scheme of labor which proved to be about the most irreligious and perhaps the most cruel of any forced labor in the world.

*Settlement of Cuba.* Cuba, as we have seen, was the first one of the Greater Antilles touched by Columbus, but it was not until

[5] Coke: "History of the West Indies," Vol. I, p. 131.
[6] Legèr: "Hayti," Ch. II.
[7] Fiske: "The West Indies," p. 45.

1511 that the first settlement was made. At that time Diego
Colon, brother of Columbus, sent Velasquez with three hundred
men, who landed on the North coast of Cuba and started a settlement at Baracoa. Cortez, of Mexico fame, was among these first
settlers. Las Cassas, who plead for the natives of Hispaniola,
tells us that due to the murder of the natives of Cuba "it lies
wholly untilled and ruined. The island of St. John and Jamaica
lie waste and desolate." "In 1524 the Cuban Indians had already
been reduced by two thirds; some yielded to the suffering, others
hastened their end by swallowing earth and gravel, or eating the
bitter manioc before being deprived of its poisonous sap. According to an official report scarcely 4,000 natives had survived
till 1532, so that in twenty-one years nearly the whole race had
completely disappeared." [8] In 1554 it is said there were only sixty
families left.

*First Slaves Introduced.* The first Negroes were introduced
into the West Indies in 1502. Sugar cane was introduced into
Hispaniola by Columbus, being brought from Cape Verde.
Others have claimed that sugar cane was introduced from the
Canary Islands by a Spaniard named Aguilan, in 1505.[9] At that
time sugar in Europe was very scarce and was considered a great
luxury. Gold not proving very plentiful, the raising of sugar
cane, cotton and tobacco soon came to be the chief occupation of
the islands. For this work the Negroes were peculiarly qualified,
so that the demand grew very rapidly. Most of the slaves up to
the middle of the sixteenth century were imported by the Portuguese, however a few of the buccaneers brought slaves, and Sir
John Hawkins made slave voyages to the West Indies in 1562,
1564, and 1567. On this last voyage Francis Drake made his
maiden trip to sea, and got his first experience in the West Indies
which he afterward visited as a British Admiral and as a
freebooter.[10]

*Other Nations Enter the West Indies.* The French captured the little island of Tortuga, north of Hayti, in 1629,
which ultimately led to their final possession of the whole
western section of the island. By 1635 they had occupied
Guadeloupe and Martinique and even earlier had sent settlers
into French Guiana. The French found that their white indentured servants were unable to do the work of farming in a tropical
country so they began importing Negroes, and by the middle of
the seventeenth century their share in the slave trade was in full
swing. The British occupied the island of Barbadoes in 1625,
and the Dutch took possession of St. Eustasius in 1635. Jamaica

[8] Keane: "The Earth and Its Inhabitants, North America," Vol. II, p. 567.
[9] Johnston: "The Negro in the New World," p. 78.
[10] Fiske: "The West Indies," p. 66.

which was colonized by the Spanish under Diego Colon in 1525 was really almost barren of Europeans until 1655 when the British planted a colony. Port Royal became a thriving town whose citizens were buccaneers and whose most welcome visitors were slave traders.[11] The Danes early took possession of a number of islands including St. Thomas and St. John,—east of Porto Rico, but these islands were scarcely worthy of note until the close of the seventeenth century when they became prosperous from sugar plantations.

Brazil was discovered in 1599, but it was more than thirty years before the Portuguese to whom it belonged by the treaty of Tordesillas, and the Pope's decree, were able to make much of their possession. Sugar cane was introduced in 1640 from whence a century later it was introduced into Barbadoes. Both the French and the Dutch attempted to share Brazil with Portugal. Dutch Guiana was held by the Dutch until the middle of the seventeenth century.

*Labor Supply in the New World.* To furnish these various possessions of the New World with a sufficient labor supply was a herculean task. Practically all the European nations had a hand in the trade. The Dutch brought many of their slaves from the Gold coast and just following 1640 from Angola, which they had captured from the Portuguese. The Portuguese brought their slaves largely from Angola and for a while following 1640 from Mozambique. The French and English began their slave trading near the Senegal River, later they established slave markets in the Congo section and on the Ivory Coast. Louis XIV held a number of shares in the Royal Senegal Company.

*Slaves not Self-Sustaining in Numbers.* Recluse estimates that 413,000 slaves were introduced into Cuba during the period of legal importation up to 1820, and that 500,000 more were smuggled in before slavery was finally abolished in 1887, a gradual process of emancipation starting in 1880. Jamaica received 610,000 slaves between 1680 and 1786 and it is altogether probable that from 1625 to 1680, and from 1786 to 1807, periods not covered by official figures, half as many more may have been landed on these shores. Carey estimates the total imports to Jamaica at 750,000.[12] So overwhelmingly were they in the majority in Jamaica that they retained almost in toto their African spirit worship, and sacrifices.[13] In Haiti alone of all the islands did the slaves seem to reproduce themselves. Here there were always more women than men and the natural increase was large  At the

---

[11] Fiske: "The West Indies," p. 210.
[12] Carey: "The Slave Trade" (1862), p. 12; cf. also, Pittman: "The Development of the British West Indies," p. 391 f.
[13] Keane: "North America," Vol. II, p. 386.

dawn of the revolution there were about 500,000 slaves in Hayti, and some 27,000 mulattoes, mostly free.  The first English settlers to the Barbadoes in 1626 took with them a few Negro slaves whom they had captured from a Spanish slaver on the way out. By 1674 the number of slaves was perhaps 100,000.[14]  Pittman says the average importations for a long period was about three thousand annually, so that perhaps over three hundred thousand slaves were imported into this island alone.[15]

There are no exact figures for many of the islands,—St. Vincent, for instance,—but we know that 6,100 slaves were imported into this island between 1784 and 1787 and 23,000 were imported into Dominica during the same period.  The total number of Negro slaves imported into the West Indies has been set at 2,130,000 by a number of authorities. ' Perhaps this is even too low an estimate.

The striking thing about the slaves in the West Indies is that they do not reproduce themselves, but showed a constant tendency to die out.  Carey says: There is no instance on record of any natural increase in any of the islands, under any circumstances." [16] Haiti seems to be an exception to this rule.  Perhaps Jamaica is as good an example of the tendency to decrease in slave population as any other.  In 1702 there were 36,000 Negroes on the island. In 1775, or seventy-two years later, there were only 194,614, or an increase of 158,614.  But during that time 497,736 Negroes had been imported and only 137,114 had been exported to other islands, leaving a net import of 360,622.  In other words, in order to get an increase of 158,614 in seventy-three years, 360,622 had to be imported.  From 1775 to 1791 there was a total net import of 113,000, but the total net increase in population was only 56,000.  Carey remarks that more than half the net importations perished under the treatment to which they were subjected.[17]

In St. Vincent the deaths and births for a series of years was as follows: [18]

|  |  |  |  |  |
|---|---|---|---|---|
| 1822 | 4205 | deaths — | 2656 | births |
| 1825 | 2106 | " | 1852 | " |
| 1828 | 2020 | " | 1829 | " |
| 1831 | 2266 | " | 1781 | " |

[14] Johnston: "The Negro in the New World," p. 212.
[15] Pittman: "The Development of the British West Indies," p. 72.
[16] Carey: "The Slave Trade," p. 11.
[17] Ibid., p. 9.
[18] Ibid., p. 12.

In British Guiana the deaths and births were as follows: [19]

| | | | | | |
|---|---|---|---|---|---|
| 1817-1820 | ...... | 7140 | deaths — | 4868 | births |
| 1820-1823 | ...... | 7188 | " | 4512 | " |
| 1823-1826 | ...... | 7634 | " | 4494 | " |
| 1826-1829 | ...... | 5131 | " | 4486 | " |
| 1829-1832 | ...... | 7016 | " | 4086 | " |

Other islands seemed to follow about this same rate of decrease so that the keeping up of this slave population necessitated constant importation of raw Negroes from Africa.

*A Typical Island Plantation Birth Record.* Phillips in his American Negro Slavery gives an extended description of Worthy Park's plantation on the island of Jamaica.[20] There were on this plantation 248 male slaves, 244 female slaves. "About eighty of the seasoned women were within the age limits of childbearing. The births recorded were on an average of nine for each of the five years covered, which was hardly half as many as might have been expected under favorable conditions. Special entry was made in 1795 of the number of children each woman had borne during her life. The number of these living at the time this record was made, and the number of miscarriages each woman had had. The total of births thus recorded was 345; of children then living 159; of miscarriages 75. Old Quasheba and Betty Madge had each borne fifteen children, and sixteen other women had borne from six to eleven each. On the other hand, seventeen women of thirty years and upwards had had no children and no miscarriages. The child-bearing records of the women past middle age ran higher than those of the younger ones to a surprising degree. Perhaps conditions on Worthy Park had been more favorable at an earlier period, when the owner and his family may possibly have been resident there. The fact that more than half of the children whom these women had borne were dead at the time of the record comports with the reputation of the sugar colonies for heavy infant mortality. With births so infrequent and infant deaths so many it may well appear that the notorious failure of the island-bred stock to maintain its numbers was not due to the working of the slaves to death. The poor care of the young children may be attributed largely to the absence of a white mistress, an absence characteristic of Jamaica plantations. There appears to have been no white resident on Worthy Park during the time of this record. In 1795 and perhaps in other years the plantation had a contract for medical service at the rate of 140 pounds a year." [21]

[19] Carey: "The Slave Trade," p. 13.
[20] Phillips: "American Negro Slavery," p. 57 f.
[21] *Ibid.,* pp. 61-62.

*Causes Assigned for Slow Increase of Slaves.* Writing of Santa Domingo, Stoddard says: "The continual dying out of the slave population in a favorable climate created much comment at the time, and many reasons for it were given. In 1764, a Governor attributed it to improper food, undue labor imposed upon pregnant women, and a very high infant mortality. The general opinion seems to have been that the Negroes were worked too hard, and Hilliard d'Auberteuil asserts that this was often deliberately done, as many masters considered it cheaper to buy slaves than to breed them. A colonial writer lays much of the trouble to immorality among the Negroes and to the ensuing ravages of venereal disease. Peytrand, perhaps the ablest student on the subject, thinks that much stress should be laid on the great nervous strain imposed by the sudden change from the careless indolence of savage existence, to a life of continuous labor." [22]

As a result of this situation the constant plaint of the planters of all the islands was for more slaves. When Colonel Modyford became governor of Jamaica in 1664 he found the planters most impatient of the import tax on slaves, and demanding a very much larger supply. "On September 20th, 1670, he enumerated a number of needs of the Island and asked Secretary Arlington that license to trade to Africa for Negroes be granted free of charge or at least at some moderate rates. Modyford admitted that the Anglo-Dutch war had been a great hindrance to Jamaica's prosperity but that the lack of Negroes since 1665 had been a much greater obstruction." [23]

*Demand for Slaves in the Barbadoes.* "In 1660 Barbadoes was in much the same condition as is true of every rapidly expanding new country. The settlers occupied as much land as they could obtain and directed every effort toward its cultivation and improvement. The growing of sugar had proved to be very profitable and every planter saw his gains limited only by the lack of labor to cultivate his lands. Every possible effort was therefore made to obtain laborers and machinery. Although the planters had little ready capital, they made purchases with a free hand, depending upon the returns from their next year's crop to pay off their debts. As a result, the planters were continually in debt to the merchants. The merchants greatly desired that Barbadoes should be made as dependent on England as possible in order that the constantly increasing amount of money which the planters owed them might be better secured. Moreover, they wished to prevent the planters from manipulating the laws of the island in such a way as to hinder the effective collection of debts. The planters, on the other hand, appreciated very keenly the ill effects

[22] Stoddard: "The French Revolution in San Domingo," p. 51.
[23] "Journal of Negro History," Vol. IV, p. 221.

upon themselves of the laws which were passed in England for the regulation of commerce. They bitterly complained of the enumerated article clause of the Navigation Act of 1660, which provided that all sugars, indigo and cotton-wool should be carried only to England. Already the planters were very greatly in debt to the merchants and they saw in this new law the beginning of the restrictions by which the merchants intended to throttle their trade. Indeed it seemed to the planters as if they were completely at the mercy of the merchants, who paid what they pleased for sugar, and charged excessive prices for Negroes,. cattle and supplies. Among those who were regarded as oppressors were the factors of the Royal Company, which controlled the Negro supply upon which the prosperity of the plantations depended." [24]

*Bitterness Over Scarcity of Slave Imports.* That little relief was given to the island can be seen from the heated protests of Governor Willoughby. Speaking of the general prohibitions on their trade, the governor exclaimed, May 12, 1666, that he had "come to where it pinches, and if your Maty gives not an ample & speedy redress, you have not onely lost Christophers but you will lose the rest, I (aye) & famous Barbadoes, too, I feare." In bitter terms he spoke of the poverty of the island, protesting that anyone who had recommended the various restraints on the colony's trade was "more a merchant than a good subject." The restriction on the trade to Guinea, he declared, was one of the things that had brought Barbadoes to its present condition; and the favoritism displayed toward the Royal Company in carrying on the Negro trade with the Spaniards had entirely deprived the colonial government of an export duty on slaves.

*Private Slave Ships Licensed.* "The decision of the company to issue licenses to private traders did not allay the storm of criticism that continued to descend on the company from Barbadoes. The new governor, as his brother had done, urged a free trade to Guinea for Negroes, maintaining that slaves had become so scarce and expensive that the poor planters would be forced to go to foreign plantations for a livelihood. He complained that the Colletons, father and son, the latter of whom was one of the company's factors, had helped to bring about this critical condition. On September 5, 1667, representatives of the whole colony petitioned the king to throw open the Guinea trade or to force the company to supply them with slaves at the prices promised in the early declaration, although even those prices seemed like a canker of usury to the much abused planters.

*Petition for Open Slave Trade.* "Following these complaints Sir Paul Painter and others submitted a petition to the House

[24] "Journal of Negro History," Vol. IV, pp. 208-209.

of Commons in which they asserted that an open trade to Africa was much better than one carried on by a company. They maintained that previous to the establishment of the Royal Adventurers, Negroes had been sold for twelve, fourteen and sixteen pounds per head, or 1,600 to 1,800 pounds of sugar, whereas now the company was selling the best slaves to the Spaniards at eighteen pounds per head, while the planters paid as high as thirty pounds for those of inferior grade. This, they declared, had so exasperated the planters that they often refused to ship their sugar and other products to England in the company's ships no matter what freight rates the factors offered." [25]

*Restricted Slave Trade and Slow Growth of Population.* There were evidently many causes for the high death rate and low birth rate of the slaves. The hot climate was certainly not conducive to a long life either of master or slave. Besides the slave had never been accustomed to regular work and the process of readjustment was a most trying one. The conversion of new Negroes into plantation laborers, a process called "breaking in," required always a mingling of delicacy and firmness. Some planters distributed their new purchases among the seasoned households, thus delegating the task largely to the veteran slaves. Others housed and tended them separately under the charge of a select staff of nurses and guardians and with frequent inspections from headquarters. The mortality rate was generally high under either plan, ranging usually from twenty to thirty per cent in the seasoning period of three or four years. The deaths come from diseases brought from Africa, such as the yaws, which was similar to siphilis; from debilities and maladies acquired on the voyage; from the change of climate and food; from exposure incurred in running away; from marked habits, such as dirt eating; and from accident, manslaughter and suicide." [26]

*Treatment of Slaves in the Islands.* That there were other causes also, such as lack of proper food, poor housing facilities, overwork, and cruelty which lay behind the running away, morbid habits, suicide, etc., it seems to me no fair investigator can doubt. In 1790-91 the British Parliament made an exhaustive investigation of conditions of slavery as it then existed and their conclusions were anything but flattering to the planters. A large number of prominent persons who had actually seen conditions in the West Indies made reports. This compilation says that the slaves went to the field at daybreak, and labored all day with the exception of thirty minutes during the morning when they ate breakfast, and two hours in the heat of the day, when they either rested or did lighter tasks, such as pulling grass for

[25] Journal of Negro History," Vol. IV, pp. 213-214.
[26] Phillips: "American Negro Slavery," p. 53.

the animals. If a hand was late in the field they were whipped on the spot.

During the crop gathering period, the hours were much longer, often 18 hours per day. The report concludes they were worked as long as they could keep going. "Sometimes they fall asleep through excess of fatigue when their arms are caught in the mill and torn off." [27]   Particularly on the sugar plantations the gathering season was most trying.   Mr. Fitzmaurice testified before the commission, that on the plantations which were under-manned—which were the majority—the Negroes were divided into two groups; one group serving at the boiling house from twelve noon to twelve midnight, and the other group serving the remainder of the twenty-four hours.   But each group must do five to six hours' work besides that at the boiling house.   The cane must be cut and brought to the mill, the stock must be cared for, grass must be cut to feed the animals, and many other chores must be done.   Men and women worked side by side in all the tasks.

*Treatment of Women.*   The conditions of women were par-ticularly pitiable. "It is impossible to pass over in silence the almost total want of indulgence which the women slaves fre-quently experience during the operations in the field.   It is asserted by Dalrymple, that the drivers in using their whip never distinguish sex.   As to pregnant women, and such as had children, Mr. Davies believed they were allowed to come into the field a little later than the rest.   They did little work after they were four months gone with child, in the experience of Mr. Duncan. Dr. Harrison also has known some overseers allow complaining pregnant women to retire from work, but he has seen them labor-ing in the field, when they seemed to have but a few months to go; they were generally worked as long as able.   Much the same work, says Mr. Cook, was expected from pregnant women as others.   He has seen them hoeing till a few hours of their delivery, and has known them receive thirty-nine lashes while in this state. Mr. Woolrich thinks the pregnant women had some little indul-gence, but it was customary for them to work in the field till near their time.   The whip was occasionally used upon them, but not so severely as upon the men.   Mr. Ross, observing the gangs at work, saw a pregnant woman rather behind the rest. The driver called her to come on, and going back struck her with the whip up toward her shoulders.   He asked another preg-nant woman, if she was forced to work like the rest, and she said, Yes.   Sir G. Young adds, that women were considered to miscarry in general from their hard field labor; and Captain Hall says that, where they had children, they were sent again

[27] "Evidence on the Slave Trade" (1791); republished 1859, pp. 63-65, *passim.*

after the month to labour with the children upon their backs, and so little time afforded them to attend their wants, that he has seen a woman seated to give suck to her child roused from that situation by a severe blow from the cart whip." [28]

*Scanty Food Allowance.* As to food it is quite clear from the general evidence that it was neither sufficient in quantity nor in variety. "The point which may be considered next may be that of the slaves' food. This appears by the evidence to be subject to no rule. On some estates they are allowed land which they cultivate for themselves at the times mentioned above, but they have no provisions allowed them, except, perhaps, a small present of salt fish, or beef, or salt pork, at Christmas. On others they are allowed provisions, but no land; and on others again they are allowed land and provisions jointly. Without enumerating the different rations mentioned to be allowed them by the different evidences, it may be sufficient to take the highest. The best allowance is evidently at Barbadoes, and the following is the account of it. The slaves in general, says General Tottenham, appeared to be ill fed; each slave had a pint of grain for twenty-four hours, and sometimes half a rotten herring, when to be had. When the herrings were unfit for the whites, they were bought up by the planters for the slaves. Mr. Davis says, that on those estates in Barbadoes where he has seen the slaves' allowance dealt out, a grown Negro had nine pints of corn, and about one pound of salt a week, but the grain of the West Indies is much lighter than wheat. He is of opinion that, in general, they were too sparingly fed. The Dean of Middleham also mentions nine pints per week as the quantity given, but that he has known masters abridge it in the time of crop. This is the greatest allowance mentioned throughout the whole of the evidence, and this is one of the cases in which the slaves had provisions but no land. Where, on the other hand, they have land and no provisions, all the evidences agree that it is quite ample to their support, but that they have not sufficient time to cultivate it. Their lands, too, are often at the distance of three miles from their houses, and Mr. Giles thinks the slaves were often so fatigued by the labor of the week as scarcely to be capable of working in them on Sunday for their own use." [29]

*The Slave Codes.* But perhaps more than anything else the severity of the slave codes tended to discourage and destroy the slaves. In 1667 Parliament passed an act to regulate the Negroes on the British plantations. It set forth that the islands could not be brought into use without slaves, then described the Negroes as of wild, barbarous, and savage nature to be controlled only

[28] "Evidence on the Slave Trade," p. 64.
[29] *Ibid.,* p. 66.

with strict severity, and followed with a long list of prohibitions. Slaves were not to leave their own plantations without a ticket or pass from their master or mistress, they were not to be away from their plantations on Sunday, they were not allowed to carry any weapons, they must not keep drums or any other instrument, such as a horn, by which they could signal to each other. If a slave struck a "Christian" he was to be severely whipped by the constable, and for a second offense he was to be branded on the face with a red hot iron. Punishments were set for murder, rape, stealing, injuring stock and incendiarism. If the state executed a slave the owner was to receive 25 pounds sterling. If the owner accidentally—without intention—whipped a slave to death or by other accident during punishment killed him—he was not liable even to fine; but if he wantonly killed his slave, he must pay into the public treasury 15 pounds. If he killed another man's slave he must pay 25 pounds. Ten years later a law was passed forbidding Quakers from assembling Negroes at their meeting houses for services.

*The French "Code Noir"*   The French "Code Noir" of 1685 is considered one of the most humane of all the codes regulating slaves. It ordered baptism and instruction of slaves in religion, made drastic rules against concubinage, and decreed that slave families might not be separated. Slaves were not allowed to carry arms, were forbidden to assemble together, could not hold property, were put to death for striking a white person, and for the offense of running away were to have their ears cut off and their shoulders branded. For a second offense they were to be branded again and hamstrung. But in spite of the more moderate and humane clauses of this code, the "French seem to have treated their slaves at times with a wanton, almost tigerish cruelty which left a deep impression on the Negro mind and tradition. Particularly after insurrection or plots, the offenders were treated with dastardly cruelty, which only sowed the seed for more discontent. Speaking of Ogè and his associates who led an insurrection during the last decade of the eighteenth century and all of whom were cruelly executed, though promised immunity if they would surrender, Johnston says: "Their arms, thighs, legs and backbones were broken with clubs on a scaffold. They were then fastened round a wheel in such manner that their face was turned upward to receive the full glare of the sun. 'Here,' ran the sentence, 'they are to remain for so long as it shall please God to preserve them alive,' after which their heads were cut off and exposed on tall poles." [30]   By such cruelty the French were laying for themselves a mine of revolt which was later to explode with terrible results.

[30] Johnston: "The Negro in the New World," p. 146.

*Spanish Treatment of Slaves.* The Spanish, contrary to their general reputation, were perhaps better to their slaves than any of the other nations working in the West Indies. The result was they had fewer insurrections and held their possessions down to 1898, when on account of certain abuses America interfered. In their earlier codes of 1540 and 1641 slaves were allowed to buy their freedom for $250 and in the case of an expectant mother twelve dollars more would free her unborn child. Owners were encouraged to free their slaves, by the priests, it being considered an act of great piety. A new code was promulgated in 1789 which was not quite so liberal but carried the following provisions:

1. Masters were to instruct their slaves in the principles of the Catholic religion.
2. A minimum of food and clothing was prescribed, and the justices were ordered to enforce this provision.
3. Definite kinds of work were forbidden children and women and the aged.
4. No work was to be demanded on the Sabbath or holy days.
5. A housing code prevented more than two slaves being lodged in one room.
6. In old age slaves must be maintained by their masters.
7. Matrimony of slaves was encouraged.
8. Industrial training must be given all slaves.
9. Severe punishments were prescribed for the violation of any of these codes, and priests and others were encouraged to inform about those disobeying.[31]

*Dutch Cruelty to Slaves.* If the Spanish were the most humane masters the Dutch were the most cruel. Johnston thinks they housed and fed slaves better than did the British, but were far more cruel and reckless in their general treatment of Negroes. "Slaves were compelled to work every day in the week if their masters wished it." The women were particularly cruel to their housemaids, often branding them to keep them from being too beautiful and forcing them to serve nude lest they should attempt concealment by their clothing. "It is recorded of a certain Miss S——— that she always had her female slaves flogged across the breasts because it caused them greater pain."[32]

*British Testimony.* That the punishments in all the islands were severe will be readily proven by the testimony before the House of Commons Committee. "In speaking of the punish-

[31] Johnston: "The Negro in the New World," pp. 42-46, *passim.*
[32] *Ibid.,* p. 113.

ments of the slaves by means of the whip and cowskin, it is impossible to pass over the frequency and severity of them as described in the evidence, as well as the lengths to which some of their owners go upon these occasions.

"On the frequency of these punishments something may be deduced from the different expressions which the different evidences adopt according to their different opportunities of observation. Many of the field slaves are said by Duncan, Dalrymple, Fitzmaurice, and Rees, to be marked with the whip. A great proportion of them is the term used by Captain Wilson. That they are marked commonly or generally, or that the generality of them are marked, are the expressions agreed in by the Dean of Middleham, Lieutenant Simpson, Captain Ross, Captain Hall (Navy), Captain Giles, Captain Smith, and Lieutenant Davison. The greater part of them, says Jeffreys, most of them, say Coor and Woolrich, bear the marks of the whip.

*Instruments of Punishment.* "With respect to the severity of these punishments, it may be shown by describing the nature of the instrument with which they are inflicted, and the power it has, and the effect it produces wherever it is seriously applied.

"The whip, says Woolrich, is generally made of plaited cowskin with a thick strong lash. It is so formidable an instrument in the hands of some of the overseers, that by means of it they can take the skin off a horse's back. He has heard them boast of laying the marks of it in a deal board, and he has seen it done. On its application on a slave's back he has seen the blood spurt out immediately on the first stroke.

"Nearly the same account of its construction is given by other evidences, and its power and effects are thus described. At every stroke, says Captain Smith, a piece of flesh was drawn out. Dalrymple avers the same thing. It will even bring blood through the breeches, says J. Terry; and such is the effusion of blood on those occasions, adds Fitzmaurice, as to make their frocks, if immediately put on, appear as stiff as buckram; and Coor observes, that at his first going to Jamaica, a sight of common flogging would put him in a tremble, so that he did not feel right for the rest of the day. It is observed also by Dr. Harrison and the Dean of Middleham, that the incisions are sometimes so deep that you may lay your fingers in the wounds. There are also wheals, says Mr. Coor, from their hams to the small of their backs. These wheals, cuts, or marks, are described by Captain Thompson, Dean of Middleham, Mr. Jeffreys, and General Tottenham, as indelible, as lasting to old age, or as such as no time can erase, and Woolrich has often seen their backs one undistinguished mass of lumps, holes, and furrows." [33]

[33] "Evidences on the Slave Trade," p. 73.

*Special Cruelty.* Extraordinary cruelty was also cited, which of course could not be taken as normal or as frequent, but showed to what enormity the system sometimes led. "Captain Ross has seen a negro woman, in Jamaica, flogged with ebony bushes (much worse than our own thorn bushes) so that the skin of her back was taken off, down to her heels. She was then turned round and flogged from her breast down to her waist, and in consequence he saw her afterwards walking upon all fours, and unable to get up.

"Captain Cook being on a visit to General Frere, at an estate of his in Barbadoes, and riding one morning with the General and two other officers, they saw near a house, upon a dunghill, a naked negro nearly suspended by strings from his elbows backwards, to the bough of a tree, with his feet barely upon the ground, and an iron weight round his neck, at least, to the appearance of fourteen pounds weight; and thus without one creature near him, or apparently near the house, was this wretch left, exposed to the noonday sun. Returning a few hours after, they found him still in the same state, would have released him, but for the advice of General Frere, who had an estate in the neighborhood. The gentlemen, through disgust, shortened their visit, and returned the next morning.

"Jeffreys, Captain Ross, M. Terry and Coor, mention the cutting off of ears, as another species of punishment. The last gentleman gives the following instance in Jamaica. One of the house-girls having broken a plate or spilt a cup of tea, the doctor (with whom Mr. Coor boarded) nailed her ear to a post. Mr. Coor remonstrated with him in vain. They went to bed, and left her there. In the morning she was gone, having torn the head of the nail through her ear. She was soon brought back, and when Mr. Coor came to breakfast, he found she had been severely whipped by the doctor, who, in his fury, clipped both her ears off close to her head, with a pair of large scissors, and she was sent to pick seeds out of cotton, among three or four more, emaciated by his cruelties, until they were fit for nothing else." [34]

*Effect of Cruelty.* These various forms of cruelty, even though they may have been infrequent, evidently tended to spread great discontent and so to dishearten the slaves that a normal length of life was not to be expected. Furthermore, it had a tendency to make slaves unhappy and willing to stir up insurrections.

*Rise of the Maroons.* When the English took possession of Jamaica in 1650, they found that their reputation for cruelty to slaves had already preceded them and practically all the slaves escaped to the mountains. These escaped slaves formed a colony

[34] "Evidences on the Slave Trade," pp. 76-77.

which came to be called the Maroons.  The word probably means mountain dwellers, from the word comia, meaning mountain top, for they were first called Cimarons, later shortened to marons, then maroons.  The "labyrinthine valleys and cockpits offered a refuge to the runaways, who found a sufficient support by clearing the forests, planting yams, and hunting the wild boar."  "Thanks to their knowledge of the locality and to the 'drum language,' by which news was rapidly spread from hill to hill, as amongst their dwalla kindred of the Cameroons on the West coast of Africa, frequent communications were kept up from one end of the island to the other; munitions and other supplies were also obtained through their secret intercourse with the plantation Negroes." [35]  A constant warfare was kept up between the planters and these maroons and the whites lived in constant terror of being robbed and murdered.  "As Jamaica came to be a great center of slave trade and her growing plantations were worked almost exclusively by slave labor under brutal taskmasters, fugitives multiplied and the community of maroons became formidable enough to produce serious trouble." [36]  In 1730 these various communities united under a powerful chief named Cudjo and so ravaged the plantations that two additional regiments of soldiers were sent out from England to protect the whites.

*Cruel Treatment of the Maroons.*  One of the cruel means of fighting the Maroons was to track them down with bloodhounds, which hounds were "provided by the church wardens of the various parishes."  In 1739 a treaty of peace was entered into between the colonists and the Maroons, by which the latter were guaranteed their independence provided they would return all fugitive slaves.  This fugitive slave law, like the one in the United States, more than a century later, created much friction and discontent.  In 1795 two Maroons were tried by the colonists for stealing a pig, and were condemned to be whipped.  This was to the Maroons a great indignity, because it was the punishment meted out to slaves.  The hot headed governor resented their complaint, surrounded their reservations, imported more bloodhounds from Cuba, overpowered the Maroons and a number were deported to Nova Scotia.  This, however, did not settle the question, for no question is ever settled until settled right.  The remaining Maroons held the action of the planters as a grievance and constant uprisings occurred.  In 1833 freedom of slaves was decreed, but just before this act was passed there was a slave uprising and much property destroyed.  The planters in retaliation, shot, hanged or brutally murdered 1,500 slaves, another

[35] Keane: "The Earth and Its Inhabitants, North America," Vol. II, pp. 386-387.
[36] Fiske: "West Indies," p. 90.

insurrection of the blacks, who were still treated as slaves, though nominally free, came in 1865, and was put down with great severity. Meanwhile, most of the white planters returned to England, leaving their estates to agents. Many of the big estates have been broken up and some of the Negroes now own their farms. The present population of 700,000, mostly Negroes, is not altogether prosperous.

*Hardships in Haiti.* As noted before Haiti, or the western third of Hispaniola, was ceded to France by the treaty of Ryswick in 1697. The French called it St. Domingue, by which name it was known until after it was declared independent, when it took the name Haiti. The eastern end of the island, still belonging to Spain, was called Hispaniola until the name Haiti was applied to the West, at which time the Spaniards changed the name of their section to Santo Domingo, by which name it is still called. The history of Haiti is one filled with cruelty and bloodshed. Beginning with Columbus and his followers, who enslaved, overworked and finally exterminated the native Indians, down to the period of independence in 1804, there is a crowded record of revolt and massacre, and retaliations. "Scarcely a single town in Haiti but recalls some siege, battle, or butchery. The very river marking the northern frontier is known by the name of Rivière du Massacre, in memory of the sanguinary conflict between the natives and the Spaniards." [37] Just as in Jamaica, cruel treatment drove many Negroes into the mountains as fugitives, so in Haiti and Santo Domingo, the high mountains and tangled tropical forests offered a safe retreat of those who desired to escape the hardships of the slave régime. It is said that one thousand slaves took to the mountains in 1620 and the constant stream of runaways built up a Maroon colony or colonies which the Colonial government recognized in 1784. These "Maroons kept constantly in touch with the enslaved Negroes and could always stir many to trouble." [38] The years of 1679, 1691, 1704 were all marked by uprisings, massacres and severe punishments. "But about 1750 there appeared a man of real ideas and powerful personality who was to become a veritable menace to the colony. This man was the famous Macandal. Macandal was an African, whether from the Senegal or Guinea is uncertain. For more than six years he abstained from active warfare against the whites while strengthening his influence over the Negroes. His power was of a religious nature, for he announced that he was the **Black Messiah, sent to drive the whites from the island.** His magic powers gave him the authority of a veritable Old Man of the Mountain, and the superstitious Negroes considered him

[37] Keane: "The Earth and Its Inhabitants, North America," Vol. II, p. 410.
[38] Stoddard: "The French Revolution in San Domingo," p. 64.

a god.  He had a clear idea of race, and concerning it, gave utterance to the following remarkable prophecy:  One day, before a numerous assembly, he exhibited a vase containing three hand-kerchiefs, colored yellow, white, and black, which he drew out in turn.  'Behold,' said he, 'the first people of San Domingo—they were yellow.  Behold the present inhabitants—they are white. Behold those who shall one day remain its masters'—and he drew forth the black handkerchief.

*The Uprising in Haiti.*  "At last, about 1758, he thought the moment come for his great stroke.  His plan rested on the whole-some use of poison.  Poison had always been the chief slave method of obtaining revenge.  It assumed the most diverse forms: poisoning of the master, of his children, his cattle, his slaves,— even self-inflicted poisoning, if the party thought himself a chattel of value.  But Macandal united poisoning to marronage for a definite end.  According to an official memoir, the plot was woven with consummate skill.  On a certain day all the water of Le Cap was to be poisoned, and, when the whites were in convulsions, Macandal and his maroon bands were to raise the waiting Negroes of the "plaine" and exterminate the colonists.  Only by the merest chance was the conspiracy discovered.  The terror among the whites was great, and Macandal was relentlessly hunted down and executed.  Yet even in death he left behind a legacy of unrest, for he prophesied that he would one day return, more terrible than before.  This was believed by many Negroes, and the colony was never free from poisonings and disturbances.

"The great negro insurrection of 1791 was thus only the coming to pass of what had been awaiting the favor of circumstance since the colony's beginning.  Its possibility had long been fore-seen.  'We have in the negroes most dangerous enemies,' writes a Governor in 1685.  A century later, a royal officer exclaims, 'A slave colony is a town menaced by assault; we are walking on barrels of powder.'  His words were true;—and sparks from the edicts of Revolutionary France were soon to fall upon those powder-barrels." [39]

*Abolition Societies.*  The rise of the English Abolition Society in 1787, followed in 1788 by the organization of a similar society in France, headed by such men as La Fayette, Mirabeau and others, together with the silly bungling of the States General on the whole question of freedom and legal rights, hastened the up-rising of the Negroes of Haiti.  At first the Negroes had no idea of setting up an independent republic.  They were only striving for a share in their self-control; but as time went on and the leadership came into the hands of the powerful Toussaint L'Ouverture, both the free people of color and the slaves were

[39] Stoddard: "French Revolution in San Domingo," pp. 65-67.

united and in 1801 independence was declared. At this stage Napoleon interfered and through the basest of intrigue, Toussaint was induced to plan a representative assembly for the island. At this proposed assembly Toussaint, who had been repeatedly assured of good faith, was seized and carried to France, where he died of neglect and starvation in a dungeon cell. The fighting for freedom by the Negroes was again taken up with renewed desperation, yellow fever helped them by destroying many of the French soldiers, and finally the French garrison at Cape Haitien surrendered and Haiti was again declared a free and independent state on January 1, 1804.

Thus cruelty, greed and mismanagement robbed France of her greatest Western possession. In all these movements the eastern or Spanish part of the island was much concerned. Its career was too checkered to receive detailed statement. For a long while under Spain, then paying allegiance to Bolivar of Colombia in 1821, it passed over to Haiti and finally became an independent republic in 1844. Its history is filled also with revolts, though not so numerous as in the other islands because, as we remarked before, the slave régime was much more kindly and humane.

*Cruelty and Revolt in Danish Islands.* The Danish West Indies, though small, were no exception to this general story of cruelty, mistreatment, insurrection and bloodshed. "The most persistent motive that led to general unrest among the slaves was lack of food. When months of drought ruined the crops of maize, sweet potatoes, and other foods which the Negroes were expected to raise for their own sustenance, the planters were obliged to buy provisions from outside sources if they were to save their Negroes' lives and prevent them from rising against their masters. In 1725-1726 the drought was unusually severe and protracted. A number of the planters let their slaves starve to death; others gave them extra holidays, with the natural result that the blacks stole right and left and became exceedingly difficult to manage. Since open resistance to the whites was the worst of crimes, it is not surprising to find rcorded in the Company's books for 1726 that seventeen slaves distributed among thirteen planters had been executed and debited to the community at a price of about 120 rdl. each. The planters secured the equivalent for their losses in fresh slaves from the next incoming Guinea cargo." [40]

In September, 1733, Governor Gardelin of St. Thomas Island issued a most drastic decree of punishments for slave crimes, including pinching with iron tweezers, burning, whipping and hanging. This aroused so much discontent that a fearful uprising soon followed. "On Monday afternoon, November 23,

[40] Westergaard: "The Danish West Indies," p. 164.

1733, a very badly frightened soldier and some panic-stricken refugees from St. John appeared in the fort at St. Thomas harbor and poured into the ears of the astonished governor and his council a most fearful tale. Early that morning twelve or fourteen of the Company's Negroes had come up the path on the mountainside to the fort overlooking Coral Bay on St. John, each of them with an armful of wood. When the sentinel shouted 'Who is there?' he received the answer, 'Negroes with wood,' and opened the door. Rushing inside, the Negroes pulled sugarcane knives (Kapmesser) out from the wood and murdered the soldier on the spot. Meantime other Negroes had assembled and together they rushed in upon the sleeping corporal and his six soldiers, killing all but one (John Gabriel), who in the early twilight managed to save himself by crawling under a bed, and later escaped through the bush and down to a canoe by the seashore. With the garrison out of the way the Negroes proceeded to raise the flag and fire three shots from the cannon at the fort. This was the signal for a general slaughter on all the plantations on the island.

*The Revenge of the Slaves.* "The ranking magistrate on St. John, John Reimert Soedimann, and his stepdaughter were among the first victims of that fateful day. A band of Negroes, including some of Soedtmann's own, routed them both out and put them to death in the early morning. Soedtmann's wife was saved by the circumstance of her being on a visit to St. Thomas. Roaming about from plantation to plantation in that dim tropic dawn they slaughtered such whites as they could find, planters and overseers, women and children. As the bloody work proceeded, the band increased their numbers. The Company's and Soedtmann's Negroes were joined by others; and by the middle of the afternoon a body of eighty desperate blacks, half of them with flintlocks or pistols, the rest with cane-knives and other murderous weapons, were ready to attack those whites that remained. Though murder was rife, its course did not run absolutely without control. One Cornelius Bodger, the surgeon on St. John, and his two young step-sons were saved,—the former because of his medical skill, the latter because the rebels hoped to make these boys their servants. Someone's intercession at the last moment saved the life of a former overseer of the Company who accepted with alacrity the invitation of the rebels to leave the island.

"The surviving planters, with such Negroes as remained faithful, had in the meantime collected at Peter Deurloo's plantation on the northwest corner of the island. The approach to 'Deurloo's Bay' was easily guarded, and the fugitive planters were within fairly easy reach of St. Thomas. While the St. Thomas officials and planters were making such preparations for their relief as they could, a small band of whites under the leadership of Captain of Militia John von Beverhoudt and Lieutenant John Charles, together with a score or more of their best Negroes, were hastening with feverish activity to prepare for the rebel onslaught.  The women and children were quickly transported to nearby islets.  A number of the planters on the south side and on the west end of the island were warned by friendly slaves in time to permit them to join the men at Deurloo's or to seek safety in their canoes." [41]

With slight variations the story of the other islands is practically the same as that of Jamaica, Haiti and the Danish West Indies.  None of them were free from a certain amount of hardness and cruelty in the treatment of slaves, and all of them reaped sooner or later the terrible harvest of uprisings and bloodshed.

*Financial Aspects in West Indies.*  Financially the West Indies can hardly be said to have yielded a satisfactory return.  Tobacco, cotton, indigo, ginger and sugar have always been the main crops, and most of these seemed to be best raised on large plantations. This was particularly true of sugar because it required a great deal of capital to provide the mill for grinding, and the apparatus for boiling and preparing the product.  A small planter could not afford this large initial outlay, but must depend on his neighbor for such machinery, which dependence, due to the shortness and emergency of the gathering season, was rather precarious. Bryon Edwards estimated that $150,000 was a minimum capital for running a sugar plantation.  This demand for a large initial outlay resulted in an overwhelming amount of absenteeism.  Most of the great estates were owned by the nobility and the rich in the mother countries, some of them, of course, being held by great companies.  Investment in a plantation in the West Indies, was to the mother countries, what investment in mining prospects in the West has been to the wealthier and more settled populations of our eastern section of the United States during the last fifty years.  A few men have made fabulous wealth out of their mining ventures, but most of those who have invested have never realized any profits and often they have lost their capital.  However, the spirit of adventure is still strong in men and on the basis of a chance men will continue to invest.  So it was with the West Indian investors.  They continued to buy land and slaves in the hope that some day they would "strike it rich."  Most of them never did.  It is due to this fact of absenteeism that so much of cruelty and hardship fell to the lot of the West Indian slave.  The overseers, managers, and slave drivers were eager to make the best showing of profits and were not looking to a long time policy of success.

[41] Westergaard: "The Danish West Indies," pp. 168-169.

*Small Cash Return—Worthy Park.* Frequently one of these large plantations yielded less than 4% on the investment; indeed, it was not uncommon for them to yield nothing. But on a year when sugar or cotton rose to high price much money was made, and thus planters were encouraged to continue their business. The extravagance, wastefulness and inefficiency of a slave plantation can best be shown by quoting from Dr. Phillips's account of Worthy Park's plantation in Jamaica. The number of slaves is far out of proportion to the number actually producing and to the income from the plantation. "Slaves of the estate at the beginning of 1792 numbered 355, apparently all seasoned Negroes, of whom 150 were in the main field gang. But this force was inadequate for the full routine, and in that year "jobbing gangs" from outside were employed at rates from 2s 6d to 3s per head per day, and at a total cost of £1,832, reckoned probably in Jamaican currency, which stood at thirty per cent discount. In order to relieve the need of this outside labor the management began that year to buy new Africans on a scale considered reckless by all the island authorities. In March five men and five women were bought; and in October 25 men, 27 women, 16 boys, 16 girls, and 6 children; all new Congoes; and in the next year 51 males and 30 females, part Congoes and part Coromantees, and nearly all of them eighteen to twenty years old. Thirty new huts were built; special cooks and nurses were detailed; and quantities of special foodstuffs were bought—yams, plantains, flour, fresh and salt fish, and fresh beef heads, tongues, hearts and bellies; but it is not surprising to find that the next outlay for equipment was for a large new hospital in 1794, costing £341 for building its brick walls alone. Yaws became serious, but that was a trifle as compared with dysentery; and pleurisy, pneumonia, fever and dropsy had also to be reckoned with. About fifty of the new Negroes were quartered for several years in a sort of hospital camp at Spring Garden, where the routine even for the able-bodied was much lighter than on Worthy Park.

*Diseases Among Slaves.* "One of the new Negroes died in 1792, and another in the next year. Then in the spring of 1794 the heavy mortality began. In that year at least 31 of the newcomers died, nearly all of them from the "bloody flux" (dysentery), except two who were thought to have committed suicide. By 1705, however, the epidemic had passed. Of the five deaths of the new Negroes that year, two were attributed to dirt-eating, one to yaws, and two to ulcers, probably caused by yaws. The three years of the seasoning period were now ended, with about three-fourths of the number imported still alive. The loss was perhaps less than usual where such large batches were bought;

but it demonstrates the strength of the shock involved in the transplantation from Africa, even after the severities of the middle passage had been survived and after the weaklings among the survivors had been culled out at the ports. The outlay for jobbing gangs on Worthy Park rapidly diminished.

*Lists of Slaves.* "The list of slaves at the beginning of 1794 is the only one giving full data as to ages, colors and health as well as occupations. The ages were of course in many cases mere approximations. The "great house Negroes" head the list, fourteen in number. They comprised four housekeepers, one of whom, however, was but eight years old, three waiting boys, a cook, two washer-women, two gardeners and a grass carrier, and included nominally Quadroon Lizette, who after having been hired out for several years to Peter Douglas, the owner of a jobbing gang, was this year manumitted.

"The overseer's house had its proportionate staff of nine domestics with two seamstresses added, and it was also head-quarters both for the nursing corps and a group engaged in minor industrial pursuits. The former, with a 'black doctor' named Will Morris at its head, included a midwife, two nurses for the hospital, four (one of them blind) for the new Negroes, two for the children in the day nursery, and one for the suckling babies of the women in the gangs. The latter comprised three cooks to the gangs, one of whom had lost a hand; a groom, three hog tenders, of whom one was ruptured, another 'distempered' and the third a ten-year-old boy, and ten aged idlers, including Quashy Prapra and Abba's Moo to mend pads, Yellow's Cuba and Peg's Nancy to tend the poultry house, and the rest to gather grass and hog feed.

"Next were listed the watchmen, thirty-one in number, to guard against depredations of men, cattle and rats and against conflagrations which might sweep the ripening cane-fields and the buildings. All of these were black but the mulatto foreman, and only six were described as able-bodied. The disabilities noted were a bad sore leg, a broken back, lameness, partial blindness, distemper, weakness, and cocobees, which was a malady of the blood.

*Working Condition of Slaves.* "A considerable number of the slaves already mentioned were in such condition that little work might be expected of them. Those completely laid off were nine superannuated ranging from seventy to eighty-five years old, three invalids, and three women relieved of work as by law required for having reared six children each.

"Among the tradesmen, virtually all the blacks were stated to be fit for field work, but the five mulattoes and the one quadroon, though mostly youthful and healthy, were described as not fit for the field.   There were eleven carpenters, eight coopers, four sawyers, three masons and twelve cattlemen, each squad with a foreman; and there were two rat-catchers whose work was highly important, for the rats swarmed in incredible numbers and spoiled the cane if left to work their will.   A Jamaican author wrote, for example, that in five or six months on one plantation "not less than nine and thirty thousand were caught."

"In the 'weeding gang,' in which most of the children from five to eight years old were kept as much for control as for achievement, there were twenty pickaninnies, all black, under Mirtilla as 'driveress,' who had borne and lost seven children of her own.   Thirty-nine other children were too young for the weeding gang, at least six of whom were quadroons.   Two of these last, the children of Joanny, a washer-woman at the overseer's house, were manumitted in 1795.

*Spring Garden Gang.*   "Fifty-five, all new Negroes except Darby the foreman, and including Blossom, the infant daughter of one of the women, comprised the Spring Garden squad. Nearly all of these were twenty or twenty-one years old.   The men included Washington, Franklin, Hamilton, Burke, Fox, Milton, Spencer, Hume and Sheridan; the women Spring, Summer, July, Bashful, Virtue, Frolic, Gamesome, Lady, Madame, Duchess, Myrtle and Cowslip.   Seventeen of this distinguished company died within the year.

*Worthy Park Gang.*   "The 'big gang' on Worthy Park numbered 137, comprising 64 men from nineteen to sixty years old and 73 women from nineteen to fifty years, though but four of the women and nine of the men, including Quashy, the 'head driver,' or foreman, were past forty years.   The gang included a 'head home wainman,' a 'head road wainman,' who appears to have been also the sole slave plowman on the place; a head muleman, three distillers, a boiler, two sugar potters, and two 'sugar guards' for the wagons carrying the crop to port.   All of the gang were described as healthy, able-bodied and black.   A considerable number in it were new Negroes, but only seven of the whole died in this year of heaviest mortality.

"The 'second gang,' employed in a somewhat lighter routine under Sharper as foreman, comprised 40 women and 27 men ranging from fifteen to sixty years, all black.   While most of them were healthy, five were consumptive, four were ulcerated, one was 'inclined to be bloated' and one was 'very weak,' and Pheba was 'healthy but worthless.'

"Finally in the third or 'small gang' for yet lighter work under Baddy as driveress, with Old Robin as assistant, there were 68 boys and girls, all black, mostly between twelve and fifteen years old. The draught animals comprised about 80 mules and 140 oxen." [42]

*West Indian Slavery a Failure.*  After giving a full account of cost of upkeep, provisions, etc., and setting over against it the amount of gross income, Dr. Phillips concludes of this great plantation, which was perhaps better than the average: "The net earnings in good years were thus less than four per cent on the investment; but the liability to hurricanes, earthquakes, fires, epidemics and mutinies would bring the safe expectations considerably lower.  A mere pestilence which carried off about sixty mules and two hundred oxen on Worthy Park in 1793-1794 wiped out more than a year's earnings." [43]

Thus the slave régime of the West Indies not only broke down of its own cruelty, hardship and bloodshed, but judging from the standpoint of financial returns, on which basis alone it had any basis of justification, we see it was weighed in the balances and found wanting.  Slavery in the islands was economically a failure.

[42] Phillips: "American Negro Slavery," pp. 57-61.
[43] *Ibid.,* p. 65.

## CHAPTER VI

# THE RISE AND FALL OF SLAVERY IN AMERICA

*Character of Early Colonists.* When the Virginia Company of London was chartered by James I in 1606, it was with the purpose of colonizing the Western World, and at the same time to open up a new source of trade for the mother country. There were two types of members in this company; first, those who subscribed money, called adventurers, and second, those who went out as colonists, called planters. The planters were thus from the start recognized as regular members of the company, who were to receive free transportation to America, maintenance for a term of years, a certain share in the profits, and a proportionate part of the land which advertisements of the company said would surely amount to five hundred acres per colonist. The call was so attractive that a great many set sail for the new land, but few of them were really laborers, or men willing to be laborers. It is said the first ship carried fifty gentlemen, various skilled workers, and only eight who acknowledged themselves to be just common laborers. The first great need of the colony, therefore, was for labor, for most of the men did not like work. In order to prevent starvation, "The whole colony was organized in 1610 as a working force. The colonists were marched to their daily work in squads and companies, under officers, and the severest penalties were prescribed for a breach of discipline or neglect of duty. A persistent neglect of labor was to be punished by galley service from one to three years. Penal servitude was also instituted; for petty offenses they worked as slaves in irons for a term of years." [1]

*Political Criminals Became Indentured Servants.* The great demand for labor caused the colonists to send a petition to the crown in 1618 which begged that he present them vagabonds and condemned men who should be sent out as slaves. The mother country, glad to get rid of a surplus of unemployed and rid herself of care of criminals, particularly political criminals, began sending the same to Virginia. As new colonists came out they brought other indentured servants. An indentured servant was a person who bound himself or herself to serve for a certain number of

[1] Ballagh: "White Servitude in the Colony of Virginia," Johns Hopkins Studies.

years on certain stipulated conditions. At the end of the time agreed upon they were set free with a certain amount of clothing and supplies. These indentured servants became a distinct class after 1619.[2] "One hundred poor boys and girls who were about to starve in the streets of London were sent in 1619, by the aid of the Mayor and Council of the city, to be bound to the tenants for a term of years, at the end of which they were to become themselves tenants-at-halves on the public lands, with an allowance of stock and corn to begin with." [3] "Apprentices soon began to be disposed of to the planters on their reimbursing the company for the charges of their outfit and transportation, and the records in several cases suggest a suspicion of speculation." [4] Most of these indentured servants were Irish, Scotch, Welsh and English, good sturdy stock, but too poor to buy a passage to the New World, with of course a goodly number of political criminals. "Of the Scotch prisoners taken at the battle of Worcester, six hundred and ten were sent to Virginia in 1651. Two years later a hundred Irish Tories were sent, and in 1685 a number of the followers of Monmouth that had escaped the cruelties of Jeffries. Many of the Scotch prisoners of Dunbar and of the rebels of 1666 were sent to New England and the other plantations." [5] Some real criminals and ne'er-do-wells came along with the rest. "In 1618 a man convicted of manslaughter and sentenced to be hanged was reprieved, 'because he was a carpenter and the plantations needed carpenters.' " [6] We are told that in Maryland the original immigrants were in the proportion of one freeman to six servants, and that in 1637 the ratio was three to seven.[7] Hardly a ship arrived at the ports of Baltimore or Annapolis that did not bring from twenty to fifty and sometimes a hundred indentured servants or convicts.[8] "The economic importance of the sevrant in developing the resources of the colonies, especially in the middle colonies, can hardly be overestimated. All the provinces were essentially agricultural, but the large tobacco plantations of Maryland and Virginia made a large supply of cheap laborers more necessary there than in the Northern colonies." [9] "Even with the large supply of servants and convicts, free labor was high and unprofitable. Laborers would not hire except for very high wages, when they could easily obtain new lands and become planters themselves." [10]

[2] Ballagh: "White Servitude in the Colony of Virginia," p. 27.
[3] Ibid., p. 28.
[4] Ibid., p. 29.
[5] Ibid., p. 35.
[6] Ibid., p. 36.
[7] McCormack: "White Servitude in Maryland," p. 28.
[8] Ibid., p. 30.
[9] Ibid., pp. 32-33.
[10] Ibid., p. 34.

*Conditions Favorable to Slavery.* The large amount of free land, the richness of the soil, and the salubrity of the climate enabled any one to make a living, hence it proved necessary, if large blocks of labor were to be concentrated, to do so by means of forced labor. The very conditions of life seemed to favor a slave régime, and the early settlers of America had little scruples in following the path which prosperity seemed to point.

Perhaps the largest number of indentured servants were brought into Virginia, Maryland and Pennsylvania, but the New England colonies also had a share in this type of servitude. These colonies were adepts in enslaving the Indians, just as the early settlers had done in the West Indies. The rigid Puritans soothed their consciences just as did the Spaniards, in the thought that those Indians who were made slaves would be brought under the influence of the Christian religion. Phillips quotes a letter of Emanuel Downing to his brother-in-law, John Winthrop, in which "Downing was in hopes of a war with the Narragansetts for two reasons, first to stop their 'worship of the devill,' and '2lie, if upon a just warre the Lord should deliver them into our hands, we might easily have men, women, and children enough to exchange for Moores (Negroes), which will be more gaynful pilladge for us than wee conceive, for I doe not see how we can thrive untill wee get into a stock of slaves sufficient to doe all our business.' " [11]  "The war against the Pequots in 1637 yielded a number of captives, whereupon the squaws and the girls were distributed among the towns of Massachusetts and Connecticut and a parcel of the boys was shipped off to the tropics in the Salem ship Desire." [12]  But the Indians did not make good slaves. They were unaccustomed to labor, they were intractable, they were morose and soon died under the restraint of slavery. Most of the tribes fled from the white man, and rather than be captured as slaves, they fought to their death.

*First Negroes Landed in America.* As no new country ever has enough labor, it is not surprising therefore that the chance landing of a Dutch slave vessel on the Virginia coast was no unwelcome event. Twenty Negroes were sold to the Virginia colonists in 1619, and the story of Negro slavery in America was begun. (cf. Chapter on The Free Negro.) Negro slavery did not grow rapidly because it was for a long time more convenient to get indentured servants from England, but this supply of labor was cut off after 1688 and Negroes were the main dependence for workers. In 1714 there were only 58,850 Negro slaves in America, distributed throughout all the colonies. In 1750 there were 220,000 Negroes; in 1760 there were 310,000;

[11] Phillips: "American Negro Slavery," p. 101.
[12] *Ibid.,* p. 100.

in 1770 462,000; in 1780 582,000; in 1790 757,000; of whom 697,000 were slaves, and in 1801 the total colored population stood at 1,007,037.

Following that by decades, the numbers of Negroes were as follows:[13]

| | |
|---|---|
| 1810 | 1,377,808 |
| 1820 | 1,771,656 |
| 1830 | 2,328,642 |
| 1840 | 2,873,648 |
| 1850 | 3,638,808 |
| 1860 | 4,441,830 |

It is evident that after 1700 the slave trade grew rapidly. Many were imported from the West Indies and many more came direct from Africa. From 1680 to 1688 the African Company with 249 ships delivered on American shores 46,396 slaves. The English imported annually from 1733 to 1766 about 20,000.[14] Wilson thinks that a total of 300,000 slaves were imported into America before the revolution.[15] The Revolution slowed down the slave trade, both because the business was precarious on account of war, and because the sentiment of freedom and self-government which burned hot in the hearts of the colonists, was not congenial to the traffic in human beings. But, as is usual after wars in which high idealism is called out, the sag in ideals came and there was soon a return to slavery because it was a scheme for securing wealth.

*The Three Cornered Trade.* European slave traders took rum, and trade goods to Africa, where they were exchanged for slaves. These were taken to the West Indies or to the South, and exchanged for sugar, molasses, tobacco, cotton, and when the sugar and molasses got to England it was in part manufactured into rum to buy more slaves. The New England ships made a similar circuit. Rum was taken to Africa and exchanged for slaves, slaves taken to the West Indies or the South and exchanged for sugar and other commodities, and then the trip home. Often a New England slaver would have a few slaves left over which he could not sell, so he took them with him to New England. Newport was the principal port for this trade and it was as a slave market that Newport gained its commercial prominence. "The rum distillery industry indicates to some extent the activity of New England in the slave-trade. In May, 1752, one Captain Freeman found so many slavers fitting out that, in spite of the large importations of molasses, he could get no rum for

[13] Census Bulletin 129, p. 8.
[14] DuBois: "The Suppression of the Slave Trade," p. 5, *passim.*
[15] Wilson: "The Rise and Fall of the Slave Power in America," Vol. I, p. 3.

his ship.   In Newport alone twenty-two stills were at one time
running continuously, and Massachusetts annually distilled 15,000
hogsheads of molasses into this chief manufacture." [16]

*A Typical Slave Voyage.*   A typical voyage is that of the
brigantine, Sanderson of Newport.   She was fitted out in March,
1752, and carried besides the captain, two mates and six men and
a cargo of 8,220 gallons of rum, together with African iron,
flour, pots, tar, sugar, and provisions, shackles, shirts and water.
Proceeding to Africa, the captain, after some difficulty, sold his
cargo for slaves, and in April, 1753, he is expected in Barbadoes,
as the consignees write.   After a stormy and dangerous voyage,
Captain Lindsay arrived, June 17, 1753, with fifty-six slaves, all
in health and fatt.   He also had 40 oz. of gold dust, and 8 or 9
cwt. of pepper.   The net proceeds of the sale of all this was
£1,324—3d.   The Captain then took on board 55 hkd of molasses
and 3 hkd, 27 bbl. of sugar, amounting to £911 17s 2½d, received
bills on Liverpool for the balance, and returned in safety to
Rhode Island.   He had done so well that he was immediately
given a new ship and sent to Africa again.[17]   The colonists'
capacity for shrewd trading found ample exercise in this ugly
traffic, as is evidenced by such instructions as the following from
a Rhode Island slaver to his captain, "Warter yr rum as much
as possible and sell as much by short mesuer as you can.'"

*Massachusetts and Slavery.*   Massachusetts in 1640 took drastic
action against a Captain Smith who attacked an African village
and brought away slaves, condemning this as man stealing, but
the large profits of the slave carrying business soon overcame
all opposition.   In 1705 she passed a law placing a £4 tax on all
importations, but remitting three quarters of the tax if the slave
was re-exported.   "It was a much less violent wrenching of moral
ideals of right and wrong," remarks Du Bois, "to allow Massachusetts men to carry slaves to South Carolina, than to allow
cargoes to come into Boston, and become slaves in Massachusetts." [18]

*Rhode Island's Slave Trade.*   Rhode Island, which was the
greatest slave trader in America, built 103 slave ships in the
decade from 1698 to 1708, and in 1770 this state alone had 150
ships engaged in the slave trade.   In 1774 a law was passed
prohibiting importation of Negroes into the colony, but slave
trading was not only not prohibited by the act but positively
encouraged.   Any slave ship which could not sell its cargo was at
liberty to bring any unsold slaves into the colony provided bond
was given to export the slave within one year's time.   Connecticut

[16] DuBois: "Suppression of the Slave Trade," p. 29.
[17] Quoted by DuBois from "American Historical Records," Vol. L, p. 315.
[18] DuBois: "Suppression of the Slave Trade," p. 31.

prohibited importation into the colony in 1774, but did not forbid participation in the slave trade by her citizens until 1788.[19]

*Participants in the Slave Trade.* Charleston, S. C., seems to have engaged heavily in the slave trade, for the South Carolina slaves grew very rapidly. In 1708 there were in the state 4,100 slaves; in 1715, 10,500; in 1723, 18,000; in 1740, 30,000; in 1749, 39,000; in 1759, 108,000. DeBow's "Industrial Resources of the South and West"[20] gives the names of all the slave ships clearing from Charleston harbor from 1804 to 1807. It includes 61 ships owned by residents of Charleston, 59 Rhode Island ships, 4 from Baltimore, 1 from Boston, 2 from Norfolk, 1 from Connecticut, 1 from Sweden, 70 from Britain, and 3 from France. Of all the owners of these ships 13 were native Charlestonians, 88 were Rhode Islanders, 91 were British, 10 were French. The British owned ships imported 19,649 slaves, the French owned imported 1,078, the Rhode Island owned, 8,238, Charleston vessels belonging to foreigners, 5,107, vessels owned by native Charlestonians, 2,006. It is thus quite evident that the slave traffic can be laid at the door of no one nation, nor at the door of any one section of our own country. Various nations and various sections of our own country eagerly competed for the wealth to be had from the slave trade.

*Early Opposition to Slavery.* Although all the early colonies, except Georgia, sanctioned and practiced slavery, there were not a few people that felt from the very beginning that it was wrong. Pennsylvania, due to her large number of Quakers, led the way in opposition to the practice. As early as 1710 the Assembly of Pennsylvania placed a restrictive duty on the importation of slaves, and in 1712 passed an act to prevent the importation of Negroes and Indians altogether. An import duty of £20 was levied, which it was considered would be prohibitive. But the British parliament quickly forbade the enforcement of these laws, and directed that the "Governor, Council, and Assembly of Pennsylvania, be an they are hereby strictly enjoined and required not to permit the said laws to be henceforward put into execution."[21] By the treaty of Utrecht, 1713, the Asiento passed into the hands of the English and they promptly began to make the most of their monopoly. The old Company pressed the colonies to buy slaves in ever increasing numbers.

*Slave Population Alarms Colonists.* The rapid growth of the slave population soon alarmed the colonists and where there was no strong moral objection there was the fear of insurrection ever present in the minds of the white settlers. But the slave

[19] DuBois, "Suppression of the Slave Trade," pp. 30-37, *passim.*
[20] DeBow: "Industrial Resources," Vol. II, pp. 340-342.
[21] Quoted by DuBois: "Suppression of the Slave Trade," p. 22.

trade, a lucrative source of wealth to the mother countries, England, France, Spain and Holland, had the hearty support of the crowned heads as well as the organized pressure of the licensed companies. The West India Company introduced Negroes into Manhattan in 1626, and constantly urged the importation of others. "Stuyvesant was instructed to use every exertion to promote the sale of slaves." [22]   The London Company saw to it that all the slaves were supplied that could be absorbed into the labor forces of the English colonists. "During the years from 1619 to the opening of the American Revolution the friends of the slave trade and of slavery controlled the government and dictated the policy of England. Her kings and queens, lords and commons, judges and attorney-generals, gave to the African slave trade their united support. Her merchants and manufacturers clamored for its protection and extension. Her coffers were filled with gold bedewed with tears and stained with blood." [23]   "Queen Anne, who had reserved for herself one quarter of the stock of the Royal African Company, that gigantic monopolist of the slave trade, charged it to furnish full supplies of slaves to the colonists of New York and New Jersey and instructed the governors of these colonies to give due encouragement to the company; and it was the testimony of Madison that the British government constantly checked the attempts of his native state 'to put a stop to this infernal traffic.'" [24]

*Virginia Protests Against More Slaves.*   Virginia in particular received large numbers. Although slavery was not recognized by statute in Virginia until 1661, it grew so rapidly that by the time of the revolution there were as many Negro slaves as there were white people. It was this condition which drew out protests from Virginia's leading men. On July 12, 1736, William Byrd wrote to Lord Egmont: "Your Lord's opinion concerning rum and Negroes is certainly very just and your excluding both of them from your colony of Georgia will be very happy. I wish, my Lord, we could be blessed with the same prohibition. They import so many Negroes here that I fear this colony will some time or other be confirmed by the name of New Guinea. I am sensible of the many bad consequences of multiplying the Ethiopians among us. They blow up the pride and ruin the industry of our white people, who, seeing a class of poor creatures below them, detest work for fear it should make them look like slaves. . . .

"But these private evils are nothing if compared to the public danger. It were, therefore, worth the consideration of the British

[22] Bancroft: "History of United States," Vol. I, p. 513.
[23] Wilson: "Rise and Fall of the Slave Power in America," Vol. I, p. 3.
[24] *Ibid.,* p. 4.

Parliament, my Lord, to put an end to this unchristian traffic of merchandise of our Fellow Creatures. At least the further importation of them into our colony should be prohibited, lest they prove as troublesome and dangerous elsewhere as they have been lately in Jamaica." [25]

*Further Protests From Virginia.* From 1726 until the Revolution almost every session of the Virginia Assembly debated the question of the restriction of the slave trade and many of its leading citizens, like Jefferson, openly advocated complete emancipation. "Again and again they had passed laws restraining importations of Negroes from Africa; but their laws had been disallowed. How to prevent them from protecting themselves against the increase of the overwhelming evil was debated by the king in council; and in December, 1770, he issued an instruction, under his own hand, commanding the governor 'upon pain of the highest displeasure, to assent to no law by which the importation of slaves should be in any respect prohibited or obstructed.' " [26] In 1772 the Virginia Assembly seriously debated this order of the king and sent a petition to him in person which read as follows: "The importation of slaves into the colonies from the coast of Africa hath long been considered as a trade of great inhumanity; and, under its present encouragement, we have too much reason to fear, will endanger the very existence of your majesty's American dominions. We are sensible that some of your majesty's subjects in Great Britain may reap emoluments from this sort of traffic; but, when we consider that it greatly retards the settlement of the colonies with more useful inhabitants, and may in time have the most destructive influence, we presume to hope that the interest of a few will be disregarded, when placed in competition with the security and happiness of such numbers of your majesty's dutiful and loyal subjects.

"Deeply impressed with these sentiments, we most humbly beseech your majesty to remove all those restraints on your majesty's governors of this colony which inhibit their assenting to such laws as might check so very pernicious a commerce." [27]

*Patrick Henry's Opinion.* In 1773 Patrick Henry wrote in a private letter to a friend the following words about slavery: "Every thinking honest man rejects it in speculation; but how few in practice, from conscientious motives! Believe me, I shall honor the Quakers for their noble efforts to abolish slavery; they are equally calculated to promote moral and political good. Would any one believe that I am master of slaves of my own purchase? I am drawn along by the general inconvenience of living without

[25] Quoted from Munford's "Virginia's Attitude Toward Slavery and Secession," p. 17.
[26] Bancroft: "History of United States," Vol. III, p. 410.
[27] *Ibid.*, p. 411.

them. I will not, I cannot, justify it; however culpable my conduct, I will so far pay my devoir to virtue as to own the excellence and rectitude of her precepts, and to lament my want of conformity to them. I believe a time will come when an opportunity will be offered to abolish this lamentable evil; everything we can do is to improve it, if it happens in our day; if not, let us transmit to our descendants, together with our slaves, a pity for their unhappy lot and an abhorrence of slavery." [28]

As the situation between Britain and her colonies grew more tense and war seemed inevitable it was suggested in Parliament that the slaves might be freed and turned against their masters. To this Edmund Burke, a far wiser and more judicious man, replied in his speech on "Conciliation with the American Colonies."

*Burke's Arraignment of the Slave Trade.* "With regard to the high aristocratic spirit of Virginia and the southern colonies it has been proposed, I know, to reduce it by declaring a general enfranchisement of their slaves. This project has had its advocates and panegyrists, yet I never could argue myself into any opinion of it. Slaves are often much attached to their master. A general wild offer of liberty would not always be accepted. History furnishes few instances of it. It is sometimes as hard to persuade slaves to be free as it is to compel freemen to be slaves; and in this auspicious scheme we should have both these pleasing tasks on our hands at once. But when we talk of enfranchisement, do we not perceive that the American master may enfranchise too, and arm servile hands in the defense of freedom? —a measure to which other people have had recourse more than once, and not without success, in a desperate situation of their affairs.

"Slaves as these unfortunate black people are, and dull as all men are from slavery, must they not a little suspect the offer of freedom from that very nation, which has sold them to their present masters; from that nation, one of whose causes of quarrel with those masters is their refusal to deal any more in that inhuman traffic? An offer of freedom from England would come rather oddly, shipped to them in an African vessel, which is refused an entry into the ports of Virginia or Carolina, with a cargo of three hundred Angola negroes. It would be curious to see the Guinea captain attempting at the same instant to publish his proclamation of liberty, and to advertise his sale of slaves." [29]

*Original Draft of Declaration of Independence and Slavery.* This attitude of the colonists toward the slave trade is clearly seen in Jefferson's words in the original draft of the Declaration

[28] Bancroft: "History of United States," Vol. III, p. 412.
[29] Burke: "Conciliation with the American Colonists," in the English Classics' Series, pp. 44-45.

of Independence: "George the Third has waged cruel war against humanity itself, violating its most sacred rights of life and liberty, in the persons of a distant people who never offended him; captivating and carrying them into slavery in another hemisphere, or to incur a miserable death in their transportation thither. This piratical warfare, the opprobrium of infidel powers, is the warfare of the Christian King of Great Britain. Determined to keep open a market where men should be bought and sold, he has prostituted his negative for suppressing every legislative attempt to prohibit, or to restrain, this execrable commerce. And that this assemblage of horrors might want no fact of distinguished dye, he is now exciting these very people to rise in arms among us, and to purchase that liberty of which he has deprived them, by murdering the people on whom he obtruded them; thus paying off former crimes committed against the liberties of one people with crimes which he urges them to commit against the lives of another." [30]

*War of Revolution Weakens Slavery.* There can be no doubt that the struggle of the colonies for political freedom produced, North and South, a great revulsion of feeling against slaves, which was in a political sense the evil against which they fought. Massachusetts twice passed a bill to prohibit slavery in 1774, but neither bill went into effect. Bills were again recommended in 1776 and 1777 but no action taken. In 1780 slavery was prohibited and in 1788 participation in the slave trade was prohibited, and actual slavery in the colony was practically extinct. Rhode Island prohibited importation of slaves in 1774 and forbade participation in the slave trade in 1787. Connecticut prohibited importations in 1774, forbade participation in the slave trade in 1788. New Hampshire excluded slavery in 1792, Vermont in 1793, and New York began a gradual abolition in 1799. Of the general attitude at this period DuBois writes: "Indeed it needed an exceptionally clear and discerning mind in 1787 to deny that slavery and the slave trade in the United States of America were doomed to early annihilation. It seemed certainly a legitimate deduction from the history of the preceding century to conclude that as the system had risen, flourished, and fallen in Massachusetts, New York, and Pennsylvania and as South Carolina, Virginia, and Maryland were apparently following in the same legislative path, the next generation would in all probability witness the last throes of the system on our soil." [31]

*Attitude of Congress Toward Slavery.* In the Continental Congress of 1784, Thomas Jefferson of Virginia, Mr. Chase of Maryland, and Mr. Howell of Rhode Island, were on a committee which recommended that "after the year of the Christian era 1800,

[30] Munford: "Virginia's Attitude Toward Slavery and Secession," pp. 19-20.
[31] DuBois: "Suppression of the Slave Trade," p. 40.

there shall be neither slavery nor involuntary servitude in any of these states, otherwise than in the punishment of crime, whereof the party shall have been duly convicted." [32]    But the Southern states did not sustain the committee and the clause was struck out. In March of 1785 "Rufus King, a delegate from Massachusetts, moved to modify the report made at the previous session, by inserting therein a total and immediate prohibition of slavery." [33] His motion failed to carry.    In July 1787, Nathan Dane, of Massachusetts, was chairman of the committee which reported the ordinance afterwards known as the ordinance of '87, by which all territory north and west of the Ohio, should, when organized, be organized as free states.    The ordinance lacked only one vote —that of Mr. Yates of New York, receiving a unanimous approval and was passed on July 13, 1787.    Thus did the moral tide of humanity rise to meet this human problem.    But when the question of further imports into the colonies came up, a new disposition was manifest.    The delegates from South Carolina and Georgia strongly opposed the prohibition of imports and threatened to withdraw if such were voted.    The economic argument came to the fore.    Pinckney and Rutledge of South Carolina declared that more slaves would mean more products and would enrich all, and Ellsworth, of Connecticut agreed that: "What enriches a part enriches the whole." [34]

*The First Compromise.*    After a long debate a compromise was struck whereby the Northern colonies agreed not to interfere with slave importations until after 1800, provided the Southern colonies would not interfere with navigation and exports.    When this was reported on the floor, Pinckney of South Carolina, seconded by Graham of Massachusetts, moved to extend the time of constitutional non-interference with slave importations to 1808.    Madison and others protested against this but it was finally carried, and the provision as finally adopted read as follows: "Art. I, Section 9. The migration or importation of such persons as any of the states now existing shall think proper to admit, shall not be prohibited by the congress prior to the year one thousand eight hundred and eight, but a tax or duty may be imposed on such importations, not exceeding ten dollars for each person."

*Three Southern States Permitting Imports.*    By this provision any state could dispose of the problem of the slave trade as it liked up to 1808.    South Carolina, Georgia and North Carolina were the only states at the time which still permitted slave importations.    Just at this time, the great revolution in Haiti which was taking place with such terrible bloodshed and cruelty, brought

[32] Wilson: "Rise and Fall of Slave Power in America," Vol. I, p. 32.
[33] *Ibid.,* Vol. I, p. 32.
[34] DuBois: "Suppression of the Slave Trade," p. 56.

a new motive to bear, or at least reëmphasized an old motive. Fear of insurrections took hold upon the minds of many of the people, so that South Carolina in 1788 prohibited the slave trade for five years, which act was extended several times and finally did not expire until 1803. North Carolina had had a very high duty on importations which was repealed in 1790, but in 1794 she passed a stringent law by which not only the slave trade was prohibited, but even personal servants could with difficulty be brought in. Georgia alone had open ports. Even that state in 1798 prohibited importations, under heavy penalties, so that legally the whole of the American coast was closed to the slave trade. The border states strengthened the prohibitory laws and the Eastern states put heavier penalties on their citizens for participation in the slave trade. Again it looked as though slavery was tottering to its fall.

*Abolition Agitation.* From 1789 to 1803 there were constant petitions presented to Congress both by abolitionists and by free Negro organizations praying for complete emancipation. Each petition brought on hot debate, the Northern states, with the exception of certain representatives from Rhode Island, standing for abolition, the Southern states, with the exception of Virginia, usually standing against it. In 1794 Congress finally passed a law against carrying slaves from the United States to any foreign port, and prohibiting citizens of the country from aiding in fitting out slave ships. A fine of $1000 for each person engaged, and of $200 for each slave carried, was imposed. In 1803 this law was reënacted and greatly strengthened, calling for the forfeiture of any ship which brought any Negro, or person of color into the states, which prohibited the same. Just at this time South Carolina brought consternation to all by reopening her slave trade. The growing certainty that the United States would prohibit the slave traffic in 1808 as soon as the constitutional prohibition expired, led South Carolina to take advantage of the few remaining years to replenish her stock of slaves for a greatly growing agriculture. Immediately a representative from Pennsylvania offered a resolution to tax imported slaves, but the bill presented was finally lost. Another event which brought consternation to those who hoped for the emancipation of slaves, was the purchase of Louisiana in 1803. A long and bitter debate as to whether slave importation should be allowed in this territory followed. It was finally decided to allow an interstate trade with Louisiana, only selling to her slaves imported before 1798. That is, slaves could not be imported and bought in Charleston and immediately reshipped to Louisiana. It is quite evident that the law was not well enforced and many fresh slaves were evidently brought into New Orleans.

*Jefferson Sends Prohibition Message to Congress.*  The abolition forces, seemingly defeated again, began marshaling their
forces to prohibit the slave trade completely by national legislation.  President Thomas Jefferson in 1806 sent a message to
Congress urging immediate action, even though the law could
not take effect until 1808.  His message ran: "I congratulate you,
fellow citizens, on the approach of the period at which you may
interpose your authority constitutionally to withdraw the citizens
of the United States from all participation in the violation of
human rights which has been so long continued on the unoffending
inhabitants of Africa, and which the morality, the reputation and
the best interests of the country have long been eager to proscribe.
Although no law you can pass can take prohibitive effect until the
first day of the year 1808, yet the intervening period is not too
long to prevent, by timely notice, expeditions which cannot be
completed before that day."  A bill was finally passed in 1807
which prohibited the slave trade.  There was practical unanimity
both North and South in the desire to prohibit the trade, for the
fear of insurrections due to incoming of free Negroes from the
West Indies, and also the fear that further importations would
work havoc with price of present slaves, whipped into line all
those who did not feel the pressure of moral and humanitarian
arguments.

*Difficulties of Legal Procedure.*  But just how to draw the bill
was one of great perplexity.[35]  If it was to be effective there
must be penalties attached.  But what must be done with the
imported slaves?  If confiscated then the government itself must
either free them or sell them.  The South could not and would
not submit to fresh savages being set free upon her soil, nor
would the Northern states relish this action.  But if sold, then
the government would, in the words of Mr. Smilie of Pennsylvania, "in attempting to put a stop to the traffic, take upon itself
the odium of being a slave trader."  Mr. Early of Georgia said
if they were freed and left in the South "not one of them would
be left alive in a year."  It was suggested they should be returned
to Africa but this amendment was voted down.  Mr. Quincy of
Massachusetts, remarked that if left in the South, the imported
Negroes would surely become slaves, and if taken to the North
they would become vagabonds.

*Question of Penalty for the Slaver.*  The question of the punishment of the slave importer was a difficult one.  The original
bill recommended that he should be put to death.  The Southern
representatives charged that most of the illegal importers would
be Northern men, but at the same time they opposed the death

[35] Cf. Wilson: "Rise and Fall of the Slave Power in America," Vol. I, Ch.
VII, *passim,*

penalty because it seemed to brand the trade as too heinous a crime. Mr. Mosely of Connecticut sharply retorted to this, that he saw no reason why the Southern representatives "should be so tender of these Northern men." Early, of Georgia, bluntly said the South would not execute the death sentence because "the Southern people do not regard the traffic as a crime." He maintained it was an evil but not a crime. Clay, of Pennsylvania, said the death penalty could not be carried into effect even in his state.

*Problem of Coastwise Trade.* The third knotty question was what to do with the coastwise trade. It was finally agreed that it should be limited to small ships of 40 tons burthen.

The final settlement agreed that:

"Neither the importer, nor any person or persons claiming from or under him, shall hold any right or title whatsoever to any Negro, mulatto, or person of color, nor to the service or labor thereof, who may be imported or brought within the United States, or territory thereof, in violation of this law, but the same shall remain subject to any regulations not contravening the provision of this act, which the Legislatures of the several states or territories at any time hereafter make, for disposing of any such Negro, mulatto, or person of color."

Thus the disposal of the imported slaves was left to the individual state. As to the punishment of the slave importers, the following provisions were made:

For equipping a slaver, a fine of $20,000 and forfeiture of the ship.

For transporting and selling Negroes a fine of $1000 to $10,000, imprisonment for 5 to 10 years and forfeiture of the ship and Negroes.

For transporting Negroes, a fine of $5000 and forfeiture of the ship and negroes.

For knowingly buying illegally imported Negroes, fine of $800 for each Negro and forfeiture.[36]

*Illicit Slave Traffic.* The long struggle for legal prohibition was thus ended, but the passage of the law did not stop the slave traffic. The Southern states were slow about passing laws for the disposal of captured slaves, and what was more serious the central government provided no adequate means for executing its law. First the customs officials were responsible for enforcement, then the Navy assumed responsibility, later on the Department of State and finally the Department of Interior. So vacillating was the policy that slave importations went forward with little

[36] Compare DuBois: "Suppression of the Slave Trade," p. 104.

molestation.   Cargoes were landed in Florida and smuggled over the Georgia line, or they were landed at Galveston and brought from thence into the states.   Du Bois estimates that 40,000 slaves were imported annually into North and South America between 1808 and 1820 and by 1837 it had reached 200,000 annually; that by 1848 it had declined to 100,000 annually, but importations continued right up to 1860.[37]   Indeed there is at this present writing a freed slave still living in Alabama, who was smuggled in through Mobile in 1860.

*Great Britain's Attitude.*   Great Britain had in 1807 abolished all slave traffic and for more than fifty years she strove earnestly to suppress the whole illicit traffic.   Again and again England attempted to get other nations to unite with her in this effort. The great obstacle which stood in the way was opposition to the right of search.   England was really the mistress of the seas and to give her the right of free search of all merchant ships was entirely too hazardous a business.   The question was earnestly discussed at the Congress of Vienna in 1814, at the Treaty of Ghent in 1815, at the Congress of Verona in 1822 and always with sympathetic attitude by the contracting nations but with the same futile results.

*Monroe Opposes Slave Traffic.*   In 1823 under the constant efforts of Monroe, a proposal was offered Great Britain in accordance with which the United States agreed to denounce the slave trade as piracy, under the law of Nations, agreed to a limited right of search, and the trial of all offenders seized was to take place under the country of the captives.   England accepted these stipulations but when the treaty was laid before the Senate it was so mutilated as to become powerless and was rejected by England.   Following this, England frequently searched ships flying the American flag without right and hence defeated successful coöperation of the nations in suppressing the slave traffic.   Little by little the traffic assumed the flag of America to shield itself, whether the ship belonged to American merchants or not.   "From 1830 to 1840 it (the illegal slave traffic) began gradually to assume the United States flag; by 1845 a large part of the trade was under the stars and stripes; by 1850 fully one half the trade, and in the decade 1850 to 1860 nearly all the traffic found this flag its best protection."[38]

*Wealth and the Survival of Slavery.*   We must now retrace our steps to see why slavery, which seemed so near to an end in 1787, was able to revive and grow.   It was primarily an economic impulse which fastened slavery so hard and fast on the South. The North did not find slavery profitable economically and so it

[37] DuBois: "Suppression of the Slave Trade," Chapters 8 and 9, *passim.*
[38] *Ibid.,* p. 143.

gradually died of its own uselessness. But it was different with the South. Here was a great rich country, with a congenial climate, and unlimited acres to be brought under the plow. The great need was for laborers. Furthermore, the crops of the South were just those that could best be cultivated on a large scale. Tobacco which was Virginia's great staple product up to the Civil War, was easily worked by slaves. Rice, which was one of the great products of South Carolina, was best raised in the marsh land where only Negroes could live. Sugar could be raised only on large plantations, for it required large capital for the machinery of grinding and manufacturing. Cotton also could be raised on a large scale, and since it was a crop that absorbed almost the whole year, it was the most profitable crop to be worked by slaves. The introduction of the cotton gin by Eli Whitney, 1793, therefore, brought a great impulse to the waning system of slavery. By the old process of seeding cotton with the fingers a slave could clean six pounds per day of the seed, but by the cotton gin, even in its earliest stages, many hundreds of pounds could be freed of its seed in a day. Not only so but the rapid improvement of machinery for the manufacture of cotton into cloth gave a great impulse to the raising of this staple.

*Increase in Cotton Crops.* The raising of cotton thus became a profitable crop for slave labor, as is indicated by the rapid rise in the amount transported. In 1785 there were 14 bags transported to Europe, in 1789—842 bags, in 1791—200,000 pounds, but in 1795 it had jumped to 6,000,000 and in 1800 it was 17,000,000 pounds.[39] In 1804 the import was said to amount to 38,000,000 pounds.[40] The value of the crop in 1800 was 24 times the value of the crop in 1790. This rapid growth of cotton culture, naturally raised the price of slaves, and fastened in the minds of the planters the idea that slaves were an absolute necessity. "Before this tremendous development of cotton culture had taken place, slavery had hardly had more than habit and the perils of emancipation to support it in the South; Southern life and industry had shaped themselves to it, and the slaves were too numerous and too ignorant to be safely set free. But when the cotton gin supplied the means of indefinitely expanding the production of marketable cotton by the use of slave labor, another and even more powerful argument for its retention was furnished. After that, slavery seemed nothing less than the indispensable economic instrument of Southern society." [41] Thus the economic aspect of slavery, concentrated into the great slave cotton raising plantations, began to dominate the thinking and the political out-

[39] DeBow: "Industrial Resources," Vol. I, pp. 120-122, *passim.*
[40] Woodrow Wilson: "Division and Reunion," p. 124.
[41] *Ibid.*, p. 125.

look of the South.   Gradually the slaves became more or less concentrated into great aggregations, and the great slave owners became the dominating factors in the political, social and economic life of this section.   Already the two sections of the country, the slave holding and the non-slave holding, had been in conflict often enough over various laws pertaining to the slave traffic to concentrate the forces of each into a fighting unity   This was particularly true in the South, for the constant attacks on the slave system had a tendency not only to unify that section but to arouse a spirit of resentment which cemented the unity all the more firmly.   "There was throughout Southern society something like a reproduction of that solidarity of feeling and of interest, which existed in the ancient classical republics, set above whose slaves there was a proud but various democracy of citizenship and privilege.   Such was the society which by the compulsion of its own nature, had always resented change and was to resist it until change and even its own destruction were forced upon it by war." [42]

*The Power of the Slave Owners.*   "The ruling class in the South was small, compact and on the whole homogeneous; it was intelligent, alert and self-conscious. . . . It had, besides, more political power and clearer notions of how it meant to use that power than any other class in the country." [43]   The leisure which slavery allowed had given time for the development of a statesman class like Jefferson, Madison, Randolph, Calhoun and a score of others who were unmatched in the rest of the country for bold and impetuous leadership.   For forty years they were able to hold their balance of power even though they were fighting what must prove a losing battle.   The admission of Missouri was the first great trial of the comparative strength of the two sections.   The issue at stake was whether the slave section should continue to have an equal voice in the national government.   With the admission of states from the Northwest territory and from the New England section, the slave states were sure to be out-voted unless new slave states could be admitted.   Maine was applying for admission into the union, of course, as a free state.   Missouri was north of the line determined upon as the Southern limit of the Northwest territory, but in order to keep a balance it was finally voted "That in all the territory ceded by France to the United States under the name of Louisiana, which lies north of thirty-six degrees, thirty minutes, north latitude, not included within the limits of the state contemplated by this act, slavery . . . shall be and is hereby forever prohibited."   Thus, "the principle of compromise had been adopted, and the southern leaders given to

[42] Woodrow Wilson: "Division and Reunion," p. 107.
[43] *Ibid.*, p. 129.

understand that, within a certain space, they had the sanction of
the general government in the prosecution of their efforts to
extend their system and their political influence." [44]

*Texas: Slave or Free.* The next great struggle arose over the
Texas question. Texas and Coahuila, had been united into a
single state under Mexico in 1824, and provision had been made
for the gradual abolition of slavery. But the state soon began
filling up with settlers from Alabama, Georgia, North Carolina,
Tennessee and even Virginia, so that in the early thirties it was
no longer a Spanish state but an American territory. Due to
oppression of the Mexican government Texas seceded in 1836 and
by a sweeping victory over Santa Anna, the Texans led by Sam
Houston, a Tennessean, declared their independence on San
Jacinto day, April 21, 1836. In their new constitution slavery
was recognized. The slave owning states were therefore eager to
recognize Texas as independent in the hope that this territory
might be added to the Union, and thus strengthen their position.
The Southern leaders were aided in their plans by the fact that
both France and England were flirting with Texas, and fear lest
one of these European nations might get possession of this broad
sweep of territory led to hurried action with regard to annexation.
The presidential election of 1844 was determined by the attitude
of the candidate toward the annexation of Texas. Clay opposed
it. James K. Polk, of Tennessee, favored it and was overwhelmingly elected. The election having settled the mind of the
country, the retiring Congress passed a joint resolution of annexation which was signed by Tyler on his last day of office, March 3,
1845. This plunged the United States into war with Mexico
over the boundary of Texas. In the treaty of Guadalupe Hidalgo
(1848) the United States agreed to pay Mexico fifteen million
dollars for lands ceded, and the Rio Grande was made the southern boundary.

*The Wilmot Proviso.* In 1846 David Wilmot had affixed an
amendment to the bill on the boundary question, which provided,
that in any territories that might be acquired from Mexico, neither
slavery nor involuntary servitude should exist except for crime,
judicially determined. This passed the House but failed by default in the Senate, and hence left the whole question of organizing the new territory open for new debates. Meanwhile the
doctrine of "squatter sovereignty" arose. Leave the question to
the settlers themselves. Let them decide whether they will come
in as free or slave territory. Thus the Missouri Compromise
laid the ground for new aggressions which were to cause endless
debates and great heart rendings. Oregon was finally organized
in 1848 as a free state but the great California, New Mexico

[44] Woodrow Wilson: "Division and Reunion," pp. 131-132.

territory was still unorganized. The stage was thus set for a great fight between the sections.

*Growth of Bitterness.* The spirit of antagonism and bitterness had been growing rapidly. Both sides were hot-headed and set. John Quincy Adams had in 1843 said that the annexation of Texas would justify dissolution of the Union, and William Lloyd Garrison had publicly advocated in Boston, that Massachusetts should lead a movement of secession from the Union. On the other hand Southern voices were not wanting, which declared if Texas were not annexed the slave holding states should withdraw. The North held to the doctrine of complete control of the new territories and the South held to the doctrine of non-interference on the part of the national government. President Taylor urged the territories to organize and express in this constitution their own preferences, and California, New Mexico and Utah did so organize.

*Clay's Compromise.* "It was under these circumstances that Henry Clay came forward, with the dignity of age upon him, to urge measures of compromise. He proposed January 29, 1850, that Congress should admit California with her free constitution; should organize the rest of the Mexican Cession without any provision at all concerning slavery, leaving its establishment or exclusion to the course of events, and the ultimate choice of the settlers; should purchase from Texas her claim upon a part of New Mexico; should abolish the slave trade in the District of Columbia, but promise for the rest, non-interference elsewhere with slavery or the interstate slave trade; and should concede to the South an effective fugitive slave law." [45]    This compromise of Clay was recommitted and three separate bills were brought back. The first known as the Omnibus Bill, provided for the admission of California as a free state, the organization of Utah and New Mexico as territories without settling the question of slavery in them, the payment of Texas for her claim on New Mexico. The second bill abolished slavery from the District of Columbia, and the third enacted a drastic fugitive slave law which put the burden of execution back on the Central government. All of these after long and bitter debate were finally passed in 1850.

*Irritation of Fugitive Slave Law.* Perhaps the most serious blunder of this famous compromise of 1850 was the Fugitive Slave Law. Up to this time the return of fugitives from justice as well as fugitives from service had rested as a responsibility upon state governments. But there had been a growing laxness on the part of the officials of free states about returning fugitive slaves. Therefore, the compromise law of 1850 put the whole

[45] Woodrow Wilson: "Division and Reunion," p. 169.

burden back on the central government.  Warrants for arrest were to be issued by United States judges or Commissioners, these warrants were to be executed by United States Marshals, all citizens were commended under heavy penalty to assist in the return of fugitives and assistance of fugitive slaves was made an offence punishable both by fine and imprisonment.  The affidavit of the master was made all that was necessary to demand a warrant for arrest of a slave.  In the putting of this law into effect a great deal of bad blood was stirred up.  Southern masters were disposed to push the law to the extreme, and Northern abolitionists were disposed to evade it wherever possible.  Perhaps more than any other one item of the famous compromise this law helped to hasten to its conclusion the tragedy of the country, bringing the settlement of the question to the arbitrament of war.

*Uncle Tom's Cabin.*   Matters now hastened to their close. Mrs. Harriet Beecher Stowe wrote her famous novel, "Uncle Tom's Cabin," in 1852 and this stirred the South with deep and bitter indignation.  Although it clearly represented what might be the extreme fruitage of the slave system, it surely did not represent the average working of the system.  It was based on exceptional cases, cases which all knew might be true, but which were by no means typical.  Nevertheless, it profoundly moved the whole North and inflamed the imagination of the opponents of slavery, and no doubt had much to do with the crystallizing of opinion in favor of the most drastic methods of ridding the country of the slave evil.

*Kansas-Nebraska Bills.*   The Kansas-Nebraska bill of 1854, repealed the Missouri Compromise, established firmly the idea of each territory, even north of thirty-six degrees and thirty minutes north latitude, having the right to decide whether it would be free or slave territory, and extended the fugitive slave law to the West.  It was a bold stroke, introduced by Stephen A. Douglas, and carried through with an audacity which stunned the North and brought great rejoicing to the slave-holding states.

*Dred Scott Decision.*   The next crisis arose over the Dred Scott decision.  An army surgeon with his body servant, Dred Scott, went from Missouri into Illinois, and later on into Minnesota. In 1838 he returned to Missouri with his slave.  Dred Scott claimed his freedom by virtue of the fact he had been taken into free territory, Illinois and Minnesota.  The case reached the Supreme Court in 1857 and the contention of the master was sustained.  But the Court went further and maintained that since slaves were property and the right of property was guaranteed by the constitution, Congress had no right to interfere with the holding of that property in the territories, any more than it had a right to interfere with the holding of any other kind of property.

Thus the flood gates were thrown open for taking slaves into any of the territories, even that north of the Missouri Compromise line, and the Missouri Compromise was declared unconstitutional.

*John Brown's Raid.* John Brown's raid of 1859, on Harper's Ferry, with the express purpose of liberating forcibly all Negroes of the South through a general insurrection, inflamed the Southern imagination, always susceptible to fear of insurrection, and added more fuel to the already hotly blazing fire of sectional suspicion.

*Presidential Election.* Rent by dissensions, the various parties met for the nomination of their presidential candidates. The Northern Democrats nominated Douglas of Illinois. The Constitutional Union party, a group of conservatives, nominated John Bell of Tennessee; the radical southern group which withdrew from the Democratic party, nominated John C. Breckenridge and the Republicans nominated Abraham Lincoln. It was a foregone conclusion that should Lincoln be elected, though the various wings of the Democratic party polled 2,823,000 popular votes against 1,866,000 cast for Lincoln. The influence on the South was momentous.

*Effect of Lincoln's Triumph.* "The South had avowedly staked everything, even her allegiance to the Union, upon this election. The triumph of Mr. Lincoln was, in her eyes, nothing less than the establishment in power of a party bent upon the destruction of the southern system and the defeat of southern interests, even to the point of countenancing and assisting servile insurrection. In the metaphor of Senator Benjamin, the Republicans did not mean, indeed, to cut down the tree of slavery, but they meant to gird it about, and so cause it to die. It seemed evident to the southern men, too, that the North would not pause or hesitate because of constitutional guarantees. For twenty years northern States had been busy passing "personal liberty" laws, intended to bar the operation of the federal statutes concerning fugitive slaves, and to secure for all alleged fugitives legal privileges which the federal statutes withheld. More than a score of States had passed laws with this object, and such acts were as plainly attempts to nullify the constitutional action of Congress as if they had spoken the language of the South Carolina ordinance of 1832. Southern pride, too, was stung to the quick by the position in which the South found itself. The agitation against slavery had spoken in every quarter the harshest moral censure of slavery and the slaveholders. The whole course of the South had been described as one systematic iniquity; southern society had been represented as built upon a wilful sin; the southern people had been held up to the world as those who deliberately despised the most righteous commands of religion. They knew that they did not deserve such reprobation.   They knew that their lives were honorable, their relations with their slaves humane, their responsibility for the existence of slavery among them remote. National churches had already broken asunder because of this issue of morals.   The Baptist Church had split into a northern and a southern branch as long ago as 1845; and 1844 had seen the same line of separation run through the great Methodist body.

"The Republican party was made up of a score of elements, and the vast majority of its adherents were almost as much repelled by the violent temper and disunionist sentiments of the Abolitionists as were the southern leaders themselves.   The abolitionist movement had had an exceedingly powerful and a steadily increasing influence in creating a strong feeling of antagonism towards slavery, but there was hardly more of an active abolitionist party in 1860 than there had been in 1840.   The Republicans wished, and meant, to check the extension of slavery; but no one of influence in their counsels dreamed of interfering with its existence in the States.   They explicitly acknowledged that its existence there was perfectly constitutional.   But the South made no such distinctions.   It knew only that the party which was hotly intolerant of the whole body of southern institutions and interests had triumphed in the elections and was about to take possession of the government, and that it was morally impossible to preserve the Union any longer.   'If you who represent the stronger portion,' Calhoun had said in 1850, in words which perfectly convey this feeling in their quiet cadences, 'cannot agree to settle the great questions at issue on the broad principle of justice and duty, say so; and let the States we both represent agree to separate and depart in peace." [46]

*Slavery Brought Its Own Penalty.*   South Carolina, Georgia, Florida, Alabama, Mississippi and Louisiana immediately withdrew from the Union.   They claimed that what they had freely entered for the purposes of common interest, they had a right to withdraw themselves from, when that Union would no longer help them to carry out their own purposes and foster their common interests.   The contention seemed reasonable enough, but it failed to recognize that although the states had started as separate entities, united into a confederacy, the inevitable growth of the country had blended them into a whole, whereby one part could not withdraw without great injury to all the others.   Slavery in the South had helped to keep the old conception of individuality and independence.   It had kept the South from entering fully into the spirit of progress and social responsibility involved in a confederation.   It was therefore overwhelmed in this hour by

[46] Woodrow Wilson: "Division and Reunion," pp. 208-210.

forces which had been growing unobserved by its citizens.  The conflict was inevitable, the calamity, the sure result of a policy of isolation.  In the Civil War the colossal system of slavery came finally to its close, and the South began again to build her life on a new and surer foundation.

CHAPTER VII

PLANTATION LIFE DURING THE SLAVE REGIME

There was a certain glory that shone round the life of the old South which none who knew it can ever forget, and those of us who have come after will do well to know and cherish the record. Whatever the evils of any age, there are usually some alleviating blessings, and even though there was hardship during slavery, there was also another side. The larger plantations were of an ample size which gave room to breathe and grow, and from them came men of great capacity in church and state. Mrs. Smedes describing the home at Elmington, located on the Chesapeake Bay and the North River in old Gloucester County, Virginia, writes:

*An Old Virginia Plantation.* "The house was of red brick, quaint and old-fashioned in design. It was built very near the water's edge. The lapping of the waves of the incoming tide was a sweet lullaby to the quiet scene, as the eye rested on the greensward of the lawn, or took in the bend of the river that made a broad sweep just below the Elmington garden. The North River is half a mile wide. On the other shore could be seen the groves and fields and gardens of the neighboring country-seats. The low gounds on the river-shore extend back a distance of a mile and three-quarters, and lie like a green carpet, dotted here and there with grand old forest-trees, and corn, wheat, rye, and tobacco fields. Far as the eye can reach stretches this fair view around Elmington. And far over, beyond field and grove and creek, rises the line of soft, round hills that mark the highlands of Gloucester.

"On the land side, the Elmington house was approached through the fields by a lane a mile and three-quarters long. It was broad enough to admit of three carriage-drives. Many of the lanes in Gloucester lie between avenues of cedar-trees, and the fields in most of the estates are divided by cedar-hedges. It was so on the Elmington lands.

"About four miles inland from the North River, in a quiet spot, surrounded by venerable oak and pine and walnut and other native trees, stands old Ware Church. It was built in colonial times, and its age is unknown. It is nearly square in form, and altogether unlike the present style of church architecture in this country. But its ancient walls are churchly, and the look of unchangeable-

139

ness is soothing to the spirit in this world unrest.  This was the
parish church attended by the North River people.  The old pew
backs at that day were so high that the occupants were invisible
to each other.  Many of them might read the names of their
deceased ancestors on the tombstones that served as a floor for
the chancel.  The floor of Ware Church was made of flagstones.
Stoves were not then in use in churches, nor was any attempt
made to heat them.  *Delicate people stayed at home in the winter,
or had warming-pans of coals carried in by their servants to put
to their feet.*

"Gloucester County had been settled by the best class of English
people who came to this country, the younger sons of noble
houses, and other men of standing, who were induced to make
their homes over here by an inherent love of change, or because
they had not the means to live in the mother-country in the
extravagant style required by their station.  These brought to
their homes in the New World the customs and manners of the
Old.  The tone of society has always been truly English in
Lower Virginia, the 'tide-water country,' as the people love to
call it.  Everybody kept open house; entertaining was a matter
of course, anything and everything was made the occasion of a
dinner-party.  The country-seats were strung along the banks of
the North River in a way to favor this.  A signal raised on one
could be seen for several miles up and down the river.  If one
of the colored fishermen, whose sole occupation was to catch fish
for the table at the Great House, as they called their master's
residence, succeeded in catching a sheephead, his orders were to
run up a signal-flag.  This was an invitation to dinner to every
gentleman in the neighborhood.  If a rabbit was caught the same
rule was observed.  Rabbits were not common, which seemed to
be the pretext for this, for they were not really esteemed as a
dainty dish.  A rabbit was served up rather as a trophy of the
hunt than as a part of the feast intended to be eaten.  But the
sheep's-head in those waters were not uncommon, and one was
taken by the fisherman of one house or another nearly every day.
At five minutes before the time for dinner the gentleman would
ride up, or come by boat to the door of the house that had the
signal flying.  If any one was unable to attend, his servant rode
up promptly with a note of regrets.  Punctuality in the observance
of all the rules of courtesy and good breeding seemed inherent in
the men and women of Gloucester society." [1]

*Description of a South Carolina Plantation.*  Olmsted in his
journey through South Carolina in the fifties stumbled into some
of these old plantations.  As he rode up the entrance way of this
plantation he describes what he saw as follows:

[1] Smedes: "A Southern Planter," p. 34.

"At the head of the settlement, in a garden looking down the street, was an overseer's house, and here the road divided, running each way at right angles; on one side to barns and a landing on the river, on the other toward the mansion of the proprietor. A negro boy opened the gate of the latter, and I entered.

"On either side, at fifty feet distant, were rows of old live oak trees, their branches and twigs slightly hung with a delicate fringe of gray moss, and their dark, shining, green foliage, meeting and intermingling naturally but densely overhead. The sunlight streamed through and played aslant the lustrous leaves, and fluttering, pendulous moss; the arch was low and broad; the trunks were huge and gnarled, and there was a heavy groining of strong, rough, knotty branches. I stopped my horse and held my breath; for I have hardly in all my life seen anything so impressively grand and beautiful. . . .

"At the upper end was the owner's mansion, with a circular court-yard around it, and an irregular plantation of great trees; one of the oaks, as I afterwards learned, seven feet in diameter of trunk, and covering with its branches a circle of one hundred and twenty feet in diameter. As I approached it, a smart servant came out to take my horse. I obtained from him a direction to the residence of the gentleman I was searching for, and rode away, glad that I had stumbled into so charming a place." [2]

*Living Condition on a Plantation.* The South was always a planter section. Men settled on their land, not with reference to the nearness of neighbors, but with reference to natural advantages. Good springs for water supply; appropriate building sites, the proper lay of land for farming, pastures and gardens, the proximity of timber for building and fuel, these were the determining factors. As a result, most of the early settlers lived in complete isolation and the plantations of necessity became more or less self-sufficient and independent little kingdoms. Everything except sugar and coffee must be grown on the land, and almost every article of use manufactured. On the larger plantations the clothing and furnishings for the "big house" were imported, but all other articles of daily use were manufactured by the slaves. Mrs. Smedes mentions 'two millers, two blacksmiths, two carpenters, a tanner and a shoemaker, together with five seamstresses and two laundresses, as continuously occupied on her father's plantation in Southern Mississippi.[3] Olmstead found plantations on which there were wheelwrights, blacksmiths, carpenters and other skilled mechanics. Fannie Kemble tells us there was a gang of coopers, blacksmiths, bricklayers, carpenters, all well ac-

[2] Olmsted's: "Seaboard Slave States," p. 417.
[3] Smedes: "A Southern Planter," p. 82.

quainted with the trade, on the Georgia plantation where she resided.[4] She also mentions engineers, and other skilled workers.[5] The plantation was a great industrial school where slaves were taught to do almost everything that was necessary to life in those simple, primitive times.

*Plantation Life Attractive.* Life on a big plantation was far from monotonous. Of course the happiness, or suffering of the slaves depended quite largely on the disposition of the master, but we are persuaded that on the average there was much more of care-free joy than there was of unhappiness. The Negro naturally had a care-free disposition and made the most of every opportunity for rejoicing. More than one Northern man coming South expecting to find the slaves a terribly dejected lot, was amazed at finding most of them not only well kept, but seemingly very happy. The reaction was usually somewhat extreme and not infrequently these men were blind to many of the real hardships. A most extreme case of this kind was that of the Rev. Nehemiah Adams, an abolitionist from New England, who coming South for health reasons found conditions so different from what he had expected that he immediately turned apologist for slavery. But the picture was not all dark even for those whose eyes were accustomed to seeing the evils that did exist.

After the work of the day the slaves who lived in quarters gathered in front of their cabins and with banjo in hand, and with imaginations that worked freely, they improvised while the children played and the young folks frolicked. During the hunting season, the men and boys accompanied the young white men in their expedition and not infrequently they were allowed to organize a " 'possum" or "coon" hunt of their own. On some of the larger plantations regular provision was made for regular days off for some workers in order that the quarters and the "big House" might be supplied with fish and game. If a fox hunt was organized there were always a few favored Negroes who followed the hounds and had as much fun as any of the white men. Dr. Moton in his autobiography tells us of his many happy hours spent with the white boys when he worked on the Virginia plantation of the Vaughans. He was no exception in this, for the children of the "big house" and the children of the quarters often found in each other most congenial company.

A marriage on the plantation was a gala day for the Negroes. All work was suspended, they shared in the rich food which had been prepared; they enjoyed the coming and going of the guests, and not infrequently they were actual observers of the sacred ceremony. But a wedding of a favorite slave was the climax of

[4] Kemble: "Journal of a Residence on a Georgia Plantation," p. 25.
[5] *Ibid.,* p. 133.

all joys. Such a wedding is described in the following terms by an old slave.

*A Plantation Wedding.* "I had a weddin'—a big weddin'—for Marlow's kitchen. Your pa gib me a head weadin',—kilt a mutton—a round o' beef—turkeys—cakes, one on t'other,—trifle. I had all de chiny off de sideboard, cups an' saucers, de table, de white table-cloth. I had on your pa's wife's weddin' gloves and slippers an' veil. De slippers was too small, but I put my toes in. Miss Mary had a mighty neat foot. Marster brought out a milk-pail o' toddy an' more in bottles. De gentlemans an' marster stand up on de tables. He didn't rush 'mongst de black folks, you know. I had a tearin'-down weddin',' to be sho'. Nobody else didn't hab sich a weddin'. Yes, Sis Abby hab a mighty nice weddin', too,—cakes an' things,—a handed roun' supper, you see. Marster promised de fust one what git married after he did a tearin'-down weddin', an' I was de fust. De whole day 'fore I was to be married Miss Mary—dat was your pa fust wife—kep' me shut up in a room. 'A bride must not be seen,' she said, An' she wouldn't lemme come out to dinner, but she sent my dinner in to me on a plate. De nex' mornin' I went to marster's and Miss Mary's room 'fore dey was up. 'Who is that?' she say. I say, 'Harriet.' 'Good-morning, Mrs. Bride. I wish you joy.'

"Oh, yes, I'se been see good times!

"In dem days I always dress my hyar very fine an' wear a high top comb in it.

"I don't nebber 'spect to see no sich times again." [6]

*Arrangement of Plantation Buildings.* The lay out of one of these old plantations was both convenient and interesting. Usually the "big house" stood far back from the road and was well shielded by a grove of live oaks, pines, cedars or maples as the case might be. To the rear were the kitchen—a separate house—the smoke house, where the meat was cured and stored, the house of the family servants, and behind these the barns. The regular "quarters" often stretched out like two great wings from the house or were sometimes further removed, in which case they usually formed a street with huts on either side and the overseer's house stood at the head of the street. A typical old plantation home of the finest type stands near Nashville, Tennessee. The Hermitage was the home of Andrew Jackson. Located amid broad rolling acres, with enough of rise and fall to break all monotony, it was one of the famous farms of the state. As one approaches the place he sees a great colonnade of cedars, planted by Jackson himself, which colonnade spreads out into the form of a fan as it approaches the house, thus screening a most beautiful circular driveway that passes the front of the house with its

[6] Smedes: "A Southern Planter," p. 55.

stately columns.  To the right and extending back of the house is one of those wonderful old gardens so common on the better plantations, in which grew lilac, old-fashioned flags, violets, roses and a score of the older flowers so typical of a southern garden. To the rear were the log cabins, stretching away for half a mile, and when the writer first saw it, old Uncle Alfred, the faithful body servant of General Jackson, still lived in his old quarter. There is a majesty and stateliness about the place which speaks of power and leadership.  These old plantations of the South were petty kingdoms in themselves and offered to their owners opportunity to develop a self-mastery, a resourcefulness and a leadership which made them the dominating figures of the nation up to the time of the Civil War.  It would have been hard to devise a system of life which tended to make clearer demarcations between the planter and the great mass of men who surrounded him.

*Slavery Stifled Growth.*  While the slave régime did develop a few masterful personalities, its fatal weakness lay in the fact that it refused to recognize the personalities of slaves and left completely undeveloped and crushed the personalities of the great mass of the poor whites.  "Of the 12,500,000 persons in the slave holding communities in 1860, only about 384,000 persons, or one in thirty-three, was a slave holder.  Since the property of a family was commonly vested in a single person, the true proportion would be about 350,000 white families out of perhaps 1,800,000; leaving out of account the white mountaineers, a fourth to a fifth of the white families in the slave holding sections had a property interest in slaves.

"A counter correction must now be made: about 77,000 owners had only one slave a piece, and 200,000 more owned less than ten slaves each; while only 2,300 families owned as many as a hundred slaves."[7]

*Small Number of Slave Owners.*  The wealth and leadership in the South was concentrated into the hands of these and a few thousand more who were owners of plantations and had from twenty-five to one hundred slaves each.  The names, Butler, Hayne, Pickney, Calhoun, Lee, Mason, Randolph, Ruffin, Dabney, Tyler, Polk, Jackson, Breckinridge, George, Claiborne, speak at once of power and influence.  It was because the leadership of the section was concentrated in a few efficient persons, who had leisure for politics and statesmanship, that the South had such a dominating influence for so long a time.

The distribution of slaves in various states follows the general average:  "More than 55 per cent of Virginia slaves in 1860 were held by owners of 1 to 20, and half of these by owners

[7] Harte: "Slavery and Abolition," pp. 67-68.

of 1 to 9. A poll of Spottsylvania County, Virginia, in 1783 showed 505 owners as possessing 4,581 slaves, the largest owner having but 159 slaves, nearly 50 per cent having between one and five slaves and only nine persons having over forty." [8] "There were 34,608 slaveholders in North Carolina in 1860, and these owned in all 331,059 slaves, or an average of 9.6 to each owner." [9] The average in Virginia was 9.4 and in South Carolina 15." [10] The number of large slaveholders in Missouri was smaller than in the states farther South and East. Trexler [11] says that in Cooper County in 1850 there was only one man, J. H. Ragland, who owned as many as seventy slaves; in St. Genevieve the largest slave owner, John Coffman, held only seventy-eight slaves; in Boone County, R. King had fifty-seven slaves, and W. C. Robinett had fifty. In Pike County, J. C. Carter had forty-three slaves, in 1859. "The Reverend Frederick Starr ('Lynceus') says that there were some plantations along the Missouri River having from 150 to 400 slaves. From the above figures it appears that a Missouri plantation with as many as 400 slaves must have been extremely rare." The average for Missouri seems to have been between four and five slaves per owner. Usually a small farmer who owned slaves held a family of husband, wife and children. These lived in very close proximity to the white family and felt much of their refining influence. The men worked side by side in the field and the women busied themselves over common tasks in the house. Except in rare cases there was little cruelty, because masters were too close to the slaves and had too much personal dealings with them. There was no absenteeism, no impersonal dealing. This always tends to ameliorate the life conditions of those who toil. Olmsted's observations convinced him that in North Carolina "The slave more frequently appears as a family servant—a member of his master's family, interested with him in his fortune, good or bad. Slavery thus loses much of its inhumanity." [12]

*No Personal Contacts on Big Plantations.* As in our modern industry, the greatest danger of exploitation arises where relations between employer and employee are impersonal. It is much easier to be harsh with a man who is known only as No. 112 than it is to be harsh with one you know as John Smith, the husband of Dinah Smith and the father of two children. On the large plantations where fifty or more Negroes were worked, there was more chance that the field hands would receive cruel treatment at the hands of the overseers. The men who were

[8] Ballagh: "A History of Slavery in Virginia," p. 105.
[9] Bassett: "Slavery in the State of North Carolina," p. 78.
[10] *Ibid.,* p. 78.
[11] Trexler: "Slavery in Missouri, p. 14 f., *passim.*
[12] Olmsted: "Seaboard Slave States," p. 367.

available as overseers were not of a very high order on the whole. The chronic complaint was that these men "were the laziest and most worthless dogs in the world," [13] that they were, because of the requirements of the law, "employed merely as a matter of form," [14] and that the Negroes were much more reliable than the overseers. Olmsted says of overseers: "Though sometimes of intelligence and piety, they were more often coarse, brutal and licentious; drinking men, wholly unfitted for the responsibility imposed on them." [15]

*Character of Overseers.* On many plantations the head man —a Negro—carried the keys and not the overseer. Fannie Kemble's report of Mr. K., the overseer on her husband's plantation in Georgia, is certainly not very flattering. She makes him out to be arbitrary, cruel, licentious, and crafty. He was a heartless wretch who knew how to squeeze profits out of the plantation, and at the same time to buy his way into the good graces of the Negroes, whom he abused, by giving out annuities from time to time like a professional ward boss. Fortunately for most of the Negroes these men were not given a free hand, but were usually held decidedly in check by the owners themselves. All planters laid down certain rules to govern their overseers, and insisted that they must not be broken. One of these rules very frequently found was that the overseer should not personally inflict corporal punishment, but should always have it done by the driver, under his personal observation. This tended to mitigate the severity of the punishment. Where the overseer was allowed to inflict punishment, it was usually limited to a specific number of lashes—say fifteen. Often he was ordered to reserve punishment for twenty-four hours in order that his anger might cool. J. W. Fowler, of Coahoma County, Mississippi, wrote as follows to his overseer in 1857:

*Rules of a Mississippi Plantation.* "The health, happiness, good discipline and obedience; good, sufficient and comfortable clothing, a sufficiency of good, wholesome and nutritious food for both man and beast being indispensably necessary to successful planting, as well as for reasonable dividends for the amount of capital invested, without saying anything about the Master's duty to his dependents, to himself and his God—I do hereby establish the following rules and regulations for the management of my Prairie Plantation, and require an observance of the same by any and all Overseers I may at any time have in charge thereof, to wit:

" 'Punishment must never be cruel or abusive, for it is abso-

---

[13] Olmsted: "Seaboard Slave States," p. 206.
[14] *Ibid.*, p. 438.
[15] *Ibid.*, p. 97.

lutely mean and unmanly to whip a negro from mere passion or malice, and any man who can do this is entirely unworthy and unfit to have control of either man or beast.

"'My negroes are permitted to come to me with their complaints and grievances and in no instance shall they be punished for so doing. On examination, should I find they have been cruelly treated, it shall be considered a good and sufficient cause for the immediate discharge of the Overseer.'" [16]

*Weston's Rules.*  P. C. Weston writes for a South Carolina plantation the following instructions for his overseer: "The Proprietor, in the first place, wishes the Overseer most distinctly to understand that his first object is to be, under all circumstances, the care and well being of the negroes. The Proprietor is always ready to excuse such errors as may proceed from want of judgment; *but he never can or will excuse cruelty, severity, or want of care towards the negroes.* For the well being, however, of the negroes, it is absolutely necessary to maintain obedience, order, and discipline; to see that the tasks are punctually and carefully performed, and to conduct the business steadily and firmly, without weakness on the one hand, or harshness on the other. For such ends the following regulations have been instituted.

"It is desirable to allow 24 hours to elapse between the discovery of the offense, and the punishment. No punishment is to exceed 15 lashes: in cases where the Overseer supposes a severer punishment necessary, he must apply to the Proprietor, or to ———— Esq., in case of the Proprietor's absence from the neighborhood. Confinement (not in the stocks) is to be preferred to whipping: but the stoppage of Saturday's allowance, and doing whole task on Saturday, will suffice to prevent ordinary offenses. Special care must be taken *to prevent any indency in punishing women.* No Driver, or other negro, is to be allowed to punish any person in any way, except by order of the Overseer, and in his presence." [17]

*Manigault's Rules.*  S. F. Clark, the overseer on Charles Manigault's plantation in Georgia, signed a contract which bears the following language:

"I will treat them all with kindness and consideration in sickness and in health. I will be at both settlements every day, and supervise all that is going on at each place, and attend personally to giving out allowance every Sunday morning and see to all other things myself." [18]

---

[16] Phillips: "Plantation and Frontier," Vol. I, p. 116.
[17] *Ibid.,* p. 118.
[18] *Ibid.,* Vol. I, p. 123.

Manigault also writes: "You had best think carefully respecting him, and always keep in mind the important old plantation maxim, viz: *'never to threaten a negro,'* or he will do as you and I would when at school—he will run.  But with such a one, . . . if you wish to make an example of him, take him down to the Savannah jail and give him prison discipline, and by all means solitary confinement, for three weeks, when he will be glad to get home again. . . .  Mind then and tell him that you and he are quits, that you will never dwell on old quarrels with him, that he has now a clear track before him and all depends on himself, for he now sees how easy it is to fix 'a bad disposed nigger.'  Then give my compliments to him and tell him that you wrote me of his conduct, and say if he don't change for the better I'll sell him to a slave trader who will send him to New Orleans, where I have already sent several of the gang for misconduct, or their running away for no cause." [19]

Other planters used prizes to get the best work out of Negroes and to keep them happy and satisfied.  The Burleigh plantation in Mississippi, owned by Charles Dabney, used this method:

*Dabney's Method of Control.*  "His plantation was considered a model one, and was visited by planters anxious to learn his methods.  He was asked how he made his negroes do good work.  His answer was that a laboring man could do more work and better work in five and a half days than in six.  He used to give the half of Saturdays to his negroes, unless there was a great press of work; but a system of rewards was more efficacious than any other method.  He distributed prizes of money among his cotton-pickers every week during the season, which lasted four or five months.  One dollar was the first prize, a Mexican coin valued at eighty-seven and a half cents the second, seventy-five cents the third, and so on, down to the smallest prize, a small Mexican coin called picayune, which was valued at six and a quarter cents.  The decimal nomenclature was not in use there.  The coins were spoken of as 'bits.'  Eighty-seven and a half cents were seven bits, fifty cents four bits, twenty-five cents two bits.  The master gave money to all who worked well for the prizes, whether they won them or not.  *When one person picked six hundred pounds in a day, a five-dollar gold-piece was the reward.*  On most other plantation four hundred pounds or three hundred and fifty or three hundred was considered a good day's work, but on the Burleigh place many picked five hundred pounds.  All had to be picked free of trash.  No one could do this who had not been trained in childhood.  To get five hundred pounds a picker

[19] Phillips: "American Negro Slavery," Vol. I, p. 271.

had to use both hands at once. Those who went into the cotton-fields after they were grown only knew how to pull out cotton by holding on to the stalk with one hand and picking it out with the other. Two hundred pounds a day would be a liberal estimate of what the most industrious could do in this manner. A very tall and lithe young woman, one of mammy's 'Brer Billy's' children, was the best cotton-picker at Burleigh. She picked two rows at a time, going down the middle with each hand. Some of the younger generation learned to imitate this. At Christmas Nelly's share of the prize money was something over seventeen dollars. Her pride in going up to the master's desk to receive it, in the presence of the assembled negroes, as the acknowledged leader of the cotton-pickers, was a matter of as great interest to the white family as to her own race." [20]

Governor Hammond, of South Carolina, used rewards instead of punishments, much to his own satisfaction.

*Profit Sharing Schemes.* Some planters, in their attempt to get good results from the slaves, had a kind of profit-sharing scheme, which seemed greatly to encourage industry.

Olmsted found on one plantation the following scheme: "At Christmas, a sum of money, equal to one dollar for each hogshead of sugar made on the plantation, was divided among the negroes. The last year this had amounted to over two dollars a head. It was usually given to the heads of families. If any had been particularly careless or lazy, it was remembered at this Christmas dole. Of course, the effect of this arrangement, small as was the amount received by each person, was to give the laborers a direct interest in the economical direction of their labor: the advantage of it was said to be very evident." [21]

*Elaborate Rules on a Mississippi Farm.* A Mississippi planter who signs himself "A Small Farmer," but who must have had a rather large number of slaves for such careful and elaborate organization, writes of his methods of work in DeBow's Industrial Resources:

"1. There shall be a place for everything, and everything shall be kept in its place.

"2. On the first days of January and July, there shall be an account taken of the number and condition of all the negroes, stock, and farming utensils of every description on the premises, and the same shall be entered in the plantation book.

"3. It shall be the duty of the overseer to call upon the stock-

[20] Smedes: "A Southern Planter," pp. 68-69.
[21] Olmsted's: "Seaboard Slave States," p. 660.

minder once every day, to know if the cattle, sheep, and hogs have been seen and counted, and to find out if any are dead, missing, or lost.

"4. It shall be the duty of the overseer, at least once in every week, to see and count the stock himself, and to inspect the fences, gates, and water-gaps on the plantation, and see that they are in good order.

"5. The wagons, carts, and all other implements, are to be kept under the sheds, and in the houses where they belong, except when in use.

"6. Each negro man will be permitted to keep his own axe, and shall have it forthcoming when required by the overseer. No other tool shall be taken or used by any negro without the permission of the overseer.

"7. Humanity on the part of the overseer, and unqualified obedience on the part of the negro, are, under all circumstances, indispensable.

"8. Whipping, when necessary, shall be in moderation, and never done in a passion; and the driver shall in no instance inflict punishment, except in the presence of the overseer, and when, from sickness, he is unable to do it himself.

"9. The overseer shall see that the negroes are properly clothed and well fed. He shall lay off a garden of at least six acres and cultivate it as part of his crop, and give the negroes as many vegetables as may be necessary.

"10. It shall be the duty of the overseer to select a sufficient number of women, each week, to wash for all. The clothes shall be well washed, ironed, and mended, and distributed to the negroes on Sunday morning; when every negro is expected to wash himself, comb his head, and put on clean clothes. No washing or other labor will be tolerated on the Sabbath.

"11. The negroes shall not be worked in the rain, or kept out after night, except in weighing or putting away cotton.

"12. It shall be the duty of the driver, at such hours of the night as the overseer may designate, to blow his horn, and to go around and see that every negro is at his proper place, and to report to the overseer any that may be absent; and it shall be the duty of the overseer, at some hour between that time and daybreak, to patrol the quarters himself, and see that every negro is where he should be.

"13. The negro children are to be taken, every morning, by their mothers, and carried to the houses of the nurses; and every cabin shall be kept locked during the day.

"14. Sick negroes are to receive particular attention. When they are first reported sick, they are to be examined by the overseer, and prescribed for, and put under the care of the nurse, and not put to work until the disease is broken and the patient beyond the power of a relapse.

"15. When the overseer shall consider it necessary to send for a physician, he shall enter in the plantation book the number of visits and to what negro they are made.

"16. When the negro shall die, an hour shall be set apart by the overseer for his burial; and at that hour all business shall cease, and every negro on the plantation, who is able to do so, shall attend the burial.

"17. The overseer shall keep a plantation book, in which he shall register the birth and name of each negro that is born; the name of each negro that died, and specify the disease that killed him. He shall also keep in it the weights of the daily picking of each hand; the mark, number, and weight of each bale of cotton, and the time of sending the same to market; and all other such occurrences, relating to the crop, the weather, and all other matters pertaining to the plantation, that he may deem advisable.

"18. The overseer shall pitch the crops, and work them according to his own judgment, with the distinct understanding that a failure to make a bountiful supply of corn and meat for the use of the plantation, will be considered as notice that his services will not be required for the succeeding year.

"19. The negroes, teams, and tools are to be considered under the overseer's exclusive management, and are not to be interfered with by the employer, only so far as to see that the foregoing rules are strictly observed.

"20. The overseer shall, under no circumstances, create an account against his employer, except in the employment of a physician or in the purchase of medicines; but whenever anything is wanted about the plantation, he shall apply to his employer for it.

"21. Whenever the overseer, or his employer, shall become dissatisfied, they shall, in a frank and friendly manner, express the same, and, if either party desires it, he shall have the right to settle and separate." [22]

Another Mississippi planter writes at length of his methods of handling his slaves, throwing some light on the general treatment of the Negro:

*Conditions on Another Mississippi Plantation.* "My first care has been to select a proper place for my 'Quarter,' well protected by the shade of forest trees, sufficiently thinned out to admit a free circulation of air, so situated as to be free from the impuri-

[22] DeBow: "Industrial Resources, etc., in the South and West," Vol. II, pp. 332-333.

ties of stagnant water, and to erect comfortable houses for my negroes. Planters do not always reflect that there is more sickness and consequently greater loss of life, from the decaying logs of negro houses, open floors, leaky roofs, and crowded rooms, than all other causes combined; and if humanity will not point out the proper remedy, let self-interest for once act as a virtue, and prompt him to save the health and lives of his negroes, by at once providing comfortable quarters for them. There being upwards of one hundred and fifty negroes on the plantation, I provide for them twenty-four houses made of hewn post-oak, covered with cypress, sixteen by eighteen, with close plank floors and good chimneys, and elevated two feet from the ground. The ground under and around the houses is swept every month, and the houses, both inside and out, whitewashed twice a year. The houses are situated in a double row from north to south, about 200 feet apart, the doors facing inwards, and the houses being in a line, about 50 feet apart. At one end of the street stands the overseer's house, workshops, tool house, and wagon sheds; at the other, the grist and saw-mill, with good cistern at each end, providing an ample supply of pure water. My experience has satisfied me, that spring, well, and lake water are all unhealthy in this climate, and that large under-ground cisterns, keeping the water pure and cool, are greatly to be preferred. They are easily and cheaply constructed, very convenient, and save both doctors' bills and loss of life. The negroes are never permitted to sleep before the fire, either lying down or sitting up, if it can be avoided, as they are always prone to sleep with their heads to the fire, are liable to be burnt and to contract disease; but beds with ample clothing are provided for them, and in them they are *made to sleep.*

*Concerning Moral Conditions.* "As to their habits of amalgamation and intercourse, I know of no means whereby to regulate them, or to restrain them; I attempted it for many years by preaching virtue and decency, encouraging marriages, and by punishing, with some severity, departures from marital obligations; but it was all in vain. I allow for each hand that works out, four pounds of clear meat and one peck of meal per week. Their dinners are cooked for them, and carried to the field, always with vegetables, according to the season. There are two houses set apart at mid-day for resting, eating, and sleeping, if they desire it, not being permitted to remain in the hot sun while at rest. They cook their own suppers and breakfasts, each family being provided with an oven, skillet, and sifter, and each one having a coffee-pot (and generally some coffee to put in it), with knives and forks, plates, spoons, cups, &c., of their own providing. The wood is regularly furnished them; for I hold it to be absolutely mean for a man to require a negro to work until daylight closes in, and then force him to get wood, sometimes a half mile off, before he can get a fire, either to warm himself or cook his supper. Every negro has his hen-house, where he raises poultry, which he is not permitted to sell, and he cooks and eats his chickens and eggs for his evening and morning meals to suit himself; besides, every family has a garden paled in, where they raise such vegetables and fruits as they take a fancy to. A large house is provided as a nursery for the children, where all are taken at daylight, and placed under the charge of a careful and experienced woman, whose sole occupation is to attend to them, and see that they are properly fed and attended to, and above all things to keep them as dry and cleanly as possible, under the circumstances. The suckling women come in to nurse their children four times during the day; and it is the duty of the nurse to see that they do not perform this duty until they have become properly cool, after walking from the field. In consequence of these regulations, I have never lost a child from being burnt to death, or, indeed, by accidents of any description; and although I have had more than thirty born within the last five years, yet I have not lost a single one from teething, or the ordinary summer complaints so prevalent amongst the children in the climate.

*Clothes and Extra Money.* "I give to my negroes four full suits of clothes with two pair of shoes, every year, and to my women and girls a calico dress and two handkerchiefs extra. I do not permit them to have 'truck patches' other than their gardens, or to raise anything whatever for market; but in lieu thereof, I give to each head of a family and to every single negro, on Christmas day, five dollars, and send them to the county town, under the charge of the overseer or driver, to spend their money. In this way, I save my mules from being killed up in summer, and my oxen in winter, by working and hauling off their crops; and more than all, the negroes are prevented from acquiring habits of trading in farm produce, which invariably leads to stealing, followed by whipping, trouble to the master, and discontent on the part of the slave. I permit no spirits to be brought on the plantation, or used by any negro, if I can prevent it; and a violation of this rule, if found out, is always followed by a whipping, and a forfeiture of the five dollars next Christmas.

*Hospital Service.* "I have a large and comfortable hospital provided for my negroes when they are sick; to this is attached a nurse's room; and when a negro complains of being too unwell to work, he is at once sent to the hospital, and put under the charge of a very experienced and careful negro woman, who administers the medicine and attends to his diet, and where they remain until they are able to work again.  This woman is, provided with sugar, coffee, molasses, rice, flour, and tea, and does not permit a patient to taste of meat or vegetables until he is restored to health.  Many negroes relapse after the disease is broken, and die, in consequence of remaining in their houses and stuffing themselves with coarse food after their appetites return, and both humanity and economy dictate that this should be prevented.  From the system I have pursued, I have not lost a hand since the summer of 1845 (except one that was killed by accident) nor has my physician's bill averaged fifty dollars a year, notwithstanding I live near the edge of the swamp of Big Black River, where it is thought to be very unhealthy.

*Land Allotment per Worker.*  "I cultivate about ten acres of cotton and six of corn to the hand, not forgetting the little wheat patch that your correspondent speaks of, which costs but little trouble, and proves a great comfort to the negroes; and have as few sour looks and as little whipping as almost any other place of the same size.

"I must not omit to mention that I have a good fiddler, and keep him well supplied with catgut, and I make it his duty to play for the negroes every Saturday night until twelve o'clock.  They are exceedingly punctual in their attendance at the ball, while Charley's fiddle is always accompanied with Ihurod on the triangle, and Sam to 'pat.'

*Religious Teaching.*  "I also employ a good preacher, who regularly preaches to them on the Sabbath day, and it is made the duty of every one to come up clean and decent to the place of worship.  As Father Garritt regularly calls on Brother Abram (the foreman of the prayer-meeting) to close the exercises, he gives out and sings his hymn with much unction, and always cocks his eye at Charley, the fiddler, as much as to say, 'Old fellow, you had your time last night; now it is mine.'

"I would gladly learn every negro on the place to read the Bible, but for a fanaticism which, while it professes friendship to the negro, is keeping a cloud over his mental vision, and almost crushing out his hopes of salvation.

"These are some of the leading outlines to my management, so far as my negroes are concerned.  That they are imperfect, and could be greatly improved, I readily admit; and it is only with the hope that I shall be able to improve them by the experience of others, that I have given them to the public.

"Should you come to the conclusion that these rules would be of any service when made known to others, you will please find them a place in the *Review*." [23]

[23] DeBow: "Industrial Resources, etc., in the South and West," Vol. II, pp. 331-332.

*Shielded from Dangerous Work.*  The slaves were shielded from the most unhealthful and dangerous work on purely economic grounds.  A good planter valued his Negroes highly and where work was apt to endanger their health or lives, he hired free labor to perform the tasks.  Thus Olmsted finds in Virginia a planter, Mr. C., who does not like the Irish but employs them to do the ditching on his place because that was considered very unhealthful.  Another planter, Mr. W., "had an Irish gang draining for him by contract.  He thought a Negro could do twice as much in a day as an Irishman.  He had not stood over them and seen them at work, but judged entirely from the amount they accomplished:  He thought a good gang of Negroes would have got on twice as fast. . . . I asked why he should employ Irishmen rather than doing the work with his own hands.  'It's dangerous work (unhealthful?) and a Negro's life is too valuable to be risked at it.  If a Negro dies it's  a considerable loss, you know.' [24]

Nor was this case of the slave simply a business arrangement. To many of the slave owners it was a personal responsibility most religiously assumed and carried out.  Mrs. Smedes tells of the intense personal interest in slaves which maintained in her household after her father moved with all his slaves from Virginia to Mississippi.  There was at first some difficulty in getting supplies.

"One of the first was the unavoidable delay in getting supplies of meat for the servants.  For two weeks after their arrival they had none.  *Sophia's sister Emmeline, Mrs. Lewis Smith, was so conscientious that she refused during this period to touch a morsel of meat, although the supply on hand was ample* to last the white families till more could be procured." [25]

*Solicitude for Slaves.*  Of the solicitude of her father for his slaves, she says:

"Until over seventy years old, he was singularly indifferent to cold or heat, or to discomforts of any sort.  But he felt compassion for his Negroes.  He knew that the warm African blood in their veins was not fitted to endure what he could stand.  He never regarded the weather for himself, but was very careful about sending them out in bad weather, and never did it unless it seemed a necessity.  On such occasions he wore an anxious look, *and said that he could not go to bed until his servants had*

---
[24] Olmsted: "Seaboard Slave States," pp. 90-91.
[25] Smedes: "A Southern Planter," p. 65.

*gotten home safely.* They were *always sure of finding a hot fire and a warm drink ready for them on their return."*[26]

*Affection for Slaves.* William Chambers, an Englishman, who made a tour through the South, in 1857 declared:

"That there frequently exists the most kindly feeling between the families of proprietors and their slave dependents, is undeniable; and it is the spectacle of this harmony between master and servants, that fascinates travellers in the South, and induces them to declare that slavery is by no means so bad a thing as it is usually represented." [27]

*Abuses of Slavery.* But in spite of all precaution as to cruelty on the part of oveseers and drivers, the very fact of complete legal control made the system susceptible of terrible abuse. Louisiana, by express statute, allowed the overseer the same authority as that vested in the master:

"The *condition of a slave* BEING MERELY A PASSIVE ONE, his subordination to his master, AND ALL WHO REPRESENT HIM, *is not susceptible of any modification or restriction* (except in what can excite the slave to the commission of crime), in such manner that he owes to his master and to *all his family* a respect WITHOUT BOUNDS and an ABSOLUTE OBEDIENCE, and he is consequently to execute all the orders which he receives from him or from them." (Martin's Digest, 616) [28]

While Louisiana was the only state having such a direct statute, it was clearly recognized by custom in other states that the slave was completely in the hands of the agent of the master.

" 'The slave is liable to be coerced or punished by the whip, *and to be tormented by every species of personal ill-treatment,* subject only to the exceptions already mentioned (i.e., the deprivation of life and limb), *by the attorney, manager, overseer, driver, and every other person to whose government and control* the owner may choose to subject him, as fully as by the owner himself. Nor is any special mandate or express general power necessary for this purpose, *it is enough that the inflictor of the violence is set over the slave for the moment, either by the owner or by any of his* delegates or sub-delegates, of whatever rank or character.' (Stephen's Slavery, p. 46)" [29]

[26] Smedes: "A Southern Planter," p. 73.
[27] Chambers: "Slavery and Colour," p. 116.
[28] Goodell: "American Slave Code," p. 198.
[29] *Ibid.,* p. 199.

*Laws to Prevent Cruelty.* To prevent excessive cruelty by masters themselves, various states passed laws prescribing how far a master might go. South Carolina, Act of 1740 reads:

" 'In case any person shall wilfully cut out the tongue, put out the eye, castrate, or *cruelly* scald, burn, or deprive any slave of any limb or member, or shall inflict any *other cruel* punishment, OTHER THAN by whipping, or beating with a horsewhip, cowskin, switch, or small stick, *or* by putting irons on, or confining or imprisoning such slave, every such person shall, for every such offense, forfeit the sum of one hundred pounds, current money.' (2 Brevard's Digest, 241.)" [30]

Louisiana law said:

" 'The slave is *entirely* subject to the will of his master, *who may* correct and *chastise him,* though not with *unusual* rigor, nor so as to maim or mutilate him, or to expose him to the danger of loss of life, or so as to cause his death.' (Civil Code of Louisiana, Art. 173)" [31]

Mississippi and a number of other states set fines for excessive punishment. The Mississippi code says:

" 'No cruel or *unusual* punishment shall be inflicted on any slave in this state. And any master or other person entitled to the service of any slave, who shall inflict such cruel or unusual punishment, or shall authorize or permit the same to be inflicted, shall, on conviction, &c., be fined according to the magnitude of the offense, at the discretion of the Court, in any sum not exceeding five hundred dollars, &c.' (Rev. Code, 379; Act of June 18, 1822)" [32]

*Punishment Unto Death Not Murder.* The murder during punishment of a slave by a master was not murder according to the statute of most of the states; but was a crime punishable by fine and in some cases imprisonment. In case the murder was deliberate and wilful the master could be tried for murder, but it must be stated in fairness that to convict a white man of murdering a Negro was practically impossible. On the big plantations there were few others than Negroes and they were not allowed to testify against a white man. Hence there was ample opportunity for severity. It is much to the credit of the good behavior of

[30] Goodell: "American Slave Code," p. 159.
[31] *Ibid.,* p. 161.
[32] *Ibid.,* p. 164.

the slaves and the benevolence of the masters that charges of cruelty were so rare. Olmsted found that public opinion was strongly opposed to cruelty.[33] He felt that slaves were usually treated with much more consideration for their physical comfort and health, than were free domestics,[34] and he bore testimony to the fact that the published reports of the suffering of slaves on the rice plantations were greatly exaggerated.[35]

*Whippings Severe.* But at least severe whippings were not uncommon. An advertisement in the Virginia *Gazette* (Williamsburg) January 13, 1774, offering a reward for a runaway Negro, unblushingly gives the following marks by which the Negro may be identified: "As I have whipped him twice for his bad Behavior, I believe Scars may be seen upon his body."[36] A Louisiana planter advertising for his runaway slave who had been committed to the work house, in 1826 writes as follows: "He is black, and has a down look, five feet, seven inches high, when committed had around his neck an iron collar with three prongs extending upward, has many scars on his back and shoulder from the whip."[37]

Andrew Jackson advertised in the Nashville *Gazette* and *Mero District Advertiser,* November 7, 1804, that he would pay a liberal reward of fifty dollars to any one returning his mulatto man slave, would pay reasonable expenses if found beyond the borders of the state, and would give "ten dollars extra for every hundred lashes any person will give him to the limit of three hundred."[38] Not infrequently in the advertisement for runaways it is stated they have a specific brand mark on the shoulder.

H. H. Johnston quotes from the Nashville *Banner* for 1834 a story of great cruelty. Phillips, an overseer for Meeks, had whipped one of the Meeks' slaves to death, and Meeks was suing Phillips for the price of the slave. The Negro had disobeyed Phillips, the overseer, and then had resisted punishment; whereupon he was knocked down, then tied and strung up and literally whipped to death. The court declared that the overseer was guilty of killing the Negro and must pay for the same, but there is no evidence in the report that Phillips was ever criminally prosecuted for the murder.[39]

*Cruelty in Punishment.* Olmsted gives an account of a severe whipping of a Negro girl by an Alabama overseer. The girl seemed to be trying to shirk work and was caught by the overseer.

[33] Olmsted: "Seaboard Slave States," p. 97.
[34] *Ibid.,* p. 421.
[35] *Ibid.,* p. 484.
[36] Phillips: "Plantation and Frontier," Vol. II, p. 81.
[37] *Ibid.,* p. 88.
[38] *Ibid.,* p. 81.
[39] Johnston's: "The Negro in the New World," p. 372.

" 'That won't do,' said he; 'get down.' The girl knelt on the ground. He got off his horse, and holding him with his left hand, struck her thirty or forty blows across the shoulders with his tough, flexible 'raw-hide' whip (a terrible instrument for the purpose). They were well laid on, at arm's length, but with no appearance of an angry excitement on the part of the overseer. At every stroke the girl winced and exclaimed, 'Yes sir!' or 'Ah, sir!' or 'Please, sir!' not groaning or screaming. At length he stopped and said, 'Now tell me the truth.' The girl repeated the same story. 'You have not got enough yet,' said he, 'pull up your clothes; lie down.' The girl without any hesitation, without a word or look of remonstrance or entreaty, drew closely all her garments under her shoulders, and lay down upon the ground with her face toward the overseer, who continued to flog her with the raw hide, across her naked loins and thighs, with as much strength as before. She now shrunk away from him, not rising, but writhing, groveling, and screaming, 'Oh, don't, sir! oh, please stop, master! please, sir! please, sir! oh, that's enough, master! oh, Lord! oh, master, master! oh, God, master, do stop! oh, God, master! oh, God, Master!' " [40]

*Extreme Cruelty Not Common.* These are very extreme cases and undoubtedly did not happen often. But they are illustrations of what the slave system made possible. No doubt there are cases of cruelty equally ugly at the present time, but the one marked difference between cruelty to the slave and cruelty to the under dog now lies in the fact that the slave had no redress or practically none, while the subject of cruelty in a free community does find redress in the courts. While our careful study of slave conditions convinces us that such cruelty as recorded above, and such as recorded in Stowe's "Uncle Tom's Cabin," are decidedly uncommon, no student of the subject should fail to see that a system which makes such occurrences possible at all without redress, is a bad system and must die of its own weight.

*Slave Housing.* The housing of the slave varied as much as his treatment. On the better plantations they were as good or better than the average for the poor whites. "Often they were built of substantial brick with a second story, inner fittings and windows of glass, far more commodious and comfortable than the average laboring free man of the South, white or black, is able to erect for himself." [41] Olmsted found plantations where the slaves were housed in brick cabins, "neatly and comfortably furnished." [42] He describes the slave quarters of Mr. X's plantation as follows:

[40] Johnston's: "The Negro in the New World," p. 373.
[41] Ballagh: "A History of Slavery in Virginia," p. 103.
[42] Olmsted: "Seaboard Slave States," p. 421.

"Each cabin was a framed building, the walls boarded and whitewashed on the outside, lathed and plastered within, the roof shingled; forty-two feet long, twenty-one feet wide, divided into two family tenements, each twenty-one by twenty-one; each tenement divided into three rooms—one, the common household apartment, twenty-one by ten; each of the others (bed-rooms), ten by ten. There was a brick fire-place in the middle of the long side of each living room, the chimneys rising in one, in the middle of the roof. Besides these rooms, each tenement had a cock-loft, entered by steps from the household room. Each tenement is occupied, on an average, by five persons. There were in them closets, with locks and keys, and a varying quantity of rude furniture. Each cabin stood two hundred feet from the next, and the street in front of them being two hundred feet wide, they were just that distance apart each way. The people were nearly all absent at work, and had locked their outer doors, taking the keys with them. Each cabin has a front and back door, and each room a window, closed by a wooden shutter, swinging outward, on hinges." [43]

The author has seen many of the old slave quarters which still stand here and there in the South, and many of them were remarkable for their comfort, space, and convenience. The furnishing in these houses was, of course, very simple. A rude bed, made of wood, with either slats or corded rope for springs, a pallet or two, a few chairs, made by hand from the hickory of the forest, the big pot which sometimes hung from a crane at the fireplace, but more usually was set on the log fire, a skillet in which bread, sweet potatoes and the delectable "possum" were baked, a few rude dishes, a wooden pail with its long handled gourd, used as a dipper, these with slight variations made up most of the furnishings of a slave's home.

*Care of Health and Comfort.* On the best plantations care was taken that the houses were kept clean and wholesome. A Mississippi planter writes his overseer: "At least once a week (especially in the summer), inspect their houses and see that they have been swept clean, examine their bedding and see that they are occasionally well aired; their clothes mended and everything attended to that conduces to their health, comfort and happiness." [44]

A Virginia planter writes that "the addition of comfort to the mere necessaries is a price paid by a master for the advantages he will derive from binding his slaves to his service, by a ligament

[43] Olmsted: "Seaboard Slave States," p. 422.
[44] Phillips: "Plantation and Frontier," Vol. I, p. 113.

stronger than chains." [45]  Mrs. Smedes says her father distributed blankets to all the Negroes every other year, and gave extra supplies to the larger families.[46]  In instructions to overseers one frequently finds references to spring house-cleaning of the quarters, sprinkling of lime about the premises, care of the water supply, attention to plenty of wood being provided for winter use, the changing of the straw in the mattresses, careful attention to extermination of bugs and insects, and many other details.  Economic interest, if not human interest, forced all careful and thoughtful planters to look well to the health and housing of their slaves.

There were undoubtedly many exceptions to this good care. Not infrequently the slave quarters were one room cabins, which gave little comfort and no privacy.  This was particularly true where the planter did not live on his land, but left an overseer in complete charge.  Olmsted describes a large plantation of this kind.

*Poor Housing.*  "There was no residence for the owner, at all, only a small cottage, or whitewashed cabin, for the overseer.  It was a very large plantation, and all the buildings were substantial and commodious, except the negro-cabins, which were the smallest I had seen—I thought not more than twelve feet square, interiorly.  They stood in two rows, with a wide street between them.  They were built of logs, with no windows—no opening at all, except the doorway, with a chimney of sticks and mud; with no trees about them, no porches, or shades, of any kind.  Except for the chimney—the purpose of which I should not readily have guessed—if I had seen one of them in New England, I should have conjectured that it had been built for a powderhouse, or perhaps an ice-house—never for an animal to sleep in." [47]

*The Butler Plantation.*  Fannie Kemble's description of the dilapidated condition of her husband's plantation quarters bears out this general statement about neglect of the slave housing where the owner was an absentee.  As is the result always in absenteeism, things go from bad to worse.

"I walked down the settlement toward the Infirmary or hospital, calling in at one or two of the houses along the row.  These cabins consist of one room, about twelve feet by fifteen, with a couple of closets smaller and closer than the state-rooms of a ship, divided off from the main room and each other by rough wooden partitions, in which the inhabitants sleep.  They have almost all of them a rude bedstead, with the gray moss of the forests for

[45] Phillips: "American Negro Slavery," p. 275.
[46] Smedes: "A Southern Planter," p. 73.
[47] Olmsted: "Seaboard Slave States," p. 386.

mattresses, and filthy, pestilential-looking blankets for covering. Two families (sometimes eight and ten in number) reside in one of these huts, which are mere wooden frames pinned, as it were, to the earth by a brick chimney outside, whose enormous aperture within pours down a flood of air, but little counteracted by the miserable spark of fire, which hardly sends an attenuated thread of lingering smoke up its huge throat. A wide ditch runs immediately at the back of these dwellings, which is filled and emptied daily by the tide. Attached to each hovel is a small scrap of ground for a garden, which, however, is for the most part untended and uncultivated. Such of these dwellings as I visited today were filthy and wretched in the extreme, and exhibited that most deplorable consequence of ignorance and abject condition, the inability of the inhabitants to secure and improve even such pitiful comfort as might yet be achieved by them. Instead of the order, neatness, and ingenuity which might convert even these miserable hovels into tolerable residences, there was the careless, reckless, filthy indolence which even the brutes do not exhibit in their lairs and nests, and which seemed incapable of applying to the uses of existence the few miserable means of comfort yet within their reach. Firewood and shavings lay littered about the floors, while the half-naked children were cowering round two or three smoldering cinders. The moss with which the chinks and cranies of their ill-protecting dwellings might have been stuffed was trailing in dirt and dust about the ground, while the back door of the huts, opening upon a most unsightly ditch, was left wide open for the fowls and ducks, which they are allowed to raise, to travel in and out, increasing the filth of the cabin by what they brought and left in every direction.

*Conditions of Slave Children.* "In the midst of the floor, or squatting round the cold hearth, would be four or five little children from four to ten years old, the latter all with babies in their arms, the care of the infants being taken from the mothers (who are driven afield as soon as they recover from child labor), and devolved upon these poor little nurses, as they are called, whose business it is to watch the infant, and carry it to its mother whenever it may require nourishment. To these hardly human little beings I addressed my remonstrances about the filth, cold, and unnecessary wretchedness of their room, bidding the elder boys and girls kindle up the fire, sweep the floor, and expel the poultry. For a long time my very words seemed unintelligible to them, till, when I began to sweep and make up the fire, etc., they first fell to laughing, and then imitating me. The incrustations of dirt on their hands, feet, and faces, were my next object of attack, and the stupid negro practice (by-the-by, but a short time since nearly universal in enlightened Europe) of keeping the babies with their feet bare, and their heads, already well capped by nature with their woolly hair, wrapped in half a dozen hot, filthy coverings.   Thus I traveled down the 'street,' in every dwelling endeavoring to awaken a new perception, that of cleanliness, sighing, as I went, over the futility of my own exertions, for how can slaves be improved?" [48]

*Treatment of Women.*   The treatment of slave women was perhaps the darkest blot on the system.   Perhaps the darkest picture of this phase of slavery is presented by the above Fannie Kemble, an English woman, an actress, who married a trifling Georgia planter who had inherited large wealth but no great amount of thrift or character.   As an abolitionist she was perhaps an unfair observer, but her facts evidently show what could happen when the owner had little strength of character, was absent most of the time and left the place to unscrupulous overseers, such as Fannie Kemble describes Mr. K. as being.   The general rule on plantations was that a woman should do three-fourths the task of an able-bodied man in the field.   In the case of becoming a mother, she worked right up to the time of the birth of her child, though the labor was lightened during the last weeks, and ordinarily she was supposed to go back to work one month after her child was born.   It seems on Mr. Butler's (the husband of Fannie Kemble) plantation, the time of rest for the mother was only three weeks.   "The women who visited me yesterday evening," she writes, 'were all in a family way, and came to entreat me to have the sentence modified, which condemned them to resume their labor of hoeing in the fields three weeks after confinement." [49]   With bitter irony the chivalry of the South is attacked:   "I think an elegant young Carolinean or Georgian gentleman, whip in hand, driving a gang of 'lusty women,' as they are called here, would be a pretty vision of the 'chivalry of the South'—a little coarse, I am afraid you will say.   Oh! quite horribly coarse, but then so true. . . ." [50]

*Indecent Treatment of Women.*   That women were sometimes punished not only cruelly, but also indecently, is clear from the testimony of Olmsted and others.   Fannie Kemble tells of an expectant mother so punished:   "I asked her what she meant by having her arms tied up.   She said their hands were first tied together, sometimes by the wrists, and sometimes, which was worse, by the thumbs, and they were then drawn up to a tree or post, so as almost to swing them off the ground, and then their clothes rolled round their waist, and a man with a cowhide stands and stripes them.   I give you the woman's words.   She did not

[48] Kemble: "Journal of a Residence on a Georgia Plantation," pp. 30, 31, 32.
[49] *Ibid.*, p. 182.
[50] *Ibid.*, p. 135.

speak of this as of anything strange, unusual, or especially horrid and abominable; and when I said, 'Did they do that to you
when you were with child?' she simply replied, 'Yes, missis.'
And to all this I listen—I, an English woman, the wife of the
man who owns these wretches, and I can not say, 'That thing shall
not be done again; that cruel shame and villainy shall never be
known here again." [51]

*More Thoughtful Masters.*   But this was only one side of the
picture.  .The best masters of the South gave every care to the
women as well as to all their other servants.   Phillips quotes
Weston's rules for care of women and children as follows:

"The pregnant women are always to do some work up to the
time of their confinement, if it is only walking into the field and
staying there.  If they are sick, they are to go to the hospital and
stay there until it is pretty certain their time is near.  'Lying in'
women are to be attended by the midwife as long as is necessary,
and by a woman put to nurse them for a fortnight.  They will
remain at the negro houses for four weeks, and then will work
two weeks on the highland.   In some cases, however, it is
necessary to allow them to lie up longer.  The health of many
women has been ruined by want of care in this particular." [52]

*Better Treatment of Women.*   Hammond's rules were as follows: "Sucklers are not required to leave their homes until sun-
rise, when they leave their children at the children's house before
going to field.   The period of suckling is twelve months.   Their
work lies always within half a mile of the quarter.   They *are
required to be cool before commencing to suckle—to wait fifteen
minutes at least in summer, after reaching the children's house
before nursing.*   It is the duty of the nurse to see that none are
heated when nursing, as well as of the overseer and his wife
occasionally to do so.   They are allowed forty-five minutes at each
nursing to be with their children.   They return three times a day
until their children are eight months old—in the middle of the
forenoon, at noon, and in the imddle of the afternoon; till the
twelfth month but twice a day, missing at noon; during the
twelfth month at noon only. . . . Pregnant women at five months
are put in the suckler's gang.   No plowing or lifting must be
required of them.   Sucklers, old, infirm and pregnant, receive the
same allowances as full-work hands.   The regular plantation midwife shall attend all women in confinement.   Some other woman
learning the art is usually with her during delivery.   The confined woman lies up one month, and the midwife remains in con-

[51] Kemble: "Journal of a Residence on a Georgia Plantation," p. 200.
[52] Phillips: "American Negro Slavery," p. 264.

stant attendance for seven days. Each woman on confinement has a bundle given her containing articles of clothing for the infant, pieces of cloth and rag, and some nourishment, as sugar, coffee, rice and flour for the mother." [53]

*Bishop Bratton's Testimony.* Bishop Bratton, whose intimate contact with slavery in his boyhood days, and whose deep interest in the race to-day make him a most intelligent interpreter, writes of the home life in these most human words:

"The women had their tasks. There were the hoe-hands—women, boys, and girls—to be taught under easy, short tasks, but with the care always required by their foremen. There was the weave-room, where cotton and wool were spun and woven into cloth for home use. The dyeing was done at home. There was the sewing room where, under the oversight of the mistress, clothing in proper quantity was cut and made for 'top and bottom' wear. There was the day nursery where the young mothers, busied with the half tasks allotted them, left their little ones under the care of the older experienced women who, under the mistress, were at times, nurses, and at other times mid-wives.

*Care of Sick.* "Some plantations also had the 'sick house' for severe cases; but, in most cases, the sick were at home, visited regularly by master or mistress or both, and by the family doctor where his attention was needed. The last was often distant, and the master and mistress were generally good substitutes, always supplied with simple remedies. The day-nursery provided the opportunity for instruction in baby-farming, which many a mistress used to great advantage. For instruction in domestic service, the 'Big House' was the school, and none better. A southern white boy would as soon have been disrespectful to his father as 'sassed' the dignified butler; a punishment would even more certainly have followed the latter, if known. And the relation of love between children and 'Mammy,' and between family and servants, is too charmingly commonplace to remark." [54]

*Care of Children.* On the best plantations children were very carefully cared for. They were kept during the day at a general nursery usually presided over by kind old Negro women who had had considerable experience with children of their own. The food for the older children was carefully prepared and everything done to insure a healthy child. Olmsted describes one of these nurseries where twenty-seven children of all ages were seen.[55] Among them were boys and girls ten years old, for children were

[53] Phillips: "American Negro Slavery," pp. 264-265.
[54] Bratton: "Wanted a Leader," pp. 104-105.
[55] Olmsted: "Seaboard Slave States," p. 423 f.

166    THE NEGRO FROM AFRICA TO AMERICA

not regularly sent to work until they were twelve and then they
were set tasks commensurate with their ability. At twelve the
regular task of a child was supposed to be one-quarter of the task
of an able-bodied man.

*Conditions of Marriage.* Perhaps the greatest hardship of
slavery lay in the possible separation of families in case of sale of
slaves. In the normal course of events it often happened that a
slave man of one plantation became attached to a slave woman of
a neighboring plantation. With the consent of both masters they
were married, or what was the equivalent, began to live with
each other. If there were any children as the result of the union,
they belonged to the master of the woman. Not infrequently
one or the other of the planters would buy the husband or the
wife in order to get them together on the same plantation. This
was done not only from a humanitarian purpose, but also in the
interest of efficiency. A slave would work much better when
happy and contented; and nothing did more to make them
happy than to provide at least the elemental beginnings of a home.
Few planters were so heartless or so mean, not to say stupid,
as not to care for the happiness of their slaves in this manner.
Nor would a planter sell slaves unless forced to by failure or
calamity. Chambers found evidence "that planters parted with
their servants with reluctance and only under the pressure of
extreme necessity."

When Thomas Dabney planned to move from Virginia to
Mississippi, his daughter (Mrs. Smedes) says he called all his
slaves together and told them he did not mean to take any Negro
who did not want to go. He further told them his plan was to
buy all husbands or wives connected with his own slaves from
other plantations, and at prices satisfactory to their owners.
"Everything should be made to yield to the important consideration of keeping families together." [56] A planter with a large
number of slaves told Olmsted he had never sold but three slaves
and these all went willingly, or were banished for exceedingly
and persistently bad conduct. However, a neighboring planter
sold a valuable man during the very week that Olmsted stayed
at this plantation.[57]

*Selling Slaves Discouraged.* A man who sold slaves undoubtedly lost caste with his neighbors, and since slavery was not only
an economic but also a social institution, only those who had
little reputation to lose could be induced to part with a slave.
However, the death of the head of the house often forced a sale
and the settling of an estate, in which case much hardship on the
slaves might result. Often, also, financial distress forced a mas-

[56] Smedes: "A Southern Planter," p. 48.
[57] Olmsted: "Seaboard Slave States," p. 485.

ter to sell slaves, so that no slave was completely safe from such a catastrophe. No more terrible threat could be held over the head of a Negro than that he would be sold down South—which to the Negro meant the far away, unknown and untried land—hence bad. There was undoubtedly much selling of slaves from the older states to the newer and more western states, as we shall see later, but this in large measure was a sale of the younger and more robust Negroes, and did not so frequently separate husband and wife as would be supposed. But simply the possibility of it, and the occasional actuality of it, made the system very odious to men, and surely not able to persist in the presence of a growing conscience.

*Summary.* The slave regime had undoubtedly some favorable aspects. It allowed the concentration of labor in a sparcely settled country; it allowed a few the leisure to develop governmental life; it built up a paternal aristocracy which developed a chivalry, narrow to be sure, but none the less a chivalry that has hardly had an equal; it took a crude and unsettled people and gave them their first lessons in industry, thrift, moral life. On the other hand, it helped to breed a listless and irresponsible white leadership; it put heavy handicaps upon the poor whites; it degraded labor both in the eyes of the whites and the Negroes; it tended to keep the Negro's ideals of morality at the same low stage that he had inherited from Africa, and the presence of a defenseless womanhood belonging to a lower social caste was a constant temptation to the reckless young men of the ruling class. All these facts were clear to hundreds of the best white people of the South long before the emancipation proclamation, for as Mrs. Smedes declares, "Very many slave owners looked on slavery as an incubus, and longed to be rid of it, but they were not able to give up their young and valuable Negroes, nor were they willing to set adrift the aged and helpless." . . . "Who can wonder that we longed for a lifting of the incubus, and that in the family of Thomas Dabney the first feeling when the war ended was of joy that one dreadful responsibility at least was removed." No one wishes back the days of the old South, but no true student of history can fail to appreciate their romance and glory as well as their cruelties and hardships.

CHAPTER VIII

## THE FREE NEGRO

No review of the life of the Negro in America would be complete which failed to consider the origin and growth of the Free Negro class, neither is it possible to get a clear view of the development of the present Negro population without seeing clearly the relation of the Free Negro to the early slave population.

*White Servitude.* As noted in a previous chapter, servitude of whites in colonial days was the fore-runner of Negro slavery. The early Plymouth company which established settlements in Virginia, raised its funds for a company of men known as adventurers, each of whom must put in the treasury 12 pounds, 10 shillings, or multiples of that amount, and who on that basis were to be joint sharers in the land and wealth of the colony. The colonists themselves were made up of those who gave their service to the company for a specific number of years, and were known as planters. These planters theoretically stood on the same basis as the adventurers and were supposed to have an equal voice in the management of the company. Because they were absent, however, from the seat of the company's government they really had no voice and became virtually servants of the company. "He (the planter), was kept by force in the colony and could have no communication with his friends in England. His letters were intercepted by the Company and could be destroyed if they contained anything to the Company's discredit." "His true position was that of a common servant working in the interest of a commercal company. In lieu of his support, or of his transportation and support, he was bound to the service of his Company for a term of years. He could be hired out by the Company to private persons or by the Governor for his personal advantage." [1]

On the basis of this practice, planters who had finished their term of service began in turn to import white men and women to settle and to cultivate the land on contracts, the condition of which demanded a term of years of service as compensation for transportation charges, board, shelter and clothing, and certain stipulated goods at the expiration of the term of contract. Soon ship captains began transporting persons who were not able to pay

[1] Ballagh: "White Servitude in the Colony of Virginia," p. 26.

for their passage, by accepting from them an agreement that their services should be sold by the captain to some planter on the ship's arrival at the colony. This practice of sale of services grew to such proportions that as early as 1619 the Assembly passed a law requiring all such contracts to be recorded, because already disputes were arising over the time of expiration of service. Thus the indenture system became a recognized form of servitude.

*First Negroes in America Not Slaves.* It was just at this time that the first Negroes were introduced into Virginia, and since they were sold to the colonists, it has usually been supposed that they immediately became slaves. It is, however, quite likely that they were sold into servitude, and not into slavery, following the custom of white purchase into servitude. That the first Negroes entered servitude instead of slavery was first suggested by Ballagh in his "History of Savagery in Virginia," and has since been fully justified by J. H. Russell in his discussion of "The Free Negro in Virginia." The line of proof is as follows: The colonists were not accustomed to slavery, and had not introduced it for white men, but had rather developed a system of time servitude and would normally be expected to follow such procedure in case of a different group being brought into the colony. Further in 1624, five years after the introduction of Negroes into Virginia, there were just twenty-three listed, and these were all held by officials of the colony, the presumption being that they were held on similar conditions to those binding the white servants of the colony, some of whom were regularly assigned to the officials. Yet again in this early listing they are not designated as slaves, but are listed as servants, just as were white indentures. "In the records of the county courts 1632 to 1661, Negroes are designated as servants, Negro servants, or simply as Negroes, but never in the records which we have examined were they called slaves." [2] The proof of Negroes being indentured servants and not slaves at the beginning is further established by specific cases in court record. Thus one May Johnson and her husband, Anthony Johnson, were by the county court of Northampton County freed from taxes because of faithful services and because they had lived in the colony for over thirty years. In other words, they must have entered the colony before 1622 and must have been free before the court decree of 1652.[3] There are records extant of Negroes being brought into the colony bound for specific terms of five, ten or other numbers of years. Russell gives another record of Emanuel Dregis and family which seems to give clear proof

[2] Russell: "The Free Negro in Virginia," p. 24.
[3] *Idem.*

that some at least of the early Negro population in the colony were not slaves but servants. In 1645 a writing of indenture of Dregis' two daughters was made to a Captain Francis Potts, one of the girls being bound to serve thirteen years and the other being bound to serve until she was thirty years of age. Seven years later (1652) there is a court record showing that Emanuel Dregis owned hogs and cattle in his own right, and the court declared he might dispose of them during his life time or at his death.[4] No slave could determine the use of property after death, hence it seems clear that Dregis could not have been a slave, but rather an indentured servant.

*Servitude Changed to Slavery. Rise of Free Negro.* But if the first Negroes entered Virginia as 'servants, their condition soon degenerated into a state of slavery. It is certain that some received their freedom after serving their term of years, but it seems certain also that others failed to receive such freedom. It was not until 1661 that the Virginia Colony legally recognized slavery, though slavery as a matter of custom had gradually been growing from the very time of the introduction of the first Negroes in 1619. Out of the first Negroes who gained their freedom after serving their term of indenture, there arose the Free Negro class. This group was added to through a law passed by the Colonial Assembly in 1662. Already there had sprung up between the English colonists and their Negro sevants illicit relations, and also children were being born of Negro mothers who had known the white seamen on the way over from Africa. It was necessary, therefore, to determine the legal status of this Mulatto offspring. Hence the Assembly decreed that all such illegitimate offspring should follow the condition of the mother. In view of the fact that there was as yet slight prejudice against color it is altogether possible that some of the indentured white servant women may have become mothers of mulatto children, who would in that case ultimately be free. That the colonists believed such was occurring is clear from the specific clauses of the law which inflicted five years of servitude upon the guilty white woman, and declared her offspring should serve until thirty years of age. "Thus by statute was originated a class, probably always small, of mulatto servants, which occupied a position midway between the slave and the ordinary bond servant, and became an ultimate source of the free Mulatto."[5]

*Slow Increase of Free Negroes.* The free Negro population did not grow rapidly, for after a century and a half of Negro residence in America, the first census of 1790 showed 677,624 slaves, and only 59,557 free Negroes, or 7.9 per cent free. Of

[4] Russell: "The Free Negro in Virginia," p. 26 f.
[5] Ballagh: "A History of Slavery in Virginia," p. 45.

this number 32,048, or slightly more than half were in the Southern states and two-thirds of this number were in Virginia and Maryland alone. Beginning with 1790 the number grew much more rapidly. The spirit of freedom was in the air. The colonists had just thrown off the yoke of foreign control and the spirit of the French revolution was making itself felt in the new world. In the new enthusiasm for liberty many of the planters set their slaves free on grounds of humanity and religious conviction. Thus Joseph Hill in 1783 makes a deed of freedom to his slaves in the following language: "I, Joseph Hill, of Isle of Wight County in Virginia, after full and deliberate consideration, and agreeable to our Bill of Rights, am fully persuaded that freedom is the natural right of all mankind, and that no law, moral or divine, hath given me a just right of property in the persons of any of my fellow-creatures, and desirous to fulfil the injunction of our Lord and Saviour, Jesus Christ, by doing to all others as I would be done by in a like situation . . . do hereby emancipate and set free all and every of the above named slaves, &c." [6]

*Manumission of Slaves.* Charles Moorman, of Campbell County, on September 1, 1789, declares:

"I, Charles Moorman, from mature consideration and the conviction of my own mind, being fully persuaded that freedom is the natural right of all mankind, and that no law, moral or divine, has given me a right to or property in the persons of any of my fellow-creatures, and being desirous to fulfil the injunction of our Lord and Saviour, Jesus Christ, by doing to others as I would be done by—do therefore declare that having under my care twenty-eight slaves (naming them), I do for myself, my heirs, executors and administrators, hereby release unto them the said slaves all my rights, interests, claims or pretensions of claims whatsoever to their persons or any estate they may acquire, &c." [7]

*Washington's Will.* George Washington in 1799 made a will looking to the freedom of his Negroes: "Upon the decease of my wife, it is my will and desire that all the slaves whom I hold in my own right shall receive their freedom. To emancipate them during her life would, though earnestly wished by me, be attended with such insuperable difficulties on account of their intermixture by marriage with the dower negroes as to excite the most painful sensations, if not disagreeable consequences to the latter, while both descriptions are in the occupancy of the same proprietor; it not being in my power under the tenure by which the dower negroes are held to manumit them."

[6] Munford: "Virginia's Attitude Toward Slavery and Secession," p. 105.
[7] *Idem.*

"The will further provides that all slaves who at the time of their emancipation are unable, by reason of old age, bodily infirmities, or youth, to support themselves, shall be cared for out of his estate, the testator declaring:

"I do moreover most pointedly and most solemnly enjoin it upon my executors hereafter named, or the survivors of them, to see that this clause respecting slaves and every part thereof be religiously fulfilled at the epoch at which it is directed to take place without evasion, neglect or delay, after the crops which may then be in the ground are harvested, particularly as it respects the aged and infirm; seeing that a regular and permanent fund be established for their support as long as there are subjects requiring it.' " [8]

*Rapid Growth of Free Negro Class 1780-1800.* The deeds and wills of southern planters so frequently contained orders of manumission that the free Negro population was practically doubled in the decade between 1790 and 1800. The total free Negro population in 1800 was 108,435, of whom 61,249 were in the South Atlantic and East South Central states. The rate of increase in the South for the decade was 91 per cent. The increase of free Negroes from 1800 to 1810 was for the whole country from 108,435 to 186,446, and the increase in the South was from 61,249 to 105,658, or 72 per cent.[9] Following 1810 the increase was not so rapid but was sufficiently substantial to bring the total number of free Negroes to 486,070 in 1860. While a large proportion of this growing number is accounted for on the basis of natural increase, the records show that there were constant additions throughout the period due to deeds and wills of manumission.

*Manumission for Services Rendered.* There were also other sources of free Negroes besides natural increase and the manumission by masters. Early in each of the colonies there arose the practice of freeing a slave who had rendered some conspicuous service to the common good, such as revealing plots, recovering runaway slaves, etc. In such cases the slave was freed by the county courts and the owners were given due compensation. In 1777 North Carolina, fearing the growth of the free Negro class, passed a law that prohibited the freeing of slaves, save on the basis of meritorious conduct. The first slave freed by legislative enactment in Virginia was in 1710 when a Negro named Will "is (declared) forever hereafter free from his slavery," because of his service in discovering a conspiracy of

---

[8] Munford: "Virginia's Attitude Toward Slavery and Secession," p. 108.
[9] Bureau of Census: Negro Population of U. S. 1790-1915, p. 57.

divers Negroes.[10] Forty pounds was the amount paid Robert Ruffin for his Negro Will.

*Negro Kitt Freed.* In 1779 the Assembly of Virginia passed the following act: "Whereas a Negro man slave named Kitt, the property of Hinchia Mabry, of the County of Brunswick, hath lately rendered meritorious service in this commonwealth, in making the first information and discovery against several persons concerned in counterfeiting money, whereby so dangerous a confederacy has been in some measure broken, and some of the offenders have been discovered and brought to trial; and it is judged expedient to manumit him for such service; *Be it therefore enacted by the General Assembly,* That the said Kitt be, and is hereby declared to be emancipated and free; any law or usage to the contrary notwithstanding." [11] In cases where Negroes were set free by the government, not only did the owner receive pay for the same, but the freed man was often allowed to remain in the state, as was not true of the manumitted slaves in most states after 1790.

*Other Notable Cases.* In 1729 there was a curious case of a Negro's obtaining his freedom for revealing an herb medicine by which wonderful cures had been effected: "Among more romantic liberations was that of Pierre Chastang, of Mobile who, in recognition of public services in the war of 1812 and the yellow fever epidemic of 1819 was bought and freed by popular subscription; that of Sam which was provided by a special act of Georgia legislature in 1834 at a cost of $1,800 in reward for his having saved the state capitol from destruction by fire; and that of Prince which was attained through the good offices of the United States government. Prince, after many years as a Mississippi slave, wrote a letter in Arabic to the American consul at Tangier in which he recounted his early life as a man of rank among the Timboo people and his capture in battle and sale overseas. This led Henry Clay on behalf of the Adams Administration to inquire at what cost he might be bought for liberation and return. His master thereupon freed him gratuitously, and the citizens of Natchez raised a fund for the purchase of his wife, with a surplus for a flowing Moorish costume in which Prince was promptly arrayed. The pair then departed, in 1828, for Washington *en route* for Morocco, Prince avowing that he would soon send back money for the liberation of their nine children." [12]

*Fighting in Master's Stead.* Still another method of a Negro getting his freedom was to serve in his master's stead in war. In 1783 the Virginia legislature passed a law setting free any Negro

[10] Russell: "The Free Negro in Virginia," p. 44.
[11] Quoted by Russell from "Henning," Vol. X, p. 115.
[12] Phillips: "American Negro Slavery," p. 428-429.

who had served in his master's stead, even though the promise
of freedom had only been a verbal one.\ In fact in all cases where
the slave appeared in court in behalf of his freedom, he was given
much consideration, his suit proceeded without cost to the slave,
and he was given the same standing in his suit as if he were
already a free Negro.

In Missouri the jury was to be instructed that the "weight of
evidence lies with the petitioner," that is the slave, and every
possible chance to establish his claim to freedom was to be
allowed.  The law of 1807 gave counsel to the slave, required that
he should have liberty to prosecute his case, and defended him
against punishment because he had brought such suit.[13]

*Buying Freedom.*  Lastly, the free population was increased
by the fact that a slave might buy his freedom.  This was made
possible by working overtime as on Sundays, or sometimes by
raising small crops in his garden, which gardens on most plantations were allotted to all heads of families.  Olmsted writes
that in "tobacco factories of Richmond and Petersburg, slaves
are at this time, in great demand, and are paid one hundred and
fifty to two hundred dollars, and all expenses for a year.  These
slaves are expected to work only to a certain extent for their
employers; it having been found that they could not be 'driven,'
to do a fair day's work so easily as they could be stimulated
to it by the offer of a bonus for all they would manufacture above
a certain number of pounds.  This quantity is so easily exceeded,
that the slaves earn for themselves from five to twenty dollars
per month." [14]

Frequently a Negro was permitted to "hire his time."  He
agreed with his master to pay a certain stipulated amount for
certain amount of time, say a year, and all he could make above
that amount was his own.  In certain of the states this practice
of "hiring one's time" was forbidden, for it led directly to emancipation.  Tennessee passed such a law, but it was generally
evaded.  "An ex-slave of Wilson County explains that the usual
method of evasion was the declaration of the employer of the
slave that he had hired the slave from the slave's master.  Sometimes the owner would pretend to keep the wages of the slave, but
really was holding them at the slave's disposal.  In this way
a number of slaves bought themselves." [15]  Washington says
"when he (the master) allowed them (the slaves) to buy their
own freedom, it was a practical recognition that the system was
economically a mistake, since the slave who could purchase his
freedom was one whom it did not pay to hold as a slave.  This

[13] Trexler: "Slavery in Missouri."
[14] Olmsted: "Seaboard Slave States," p. 127.
[15] "Journal of Negro History," Vol. IV, p. 258.

fact was clearly recognized by a planter in Mississippi who declared that he had found it paid to allow the slaves to buy their freedom. In order to encourage them to do this he devised a method by which they might purchase their freedom in instalments. After they had saved a certain amount of money by extra labor, he permitted them to buy one day's freedom a week. With this much capital invested in themselves, they were then able to purchase, in a much shorter time a second, a third and a fourth day's freedom, until they were entirely free. A somewhat similar method was sometimes adopted by certain freedmen for purchasing the freedom of their families. In such a case the father would purchase, for instance, a son or a daughter. The children would then join with their father in purchasing the other members of the family." [16]

*Struggles to Buy Freedom.* "Accounts are on record of most heroic and pathetic sacrifices on the part of relatives to liberate slaves. That of George Kibby of St. Louis and his wife Susan is very instructive. In 1853 Kibby entered into a contract with Henry C. Hart and his wife Elizabeth L. Hart to purchase their negress named Susan, whom he wished to marry. The price was eight hundred dollars. The contract is devoid of all sentiment and is as coolly commercial as though merchandise was the subject under consideration. Kibby had two hundred dollars to pay down. He was to pay the remainder in three yearly installments, and upon the fulfilment of the contract Susan was to receive her freedom. In the meantime Kibby was to take possession of Susan under the following conditions: 'Provided however said Kibby shall furnish such security as may be required by the proper authorities, to such bond as may be required for completing such emancipation, so as to absolve . . . Hart and wife from all liability for the future support and maintenance of said Susan and her increase. This obligation to be null and void on the part of said Hart and wife, if said Kibby shall fail for the period of one month, after the same shall become due and payable, to pay to said Hart and wife said sums of money as hereinbefore specified, or the annual interest thereon, and in the event of such failure, all of the sum or sums of money whether principal or interest, which may have been paid by the said Kibby sahll be forfeited, and said Kibby shall restore to said Hart and wife said negro girl Susan and such child or children as she may then have, such payments being hereby set off against the hire of said Susan, who is this day delivered into the possession of said Kibby. And said Kibby hereby binds himself to pay said sums of money as hereinbefore specified, and is not to be absolved therefrom on the death of said Susan, or any other contingency or plea what-

[16] Washington: "The Story of the Negro," Vol. I, p. 194.

ever.  He also binds himself to keep at his own expense a satisfactory policy of insurance on the life of said Susan, for the portion of her price remaining unpaid, payable to T. J. Brent, trustee for Mrs. E. L. Hart, and that said Susan shall be kept and remain in this County, until the full and complete execution of this contract.'

"Attached to the back of this contract are the receipts for the installments.  The first reads thus: 'Received of George Kibby one mule of the value of sixty-five dollars on within contract Feb. 1st, 1854, H. C. Hart.'  The fifth and last payment was made on December 3, 1855—two years lacking six days following the date of the contract.  Accompanying the contract is the deed of manumission of Susan, likewise dated December 3.  Thus Kibby fulfilled his bargain in less than the time allowed him." [17]

*Novel Schemes for Giving Freedom.*  Numerous planters worked out novel schemes by which the slave might purchase his freedom.

"John McDonogh, the most thrifty citizen of New Orleans in his day, made a unique bargain with his whole force of slaves, about 1825, by which they were collectively to earn their freedom and their passage to Liberia by the overtime work on Saturday afternoons.  This labor to be done in McDonogh's own service, and he was to keep account of their earnings.  They were entitled to draw upon this fund upon approved occasions; but since the contract was with the whole group of slaves as a unit, when one aplpied for cash the others must draw their *pro rata*, thereby postponing the common day of liberation.  Any slaves violating the rules of good conduct were to be sold by the master, whereupon their accrued earnings would revert to the fund of the rest.  The plan was carried to completion on schedule, and after some delay in embarkation they left America in 1842, some eighty in number, with their late master's bendiction.  In concluding his public narration in the premises McDonogh wrote: 'They have now sailed for Liberia, the land of their fathers.  I can say with truth and heartfelt satisfaction that a more virtuous people does not exist in any country.' " [18]

*Chambers' Comment.*  Chambers, however, felt as he traveled through America, that the slaves were not given as good a chance to earn money to buy their freedom as were the slaves in Brazil or the West Indies.  "In the United States," he says, 'the slaves can legally claim no holidays; though a week at Christmas is usually granted and in most quarters they are allowed to be at

[17] Trexler: "Slavery in Missouri," pp. 221-222.
[18] Phillips: "American Negro Slavery," pp. 427-428.

rest on Sunday. This denial of the power of laboring to buy
themselves from their owners, forms a feature in American
slavery which distinguishes it from aught in ancient or modern
times." [19] Just how he arrived at such conclusions is a little hard
to tell, though, of course, the time of his writing (1857) may
somewhat account for it. The slavery struggle was at white heat
and masters were perhaps much more strict than they had been
in earlier decades. The rapid growth of free Negroes as noted
above indicates that by purchase and by manumission a very
large number were annually added to the free list.

*Plans for General Emancipation.* Plans for general emancipation were considered from time to time by various states. In
1820 Elihu Embree, published at Jonesboro, Tennessee, the "Eman-
cipator," the first abolition journal ever published in the United
States. In 1834 the Constitutional Convention met in Nashville,
Tennessee, and so general was the desire for gradual emancipation, that it was only kept out of the written constitution by the
most desperate struggle on the part of the West Tennessee planters. In North Carolina both the Quakers and the Methodists
were active in the work of emancipation. Slaves were often transferred to the trustees of a church with the virtual intent of making them free, without the embarrassment of legal procedure. [20]

In Virginia three well formed plans for gradual emancipation
were brought forward. The first was by Thomas Jefferson in
1779, and included two main provisions, (1) the freeing of all
slaves born after a certain time, especially females, (2) and the
gradual colonization of all free Negroes. Jefferson boldly advocated that these slave children should be paid for by the state,
and that they should be forced to stay with their parents until
they were of age, that they were to be taught tillage, arts, and
sciences, and then colonized under the protection of the state.

The second plan was that proposed by Tucker. "Tucker's
plan, consequently, was partly made up from Jefferson's and
partly from those of other states. It provided that after the
adoption of the plan, (1) every female born and her issue should
be free, but should remain with the family as servants for twenty-
eight years and then receive appropriate freedom dues for a start
in life, being treated during their servitude in all respects as white
servants and apprentices; (2) civil slavery should be retained,
and officeholding, action as an attorney, juror or witness except
in cases between blacks, franchises, or interests in lands greater
than a twenty-one year lease should be prohibited. And further
the emancipated were not to keep or bear arms, except under legal
limitations; nor to marry a white; nor to be an executor or ad-

[19] Chambers: "Slavery and Colour," p. 117.
[20] Bassett: "Slavery in the State of North Carolina," Ch. II.

ministrator; nor to be capable of making a will or acting as a trustee; nor of maintaining any real action, but they were to be tried in criminal cases as free Negroes and mulattoes were at that time entitled to be. This provision was a compromise to prejudice, but with a distinct object. The privileges were to be enlarged as occasion demanded, and the personal rights and property of the servants, though limited, were to be protected by law. 'By denying them,' said Tucker, 'the most valuable privileges which civil government affords I wish to render it their interest to seek those privileges in some other climate.' He seems to have had Spanish territory in view, and hoped the cutting off of ambition, power of resentment, and landed property would be sufficient to induce emigration as a substitute for colonization." [21]

The matter came to sharp issue in the Virginia Assembly 1831-2, when Thomas Jefferson Randolph, a nephew of Jefferson, proposed a different plan: "This not only denied the master's property right according to the principle *partus sequitur ventrem,* but put upon him the obligation of raising and maintaining the child till of age at eighteen or twenty-one years. The assumption was that the labor of the child after twelve or fourteen years would offset the cost of the preceding years. The proposition was to emancipate all born after 1840 and that the freedman should earn and pay his own transportation from America. To do this he was to be hired out after becoming of age till he accumulated enough for his passage." [22]

But growing difficulties in the way of emancipation defeated all attempts and gradually efforts at the same became less frequent and less popular. There were perhaps three influences which contributed most to this attitude toward freeing the slaves.

*Objections to Free Negroes.* The earliest objection to the free Negro came from the fear that he would stir up insurrection by making the slaves dissatisfied. Russell thinks that the early practice of freeing Negroes for meritorious service, especially for revealing plots, was not in any sense an expression of the growth of a sentiment for freedom, but on the other hand, an attempt to discourage in slaves that which "most free Negroes were suspected of encouraging, namely, insubordination and a disposition to plot mischief." [23]

As early as 1711, Governor Gibbes, of South Carolina, became alarmed at the large number of Negroes coming into that colony and addressed the legislature as follows: "Gentlemen, I desire you will consider the great quantities of Negroes that are daily brought into the government, and the small number of whites

[21] Ballagh: "A History of Slavery in Virginia," p. 134.
[22] *Ibid.,* p. 138.
[23] Russell: "The Free Negro in Virginia."

that come amongst us; how insolent and mischievous the Negroes are become, and to consider the Negro Act already made, doth not reach up to some of the crimes they have lately been guilty of; therefore, it might be convenient by some additional clause of said Negro Act, to appoint either by gibbets or some such like way, that after executed they remain more exemplary than any punishment that hath been inflicted on them." [24]

*Insurrections.* In 1712 a slave plot in New York brought consternation and fear to the hearts of all the whites. The Negroes had planned to kill all the white people. The plot was accidentally discovered, and the loss of life was only eight killed and twelve wounded. "In 1722 about two hundred Negroes near the mouth of the Rappahannock River, Virginia, got together in a body, armed with an intent to kill the people in church, but were discovered and fled." [25] The excitement caused by fear of the Negroes was not at all confined to the South in these early days. In 1723 it is said of Boston: "So great at that time were the alarm and danger in Boston occasioned by the slaves, that in addition to the common watch, a military force was not only kept up, but at the breaking out of every fire, a part of the militia were ordered out under arms, to keep the slaves in order." [26] Coffin collected accounts of twenty-four insurrections occuring between 1712 and 1832. Harte tells us there were twenty-five insurrections before the Revolution.[27] Among the most terrible of these was the one in Charleston, 1739, in which twenty-five whites were killed, thirty-four Negroes were shot, and many others hanged or shot. Another terrible insurrection came in New York in 1741, after which eighty Negroes were transported and thirteen condemned and burned at the stake. In 1800 came the Gabriel insurrection in Richmond, Virginia, which stirred the whites of the state as nothing of the kind had ever done. Thirty-six or more Negroes were executed, including Gabriel himself. An account of the "Times" says: "The city of Richmond and the circumjacent country are in arms and have been for ten or twelve days. The patrollers are doubled through the state, etc." [28]

*Vesey Plot.* In 1822 the free Negro, Denmark Vesey, headed a revolt in Charleston which it was planned should completely exterminate the white inhabitants of that city. The plot was revealed by a slave, Vesey was caught and tried, and together with thirty-four others was executed. This stirred the fear of the whites so thoroughly that it influenced their attitude right up to the Civil War.

[24] Joshua Coffin: "Slave Insurrections," p. 10 (a pamphlet compiled and published 1860).
[25] *Ibid.,* p. 11.
[26] *Ibid.,* p. 12.
[27] Harte: "Slavery and Abolition," p. 51.
[28] Coffin: "Slave Insurrections," p. 25 f.

Dr. John B. Adger, a Charlestonian, who "when a boy eleven years old saw twenty-two of these Negroes hanging on one gallows" found that his work as a missionary to the Negroes twenty-five years later was greatly hampered because of the fear aroused at this time.[29]

*Turner's Rebellion.* The last terrible rebellion was known as Nat Turner's Rebellion, which occurred at Southampton, Va., in 1831. Nat Turner was a preacher—perhaps a bit unbalanced—who believed himself a prophet called of God to deliver his people from bondage. He collected a number of slaves around him, killed sixty white people, and was finally captured. Twelve Negroes were sold out of the state, twenty were hanged, including Nat Turner and one woman.

While all the leaders of these insurrections were not freemen, they were charged up to the spirit and work of the free Negroes, and each insurrection drew tighter and tighter the lines of control and restraint of the free Negro class.

*Fear of Insurrections.* That fear of insurrections and insubordination was one of the dominant factors in the social reactions of the South during the entire period before the war cannot be doubted. It influenced every political action; it controlled to a large extent social customs, it dominated educational policies, and laid a heavy hand on economic progress. No one can understand the pre-Civil War South without reckoning with this psychic fact, nor can one understand the present social response of the South without a knowledge of this background. In Washington, D. C., Olmsted found the magistrates who tried Negro cases, were "actuated by a well-founded dread of secret conspiracies, inquisitions and persecutions." [30]    Harte says of the Vesey plot in South Carolina, that "the desperate plan was so nearly successful that it left an ineradicable distrust of the free Negroes and a desire to get them out of the country." [31]    It was this fear of the free Negroes which caused Florida to write into her constitution a clause denying to the legislature the power to free slaves, and giving it the power to prevent free Negroes immigrating into the state, or from being discharged from ships on to her shores." [32]

Southern representatives in Congress defended this constitution on the basis that the new state had a right to take steps for its own self preservation, implying thereby that the presence of free Negroes was in their opinion a source of danger in any slave holding state. Mr. Besler, of Alabama, maintained that no slave state was safe without such provision, as "free Negroes would go there with no peaceable intentions, but with firebrands in their

[29] Adger: "My Life and Times," p. 165.
[30] Olmsted: "Seaboard Slave States," p. 15.
[31] Wilson: "Rise and Fall of the Slave Power in America," Vol. II, p. 2.
[32] Harte: "Slavery and Abolition," p. 163.

hands, to excite disaffection among the slaves." [33]    Chambers, traveling in America, writes "Slave owners over the whole South are less or more under a constant apprehension of outbreak, the best evidence of their uneasiness being the rigorous measures of coercion by which the power is sustained," [34] and he adds that one can tell when he has passed from the North into the slave holding states "by the appearance for the first time, of soldiers on guard in the evenings at public buildings." [35]    The same writer claims that in 1854, "Virginia expended for the education of poor children $69,404; for the maintenance of a public guard $73,189." [36]    Dr. Washington, with that keen insight which characterized most of his utterances, declares: "The great slave insurrection which during the whole period of slavery, was frequently expected, and always feared, never actually took place, but the fear of such a general outbreak always haunted the South and helped to harden the hearts of the Southern people against the Negro race.  This was responsible, for instance, for the passage of laws which made it difficult, if not impossible, in many of the Southern States for a master to emancipate his slaves; made it a crime for him to teach his slaves to read and write, and imposed such limitations and burdens on the free Negro as reduced that unfortunate class to a condition often counted worse than that of slavery.  The master frequently trusted his slave, usually cared for and protected him, and had for him in many instances a feeling of genuine affection.  And yet, the slaveholder was never able to shake off his sense of danger of an uprising of the slaves." [37]

Speaking of the strong opposition to the Quaker attitude toward emancipation in North Carolina, and of the action of courts frustrating their attempt to give individual Negroes to the guardianship of church wardens, Bassett says: "In all these cases the cast-iron necessity of keeping slavery unendingly confined to its present condition, cutting off the least tendency to amelioration, is clearly seen.  Slavery absolute—nothing short of it—and as few free Negroes as possible was the idea." [38]

*Legislation Against Manumission.*  Due to this fear of insurrection, and because the free Negro could not be controlled, and hence might become a spreader of sedition, Virginia as early as 1691 passed restrictive legislation against manumission.

"The increasing frequency of manumissions created apprehensions as to the consequences of allowing the practice to continue, and restrictive legislation was deemed expedient.  The preamble

[33] Wilson: "Rise and Fall of Slavery in America," Vol. II, p. 2-3.
[34] Chambers: "Slavery and Colour," p. 118.
[35] *Ibid.*, p. 119.
[36] *Ibid.*, p. 151.
[37] Washington: "The Story of the Negro," Vol. I, p. 178.
[38] Bassett: "Slavery in the State of North Carolina," p. 33.

of the restrictive act, which was passed in 1691, declared a law to be necessary to prevent manumissions, because "great inconvenience may happen to this country by setting of negroes and mulattoes free by their either entertaining negro slaves or receiving stolen goods or being grown old bringing a charge upon the country.' Under the provisions of this act no negro or mulatto was to be set free unless the person so doing should pay the charges for transporting the manumitted negro beyond the limits of the colony. Thus was devised a scheme which would offer three obstacles to the increase of the free Negro class : A charge of transportation would restrain the master; the prospect of banishment would restrain the desire of the slave to be free. Should both of these restraints fail in any case, removal would prevent addition to the free colored class." [39]

This act of 1691 was further strengthened in 1723 by an act which forbade free Negroes to carry firearms, or to visit slaves, or be present at their meetings. These laws were in effect up to 1782 when the spirit of the Revolution made it possible to repeal them. Thomas Jefferson had attempted to get them repealed in 1769 but to no effect. We have noted before that the Revolution gave a great impetus to the movement for manumission, so that the number of free Negroes increased very rapidly until about 1800. During this period there was noticeable a growing uneasiness on the part of the whites which gave rise to an act of 1793, forbidding free Negroes to come into the state. This feeling found further expression just after the Gabriel plot, for the Virginia House of Delegates in secret session on December 21, 1800, "Resolved that the Governor (Monroe) be requested to correspond with the President of the United States, on the subject of purchasing land without the limits of this state whither persons obnoxious to the laws, or dangerous to the peace of society may be removed." [40] In 1805 the Assembly of Virginia again in secret session "Resolved that the senators of this state in the Congress of the United States be instructed and the representatives be requested, to exact their best efforts for the obtaining from the General Government a competent portion of territory in the country of Louisiana, to be appropriated to the residence of such people of color as have been or shall be emancipated, or may hereafter become dangerous to the public safety, etc." [41] All efforts to secure a colony having failed, Virginia passed a law in 1805, by which all slaves manumitted after May 1, 1806, were required to leave the state within twelve months after receiving their freedom, on the penalty of being sold again into

[39] Russell: "The Free Negro in Virginia," p. 51.
[40] Coffin: "Slave Insurrections," p. 28.
[41] *Ibid.*, p. 29.

slavery, and the proceeds used for the poor of the county in which such slaves were apprehended. As early as 1777 Tennessee passed a law that made assent of the state necessary to render valid deeds or wills of manumission.[42] According to the law of 1826 a slaveholder might petition the county court and get permission to emancipate a slave. In 1831 a law was passed making it obligatory upon the slave to leave the state, and those who desired to emancipate their slaves must give bond to guarantee such removal. By this same act free Negroes were forbidden to enter the state.[43]

*Alabama Law. Other States.* In Alabama a master could free his slaves by petitioning the county court, but meritorious service must be proved, and the freed Negro must leave the state at once.[44] In Louisiana the slave must be thirty years of age, and must have behaved well for four years preceding his emancipation. If a slave saved the life of his master or any of the family, he could be emancipated on meritorious conduct at any age. The child of a slave mother, who had acquired the right of future freedom, became free on the death of the mother.[45] In all states creditors were protected against freeing of slaves, as were also the widows protected in their dower. Thus if a slave owner set free his Negroes and it was found that he had debts contracted before such manumission, the Negroes could be resold into slavery to satisfy such creditors. Debts against the master were satisfiable by the sale of the slave even though the slave might have bought himself from his master, provided such purchase of freedom came after the contracting of the debt. In other words, a debtor master could not alienate any of his property to avoid the payment of his debts.[46] In North Carolina the restrictions on manumission were gradually tightened until in 1830 when it was decreed that "the petitioner must notify his intention at the court house and in the *State Gazette* six weeks before the hearing of the petition; he must give bond with two sureties for $1000 that the said slave should conduct himself well as long as he or she remained in the State, that the slave would leave the State within ninety days after liberation, and the said liberation should invalidate the rights of no creditor. Executors of wills by which slaves were directed to be liberated must secure consent of the courts and take steps to send the negroes out of the State and guard against the loss of creditors. A slave more than fifty years old might be liberated for meritorious conduct to be approved by the Court without subsequently leaving the

[42] Goodell: "American Slave Code," p. 343.
[43] "Journal of Negro History," p. 260.
[44] Goodell: "American Slave Code," p. 343.
[45] *Ibid.*, pp. 343-344.
[46] *Ibid.*, p. 344.

State, provided that the master swore that the emancipation was not for money and that he gave bond that the negro would conduct himself well and not become a charge on the county. No slave was to be liberated except by this law."[47]

*Basis of Restrictions.* All these restrictions on manumission arose primarily out of the dread of a free Negro class which it was felt had a tendency to make the slaves restless and insubordinate. Many of the leading men of the South felt that black and white could not live side by side on the common basis of freedom. Jefferson said it was impossible to "retain and incorporate the blacks into the state. Deep rooted prejudice of the whites, ten thousand recollections of the blacks of injuries sustained, new provocations, the real distinction nature has made, and many other circumstances will divide us into parties and produce convulsions which will probably never end but in the extermination of one or the other race." [48]

*Attitude of Northern States.* Not only did the laws of the Southern states impede the progress of manumission, but many of the free states passed similar impeding laws. Garrison wrote in 1831, "Every place that I visited gave fresh evidence of the fact that a greater revolution in public sentiment was to be effected in the free states and particularly in New England than in the South. I found contempt more bitter, detraction more relentless, prejudice more stubborn, and apathy more frozen, than among slave owners themselves." [49] Ohio became restless about so many colored people coming into the state and passed laws intended to stop the same. A law of 1807 prohibited any free Negro entering the state unless he could give bond of five hundred dollars for good behavior and as a guarantee that he would not become a pauper on the state. Even when free Negroes could furnish such bond it was not certain they would be allowed to settle peaceably. John Randolph, of Roanoke, Va., died in 1833 and left a will which called for the freeing of his slaves under the direction of Judge Leigh, his executor. "In 1846 Judge Leigh, of Virginia, purchased 3,200 acres of land in this settlement (Ohio) for the freed slaves of John Randolph, of Roanoke. These arrived in the summer of 1846 to the number of about four hundred, but were forcibly prevented from making a settlement by a portion of the inhabitants of the county. Since then acts of hostility have been commenced against the people of this settlement and threats of greater violence held out if they do not abandon their lands and homes.' "

[47] Bassett: "Slavery in the State of North Carolina," p. 30.
[48] Ballagh: "History of Slavery in Virginia," p. 132.
[49] Quoted from Wilson's "Rise and Fall of the Slave Power in America," Vol. I, p. 182.

" 'From a statement in the county history issued in 1882 we see that a part of the Randolph Negroes succeeded in effecting a settlement at Montezuma, Franklin Township, just south of the reservoir.' " [50]

Of the reception of Negroes into this state Munford says: "The facts are meager with respect to the reception accorded these Negroes and the measure of success which attended the colonization. From the best information obtainable, it seems they were treated in no very friendly manner and that, in time the Negroes lost most of the lands provided by their former owners." [51]

Delaware in 1857 prohibited the immigration of free Negroes into the state from any other state save Maryland. Indiana in the same year "prohibited free Negroes and mulattoes from coming into the state, and fined all persons who employed or encouraged them to remain in the state, between ten and five hundred dollars for each offense." [52]

*Illinois' Attitude.* "Illinois in 1853, made it a misdemeanor for a Negro to come into the state with the intention of residing there and providing that persons violating this law should be prosecuted, and fined, or sold for a time to pay the fine." [53] The South feared the free Negro lest he become a trouble-maker and an inciter of insurrection, the North feared him lest he should become a charge on the charity of the state. Between the two the free Negro had a hard life, and the slave master who desired to free his slaves found real difficulty. He could not keep his freed Negroes in his own state, and to send them into free territory meant to subject them to many disabilities and hardships, in addition to the fact that they would be without friends or those who took personal interest in their lives. It was indeed a trying situation, and easily accounts for the lessening of the number of manumitted slaves.

*Economic Considerations.* A second cause which tended to lessen the enthusiasm for manumission was the growing importance of the cotton industry. The old, hard process of seeding cotton was so very slow as to render the economic value of cotton culture decidedly questionable. But the introduction of the cotton gin in 1793 immediately had a great influence on the problem of slavery. By this new invention an unskilled slave could cleanse a thousand pounds of lint from the seed, whereas by the old process the cleansing of four to six pounds was considered a day's work. "Almost at a single bound the South became the

[50] Quoted by Munford from Hawes' "Historical Collection of Ohio," Vol. II, p. 505.
[51] Munford: "Virginia's Attitude Toward Slavery and Secession," p. 66.
[52] Stephenson: "Race Distinction in American Law," p. 37.
[53] *Ibid.*, p. 125.

chief cotton field of the world." [54]    The exportation of cotton
in 1792 was 138,328 pounds, in 1804 it was 38,118,041 pounds,
and in 1820 it was 127,860,152 pounds. "When the cotton gin
supplied the means of indefinitely expanding the production of
marketable cotton by the use of slave labor, another and even
more powerful argument for its retention was furnished. After
that slavery seemed nothing less than the indispensable economic
instrument of Southern society." [55]    That slavery was a real
economic asset we may have reason to doubt, as will be shown
in a later chapter, but that it was considered as an asset by the
slave owners, or at least by most of them, cannot be doubted.
Anything, therefore, which tended to disturb this economic factor
would naturally be opposed. Free Negroes seemed to be such
a disturbing factor and hence the pressure against the manumission of slaves.

*Interference Resented.*    A third factor which it seems clear militated against the freeing of slaves was the growing sensitiveness
of the South to outside interference. Randolph, of Virginia,
expressed clearly this feeling as follows: "After the adjourn-
ment of the Legislature in 1753, the question was discussed before
the people fairly and squarely, as one of the abolition of slavery.
I was reëlected on that ground in my county. The feeling
extended rapidly from that time in Virginia, Kentucky and Missouri until Northern abolitionism reared its head. Southern
abolition was reform and an appeal to the master; Northern
abolition was revolution and an appeal to the slave. One was
peaceful and the other mutually destructive of both races by a
servile insurrection. The Southern people feared to trust to the
intervention of persons themselves exempt by position from the
imagined dangers of the transition." Professor Tucker, of the
University of Virginia, expressed it thus: "This is not the place
for assailing or defending slavery; but it may be confidently
asserted that the efforts of Abolitionists have hitherto made
the people in the slave-holding states cling to it more tenaciously.
Those efforts are viewed by them as intermeddling in their domestic concerns that is equally unwarranted by the comity due
to sister states, and to the solemn pledges of the Federal compact.
In the general indignation which is thus excited, the arguments
in favor of Negro emancipation, once open and urgent, have
been completely silenced, and its advocates among the slaveholders, who have not changed their sentiments, find it prudent to
conceal them. . . . Such have been the fruits of the zeal of
Northern Abolitionists in those states in which slavery prevails;
and the fable of the Wind and the Sun never more forcibly illus-

[54] Wilson: "Division and Reunion," p. 124.
[55] *Ibid.,* p. 125.

trated the difference between gentle and violent means in influencing men's wills." And President Henry Ruffner, of Washington College, wrote of the abolition influence as follows: "But this unfavorable change of sentiment is due chiefly to the fanatical violence of those Northern anti-slavery men usually called Abolitionists. . . . They have not, by honorable means, liberated a single slave, and they never will by such a course of procedure as they have pursued. On the contrary, they have created new difficulties in the way of all judicious schemes of emancipation by prejudicing the minds of slaveholders, and by compelling us to combat their false and rash schemes in our rear; whilst we are facing the opposition of men and the natural difficulties of the case in our front."

*Extreme Abolition Harmful to Cause.* That the immoderate and abusive language of Abolitionists like Garrison aroused not only the indignation of southern people, but also the apprehension of northern men, even his sympathizers, is indicated by his own statement. "It is pretended," he says, "that I am retarding the cause of emancipation by the coarseness of my invectives and by the precipitancy of my measures." [56] "Were it not for the din and clamor of Northern invectives against slavery," writes Nehemiah Adams, himself an Abolitionist, "we should hear more distinctly the candid expression of our Southern friends in regard to evils in the system." [57] "I believe slavery is a curse to the South, and many others believe it, who will not own it, on account of the fanatic efforts of the Abolitionists." [58] Writing still further of the cause of reaction against manumission, Adams says:

"A traveling agent of a northern society was arrested, and, on searching his trunk, there were found some prints, which might well have wrought, as they did, upon the feelings of the southern people. These prints were pictorial illustrations of the natural equality before God of all men, without distinction of color, and setting forth the happy fruits of a universal acknowledgment of this truth, by exhibiting a white woman in no equivocal relations to a colored man. Incendiary sentiments and pictures had for some time made their appearance on northern handkerchiefs, for southern children and servants. The old-fashioned, blue-paper wrappers of chocolate had within them some eminently suggestive emblems. When these amalgamation pictures were discovered, husbands and fathers at the south considered that whatever might be true of slavery as a system, self-defence, the protection of their households against a servile insurrection, was

[56] Wilson: "Rise and Fall of the Slave Power in America," p. 183.
[57] Adams: "A South Side View of Slavery," p. 90.
[58] *Ibid.*, p. 99.

their first duty.   Who can wonder that they broke into the post office, and seized and burned abolition papers; indeed, no excesses are surprising, in view of the perils to which they saw themselves exposed.   Then ensued those more stringent laws, so general now throughout the slaveholding states, forbidding the slaves to be publicly instructed.   Those laws remain to the present day; they are disregarded, indeed, to a very great extent, by the people themselves; but they remain in order to be enforced against northern interference.

"Yet the paralyzing influence of the causes which led to such legislation continues.  We wonder at it, and so do our southern friends.   To the question why various things are not done to improve the condition of the blacks, the perpetual answer from men and women who seek no apology for indolence or cupidity is, 'We are afraid of your Abolitionists.   Whoever moves for redress in any of these things is warned that he is playing into the hands of northern fanatics.'   They seem to be living in a state of self-defense, of self-preservation, against the north." [59]

Nothing forces itself more constantly upon the thoughts of a Northerner at the South, who looks into the history and present state of slavery, than the vast injury which has resulted from northern interference." [60]   "The South was just on the eve of abolishing slavery; the abolitionists arose, and put it back within its innermost intrenchments." [61]   "Remember what they said and did before we drove them to personal self-defense.   Mingle with them as friends, and not as antagonists; hear them preach and pray; talk with them as you loiter in the woods, or ride, or sail; and let them tell you, as they will be sure to do, all their burden on this subject, and compare it with what you see in the streets, and in families, and in all the unconstrained intercourse of society; and you will be sure to feel that the greatest kindness which we at the North can bestow upon the slaves is to be no longer the seeming enemies, the censors, the civil and ecclesiastical judges of the masters." [62]

*Lincoln's Attitude.*   On this point Lincoln himself wrote: "Resolutions upon the subject of domestic slavery having passed both branches of the General Assembly at its present session, the undersigned hereby protest against the passing of the same.

"They believe that the institution of slavery is founded on both injustice and bad policy, but that the promulgation of abolition doctrines tends rather to increase than abate its evils." [63]   This statement was signed by both Abraham Lincoln and Dan

[59] Adams: "A South-Side View of Slavery," pp. 107-108.
[60] *Ibid.,* p. 110.
[61] *Ibid.,* p. 115.
[62] *Ibid.,* p. 148.
[63] Munford: "Virginia's Attitude Toward Slavery and Secession," p. 54.

Stone. William Ellery Channing in 1835 said of the abolition movement: "Its influence at the South has been almost wholly evil. It has stirred up bitter passions and a fierce fanaticism which have shut every ear and every heart against its arguments and persuasions. These effects are more to be deplored because the hope of freedom to the slaves lies chiefly in the disposition of his master. The Abolitionist proposed indeed to convert the slaveholders; and for this reason he approached them with vituperation and exhausted upon them the vocabulary of reproach. And he has reaped as he sowed. . . . Thus, with good purpose, nothing seems to have been gained. Perhaps (though I am anxious to repel the thought) something has been lost to the cause of freedom and humanity." [64]

*Summary of Causes.* Thus we see a three-fold influence which dried up the springs of good will and almost stopped the flow of the stream of manumissions—fear of the free colored people, lest they become trouble-makers and insurrectionists; the tightening of the supposed economic demands, and the opposition to outside interference caused the masters to desist from manumission until at the close of the ante-bellum régime,—there was only a small increase of free people in each decennial period. Perhaps a careful study of these facts should lead us to act thoughtfully in all modern movements for reform.

*Legal Status.* We turn now to the legal status of the free Negro. In the early years of the Negro's sojourn in America, he seems to have been given the same economic and political status that the white indentured servants held. In Virginia during the seventeenth century, in fact up to 1723, the free Negro was allowed to vote, he entered freely into economic relations and aside from intermarrying with whites, seemed to suffer little from race prejudice. "The denial to him, by laws passed in 1723, of the right to vote, the right to bear arms, and the right to bear witness, is proof of the fact that prejudice had extended beyond a demand for race separation and race purity to an imposition upon the Negro of a low and servile station." [65] Harte claims that in all the colonies except Georgia and South Carolina free Negroes who had sufficient property qualifications were allowed to vote up to the time of the Revolution.[66] In 1715 North Carolina passed a law that no Negro, Indian or mulatto should have the right to vote for a member of the Assembly.[67] This law was later repealed and it seems the privilege of voting was left open to Negroes, but whether they availed themselves of the privilege or not is not known. When the new constitution was drawn in 1835, the question of suffrage for free Negroes

[64] Munford: "Virginia's Attitude Toward Slavery and Secession," p. 53.
[65] Russell: "The Free Negro in Virginia," p. 125.
[66] Harte: "Slavery and Abolition," p. 53.
[67] Bassett: "Slavery and Servitude in the Colony of North Carolina," p. 67.

was raised. The friends of this suggestion tried to carry it by restricting the privilege to the more industrious who could show property to the value of $250. They agreed this would put a premium on industry and sobriety, and would thus benefit the state. In the course of the long discussion Judge Gaston, one of the most influential members of the convention, said of the free Negroes: "Let them know that they are a part of the body politic, and they will feel an attachment to the form of government, and have a fixed interest in the prosperity of the community, and will exercise an important influence over the slaves." But the vote went against the right of the free Negro sixty-five to sixty-two and the final draft of the constitution read: "No free Negro, free Mulatto, or free person of mixed blood, descended from Negro ancestors to the fourth generation inclusive (though an ancestor of each generation may have been a white person), shall vote for members of the senate or house of commons." [68]

*Tennessee and New Jersey Law.* The first constitution of Tennessee (1796) granted the vote to the free Negroes, but the constitution of 1834 restricted the right of voting to "free men who should be competent witnesses against a white man in a court of justice." [69] In New Jersey a free Negro was allowed to vote. The constitution of 1776 states that "all inhabitants of this colony, of full age, who are worth fifty pounds and have resided within the county" for twelve months were entitled to vote. This continued true until 1844,[70] when the franchise was restricted to whites.

*Delaware and New York Law.* Delaware in 1752 passed a law which "provided that no free Negroes should have the right to vote or to enjoy any rights of a freeman other than to hold property, or to obtain redress in law and in equity for any injury to his or her person or property." [71] New York permitted all white men of age to vote, but required a $250 property qualification of free Negroes.[72] Speaking of the general exclusion from the elective franchise of free Negroes in the non-slaveholding states, William Jay says: "Were this exclusion founded on the want of property, or any other qualification deemed essential to the judicious exercise of the franchise, it would afford no just cause of complaint; but it is founded solely on the color of the skin, and is therefore irrational and unjust. That taxation and representation should be inseparable, was one of the axioms of the Fathers of our Revolution, and one of the reasons they assigned for their revolt from the crown of Britain. Now, it is deemed a mark

[68] Bassett: "Slavery in the State of North Carolina," p. 42.
[69] "Journal of Negro History," Vol. IV, p. 261.
[70] Cooley: "A Study of Slavery in New Jersey," p. 54.
[71] Stevenson: "Race Distinctions in American Law," p. 37.
[72] William Jay: "Miscellaneous Writings on Slavery," p. 375.

of fanaticism to complain of the disfranchisement of a whole
race, while they remain subject to the burden of taxation.  It is
worthy of remark, that of the thirteen original states, only *two*
were so recreant to the principles of the Revolution, as to make
a *white skin* a qualification for suffrage.  But the prejudice has
grown with our growth, and strengthened with our strength;
and it is believed that in every State constitution subsequently
formed or revised (excepting Vermont and Maine, and the revised constitution of Massachusetts), the crime of a dark complexion has been punished, by debarring its possessor from all
approach to the ballot-box." [73]

Thus it will be seen that the free Negro had no voice in government within the slave states or in the free states.

*Other Disabilities.*  There were many other disabilities placed
on free Negroes besides that of lack of the franchise.  In Virginia the law of 1723 forbade him to bear arms, or to bear
witness against a white man.  After the Gabriel insurrection in
1800 the free Negro was denied educational advantages.  In 1832
free Negroes were forbidden to teach, preach, or practice medicine, nor were they allowed to keep an inn, lest it might become
an assembling place for insurrectionists.  The laws of North
Carolina show similar history.  "At first they had most of the
rights and duties of the poor white man; they fought in the
Revolutionary armies, mustered in the militia, voted in the elections, and had the liberty to go where they chose.  At length
they lost their right to vote; their service in the militia was
restricted to that of musicians; and the patrol came more and
more to limit their freedom of travel.  Taxes and road duty
alone of all their functions of citizenship were at last preserved.
The story of the appearance of these progressive limitations is not
a pleasant one.

"The same law forbade a free negro to marry or to cohabit
with a slave without the written consent of the master, and in
1830 (chap. 4, sec. 3) such relations were forbidden even though
the master gave his written consent, and the penalty for violation
was thirty-nine lashes.  In 1795 (chap. 16) free negroes who
settled in the State were required to give bond of two hundred
pounds for their good behavior, in default of which they were
sold by the sheriff for the benefit of the public.  In 1826
(chap. 13) a free negro was forbidden to be on a ship at night,
or on Sunday, without a pass from a justice of the peace, unless,
indeed, he were employed there; but the punishment for a violation of this law fell on the captain of the ship.  Neither must a
free negro trade with a slave, and a free negro must have a
license from the County Court to hawk or peddle.

[73] Jay: "Miscellaneous Writings on Slavery," p. 374.

"In 1826 (chap. 21) the relation of the free negro to the State was pretty thoroughly restated by law. With free negroes were now to be included all persons of negro blood to the fourth generation inclusive, though one ancestor in each generation may have been white.

*Vagrancy Laws.* "Any able-bodied free negro 'found spending his or her time in idleness and dissipation, or having no regular or honest employment,' was to be arrested and made to give bond for good behavior, in default of which he or she was to be hired out for such a term as the court might think 'reasonable and just and calculated to reform him or her to habits of industry or morality, not exceeding three years for any one offense.' Furthermore the Courts might bind out the children of such free negroes who were not industriously and honestly employed.

*Less Than a Freeman.* "The legal status of the free negro was peculiar. Was he a freeman, or was he less than a freeman? The former he was by logical intent; yet he was undoubtedly denied, as has just been stated, many rights which mark the estate of freemen. At any time in the eighteenth century, I suppose, there would have been no question about the free negro being equally a freeman with the whites. After the severe laws of the third and fourth decades of the nineteenth century opinion changed. It was thus that it was as late as 1844 that the Supreme Court undertook to fix the status of free negroes. It then declared that 'free persons of color in this State are not to be considered as citizens in the largest sense of the term, or if they are, they occupy such a position as justifies the Legislature in adopting a course of policy in its acts peculiar to them, so that they do not violate the great principles of justice which lie at the foundation of all law.' This position is further illustrated by the opinion of the Court in regard to the free negro's right to defend himself against physical force. It was held in 1850 that insolence from a free negro to a white man would excuse a battle in the same manner and to the same extent as insolence from a slave. In 1859 the Court became more explicit. It declared that a free negro was in the peace of the State, and added at length: 'So while the law will not allow a free negro to return blow for blow and engage in a fight with a white man under ordinary circumstances, as one white man may do with another or one free negro with another, he is not deprived absolutely of the right of self-defense, but a middle course is adopted, 'by which he must prove 'that it became necessary for him to strike in order to protect himself from great bodily harm or grievous oppression.' " [74]

*Free Negroes Not Desired.* In Tennessee a free Negro who

[74] Bassett: "Slavery in the State of North Carolina," pp. 34-38.

was allowed to stay in the state must after 1836 present a petition
to the county court of his county each three years, must have
with him at all times his free papers filled out by the clerk of
the court and giving full details for his identification. In the
courts he could witness in cases between colored persons, but
not when a white man was concerned. He was not allowed to
keep firearms, he could not sell whiskey, he could not keep an
inn, he could not meet with assemblages of slaves, he could not
marry a slave without the consent of the master, which was not
freely given.

"In Louisiana it is gravely set forth, by express statute, that
*free* people of *color* ought never to insult or strike *white* people,
nor presume to conceive themselves *equal* to the whites; but, on
the contrary, they ought to *yield to them on every occasion,* and
never speak or answer them but with respect, but, under penalty
OF IMPRISONMENT, according to the nature of the offense." [75]

"In Georgia a WHITE man is liable to a fine of *five hundred
dollars* for teaching a FREE negro to read or write. If one
free negro teach another, he is fined *and* whipped, at the discretion of the Court! Should a free negro presume to preach to
or exhort his companions, he may be seized without warrant, and
whipped thirty-nine lashes, and the same number of lashes may
be applied to each one of his congregation." [76]

*Jay's View.* William Jay in his "Miscellaneous Writings"
gives ten impediments put in the way of free Negroes in the
non-slaveholding states. "(1) General exclusion from the elective
franchise; (2) denial of the right of locomotion; (3) denial of
the right of petition; (4) exclusion from the army and militia;
(5) exclusion from all participation in the administration of
justice; (6) impediments to education,; (7) impediments to
religious instruction; (8) impediments to honest industry; (9)
liability to be seized and treated as slaves; (10) subject to insult
and outrage." [77]

This is certainly a formidable array of charges, and each
charge is backed up by ample illustrations and citations. Quoting
from Jay's "Inquiry," the American Slave Code says:

*Hardships of Free Negroes.* "A citizen of New York, if he
happens to be colored, may not visit a dying child in Maryland
without incurring a penalty of fifty dollars for every week he
remains; and if he is unable to pay the fine, why, then he is to be
*sold by the sheriff* at public sale, for such a time as may be
necessary to cover the aforesaid penalty. But if a free negro

[75] Phillips: "American Slave Code," p. 357.
[76] *Ibid.,* p. 359.
[77] Jay: "Miscellaneous Writings on Slavery," pp. 374-393.

is sold for a limited time, he is in reality sold for life. During the term for which he is sold, he is sold as *a chattel,* and may be transported at the pleasure of his master; and when the ex- piration of his term finds him in a cotton-field in Missouri, or a sugar-mill in Louisiana, who is to rescue him from interminable bondage?

"It is known that such cases have occurred, and that free negroes taken up as fugitives in the Federal District have been sold to the slave traders and sent to the far South. A case is narrated in a petition to Congress, signed by Judge Cranch and nearly eleven hundred citizens of the Federal District in 1828. And the advertisements of free negroes for sale by the marshal and sheriff, appear frequently in the public journals. Mr. Miner, in the U. S. House of Representatives, in 1829, stated that in 1826-7 no less than *five* persons in the Federal District were thus sold into perpetual bondage for jail fees!

"A free colored man living near the line of the District of Columbia, petitioned the House of Delegates of Maryland for leave to bring his grandchild from the city of Washington. The child had probably been left an orphan, and he naturally wished to take it to his own house. The petition was rejected." [78]

Phillips gives a number of cases of freemen in the North enticed into slavery or kidnapped. "Solomon Northrup had been a raftsman and farmer about Lake Champlain until in 1841, when on the ground of his talent with the fiddle two strangers offered him employment in a circus which they said was then in Washington. Going thither with them, he was drugged, shackled, despoiled of his free papers, and delivered to a slave trader who shipped him to New Orleans. Then followed a checkered experience as a plantation hand on the Red River, last- ing for a dozen years until a letter which a friendly white carpen- ter had written for him brought one of his former patrons with an agent's commission from the governor of New York. With the assistance of the local authorities Northrup's identity was promptly established, his liberty procured, and the journey ac- complished which carried him back again to his wife and children at Saratoga.

"A third instance, but of merely local notoriety, was that of William Houston, who, according to his own account, was a British subject who had come from Liverpool as a ship steward in 1840 and while at New Orleans had been offered passage back to England by way of New York by one Espagne de Blanc. But upon reaching Martinsville on the up-river voyage de Blanc had ordered him off the boat, set him to work in his kitchen, taken away his papers and treated him as a slave. After five

[78] Goodell: "American Slave Code," p. 360.

years there Houston was sold to a New Orleans barkeeper, who
shortly sold him to a neighboring merchant, George Lynch, who
hired him out.   In the Mexican war Houston accompanied the
American army, and upon returning to New Orleans was sold
to one Richardson.   But this purchaser, suspecting a fault of
title, refused payment, whereupon in 1850 Richardson sold
Houston at auction to J. F. Lapice, against whom the negro now
brought suit under the ægis of the British consul.  While the trial
was yet pending a local newspaper printed his whole narrative that
it might 'assist the plaintiff to prove his freedom, or the defendant to prove he is a slave.' " [79]

*Disabilities in South Carolina.*  Speaking of disabilities of free
Negroes in South Carolina Mehlinger says:

"Conditions in that State, however, forced some free Negroes
to emigrate to foreign soil.   A number of free colored people
left Charleston, and settled in certain free States.  After residing
two or three years in the North they found out that their condition
instead of improving had grown worse, as they were more despised, crowded out of every respectable employment, and even
very much less respected.   They, therefore, returned to their former home.   On reaching Charleston, however, they were still
dissatisfied with their condition.   Changes, which had taken place
during their absence from the State, made it evident that in this
country they could never possess those rights and privileges which
all men desire.   Some of them resolved, therefore, to try their
fortunes in Liberia." [80]

*A Few Negroes Voluntarily Become Slaves.*  In the light of
these facts it is no wonder that free Negroes sometimes preferred
the condition of slavery and deliberately reassumed that status.
In view of this situation most of the southern states, notably
Virginia and Tennessee, made provision by law for a free person
to reassume the slave status.   "Possibly the most extraordinary
legal right possessed by free negroes at any time during the
continuation of slavery was the right to choose a master and
to go into voluntary bondage.   Liberty to become a slave was
one variety of liberty which a white man could not have exercised had he wished to do so.   One might surmise that this right
possessed for a while by free negroes was of a higher class of
rights than the fundamental, inherent rights spoken of by the
constitutional fathers; for a free negress who exercised it deprived and divested her posterity of liberty, and subjected both
herself and it to perpetual tyranny.

"Regardless of what may be said of the nature of this very
unusual right, it is a fact that free Negroes did not possess it

[79] Phillips: "American Negro Slavery," pp. 444-445.
[80] "Journal of Negro History," Vol. I, p. 281.

until near the end of the slavery régime.  Before 1856 a special act was deemed necessary to render legal the slavery of a free Negro who of his own will selected a master.  A number of such private acts, making it lawful for certain free Negroes, whose names were mentioned in the acts, 'to select a master or mistress,' were passed in the first half of the decade of the fifties.  In 1856 a general act was passed making it lawful for any free colored man over twenty-one and any free colored woman over eighteen years of age to select a master or a mistress.  A free Negro desiring so to alter his status could file a signed petition with the circuit judge stating the name of the proposed master or mistress. The petition would be posted for one month at the door of the court-house; if the judge was satisfied that there was no fraud, he would grant the request and fix a value on the petitioner. When one-half of the designated price was paid into the public treasury, the petitioner became as much the absolute property of his chosen master as if he had been born a slave.  The rule that the status of a child followed the status of the mother at the time of the birth of the child was applicable to the offspring of free colored females who elected to be slaves.

"Hard as was the lot of some free Negroes in Virginia between 1856 and 1861, the courts had not many petitioners seeking the refuge of slavery." [81]

*Exceptional Cases of Self-Enslavement.*  Numerous instances of voluntary enslavement occur, in spite of the fact that freedom was the highest ideal of most of the slaves: "A few others voluntarily converted themselves into slaves.  Thus Lucinda who had been manumitted under a will requiring her removal to another state petitioned the Virginia legislature in 1815 for permission, which was doubtless granted, to become the slave of the master of her slave husband, 'from whom the benefits and privileges of freedom, dear and flattering as they are, could not induce her to be separated.'  On other grounds William Bass petitioned the South Carolina general assembly in 1859, reciting 'That as a free Negro he is preyed upon by every sharper with whom he comes in contact, and that he is very poor, though an able-bodied man, and is charged with and punished for every offense, guilty or not, committed in his neighborhood; that he is without house or home, and lives a thousand times harder and in more destitution than the slaves of many planters in this district.'  He accordingly asked permission by special act to receive him if he could lawfully  do so." [82]

*Prosperity of Free Negroes.  Lane's Case.*  In spite of all the hardships put upon free Negroes, many of them did prosper

---

[81] Russell: "The Free Negro in Virginia," p. 108.
[82] Phillips: "American Negro Slavery," p. 446.

and not only became good citizens but amassed considerable fortunes. "Lunsford Lane was a slave of Mr. Sherwood Haywood, a prominent citizen of Raleigh, N. C. His parents, of pure African descent, had been kept in the town for family service, and thus their offspring had opportunities beyond the other Negroes. Lunsford early learned to read and write, a privilege that would not legally have been allowed him a few years later.

"He waited on La Fayette when he passed through Raleigh in 1824, and was greatly impressed by the distinguished Frenchman's devotion to liberty. Once he heard Dr. McPheeters, the Presbyterian minister in Raleigh, say: 'It is impossible to enslave an intelligent people.' This made an impression which he never forgot. His desire to gain his freedom grew daily, and all the spare money that he received as fees from his master's guests was put away toward that end.

"Lunsford had been taught by his father the secret of making a superior kind of smoking tobacco, and this the father and son now began to manufacture for the market. To have free opportunity for this he hired his time, paying for it from $100 to $120 a year. It was some time near this date that his master died. Mr. Haywood had been an indulgent master. He had assured Lunsford that he should be allowed to buy himself. Lunsford now found himself the property of his former master's widow, and he feared that she would not be willing to fulfill the promise. He says, however, that she valued the good opinion of her neighbors, and that they would expect the fulfillment of Mr. Haywood's promise. Stifling his doubts, he worked all the harder. The demand for his tobacco was growing. He enlarged his plant and made arrangements to sell the product in the neighboring towns of Fayetteville, Salisbury and Chapel Hill. At the end of about eight years he had saved $1,000. With much anxiety he approached his mistress to propose the purchase of his liberty. Of this negotiation he says: 'I casually asked her price, provided I should desire my freedom. She said she would be satisfied with $1,000. I then very frankly told her I greatly desired my freedom, and asked if she was ready to execute the deed, provided I could find some person whom I could trust by whom the purchase in my behalf could be made.' A slave, it should be said, had no standing in law, and could not make a contract. Lunsford, therefore, had to get some trusted white man to buy and then emancipate him. He decided to entrust the affair to Mr. Smith, his wife's master. That gentleman, after making the purchase, applied to the courts for leave to emancipate Lane. Now by law slaves could be freed for meritorious services only. No such service could be shown in this case, and the application was refused. Mr. Smith, who was a merchant, then proposed that Lane should accompany him on his next trip to the North and have the freedom papers issued there. This was agreed to, and a year later the emancipation papers of Lunsford Lane were recorded in New York City.

"The business sense of Lane now began to expand his lines of labor. Although he kept to the manufacture of tobacco, he added the making of pipes, and began to sell almost everything kept in an ordinary village store. He also opened a wood yard, and bought horses and wagons for use in connection with it. He was patronized by whites as well as by blacks.

"All this prosperity was beginning to attract the notice of the whites. Several other Negroes in the place were making progress in the same way. Some of the whites thought this was likely to have a bad effect on the slaves generally. Fearing something like this, Lunsford had been careful, as he said, not to intrude his intelligence, but to seem to know less than he did know. He dressed as poorly and fared as simply as if he were still a slave. He also said that he was careful never to do anything which looked like leadership of the other Negroes, that he had done nothing disorderly, and that he had never plotted to free the slaves. The good opinion in which he was held by some of the best men in the place is evidence that this is true. On the evidence of his biographer none of these things were alleged against him. Everything indicates that he devoted himself quietly to the one object of purchasing his family.

"To one class of whites, however, his presence and his success were becoming exceedingly objectionable. These were the younger and more adventurous members of the community. . . . They became alarmed, and soon convinced themselves that it would be a great calamity if every Negro could buy himself and his family at the good round prices that Lane had paid." [83]

Lane was finally driven out of the state, went North, became a lecturer and worker in the cause of freedom.

*Rev. Evans.* Bishop Capers wrote of a famous free Negro preacher whom he knew as follows: "But the most remarkable man in Fayetteville when I went there, and who died during my stay, was a negro, by the name of Henry Evans. I say *the most remarkable* in view of his class; and I call him *negro* with unfeigned respect. He was a negro: that is, he was of that race, without any admixture of another. The name simply designates the race, ánd it is vulgar to regard it with opprobrium. I have known and loved and honored not a few negroes in my life, who were probably as pure of heart as Evans, or anybody else. Such were my old friends, Castile Selby and John Boquet, of Charleston, Will Campbell and Harry Myrick, of Wilmington, York Cohen,

[83] Bassett: "Anti-Slavery Leaders of North Carolina," pp. 61-67.

of Savannah, and others I might name. These I might call remarkable for their goodness. But I use the word in a broader sense for Henry Evans, who was confessedly the father of the Methodist Church, white and black, in Fayetteville, and the best preacher of his time in that quarter; and who was so *remarkable*, as to have become the greatest curiosity of the town; insomuch that distinguished visitors hardly felt that they might pass a Sunday in Fayetteville without hearing him preach. Evans was from Virginia; a shoemaker by trade, and, I think, was born free. He became a Christian and a Methodist quite young, and was licensed to preach in Virginia. While yet a young man, he determined to remove to Charleston, S. C., thinking he might succeed best there at his trade. But having reached Fayetteville on his way to Charleston, and something detaining him for a few days, his spirit was stirred at perceiving that the people of his race in that town were wholly given to profanity and lewdness, never hearing preaching of any denomination, and living emphatically without hope and without God in the world. The town council interfered, and nothing in his power could prevail with them to permit him to preach. He then withdrew to the sand-hills out of town, and held meetings in the woods, changing his appointments from place to place. No law was violated, while the council was effectually eluded; and so the opposition passed into the hands of the mob. These he worried out by changing his appointments, so that when they went to work their will upon him, he was preaching somewhere else. Meanwhile, whatever the most honest purpose of a simple heart could do to reconcile his enemies, was employed by him for that end. He eluded no one in private, but sought opportunities to explain himself; avowed the purity of his intentions; and even begged to be subjected to the scrutiny of any surveillance that might be thought proper to prove his inoffensiveness; anything, so that he might but be allowed to preach. Happily for him and the cause of religion, his honest countenance and earnest pleadings were soon powerfully seconded by the fruits of his labors. One after another began to suspect their servants of attending his preaching, not because they were made worse, but wonderfully better. The effect on the public morals of the negroes, too, began to be seen, particularly as regarded their habits on Sunday, and drunkenness. And it was not long before the mob was called off by a change in the current of opinion, and Evans was allowed to preach in town. At that time there was not a single church edifice in town, and but one congregation (Presbyterian), who worshipped in what was called the State-house, under which was the market; and it was plainly Evans or nobody to preach to the negroes. Now, too, of the mistresses there were not a few, and some masters, who were brought to think that the preaching which had proved so beneficial to their servants might be good for them also; and the famous negro preacher had some whites as well as blacks to hear him.

*Evans Preaches to Whites.* "Seats, distinctly separated, were at first appropriated to the whites, near the pulpit. But Evans had already become famous, and these seats were insufficient. Indeed, the negroes seemed like to lose their preacher, negro though he was, while the whites, crowded out of their appropriate seats, took possession of those in the rear. Meanwhile Evans had respresented to the preacher of Bladen Circuit how things were going, and induced him to take his meeting house into the circuit, and constitute a church there. And now, there was no longer room for the negroes in the house when Evans preached; and for the accommodation of both classes, the weather-boards were knocked off and sheds were added to the house on either side; the whites occupying the whole of the original building, and the negroes those sheds as a part of the same house.

*Capers Preaches to Negroes.* "It was my practice to hold a meeting with the blacks in the church directly after morning preaching every Sunday. And on the Sunday before his death, during this meeting, the little door between his humble shed and the chancel where I stood was opened, and the dying man entered for a last farewell to his people. He was almost too feeble to stand at all, but supporting himself by the railing of the chancel, he said: 'I have come to say my last word to you. It is this: None but Christ. Three times I have had my life in jeopardy for preaching the gospel to you. Three times I have broken the ice on the edge of the water and swum across the Cape Fear to preach the gospel to you. And now, if in my last hour I could trust to that, or to anything else but Christ crucified, for my salvation, all should be lost, and my soul perish forever.' A noble testimony! Worthy, not of Evans only, but St. Paul. His funeral at the church was attended by a greater concourse of persons than had been seen on any funeral occasion before. The whole community appeared to mourn his death, and the universal feeling seemed to be that in honoring the memory of Henry Evans we were paying a tribute to virtue and religion. He was buried under the chancel of the church of which he had been in so remarkable a manner the founder." [84]

*Charleston Free Negroes.* "In the city of Charleston, South Carolina, there was a colony of 'free persons of colour,' who were proud of the fact that they sprang from a generation of free ancestors going back to before the Revolutionary War. In the list of taxpayers in the city of Charleston for 1860 the names

[84] Wightman: "Life of Bishop Capers," pp. 124-129.

of three hundred and sixty 'persons of colour,' whose property was assessed in that year are given. They owned real estate which was valued for taxation at $724,570. Of these three hundred and sixty taxpayers, one hundred and thirty owned slaves, aggregating three hundred and ninety in number. The largest number of slaves held by a coloured person was fourteen. In this list of 'persons of colour' thirteen are classed as Indians, but it is quite certain that these so-called Indians were largely mixed with Negro blood. Like so many other communities, there were Indians in Charleston who had been but partially absorbed by coloured people with whom they had been associated. . . .

"There were a number of other slaves held in trust by the free coloured people of Charleston. The wealthiest family in Charleston, among the free coloured people, were the Westons. They had among the various members of the family taxable property to the amount of $80,000. They also owned thirty-six slaves, nine of whom they held as trustees. It is said that the number of slaves held by St. Philip's Church, which was the aristocratic church of the city, amounted to something over one hundred. These consisted for the most part of slaves who had actually bought their freedom and whom the church held in trust." [85]

*Louisiana Free Negroes Prosperous.* In his visits through Louisiana Frederick Law Olmsted found "a large number of free colored planters. In going down Cane River, the Dalman called at several of their plantations, to take on cotton, and the captain told me that in fifteen miles of a well-settled and cultivated country, on the bank of the river, beginning ten miles below Nachitoches, he did not know but one pure-blooded white man. The plantations appeared no way different from the generality of those of the white Creoles; and on some of them were large, handsome, and comfortable houses. These free-colored people are all descended from the progeny of old French and Spanish planters, and their Negro slaves. Such a progeny, born before Louisiana was annexed to the United States, and the descendants of it, are entitled to freedom.

"The colored planters, within their knowledge (i. e., certain merchants), had large and healthy families; they were honest, and industrious, and paid their debts quite as punctually as the white planters, and were, so far as they could judge, without an intimate acquaintance, good citizens, in all respects. One of them had lately spent $40,000 in a law suit, and it was believed that they were increasing in wealth. If you have occasion to call at their houses, I was told, you will be received in a gentlemanly manner, and find they live in the same style with white

[85] Washington: "The Story of the Negro," pp. 205-207.

people of the same wealth. They speak French among themselves, but all are able to converse in English also, and many of them are well educated." [86]

A German planter whom Olmsted met spoke quite favorably of the free Negroes in the vicinity of Washington, Louisiana. "Often," he said, "they were wealthy and thriving, and they owned some of the best of the cotton and sugar plantations. Some of them were educated; he did not know how or where. One planter that he did business with, kept his books and wrote business-letters in a better manner than most white planters." [87]

Another visitor whom Olmsted met at Washington reported that "The best house and most tasteful grounds that he had visited in the State, belong to a nearly full-blooded negro—a very dark man. He and his family are well educated, and though French is their habitual tongue, they speak English with freedom; and one of them with much more elegance than most liberally educated whites in the South. They had a private tutor in their family. They owned, he presumed, a hundred slaves." [88]

*Number of Free Negroes, 1860.* Dr. Washington estimates that 262,000 free Negroes in the South in 1860 owned twenty-five million dollars' worth of property,[89] which, if correct, would be a sure indication of wonderful perseverance and industry on the part of a group so greatly handicapped.

*Respect for Certain Free Negroes.* While there is much abusive language recorded concerning the free Negro, in which he was called "lazy," "incompetent," and "dangerous," it is quite evident that a considerable number of that class were an economic asset to the communities. Thus after laws were passed forcing all masters to send their freed slaves out of the state, there appear numerous petitions both from free colored men and from groups of white men, begging that these persons be allowed to remain in the state. "The protests are hardly less significant because they attempt to have only individuals excepted from the operation of the law than if they aimed at saving the entire class. In 1810 sixty persons prayed the legislature (of Virginia) to allow a free negro wheelwright, 'who will benefit the whole country' to remain in the State and the county; and in the same year citizens of Petersburg declared to the Assembly that the town could not spare without loss one Uriah Tyner. In 1812 a large number of citizens of Berkeley and Frederick counties told the legislature that 'there is not a human being in this part of the country where they (Jerry and Susanna, free colored) reside who is opposed to their remaining in Virginia.' The plea of the inhabitants of

Lynchburg for Pleasant Rowan, a free colored carpenter and mechanic, was that 'his loss would be felt in the community;' for Frederick Williams that he was a much needed barber; and for Ned Adams, that he was an almost indispensable cooper. The people of Henrico County, petitioning for John Hope, a free negro, said that he was a cooper 'who would be useful in any community.' The same thing was said of Daniel Warner, a free negro barber of Warrenton, by one hunded and twenty white petitioners. Ninety-five citizens of Accomac County declared to the legislature in 1838 that the services of John, a free negro sawyer, 'are much required in his neighborhood.' Henry Parker of Loudoun County was considered by his white neighbors as 'a good and useful man,' desirable in the community as a day laborer. No better example of the economic value placed upon the free negro could be found than the following petition from thirty-eight citizens of Essex County: 'We would be glad if he (Ben, a free negro) could be permitted to remain with us and have his freedom, as he is a well disposed person and a very useful man in many respects, he is a good carpenter, a good cooper, a coarse shoemaker, a good hand at almost everything that is useful to us farmers.'

"In behalf of Harriet Cook, free colored, nearly one hundred white persons, among whom were seven justices of the peace, five ex-justices, sixteen merchants, six lawyers, and one postmaster, made to the legislature this petition: 'It would be a serious inconvenience to a number of the citizens of Leesburg to be deprived of her services as a washerwoman and in other capacities in which, in consequence of her gentility, trustworthiness, and skill she is exceedingly useful.' In a similar manner Fortune Thomas, free colored, had rendered her services indispensable to the town of Halifax by baking cakes and tarts and making candies. 'In fact,' say the petitioners in her behalf, 'she has been earnestly assured by the ladies that they can in no measure dispense with her assistance and that no party or wedding can well be given without great inconvenience should her shop be broken up and discontinued.' But rarely were protests uttered against favorable legislation in aid of a free negro who sought permission to remain in a community." [90]

Thus in spite of the fact that the slave owners of the South feared lest the free Negro would become a disturber of the peace, and hence there was a general desire to get rid of him, nevertheless because he was a good laborer and often a skilled mechanic, because he often became a good farmer and a prosperous neighbor, he was frequently allowed to remain in the South, where in increasing measure he won the respect and protection of the slave owning class.

[90] Russell: "The Free Negro in Virginia," pp. 152-154.

CHAPTER IX

# THE ECONOMIC FAILURE OF SLAVERY

*Conditions Favorable to Slavery.* Professor Jerome Dowd lays down three conditions which make the development of slavery seem necessary and profitable: First, a country favored by the bounty of nature, and thus able to produce enough to provide for the laboring slaves and for the idle, non-producing masters. Second, a country where the labor necessary for production is disagreeable and to be shirked if possible. Third, a country where there is plenty of free land; for, as Professor Dowd suggests, where there is free land no man will work for another on wages, —he must be forced to work.[1] It seems necessary to add to this list the fact that a sparse population, where conditions of life are such that each man can provide for his own wants, seems to make it necessary to have slavery in order that enough labor supply may be mobilized for carrying out any large schemes of production. We have referred before to Sumner's idea of the basis of slavery as fourfold: (1) hatred of members of other tribes, (2) desire to get something for nothing, (3) love of dominion, and (4) hatred of work.[2]

*South Better Fitted for Slavery Than North.* In a preceding chapter we have pointed out that slavery did not prove profitable in the North because the climate was hard and hence the yield of nature not bounteous, and good land was at a premium. Furthermore, usable land was not to be found in large tracts, so that a plantation system could not be established on a large scale. On the other hand the South had a congenial climate, nature was most bounteous, yielding more than one crop per year, land was plentiful and accessible in large tracts, labor was scarce in the early days, and it must be confessed that the early colonists were not any too eager for hard work. It was also true that labor was most irksome in certain sections, where both the heat of the sun and the malaria of the marsh made hard labor a source of physical danger. It would seem that slavery would succeed here if it could succeed anywhere in the world. All the conditions at least seemed favorable for its economic success.

"The economic importance of the servant in developing the

[1] "Journal of Negro History," Vol. II, p. 1 f.
[2] Cf. Chapter III, "Folkways," p. 280.

resources of the colonies, especially in the middle colonies, can hardly be overestimated. All the provinces were essentially agricultural, but the large tobacco plantations of Maryland and Virginia made a large supply of cheap laborers more necessary there than in the northern colonies. . . .

"No system of free labor could have been maintained in the plantation colonies until a comparatively late date. In the first place, the poor of Europe would not have been able to come to America, had they been obliged to pay for their passage in advance. On the other hand, the planters could not afford to pay the wages of free laborers. Even with the large supply of servants and convicts, free labor was high and unprofitable. Laborers would not hire, except for very high wages, when they could easily obtain new lands and become planters themselves. Winthrop records an instance of the seventeenth century which illustrates the conditions in a colony which depended very largely on free labor.

"I may upon this occasion report a passage between one Rowley and his servant. The master, being forced to sell a pair of his oxen to pay his servant his wages, told his servant he could keep him no longer, not knowing how to pay him next year. The servant answered him, he would serve him for more of his cattle. But how shall I do (saith the master) when all my cattle are gone? The servant replied, you shall then serve me, and so you may have your cattle again.' (Winthrop, Hist. of New Eng. II. 219, 220.) It was the scarcity of laborers that made the sale of convicts easy, in spite of the sentiment against them." [3]

*Tobacco Raising by Slaves Profitable.* Tobacco was the first staple crop raised by the early settlers in Virginia and used as a money crop. In fact, tobacco was for most of the seventeenth century the real medium of exchange. As early as 1619 Governor Yeardley urged the colonists to plant tobacco for profit, and its importance in early Virginia can scarcely be exaggerated. In 1619 Virginia exported 20,000 pounds of tobacco. Twenty years later, 1639, she exported 1,500,000 pounds, and in 1753 the exports amounted to 53,862,300 pounds.[4] It will thus be seen that the culture of tobacco was a steadily growing industry. Arnold tells us that as late as 1860 tobacco "furnished a produce whose value was 24 per cent of that of the whole state." [5]

Tobacco culture could be carried on profitably by slaves, for it involved a great amount of pure routine work. The seeds were bedded in the winter, and while the plants were growing

[3] McCormac: "White Servitude in Maryland," p. 32-34.
[4] Cf. Arnold: "History of the Tobacco Industry in Virginia," p. 11.
[5] *Ibid.*, p. 13.

the land was thrown up into long hills such as are often used at present for planting sweet potatoes. When the plants were three inches high they were transplanted to the field, care being taken to do this work when the land was thoroughly moist after rains. Then followed the routine process of hoeing, plowing, worming, topping and stripping of superfluous leaves. In the late summer or early fall the plants must be cut close to the ground, carried to the curing barns, where the process was slow and tedious. When fully cured it must be sorted into the several types of leaves, and packed in hogsheads. All this work could be more profitably done on a large scale than on a small one, so that the concentration of large numbers of workers on individual plantations favored the growth of slavery. The same influence that has held cotton as the one staple crop in the far South and Southwest, namely a ready cash market, made tobacco the king of Virginia agriculture. Maryland and North Carolina early engaged in the tobacco growing business, as did Kentucky and Tennessee a little later on. All of these states secured much of their cash revenue from tobacco alone.

*Wealth From Tobacco Culture.* That some men were able to make considerable fortunes out of tobacco culture is evidenced in an account quoted by Chambers from a Richmond paper in 1854.

" 'I have thought for some time I would write for your paper something in relation to the richest man in Virginia, and the largest slaveholder in the Union, and perhaps in the world, unless the serfs of Russia be considered slaves; and the wish expressed in your paper, a few days ago, to know who was so wealthy in Virginia, induces me to write this now. Samuel Hairston, of Pittsylvania, is the gentleman. When I was in his section a year or two ago, he was the owner of between 1,600 and 1,700 slaves, in his own right, having but a little while before taken a census. He also has a prospective right to about 1,003 slaves more, which are now owned by his mother-in-law, Mrs. R. Hairston, he having married her only child. He now has the management of them, which makes the number of his slaves reach near 3,000. They increase at the rate of nearly 100 every year: he has to purchase a large plantation every year to settle them on. A large number of his plantations are in Henry and Patrick counties, Virginia. He has large estates in North Carolina. His wealth is differently estimated at 3,000,000 to 5,000,000 dollars; and I should think it nearer the latter. You think he has a hard lot; but, I assure you, Mr. Hairston manages all his matters as easy as most would an estate of 10,000 dollars. He has overseers who are compelled to give him a written statement of what has been made and spent on each plantation, and his negroes are all clothed and fed from his own domestic manufacture; and raising his own tobacco-crop, which is immensely large, is so much clear gain every year, besides his increase in negroes, which is a fortune of itself. And now for his residence. I have traveled over fifteen states of this Union, and have never seen anything comparable to his yard and garden, except some of those in the Mississippi delta, and none of them equal to it. Mrs. Hairston has been beautifying it for years: and a good old minister, in preaching near the place, and describing paradise, said, 'it was as beautiful as Mrs. Hairston's;' or, as a friend who visited Washington city for the first time, remarked that 'the public grounds were nearly as handsome as Samuel Hairston's.' He is a plain, unassuming gentleman, and has never made any noise in the world, though he could vie with the Bruces, M'Donoughs, and Astors; and it is strange, that while their wealth is co-extensive with the Union, he is not known 100 miles from home. I believe he is now the wealthiest man in the Union, as William B. Astor is only worth about 4,000,000 dollars, and the estates of city people are vastly overrated, while Mr. Hairston can shew the property that will bring the cash at any moment. Mr. Hairston was raised within a few miles of where he now lives, in Henry county. He has several brothers, who are pretty well to do in the world. One of them, Marshall Hairston, of Henry, owns more than 700 negroes; Robert Hairston, who now lives in Mississippi, near 1,000; and Harden Hairston, who has also moved to Mississippi, about 600 slaves. George Hairston, of Henry, has given almost all of his property to his children, reserving only about 150 slaves for his own use. This, I believe, is a correct statement of the circumstances of the Hairston family.' " [6]

*Dangers in Raising Tobacco Alone.* That even tobacco was not always a lucrative crop is made clear from a letter of a Mr. Calvert to Lord Baltimore, dated October 26, 1729:

"In Virginia and Maryland Tobacco is our Staple, is our All, and Indeed leaves no room for anything Else; It requires the Attendance of all our hands, and Exacts their utmost labour, the whole year round; it requires us to abhor Communitys or townships, since a Planter cannot Carry on his Affairs, without Considerable Elbow room, within his plantation. When All is done, and our Tobacco sent home, it is perchance the most uncertain Commodity that Comes to Markett; and the management of it there is of such a nature and method, that it seems to be of all other, most lyable and Subject to frauds, in prejudice to the poor

[6] Chambers: "Slavery and Colour," pp. 194-195.

Planters.  Tobacco Merchants, who deal in Consignments, get great Estates, run no risque, and Labour only with the pen; the Planter can scarce get a living, Runs all the risques attendant upon trade, both as to his negroes and Tobacco, and must work in variety of Labour.  I write not this in malicious Envy to the Merchts, nor do I wish them less success in business; but I heartily wish the Planters Lay was better.  When our Tobacco then is sold at home, whatever is the product of it returns not to us in Money, but is either converted into Apparell, Tools or other Conveniences of life, or Else remains there, as it were Dead to us; for where the Staple of a Countrey, upon forreign Sale, yields no returns of money, to Circulate in such a Country, the want of such Circulation must leave it almost Inanimate." [7]

*Cotton Culture; Large Plantations.*  In the states of the lower South, cotton early became the chief product of agriculture. Phillips gives a full account of the Telfair estate in Jefferson County, Georgia, known as Retreat.  With an average of about eighty slaves on the estate, it yielded from $4,000 to $21,300 gross income for various years from 1834 to 1853.

"From 1834 to 1841 the gross earnings on Retreat ranged between eight and fifteen thousand dollars, of which from seven to twelve thousand each year was available for division between the owners.  The gross then fell rapidly to $4000 in 1844, of which more than half was consumed in expenses.  It then rose as rapidly to its maximum of $21,300 in 1847, when more than half of it again was devoted to current expenses and betterments. Thereafter the range of the gross was between $8000 and $17,000 except for a single year of crop failure, 1856, when the 109 bales brought $5750.  During the 'fifties the current expenses ranged usually between six and ten thousand dollars, as compared with about one third as much in the 'thirties.  This is explained partly by the resolution of the owners to improve the fields, now grown old, and to increase the equipment.  For the crop of 1856, for example, purchases were made of forty tons of Peruvian guano at $56 per ton, and nineteen tons of Mexican guano at $25 a ton. In the following years lime, salt and dried blood were included in the fertilizer purchases." [8]

*The Hammond Estate.*  Of the Hammond estate in South Carolina he gives the following facts:

"At Silver Bluff, the 385 acres in cotton were expected to yield 330 bales of 400 pounds each; the 400 acres in corn had an

[7] Phillips: "Plantation and Frontier," Vol. I, p. 282-283.
[8] Phillips: "American Negro Slavery," p. 238.

expectation of 9850 bushels; and 10 acres of rice, 200 bushels. At Cathwood the plantings and expectations were 370 acres in cotton to yield 280 bales, 280 in corn to yield 5000 bushels, 15 in wheat to yield 100 bushels, 11 in rye to yield 50, and 2 in rice to yield 50. In financial results, after earning in 1848 only $4334.91, which met barely half of his plantation and family expenses for the year, his crop sales from 1849 to 1853 ranged from seven to twenty thousand dollars annually in cotton and from one and a half to two and a half thousand dollars in corn. His gross earnings in these five years averaged $16,217.76, while his plantation expenses averaged $5393.87, and his family outlay $6392.67, leaving an average 'clear gain per annum,' as he called it, of $4431.10. The accounting, however, included no reckoning of interest on the investment or of anything else but money income and outgo." [9]

*Cotton Alone Produced Small Income.* It is quite evident from these facts, which seem to be typical, that no enormous fortunes would easily be built up. The slaves could hardly have earned one hundred dollars each, even with no charge for interest on land and the deterioration thereof.

*Cost of Producing Cotton.* Cotton, of course, varied in price, and one result of slave labor was that it could not readily be shifted to other forms of production to prevent overproduction, because the slave could not quickly be taught a new method of work. DeBow, in his Industrial Resources, gives the following account:

"COTTON—Cost of Producing, &c.—We have seen within a short time various statements published in regard to the cost of producing cotton and what should be its natural price. A writer in the *Carolinian* declares 5 cents will not pay in that state any profit. He takes an estate well managed, inferior to none in productiveness, and affording more than an average yield in the state. The winter but not summer clothing was manufactured at the place. The number of acres was 550, much of which, four years ago, cost $25 per acre, number of slaves forty, one-half field hands. Estimating the negroes at $300 each, and the land at $12, with stock etc. the investment will be $20,000.

[9] Phillips: "American Negro Slavery," p. 218.

## Income 1848

| | |
|---|---:|
| Bales of cotton 120; 350 lbs. equals 42,500 lbs. at 5¢ | $2,100.00 * |
| Increase in negroes ......................... | 200.00 |
| | $2,300.00 |
| Deduct expenses, etc. ....................... | 1,383.00 |
| | 917.00 |
| Value planter's superintendence ............... | 417.00 |
| Net income (or 2½ per cent) ................. | 500.00 |

## Expenses and loss for 1848

| | |
|---|---:|
| Wages of overseer .......................... | 300.00 |
| Blacksmith's account, iron included ............. | 35.00 |
| Medicine and medical attendance .............. | 30.00 |
| Bagging, rope and twine for 120 bales cotton ..... | 150.00 |
| Blankets, thirty in number, at $1.12½ each ...... | 33.75 |
| Shoes, twenty-five pairs, say $1.25 per pair....... | 31.25 |
| Cotton Osnaburgs, 300 yards, at 8¢ per yard..... | 24.00 |
| Taxes, (state, poor, and bridge) say............ | 30.00 |
| Salt, six sacks, at $2 each..................... | 12.00 |
| Nails, 100 lbs. at 5¢ per lb.................... | 5.00 |
| Hoes, 1 dozen ............................... | 4.50 |
| Sugar and coffee for sick, 75 lbs., at 10¢ per lb.... | 7.50 |
| Annual wear and tear of land, say 5 per cent upon estimated value (6,600) ..................... | 330.00 |
| Contingencies, such as re-stocking the place with mules, wear and tear of wagons, etc........... | 200.00 |
| Cost of transporting 120 bales cotton to market, at 75¢ per bale ............................... | 90.00 |
| Loss by death of old negro, say................ | 100.00 |
| Whole expenses and loss ..................... | $1,383.00"[10] |

* This error appears in the Original; it should be $2,125.00.

DeBow's Industrial Resources gives another record which is worth quoting:

*Robinson's Figures on Cotton Cost.* "Mr. Solon Robinson, a very observant agriculturist, who has been traveling extensively in the South, furnishes some statistics to the same effect. He presents the case of Col. Williams's plantation, at Society Hill, S. C.

[10] DeBow: "Industrial Resources, Etc., in South and West," Vol. I, pp. 161-162.

## Capital Invested

| | |
|---|---|
| 4,200 acres of land (2,700 in cultivation) at $15 .... | $63,000.00 |
| 254 slaves, at $350 each, average old and young..... | 89,900.00 |
| 60 mules and mares, and one jack, and one stud, average $60 ............................. | 3,720.00 |
| 200 head of cattle, at $10 ...................... | 2,000.00 |
| 500 head of hogs, at $2 ......................... | 1,000.00 |
| 23 carts and 6 wagons ......................... | 520.00 |
| 60 bull-tongue plows, 60 shaving do., 25 turning do., 15 drill do., 15 harrows, at an average of $1.50 each. | 262.00 |
| All other plantation tools estimated, worth ......... | 1,000.00 |
| | $161,402.00 |

## Crop

| | |
|---|---|
| 13,500 lbs. of bacon, taken for home place and factory | 675.00 |
| Beef and butter for ditto and sales ............... | 500.00 |
| 1,100 bushels of corn and meal for ditto and sales.... | 550.00 |
| 80 cords of tan bark for his tan yard ............. | 480.00 |
| Charges to others for blacksmith work ........... | 100.00 |
| Mutton and wool for home use and sales ......... | 125.00 |
| | 2,430.00 |
| Cotton 331,000 lbs. @ 4.7¢ ...... | 15,464.00 |
| | $17,894.00 |

## Expenses

| | |
|---|---|
| Interest is only counted on the first five items, $158,620, at seven per cent .................. | $11,103.00 |
| 3,980 yards Dundee bagging, at 16¢ (5 yds. to a bale) | 536.80 |
| 3,184 lbs. of rope, at 6 cents .................... | 191.04 |
| Taxes on 254 slaves, at 76 cents ................. | 193.04 |
| Taxes on land .................................. | 70.00 |
| Three overseers' wages ......................... | 900.00 |
| Medical attendance, $1.25 per head .............. | 317.50 |
| Bill of yearly supply of iron, average ........... | 100.00 |
| Plows and other tools purchased, annual average.... | 100.00 |
| 200 pairs of shoes, $175; annual supply of hats, $100 | 275.00 |
| Bill of cotton and woolen cloth ................. | 810.00 |
| 100 cotton comforters, in lieu of bed blankets....... | 125.00 |
| 100 oil-cloth capotes (New-York cost)........... | 87.50 |
| 20 small woolen blankets for infants ............. | 25.00 |
| Calico dress and handkerchief for each woman and girl (extra of other clothing) ................ | 82.00 |
| Christmas presents, given in lieu of "negro crop".... | 175.00 |

| | |
|---|---:|
| 50 sacks of salt .............................. | $80.00 |
| Annual average, outlay for iron and wood work for carts and wagons ........................... | 100.00 |
| Lime and plaster bought last year ................ | 194.00 |
| Annual average outlay for gin, belts, etc............ | 80.00 |
| 400 gallons of molasses ......................... | 100.00 |
| 3 kegs tobacco, $60; 2 bbls. of flour, $10............ | 70.00 |
| 3/8 of a cent a pound on cotton for freight and commission .................................. | 2,069.60 |
| | 17,894.48 |
| Deduct other products than cotton............... | 2,430.00 |
| | $15,464.48 |

"Showing the average cost of producing cotton per lb. a little less than 4 cents and 7 mills. Had this cotton sold at 6 cents, the profits would have been $1,973.68, at 7 cents, $5,385.04, which was about what it brought, being little more than 3 per cent." [11]

*Olmsted's Studies on Cotton Cost.* Frederick Law Olmsted made long and faithful inquiry as to the cost of cotton raised by slaves and came deliberately to the conclusion that it was far more expensive than would permit of reasonable profits.[12]

"Give the South a people moderately close settled, moderately well-informed, moderately ambitious and moderately industrious, somewhat approaching that of Ohio, for instance, and what a business it would have! Twenty double-track railroads from the Gulf to the lakes, and twenty lines of ocean steamers would not sufficiently meet its requirements. Who doubts, let him study the present business of Ohio, and ask upon what in the natural resources of Ohio, or its position, could, forty years ago, a prediction of its present wealth and business have been made, of its present supply and its present demand have been made, which would compare in value with the commercial resources and advantages of position possessed today by any one of the western cotton States?" [13]

*Rice Culture.* Rice culture in South Carolina and Georgia engaged a large number of slaves. A typical rice plantation, well-managed and of fair size, was that of Manigault on the Savannah River, near the city of Savannah.[14] This estate in 1833 comprised 220 acres in rice, 80 acres uncultivated, a rice mill, 50 Negroes—

[11] DeBow: "Industrial Resources, etc., in the South and West," Vol. I, p. 162.
[12] Olmsted: "A Journey in the Back Country," pp. 337-354.
[13] *Ibid.*, p. 354.
[14] Phillips: "Plantation and Frontier," Vol. I, p. 134 f.

for all of which Manigault paid $40,000—$25,000 for the estate and $15,000 for the Negroes. In 1839 he listed 57 Negroes and bought 16 additional at the average of $640 each, or $10,640. The records of the plantation for six years, 1833 to 1838 inclusive, showed a total of 2365 barrels of rice, or 1,419,000 pounds, which at an average of 3 cents per pound yielded $42,570. The expense he estimated for the six years at $12,000, giving a revenue for the six years of $30,570 or a little over $5000 per year. In 1839 the rice crop was 578 barrels, and sold for $15,239, of which amount $10,240 was turned into new slaves. Each of the 57 old slaves cost $21 for upkeep, and the overseer must be paid. The records show that 19 more slaves were bought in 1857 at the cost of $11,850, indicating the constant outlay of money to keep the slave population up to standard. In spite of this fact the slave population seems decidedly diminished in this record of 1860, due perhaps to deaths and some runaways which he notes. Manigault also owned a second estate, called East Hermitage. On the two estates he made in 1855 a total of $15,637.19, but in the following year, due to floods and storms, also to cholera among the Negroes, the net yield was only $3,141.62. In 1858 the proceeds for the two plantations were $3,286.26, and in 1859 they were $5,938.54. As one reads these facts he must conclude that the average return from 100 or more Negroes' labor and some six hundred acres of land in the two plantations was meager indeed. The entry of 1857 in Manigault's diary would bear out this same impression:

*Manigault's Rice Plantation.* "Upon the death of my Overseer (19th Dec'r, 1855) I was left alone on the plantation. We soon finished threshing the Crop & I went to work preparing the lands for the next year. There were many applications, as Overseers, for this place, but none pleased us. The latter part of February was now approaching, still we had no Overseer. At last we were recommended (by Mr. Wm. Bull Pringle of Charleston, S. C.) a young man who had acted as Sub-Overseer for 2 or 3 years upon his Brother's (Mr. R. Pringle's) Plantation on Black River, about 20 miles from Georgetown, So. Ca. Mr. Leonard F. Venters, 24 yrs. of age reached this on 21st Feb'y, 1856. He struck me as being very young; I explained however all Concerning our mode of 'water Culture' & how our Crops were treated on Savannah River, a very different method being used here from what, I was told, they used on other rivers, where black soil could not stand the water which these stiff clay lands did, &c. We commenced planting on the 15th March, & finished the entire tract of 638 Acres (all Open plant) on 3d May, when we began to hoe Rice and I left the plantation for the summer. Venters made two great and fatal mistakes. He drew off his "Sprout Water" too rapidly, prostrating his rice to the ground, & again he kept his fields dry too long, before he could get at them to give first hoeing. His rice was all stunted, sickly, and grass took him. We have made one half a Crop. He says 'he will do better another year, that now he sees into it,' and as is well known, 'Never change an Overseer if You can help it.' We try him once (but only once) more. We have purchased 19 Negroes; amongst them 13 prime hands Costing in all $11,850. Also 771 Acres High Land on Georgia Main, for Cholera Camps, Children's Summer residence, &c. Costing $2,195. We have been blessed with health during the past year & now as hope ever bears us onward, I try to forget the past, looking forward with brighter expectations for the Coming Season, that We may be blessed with 'the kindly fruits of the Earth so that in due time we may enjoy them.'

"Gowrie, (Savannah River), 1st February, 1857." [15]

*Sugar Culture.* Tobacco, cotton, rice and sugar were the four great staple crops of the slave régime.

"The manufacture of cane into sugar does not appear to have commenced before 1764, when samples were sent to the mother country from the estate of Chevalier de Mazan, near the city (New Orleans) on the opposite bank. The yield per acre was then stated to have been 3,000 lbs. and the quality was pronounced to be equal to that of St. Domingo moscovado.

*Louisiana as a Sugar State.* "The cession of Louisiana to Spain, at that epoch appears to have put a stop to that industry, for no farther traces of sugar-making are to be found until 1791, when the first sugar-house, under the Spanish government, was erected by a Mr. Solis, at Terre-au-Beaufs, in the parish of St. Bernard. The next was established in 1796, on a plantation situated where now stands Carrollton, and belonging to a Mr. Bore; it produced a crop of $12,000, a sum considered at that epoch as very large. This result may be said to have laid the foundation of the sugar industry in Louisiana. Its progress, however, was at first extremely slow; and at the epoch of the cession of Louisiana to the United States, the number of sugar estates was very small, no doubt owing to the want of capital.

"The statistics from 1803 to 1817 are so deficient, that it is extremely difficult to arrive at any correct data as to the progressive annual increase of the sugar crop during the above period.

"The crop in 1818 had attained 25,000 hogsheads. Cattle was the only power, used up to that period.

"In 1822, steam power was introduced; the first engines and mills cost about $12,000, and were chiefly imported by Gordon

[15] Phillips: "Plantation and Frontier," Vol. I, pp. 142-144.

and Forstall.  This power, however, was used but by very few, until our own foundries placed it within the reach of all, by reducing its cost to $5,000 or $6,000." [16]

*Large Capital Required for Sugar Raising.*  Most of the sugar was raised in Louisiana and lower Mississippi.  Sugar growing required much more capital than either of the other staples, and hence was concentrated in the hands of a smaller number of planters.  "In 1849 there were 1474 sugar estates in Louisiana, producing 236,547 hogsheads of sugar, but it is thought that half of this quantity was produced on less than 200 estates, that is, one-eighth of the plantations produced one-half of the sugar.  The sugar works on some of the large estates cost over $100,000, and many of them manufactured 1,000,000 pounds per annum.  The profits on these in a favorable season are immense." [17]  Sugar was a staple which required almost the whole year to produce, hence most profitable for slave labor.  The winter and early spring were used in preparing the ground for the planting, one-third of the crop being replanted each year, the other two-thirds being grown from the stubble of the year before.  Each year at the cutting season about one-twelfth of the entire crop was mattressed low in heavy piles on the ground, where during the early spring it began to sprout.  It was then transferred to the furrows, two stalks being laid side by side for the full length of the furrows, but so placed that the joints or sprouting points were not together.  These stalks were lightly covered with 'dirt and from them came a full stand of cane which would not have to be replanted until the third year thereafter.  After the cane had well sprouted, the hoeing and plowing process began, in April, and continued until July when the cane had grown sufficiently to shade the whole ground by over-arching leaves.  The crop was then "laid by," and all hands were concentrated on getting out wood for the boiling, repairing the machinery, and getting everything in readiness for the grinding season.  The grinding season began about October and lasted for two or three months.  During this time every man, woman and child worked to the limit, often eighteen hours per day,—for there was always danger that a heavy frost would destroy the cane and thus render useless the work of the whole year.  This rush of work made it necessary for each planted to have his own cane mill, for no time was to be lost when the season for grinding arrived, and waiting on a "custom mill" might endanger his entire crop.  Hence it was estimated that no man with less than $150,000 capital should embark in the sugar raising business.  One-third of this was probably required for

[16] E. J. Forestall, in DeBow's "Industrial Resources," Vol. III, p. 275.
[17] Olmsted: "Seaboard Slave States," p. 669.

machinery. Olmsted thought that these sugar plantation owners were "among the most intelligent, enterprising, and wealthy men of business in the United States." [18]

*Process of Manufacture.* "The first operation in the manufacture of sugar from cane is, to express the saccharine juice it contains; this is done by passing it twice between rollers, on the same plan that apples are crushed in our best cider-mills. A great deal of ingenuity has been applied to the construction of the mills for this purpose, and they have been, from time to time, improved, but are yet far from satisfactory in their operation, as it is known that the crushed cane still retains nearly one-third of its original moisture, with a large share of the saccharine principle which belonged to it before it was passed between the rollers. No plan has yet been devised by which this can be economically secured.

*Boiling Process.* "The expressed juice is strained into a vessel, in which it is heated to a temperature of about 140° F., when it is clarified by the application of lime, the chemical action of which is now, I believe, perfectly understood; the effect is, to cause a precipitate of impurities, and to give a yellow color to the juice. In addition to this, the juice is sometimes further clarified by filtration. The next operation is the reduction of the cane-juice by the evaporation of the greater part of its constituent water—to syrup. This is effected by the action of heat, which is applied in different ways, according to the apparatus used. There are seven different forms of this, in general use in Louisiana. In the simplest and rudest, the juice is boiled in open kettles; in the most improved, it is boiled in vacuo, on the principle that liquids boil at lower temperature, as the pressure of the atmosphere is removed. The sugar made by the latter process is much superior to that made by the former, which is always much burnt, and less pure, and it is also obtained at a much less expenditure of fuel.

*Granulation of Sugar.* "The syrup having reached the proper degree of concentration, is next drawn off into vessels, in which it remains until granulation takes place. To separate the uncrystallizable syrup from the granulated sugar, in the more usual method, the mass of saccharine matter is placed in hogsheads, in the bottoms of which are holes, in which are inserted pieces of cane, which reach above the contents. As the granulation proceeds, a contraction takes place, which leaves an opening about the canes, by which the remaining liquid drains to the bottom, and, the canes being loosely inserted, it flows through the holes, out of the hogshead, leaving the comparatively dry sugar now completely granulated. The hogsheads are set upon a staging, or loose floor, over a large vat, in which the drainage is collected. This drainage is molasses. It is afterwards pumped out of the tanks into barrels,

[18] Olmsted: "Seaboard Slave States," p. 670.

for market; commonly the purchaser buys it in the tank and provides barrels for its removal. Seventy gallons of molasses for each hogshead of sugar is considered a large estimate. The sugar is now in the condition known as 'Muscovado,' or raw brown sugar. Its color and quality depend on the caution and skill that have been used in the manufacture, and the excellence of the apparatus employed. The best Louisiana sugar is not inferior to any other plantation sugar of the world." [19]

*Average Yield of Sugar.* It was usually estimated that a sugar plantation ought to yield one hogshead of sugar to each slave employed, though on Mr. R.'s plantation visited by Olmsted in 1856, the average yield had been more than two hogsheads per slave.[20] In 1846 forty-eight planters in St. Mary's Parish had estimated for the Secretary-Treasurer of the United States that any plantation which might reasonably be expected to yield an average of one hunded hogsheads of sugar per annum, valued at $3650, at a cost of $1625, would leave a meager profit of $2000. On such a plantation there would probably be thirty slaves, but with not more than fifteen able-bodied field hands. Another estimate made at the same time for a plantation of 100 working slaves (total of 250 slaves, producing from 400 to 500 hogsheads of sugar, places the average yield at about $15,000 and the expense at $7560. Another estimate by the Agricultural Society indicates that one slave could cultivate five acres, producing 5000 pounds of sugar valued at 18 cents per gallon, or $297.50 total. The annual expense was estimated at $105. The capital investment on a large plantation of 1200 acres was about $150,000. Counting interest and expenses, it was claimed by the Society that a net yield of 10-3.7 per cent ought to be secured.[21]

*Net Returns.* This seems a rather high estimate compared with others. Valcour Aime's estate, sixty miles above New Orleans, contained 15,000 acres, 800 in cane, 300 in corn, 150 in slave crops. There were 215 slaves on the estate. The land was valued at $360,000, the buildings at $100,000, slaves at $170,000, live stock at $11,000 and machinery at $60,000, total $701,000. The returns on this place for 1852 were 1,300,000 pounds of sugar and 60,000 gallons of syrup—yielding a gross return of $119,000, or a net return of perhaps $100,000, or about 7 per cent.[22] All of these estimates are high, for there is no doubt that 4% was nearer the income on sugar plantations than the above percentages.

"I must confess that there seems to be room for grave doubt if

[19] Olmsted: "Seaboard Slave States," p. 670-672.
[20] *Ibid.*, p. 660.
[21] *Ibid.*, pp. 686-688.
[22] Cf. Phillips: "American Negro Slavery," pp. 242-243.

218    THE NEGRO FROM AFRICA TO AMERICA

the capital, labor, and especially the human life, which have been
and which continue to be spent in converting the swamps of
Louisiana into sugar plantations, and in defending them against
the annual assaults of the river, and the fever and the cholera,
could not have been better employed somewhere else.   It is claimed
as a great advantage of Slavery, as well as of Protection, that
what has been done for this purpose never would have been done
without it.   If it would not, the obvious reason is, that the wages,
or prospect of profit would not have been sufficient to induce free
men to undergo the inconveniences and the danger incident to
the enterprise.   There is now great wealth in Louisiana; but I
question if greater wealth would not have been obtained by the
same expenditure of human labor, and happiness, and life, in other
directions." [23]

*Basis of Small Returns—Idle Labor.*   The reasons for small
incomes on all staple products is not far to seek.   The first great
handicap of slavery lay in the fact that it prevented mobilization
of labor.   Contrary to general belief, it was not easy to transfer
labor from where it was overabundant to where it was really
needed.   Olmsted found that in the Red River cotton plantations
a great deal of cotton was allowed to waste because there was no
extra supply of labor to pick it.   Each planter must rely on his
own slaves to pick all they could raise, which was quite impossible.
"I much doubt," he adds, "if the harvest demand of the principal
cotton districts of Mississippi adds five per cent. to their field
hand force." [24]    Many a planter, as his lands deteriorated and
needed rest, found it impossible to employ all his force on his
plantation, and since there was a decided prejudice against hiring
out slaves they became a liability instead of an asset.   John B.
Lamar, who managed the plantation of Howell Cobb, his brother-
in-law, writes May 16, 1847:

"You have a large and effective force of hands, more effective
than any of the same number I know of in the State.   But they
cultivate a large proportion of poor land, and there is not
enough of even poor land in Baldwin for them to be properly
employed.   This will not, must not be, much longer!   Thirty good
hands are sufficient to cultivate all the rich spots on these old places
in Baldwin.   That number could be employed as profitably there
as anywhere else, as there is some land there that is rich.   Now
think of your having nearly 90 hands that work out, only one third
paying any profit, while all the rest have to be fed, clothed, &c.
just as expensively as if they were at work on good land.   At low
prices for cotton such a system will not much over pay expenses.

[23] Olmsted: "Seaboard Slave States," p. 664-665.
[24] Olmsted: "A Journey in the Back Country," p. 346.

At high prices it will pay just enough to make a body sigh over what they could do if the remaining two thirds were profitably employed, in place of being an expense." [25]

*Large Percentage of Slaves Unproductive.* The system was further wasteful of labor because such a large proportion of the slaves were really occupied at nothing productive. Charles Lyell reports that an Alabama planter said to him: "Half the population of the south is employed in seeing that the other half do their work, and they who do work, accomplish half what they might do under a better system." "We can not," said another, "raise capital enough for new cotton factories, because all our savings go to buy negroes, or, as has lately happened, to feed them, when the crop is deficient." [26]

In his report on the Belmeade Plantation, near Richmond, in 1854, Phillips estimated that of the 127 slaves on the plantation about one-half constituted the working force. "A gentleman, with whom I was conversing on the subject of the cost of slave labor, in answer to an inquiry—what proportion of all the stock of slaves of an old plantation might be reckoned upon to do full work?—answered, that he owned ninety-six negroes; of these, only thirty-five were field-hands, the rest being either too young or too old for hard work. He reckoned his whole force as only equal to twenty-one strong men, or *'prime* field-hands.'" [27]

*Labor Wastage on the Butler Estate.* Fannie Kemble described the "Big House" in which she lived on a Georgia plantation as a very crude six-roomed pine house, with the barest furnishing, and 'more devoid of conveniences than anything she had ever taken up her abode in,' [28] and yet in this meager residence she had a man cook, a dairy maid, two footmen or butlers. She also had a personal attendant who acted as her boatman when rowing and her guard when riding. In addition, there were probably several other Negroes employed or loafing around the house, whom she declares 'lounge in and out of the dirt floored kitchen like a pack of hungry hounds.' [29] The number of slaves used to keep the plantation afloat was out of all proportion. Mrs. Smedes tells us that "at Burleigh there were two carpenters in the carpenter shop, two blacksmiths in the blacksmith-shop, two millers in the mill, and usually five seamstresses in the house. In the laundry there were two of the strongest and most capable women on the plantation and they were perhaps the busiest of the corps of house servants. Boys were kept about ready to ride for the mail or to

[25] Phillips: "Plantation and Frontier," Vol. I, p. 178.
[26] *Ibid.*, Vol. II, p. 46.
[27] Olmsted: "Seaboard Slave States," p. 57.
[28] Phillips: "Plantation and Frontier," Vol. I, p. 208.
[29] Kemble: "Journal of a Residence on a Georgia Plantation," pp. 23, 25, 26, *passim.*

take notes around the neighborhood.  There was no lack of numbers to fill every place; the trouble was rather to find work for supernumeraries.  There were twenty-seven servants in the service of the house." [30]

A glance at this list shows its extravagance.  It is preposterous to suppose that two millers were needed to grind corn and wheat for one hundred people or less, even with the crude machinery of that day, and that two of the best women on the place needed to be occupied continually in doing the laundry of less than a dozen white people was even more foolish.

*Surplus of House Servants.*  "The number of servants usually found in a southern family, of any pretension, always amazed a northern lady," wrote Olmsted.  "In one that I visited, there were exactly three Negroes to each white, and this in a town, the Negroes being employed solely in the house." [31]  On the average plantation it was a fair estimate that only one-third of the slaves were actually in the fields.  Perhaps a second third were used as skilled laborers and as house servants, and the remaining third were sick, crippled, too old or too young to work.  The extravagance and wastefulness of the system was beyond the comprehension of those who traveled through the South as visitors.

*Slave Labor Inefficient.*  Slave labor was expensive because it was crude and careless and must therefore use crude and clumsy tools.  Olmsted estimated that the tools used on certain plantations in Virginia added at least ten per cent. to the amount of energy used in doing a piece of farm work.  He was assured that anything lighter would not "last out a day in a Virginia corn field." [32]  On visiting a Louisiana plantation he likewise "expressed surprise at the clumsiness of the hoes, particularly as the soil was light, and entirely free from stones.  'Such hoes as you use in the North would not last a Negro a day,' said the planter." [33]  In South Carolina Olmsted found gangs of slaves working with hoes, where plows would have done ten times as much, and much more efficient service with the same expenditure of time and labor.  "The fact is," he says, "in certain parts of South Carolina a plow is yet an almost unknown instrument of tillage." [34]

*No Improved Machinery.*  "The constant misapplication and waste of labor on many of the rice plantations, is inconceivably great.  Owing to the proverbial stupidity and dogged prejudice of the negro (but peculiar to him only as he is more carefully poisoned with ignorance than the laborer of other countries), it is exceedingly difficult to introduce new and improved methods

[30] Smedes: "A Southern Planter," pp. 82-83.
[31] Olmsted: "Seaboard Slave States," p. 195.
[32] *Ibid.*, p. 195.
[33] *Ibid.*, p. 666.
[34] *Ibid.*, p. 397.

of applying his labor.  He always strongly objects to all new-fashioned implements; and, if they are forced into his hands, will do his best to break them, or to make them only do such work as shall compare unfavorably with what he has been accustomed to do without them.  It is a common thing, I am told, to see a large gang of negroes, each carrying about four shovelsful of earth upon a board balanced on his head, walking slowly along on the embankment, so as to travel around two sides of a large field, perhaps for a mile, to fill a breach—a job which an equal number of Irishmen would accomplish, by laying planks across the field and running wheelbarrows upon them, in a tenth of the time.  The clumsy iron hoe is, almost everywhere, made to do the work of pick, spade, shovel, and plow.  I have seen it used to dig a grave. On many plantations, a plow has never been used; the land being entirely prepared for the crop by *chopping* with the hoe, as I have described.  There is reason, perhaps, for this, on the newly-cleared rice-ground, encumbered, as it is, with the close-standing stumps and strong roots and protuberances of the late cypress swamp; though, I should suppose, it would be more economical to grub these by hand, sufficiently to admit of the use of a strong plow.  On old plantations, where the stumps have been removed, the surface is like a garden-bed—the soil a dark, rich, mellow, and exceedingly fine loam, the proportion of sand varying very much in different districts; but always considerable, and sufficient, I must think, to prevent an injurious glazing from the plow, unless the land is very poorly drained.  Yet, even on these, the plow is not in general use." [35]

*A Slave's Daily Output.*  The daily output of a slave hand was amazingly small.  This was not only due to crude tools, but to the ignorance and clumsiness of the workers and also to the lack of incentive.  Colonel Langdon Carter in his diary August 16, 1771, writes:

"Col. Brockenbrough came here last night.  He says he never got above a bushel a day of wheat whipped out by any hand he had; and he declared that those who boast otherwise must measure chaff and all.  I have spent a day at it with my overseer, and it was as much as 8 hands could produce 8 bushels." [36]

Chambers, while visiting the South, observed this same disability and remarked: "Skilled labor infers education, and that is totally irreconcilable with slavery, by maintaining which, the South restricts itself to the rudest kind of unskilled operations." [37]

[35] Olmsted: "Seaboard Slave States," p. 481-482.
[36] Phillips: "Plantation and Frontier," Vol. II, p. 33.
[37] Chambers: "Slavery and Colour," p. 155.

"Mr. O————," an overseer, writes Fannie Kemble, "stated un-equivocally his opinion that free labor would be more profitable on the plantation than the work of slaves, which, being compulsory, was of the worst possible quality and the smallest possible quantity." [38]  Dr. Thomas Cooper, President of South Carolina College, said during the first quarter of the nineteenth century: "Slave labour is undoubtedly the dearest kind of labour; it is forced, and forced too from a class of human beings who have the least propensity to voluntary labor, even when it is to benefit themselves alone." [39]  "Slave labor in each individual case and for each small measure of time," wrote Edmund Ruffin, of Virginia, "is more slow and inefficient than the labor of a free man." [40]  Harrison, of Virginia, declared: "Slave labor is dearer than free, because of its lack of incentive." [41]  "Slavery merely serves to appropriate the wages of labor,—it distributes wealth but cannot create it," wrote Goodloe of North Carolina in 1846.[42]

*Slavery Discouraged Free Mechanics.*  Furthermore slave labor either drove out or discouraged the development of mechanical skill on the part of whites.  If a skilled trade was to be followed by white men, artificial means must be used to prevent slaves being employed in the same form of labor.  Charles Lyel in his journeys observed this at Columbus, Georgia:

"The water-power at the rapids has been recently applied to some newly-erected cotton mills, and already an anti-free-trade party is beginning to be formed.  The masters of these factories hope, by excluding colored men—or, in other words, slaves—from all participation in the business, to render it a genteel employment for white operatives; a measure which places in a strong light the inconsistencies entailed upon a community by slavery and the antagonism of races, for there are numbers of colored mechanics in all these southern states very expert at trades requiring much more skill and knowledge than the functions of ordinary work-people in factories.  Several New Englanders, indeed, who have come from the north to South Carolina and Georgia, complain to me that they can not push on their children here, as carpenters, cabinet makers, blacksmiths, and in other such crafts, because the planters bring up the most intelligent of their slaves to these occupations.  The landlord of an inn confessed to me, that, being a carrier, he felt himself obliged to have various kinds of work done by colored artisans, because they were the slaves of planters

[38] Kemble: "Journal of a Residence on a Georgia Plantation," p. 131.
[39] Quoted from Phillips: "American Negro Slavery," p. 348.
[40] *Ibid.*, p. 352.
[41] *Ibid.*, p. 349.
[42] *Idem.*

who employed him in his own line. 'They interfere, said he, 'with the fair competition of white mechanics, by whom I could have got the work better done.' " [43]

*Slavery Discouraged Manufacture.* "Slavery discourages arts and manufactures," [44] declared Colonel Mason before the Constitutional Convention of Virginia. "Wherefore then object to slavery?" said Thomas Marshall before the Virginia legislature of 1832. "Because it is ruinous to the whites, retards improvements, roots out an industrious population, banishes the yeomanry of the country, deprives the spinner, the weaver, the smith, the shoemaker, the carpenter, of employment and support." [45]

*Slavery Absorbed All Capital.* Slavery absorbed all free capital and thus made it impossible for the South to accumulate enough surplus wealth to enter largely into manufacturing. The result was that her own cotton must be sent north or to England and then manufactured into cloth and sold back to her with the added cost of transportation and profits for those who acted as the middle men. "Outside of the plantation buildings and moderate accumulation of buildings and stocks of goods in a few cities, the South knew but two forms of wealth, land and slaves." [46] Traveling through Virginia, Olmsted was amazed at the lack of industrial plants, for he observed plenty of water power, he saw the raw material about him, and he knew the great expense of transportation from the North. Of this importation he writes: "No man can form an adequate idea of the extent of this trade unless he travel through the southern states. Scarcely a broom, a clock, a boot, or shoe, or anything of the kind is used in the South that is not manufactured by northern industry; and yet all articles used can be readily manufactured here as well as there, and, if taken hold of by some enterprising men, would be found most profitable." [47]

*South Lacking in Manufactures.* The census reports of the four or five decades preceding the Civil War showed that the South had only a fifth to a tenth of her proportionate amount of manufacturing. A high flown speech delivered at the Southern Commercial Convention in New Orleans, 1855, ran as follows:

"It is time that we should look about us, and see in what relation we stand to the North. From the rattle with which the nurse tickles the ear of the child born in the South, to the shroud that

[43] Phillips: "Plantation and Frontier," Vol. II, p. 337.
[44] Helper: "The Impending Crisis," p. 209.
[45] *Ibid.,* p. 211.
[46] Harte: "Slavery and Abolition," p. 55.
[47] Olmsted: "Seaboard Slave States," p. 175.

covers the cold form of the dead, everything comes to us from the North. We rise from between sheets made in Northern looms, and pillows of Northern feathers, to wash in basins made in the North, dry our beards on Northern towels, and dress ourselves in garments woven in Northern looms; we eat from Northern plates and dishes; our rooms are swept with Northern brooms, our gardens dug with Northern spades, and our bread kneaded in trays or dishes of Northern wood, or tin; and the very wood which feeds our fires is cut with Northern axes, helved with hickory brought from Connecticut and New York." [48]

*Land and Slaves Absorbed all Money.* If a large planter made money in good years, he was almost sure to buy more land, which demanded more slave labor, and so his capital was all eaten up. The bank capital in the sixteen free states in 1855 was $230,000,-000, that in fifteen slave states was $102,000,000.[49] The capital employed in manufacturing for the same year was for the free states $430,000,000 and for the slave states $95,000,000. The corresponding value of products was for the free states $842,-586,000, and for the slave states $165,413,000.[50]

*Concentration of Land-Ownership.* Chambers observes of Alabama in 1857 that the wealthier planters were buying out their poorer neighbors, "extending their plantations and adding to their slave force. Of the 20,000,000 of dollars annually realized from the sales of cotton crop of Alabama, nearly all not expending in supporting the producers is reinvested in land and negroes." [51] Chambers adds that all efforts to establish in the South harbors, shipping and commerce were failures because of lack of capital.[52]

*Slave Investments.* It will readily be seen why there was no free capital when one realizes how much money was invested in slaves. The following figures were compiled by Hinton R. Helper, a North Carolinian in 1857. The value of personal property and real estate exclusive of slaves in the fifteen southern states was in 1850, $1,655,945,137, and the value of slaves in the same states was $1,280,145,600. In five of the states the slave values, estimated at $400 per slave, were in excess of all other real and personal property values. The comparative amounts for these states were: Alabama, slaves $137,137,600; other property $81,-066,732; Florida, slaves $15,724,000, other property $7,474,734; Mississippi, slaves $123,957,200, other property $105,000,000; North Carolina, slaves $115,419,200, other property $111,381,-

[48] Olmsted: "Seaboard Slave States," p. 544.
[49] Helper: "The Impending Crisis," p. 286.
[50] *Ibid.,* p. 284.
[51] Chambers: "Slavery and Colour," p. 9.
[52] *Ibid.,* p. 94.

272; South Carolina, slaves $153,994,600, other property $134,-264,094.[53] In Virginia the two amounts were nearly equal. In the North, therefore, a man who owned $100,000 would in all probability have twice as much free capital as the man who lived in a slave state, having an equal fortune.

*Slaves not Trained for Industry.* Nor were slaves, the only available labor, well suited to manufacturing work. We have seen before that crude tools were constantly used on the plantations because ignorance, carelessness, and lack of incentive inherent in the system seemed to indicate—at least so the masters thought— that better tools would be broken and destroyed so quickly as to render them uneconomic. If this was true of the farm tools, how much more true would it be of the complicated machinery of a cotton factory. However, certain manufacturers did try slave labor with varying success. Speaking of one such factory in the South DeBow's Industrial Resources gives the following account:

"The factory in question ($100,000 capital) employs 98 operatives, or 128 including children. They are all slaves; and a large proportion of them are owned by the company. The mill runs 5,000 spindles and 120 looms. The fabrics manufactured are heavy brown shirting and southern stripe, a coarse kind of colored goods for house servants. The superintendent is decidedly of the opinion that slave labor is cheaper for cotton manufacture than free white labor. The average cost per annum of those employed in this mill, he says, does not exceed $75. Slaves not sufficiently strong to work in the cotton fields can attend to the looms and spindles in the cotton mills; and most of the girls in this establishment would not be suited for plantation work. . . . At the best, the work in a cotton mill is consumptive of lungs as well as cotton. We have been through the mills of Lowell and other places in the north; the general appearance of the female operatives is neat and cleanly, but their prevailing complexion is an unhealthy pallor. Not many die at the mills, because they are young, and when they fall sick, they, if possible, return home. But the life of an operative in a cotton mill is a consumptive business at best.

"Mr. Graves is of the opinion that the blacks can better endure the labor of the cotton mills than the whites. The slaves in this factory, male and female, appear to be cheerful, well fed, and healthy. The mill has been worked by slave operatives (requiring only one white overseer) for two years past, and the result, we are informed, is in favor of slave operatives;

[53] Helper: "The Impending Crisis," p. 306.

Average cost of a white operative, at least............ $116.00
Average cost of a slave operative per annum........... 75.00

Difference .................................. $41.00
Or over thirty per cent. saved in the cost of labor alone." [54]

*Items in Cost of Slave Labor.* The real difficulty with this calculation which seems to indicate a saving in slave labor is three fold: First, most of the extant records indicate that $100 was the average or perhaps minimum paid for a slave's wages per year; an ablebodied man often received $200. Second, the slave had to be clothed in addition to being fed—an average of $21 per year per slave—and we take for granted that the $116 estimated for white labor did not include clothing, though perhaps it did include food; and third, when the slave was sick his time went on, while in the case of free labor at that time very few manufacturers made any provision for their maintenance.

Discussing the problem of slave labor in factories, an Englishman, J. S. Buckinham, wrote:

"There is no difficulty among them on account of color, the white girls working in the same room and at the same loom with the black girls; and boys of each color, as well as men and women, working together without apparent repugnance or objection. . . . The negroes here are found to be quite as easily taught to perform all the required duties of spinners and weavers as the whites, and are just as tractable when taught; but their labor is dearer than that of the whites, for whilst the free boys and girls employed receive about 7.00 dollars per month, out of which they feed themselves, the slaves are paid the same wages (which is handed over to their owners) and the mill-owner has to feed them all in addition; so that the free labor is cheaper to him than the slave; and the hope expressed by the proprietor to me was, that the progressive increase of white population by immigration, would enable him to employ wholly their free labor, which, to him would be more advantageous." [55]

*Southern Defense of Slave Labor.* If one reads a file of newspapers of the period preceding the Civil War, he will find many articles declaring that slave labor is profitable and that the South ought to manufacture its own cotton. However, most of the attempts were failures, partly perhaps because of unskilled management, and partly perhaps because of poor labor. In 1828 a

[54] DeBow: "Industrial Resources, etc., in the South and West," Vol. II, p. 127.
[55] Phillips: "Plantation and Frontier," Vol. II, p. 357.

Mr. Nightingale was manufacturing a coarse cotton cloth in Maûry County, Tennessee, using slave labor.[56]

Phillips cites from DeBow's Industrial Resources the case of the Saluda Factory near Columbia, South Carolina, where in 1848 Negroes were worked by a Mr. J. Graves as manager:

" 'They are easily trained to habits of industry and patient endurance," he (Mr. Graves) said, 'and by the concentration of all their faculties . . . their imitative faculties become cultivated to a very high degree, their muscles become trained and obedient to the will, so that whatever they see done they are quick in learning to do.' The company was impelled by Graves' enthusiasm to resort to slave labor exclusively, partly on hire from their owners and partly by purchase. At the height of this régime, in 1851, the slave operatives numbered 158. But whether from the incapacity of the negroes as mill hands or from the accumulation of debt through the purchase of slaves, the company was forced into liquidation at the close of the following year." [57]

An article in the Charleston *News*, July 1855, gives the impression that the use of slave labor was a handicap against which the South could not successfully battle:

"A large cotton factory has been in operation here about three years, but is now about being closed, and to-day will probably terminate its existence. It unpleasantly reminded us of a fate of a similar enterprise which so signally failed, after a brief career, in our own city, Why is it so? It would seem to be reasonable, at least that, surrounded with the raw material, unencumbered with the cost of transportation to Northern cities, Southern manufactories should not only compete, but successfully maintain a higher position than those so far removed from the cotton-growing region. But so it is, with few exceptions, our own Graniteville being among them." [58]

Whatever may have been the causes, industrial interests in the South lagged far behind that of the North right up to the time of the Civil War, though her water power and raw· material would seem to have given her the advantage.

*Slavery Depleted the Land.* Perhaps a more serious charge against slavery than any of the foregoing was the fact that it destroyed the land which was the very economic foundation of the civilization of which slavery was a part. The soil of the South

[56] *Ibid.*, p. 258.
[57] Phillips: "American Negro Slavery," p. 379.
[58] Quoted from Olmsted: "Seaboard Slave States," p. 543.

is light, but very fertile. If properly treated it will produce as copiously as any land in America. Furthermore the seasons are long and facilitate making more than one crop per year. However, if this light land is cultivated year after year in only one crop, it soon loses its power of production. It was just this one-crop system that the slave régime superinduced. In Virginia and parts of North Carolina it was tobacco alone; in South Carolina, Georgia, and Mississippi it was cotton alone; in Louisiana and certain sections of Mississippi it was sugar cane alone, and in parts of Georgia and South Carolina it was rice alone. In almost no section of the South was a farmer or planter self-sustaining. He put almost all his energy on one crop and imported from the North his manufactured products, and from the West his food and feed products. "The average importation of corn into Charleston," said DeBow, "is about 400,000 bushels, of which the railroad now brings one-half from the interior of the state. Importations of oats average 50,000 or 60,000 bushels. Average bales of hay 20,000 to 25,000. Imports sugar, average hogsheads, 8,000, tierces 200, barrels, 2,000, boxes 1,000; molasses, hogsheads, 5,000, (of late) barrels, 5,000; average coffee, bags 28,000; salt, sacks about 100,000, and 20,000 bushels." [59] Up to the time of the Civil War the South was not a self-sustaining region. Not only was hay, corn, wheat and oats imported, but great quantities of hams and bacon, which should have been raised in its own corn fields. By the raising of food crops the land could have been rested by rotation; by raising more animals to which the hay and corn could have been fed much of the fertilization could have been restored to the land; and furthermore, enormous sums of money paid out for freights could have been saved. The program of the individual planter was not to farm his land but to mine it. He dug out of it every ounce of producing power it possessed and then moved on to new lands. Lamar of Georgia, (1847) writing Howell Cobb, whose estate he managed, says:

*Lamar of Georgia on Soil Destruction.* "Lord, Lord, Howell, you and I have been too used to poor land to know what crops people are making in the rich lands of the new counties. I am just getting my eyes open to the golden view. On those good lands, when cotton is down to such a price as would starve us out, they can make money. I have moved 1/3d of my force to Sumpter. I shall move another 1/3d this fall or winter, leaving the remaining 1/3d to cultivate the best lands on my Bibb place. This year I shall do better than I ever have done, & next I shall do better than I ever expected to do. This year I shall cultivate very little poor land & next year I shall not waste labour on a

[59] DeBow: "Industrial Resources, Etc., in the South and West," Vol. I, p. 247.

foot of unprofitable soil. All will be of the 1st quality. When I work through I will try & help you onward to the promised land. But for 2 years after the present one, I shall be up to my chin in responsibility. I hate responsibility, but I have figured it out, that unless I take some as other prudent folks do I shall be like John Grier of Chack farm cultivating poor land all my life, which I am resolved not to do." [60]

*Negro Comments on Soil Destruction.* Of the devastation of Virginia lands Charles Ball, a Negro, writes rather fulsomely:

"The ground over which we had traveled since we crossed the Potomac, had generally been a strong reddish clay, with an admixture of sand, and was of the same quality with the soil of the counties of Chester, Montgomery and Bucks, in Pennsylvania. It had originally been highly fertile and productive, and had it been properly treated, would doubtlessly have continued to yield abundant and prolific crops; but the gentlemen who became the early proprietors of this fine region, supplied themselves with slaves from Africa, cleared large plantations of many thousands of acres—cultivated tobacco—and became suddenly wealthy; built spacious houses and numerous churches, such as this; but regardless of their true interest, they valued their lands less than their slaves; exhausted the kindly soil, by unremitting crops of tobacco, declined in their circumstances, and finally grew poor, upon the very fields, that had formerly made their possessors rich; abandoned one portion after another, as not worth planting any longer; and, pinched by necessity, at last sold their slaves to Georgian planters to procure a substistence; and when all was gone, took refuge in the wilds of Kentucky; again to act the same melancholy drama; leaving their native land to desolation and poverty." [61]

*Olmsted on Soil Destruction.* The same process was going on in Mississippi, as reported by Olmsted:

"I passed during the day four or five large plantations, the hill-sides gullied like icebergs, stables and negro quarters all abandoned, and given up to decay.

"The virgin soil is in its natural state as rich as possible. At first it is expected to bear a bale and a half of cotton to the acre, making eight or ten bales for each able field-hand. But from the cause described its productiveness rapidly decreases.

"Originally, much of the country was covered by a natural

growth of cane, and by various nutritious grasses.  A good northern farmer would deem it a crying shame and sin to attempt to
grow any crops upon such steep slopes, except grasses or shrubs
which do not require tillage.  The waste of soil which attends the
practice is much greater than it would be at the North, and, notwithstanding the unappeasable demand of the world for cotton, its
bad economy, considering the subject nationally, cannot be doubted.

"If these slopes were thrown into permanent terraces, with
turfed or stone-faced escarpments, the fertility of the soil might
be preserved, even with constant tillage.  In this way, the hills
would continue for ages to produce annual crops of greater value
than those which are at present obtained from them at such
destructive expense—from ten to twenty crops of cotton rendering
them absolute deserts.  But with negroes at $1000 a head and
fresh land in Texas at $1 an acre, nothing of this sort can be
thought of.  The time will probably come when the soil now
washing into the adjoining swamps will be brought back by our
descendants, perhaps on their heads, in pots and baskets, in the
manner Huc describes in China, which may be seen also in the
Rhenish vineyards, to be relaid on the sunny slopes, to grow the
luxurious cotton in." [62]

Surprising as it may seem, the greedy planter was never satisfied, but continued to move further and further West.  When
Olmsted crossed the Neches River and went westward through
Texas he continued to see plantations which had been left for
newer fields:

"Deserted plantations appeared again in greater numbers than
the occupied.  One farm, near which we stopped, was worked by
eight field hands.  The crop had been fifty bales; small, owing to
a dry season.  The corn had been exceedingly poor.  The hands,
we noticed, came in from the fields after eight o'clock.

"The deserted houses, B. said, were built before the date of
Texas Independence.  After Annexation the owners had moved
on to better lands in the West." [63]

*Kemble on Soil Destruction.*  Fannie Kemble from her Georgia
plantation bears testimony to the same sad fact:

"When Major ———, Mr. ———'s grandfather, first sent the
produce of this plantation where we now are to England, it was
of so fine a quality that it used to be quoted by itself in the
Liverpool cotton market, and was then worth half a guinea a

[62] Olmsted: "A Journey in the Back Country," p. 19-20.
[63] Olmsted: "Texas Journey," p. 82.

pound; it is now not worth a shilling a pound. This was told me by the gentleman in Liverpool who has been factor for this estate for thirty years. Such a decrease as this in the value of one's crop and the steady increase at the same time of a slave population, now numbering between 700 and 800 bodies to clothe and house, mouths to feed, while the land is being exhausted by the careless and wasteful nature of the agriculture itself, suggests a pretty serious prospect of declining prosperity; and, indeed, unless these Georgia cotton-planters can command more land, or lay abundant capital (which they have not, being almost all of them over head and ears in debt) upon that which has already spent its virgin vigor, it is a very obvious thing that they must all very soon be eaten up by their own property. The rice plantations are a great thing to fall back upon under these circumstances, and the rice crop is now quite as valuable, if not more so, than the cotton one on Mr. ———'s estates, once so famous and prosperous through the latter." [64]

*Plea for Diversified Crops.* The plea for diversification of crops can be found in all the reports of the old agricultural societies, and reading many of these reports sounds like listening to the speeches of the farmers' institutes in the South at the present day. The Wateree Agricultural Society in South Carolina in 1843 reported:

"For many years, while our chief marketable product, cotton, bore a high price, many of us were in the habit of raising that almost exclusively, and depending upon supplies of bread and meat from abroad, which the cotton crop had to pay for—as well for the animal power necessary on the plantation; a most pernicious practice, which has impoverished the State by millions, and been the ruin of many planters. It is believed that stern necessity has forced the planter to abandon this system measurably. It is unusual for any one in this neighborhood to purchase either meat or bread; and we are rapidly becoming raisers of our own animal power on the plantations.

"It is believed that we are as successful as any body of planters in the State, on the same character of lands, in the mode of our culture. Certainly we have pressed too far the old, and seemingly well established doctrine; to wear out the land by cropping without manure, and then open new lands. But this system is also giving way to the sober light of experience; which teaches, that one acre well manured and taken care of, will produce more in the average of years, than two acres even of fresh land, not manured." [65]

[64] Kemble: "Journal of a Residence on a Georgia Plantation," pp. 163-164.
[65] "Documentary History," Vol. 1, p. 290.

This wasteful process of mining the land for a few years in a one-crop system robbed the South of millions of acres of its richest land, and the economic resources of the South are to this good day still hampered by the profligacy of the slave régime.

*Slavery Degraded Free Labor.* Once more slavery degraded the free laborer and reduced the landless white class to that which was well described as "poor white trash." William Jay, in an open letter concerning the admission of California and Mexico as free or slave states, says:

"Whenever the great mass of the laboring population of a country are reduced to beasts of burden, and toil under the lash, bodily labor,' as Chancellor Harper expresses it, must be disreputable, from the mere influence of association. Hence it is that *white* laborers at the South are styled 'mean whites.' At the North, on the contrary, labor is regarded as the proper and commendable means of acquiring wealth; and our most influential men would in no degree suffer in public estimation, for holding the plough, or even repairing the highways. Hence no poor man is deterred from seeking a livelihood by honest labor from a dread of personal degradation. The different light in which labor is viewed at the North and the South is one cause of the depression of industry in the latter." [66]

Fannie Kemble, who was an English woman, and therefore, had no squeamishness about using her hands for useful work, describes the amazement of her slaves when they saw her rowing her own boat:

"Considering that they dig, delve, carry burdens, and perform many more athletic exercises than pulling a light oar, I was rather amused at this; but it was the singular fact of seeing a white woman stretch her sinews in any toilsome exercise which astounded them, accustomed as they are to see both men and women of the privileged skin eschew the slightest shadow of labor as a thing not only painful, but degrading." [67]

*Poor Whites of the South.* ". . . But the effect on the poorer whites of the country is terrible. I speak now of the scattered white population, who, too poor to possess land or slaves, and having no means of living in the towns, squat (most appropriately is it so termed) either on other men's land or government districts—always near swamp or pine barren—and claim masterdom over the place they invade till ejected by the rightful proprietors. These wretched creatures will not, for they are whites (and

[66] Jay: "Miscellaneous Writings on Slavery," p. 507.
[67] Kemble: "Journal of a Residence on a Georgia Plantation," p. 52.

labor belongs to blacks and slaves alone here), labor for their own subsistence. They are hardly protected from the weather by the rude shelters they frame for themselves in the midst of these dreary woods. Their food is chiefly supplied by shooting the wild-fowl and venison, and stealing from the cultivated patches of the plantations nearest at hand. Their clothes hang about them in filthy tatters, and the combined squalor and fierceness of their appearance is really frightful.

"This population is the direct growth of slavery. The planters are loud in their execrations of these miserable vagabonds; yet they do not see that so long as labor is considered the disgraceful portion of slaves, these free men will hold it nobler to starve or steal than till the earth, with none but the despised blacks for fellow-laborers." [68]

*Stigma of Work.* "The white man who works down here is worse than a nigger," said a Louisiana sugar planter to Mr. Douglass of the American Missionary Society, and that sums up a modern attitude toward labor inherited from the slave régime and which, because it has not yet been completely outlived, has been one of our greatest economic handicaps, and has kept the laboring man from coming into his own. It was this fact of the degradation of labor that kept white immigrants from coming to the South, and still continues to keep that element from entering into competition with the Negro of the South. If our study of slavery teaches us anything, it surely must teach us that the labor of one man cannot be considered as degrading and menial without dragging the same labor of all men into the common mire.

*Walker's Indictment of Slavery.* Robert J. Walker, who served as Senator from Mississippi from 1836 to 1845, was Secretary of the Treasury during James K. Polk's administration, and later Commissioner to China, compiled a volume of statistics on "Slavery and Finance," [69] which was published during the progress of the Civil War, and which proved to his satisfaction at least that slavery was economically a failure. First, he compares Maryland with Massachusetts, the one a slave state, the other a free state. In 1790 Maryland contained one-twelfth, or 8½ per cent., of the population of the United States, and Massachusetts contained 10 per cent. But in 1860 Maryland contained only 2 per cent. of the total population while Massachusetts contained 4 per cent. [70] Maryland had 11,124 square miles, while Massachusetts contained only 7,800, which would seem to be an element in favor of Maryland. Maryland had a shore line including navigable rivers to head of tide water of

[68] Kemble: "Journal of a Residence on a Georgia Plantation," p. 76.
[69] Walker: "Slavery and Finance," published by William Ridgway, London, 1863.
[70] Walker: "Slavery and Finance," Letter III, p. 5 ff.

1336 miles, while Massachusetts had only 764. He thinks Maryland had the greater advantage in manufacturing due to milder climate, cheaper food, more coast line, more water power, and more fertile soil for producing raw material. But the products from Massachusetts, 1860, were $235 per capita and those of Maryland were $96 per capita.[71] Bank capital in Massachusetts in 1860 was $64,519,200; that of Maryland $12,568,962.[72] He concludes his argument as to the advantages of free labor over slavery as seen in the comparison of Maryland and Massachusetts, with the following rather oratorical statement:

"The census, then, is an evangel against slavery, and its tables are revelations proclaiming laws as divine as those written by the finger of God at Mount Sinai on the tables of stone.

*Census Returns Discredit Slavery.* "For seventy years we have had these census tables, anonuncing these great truths more and more clearly at each decade. They are the records of the nation's movement and condition, the decennial monuments marking her steps in the path of empire, the oracles of her destiny. They are prophecies, for each decade fulfils the predictions of its predecessor. They announce laws, not made by man, but the irrevocable ordinances of the Almighty. We cannot, with impunity, refuse to obey these laws. For every violation, they enforce their own penalties. From these there is no escape in the present or the past, nor for the future, except in conformity to their demands. These laws condemn slavery; and the punishment for disobedience is recorded in the result of every census, and finally culminated in the rebellion. Slavery and freedom are antagonistic and discordant elements; the conflict between them is upon us; it admits of no neutrality or compromise, and one or the other system must perish." [73]

*Comparison of Slave and Free States.* Walker then proceeds to compare New York with Virginia, Illinois with Missouri, Pennsylvania with Virginia, Rhode Island with Delaware, and lastly Kentucky with Ohio. In every case the comparison seems most disparaging to the slave-holding state, though seemingly there were certain natural advantages on the part of the slave state. Helper, from whom we have quoted earlier, made similar comparisons in his "Impending Crisis." Both Walker and Helper were southern men,—the one from Mississippi and the other from North Carolina, and the facts seem to prove that slavery was not

[71] Walker: "Slavery and Finance," Letter III, p. 15.
[72] *Ibid.*, p. 16.
[73] Walker: "Slavery and Finance," "American Finances and Resources, Letter No. III," pp. 19-20.

an economic success. In the case of a few great slave-holding families it seemed to bring great wealth and luxury, but society at large was forced to pay the bills in the form of destroyed soil, degraded labor, impoverished industrial life and retarded institutions. With the gradual using up of all the new land there must soon have come a time—even without the war—when the good sense of the great majority would have asserted itself and thrown off the yoke of bondage which made the white South more of slaves than the black slaves themselves.

*Slave Owners See Its Weakness.* Even many of the slave-owning families recognized their slaves as expensive luxuries, and would gladly have been rid of them but for the sentiment attached to their own people, and a bewilderment as to how to accomplish manumission. Fithian quotes Mrs. Robert Carter of Virginia as saying, 1774, that "if in Mr. Carter's or in any other gentleman's estate all the negroes should be sold and the money put to interest in safe hands, and let the lands which the Negroes now cultivate lie wholly uncultivated, the bare interest of the price of the Negroes would be a much greater yearly income than what is now received from their working the lands, making no allowance at all for the trouble and risk of the masters as to crops and Negroes." [74] Phillips quotes John Randolph as saying in 1814, "it is notorious that the profits of slave labor have been for a long time on the decrease, and that on a fair average it scarcely reimburses the expense of the slave." [75] If this was true when slaves were comparatively cheap, how much more true it must have been during the forties and fifties of the last century when slaves had more than doubled in price and land had become more scarce and hence very high.

It can hardly be doubted that many of the old and influential families continued to hold their slaves, partly because, as we have said, there was a sentiment against a gentleman selling a slave out of the family. Furthermore, slaves were held as a mark of dignity and prestige. Social standing, political prestige and position of leadership in the old southern régime were determined quite largely by the amount of land a man owned and the number of slaves he maintained upon it. Slowly but surely, as we have seen, the system was breaking under the weight of its own inefficiency.

[74] Fithian: "Journal and Letters," p. 144.
[75] Phillips: "American Negro Slavery," p. 391.

## Chapter X

## PRESENT ECONOMIC CONDITIONS

The basic factor in civilization is economic efficiency. No people can make progress in moral, social, and cultural life that does not have a sound economic system. In order to have time for leisure and culture, there must be a scheme of production and distribution which will meet the physical needs of a people and leave some surplus, so that time may be taken to devote to these other phases of life. Where dire poverty reigns, culture will be at low ebb, and although wealth will not of necessity bring culture and civilization, it at least gives opportunity for acquiring both. In the study of the progress of any people the economic factor is therefore basic.

*African Negro without Economic Training.* As seen in a former chapter, the Negro in Africa, at least that portion of them from which most of our slaves were recruited, had not learned much of economic efficiency. Nature was bountiful, the climate was mild or even torrid, life was extremely simple. Food could be had for the gathering, and fishing and hunting were somewhat of a pleasure. Clothing was hardly needed, and houses were decidedly crude. When the Negro came to America he did not bring with him a well established habit of labor. Dr. Booker T. Washington has well pointed out that slavery did three fundamental things for the slave.[1] First, it taught him to wear clothes, for both the climate into which he came demanded clothes for protection, and the social ideals of the white people demanded them for the sake of decency. Second, slavery taught the Negro to live in a house. He had lived in a thatched hut in Africa, but it could hardly be called a house. And third, slavery taught him to work. "Notwithstanding the fact that in most cases, the element of compulsion entered into the labor of the slave, and the main object sought was the enrichment of the owner, the American Negro had, under the régime of slavery, his first lesson in anything like continuous, progressive, systematic labor."[2] Not only did he learn to work, but since each plantation must, because of isolation, furnish practically every commodity of life, there was

[1] Washington: "The Negro in the South," Ch. I, *passim.*
[2] *Ibid.*, p. 21.

a demand for skilled labor, so that each plantation became a training school for skilled workmen. "I do not overstate the matter,"
says Washington, "When I say that I am quite sure that in one
county in the South during the days of slavery, there were more
colored youths being taught trades than there are members of
my race now being taught trades in any of the larger cities of the
North." [3]

*Slavery as a School for Mechanics.* One who got his training
under an ex-slave mechanic writes most enthusiastically about the
skill of the Negro slaves:

"One only needs to go down South and examine hundreds of
old Southern mansions, and splendid old church edifices, still
intact, to be convinced of the fact of the cleverness of the Negro
artisan, who constructed nine-tenths of them, and many of them
still provoke the admiration of all who see them, and are not to
be despised by the men of our day. . . .

"The Negro machinists were also becoming numerous before
the downfall of slavery. The slave owners were generally the
owners of all the factories, machine shops, flour-mills, saw-mills,
gin houses and threshing machines. They owned all the railroads
and the shops connected with them. In all of these the white
laborer and mechanic had been supplanted almost entirely by the
slave mechanics at the time of the breaking out of the civil war.
Many of the railroads in the South had their entire train crews,
except the conductors, made up of the slaves—including engineers
and firemen. The 'Georgia Central' had inaugurated just such a
movement, and had many Negro engineers on its locomotives and
Negro machinists in its shops. So it will be seen at once that
the liberation of the slaves was also the salvation of the poor
white man of the South. It saved him from being completely
ousted, as a laborer and a mechanic, by the masters, to make place
for the slaves whom they were having trained for those positions.
Yet, strange as it may seem to us now, the great mass of poor
white men in the South who were directly and indirectly affected
by the slave mechanic—being literally forced out of the business,
took up arms and fought against the abolition of slavery! . . .

"Much has been said of the new Negro for the new century,
but with all his training he will have to take a long stride in
mechanical skill before he reaches the point of practical efficiency
where the old Negro of the old century left off." [4]

*Relics of Slave Workmanship.* The writer has crossed many
of the old bridges in the South built by Negro artisans, put to-

[3] Washington: "The Negro in the South," p. 24.
[4] The Negro Artisan: "Atlanta University Studies," pp. 16, 17, 18.

gether mostly with pegs, which are still almost perfectly preserved. He has personally inspected not a few old mills propelled by overshot water wheels, and the workmanship, while somewhat crude, was decidedly substantial and efficient. The result of all this training was that at the opening of the Civil War the Negroes held well nigh the monopoly of all forms of mechanical and skilled labor in the South.

*Slaves Learned to Hate Work.* "But it must be remembered that slavery had another side in relation to the economic training of the Negro. While it did train him to work, it nevertheless taught him to connect all labor with the condition of slavery. It was inevitable that he should feel that labor was degrading, since he saw the slave owners keeping free from manual toil. The outcome was natural—that when he attained freedom he turned his back on all manual labor. The race has not yet been able to overcome this false conception, and it is not to be required that it should have done so in two generations. Those of us who are disposed to condemn the Negro in a wholesale manner, for his laziness and unwillingness to work systematically, need to remember the time in our own childhood when labor was a nightmare, though we would readily have done the same things had they been called play. It was the word 'work' that annoyed and bullied us; one needs only to know boys today to see the dread inspired by that word." [5]

*Present Aversion to Work.* Nor has the white South yet overcome its aversion to manual labor which arose in slave days. Not a few white people have a shrinking from and dread of toil lest it degrade them to the station of a slave. Some years ago at Blue Ridge, North Carolina, a college girl who was attending a conference there came to me in distress and said she was short of money and needed work to pay for her entertainment. We did not need another worker, but to help her we opened the way for her to join the other college girls who were serving in the dining hall. She prepared her table for the first meal, but when the guests were seated there was no waitress. She had disappeared. When found her only explanation was that she simply could not do it—that is, she could not do what had once been the office of slaves—and in her own home had always been the task of Negro maids. There is still more of this false attitude toward work among the white people than most of us are willing to admit. Perhaps no one will ever be able to know how much this feeling has retarded the economic progress of the South.

*Ex-Slaves as Skilled Workers.* After the Civil War ex-slaves were for many years the main sources of skilled labor. The southern white man had turned to slaves to have his shoes made, his

[5] The author's: "Negro Life in the South," p. 34.

suits tailored, and his houses built, and after freedom came he continued to turn to these Negro artisans. Dr. Booker T. Washington, writing in 1907, said if one would go into colored Methodist or Baptist churches and ask their pastors to point out to him the most reliable, progressive and leading colored man in the community, the man who is most given to putting his religious teachings into practice in his daily life, in a majority of cases one will have pointed out to him a Negro who learned a trade or got some special economic training during the days of slavery." [6]

*Hiring Out of Mechanics.* Before the Civil War it was often more profitable to the master to hire out his skilled mechanic slave than to keep him on the plantation—hence many of these skilled workers were already concentrated in the towns. After the war this concentration was greatly accelerated. Most of these artisans entered the towns and undertook to set up business for themselves. This, however, was a more difficult undertaking. Formerly they had been taught to work under the general direction of the white contractor, and they had had practically no training in making or carrying out contracts. They were, therefore, greatly handicapped under the new conditions. Then again, after the war, there arose rapidly a group of white mechanics. Slavery had tended to keep all white men out of the trades, but economic necessity forced them in when other resources were swept away by the war.

*The Ex-Slave and Politics.* Politics became another disturbing factor. Scheming white men stirred up the Negro to such a degree that he spent more time on politics than his economic well being would permit, and at the same time aroused a great deal of antagonism and race suspicion. This made it more difficult for him to compete with the rising class of white artisans, since he no longer had an influential white man to guarantee his work, or to protect him in any litigations that might arise. It was, therefore, only normal that the Negro should have lost much of his prestige in the trades, due to no fault of his own, nor to relative inefficiency, but due to the severe handicap under which he labored. It has often been said that he lost his standing in the skilled labor market because he was inefficient, and undoubtedly this is partly true, but it is not the whole truth. Had he been far more efficient than the white laborers the political and social conditions would have put him under a great handicap. But the greatest handicap lay in his lack of general education. He had been a good worker by rule of thumb, when the economic organization was simple and skill required was largely practical. But as industry began to expand and there arose a demand for exact and scientific workmanship, the Negro worker had not sufficient knowledge of

* Washington: "The Negro in the South," p. 29-30.

mathematics and the sciences to keep abreast with the growing difficulties of his trade. This education he had not been allowed to secure during slavery and the poverty and prejudice of the South long delayed his securing it after slavery was gone.

*Ex-Slave Loses Leadership.* Because of these various forces working against him, the Negro did lose his leadership in skilled trades. Thus in Louisiana the census of 1850 gives 2809 free Negro males over fifteen years of age who were employed in fifty-seven different occupational pursuits, most of which were semi-skilled or semi-professional, but in 1890 the total number of Negro males in Louisiana engaged in semi-skilled or semi-professional work was only 14,500. The little group of free Negroes in 1850 held more than one-fifth as many semi-skilled positions as the whole Negro population in 1890. The occupational statistics by states is not available for 1920, but it is certain that the skilled labor class is not as large as it should be, although it is growing. In 1890 30 per cent. of Negro males gainfully employed were in pursuits other than farming, while in 1910 the percentage was 37.1[7] The census report of 1910 showed ninety-four different classifications of laborers in the steam railway business, and it is most interesting to note that in ninety of these classifications Negroes appear as workers.[8] It seems evident that the Negro is now slowly gaining back some of the skilled leadership which he lost following the Civil War, but it is fairly certain he will never again bulk so large in the skilled labor field as he did in the pre-war period.

*Negroes Gainfully Employed.* Of the Negro population ten years of age and over in 1910, 71 per cent. or 5,792,535 were gainfully employed. This is a decided increase over the two previous census returns, that for 1890 being for males 79.4 per cent., for females 36.2 per cent. The figures for 1900 were for males 84.1 per cent., for females 40.7 per cent. For 1910 the figures were for males 87.4 per cent., for females 54.7 per cent. The number of males engaged in agricultural pursuits during these decades remained practically constant at fifty per cent. (1890, 49.2; 1900, 49.1; 1910, 50.3), while the percentage of females engaged in agricultural pursuits rose from 15.9 to 26.6, or almost double. This was perhaps in part due to the introduction of more truck farming and poultry farming, and other similar types of small or home farms. Nearly one million women work on such farms in America, of which number the Negro women furnish a disproportionate per cent.

*Diversification of Occupation.* The diversification of occupations of Negroes can well be seen by following the tabulation of

[7] U. S. Census—Negro Population, 1790-1915, p. 504.
[8] *Ibid.,* p. 502.

workers in the census digest.[9]   Thus we find 40,584 Negro males
and 39 females engaged in the mining and quarrying industry,
594 males and 2 females engaged in manufacturing agricultural
implements, 559 males and 10 females in automobile factories,
3174 males and 274 females in bakeries, 73 males and 14 females
engaged in paper factories, 18,124 males and 96 females in blast
furnaces, 74 males and 21 females in paper box factories, 1545
males and 65 females in wooden box factories, 365 males and
5 females in brass mills, 18,703 males and 111 females in brick
and tile factories, 242,387 males and 45,754 females in building
trades, and large numbers in butter and cheese factories, button
factories, candy factories, car and railroad shops, carpet mills,
coal and coke works, chemical factories, cigar and tobacco factories (14,717 and 10,746 respectively), clock and watch factories,
clothing factories, cooper factories, corset factories, cotton mills
(6,333 men and 883 women), distilleries, electric plants, electrical
supply factories, fertilizer factories, flour and grain mills, food
factories, canning factories, furniture factories (4,090 men, 164
women), gas works, glass factories, glove factories, gold and
silver factories, harness factories, hat factories, iron and steel
factories, iron foundries (6,140 men and 32 women), knitting
mills, lace and embroidery factories, laundries (3,027 men, 12,332
women), lead factories, leather belt factories, lime and cement
works, linen mills, marble yards, metal industries, oil refineries,
paint factories, pulp mills, potteries, powder mills, printing establishments (3,543 men and 515 women, of whom 169 men and 4
women are proprietors), rope factories, rubber factories, together
with twenty-one other manufacturing industries in each of which
Negroes are employed to the total number of 692,506 persons.
Added to this there were 255,969 in transportation trades, 22,382
in public service.

   *Wide Variety of Negro Occupations.*   A glance down the
columns of classification will convince any person that Negroes
have a very great diversity of occupations.   Many of these workers are doing manual labor, but in every case many are in the
skilled and semi-skilled departments of the plants.   There were
234,063 Negro males and 840,480 Negro females in domestic
service.   A little more than one million out of the five million
Negroes ten years old and over who are gainfully employed are
thus in personal or domestic service.   In this connection it is very
interesting to note the proportion of persons gainfully employed
in various sections of the country who were in personal or domestic service.   In most northern and western cities the number
of workers in domestic service was from five to twelve per cent of
all women, while in the South the corresponding number runs

[9] U. S. Census—Negro Population 1790-1915, p. 529 f.

from twelve to twenty-eight per cent. Only a few southern cities fall below twelve per cent., Richmond 8.8 per cent., Winston-Salem 8.5 per cent. being outstanding exceptions. Chattanooga employs 19.2 per cent. of its wage-earning population in personal or domestic service, Augusta, Georgia, 22.8 per cent., Montgomery 28.8 per cent., Macon 23.9 per cent., Jacksonville, Florida 24.6 per cent., Asheville, North Carolina, 26 per cent.[10] This fact may have its bearing on the relative increase of wealth of the two sections in North and South.

*Dr. Haynes on Negro Occupations.* Commenting on the occupation of Negroes in General and those of New York City in particular, Dr. Haynes says: "While most of the wage earners have engaged in domestic and personal service occupations, figures that are available warrant the inference that the Negro is slowly but surely overcoming the handicaps of inefficiency and race prejudice and is widening the scope of employment year by year." [11] The fact that the Greeks have run the Negro out of the shoe polishing business, and that South Europeans have displaced him as a waiter in most big hotels North, does not mean that he has lost out economically.

*Chicago Race Commission.* The Chicago Race Commission investigated 69 manufacturing plants in which whites and Negroes were employed and found 12,854 Negro workers out of a total of 79,354, or 16 per cent., thus showing a large distribution of occupation, but of these workers less than 10 per cent. were doing skilled labor.[12]

"The number of workers in certain occupations reported by a few establishments is suggestive of the fields recently opened to Negroes in Chicago. In 1910 there were only thirty-one Negro molders in Chicago, while in 1920 there were 304 reported by ten establishments. In 1910 there were but twenty-eight factory sewers or machine operators, while in 1920 there were 382 in twelve factories. In 1910 there were 934 Negroes employed in clerical occupations as compared with 1,400 in two concerns in 1920. In 1910 there were but 287 Negro laundry operatives in Chicago, while there were 764 reported by twenty laundries in 1920." [13]

*Negro Efficiency.* Is the Negro skilled worker efficient? Of the 139 employers having five or more Negroes among their workmen in Chicago, and answering this question asked by the Chicago Race Commission, 118 said they were and 19 said they were not.[14] Most employers complained that the unskilled labor

[10] Advance Occupational Statistics, U. S. Census of 1920.
[11] Haynes: "The Negro at Work in New York City," p. 145.
[12] "The Negro in Chicago," pp. 362-364.
[13] *Ibid.,* p. 365.
[14] *Ibid.,* p. 373.

fresh from the South would not work regularly,[15] but the 118 plants whose managers claimed they were satisfactory had 12,373 workers, the vast majority of whom were unskilled and many of whom were fresh from the South.[16]

"Comparing the efficiency of the Negro worker and the white worker, seventy-one employers interviewed (thirty-four manufacturing and thirty-seven non-manufacturing establishments) considered the Negro equally efficient, and twenty-two employers (thirteen manufacturing and nine non-manufacturing) considered the Negro less efficient. (Representatives of a number of the 101 establishments visited did not. feel able to make a comparison between the Negro and white workers.)

"The seventy-one establishments which reported Negro labor as equally efficient as white labor included all of the large employers of Negro labor, with very few exceptions. Ability shown by Negro workers in widely dissimilar occupations and industries was commented upon." [17]

On the question of whether Negroes needed more supervision than whites, out of 92 employers 63 felt they did not and 28 felt they did.[18]

*Skilled Labor in Nashville, Tenn.* Mr. Hardwick's investigations of skilled Negro labor in Nashville, Tennessee, indicated that 20% of the bricklayers of the city were colored, and 60% of the plasterers were colored. In each case the Negro workers were sufficiently numerous and sufficiently skilled to force the unions to admit them in order to keep them from interfering with the union programs. In the Stone Masons' Union the Negroes work in hard stone and the whites in soft stone,—though white masons admitted many Negro masons were fully qualified to work soft stone.[19]

*War-Time Studies of Skilled Labor.* In a war-time investigation made by the Department of Negro Economics, under the United States Department of Labor, skilled workers, white and colored, were studied in ten manufacturing plants, semi-skilled workers in twenty-five plants, and unskilled workers in fifty-two plants. Each plant was called a unit of comparison. Among skilled workers three units showed longer hours by Negroes and larger pay; three showed lower hours of labor per week, and five showed lower pay. Among semi-skilled workers eight units showed longer hours and larger pay for Negroes, 5 units showed lower number of hours of work and lower average pay for Ne-

[15] "The Negro in Chicago," p. 372.
[16] *Ibid.*, p. 374.
[17] *Ibid.*, p. 374.
[18] *Ibid.*, p. 376.
[19] Economic Conditions Among Negroes—Nashville—Master's Thesis—Southern College of Y. M. C. A., 1921.

groes, and 12 units showed the same average number of hours and the same average pay.

"Taking the 52 units of comparison of unskilled occupations as a whole, Negro workers showed a higher average number of hours worked per week than white workers in 23 units, nearly one-half of the total and a higher average earnings per week in 18 units, a little more than one-third of the total number. They showed a lower average number of hours worked per week than white workers in 16 units, or a little less than one-third of the total number, and a lower average earnings per hour in 22 units or about two-fifths of the total number. Negro workers showed the same average number of hours worked per week as white workers in 13 units, or about one-fourth of the total number, and the same average earnings per week as white workers in 12 units of unskilled occupations, or less than one-fourth the total number." [20]

*Negro Not Deficient.* These facts seem to indicate that Negro workers are not greatly deficient in capacity and practice when compared with the white men by whom they work.[21] A Negro named A. J. Webster, a coal miner at Buxton, Iowa, recently broke the record for fourteen days' earnings, on the basis of coal mined. He is said to have made $214.06 in the two weeks. Alonzo Horshow, of Wilkes-Barre, Pennsylvania, it is claimed, was in 1918 the champion bricklayer of the country, being able on the testimony of his company to lay 60,000 brick in one day. A Negro crew of pile drivers at Hog Island Ship Construction Yard (Pennsylvania) broke the record for driving piles with 220 sixty foot piles driven in 9 hours and 5 minutes. Charles Knight and a crew of seven Negroes at the Bethlehem Ship Building Company, Sparrow Point, Maryland, drove 4,875 rivets in a nine hour day in 1918, thus breaking the previous world record of 4,442 made by a Scotch crew. For this feat Knight received the $125 prize offered by the *London Daily Mail* for the highest record.[22]

While the Negro has comparatively fewer skilled and semi-skilled workers than the whites, those Negroes who do attain seem to be able to hold their own rather well in competition with white labor.

*Pay of Skilled Workmen.* Do skilled Negro laborers receive the same pay as skilled white workers? The investigation of the Department of Negro Economics during the war seemed to indicate they did. The following table throws light on the question:

[20] Haynes: "The Negro at Work During the World War and During Reconstruction," p. 44.
[21] *Ibid.*, pp. 42-44, *passim.*
[22] "Negro Year Book, 1918-19," p. 14.

## SLAUGHTERING AND MEAT PACKING [23]

| Occupation | Average earnings per hour | |
| --- | --- | --- |
| | White | Negro |
| Backers .......................... | $ .7249 | $ .7264 |
| Bronze trimmers ................. | .4450 | .4450 |
| Caul pullers ..................... | .4949 | .4945 |
| Droppers (hoist) ................ | .4301 | .4302 |
| Fell beaters ..................... | .4450 | .4450 |
| Gutters .......................... | .5000 | .5004 |
| Headers .......................... | .5697 | .5696 |
| Knockers ......................... | .4750 | .4650 |
| Laborers ......................... | .4001 | .4000 |
| Leg breakers ..................... | .4751 | .4827 |
| Pritchers-up ..................... | .4300 | .4301 |
| Rumpers .......................... | .6654 | .5148 |
| Rump sawyers ..................... | .5000 | .5000 |
| Splitters ........................ | .7951 | .7951 |
| Switchers-on rail ................ | .4301 | .4485 |
| Truckers ......................... | .4301 | .4300 |
|   Beef casings: | | |
|     Gut runners .............. | .5197 | .5200 |
|     Laborers ................. | .4000 | .3999 |
|     Machinemen ............... | .4300 | .4301 |
|     Strippers ................ | .4551 | .4551 |
|   Dry salt: | | |
|     Dippers .................. | .4301 | .4294 |
|     Graders .................. | .4298 | .4292 |
|     Nailers .................. | .4151 | .4300 |
|     Packers .................. | .4349 | .4297 |
|     Pilers ................... | .4296 | .4239 |
|     Rubbers .................. | .4150 | .4145 |
|     Truckers ................. | .4000 | .4002 |
|   Hog heads: | | |
|     Laborers ................. | .3998 | .4000 |
|     Skin heads ............... | .4452 | .4452 |
|   Hog killing | | |
|     Laborers ................. | .4003 | .4000 |
|     Shave sides .............. | .4547 | .4547 |
|     Snatchers ................ | .4597 | .4610 |
|   Sausage-making: | | |
|     Laborers ................. | .4000 | .3999 |
|   Beef killing: | | |
|     Backers .................. | .7909 | .7909 |

[23] Haynes: "The Negro at Work During the World War," pp. 45-47.

| Occupation | Average earnings per hour White | Negro |
|---|---|---|
| Fell beaters | .4800 | .4800 |
| Fell cutters | .5619 | .5618 |
| Foot skinners | .4857 | .4809 |
| Gullet raisers | .4587 | .4739 |
| Gutters | .5455 | .5426 |
| Headers | .6181 | .6193 |
| Knockers | .5073 | .5073 |
| Laborers | .4347 | .4349 |
| Leg breakers | .5194 | .5197 |
| Rump sawyers | 5444 | .5454 |
| Splitters | .8673 | .8673 |
| Repair department: | | |
| Steamfitters | .5735 | .5752 |
| Canning department (bacon): | | |
| Butchers | .4487 | .4540 |
| Laborers | .4317 | .4306 |
| Nailers | .4414 | .4427 |
| Beef coolers: | | |
| Knifemen | .4218 | .4294 |
| Laborers | .3988 | .3987 |
| Pieceworkers | .7830 | .6436 |

## AUTOMOBILES

| Occupation | Average earnings per hour White | Negro |
|---|---|---|
| Boiler room | $ .4514 | $ .4514 |
| Connecting rod department | .6000 | .4560 |
| Enamel rubbers | .7150 | .4950 |
| Lathe department | .6000 | .6000 |
| Machine shop | .6000 | .6000 |
| Motor assembling | .7750 | .7750 |
| Piston department | .6000 | .6000 |
| Sand-blast room | .6600 | .6600 |
| Stock tracers | .4158 | .4158 |
| Core makers | .6100 | .6100 |
| do | .5200 | .5200 |
| Heaters | .4800 | .4800 |
| Inside laborers | .4400 | .4400 |
| Janitors | .4200 | .4200 |
| Stock handlers | .4800 | .4800 |
| Truck drivers | .4800 | .4800 |

| Occupation | *Average earnings per hour* | |
| --- | --- | --- |
| | *White* | *Negro* |
| Truckers ........................ | $ .4200 | $ .4200 |
| Chippers ........................ | .4800 | .4800 |
| Machine molders ................ | .6000 | .6000 |
| Grinders ........................ | .4800 | .4800 |
| Mold rammers ................... | .6000 | .6000 |
| Molders ........................ | .8000 | .8000 |
| Janitors ........................ | .4500 | .4500 |
| Laborers ........................ | .4500 | .4500 |
| Sweepers ........................ | .4500 | .4500 |
| Truckers ........................ | .4500 | .4500 |

## COKE OVENS

| Occupation | *Average earnings per hour* | |
| --- | --- | --- |
| | *White* | *Negro* |
| Battery-door hoisters ............. | $ .4908 | $ .4887 |
| Battery-house laborers ........... | .4777 | .4717 |
| Battery laborers ................. | .4582 | .4668 |
| By-product labor ................ | .4708 | .4729 |
| Coal unloaders .................. | .4922 | .4614 |
| Coke loaders .................... | .4812 | .5106 |
| Crane engineers ................. | .6173 | .5984 |
| Door cleaners ................... | .4638 | .4736 |
| Dryermen ....................... | .4813 | .4764 |
| Firemen ........................ | .4861 | .4862 |
| Foremen ........................ | .6319 | .6216 |
| Gas tenders ..................... | .5066 | .5053 |
| Laborers ........................ | .5110 | .5530 |
| Larrymen ....................... | .4900 | .4902 |
| Lidsmen ........................ | .4814 | .4806 |
| Luttermen ...................... | .4825 | .4816 |
| Patchers ........................ | .4717 | .4725 |
| Pencilmen ...................... | .4656 | .4708 |
| Pushers ........................ | .4908 | .4905 |
| Salt wheelers ................... | .4748 | .5387 |
| Standpipe men .................. | .4807 | .4835 |
| Sulphate laborers ............... | .4736 | .4710 |
| Water tenders .................. | .5387 | .5396 |

## IRON AND STEEL AND THEIR PRODUCTS

| | Average earnings per hour | |
|---|---|---|
| *Occupation* | *White* | *Negro* |
| Transportation: | | |
| Switchmen ...................$ .5590 | | $ .5589 |
| Plate mill: | | |
| Cindersnappers .............. | .5007 | .5057 |
| Hookers .................... | .4764 | .4726 |
| Laborers ................... | .4644 | .4304 |
| Pushers .................... | .7046 | .6811 |
| Scrapmen ................... | .7007 | .6894 |
| Shear helpers ............... | .6705 | .7103 |
| Blast furnace: | | |
| Cinder laborers ............. | .4909 | .4909 |
| First helpers ............... | .4895 | .4896 |
| Handymen .................. | .5775 | .5725 |
| Keepers, furnace ............ | .5523 | .5493 |
| Laborers ................... | .4657 | .4697 |
| Larrycar helper ............. | .4890 | .4905 |
| Larrycar operators ........... | .5555 | .5250 |
| Stockhouse laborers .......... | .4798 | .4678 |

*Many Unskilled Workers Receive Less Pay.* But perhaps this is not quite normal. It is certain that many Negroes, particularly unskilled workers, are handicapped in wage by color. Mr. Hardwick's Nashville investigations showed that the wage scale for white masons was 90 cents per hour and colored masons 75 cents per hour, though the latter worked in hard stone, a more exacting class of work, and were acknowledged to have capacity to do the same work as white masons.[24]

The Chicago Race Commission found little complaint about inequality of wages, but some discrimination against Negroes in advancement in position:

"The period of this industrial investigation—the spring and summer of 1920—was one of exceptional demand for labor and high wages. Employers were glad to get workers of any sort at high pay. In branches of employment where Negroes were permitted to work, their wages were generally the same as those of the white workers. In interviewing many Negro workers the Commission's investigators found practically no complaints of discrimination in wages on the same tasks. And the Chicago Urban League, which, through its industrial department, places more Negroes in employment than any other agency in Chicago,

[24] "Economic Conditions Among Negroes in Nashville."

reported that it had very few complaints of such discrimination.

*Discrimination Against Negroes.* "Some discrimination was practiced by foremen in placing or keeping Negroes at work on processes that yielded smaller returns than those to which white workers were assigned. In the field of common labor, where the largest number of Negroes are employed, some kinds of piece-work yield greater returns than others. The tendency of foremen in some plants was to place Negroes on those processes yielding the smallest returns. The following are instances of such discrimination in favor of the white workers in the same plants.

"In two large foundries white molders were given standard patterns, which remain the same throughout the year and permit the working up of speed; while patterns that were changed frequently, and made production slower, were given to the Negroes. As speed determined the piecework earnings, the Negroes could not earn as much as the white molders in the same foundry.

"In several plants the white workers were favored in the distribution of overtime work; or Negroes were not permitted to work at all on overtime at 'time and a half' rates or on Sundays at 'double pay' as long as white workers were available.

"While in the larger industries there was seldom any complaint about inequality in the basic rate of pay for common labor, restrictions upon the promotion and advancement of Negroes frequently prevented them from earning higher wages. In one department of a large food-products plant Negroes reached the maximum rate of 61 cents per hour after a few months' employment. No further advancement could be had because the superintendent was not willing to place Negro foremen over white workers. A Negro in the starch-mixing department held a skilled position as starch-tester. It became apparent that in carrying out his duties many of the starch mixers would be subject to his immediate direction. The foreman apparently did not approve of this and ordered him to teach his duties to a Polish workman. The Negro declined to do this, and the matter was referred to the general superintendent. After an investigation it was decided to permit the Negro to retain his position as tester, but he was given no authority over the men." [25]

*Low Wages for Unskilled Labor.* In unskilled positions and particularly in positions of domestic service Negroes get very low wages on the average. Dr. Haynes, in his Columbia University studies of New York City (1912) found that of 682 Negro males 513 received less than $6 per week, 141, or 20.7% received be-

[25] "The Negro in Chicago," pp. 365-366.

tween $6 and $9 per week, and only 4.1% received $9 per week or over.    Out of 2,138 females investigated, 92% received less than $6 per week and more than half of these received less than $5 per week.    Unskilled labor in the South falls largely to the lot of the Negro and low wages is the prevailing custom.    Due to this fact thousands of Negroes are moving North where wages for both white and colored are higher, but where the Negro in particular has a better chance to win a living.

*Labor Unions and the Negro.*    One reason the Negro has had a poorer wage than the white man has been his unwillingness to organize in order that he might not have underbidding in his own group.    It is well known that there are many Negro laborers who are opposed to labor unions.    The Negro has been an individualist up to the present time.    The American Federation of Labor scarcely paid any real attention to the Negro laborer until following 1910.    In that year President Gompers, speaking in St. Louis, was quoted by the press as reading the Negro out of the Federation.    President Gompers strongly resented this statement and so expressed himself on the floor of the convention the following day.[26]    The convention itself took official action in the following words:

"St. Louis, Mo., November 26, 1910.
To the officers and delegates of the Thirtieth Annual Convention of the American Federation of Labor:

"Greeting:—In view of the very grave misrepresentation by the press of the statement upon the negro question, made by President Gompers in an address which he delivered in this city on the evening of November 17, and in addition to the refutation which he made on the floor of this convention on the following day, we feel that it is due the American Federation of Labor and the great cause of labor which we represent that we, as your duly constituted officers, should take cognizance thereof.

"Numerous telegrams and letters, newspaper clippings and editorials, from every section of the country, all protesting against the declaration which he was alleged to have made, have been received by President Gompers, thus demonstrating that the misrepresentation of his statement has been given wide publicity, something which is not only a grave injustice to him but a great wrong to our cause, the organized labor movement of the country, which this convention of Federated labor has the honor to represent.

"It is inconceivable that in view of President Gompers' record of long years of life devoted to the cause of the wage-earners, of those who toil, that he, and through him the American Fed-

[26] Cf. "Report of Proceedings Thirtieth Convention, 1910," p. 237.

eration of Labor, should be placed before the world in the position of declaring that any class of wage-earners, no matter of what race, creed, sex, or nationality, should be 'read' out of the labor movement.

"So far from closing the doors of the organized labor movement against any wage-earner, no matter of what creed, of what color, of what nationality, of what calling, of which sex, the American Federation of Labor annually exerts its efforts and spends large sums of money in spreading the gospel of trade unionism among all who toil in the endeavor to bring within the beneficent fold of the trade union movement every toiler of every trade and calling without respect to color or sex, religion or nationality. Reference to the report of our secretary from year to year, showing the amounts spent annually in organization work, will confirm us in this statement.

"The conventions of the American Federation of Labor have repeatedly declared for the organization of all wage-earners without regard to class, race, creed, religion, sex or politics. This declaration is embodied in some of the literature which is kept constantly on hand at our headquarters and which is widely distributed from year to year.

*A. F. L. Constitution on Negro Unions.* "The Constitution of the American Federation of Labor, Article 11, Section 6, provides that:

"Separate charters may be issued to Central Labor Unions, Local Unions, or Federal Local Unions, composed exclusively of colored members, where, in the judgment of the Executive Council it appears advisable and to the best interest of the Trade Union Movement to do so.

"There are now affiliated to the A. F. of L. under that provision a number of local unions of colored workmen and a number of city central bodies composed entirely of the representatives of local unions of colored workmen. There are a number of colored workmen, members in good standing of the unions of their trades, holding commissions as organizers for the A. F. of L. They keep in constant touch with headquarters, and are doing good work among the toilers of their race.

"President Gompers has accepted an invitation to address the colored people of the First Baptist church of this city to-morrow evening, so that there may be afforded still further opportunity of correcting the great wrong which has been done him and our movement.

"In view of all this we recommend that this convention shall again reiterate its often repeated declaration that the American Federation of Labor, in its endeavor to organize all the toilers of our country so as to protect and advance their rights and interests, knows no race, no color, no creed, no nationality, no political party.

"Fraternally submitted,

> "Samuel Gompers,
> "James Duncan,
> "John Mitchell,
> "James O'Connell,
> "Denis A. Hayes,
> "William D. Huber,
> "Joseph F. Valentine,
> "John R. Alpine,
> "H. B. Perham,
> "John B. Lennon,
> "Frank Morrison." [27]

*Action of 1916 A. F. L. Convention.* No further reference to Negro Unionism seems to have been made in the annual conventions of the A. F. L., until 1916, when resolution 111 was adopted, reading as follows:

"RESOLVED, That this, the Thirty-sixth Annual Convention of the American Federation of Labor, instruct the President and the Executive Council to inaugurate a movement looking toward the organization of these (Southern Negroes) men in the Southern States, to the end that they may be instructed and educated along the lines of the trade-union movement, and thereby eliminate this menace to the workers in the Northern States." [28]

*1917 Convention.* In the 1917 Convention of the A. F. L., the colored delegates from Virginia petitioned that colored organizers be appointed to instruct colored men of Virginia and sections further South in the values and purposes of organized labor. This resolution was adopted and referred to the executive committee for action.[29] At the same Convention a resolution was passed recommending to the executive committee the appointment of a special colored organizer for the railroad men of the Southeastern territory.[30]

*1918 Convention.* In the A. F. L. Convention of 1918, there was introduced a letter to President Gompers, signed by a number of prominent Negroes and leading Southern white men interested in Negro labor. This letter asked President Gompers to make a statement concerning the attitude of the A. F. L. on· points as follows:

[27] "Report of the Proceedings of the Thirtieth Annual Convention of The American Federation of Labor," pp. 333-334.
[28] "Report Proceedings A. F. L., 1916," p. 255.
[29] "Report of Proceedings A. F. L., 1917," p. 278.
[30] *Ibid.,* p. 280.

"This statement, in our judgment, should contain a clear exposition of the reasons why certain internationals may exclude colored men as they do by constitutional provision and still be affiliated with the A. F. of L., whose declared principles are opposed to such discrimination. This we think necessary because the stated facts above alluded to will be familiar to the leaders among the colored people, particularly to editors and ministers whose coöperation it is essential to secure if the best results are to be obtained.

"We would suggest further that you consider the expediency of recommending to such Internationals as still exclude colored men that their constitutions be revised in this respect.

"Second, that a qualified colored man to handle men and organize them be selected for employment as an organizer of the American Federation of Labor, his salary and expenses, of course, to be paid by the American Federation of Labor.

"Third, that for the present we meet at least once a quarter to check up on the results of our coöperative activities and to plan for further extension of the work, if satisfactorily conducted.

"Fourth, that you carry out your agreement to have your Executive Council voice an advanced position in its attitude towards the organization of Negro workingmen and have these sentiments endorsed by your St. Paul convention in June, and this action be given the widest possible publicity throughout the country." [31]

*Special Report on Organization of Negro Into Unions.* The Convention adopted the report of its committee on this subject, as follows:

"It is with pleasure we learn that leaders of the colored race realize the necessity of organizing the workers of that race into unions affiliated with the American Federation of Labor, and your committee recommends that the President of the American Federation of Labor and its Executive Council give special attention to organizing the colored wage workers in the future. We wish it understood, however, that in doing so no fault is or can be found with the work done in the past, but we believe that with the coöperation of the leaders of that race much better results can be accomplished." [32]

*1919 Convention.* Five separate resolutions came before the Convention of the A. F. L. meeting at Atlantic City in 1919. These referred to new scales of wages for colored labor union men, to right of colored men to join the union, to colored repre-

[31] "Report of Proceedings of A. F. of L., 1918," p. 199.
[32] *Ibid.*, p. 205.

sentation among the officials of the Railway Clerks' Union, to unwillingness on the part of certain white locals to have colored locals organized in the same field, and lastly to the need of special Negro organizers for Southern States.   The Convention put itself squarely behind the Negro as an integral part of the laboring group and referred all these resolutions favorably to the Executive Committee with power to act.[33]

*1921 Convention.*   The Convention of 1921, held at Denver, went on record for giving full privileges of the Unions to all men without respect to race,[34] and there was reported to the 1922 Convention a new clause in the constitution of the Railway Carmen Union as follows: "On railroads where the employment of colored persons has become a permanent institution, they shall be admitted into membership in separate lodges.   Where these separate lodges of Negroes are organized they shall be under the jurisdiction of the nearest white local, and shall be represented in any meeting of Joint Protective Board, Federation meeting or convention where delegates may be seated by white men." [35]

It thus appears that the Negro has won from the American Federation a measure of recognition of the rights of Negroes either to join the central union or to have branch unions with full power of representation.   Many national unions do not yet recognize the Negro as members of the central unions, but the following do admit members on the same footing as white men:

"International Ladies' Garment Workers, Amalgamated Meat Cutters and Butcher Workmen, Tunnel and Subway Workers, Amalgamated Association of Street and Electric Railway Employes, International Typographical Union, Brick and Clay Workers, Hod Carriers and Building Laborers, Leather Workers, Blacksmiths, Motion Picture Players' Union, American Federation of Musicians, Bakers, Postal Employes, American Federation of Teachers, Steam and Operating Engineers, Painters, Decorators and Paperhangers, Hotel and Restaurant Employees, Glass Bottle Blowers, National Association of Federal Employees, Barbers' International Union, Metal Polishers, Stereotypers and Electrotypers, Boot and Shoe Workers, Molders, Quarry Workers, Letter Carriers, International Fur Workers, Civil Engineers' Association of Boston, Firemen and Oilers." [36]

*Non-Union Negro and Riots.*   Much of the trouble between white and black in northern and western cities, such as St. Louis or Washington, has arisen because the Negro did not belong to

[32] "Report of Proceedings of A. F. L., 1919," pp. 304-306.
[34] *Ibid.*, 1921, p. 367.
[35] *Ibid.*, 1922, p. 118.
[36] "Report of Proceedings of A. F. L. Convention, 1919," p. 305.

the unions and hence could be brought in as a strike breaker. The St. Louis massacre was primarily a labor clash and not a race clash, though the fact of race difference evidently added to ferocity of the conflict. This same general situation maintained in Chicago in 1919 when the Negro population which had more than doubled the pre-war number seemed to be a growing menace to white laborers. In order to obviate further difficulties leading Negroes agreed with representatives of the meat packers to abide by the following general principles of labor:

"1. That whenever we are attempting to introduce negro workers into trades in which white workers are unionized, we must urge the negroes to join the unions.

"2. That when we are introducing negro labor into industries in which the white workers are not unionized, we advise negroes, in case the effort is made to unionize the industry, to join with their white comrades.

"3. That we strongly urge the organizers of all the unions in industries which may be opened to colored labor, not only to permit, but actively to assist in incorporating negroes into the unions.

"4. In cases where negroes are prevented from joining the unions, the right is reserved of complete liberty of action as to the advice that will be given to negro working men." [36a]

*Type of Union Demanded.* One of the Negro union leaders claimed that "men who work together in mixed gangs of white and colored workers believe their trade union ought to be organized just like the work gang " [37] In this center at least the Negroes do not want separate unions, but desire to be taken into the "bona fide" labor unions,—that is, the unions of all laborers— in a particular field. The white laborers seem to favor this since it is the only effective way of preventing the Negroes stepping in and taking places left open by white men on strike. In Nashville, Tennessee, Mr. Hardwick felt that the separate Negro unions were not as effective as those where the Negroes were part of the general union, such as the Plasterers and Brick Layers' Unions. Separate Negro unions are deterred from aggressive policies by the attitude of white employees, the Negroes themselves are not as loyal to the separate unions, and attend the meetings very poorly, the membership shifts rapidly, one-fourth going out each year, and the workers are less likely to live up to their pledge of membership, not to work for less than a standard wage or with non-union men.[38] "A Negro," said a colored brick-

[36a] Carl Sandburg: "The Chicago Race Riots," p. 44.
[37] *Ibid.*, p. 45.
[38] Hardwick: "The Economic Conditions of the Negro in Nashville," Mss. copy in Southern College Library, pp. 14-16.

layer to Miss Ovington,[39] "has to be extra fit in his trade to retain his membership, as the eyes of all the other workers are watching every opportunity to disqualify him, thereby compelling a super-efficiency." If this be true, then membership in a mixed union tends to spur the colored man to his best endeavor. All the facts seem to show that the Negro, perhaps due to the attitude of the unions, is not primarily a good unionist. He can be too easily persuaded to work for less than the standard wage, he is not willing to go out on strike when he needs food, and on the whole seems less willing to see the advantages that will come to him by standing for the union. It would hardly be expected that he would have developed a full social consciousness which would enable him to work in team with large groups of men, some of whom, white men, he suspects of not really being interested in his welfare. If, however, the union becomes as strong in the South as it is in other parts of the country, the one hope the Negro will have of sharing in skilled employment will be to unite with other workers in his own field of service. To stay out of the unions will ultimately mean that he will be relegated to menial tasks.

*Negro Women as Laborers.* A more serious problem of Negro labor is that of its womanhood. A very much larger proportion of Negro women than of whites are gainfully employed. A survey some years ago of the Negro women of Nashville, Tennessee, showed that 47 per cent of all Negro women between 15 and 45 years of age were working away from their homes. A similar study made by Miss Ruth Reed in Gainesville, Georgia, 1920, showed that 46 per cent of the Negro women worked away from home.[40] Most of these women were in domestic service, where the hours are extremely long and the pay quite low. Before the world war three to four dollars per week was a good average with meals included, and often room where desired. Since the war the house woman receives from five to ten dollars per week with the average standing raised six or seven dollars. In some sections of the South the wage is not quite so high. The hours of work are usually from 7 A. M. to 8 P. M., with Sunday afternoon off and half a day off during the week. The custom is growing of giving the whole of Sunday, but, of course, has much opposition, since Sunday throughout the South is a day of great social fellowship, and few housekeepers are willing to part with cooks and maids when guests are to be entertained. The long hours become all the more irksome because of their isolation. In the great majority of southern homes one woman domestic alone is employed. After serving the family she sits down in the

[39] Ovington: "Half a Man," p. 99.
[40] Phelps-Stokes: "Fellowship Studies, No. 6," p. 22.

kitchen and eats her food alone, and most of her work of the day is without any companionship. Of course this is not true in the wealthier families where several workers are employed. This in part accounts for the greater ease of retaining domestic help in the wealthy homes. In an investigation of house servants in three sections of Nashville for the year 1921, it was found that the average length of service in a home was nearly twice as great on West End, the wealthiest section of the city, as it was in certain other sections not far removed in distance but quite decidedly removed as to wealth.[41]

*Isolation of Domestic Service.* The isolation of work also accounts for the desire of workers to keep rooms rented in the congested Negro district where they may spend their "nights off" and find fellowship with their own people. Many white people have failed to understand why a domestic worker refuses to live on the premises of the employer. Isolation alone would account for it, but added to this is the fact that too easy access may increase the length of working hours.

There is a growing aversion to domestic service in the South, which is often misjudged. It does not indicate, I believe, less of willingness to work on the part of Negro women, but is rather due to a growing ideal of home life. As the man of the home makes more money he rightly desires his wife and daughters to remain at home and make for him a real home. This is right and proper and white people should rejoice in that growing sense of manhood which demands this of its women. Then, too, as the moral sense of the race develops, Negro mothers are increasingly desirous of giving to their daughters that protection which white mothers give to theirs. This can not well be done where a young girl works as a domestic. She nearly always works until after dark and then must go home, often through unlighted streets near her own home, without escort or protection.

*Employers Careless of Negro Girls' Morals.* Further candor forces one to admit that many white families take no thought of protecting the girl who works in their home. I asked a leading physician friend in whose home I was staying where the maid in his house lived. He said she had a nice room over the garage. When asked where his chauffeur lived he said he had a room also over the garage. One stairway led to these two rooms, where an unmarried girl and an unmarried man lived side by side. The doctor admitted he would not allow a white girl to live under similar conditions, but said it had never occurred to him that there was anything wrong about it for the colored girl. This wanton neglect of proper protection of colored girls is making it harder and harder to get domestic workers. Negro

[41] Hardwick: "The Economic Condition of the Negro in Nashville," p. 34.

mothers also feel that at times a Negro girl has to face improper attitudes toward her on the part of men in the homes. Therefore the Negro mother who desires to rear her daughter in decency and honor hesitates and rightly hesitates to send her out into domestic service unless she knows personally the people in whose home she is to work and the attitude they have toward those who work for them. If the white people desire better service they must offer better protection and better attitudes.

*Bad Conditions in North.* The conditions of working Negro women who go North is no better than that of their sisters in the South. The living conditions are apt to be very cramped, and in the worst sections of the city; the pay, while much higher, is apt to prove inadequate for decency; the temptations to vice are very great. Recognizing this, "The National League for the Protection of Colored Women was organized in 1906. An investigation of employment agencies in several northern cities had revealed abuses connected with the emigration of Negro women from the South to northern cities, where large opportunities were promised. These women were the easy prey of dishonest and immoral persons, both on their journey and after arriving at their destination." [42] This league keeps workers at Memphis, Norfolk, Philadelphia, Baltimore, New York, and other cities, who assist the Negro women in travel and in finding decent homes and proper work.

*Negro Women in Southern Industry.* The conditions of Negro industrial women in the South is often bad. Not enough care has been exercised by investigators to indicate how much worse if any these conditions are among colored women than they are among whites. Our observation proves to us that frequently the conditions are not so good for Negroes as for whites even in the same factory, and a number of industries employ Negro women only because white women will not submit to the long hours and the conditions of labor. I have followed most of the reports of the U. S. Department of Labor on working conditions among women, and rarely do they specify the conditions for white and colored. In almost every case note is made of the number of native born and foreign born, but not of white and colored. It may be the conditions did not warrant careful note of the work and treatment of the two classes of white and colored. In the study of the Oyster and Shrimp Canning Communities of the Gulf Coast,[43] Paradise found decidedly ugly conditions. The children included in the investigation were 473 colored, and 868 white, or almost two to one white. Mothers and children work side by side, at most unseasonable hours and under very bad

[42] National League for Protection of Colored Women: Report of 1910-1911.
[43] U. S. Dept. of Labor: Report No. 98, 1922.

conditions. The oysters are brought in to the packing houses in tram cars and after being steamed the workers stand by the sides of these low cars and shuck the oysters. "From the steam box the cars run on tracks into the shed. Here the shuckers take their places at the sides of the cars and attach containers, which they call their cups, to the sides of the car. The shucker takes from the car a cluster of oysters, breaks the cluster apart, with a knife opens the shell of each oyster, which the steaming process has partly opened, and removes the oyster meat, cutting it out so that the eye is left in the shell. The empty shells drop to the floor. No seats are provided for the workers. The women and children stand at these cars, swaying back and 'orth as they work, and bending over farther and farther to reach the oysters as they empty the cars. As the shells accumulate on the floor standing becomes more and more uncomfortable and bending to get the oysters more arduous. . . .

"The packing is usually done by women or older girls at a long table at which the workers stand, usually on a narrow platform of boards raised from the wet floor. On the table before the packer is a scale weighted on one side with a pan filled with oyster meat. The packer places an empty can on the other side of the scale, picks up some oyster meat with her hand and drops it into the can until the scale balances. She then places the can on a belt, which carries it through the 'briner,' a mechanical device which pours a certain amount of brine into each can."

*Child Labor.* Paradise found these children, both white and black, as young as four, five, and six, helping in the shucking and packing of the oysters. This was, of course, against the law, but the children were instructed to be on their guard against the inspector, and as soon as any stranger appeared they ran and hid.

While the great majority of Negro women workers are in domestic service, there is a growing number entering into industry. The following page gives a table of workers in New York City which is typical of this growing tendency.[44]

*U. S. Dept. of Labor Report.* The Women's Bureau of the Department of Labor in an investigation of Negro women in industry found the majority of employers felt that Negro women were as efficient as the white women of similar class and experience. Most employers claimed they would continue to employ Negro women, and added they were as reliable as the white women in their establishments. Perhaps some of these employers prefer Negro women to whites because they will work a bit cheaper. This is evidently the case in many of the large com-

[44] "Negro Year Book, 1921-1922," p. 316,

| Industry | Factories | Colored Women Workers |
|---|---|---|
| Needle Trades ............... | 121 | 892 |
| Toys ...................... | 10 | 194 |
| Buttons ................... | 9 | 120 |
| Candy .................... | 4 | 196 |
| Leather Goods ............. | 9 | 96 |
| Marabou ................... | 5 | 66 |
| Paper Boxes and Bags........ | 10 | 58 |
| Millinery ................. | 6 | 30 |
| Flowers and Feathers........ | 6 | 17 |
| Miscellaneous ............. | 37 | 516 |
| Total ................... | 127 | 2,185 |

mercial laundries in the South. Unfortunately most of the reports of the Women's Bureau of Labor do not discriminate in their figures between white and colored, but only between native and foreign born, so that full figures cannot be secured.

*Chicago Conditions.* Of the condition of Negro women industrial workers in Chicago, the Commission appointed by the Governor reports as follows:

"Negro women employed in thirty-one industrial establishments worked, in five of them forty-four hours a week, in fifteen of them forty-eight hours, in seven of them forty-nine hours, and in four of them fifty-one hours. The weekly pay ranged from $9.00 to $15.00 a week as clothing folders, to as high as $20.00 to $35.00 a week as clothing drapers or finishers. Map mounting paid $15.00 a week, book binding $15.00, paper-box making $13.00, tobacco stripping $16.40, core making (foundry work) $16.40, twine weaving $17.40, silk-shade making $10.00 to $18.00, food packing $12.00 to $15.00, mattress making $12.00 to $22.00, riveters (canvas) $15.00, paper sorters $12.00, steam laundry workers (unskilled) $13.00 to $16.00, steam laundry hand workers $18.00 to $29.00, power-machine operators on men's caps $15.00 to $18.00, on aprons $14.00 to $18.00, on dresses $15.00 to $18.00, on overalls (union shop) $18.00 to $25.00, and on overalls (non-union shop) $15.00 to $18.00.

"Of fourteen companies employing colored girls as operators, five paid on a piecework basis only. Two paid from $12.00 to $18.00 per week, depending on the skill of the operator, two companies paid $14.00 per week to beginners, one paid $15.00 per week to beginners, three paid $12.00 per week to beginners, one paid $18.00 per week to beginners, the latter being a union shop." [45]

[45] "The Negro in Chicago," p. 367.

This Commission in Chicago found four large concerns employing many hundreds of women, two of them mail order businesses and one a large wholesale millinery concern. Reports from these concerns as to the ability of the Negro women were most encouraging: "Although a long period of training is necessary in order to become a skilled milliner (four years for hand sewers, eight years for machine operators), Negro women were keen to learn the trade and willing to accept the low wages paid to beginners. Of the forty-seven Negro women employed on the day of the investigator's visit, thirty-three received less than $12.00 a week and forty-two received less than $15.00 a week. These women were all employed as hand sewers, and in the opinion of the superintendent they had done 'just as well as the white. They learn as quickly and are as persevering, and in every respect equal to the whites as far as their work is concerned. We are absolutely satisfied with their work.'" [46]

*Negro Women in Professional Service.* The number of Negro women entering professional service is growing. There is a widespread demand for Negro trained nurses. Physicians say that Negro women are peculiarly adapted to the nursing profession. They are in great demand in white homes because of their efficiency, because they will lend a hand at other tasks in the home, and because they demand a smaller wage than white graduate nurses.

A few Negro women find employment as professional musicians. Recently at Tuskegee I heard a Miss Hagan, a Negro woman, give a piano concert. She is a woman of rare skill and great musical ability and gave a concert fully the equal of the best I have heard from the leading white musicians in our cities. The place of the Negro in art will be discussed in a later chapter. It is only noted here that a growing number of Negro women as well as men are entering these professional fields.

*The Negro in Business.* Perhaps the most striking progress of the Negro in the field of economic endeavor is shown in his development of business ability. The National Business League was organized in 1900, Dr. Booker T. Washington being the moving spirit. At that time there were only four Negro banks in the country; there were in 1922, 74 Negro banks with a total capital of $6,250,000 and doing an estimated business of $100,000,000 annually. In 1900 there were fifty Negro drug stores; to-day there are probably between four and five hundred. Insurance companies have grown rapidly. Negro companies are now writing $75,000,000 in policies yearly, and $9,000,000 in benefits was paid out in 1922.[47] Monroe N. Work asserts that there were only 40 types of Negro business pursued in 1867, with

[46] "The Negro in Chicago," p. 383.
[47] "Negro Year Book, 1921-1922," p. 342.

4,000 workers, but in 1922 he finds 200 classifications of business with 50,000 Negro workers.[48] The list of business concerns includes almost every type of legitimate business pursued in this country. Twenty-nine types of business, such as banking, insurance, drug stores, undertakers, grocers, etc., employ 38,210 workers, and the amount of business done runs into many hundreds of millions of dollars. In all this progress the National Business League has taken the lead, lending encouragement, holding up conspicuous examples of success, and making the race conscious of its business ability as well as its business opportunity.

*The Negro in Agriculture.* Of all the Negro population gainfully employed, 50.3%, or 2,600,000 were working in agriculture in 1910. Therefore the prosperity of this group vitally affects the economic welfare of the whole race. There were 893,370 Negro farmers in the United States that year. Of these Negro farmers 187,797 owned their farms, of which number 179,418 lived in the South. The number of Negroes operating farms in the South increased 20.2% between 1900 and 1910. The number of Negro farmers in Georgia increased 48% during this decade, in Arkansas 35%, in Mississippi 28%, in North Carolina 19%, and in Alabama 17%. It is evident from these figures that farming is still attractive to the Negro race. Monroe Work thinks that 40% of the cotton raised in the South is raised by Negro farmers, and 10% of all the tobacco is raised by the Negro group. This does not include the cotton and tobacco raised by white farmers with Negro labor. The Negro farmer is undoubtedly working out for himself a new economic status. At the close of the civil war he owned a very small amount of land, and for the first quarter of a century he seemed unable to buy land. But the last two decades have seen a wonderful change. In 1916 I wrote each one of the United States farm demonstration agents in the South, about nine hundred of them, and asked if Negroes were buying land, and the affirmative answer was almost unanimous. In a few counties in one or two states there was opposition and little land was being acquired by Negroes. The white farm agents not only said Negroes were buying land but most of them said there was no opposition on the part of the whites, and that Negroes made very much better farmers and better citizens where they became land owners. Negroes now own more than 16,000,000 acres of farm land, they farm as tenants some 26,000,000 acres, and are day laborers on perhaps 60,000,000 acres more. Writing in 1913 Dr. Branson, one of the best authorities on Rural Economics in the country, said:

"But during the last thirty years the negroes of the South have come to feel that bank books and barns are more important than ballot boxes. At all events they appear in the 1910 census not as farm workers or farm tenants merely, but as farm owners in large numbers.

"Nearly one-fourth of all the negro farmers in the South own the farms they cultivate. In Florida they own nearly one-half of them, in Maryland and Virginia more than three-fifths of them, and in West Virginia nearly four-fifths of them. Altogether his farm properties are valued at nearly $500,000,000. Negro landholdings in the aggregate make an area a little larger than the State of South Carolina. The Russian serfs, after fifty years of freedom, have not made greater headway. They have not done so well indeed in their conquest of illiteracy." [49]

*Farm Wages.* The wages for farm hands in the South are meager as compared with wages in other sections. Thus in 1920 the average wage including board was for the North Atlantic States $51.92 per month, North Central States, $51.49 per month, North Central west of the Mississippi River, $59.63 per month, in the Far Western States, $73.21 per month, and in the South Atlantic only $35.75 per month.[50] This is considerably more than is paid the average Negro farm worker. No wonder the farm laborers are leaving the South rapidly at the present time. There seems to be no adequate reason why farm labor should be so poorly paid in the South. It is amazing how nearly the product per acre of southern farms parallels that per acre from northern and western farms. Thus the 1920 product per acre in Wisconsin was $33.40, Minnesota $17.00, Iowa $20.00, Georgia $21.60, Tennessee $30.00, Mississippi $21.00, and Texas $24.00.[51]

*Negro Tenancy.* Tenancy is growing in the South and although many Negroes are buying farms and thus rising out of tenancy, there are overwhelming numbers of Negro tenants. "After the war the old plantation owner began to divide his farm up into smaller plots and rent each plot to a family for cultivation. He had no other recourse, for he did not have enough surplus cash to hire labor to do the work, and besides, hired labor was very unreliable and scarcely to be had. Many of the old slaves stayed on the plantation and the owner aided them to the best of his ability by standing for their credit at the store where they got provisions and seed to carry them until the crop could be made. In this way there gradually grew up in the South a tenant system. The terms of tenantry are of three kinds: First, a cash tenant or renter; second, one who pays a fixed amount of produce; and third, the sharer or cropper who pays one-half or one-fourth of what he

[49] "The Human Way," p. 43.
[50] Cf. "U. S. Dept. of Agriculture Year Book 1920," Table 314, p. 819.
[51] *Ibid.,* Tables 299 and 300.

makes in accordance with whether or not the landlord furnishes
stock and seed, or whether these are furnished by the cropper.
The grades of a negro farmer, therefore, are considered to stand
in the following order: (1) Owner, (2) cash renter, (3) fourth
cropper, (4) half cropper. Many of the Negroes begin at No. 4
and go toward No. 1 as rapidly as possible. The number of farms
worked by tenants throughout the United States in 1910 was
2,349,254, or 37.1 per cent of all farms, an increase of 2 per cent
over 1900. In Mississippi 66 per cent of the farms are worked
by tenants, likewise nearly 66 per cent in Alabama, 40 per cent in
North Carolina and Tennessee, in Kentucky 24 per cent and in
Virginia 27 per cent. It will be noted that those States—Mississippi, Georgia and South Carolina—where the Negro population is
very large are the States where the tenantry system is most prevalent. Therefore, it is seen at once that the Negro is the greatest
sufferer from this type of farming. This problem demands careful
thought." [52]

*Weakness of Tenancy.* Tenant farmers often raise more produce per acre than Negro farmers who own their own land, because
the tenant is usually under the close supervision of the white land
owner, and many Negroes are not sufficiently trained to farm well
on their own account. However, it is very doubtful whether the
net returns are as great in the case of the tenant. The land is
abused and soon deteriorates and the tenant is much less apt to
save his money and invest it wisely.

Tenancy superinduces the one-crop system, because the land
owner desires a crop which can be turned into ready cash. This
means in the South usually cotton or tobacco. Under the one-crop
régime the fertility of the soil is soon exhausted and thousands
of impoverished acres in the South to-day tell the story of this
wasteful process. This one-crop system also is wasteful of labor.
In order that farming may be remunerative it is necessary to have
enough variety of work to keep the workers busy for most of the
year. If the crops are such that whole months are wasted, of
course the income to the farmer will be proportionately reduced.
This was one of the serious problems of slavery. Too much time
was wasted. Slaves had to eat whether they were kept at work or
not, and the same is true of the modern farmer. The figures
of percentage of the year's work done each month is most
illuminating.[53] See facing page 265.

It will be seen from the above table that in the southern cotton
states more than two-thirds of the work of year is concentrated
in the six months: April, May, June, July, September and October. In these six months there is twice as much work done on

[52] The Author's: "Present Forces in Negro Progress," p. 97.
[53] Cf. "U. S. Dept. of Agriculture Year Book, 1920," Table 319.

| State | Jan. | Feb. | Mar. | Apr. | May | June | July | Aug. | Sept. | Oct. | Nov. | Dec. |
|---|---|---|---|---|---|---|---|---|---|---|---|---|
| N. C.. | 2.7 | 3.5 | 6.8 | 10.1 | 12.2 | 15.6 | 11.5 | 2.4 | 8.4 | 10.0 | 28.0 | 4.0 |
| S. C.. | 3.0 | 4.1 | 8.0 | 11.3 | 13.3 | 14.2 | 8.9 | 5.4 | 8.3 | 11.1 | 8.9 | 3.5 |
| Tenn.. | 2.3 | 3.6 | 6.9 | 11.6 | 14.2 | 16.0 | 10.1 | 6.8 | 8.2 | 9.8 | 7.2 | 3.3 |
| Ga.... | 3.8 | 5.2 | 8.4 | 11.4 | 13.2 | 13.2 | 8.6 | 5.2 | 9.3 | 10.3 | 7.6 | 3.8 |
| Miss.. | 2.7 | 4.1 | 9.0 | 12.1 | 13.1 | 13.7 | 10.2 | 5.9 | 7.3 | 10.3 | 8.2 | 3.4 |
| Ill.... | 2.0 | 2.5 | 5.2 | 9.0 | 12.5 | 13.5 | 14.2 | 10.8 | 9.4 | 8.7 | 8.6 | 3.6 |
| Wis... | 2.5 | 2.6 | 3.7 | 9.5 | 12.5 | 11.7 | 15.1 | 13.7 | 12.0 | 8.7 | 4.9 | 3.1 |
| Iowa.. | 2.4 | 2.5 | 5.0 | 10.7 | 12.1 | 11.4 | 12.8 | 11.8 | 9.6 | 8.9 | 9.1 | 3.7 |
| Nebr.. | 2.5 | 2.5 | 4.8 | 8.1 | 10.7 | 12.1 | 14.3 | 13.2 | 10.4 | 9.2 | 8.0 | 4.2 |

the farms as during the other six months of the year. This means that the farmer is overcrowded and overworked for half of the year, or else he has a surplus of labor for the slack half of the year. This situation is greatly exaggerated where one crop alone is raised, for it must all be handled at once. Of course, cotton can be handled over a considerable period of time. It is not like wheat or oats, which must be harvested at once when ready. Still the heavy season for gathering cotton is September and October, and too long delay in gathering damages the product.

*Evils of the One-Crop System.* The one-crop system also brings on another evil known as the crop lien system, or the credit system. The farmer does not get his income distributed through the year, and few small farmers are provident enough to get ahead so they can carry themselves until the crop is sold. Hence they must go to the merchant, or if they are tenants, they must go to the plantation store, and buy supplies on credit. Thus in Texas the income per month from the farm beginning with January runs 3.9 per cent of the year's income on the average farm, February 2.1, March 2.4, April 2.6, May 0.7, June 1.2, July 2.9, August 3.8, September 17.7, October 25.8, November 21.4, December 15.5. It is seen from these figures that 80.4 per cent of the income from the average Texas farm comes in during the last four months of the year, and during the other eight months only 19.6 per cent. of the income is obtained. Cotton, which is the great staple crop of Texas, is marketed almost completely during these last four months. The small farmer mortgages his crop before it is raised, pays very high for the necessaries of life while his crop is maturing, and if he makes a poor crop finds himself still in debt after he has marketed his cotton. If on the other hand he makes a good crop and has a considerable amount of money in his pocket at the end of the year, there is great temptation to spend it freely and have nothing left for running the remainder of the year. Thus the vicious wheel of poverty and debt is kept going.

*One-Crop System Expensive.* Another serious effect of the

one-crop system is the fact that those who are its victims must import all of the necessities of life.  Thus in North Carolina a few years since the people marketed in round figures $100,000,000 worth of cotton, but were forced to ship into the State from the Middle West $94,000,000 worth of hay, corn and other feed and food stuff.  The high freights and the middle man's profits ate up most of the earnings of the North Carolina farmers that year.  No farmer can accumulate wealth who must spend 95 per cent. of his income on feed and food.  It will readily be seen, therefore, that the small Negro farmer, particularly the tenant, is working in a vicious circle, which is difficult to break.

*Farm Demonstration Work.*  There can be no doubt that progress is being made.  The Farm Demonstration movement, started by Dr. Seaman A. Knapp, has brought new life and hope to thousands of small farmers.  These demonstration agents are men of some scientific training and some experience who, under the direction of the Department of Agriculture, try to train the farmers of their respective counties in scientific farming.  The results have been beyond belief.  I have visited Negro farms in many counties of various southern states where such work was being done, and have constantly been amazed at the results.  I once went with Mr. Blanton, the Negro farm demonstration agent on Saint Helena Island, South Carolina.  We visited a Negro man named Green, who had raised the banner crop of corn on the island that year.  The yield had averaged 57 bushels per acre, and Green told me he had usually raised five bushels per acre before the agent taught him better methods.  In company with John B. Pierce, the Virginia State Agent for Negroes, I visited the farm of William Keaton in Nottoway County.  His crop of corn was ready to be gathered, and would yield perhaps forty bushels per acre, though Keaton said twelve bushels per acre had been his average before the demonstration agent came to him.  On this same little farm, I found blooded hogs, a pure Jersey cow, good mules, and a new home, all the results of scientific methods.  As I left the place Keaton remarked that the agent had brought to him a new life—and it was evidently true.  By means of these advanced methods, as well as by increase in acreage, the quantity and value of farm crops almost doubled between 1910 and 1920.  In some states the increase was more than double.  In this forward economic movement none have profited more than the Negro.  He is a good follower and readily accepts help.  Many of the demonstration agents say he learns more quickly than white farmers because he feels his inadequate preparation, while the white farmer is apt to think he knows better than the agent.  The heroic struggle which thousands of

Negro farmers are making to buy their farms, get out of debt, build better homes, and improve their methods of farming would make a volume more fascinating than any novel. It is a romance of real life.

*Boy and Girl Clubs.* In this connection the work for the farm boy and girl must be mentioned. The corn and pig clubs are doing a great work, not only in teaching country boys and girls how to work efficiently, but also in helping them to value aright their rural surroundings. Above all it is giving them new ideals and ambitions.

" 'I cannot begin to tell how much help club work has been to me. It not only gave me credit for a semester's work in clothing, but also created my desire for a college education,' wrote a Kansas club girl who was permitted to take a final examination for the first semester in college on the strength of her three years' experience in club work. Club work often leads boys and girls to seek a fuller knowledge of agriculture and stimulates an ambition to secure a broader education. Of those taking the regular course in agriculture and home economics in the State colleges last year over 1,800 were boys and girls who had been in club work, while over 3,300 club boys and girls took short courses at the colleges, 730 having scholarships won through their club work. . . .

"Through club work, boys and girls are led to realize the possibilities of farm life and to look upon it as worthy of their best thought and effort and as offering opportunities for success and happiness second to no other occupation. How it helps to keep the boys on the farm is indicated by the experience of a Wisconsin boy who joined the calf club and raised a prize-winning Holstein calf. To use his own words, 'Club work has completely changed my life plan, as my parents always encouraged me to get a mechanical education, thinking that I am best fitted for that. I thought so myself until I became interested in club work and found out what I could do.' " [54]

*Summary.* When one surveys the economic progress of the Negro race he is amazed at its proportions. In Virginia the assessed value of the property was in 1921, $52,505,951, in Georgia for the same year it was $68,628,514, and it has been estimated that the total property value of Negroes was in this same year one billion five hundred million dollars. He has made great progress in buying farm lands and also in securing homes. In 1910 he owned 120,738 farm homes, and 143,550 city homes. This number more than doubled during the decade of 1910-1920. [55]

[54] "U. S. Dept. of Agriculture Year Book, 1920," pp. 485, 486.
[55] Cf. "Negro Year Book, 1922," p. 13 f.

From the number of occupations he pursues, from the number of business firms he controls and runs, from the amount of capital he has accumulated, and from the number of homes he has built, one must conclude that his economic progress is not only gratifying but far beyond what any one could have dreamed who saw him start from slavery in 1865.

## Chapter XI

## HEALTH AND HOUSING OF NEGROES IN RELATION TO GROWTH OF POPULATION

During the period of slavery the problem of health of the Negro was a most vital one. There are few subjects discussed more often in the magazines of the time, such as *DeBow's Review* and *Niles Register,* than is that of health. Housing being so closely related to the whole question of health also comes in for its full share of comment. There is a popular error that the slave Negroes were all healthy, both because they worked in the open air and because they were carefully guarded from excesses and promptly attended when any sickness arose. In part this is true, but we find in the old records almost every disease among Negroes to which flesh is heir. Here is an extract from a letter signed "A Small Farmer" and published in *DeBow's Review,* which sets forth the writer's conception of the relation of housing and food to health:

"The public may desire to know the age of the writer, the length of time he has been managing negroes, and how long he has tried the mode of management he recommends. It is sufficient to say, I have had control of negroes in and out of the field for thirty years, and have been carrying out my present system, and improving it gradually, for twenty years. . . .

*Housing in Mississippi.* "Housing for negroes should be good; each family should have a house, 16 by 18 feet in the clear, plank floor, brick chimney, shingle roof; floor elevated two feet above the earth. There should be no loft, no place to stow away any thing, but pins to hang clothes upon. Each house should be provided with a bedstead, cotton mattress, and sufficient bed-clothes for comfort for the heads of the family, and also for the young ones.

"Clothing should be sufficient, but of no set quantity, as all will use or waste what is given, and many be no better clad with four suits than others with two. I know families that never give more than two suits, and their servants are always neater than others with even four. . . .

"Food is cooked by a woman, who has the children under her charge. I do not regard it as good economy, to say nothing of any feeling, to require negroes to do any cooking after their day's labor is over.

*Food Supply.* "The food is given out daily, a half pound to each hand that goes to the field, large and small, water carriers and all; bread and vegetables without stint, the latter prepared in my own garden, and dealt out to the best advantage, endeavoring to have something every day in the year. I think four pounds of clear meat is too much. I have negroes here that have had only a half pound each for twenty years, and they bid fair to outlive their master, who occasionally forgets his duty, and will be a gourmand. I practise on the plan, that all of us would be better to be restrained, and that health is best subserved by not over-eating. . . .

*Hours of Labor.* "My hours of labor, commencing with pitching my crop, is from daylight until 12 M.; all hands then come in and remain until 2 o'clock P.M., then back to the field until dark. Some time in May we prolong the rest three hours; and if a very hot day, even four hours. Breakfast is eaten in the field, half an hour to hour being given; or they eat and go to work without being driven in and out—all stopping when my driver is ready.

"I give all females half of every Saturday to wash and clean up, my cook washing for young men and boys through the week. The cabins are scoured once a week, swept out every day, and beds made up at noon in summer, by daylight in winter. In the winter, breakfast is eaten before going to work, and dinner is carried to the hands. . . .

"It is not possible in my usual crude way to give my whole plans, but enough is probably said. I permit no night-work, except feeding stock and weighing cotton. No work of any kind at noon, unless to clean out cabins, and bathe the children when nursing, not even washing the clothes." [1]

*Prejudice Against Free Negroes.* There was a strong prejudice during the slave régime against free Negroes and against mulattoes. This prejudice was undoubtedly father to the thought that neither of these classes was as strong or as long lived as were the slave Negroes. I have not been able to get any statistics which proved that this was or was not so. However, one finds frequent opinions expressed, not only by slave owners, but often by physicians that such was the case. Here are extracts printed by DeBow from the pen of a physician, bearing on this point:

"A writer in the Boston Medical and Surgical Journal, November, 1842, under the signature of 'Philanthropist,' who seems to be an earnest seeker after truth, uses the following language:

[1] DeBow's: "Industrial Resources," Vol. II, pp. 336-337.

" 'From authentic statistics and extensive corroborating information, obtained from sources to me of unquestionable authority, together with my own observations, I am led to believe that the following statements are substantially correct:

*Influence of Freedom on Health.* " 'ist. That the longevity of the Africans is greater than that of the inhabitants of any other part of the globe.

" '2d. That mulattoes, i.e., those born of parents one being African and the other white or Caucasian, are the shortest lived of any class of the human race.

" '3d. That the mulattoes are not more liable to die under the age of 25 than the whites or blacks; but from 25 to 40 their deaths are as 10 to 1 of either the whites or blacks between those ages; from 40 to 55, the deaths are as 50 to 1 ; and from 55 to 70, 100 to 1.

" '4th. That the mortality of the free people of color is more than 100 per cent greater than that of slaves.

" '5th. That those of unmixed extraction in the free states are not more liable to sickness or premature death than the whites of their rank and condition in society; but that the striking mortality so manifest among the free people of color, is in every community and section of the country invariably confined to the mulattoes.

" 'It was remarked by a gentleman from the south, eminent for his intellectual attainments and distinguished for his correct observation, and who has lived many years in the southern states, that he did not believe that he had ever seen a mulatto of 70 years of age.

" 'From a correspondence published in the Boston Spectator, in April last, are taken the following statistics :

" 'In a colored population of 2,634,348, including free blacks, there are 1,980 over 100 years of age; whereas there are but 647 whites over 100 in a population of 14,581,000.

" 'In Boston, the number of deaths annually among the colored population is about 1 in 15, and there are fewer pure blacks in this city than any other. The same comparative mortality between mulattoes and blacks exists in the West Indies and in Guiana, where unfavorable social causes do not operate against the mulattoes as in the United States.' "

*Dr. Nott's Comment on Health of Mulattoes.* "Dr. Nott, a physician of the South, comments on the above statement as follows :

"Though they do substantially, my observations at the south will not fully corroborate all the above conclusions of 'Philanthropist.'

My belief is that the mulattoes do die more than whites or blacks under 25, as they certainly do above this age, and that the pure blacks are destroyed by cold climate as well as the mulattoes, though the latter may be most sensitive.

"I will here give the results of my own professional observation during twenty years at the south, which I feel assured time and experience will substantially confirm. The facts were forced upon me during my intercourse with the colored class, and attracted my attention long before I had formed any theory on the subject, and at a time when my convictions were the opposite of what they now are.

"1st. The mulattoes are intermediate in intelligence between the blacks and whites.

"2nd. They are less capable of enduring fatigue, exposure, and hardships of all kinds, than either blacks or whites.

"3rd. The mulatto women are peculiarly delicate, and more subject to a variety of chronic diseases peculiar to females.

"4th. The women are bad breeders and bad nurses—many do not conceive, and most are subject to abortions, or premature births.

"5th. The two sexes, when they marry, are less prolific than when crossed on one of the parent stocks.

"6th. The specific difference of the races is strongly illustrated in the exemption of the negroes from yellow and congestive fevers; not only the negro, but the quarteroon, though a native of a cold latitude, is to a great extent exempt; there are occasional exceptions, and it is well known that yellow fever, like cholera, has often been fatal to domestic animals." [2]

*Better Health During Slavery.* The oft repeated statement that the Negro was much healthier during slavery than now finds some corroboration. He was not allowed to dissipate, he was kept regularly at work, and he did have regular meals and well cooked food. The master naturally saw to this. The statistics of mortality in Charleston, printed in *DeBow's Review*, seem to indicate that the death rate of Negroes from 1830 to 1845 was lower than that of whites save on the years when yellow fever was raging. One is inclined to doubt whether all the deaths for Negroes were registered or not, and whether the desire to show the good health of the slaves did not somewhat influence the way in which the facts were secured, but whatever the situation, the facts given are as follows:

[2] DeBow's: "Industrial Resources," Vol. II, p. 297.

"Mortality in Charleston

| Years | Whites | Blacks | |
|-------|--------|--------|---|
| 1830 .............. | 1 in 39.4 | 40.0 | |
| 1831 .............. | 1 in 46.6 | 37.9 | |
| 1832 .............. | 1 in 51.9 | 55.3 | |
| 1833 .............. | 1 in 55.0 | 55.7 | |
| 1834 .............. | 1 in 42.1 | 44.1 | Y. Fever |
| 1835 .............. | 1 in 43.1 | 46.4 | " |
| 1836 .............. | 1 in 40.6 | 19.6 | Cholera |
| 1837 .............. | 1 in 47.3 | 46.7 | |
| 1838 .............. | 1 in 18.3 | 33.0 | Y. Fever |
| 1839 .............. | 1 in 29.9 | 39.0 | " |
| 1840 .............. | 1 in 50.7 | 46.6 | |
| 1841 .............. | 1 in 65.1 | 44.8 | |
| 1842 .............. | 1 in 50.3 | 47.8 | |
| 1843 .............. | 1 in 60.8 | 32.9 | |
| 1844 .............. | 1 in 69.3 | 43.3 | |
| 1845 .............. | 1 in 52.9 | 48.5" [3] | |

Nassau tells us, "Most of the deaths I have known in Negro Land were from pulmonary diseases," so that pneumonia and tuberculosis seem common in Africa.[4]

One is still more convinced that a case was being made when one finds printed side by side with the above statistics similar statistics from Philadelphia and Baltimore:

"Mortality in Philadelphia

| Years | Whites | Blacks |
|-------|--------|--------|
| 1831 .............. | 1 in 39.6 | 33.6 |
| 1832 .............. | 1 in 28.8 | 22.6 |
| 1833 .............. | 1 in 47.3 | 35.2 |
| 1834 .............. | 1 in 41.4 | 33.3 |
| 1835 .............. | 1 in 38.3 | 31.2 |
| 1836 .............. | 1 in 43.8 | 21.4 |
| 1837 .............. | 1 in 45.1 | 32.7 |
| 1838 .............. | 1 in 45.0 | 29.2 |
| 1839 .............. | 1 in 49.4 | 31.3 |
| 1840 .............. | 1 in 52.2 | 38.6 |

"We have the authority of Dr. Niles, then a citizen of New York (now of Paris) in a pamphlet published by him in 1827, for giving the mortality of Baltimore in 1823-24-25, as follows:—

[3] DeBow's: "Industrial Resources," Vol. II, p. 294.
[4] Nassau: "Fetichism in West Africa," p. 228.

Whites, 1 in 44; free blacks, 1 in 32; slaves, 1 in 77-8. This result is probably attributable to two causes—1st, there is a large proportion of mulattoes among the free colored; 2d, the physical wants of the slaves are better supplied, and they are infinitely more cheerful and happy than the free colored." [5]

*Mortality in Charleston.* Writing somewhat later of the mortality in Charleston, the editor shows that Charleston is a city of good health for the Negro:

"We will remark, in passing, the low degree of mortality amongst children in Charleston compared with northern cities. In Charleston, the mortality under five years is 31 per cent, while in Boston it is 46, and in other northern and European cities the per centage is still greater.

"The average mortality for the last six years in Charleston for all ages is 1 in 51, including all classes. Blacks alone, 1 in 44; whites alone, 1 in 58, a very remarkable result, certainly. This mortality is perhaps not an unfair test, as the population during the last six years has been undisturbed by emigration and acclimated in a greater proportion than at any former period." [6]

It is a common opinion that consumption was unknown among Negroes before the Civil War. That there was little scientific study of consumption among Negroes is very evident from reports which were published at the time:

*Consumption Among Negroes.* "Negro consumption is a disease almost unknown to medical men of the northern states and Europe. A few southern physicians have acquired some valuable information concerning it from personal experience and observation; but this knowledge is scattered in fragments about, and has never been condensed in a form to make of much practical utility. Some physicians, looking upon negro consumption through northern books, suppose it to be a variety of phthisis pulmonalis; but it has no form of resemblance to the phthisis of the white race, except in the emaciation, or when it is complicated with the relics of pneumonia of a badly cured pleurisy. Others regard it as a dyspepsia or some disease of the liver or stomach; the French call it mal d'estomac. But dyspepsia is not a disease of the negro; it is, par excellence, a disease of the Anglo-Saxon race. I have never seen a well marked case of dyspepsia among the blacks. It is a disease that selects its victims from the most intellectual of mankind, passing by the ignorant and unreflecting.

[5] DeBow's: "Industrial Resources in the South and West," Vol. II, p. 294.
[6] *Ibid.*, Vol. III, p. 91.

*Causes of "Negro Consumption."* "The popular opinion is that negro consumption is caused by dirt-eating. The eating of dirt is not the cause, but only one of the effects—a mere symptom, which may or may not attend it. As in pica, there is often a depraved appetite for substances not nutritious, as earth, chalk, lime, etc.; but oftener, as in malacia, a depraved appetite for nutritious substances, to a greater degree than for non-nutritious. In negro consumption the patients are generally hearty eaters of all kinds of food; but there are exceptions." [7]

*Health of Slaves Guarded.* In an earlier chapter we have seen that many planters would not allow their slaves to do such work as ditching and draining, lest the exposure might be detrimental to the health of the slave. There was a feeling that the Negro had weak lungs and could not be exposed in this way without heavy loss of life. That the Negro might be more subject to pneumonia and tuberculosis from lack of proper ventilation than from over exposure to cold never seemed to occur to most of the planters. Most of the ignorant Negroes today are just as much afraid of "night air" in their sleeping rooms as the slaves were. It is the rarest servant that will open windows at night, even in the spring time. I have no doubt that the constant habit of sleeping without proper ventilation is a large contributing cause for tuberculosis at the present time. While many of the cabins in which the slaves lived had plenty of "air holes" to give proper ventilation, still many other cabins, such as the well chinked log huts, the adobe houses and the brick houses were not so provided. The results were evident in the diseases of the Negro of slave days.

*Pneumonia.* "One of the most formidable complaints among negroes, more fatal than any other, is congestion of the lungs; or what European writers would call false pleurisy, or peri-pneumonia notha. It is often called cold plague, typhus pneumonia, bilious pleurisy, &c., according to its particular type and the circumstances attending it; sometimes the head complains more than any other part, and it then bears the misnomer, 'head pleurisy.' It occurs, mostly, in winter and spring, but is met with at every season of the year, when cold nights succeed warm days. It is more common among those who sleep in open houses, without sufficient fires to keep them warm and comfortable. It is seldom observed among negroes who inhabit log cabins, with cemented or clay floors, or warm houses made of brick, or any material to exclude the cold wind and air. The frame houses, with open weather-boarding and loose floors, admitting air both at the sides and from below, are buildings formed in ignorance of the peculiar physiological laws of the negro's organization, and are the fruitful sources of many of his most dangerous diseases.

*Exposure as Basis of Ill Health.* "Want of sufficient fires and warm blankets is also another cause of thoracic complaints. The negro's lungs, except when the body is warmed by exercise, are very sensitive to the impressions of cold air. When not working or taking exercise, they always crowd around a fire, even in comparatively warm weather, and seem to take a positive pleasure in breathing heated air and warm smoke. In cold weather, instead of sleeping with their feet to the fire, as all other kinds of people do, whether civilized or savage, they turn their head to the fire—evidently for the satisfaction of inhaling warm air, as congenial to their lungs, in repose, as it is to infants. In bed, when disposing themselves for sleep, the young and old, male and female, instinctively cover their heads and faces, as if to insure the inhalation of warm, impure air, loaded with carbonic acid and acqueous vapor. The natural effect of this practice is, imperfect atmospherization of the blood—one of the heaviest chains that binds the negro to slavery. In treating, therefore, their pulmonary affections, the important fact should be taken into consideration, that cold air is inimical to the lungs of healthy negroes when the body is in repose and not heated by exercise, and consequently more prejudicial in the diseases of those organs. A small, steady fire, a close room, and plenty of thick blanket covering, aided with hot stimulating teas, are very essential means in the treatment of the pulmonary congestions to which their lungs are so prone." [8]

*Yaws and Other Sex Disorders.* Although the Negroes were not exposed to indiscriminate sex vice during slavery as they are now, and there were probably few Negro prostitutes in the very nature of the case, nevertheless there was considerable prevalence of disease on account of sex indulgence—notwithstanding popular opinion to the contrary. "Yaws" was a form of venereal disease rather common among Negro slaves, as indeed it was common among the African people from whom the slaves were secured. The African people were much given to immorality. Ellis tells us [9] that in Dahomi the Negro priestesses are prostitutes, that every town has its group of girl priestesses, and that women often enter these institutions to gratify their own vicious natures. It is a well known fact that chastity is seldom preserved among the women of the savage tribes of Africa. It could not be expected, therefore, that the slaves with this background, and with the loose family life fostered by slavery, would be free from diseases of sex vice.

[8] DeBow's: "Industrial Resources in the South and West," Vol. II, pp. 318-319.
[9] Ellis: "Ewe-Speaking Peoples," p. 141 f.

"The Frambæsia Pian, or Yaws, is a disease thought to be peculiar to negroes. I have seen it in its worst form in the West Indies. I have occasionally met with it in its modified form in the states of Mississippi and Lousiana, where it is commonly mistaken for syphilis. It is a contagious disease, communicable by contact among those who greatly neglect cleanliness. Children are liable to it as well as adults. It is supposed to be communicable in a modified form to the white race, among whom it resembles pseudo-syphilis, or some disease of the nose, throat, or larynx. Further observations are wanting in regard to it. It is said to be very prevalent in Temaupipas in Mexico, attacking the nose and throat, in the first instance, very similar to secondary syphilitic affections, without ever having appeared on the genital organs at all, except in the shape of a slight herpes preputialis." [10]

*Children Weakened from Sex Vice of Parents.* Sex vice must have affected many of the slaves by inheritance. It is a well known fact that scrofula among children is often due to sex indulgence on the part of parents. This disease was very common among the slaves.

"Like children, negroes are very liable to colics, cramps, convulsions, worms, glandular and nervous affections, sores, biles, warts, and other diseases of the skin. Scrofula is very common among them. Rickets, diseases of the spine and hip-joint, and white swellings are not uncommon. They are also subject to the goitre. All very fat negroes, except women who have passed the prime of life, are unhealthy and scrofulous. The great remedy for the whole tribe of their scrofulous affections, without which all other remedies do very little good, is *sunshine*." [11]

*Slaves Subject to Fevers.* Contrary to popular opinion, fevers were not uncommon among slaves.

"The next class of complaints to which they are mostly liable, are bilious and adymanic fevers—remittents and intermittents. Evacuating the stomach and bowels by a mild emetico-cathartic, combined with a weak anodyne carminative, to prevent its excessive action, is generally the best medicine to begin with; for, whatever be the type of the fever, as negroes are hearty eaters, it will be an advantage, in the after treatment of the case, to have the primoe vioe cleared of their load of undigested food, and the superabundant mucosities poured out into the alimentary canal, of a people so phlegmatic, when attacked with a fever suspending digestion and interrupting absorption." [12]

These facts point conclusively to the belief that slavery was no guarantee of health or morality. Too frequently we have de-

[10] DeBow's: "Industrial Resources," Vol. II, p. 320.
[11] *Ibid.*, p. 319.
[12] *Idem.*

sired to whitewash an institution which all now recognize as bad
by showing its good influences.  These influences will hardly
stand the light of day.  One must not forget, of course, that economic interest, and a humanitarian sense of responsibility for their
slaves did mean that masters and mistresses gave real care to
their slaves in most cases.  Perhaps the Negro was healthier
during slavery—for he had more regular hours, and ate much
more regularly than the poorer Negroes do at the present time.
But that he was a paragon of health can hardly be made out.

But if the Negro was carefully guarded as to his health during
slavery, it is certain that little attention has been paid to him
since the Civil War.  Indeed, some have even expressed the hope
that he would die out and thus solve the "race problem" in the
South.

*Is the Negro Dying Out?*  In 1905 Professor W. B. Smith,
of Tulane University, wrote a book called "The Color Line," in
which he argued that the Negro was a rapidly diminishing factor
in American life and would continue progressively as a smaller and
smaller influence in the nation.  Yet the whole book seemed to
have a severe tone of criticism about it lest some might think
the Negro was the equal of the white, which he was completely
unwilling to admit, and even in the field of labor he denied that
the Negro would ever be able to enter into competition with the
white man's skill.[13]  The book had value in that it called attention
to the fact that the Negro was not holding his own in numbers,
though little explanation save that of inferior heritage was given
for this fact.  However, the prophecies of his book as to diminishing increase seem to be all too true according to the two cen-
suses which have been taken since its appearance.  In spite of
the fact that millions of immigrants have come to American
shores, the white population has increased more slowly with each
succeeding decade, but the Negroes have increased still more
slowly yet.  Taken by double decades in order to obviate to some
extent the errors of certain census returns, the growth of white
and colored populations are as follows (see page 279).

It will be seen from this table (1) that the Negro has increased
only 40% as fast as has the white population during the last
double decade, 1900 to 1920.  The facts are even more striking
when one sees the comparisons of the last decade, 1910 to 1920,
for the whites have increased during this period 16%, the colored
have increased 6.5%, and during this decade immigration was
almost entirely cut off for the whites following 1914.

*Present Negro Population.*  The increase of Negro population
from 1890 to 1900 was 18%, from 1900 to 1910, 11.2%; 1910
to 1920, 6.5%.  The increase of Negroes for the chief geograph-

[13] Smith: "The Color Line," p. 168, *passim*.

TABLE I [14]

| | White | Increase | Colored | Increase |
|---|---|---|---|---|
| 1790 | 3,172,006 | | 757,208 | |
| 1810 | 4,306,444 | 35.7% | 1,002,037 | 31. % |
| 1820 | 7,866,797 | 82.6% | 1,771,656 | 76.8% |
| 1840 | 14,189,705 | 80.3% | 2,875,448 | 62.2% |
| 1860 | 26,922,537 | 83. % | 4,441,830 | 56.6% |
| 1880 | 43,402,970 | 61.2% | 6,580,793 | 48.2% |
| 1900 | 66,809,196 | 53.9% | 8,833,994 | 34.2% |
| 1920 | 94,822,432 | 42. % | 10,463,013 | 17.3% |

ical divisions from 1910 to 1920 were as follows: The South, 1.9%; the North, 43.3%; the West, 55.1% [15]. The large drop in the relative Negro increase in the South is largely due to the migration of Negroes during the period of the war, five southern states having actually lost Negro population during the decade. Mississippi's Negro population dropped from 1,009,487 in 1910 to 935,184, an actual decrease of 74,303, or 7% of the total in the earlier period. Kentucky Negro population dropped during the same period from 261,656 to 235,938, a net loss of 24,718, or 9.4%. Tennessee's Negro population dropped from 473,088 to 451,758, a total loss of 21,330, or 4.5%. Louisiana's Negro population dropped from 713,874 to 700,257, a total loss of 13,617, or 1.8%. Alabama's Negro population dropped from 908,282 to 900,257, a total loss of 7,630, or .8%. Seven other southern states: Texas, Oklahoma, Arkansas, Florida, Georgia, North Carolina, and South Carolina, all combined gained only 237,433 in Negro population, or 5.3% over the 1910 census. The largest numerical gain in this group was that of North Carolina, where the 1920 census returns showed an addition of 65,564, or 9.4% gain over the former returns. The State of Virginia gained 18,931, or 2.8%. Maryland gained 12,229, or 5.3%, while Delaware lost 846, or 2.7%. Thus the losses and gains in the southern states almost equalized themselves.

*Detailed Statement of Mississippi Negroes.* One can visualize more clearly what this means when one state is examined in detail. Mississippi has 82 counties; 71 of these counties had a smaller percentage of Negroes with reference to the total population in 1920 than they had in 1910. Two counties remained stationary in percentage of Negroes; six counties alone increased in percentage of Negroes; percentages in three counties not given. Of the 71 counties which lost in percentage of Negro population, 62 lost in actual numbers. In other words, 71 counties in Missis-

[14] Cf. Census: Negro Pop. 1790-1915 and Advanced sheets, 1920 Census.
[15] Cf. "Fourteenth Census of U. S., Population 1920," p. 5.

sippi have grown whiter, and 62 have actually fewer Negroes now than they had in 1910. The total State is 52 per cent colored now, while it was 56 per cent colored in 1910.

*Migrations Nothing New.* Race migrations are no new phenomena; they are as old as the human race itself. From the time of the rise of the Neanderthal man in Europe during the fourth glacial period down to the present time—a period of many thousands of years—we have clear evidences of movement and counter movement of groups of men throughout Europe. We find the same to be true of tribes in Africa, and we should not be surprised to find large racial movements in our country. The great migration of Negroes in the past decade is not the first to take place among the Negro peoples of America. In 1879 there was what was called a Negro Exodus from the South due partly to the changing conditions by which Negroes were cut off from any participation in politics, partly to ill treatment following in the wake of the Ku Klux movement, and partly to economic pressure.

"A general convention of Negroes held in Nashville in May, 1879, adopted a report that set forth their grievances and encouraged emigration to the North and West, where rights would not be denied. Thousands now left their homes in the South, going in greatest numbers to Kansas, Missouri, and Indiana. Within about twenty months Kansas alone thus received an addition to her population of 40,000 Negroes. Many of these arrived at their destination practically penniless and with no prospect of immediate employment. Large sums of money for their relief were raised through the North, however, and gradually they found a place in their new homes. In the Southeast there was also some movement in the same direction. One account says that in one noteworthy week about 5,000 Negroes removed from South Carolina to Arkansas." [16]

*Leaders of Negro Migrations.* The two outstanding leaders of this exodus were Henry Adams, of Shreveport, Louisiana, and 'Pap' Singleton of Tennessee.

"Henry Adams of Shreveport, Louisiana, an uneducated negro but a man of extraordinary talent, organized that year (1879) a colonization council. He had been a soldier in the United States Army until 1869 when he returned to his home in Louisiana and found the condition of negroes intolerable. Together with a number of other negroes he first formed a committee which in his own words was intended to 'look into affairs and see the true condition of our race, to see whether it was possible we could stay under a people who held us in bondage or not.' This committee grew to the enormous size of five hundred members. One

[16] Brawley: "The History of the American Negro," p. 129 f.

hundred and fifty of these members were scattered throughout the South to live and work among the negroes and report their observations. These agents quickly reached the conclusion that the treatment the negroes received was generally unbearable. Some of the conditions reported were that land rent was still high; that in the part of the country where the committee was organized the people were still being whipped, some of them by their former owners; that they were cheated out of their crops and that in some parts of the country where they voted they were being shot." . . .

"About the same time there was another conspicuous figure working in Tennessee—Benjamin or 'Pap' Singleton, who styled himself the father of the exodus. He began the work of inducing negroes to move to the State of Kansas about 1869, founded two colonies and carried a total of 7,432 blacks from Tennessee. During this time he paid from his own pocket over $600 for circulars which he distributed throughout the southern States. 'The advantages of living in a free State' were the inducements offered." [17]

*Other Migrations.* There was also a westward movement in 1872, and still another movement for Liberia in 1877. There has been a gradual movement North from decade to decade. As early as 1890 there were 241,000 southern-born Negroes living in the North and West. In 1900 this number had grown to 349,000; in 1910 it had grown to 440,534, and in 1920 to 780,794. In 1900 fifteen per cent (15.6%) of all Negroes born in the United States were living in other States from those in which they were born; in 1910 this percentage was 16.6, and in 1920 it was 19.9. In the year 1920 there were 2,054,242 Negroes living in other states from those in which they were born. The Negro population of both Ohio and Illinois increased 67.1 per cent, that of Pennsylvania 46.7 per cent, while that of Michigan increased 251 per cent.

*Cityward Movements.* Another movement of Negroes has been from the country to the city. Of the total urban population of the country, 6.6 per cent were Negroes in 1900, 6.4 per cent in 1910, and 6.6 per cent in 1920. It will thus appear that he is just holding his own in urban percentages. This is also largely due to the northern and western migration, for almost all the migrants go to the cities. A most interesting fact has developed during the decade, namely, that in almost every northern city the Negro has gained on the whites in percentage of population, while in almost every southern city the whites have gained over the Negroes in percentage of population. Table II sets forth these facts.

[17] Scott: "Negro Migration During the War," pp. 4 and 5.

TABLE II

| Name of Northern City | Percentage of White Population | | Name of Southern City | Percentage of White Population | |
|---|---|---|---|---|---|
| | 1910 | 1920 | | 1910 | 1920 |
| Rochester, N.Y. | 99.6 | 99.4 | Jacksonville, Fla. | 49.1 | 54.6 |
| Newark, N.J. | 97.2 | 95.8 | Tampa, Fla. | 66.2 | 77.6 |
| Jersey City | 97.7 | 97.3 | Mobile, Ala. | 55.8 | 60.7 |
| Atlantic City | 78.5 | 78.3 | Montgomery, Ala. | 49.3 | 54.4 |
| New York City | 98 | 97.1 | | | |
| Cincinnati | 94.6 | 92.6 | | | |
| Cleveland | 98.4 | 95.6 | Little Rock, Ark. | 63.3 | 73.2 |
| Columbus | 92.9 | 90.6 | Atlanta, Ga. | 66.4 | 68.7 |
| Dayton | 95.8 | 94.1 | Augusta, Ga. | 55.2 | 56.9 |
| Minneapolis | 99.1 | 98.9 | Macon, Ga. | 55.4 | 56.4 |
| St. Louis | 93.5 | 90.9 | Oklahoma City | 89.5 | 90.7 |
| Kansas City | 90.5 | 90.5 | Louisville | 81.9 | 82.9 |
| Detroit | 98.7 | 95.7 | New Orleans | 73.6 | 73.8 |
| Boston | 97.8 | 97.7 | Nashville, Tenn. | 59.9 | 62.3 |
| Baltimore, Md. | 84.8 | 85.2 | Memphis | 66.9 | 69.9 |
| Indianapolis | 90.6 | 88.9 | Dallas, Tex. | 80.4 | 84.8 |
| Gary, Ind. | 97.6 | 90.4 | Houston, Tex. | 69.6 | 75.5 |
| East St. Louis | 89.9 | 88.8 | Richmond, Va. | 63.4 | 68.5 |
| Chicago | 97.9 | 95.8 | Norfolk | 62.8 | 62.4 |
| Philadelphia | 94.5 | 92.6 | Roanoke | 77.3 | 81.7 |

*Negroes Going North.* From Table II it appears that most of the southern cities are growing whiter and most of the northern cities are growing blacker. Of course there are exceptions in both cases. The fact that the urban population has not grown as fast for Negroes as for whites throws light on another type of movement—that is from the country to the city. It appears that the Negro is staying in the country better than the white man, as was the case between 1900 and 1910. But, of course, both whites and colored have been moving to the city. Practically 78 per cent of the Negroes in the South still live in rural communities.

What are the conditions which led to this large migration of Negroes out of the South, and what are the possible bases of the great decrease in relative population for the decade?

*Causes of Northern Migration.* The prime cause of the northern migration was evidently economic. A series of factors entered into this economic motive. Perhaps most acute among those in the South were the ravages of the boll weevil. This pest had been gradually moving eastward and northward, and almost

wiped out the cotton crops of Mississippi, Alabama, and Louisiana
in the years from 1915 on. In travelling through these states
one found not only the Negroes discouraged, but the white
planters deeply pessimistic about the future of farming in that
region. One Louisiana planter told the writer in 1920 that he
had not cleared expenses for four successive years, and he planned
to try it only one more year, unless things changed for the better.
One talked with many planters who believed that the weevil
could never be destroyed. Most of these men did not know how
to raise anything but cotton, and had poor markets for most
other products that they could raise. One Alabama planter known
to the writer continued to try cotton with almost no success, just
raising enough feed and food to keep his plantation going. It
seemed pitiable to hear him talk of having raised as high as
$50,000 worth of cotton in one year, and see his crop which
would not bring more than a thousand or fifteen hundred dollars.
"Some planters in (both) Alabama and Mississippi advised their
tenants to leave and assisted them." [18] Other crop disasters such
as floods and storms, particularly in Mississippi and Alabama,
added to the general economic depression. Professor Leavell
in his report to the Department of Labor emphasizes also the
fact that many farm laborers had been thrown out of work by
the reorganization of agriculture to meet changed conditions;
for instance, many planters ceased raising cotton and turned their
farms into stock farms, which needed a comparatively smaller
number of workers.[19] That there was actual want in Mississippi
due to crop failures Professor Leavell thinks is clearly established by the rapid rise in the number of deaths from pellagra,
superinduced by malnutrition. These deaths were just three
times as prevalent in 1915 as they were in 1912, which was a
good crop year in Mississippi.

Substantially the same conditions held in Alabama as in Mississippi. Professor Snavely in his report to the Department of
Labor on the farming conditions in Alabama, writes as follows:

"For both landowners and tenants the period of transition in
farming during the past two or three years has been one of great
uncertainty, instability, and unrest. The period was preceded and
attended by two other unfortunate conditions which brought
financial ruin to many planters, merchants, tenants, etc. One
of these was the low price of cotton and the other was the inability to borrow money at a reasonable rate of interest. 'The
exodus,' said one of the most successful business men of the
State, 'originated in the low prices paid for cotton in 1913 and

[18] Scott: "Negro Migration During the War," p. 15.
[19] "Negro Migration in 1916-1917," p. 21.

1914. The farmers have not been prosperous; they have been exceedingly unprosperous. The present conditions grew out of the failure of a paying crop."

"One of the underlying causes of the migration, therefore, may be characterized as the changed conditions incident to the transition from the old system of cotton planting to stock raising and the diversification of crops." [20]

Similar conditions maintained in Georgia and other southern states. So that the migration movement had its initial impulse from the economic depression of agricultural life in the lower South.

*Northern Demand for Labor.* Simultaneous with this agricultural depression in the South came a great demand for unskilled and semi-skilled labor in the North. The world war had made a heavy demand for munitions and arms, together with all the necessities of warring peoples. Numerous industrial plants sprang up in the North, calling for a great mass of labor. The white immigrants who had for many years done the unskilled and semi-skilled labor in that section were rapidly drawn into these new manufacturing plants at high wages, leaving a vacuum in the unskilled field. Railroads and other organizations which worked large numbers of rough laborers became desperate. They offered higher wages and naturally turned to the South where was to be found the largest single body of unskilled laborers in the country. The Negro, who was in great economic need, responded readily in spite of his conservatism and hesitancy to risk the chances of a move.

*Labor Agents in the South.* Seeing the opportunity to secure labor from the South, many large corporations sent labor agents into the section to locate workers. These agents were forced to work clandestinely because of the strong opposition on the part of employers in the South. Laws and ordinances were passed fixing impossible license fees for labor solicitors and assessing exorbitant fines on those who failed to comply. In other places those suspected of being labor agents were summarily run out of town. The City Council of Jacksonville, Florida, fixed a license fee of $1,000 for labor agents, and Macon, Georgia, placed it at $25,000.[21] In spite of these handicaps the agents continued their work, with seeming good success. In this they were greatly aided by the Negro press. One paper, *The Chicago Defender,* carried among others the following advertisements:

"Wanted—10 molders. Must be experienced. $4.50 to $5.50 per day. Write B. F. R. *Defender* Office."

[20] "Negro Migration in 1916-1917," p. 59.
[21] Scott: "Negro Migration During the War," p. 73.

"Wanted—25 girls for dishwashing. Salary $7 a week and board. John R. Thompson, Restaurant, 314 South State Street. Call between 7 and 8 a.m. Ask for Mr. Brown."

"Wanted—25 young men as bus boys and porters. Salary $8 per week and board. John R. Thompson, Restaurant, 314 State Street. Call between 7 and 8 a.m. Ask for Mr. Brown."

"Molders wanted. Good pay, good working conditions. Firms supply cottages for married men. Apply T. L. Jefferson, 3439 State Street."

"Ten families and 50 men wanted at once for permanent work in the Connecticut tobacco fields. Good wages. Inquire National League on Urban Conditions among Negroes, 2303 Seventh Avenue, New York City, New York."

"Molders wanted. A large manufacturing concern, ninety miles from Chicago, is in need of experienced molders. Wages from $3 to $5.50. Extra for overtime. Transportation from Chicago only. Apply Chicago League on Urban Conditions among Negroes. T. Arnold Hill, Executive Secretary, 3719 State Street, Chicago."

"Laborers wanted for foundry, warehouse and yard work. Excellent opportunity to learn trades, paying good money. Start $2.50—$2.75 per day. Extra for overtime. Transportation advanced from Chicago only. Apply Chicago League on Urban Conditions among Negroes, 3719 South State Street, Chicago."

"Experienced machinists, foundrymen, pattern makers wanted, for permanent work in Massachusetts. Apply National League on Urban Conditions among Negroes, 2303 7th Ave., New York City."

"3,000 laborers to work on railroad. Factory hires all race help. More positions open than men for them."

"Men wanted at once. Good steady employment for colored. Thirty and 29½ cents per hour. Weekly payments. Good warm sanitary quarters free. Best commissary privileges. Towns of Newark and Jersey City. Fifteen minutes by car line offer cheap and suitable homes for men with families. For out of town parties of ten or more cheap transportation will be arranged. Only reliable men who stay on their job are wanted. Apply or write Butterworth Judson Corporation, Box 273, Newark, New Jersey, or Daniel T. Brantley, 315 West 119th Street, New York City."

"3.60 per day can be made in a steel foundry in Minnesota, by strong, healthy, steady men. Open only to men living in Chicago. Apply in person. Chicago League on Urban Conditions among Negroes, 3719 South State Street, Chicago, Illinois." [22]

[22] Quoted from "Negro Migration During the War," pp. 17-18.

*Movement Self-Propagating.* The movement once under way became self-propelling. A laborer from a community who went North and made a success wrote back glowing letters and often sent money back to relatives in order that they, too, might go north. These letters were the very best of all recruiting agents, often being read aloud in gatherings of Negroes, where much enthusiasm was worked up.

"One of the chief stimuli was discussion. The very fact that negroes were leaving in large numbers was a disturbing factor. The talk in the barber shops and grocery stores where men were wont to assemble soon began to take the form of reasons for leaving. There it was the custom to review all the instances of mistreatment and injustice which fell to the lot of the negro in the South. It was here also that letters from the North were read and fresh news on the exodus was first given out. In Hattiesburg, Mississippi, it was stated that for a while there was no subject of discussion but the migration. 'The packing houses in Chicago for a while seemed to be everything,' said one negro. 'You could not rest in your bed at night for Chicago.' Chicago came to be so common a word that they began to call it 'Chi.' Men went down to talk with the Chicago porters on the Gulf and Ship Island Railroad which ran through the town. They asked questions about the weather in Chicago. The report was that it was the same as in Hattiesburg." [23]

*Churches and Pastors Help the Movement.* In a Nashville church where the whole matter was discussed on a Sunday night, a Negro woman who spoke in opposition to the movement was bitterly attacked by the others, being called a "white folks Negro," a truckler, and other similar names. This same woman was swept into the tide in less than two months and went herself to Chicago. The psychology of the situation was all in favor of movement.

" 'You could see a man today,' said one Negro, 'and he would be calling the people who were leaving all kinds of names; he could even beat you when it came to calling them fools for going north. The next day when you met him he wouldn't talk so loud and the next day he wouldn't let you see him. That would be the last of him, because, unless you went to the depot, you wouldn't see him again. Whenever I saw them shying off from me, I always knew what they had up their sleeves.' It was 'just naturally fashionable' to leave for the North." [24]

*Grievances Exaggerated.* The more the matter was discussed the more grievous did the handicaps of the Negro in the South seem to be. In the excitement every report of success north was multiplied and exaggerated, and every report of hardships in the

[23] Scott: "Negro Migration During the War," p. 26.
[24] *Ibid.*, p. 39.

South was added to until it became more than tragic in details. There were comparatively few leaders who were able to keep a cool judgment under the influence of this mass psychology. In the ealier stages of the migration, the author sent out letters to about one hundred of the leading Negroes of the South, asking them to give what seemed to them the chief causes of the movement. Almost all of these men answered in full, giving economic conditions as one leading cause, but adding many others. Among these others were: desire for better school facilities, resentment of discrimination on street cars and other public carriers, fear of mob violence, injustice in the courts and civic disabilities. There can be no doubt that these general conditions had even more to do with the later stages of the migration than the economic motives, though the latter was undoubtedly the most powerful, and perhaps almost the sole motive in the earlier stages of the movement. The Negro press kept all these grievances clearly before the people, and thus helped forward the migration, even though in some instances they felt it was wiser for the Negro to stay in the South. The *Savannah Tribune* commented on the migration as follows:

*One Newspaper's Comment.* "The young Negro is leaving for the cities or for the North, where better conditions, embracing good schools, better wages, safety of person and property and wider social opportunity await him. It is well established that the right and privilege to spend a dollar at highest purchasing power must go along with the chance to earn it.

"The Negro preacher and teacher and merchant are leaving because their business is gone. These leaders of the group have preached the doctrine of law and order and thrift as means of insuring justice and protection, only to see their doctrines proved to be idlest folly by severest oppression and persecution on every hand. They too have only acted normally wherever they have moved to healthier conditions.

"There is no white man in the south, who has investigated it, who does not know that the charges alleged against Negroes by the rough-necks of rural communities where mobs are made, are mostly false and always highly colored. A Savannah policeman, his imaginative faculty doing over-time, conjured up in his brain a terrible situation at the Union Station a few days ago. He sent in a riot call, which caused much excitement. Upon investigation, no one saw any semblance of riot save himself. Such vivid imaginations breed trouble. In the rural districts the slightest occurrence is fanned into a consuming flame of hate, destruction and death, by such men. And there are thousands of them all over the land, and they have the thinkers and those who would do justice backed off. They put words into the mouths of the law-abiding and keep them silent and unthinking.

"What are we coming to?

"Lynching is increasing by numbers and in brutality. Lynching is the penalty for any charge. All the Negroes are terrorized or driven from their homes in a given community for the infraction of an individual. Prosperous self-respecting Negroes conceded to be good citizens by all are ordered to sell their possessions and get out.

"And the law-abiding white citizens, few and unassertive, do not dare to raise their hands and they speak safely and fearfully, if at all.

"This is just where the alarm comes in. It would seem that the fair and just and human personnel of the white south is 'on the run' or subdued. Many of these, hitherto at least fair, have been whipped into the ranks of those who abuse, take advantage and oppress.

"Many Negroes, now including those who have accumulated competencies and modest fortunes and reared fine families, are leaving to settle in northern centers, where there is at least a fighting chance to survive the mob, and where innocent men, women and children are not slaughtered." [25]

*The Louisville News Comment.* The *Louisville News* commented as follows:

"Talks with progressive members of the Race who are passing this way leaving the South bring out the startling revelations that there is a propaganda in the South against the intelligent, property-owning, well-to-do black man.

"It has been thought heretofore that lynching, horsewhipping, chain-ganging and such methods of 'Southern justice' were practiced only on the shiftless, worthless, ignorant and vicious 'Negro.' But it develops that this is the kind of Colored men wanted.

"Arkansas, Alabama and Mississippi daily furnish examples of fraud and persecution of the black man who has something, who knows something and who stands for something. A common ruse is to charge a man of means and property with improper relations with a white woman. He is then hounded out of town and his property sold at a sacrifice or completely confiscated. Appeals to leading whites are of no avail, for they are aiding and abetting the whole thing. What the answer is we cannot say. Surely the worm will turn. It means that not only will Colored labor leave the South, but Colored capital as well,

[25] Kerlin: "The Voice of the Negro," p. 129-131.

and, strange as it may seem, Colored capital is no inconsiderable thing in the South." [26]

*The Norfolk Journal's Comment.*    The *Norfolk Journal and Guide* added:

"The dissatisfaction and unrest that is so often and so unfortunately manifesting itself, and that is beginning of late to express itself in armed resistance to violence, had its first real expression in the wholesale migration of Afro-Americans from the South during 1916 and 1917.    Southern papers then said it was the lure of high wages and promises of 'social equality' that caused them to move out of the South in such large numbers, but as usual the press was mistaken.    The Negroes arose without leaders and with no other objective in view except freedom and marched away from lynching and mob violence, starvation wages, peonage, poor schools, injustice in the courts and other oppressive conditions, because they could no longer endure these conditions and no longer feel that their lives were safe in the Southland. True, their presence in the North in large numbers is causing race riots in many instances, and in some instances they are meeting conditions not much better than those they fled to escape, but their flight is going to ultimately awaken the conscience of this nation to the wrongs they suffer or bathe a good portion of it in blood." [27]

*Chicago Migrants.*    In the exhaustive study made by the Chicago Commission on Race Relations, the following causes for the migration were elicited from the Negroes who had settled in Chicago: low wages in the South, the boll weevil, lack of capital on which to carry Negroes while making crops, unsatisfactory living conditions, lack of school facilities, cessation of immigration from Europe leaving the North short on labor, lack of protection from mob violence in the South, injustice in the courts, inferior transportation facilities, etc.    All of these causes are amplified in the report.[28]

The following twenty-one answers from that many Negroes in Chicago were secured by the investigators who asked this question:  Do you feel greater freedom and independence in Chicago?  In what ways?

"1.  Yes.    Working conditions and the places of amusement.
2.  Yes.    The chance to make a living; conditions on the street cars and in movies.

[26] Kerlin: "The Voice of the Negro," p. 131.
[27] *Ibid.*, p. 141.
[28] "The Negro in Chicago," pp. 80-86.

3. Going into places of amusement and living in good neighborhoods.
4. Yes. Educationally, and in the home conditions.
5. Yes. Go anywhere you want to go; voting; don't have to look up to the white man, get off the street car for him, and go to the buzzard roost at shows.
6. Yes. Just seem to feel a general feeling of good-fellowship.
7. On the street cars and the way you are treated where you work.
8. Yes. Can go any place I like here. At home I was segregated and not treated like I had any rights.
9. Yes. Privilege to mingle with people; can go to the parks and places of amusement, not being segregated.
10. Yes. Feel free to do anything I please. Not dictated to by white people.
11. Yes. Had to take any treatment white people offered me there, compelled to say 'yes ma'am' or 'yes sir' to white people, whether you desired to or not. If you went to an ice cream parlor for anything you came outside to eat it. Got off sidewalk for white people.
12. Yes. Can vote; feel free; haven't any fear; make more money.
13. Yes. Voting; better opportunity for work; more respect from white people.
14. Yes. Can vote; no lynching; no fear of mobs; can express my opinion and defend myself.
15. Yes. Voting, more privileges; white people treat me better, not as much prejudice.
16. Yes. Feel more like a man. Same as slavery, in a way, at home. I don't have to give up the sidewalk here for white people as in my former home.
17. Yes. No restrictions as to shows, schools, etc. More protection of law.
18. Yes. Have more privileges and more money.
19. Yes. More able to express views on all questions. No segregation or discrimination.
20. Sure. Feel more freedom. Was not counted in the South; colored people allowed no freedom at all in the South.
21. Find things quite different to what they are at home. Haven't become accustomed to the place yet." [29]

*Social Causes of Migration.* That social causes had much to do with the migration is proven by the fact that those plantations and those industrial institutions which gave the Negroes better treatment and better living conditions did not lose nearly so many

[29] "The Negro in Chicago," pp. 98-99.

of their laborers as did those where conditions were bad.  Thus the American Cast Iron Pipe Company in Birmingham, Alabama, which for years had given special attention to the welfare of its workers, both white and colored, found its labor difficulties very much minimized during the migration north, as one of the chief officials reported to the writer.  Professor Leavell, in his investigations in Mississippi, found that planters who had dealt not only fairly but generously with their labor had been able to retain most if not all of the workers during this period.[30]

*The South Stirred by the Migration.*  All the evidence makes it perfectly clear that the South, in order to retain its Negro laborers, without whom economic progress cannot be made, must see to it that economic conditions for the Negro are improved, that justice and fair play are meted out to him, and that he shall come to feel that he is both respectable and respected. The distribution of a part of the Negro population throughout the nation will do no harm.  It will relieve the congestion in certain southern sections, will give the Negro a larger sense of freedom, will make the whole country feel the responsibility for improving the living conditions of the Negro, and will help the southern white man, who might otherwise be inactive, to see that the Negro gets a larger opportunity to reap the benefits of his labor here in the section where he has always lived, where he is most needed, and where perhaps he can make the greatest progress.

*Migration and Population Increase.*  When one turns to ask why the Negro population has increased so little during the last decade, the above facts of migration immediately suggest themselves as one of the causes.  A greater number of unmarried people migrated because they were free to move.  But in many cases husbands went and left their wives until they could secure enough money to set up house keeping in the new location.  These facts are evident from the comparative number of men and women in various cities in 1920.  In most of the southern cities women predominated—as in Nashville, Tennessee, where the census showed 47.7 per cent males and 52.3 per cent females.  Of course other causes than Negro migration may have entered in.  In northern cities males predominated, as in East St. Louis—52.5 per cent males, 47.5 per cent females; Gary, Indiana, 57.5 per cent males, 42.5 per cent females; Detroit, Michigan, 54.4 per cent males, 45.6 per cent females.  A similar conclusion might be drawn from the investigations of the Chicago Commission, which discovered of 274 families investigated 170, or 62 per cent, had lodgers.  As one reads the report one feels that the number of

[30] "Negro Migration in 1916-1917," p. 42 f.

unattached Negroes in Chicago is exceedingly large.[31]    It would
doubtless be so in other cities.  The general unrest caused by the
migration, the separation and temporary break-up of homes, the
difficulty of finding satisfactory living quarters in the new city
must have had considerable influence on the growth of population
during thè last five years of the last decade.

*City Dwelling Lowers Population Increase.*  Another explanation of the decreasing ratio of Negro population is found in the
cityward movement.  While Negroes have not moved to the city
as rapidly as have the white people, the influence of the city on
those who go is much more destructive to the Negro than to the
whites.  Mr. C. A. Williams while a graduate student in Southern
College of Young Men's Christian Associations (1920) prepared
a master's thesis on the influence of the city on the Negro family.  He personally investigated two hundred homes in Nashville,
Tennessee, found out the number of children born to the mothers
in those homes, and the numbers born to the grandmothers on
the mother's side.  Careful tabulation proved that those families
which had lived in the country until the children were well advanced not only had more children born than city families, but
that the number of children reared to maturity was far in excess
of the number in city bred families.[32]

*High Death Rate in Cities.*  According to the census report of
1915, city dwelling increased the death rate among Negroes from
18.3 (the rural rate) to 29.3 per thousand population, while city
dwelling increased the death rate among whites from 11.9 (the
rural rate) to 16.8.  Life in the city is, therefore, 60 per cent
more conducive to mortality among Negroes and 40 per cent more
conducive to death among whites than is life in rural sections.[33]
On the other hand city dwelling decreased the birth rate for
both whites and blacks, but the blacks suffered more than the
whites.  The number of children five years and under to each
one thousand women of motherhood age was in 1910 for whites
outside cities of 25,000 and over, 552, and for Negroes 596.  In
cities of over 25,000 inhabitants both groups are much smaller
but the Negroes show much greater decline.  The figures are
368 children for each 1000 white women, and 239 for this number
of colored women.  It is clearly seen, therefore, that cityward
movements militate more heavily against the colored population.[34]

*Health Conditions in Cities.*  The causes for such a disparity
are not far to seek.  To begin with, the housing conditions in
the cities are far from favorable to the rearing of a family.  Be-

[31] "The Negro in Chicago," Ch. V, *passim*.
[32] Cf. Mss. in Southern College Library.
[32] "Negro Population in U. S., 1790-1915," p. 315.
[34] *Ibid.*, p. 290.

cause rents are high and income small, there is almost always overcrowding. Lodgers are taken in to help pay the house rent. Miss Ovington found that in New York "the shelter afforded is poorer than that given the white resident whose dwelling touches the black, the rents are a little higher, and the landlord fails to pay attention to the ragged paper, or to the ceiling which scatters plaster flakes upon the floor." [35] . . . This overcrowding and poor housing, of course, influence the mortality statistics.

The "Chicago Commission" made "a rough classification of Negro housing according to types, ranging from the best, designated as 'Type A,' to the poorest, designated as 'Type D.'" 238 blocks were intensively investigated covering almost all the Negro residence sections of the city. "Approximately 5 per cent of Chicago's Negro population live in 'Type A' houses, 10 per cent in 'Type B,' 40 per cent in 'Type C,' and 45 per cent in the poorest, 'Type D'." [36] Notations in the investigators' reports on housing conditions ran like the following:

"No gas, bath, or toilet. Plumbing very bad; toilet leaks; bowl broken; leak in kitchen sink; water stands in kitchen; leak in bath makes ceiling soggy and wet all the time. Plastering off in front room. General appearance very bad inside and out. Had to get city behind owner to put in windows, clean, and repair plumbing. Heat poor; house damp. Plumbing bad; leaks. Hotwater heater out of order. Needs repairing done to roof and floors. In bad repair; toilet in yard used by two families. Toilet off from dining-room; fixtures for gas; no gas; just turned off; no bath; doors out of order; won't fasten. Sanitary condition poor; dilapidated condition; toilet won't flush; carries water to bathtub. Plumbing bad; roof leaks; plastering off in toilet; window panes broken and out; no bath or gas. Plastering off, water that leaks from flat above; toilet leaks; does not flush; washbowl and bath leak very badly; repairs needed on back porch; rooms need calcimining. No water in hydrant in hall; no toilet, bath, or gas; general repair needed. Water not turned on for sink in kitchen; water for drinking and cooking purposes must be carried in; toilet used by four families; asked landlord to turn on water in kitchen; told them to move; roof leaks; stairs and back porch in bad order. Sewer gas escapes from basement pipes; water stands in basement. House dirty; flues in bad condition; gas pipes leak; porch shaky. No heat and no hot water; no repairing done; no screens; gas leaks all over house; stationary tubs leak. Water pipes rotted out; gas pipes leak. Toilet leaks;

[35] Ovington: "Half a Man," p. 36.
[36] "The Negro in Chicago," p. 186.

plastering off; windowpanes out.  Plastering off; large rat holes all over; paper hanging from ceiling." [37]

*Philadelphia Conditions 20 Years Ago.*  Twenty years ago DuBois made an exhaustive study of the Philadelphia Negro, and found 829 families living in one room per family, and only 334 families out of 2441 investigated having access to a bath room.  He notes that the "bad sanitary conditions are shown in the death rate."  "Of 1751 families making returns 932 had a private yard 12 x 12 feet or larger; 312 had a private yard smaller than 12 x 12 feet, 507 had either no yard at all or a yard and outhouse in common with the other denizens of the tenement or alley." [38]  Speaking of the seventh ward he says: "Over 20 per cent and possibly 30 per cent of the Negro families of this ward lack some of the very elementary accommodations necessary to health and decency." [39]  Philadelphia had 84,000 Negroes in 1910, and 134,000 in 1920, so that crowding and bad housing soon became critical.  "Numbers of these immigrants died from exposure during the first winter, and others who died because of the inability to stand the northern climate made the situation seem unusually alarming." [40]  Conditions which are found in New York, Chicago, and Philadelphia can perhaps be duplicated to an extent in all the larger cities of the North.  The Negro certainly does not have a fair chance at health and life.

*Conditions Bad in Southern Cities.*  The conditions in southern cities are hardly less difficult.  Anyone who knows southern cities will readily recognize the fact that large numbers of Negroes live on back alleys, under viaducts and bridges, near the dump heaps, on the river banks, in back yards and other unsanitary and unhealthful places.  The best streets in the city are not available for Negro homes, however much money the Negro may possess.  There is less of sewerage, poorer street paving and cleaning, less drainage, and poor sanitary conditions in every way. One of my students, investigating housing conditions in Nashville, found one block with two intersecting alleys running through it, and on these alleys 33 Negro shanties stood.  Another block had one alley running thorugh it and two blind alleys, and a blind street; on these four there were housing spaces for 126 families. Needless to say the houses were all small frame buildings, standing flush with the alley, and not separated by more than three or four feet of space.  These are not extreme cases.  One has seen

[37] "The Negro in Chicago," p. 153.
[38] DuBois: "The Philadelphia Negro," pp. 292-293.
[39] *Ibid.*, p. 293.
[40] Scott: "Negro Migration During the War," pp. 135-136.

scores of such situations in practically every southern city. Under such conditions no wonder the population does not increase rapidly.

*High Infant Mortality.* The high rate of infant mortality among Negroes accounts in part for the slow increase of the Negro population. This matter will be treated more fully under the chapter on health, but it is necessary here to note that nowhere does crowding and poor sanitation show its effect more quickly than in the death rate of babies. But the most important cause of infant mortality is poor care and poor feeding. Negro mothers in great numbers work away from home, leaving their children to the care of older brothers and sisters, often under ten years of age, or sometimes under the care of aged grandparents who are too ignorant and too old to give the children proper attention. Ovington tells us that 31.4 per cent of the married women of New York in 1900 were self-supporting, while of the white married women only 4.2 per cent were bread winners. An investigation in Nashville, Tennessee, some years since showed that 47 per cent of all Negro women of motherhood age were bread winners. In 1900, 40.7 per cent of all Negro women in the South were bread winners, and only 11.8 per cent of white women. "In a tour of investigation in Columbia, S. C., recently, I found a home of six children where the mother cooked for a white family. She had a three-months-old baby and had been away from it continually during the day hours since the child was one week old. She simply gave it a sugar bag to suck, and, locking the door, left it in the house alone all day, coming home once during the day to nurse it. The other children were away at school or at work. It would be nothing less than a miracle if this child should grow into a healthy youth, and yet this condition is found in many of the negro homes." [41] Children need the care of their mothers if they are to grow strong, healthy and moral. No race can hope to make great progress until its motherhood can stay at home and make a home. In cases where Negro mothers are forced to work out for a living provision should be made for the care of their children in day homes handled by competent persons.

*Poor Food and High Death Rate.* Poor food, and insufficient food, due to low wages, undoubtedly accounts for a part of the high death rate.

Martin, in his investigation of the Negro population of Kansas City, estimated that fully 25 per cent were underfed.[42] Fried foods are almost exclusively eaten by the working class, and Negro children of this class eat very irregularly and poorly pre-

[41] Weatherford: "Present Forces in Negro Progress," p. 69.
[42] Martin: "Our Negro Population," p. 68.

pared food. All these things go to undermine the health of the
Negro people. The death rate in Kansas City for 1912 was 15.5
for whites, and 31.2 for Negroes.[43]

*Tuberculosis Prevalent.* Due to these living conditions and
lack of nourishment, certain diseases make great ravages among
the Negro peoples. Martin found that tuberculosis claimed 6.2
Negro deaths out of every thousand of the Negro population,
and 1.1 whites for each thousand. This means that nearly six
times as many Negroes per thousand die from this disease in
Kansas City as are claimed from whites. Pneumonia claimed
three times as many Negroes as whites out of every thousand of
each rate in this city.[44]

Crowding in homes makes for immorality, and that in turn
makes for a high death rate. Due to venereal disease the birth
rate is cut down, and thousands of Negro children inherit a
debilitated constitution. It is a well known fact that still births
are more common among colored people than among whites,
partly due to exposure of Negro women while at work, partly
due to sexual dissipation. The death rate of children during the
first month after birth is three times as high as in any other similar
period after. The rate for Negro children this age is nearly twice
as great as for white children, the respective rates for children
under one year of age in 1910 being 261 for Negroes and 129 for
whites.[45]

*Premature Birth.* In the entire registration area of cities over
100,000 population and having as many as 2500 Negro population
in 1910, "premature birth is given as the cause of death in 247
out of 397 cases of infant mortality under one day, the other chief
causes of death under one day being congenital debility, injuries
at birth and malformations. Premature birth is the most frequent cause of death in the age period 'one day under one week,'
congenital debility becoming an important cause in this period,
and the most frequent cause in the period 'one week under one
month.' Diarrhea and enteritis become the predominant causes
of death among infants more than one month old, other important
causes after the first month being broncho-pneumonia, pneumonia, and in the earlier months congenital debility." [46] The
immoral conditions superinduced in part at least by poverty
and overcrowding has much to do with this infant death rate.
Whatever the causes of infant mortality, it militates against the
growth of Negro population. Monroe N. Work claims that pure
food, pure air, pure water, would decrease the Negro death rate

[43] Martin: "Our Negro Population," p. 114.
[44] *Ibid.*, p. 115.
[45] "Negro Population of U. S. from 1790-1915," p. 315.
[46] *Ibid.*, p. 318.

one-fourth and would reduce the number of Negro deaths by 100,000 per year.[47]

*Negroes Die Twice as Fast as Whites.* The general death rate among Negroes is far in excess of that among whites. The death rate of Negroes enumerated in 1900 was, for the decade between 1900 and 1910, seventeen per cent, and the corresponding figure for whites was 9.9 per cent. This higher death rate is due to environmental causes, including housing, food, occupation, morality, etc. The census return points out "that the inference certainly is not in any degree warranted by the data that the differences in mortality between Negroes and other classes are racial or natural differences in the sense that they would persist under different environmental and economic conditions for these classes. Until the contrary fact is established the probability is rather on contrary, that the differences in mortality represent environmental factors which may be remedied by gradual improvement in the social, economic and hygienic status of the Negro population.

"That such improvement shall be achieved is unquestionably of vital importance to the Negro race, and there is no obvious reason why it should not be rapid and complete, provided a concerted and persistent social effort on the part of the Negro race is made for its achievement.[48]

*Responsibility on Both Whites and Blacks.* While the census commentator is right in placing the responsibility for better environmental conditions on the shoulders of the colored people themselves, it nevertheless remains true, and every fair minded white man recognizes it as true, that much of this improvement can only be brought about by the active coöperation of both races. It is certainly to the mutual advantage of both that there shall be a healthy, happy and efficient citizenship, and that can be true only when all the people, both white and black, are happy and efficient. Instead, therefore, of rejoicing in the comparative decrease of the Negro race, it behooves the white people to do everything possible to maintain this race as a productive agency in the country whose resources are so boundless as to be limited only by the supply of efficient workers who can make it yield up its fruitage for a larger comfort and a fuller life for all the people. But the real basis of interest in Negro health is one of pure humanity and Christian brotherhood.

[47] "Negro Year Book, 1917," pp. 338-342.
[48] "Negro Population in U. S., 1790-1915," p. 300.

CHAPTER XII

THE RELIGIOUS LIFE OF THE NEGRO

*African Background.* When the slave was brought to America he brought with him an intense religious consciousness,
albeit his religion was largely, as we have seen, a mixture of
superstition, magic, and fear of evil spirts. He had, however,
been schooled as a race for long centuries in religious responses.
He promptly transferred to America his religious rites, and set
up for himself a religious ceremonial. A new priesthood sprang
up in the form of the Hoodoo man and the Conjure woman.
This new priesthood was decidedly hampered in its movements
because of the attitude of the Christian masters. The whites,
while not overburdened with passion for Christianity, were at
least strongly opposed to pagan rites, hence the Negro religion
immediately began to undergo radical changes. The Negro was
introduced early to the Christian church and soon a definite provision was made for his attendance through the building of galleries where the family servants were regularly housed. The
more conscientious masters early began giving instruction to the
slaves of their entire plantation. As early as 1623, only four
years after the first Negroes were introduced into the colonies,
a list of names of families and their servants contains that of
Captain William Tucker and his Negroes. Among other persons
named are: "Antoney Negro; Isabell Negro; and William their
child Baptised." [1] In 1461 we read of a John Graween—a Negro
who was eager that his child "should be made a Christian, and
brought up in the fear of God and in the knowledge of religion
taught and exercised in the Church of England." [2] In 1645
Francis Pott, of Northampton County, Virginia, bought two
children of Emanuel Dregis, an indentured Negro, one of the
conditions of the sale being that the children in question should
be reared in the fear of God and the knowledge of Jesus Christ.[3]
Thus from the very beginnings of the life of the Negro in
America, religion was an elemental part of his training. Here
in reality he began to receive what the early Portuguese slaves

[1] Earnest: "The Religious Development of the Negro in Virginia," p. 16.
[2] *Ibid.,* p. 17. ·
[3] *Ibid.,* p. 18.

298

claimed they desired to give—instruction in a true religion and in the knowledge of the Christian's Bible.

*Early Slaves Baptised Before Transport.* As noted before, the early Spanish rulers insisted that all African slaves shipped to the West Indies must be taken by way of the continent where they could be "Christianized," and only when the demand became so insistent for more labor that this delay became inconvenient was it made possible to ship direct from Africa to the colonial islands. Strange enough, the early English settlers in Virginia found themselves in a dilemma because many of their slaves did promptly become Christians, at least in name. To many of the conscientious colonists it was inconsistent to hold a Christian as a slave, and yet since America was the land of religious liberty, it seemed equally inconsistent to refuse their slaves the chance of salvation. Like many of their modern descendants, they tried to settle a moral question by legal procedure, salving their conscience, and saving their property by putting on their statute books in 1667 the following statement:

*Baptism Did Not Free Slaves.* "Whereas some doubts have risen whether children that are slaves by birth, and by the charity and piety of their owners made partakers of the blessed sacrament of baptisme, should by vertue of their baptisme be made ffree; *It is enacted and declared by this grand assembly, and the authority thereof,* that the conferring of baptisme doth not alter the condition of the person as to his bondage or ffreedome; that divers masters, ffreed from this doubt, may more carefully endeavor the propagation of Christianity by permitting children, though slaves, or those of greater growth if capable to be admitted to that sacrament." [4]

In 1670 the Virginia Assembly, to protect the economic interests of the colonists and to enable them to purchase slaves without fear of losing them, passed a law that "all servants not being Christians imported into the colony by shipping shall be slaves for their lives." The term "by shipping" was a means of distinguishing between Negro slaves brought in from Africa and Indians brought in by land. The Negro Church [5] thinks that witchcraft spread rapidly among the Negro slaves because "no effort was made by the masters to offer anything better. The reason for this was the widespread idea that it was contrary to law to hold Christians as slaves." [6] The colony of North Carolina early passed a law which read: "Since charity obliges

[4] Earnest: "The Religious Development of the Negro in Virginia," p. 22. (Quoting Hening, Vol. II, p. 260.)
[5] *Atlanta University Publications, No. 8.*
[6] "The Negro Church"—Atlanta University Publications, p. 6.

us to wish well to the souls of all men, and religion ought to alter nothing in a man's civil estate or right, it shall be lawful for slaves as well as for others to enter themselves and to be of what church or profession any of them shall think best, and thereof be as fully members as any freeman. But yet no slave shall hereby be exempted from the civil dominion his master hath over him, but be in all things in the same state and condition he was in before." [7] The revised constitution of North Carolina, 1698, retained this clause. Maryland declared in 1671 that baptism did not give manumission in any way to slaves.

*Religious Rights Had No Legal Force.* In spite of all these enactments setting forth the religious rights of slaves, Goodell, in his Slave Code, published shortly before the Civil War, wrote:

"But chattels have no literary or religious rights. He is a chattel 'to all intents, constructions, and *purposes* whatsoever.' He is 'in the power of a master, to whom he belongs'—'entirely subject to the will of his master'—'not ranked among *sentient beings,* but among *things.*' It would be an absurdity for *such* a code to recognize the slave as possessing religious rights. It is free from any such absurdity.

"Except the provisions, in some of the States, for the *'baptism'* of slaves, and for their 'spiritual assistance when *sick,'* we have found no recognition of their religious wants, their religious natures, or immortal destinies. Even *here* they seem to be considered passive beings, whose salvation is to be bestowed by their masters. The American Slave Code, from beginning to end, knows no rights of conscience in its subjects. The master is to be implicitly obeyed. His will is to be law. The slave is allowed no self-direction, no sacred marriage, no family relation, no marital rights—none that may not be taken away by his master.

*Slavery Abrogated All Real Rights.* "Religion and its duties are based on human relations, including family relations. *These* relations, the 'relation of slave ownership' and chattelhood abrogates. Religion requires and cherishes self-control; but the 'owner's' authority supersedes and prohibits self-control. Religion implies free agency; but 'the slave is *not* a free agent.' His 'condition is merely a passive one.' So says the Slave Code, and so says ecclesiastical law, and therefore releases him from the obligations of the seventh commandment. Witness the decision of the Savannah River Baptist Association, while allowing its slave members, without censure, to take second or third companions, in obedience to their masters, by whom their original connections had been severed!" [8]

[7] Quoted from Bassett: "Slavery and Servitude in the Colony of North Carolina," p. 45.
[8] Goodell: "American Slave Code," p. 252-253.

*Slave Owners Encouraged Religion.*  Whatever the legal status of the Negro with reference to religion, it is certain that great numbers of slave owners were intensely in earnest to see that the Negro had a chance to know the Bible and to enter into religious life.  Of course, there were many masters who were not interested in religion at all, either for themselves or for their slaves.  There were others who feared any form of advancement or education for their slaves lest it make them dissatisfied with their position as slaves.  But the truth remains evident that many did desire their slaves to become Christians.  The attitude of planters was much like the attitude of manufacturers today, and I believe from careful study would compare favorably with the interest shown by modern employers in the religious development of their workers.

*Society for Propagation of the Gospel.*  In 1701 the Society for the Propagation of the Gospel in Foreign Parts was incorporated under the patronage of William III.  The first meeting was held on June 27, 1701.  The first purpose of this organization was to send ministers to the American colonies who would serve the white colonists who were members of the Church of England. The second motive was to extend the Gospel to Indians and Negroes.  This society entered with zeal and enthusiasm into its task.  Reverend George Keith and Reverend John Talbot were sent out as traveling preachers, who traveled from New England to North Carolina, along the coast, and preached whenever opportunity offered, over a period of two years.  Reverend Samuel Thomas was the first missionary sent to the Negroes.  He went to South Carolina in 1702.  He was originally designated for Indian mission work, but due to the influence of the Governor, Sir Nathaniel Johnson, he made his residence at Goose Creek, and worked for four years until his death among the slaves.  His first report to the Society claimed "he had taken much pains in instructing the Negroes and had learned twenty of them to read." In 1705 he writes: "I have here presumed to give an account of one thousand slaves so far as they know of it and are desirous of Christian knowledge and seem willing to prepare themselves for it, in learning to read, for which they redeem the time from their labor.  Many of them can read the Bible distinctly and great numbers of them were learning when I left the province." [9]

In 1706, on the death of Reverend Thomas, Dr. LeJeau succeeded to the work, and reported he found "parents and masters indued with much good will and a ready disposition to have their children and servants taught the Christian religion."  In 1714 he reported seventy English and eighty Negroes as communicants

[9] "The Journal of Negro History," Vol. I, p. 350.

of the church.[10]   Dr. LeJeau died in 1717 and was succeeded by Reverend Mr. Ludlam, who reported to the Society that:

"There were in his parish a large number of negroes, natives of the place, who understood English well.   He took good pains to instruct several of them in the principles of Christian religion, and afterward admitted them to baptism.   He said if the masters of them would heartily concur to forward so good a work, all those who have been born in the country might without much difficulty be instructed and received into the Church.   Mr. Ludlam continued his labors among the negroes and every year taught and baptized several of them; in one year eleven, besides some *mulattoes*." [11]

*Difference in Attitude of Various Masters.*   That there was both opposition on the part of some masters, and favorable coöperation on the part of others, is clearly indicated from the report of Reverend E. Taylor, who was sent as a missionary to South Carolina in 1713:

"As I am a minister of Christ and of the Church of England, and a Missionary of the most Christian Society in the whole world, I think it my indispensable and special duty to do all that in me lies to promote the conversion and salvation of the poor heathens here, and more especially of the Negro and Indian slaves in my own parish, which I hope I can truly say I have been sincerely and earnestly endeavoring ever since I was a minister here where there are many Negro and Indian slaves in a most pitifull deplorable and perishing condition tho' little pitied by many of their masters and their conversion and salvation little desired and endeavored by them.   If the masters were but good Christians themselves and would but concurre with the ministers, we should then have good hopes of the conversion and salvation at least òf some of their Negro and Indian slaves.   But too many of them rather oppose than concurr with us and are angry with us, I am sure I may say with me for endeavouring as much as I doe the conversion of their slaves. . . . I cannot but honour Madame Haigue. . . . In my parish a very considerable number of Negroes . . . were very loose and wicked and little inclined to Christianity before her coming among them.   I can't but honor her so much . . . as to acquaint the Society with the extraordinary pains this gentlewoman and one Madm. Edwards, that came with her, have taken to instruct those negroes in the principles of the Christian Religion and to instruct and reform them: And the wonderful success they have met with, in about a half a year's time in this

[10] Harrison: "The Gospel Among the Slaves," p. 41.
[11] *Idem.*

great and good work.  Upon these gentle women's desiring me to come and examine these negroes. . . . I went and among other things I asked them, Who Christ was.  They readily answered. He is the Son of God and Saviour of the world and told me that they embraced Him with all their hearts as such, and I desired them to rehearse the Apostles' Creed, and the Ten Commandments and the Lord's Prayer, which they did very distinctly and perfectly.  Fourteen of them gave me so great satisfaction, and were so very desirous to be baptized, that I thought it my duty to baptize them and therefore I baptized these 14 last Lord's Day.  And I doubt not but these gentlewomen will prepare the rest of them for Baptism in a short Time." [12]

*Opposition to Established Church.*  It is altogether likely that part of the opposition of the Carolina planters to the work of missionaries among their slaves lay not in opposition to the slaves becoming Christians, but in opposition to the established church which the Society for the Propagation of the Gospel in Foreign Parts represented.  Sir Nathaniel Johnson, the Governor of South Carolina, had by trickery secured the passage of a test act in 1704, by which act all members of the Assembly were to subscribe to the doctrines and usages of the Church of England.  This raised a storm of protest from the inhabitants in general, and this opposition would of necessity react against the work of the missionaries who represented the Church of England.[13]

Reverend John Blair, sent out to North Carolina in 1704, failed in his mission, partly because the settlements were so scattered. Other missionaries, however, followed and considerable work was done.  Opposition to the Church of England was also strong here, and some masters feared that instruction of every kind, even religious, would make their slaves restless, or might legally make them free.  "In the course of time, when the workers overcame the prejudice of masters, a missionary would sometimes baptize fifteen to twenty-four in a month, forty to fifty in six months, and sixty to seventy in a year." [14]

The Society seems to have done little work in Virginia, but did carry forward an aggressive work in Maryland, Pennsylvania, and New York.

*Work in Pennsylvania.*  "Rev. Mr. Pugh, a missionary at Appoquinimmick, Pennsylvania, said, in a letter to the Society in 1737, that he had received a few blacks and that the masters of the Negroes were prejudiced against their being Christians.  Rev.

[12] "The Journal of Negro History," Vol. I, p. 351.
[13] Cf. Weeks: "Religious Development of the Province of North Carolina," p. 43 f.
[14] Quoted by "Journal of Negro History," Vol. I, p. 353, from Digest of Records of Society for Propagation of the Gospel.

Richard Locke christened eight Negroes in one family in Lancaster in 1747 and another Negro there the following year.   In 1774 the Rev. Mr. Jenney reported that there was 'a great and daily increase of Negroes in this city who would with joy attend upon a catechist for instruction'; that he had baptized several, but was unable to add to his other duties; and the Society, ever ready to lend a helping hand to such pious undertakings, appointed the Rev. W. Sturgeon as catechist for the Negroes at Philadelphia. The next to show diligence in the branch of the work of the Society was Mr. Neill of Dover.   He baptized as many as 162 within 18 months.

*Work in New York.* "The most effective work of the Society among Negroes of the Northern colonies was accomplished in New York.   In that colony, the instruction of the Negro and Indian slaves to prepare them for conversion, baptism, and communion was a primary charge oft repeated to every missionary and schoolmaster of the Society.   In addition to the general efforts put forth in the colonies, there was in New York a special provision for the employment of sixteen clergymen and thirteen lay teachers mainly for the evangelization of the slaves and the free Indians.   For the Negro slaves a catechizing school was opened in New York City in 1704 under the charge of Elias Neau." [15]

*Conspiracy of 1712—Effect on Mission Work.*   In 1712 there was a conspiracy of slaves in New York.   The Negroes started a fire at night and planned to kill all the English as they ran to the fire.   The conspiracy was promptly quelled, but the religious instruction of Mr. Neau was charged with causing the conspiracy:

"This wicked conspiracy was at first apprehended to be general among all the negroes, and opened the mouths of many to speak against giving the negroes instruction.   Mr. Neau durst hardly appear abroad for some days; his school was blamed as the main occasion of this barbarous plot.   On examination, only two of all his school were so much as charged with the plot, and on full trial the guilty negroes were found to be such as never came to Mr. Neau's school; and what is very observable, the persons, whose negroes were found to be most guilty, were such as were the declared opposers of making them Christians.   However, a great jealousy was now raised, and the common cry very loud against instructing the negroes." [16]

Pierre says: "The missionaries met with more opposition than encouragement in New England.   The Puritans had no serious

[15] "Journal of Negro History," Vol. I, pp. 355 and 356.
[16] Coffin: "An Account of Some of the Principal Slave Insurrections," p. 11.

objection to seeing the Negroes saved, but when conversion meant the incorporation of the undesirable class into the state, then so closely connected with the church, many New Englanders became silent." [17]

In 1727 the Bishop of London wrote 'letters to Masters and Mistresses of Families in the colonies, exhorting them to encourage and promote the instruction of their negroes in the Christian faith,' and also letters to the missionaries exhorting zeal in the work for this neglected group.[18] These letters bore good fruit.

*Zinzendorf's Interest.*  In 1737 Count Zinzendorf had met Oglethorpe, the founder of the Georgia colony.  In their converse together Zinzendorf's interest was greatly aroused on behalf of the Indians and Negroes of America.  Oglethorpe and others urged Zinzendorf to send them missionaries.  The Count conferred with the Archbishop of Canterbury as to whether Moravian missionaries would be acceptable to the Church of England.  Being assured that they would, Peter Boehler and George Schulius set out for Georgia in 1738.  They were, however, met with many obstacles and finally turned North to Pennsylvania, where Count Zinzendorf himself three years later arrived for a mission.

"In 1747 and 1748 some Brethren belonging to Bethlehem undertook several long and difficult journeys through Maryland, Virginia, and the borders of North Carolina in order to preach the gospel to the negroes, who, generally speaking, received it with eagerness.  Various proprietors, however, avowing their determination not to suffer strangers to instruct their negroes, as they had their own ministers whom they paid for that purpose, our brethren ceased from their efforts.  It appears from the letters of Brother Spangenberg, who spent the greater part of the year 1749 at Philadelphia, and preached the gospel to the negroes in that city, that the labors of the Brethren amongst them were not entirely fruitless.  Thus he writes in 1751: 'On my arrival in Philadelphia I saw numbers of negroes still buried in all their native ignorance and darkness, and my soul was grieved for them. Soon after some of them came to me, requesting instruction, at the same time acknowledging their ignorance in the most affecting manner.  They begged that a weekly sermon might be delivered expressly for their benefit.  I complied with their request, and confined myself to the most essential truths of Scripture.  Upward of seventy negroes attended on these occasions, several of whom were powerfully awakened, applied for further instruction and expressed a desire to be united to Christ and his Church by the sacrament of baptism, which was accordingly administered to them.' " [19]

[17] "Journal of Negro History," Vol. I, p. 359.
[18] Cf. Harrison: "The Gospel Among the Slaves," p. 44.
[19] *Ibid.,* p. 48.

Thus the English Church and the Moravians paved the way for a fuller and more complete work of evangelization by the Episcopalian, Presbyterian, Methodist, and Baptist churches.

*Wesley's American Journey—Methodist Opposition to Slavery.* John Wesley's visit to America in 1737 had paved the way for the introduction of Methodism into the colonies. "In 1766 a little group of Methodist families that had found one another out among the recent comers in New York . . . formed themselves into a class and promised to attend at future meetings." [20]   In 1769 in response to earnest entreaties from America, two of Wesley's itinerant preachers, Boardman and Pilmoor, arrived with his commission to organize an American itinerancy.[21]   Frances Asbury, the pioneer of American Methodism, arrived in 1771, and in 1784 with the arrival of Bishop Coke, and the consecration of Asbury as Bishop, Methodism became an organized church movement. Even before the church was fully organized, there was a strong sentiment among its members against slavery, and Bacon calls the Methodist Society the "great anti-slavery society of the period."   As early as 1780 the gathering of Methodist itinerants declared: "that slavery is contrary to the laws of God, man, and nature, and hurtful to society; contrary to the dictates of conscience and pure religion, and doing that which we would not that others should do to us and ours." [22]   The early evangelistic meetings of this society extended both to whites and blacks.   In Virginia and the Carolinas the Methodists and Episcopalians won many converts among the Negroes between 1770 and 1780—a period of evangelistic zeal.   One letter of this period describes a meeting in which "the chapel was full of whites and blacks." [23] Another letter says: "Hundreds of Negroes were among them, with tears streaming down their faces." [24]

*Religious Gatherings of Negroes.*   At the eighth conference in Baltimore, 1780, the question was asked: "Ought not the assistant to meet the colored people himself and appoint as helpers in his absence proper white persons, and not suffer them to stay late and meet by themselves?" [25]   The first enumeration of members as colored and white is returned in 1786 as follows: 1890 colored, 18,791 white.   In 1787 there are 3803 colored members reported and the conference took the following action:

"Question 17.   What directions shall we give for the promotion of the spiritual welfare of the colored people?   Answer.   We

[20] Bacon: "History of American Christianity," p. 199.
[21] *Ibid.,* p. 200.
[22] Townsend: "New History of Methodism," p. 79.
[23] Harrison: "Gospel Among the Slaves," p. 53.
[24] *Idem.*
[25] *Idem.*

conjure all our ministers and preachers by the love of God and the salvation of souls, and do require them by all the authority that is invested in us to leave nothing undone for the spiritual benefit and salvation of them within their respective circuits or districts; and for this purpose to embrace every opportunity of inquiring into the state of their souls, and to unite in society those who appear to have a real desire of fleeing from the wrath to come; to meet such in class, and to exercise the whole Methodist discipline among them." [26]

*Colored Methodists.* Ten years later in 1797 the Methodists reported colored members as follows: Massachusetts 8, Rhode Island 2, Connecticut 15, New York 238, New Jersey 127, Pennsylvania 198, Delaware 923, Maryland 5106, Virginia 2490, North Carolina 2071, South Carolina 890, Georgia 148, Tennessee 42, Kentucky 57, a total of 12,215, or one-fourth of the entire membership of the church. [27]

*First Negro Bishop.* In 1800 the Methodist Conference authorized the bishops to ordain "African Preachers," and "Richard Allen, of Philadelphia was the first colored man who received orders under this rule." [28]  In 1816 the Methodists reported 42,304 colored members. This was less than in 1815, because Richard Allen had withdrawn his congregation of more than one thousand Negroes and established an independent church known as the African Methodist Episcopal Church. In 1819 the colored Methodists of New York, including 14 local preachers and 929 members, also seceded and entered the African Church. [29]

*Negro Evangelism.* The interest in Negro evangelization was most intense in the Carolinas where Dr. Capers, afterwards bishop, was one of the circuit riders, covering twenty-four appointments on a route of three hundred miles. He reports that in 1810 the South Carolina Conference had seventy-four preachers, seventeen thousand seven hundred and eighty-eight white members, and eight thousand two hundred and two colored members. [30] We have in an earlier chapter noted Caper's interest in the religious life of the Negro and given his description of Henry Evans, a Negro preacher. In 1828 the General Conference held at Pittsburgh elected Dr. Capers as fraternal delegate to the British Methodist Church. There was much opposition to him because he was a slave owner, but Bishop Seoul and Bishop McKendree, both southern bishops, insisted that his interest in the religious in-

[26] Harrison: "Gospel Among the Slaves," p. 54.
[27] *Ibid.,* p. 63.
[28] *Idem.*
[29] *Ibid.,* p. 67.
[30] Wightman: "Life of Bishop Capers," p. 132.

struction of the Negro showed his real spirit.[31]   On Capers' return from England he resumed his duty as Presiding Elder of the Charleston district.   His active interest in the religious life of the slaves is not only clear from the inscription on his tomb: "William Capers, the founder of missions to the slaves," [32] but from the fact that three Episcopalian planters appealed to him to furnish them missionaries to their Negroes.   Wightman's account of the occurrence is as follows:

*Capers Begins Work for Slaves.*   "After his return from England, Mr. Capers was waited on by the Hon. Charles C. Pinckney, a gentleman who had a large planting interest on Santee, to ascertain whether a Methodist exhorter could be recommended to him as a suitable person to oversee his plantation.   Mr. Pinckney stated, as the reasons for this application, Mr. Capers's known interest in the religious welfare of the colored population, and the fact that the happy results which had followed the pious endeavors of a Methodist overseer on the plantation of one of his Georgia friends, had directed his attention to the subject.   Mr. Capers told Mr. Pinckney that he doubted whether he could serve him in that particular way, but that, if he would allow him to make application to the Bishop and Missionary Board at the approaching session of the Conference, he would venture to promise that a minister, for whose character he could vouch fully, should be sent to his plantation as a missionary, whose time and efforts should be devoted exclusively to the religious instruction and spiritual welfare of his colored people.   To this proposal Mr. Pinckney gave his cordial assent.   Soon after, Col. Lewis Morris and Mr. Charles Baring, of Pon Pon, united in a similar request. These were gentlemen of high character, who thus took the initiative in a course of missionary operations which may justly be termed the glory of Southern Christianity.   They were members of the Protestant Episcopal Church, but availed themselves of the earliest opening which the peculiar itinerant organization of the Methodist Church afforded, for furnishing religious instruction to their slaves at the hands of men deemed competent and safe in the judgment of Mr. Capers." [33]

*First Methodist Missionaries to Slaves.*   Reverend John Honour and Reverend John H. Massey were appointed as the first missionaries of the Conference to serve on these plantations, and Dr. Capers undertook to supervise the work in addition to his duties as Presiding Elder.[34]   "The operation of the first year gath-

[31] Wightman: "Life of Bishop Capers," p. 258 f.
[32] McTyiere: "History of Methodism," p. 584.
[33] Wightman: "Life of Bishop Capers," p. 291.
[34] McTyiere: "History of Methodism," p. 584.

ered four hundred and seventeen church members. Foothold was gained. The experiment, eyed with distrust by most of the planters, denounced by many as a hurtful innovation upon the established order of things, favored by very few, was commenced. . . . The second year the membership of these missions more than doubled itself." [35] The growth of these missions is summarized by Wightman as follows:

"Nearly a generation has passed away since the commencement of these missionary operations among the blacks. It is interesting to trace their expansion and results through a quarter of a century. That there has been a large development is proved by the statistics published from year to year by the Missionary Society. In 1833 two additional mission stations were established. In 1834, they numbered six; in 1835, eight; in 1836, nine; in 1837, ten; and ten years afterwards, viz., in 1847, there were seventeen missions, served by twenty-five efficient preachers of the Conference. At the death of Bishop Capers, there were twenty-six missionary stations in South Carolina, on which were employed thirty-two preachers. The number of Church members at that time was 11,546 on these mission stations. The missionary revenue of the Conference had risen from $300 to $25,000. These are very substantial results, so far as statistics go.

"Beyond all this, several important consequences may be observed. That the religious sentiment of the country should be directed, clearly and strongly, in favor of furnishing the colored population with the means of hearing the gospel of their salvation, and of learning their duty to God and their accountability in a future life, is a very cheering aspect of the whole subject. The history of these missions brings out the fact that the Christian minister has been welcomed on the plantations; that chapels have been built; liberal contributions been furnished by the planters; master and servant are seen worshiping God together: the spirit of Christian light and love has reacted upon the one, while it has directly benefited the other. How important is a growing public sentiment which shows itself in such aspects as these!" [36]

*Presbyterians Work for Slaves.* The Presbyterian Church entered America in 1705 or 1706, when the first Presbytery was established at Freehold, New Jersey.[37] Virginia in these early days had strict laws of conformity in religion, but the Presbyterians streamed down the Shenandoah Valley from Pennsylvania, and formed a line of defense against the western Indians, so they

[35] McTyiere: "History of Methodism," p. 585.
[36] Wightman: "Life of Bishop Capers," p. 296.
[37] Gillett: "History of Presbyterian Church," Vol. I, p. 18.

were left rather free as to their worship. Visiting ministers came down from Pennsylvania from time to time to edify the people. In 1738 John Craig was sent to the Shenandoah Valley as a regular minister. In 1747 Samuel Davies came into Virginia with "license for four meeting houses." [38] The counties in which he labored were Hanover, Henrico, Goochland, Carolina, and Louisa. Reverend Mr. Davies began at once to preach to the Negroes, for Jonathan Edwards writes in 1749: "I heard lately a credible account of a remarkable work of conviction and conversion among whites and Negroes at Hanover, Va., under the ministry of Mr. Davies." [39] In 1755 Davies appealed for help to the London Society for Promoting Christian Knowledge Among the Poor:

"The poor, neglected negroes, who are so far from having money to purchase books that they themselves are the property of others; who were originally African savages, and never heard of the name of Jesus and his gospel until they arrived at the land of their slavery in America; whom their masters generally neglect, and whose souls none care for, as though immortality were not a privilege common to them as with their masters—these poor, unhappy Africans are objects of my compassion, and I think the most proper objects of the society's charity. The inhabitants of Virginia are computed to be about 300,000 men, one-half of which number are supposed to be negroes. The number of those who attend my ministry at particular times is uncertain, but generally about three hundred who give a stated attendance; and never have I been so struck with the appearance of an assembly as when I have glanced my eye to that part of the meeting-house where they usually sit, *adorned* (for so it has appeared to me) with so many black countenances, eagerly attentive to every word they hear, and frequently bathed in tears. A considerable number of them (about a hundred) have been baptized, after a proper time for instruction, having given credible evidence not only of their acquaintance with the important doctrines of the Christian religion, but also a deep sense of them in their minds, attested by a life of strict piety and holiness. As they are not sufficiently polished to dissemble with a good grace, they express the sentiments of their souls so much in the language of simple nature and with such genuine indications of sincerity that it is impossible to suspect their professions, especially when attended with a truly Christian life and exemplary conduct. There are multitudes of them in different places who are willing and eagerly desirous to be instructed and to embrace every opportunity of acquainting

[38] Gillett: "History of Presbyterian Church," Vol. I. p. 116.
[39] *Ibid.*, p. 120.

themselves with the doctrines of the gospel; and though they have generally very little help to learn to read, yet to my agreeable surprise many of them, by dint of application in their leisure hours, have made such progress that they can intelligibly read a plain author, and especially their Bibles; and pity it is that any of them should be without them." [40]

*Rev. Henry's Work for Slaves.* Another faithful worker of the Presbyterian Church in Virginia was Reverend Mr. Robert Henry:

"This man judiciously turned much of his attention to the negroes, and to them his ministry was attended with abundant success. Many were converted and gathered into the Church at Cub Creek. As this congregation was situated on the northern bank of Staunton River, where the land is very fertile, there were several large estates, possessing many slaves, within reach of the house of worship where he preached.

"The Rev. Henry Lacy succeeded Mr. Henry, during whose ministrations at Cub Creek about two hundred were added to the Church. There were sixty belonging to the Church under the care of Mr. Cob. (Rev. W. S. Plumer's report.)" [41]

*145 Methodist Missionaries in 1857.* The Annals of Southern Methodism for 1857 reports 172 missions for Negroes, with 145 white missionaries in charge. Letters from Bishop Andrews, who visited the rice plantations of South Carolina during this year, throw light on this work. We quote scattered passages: [42]

"On Sabbath morning Brother K. and myself went forth to do a Sabbath day's work among the negroes of the rice-fields. We rode some five miles to Stono, a chapel built by the planters for their slaves to worship God in. In consequence of some confusion in the arrangement, the congregation was rather small. Indeed, I thought at first we should have scarcely any hearers, but they kept dropping in till we had a very tolerably-sized congregation of blacks, and some half-dozen whites, to whom I preached, as I was able, the word of God.

"When preaching was over, we hurried off to reach another appointment, several miles distant. When we reached the place, we saw quite a number of carriages, and heard the negroes, who were waiting for us, singing hymns most lustily. We had quite a large congregation of blacks; and I suppose some twenty or more whites. . . .

[40] Harrison: "Gospel Among the Slaves," p. 50 f.
[41] *Ibid.*, p. 57.
[42] Deems: "Annals of Southern Methodism," 1858, pp. 296-307, *passim.*

"After closing this service, we had to take the road immediately for another appointment, a few miles distant. We stopped on the road to take lunch, and then proceeded to the church, where we found a large congregation of blacks, and some twenty or thirty white persons. Several of the planters and their families were present, and among my hearers was the Rev. Mr. P., pastor of the Wiltown parish. . . .

"Mr. L. has been a firm friend to our missions, and has lately built a very neat-looking chapel for his negroes. After an hour's pleasant conversation, I returned to Mrs. Smith's to dinner. Mrs. S. appears to feel a deep interest in the religious instruction of her people. After dinner we had a clever company of negroes of the estate collected in their chapel, to whom I gave a plain and friendly talk. My congregation seemed much affected, and expressed a great deal of thankfulness, and gave the preacher many a hearty squeeze of the hand. We may observe, by the way, that it is an invariable rule among the negroes on the missions, at the close of service, to shake hands with the preacher; and if he attends to catechize the children, every little fellow among them claims the right to receive this token of recognition from the preacher. I was frequently compelled to grasp three or four hands at once.

". . . After finishing these services, we went to Bro. Thomas's to dinner, and then went on to Mr. James Heyward's. Here we catechized a class of little negroes, and were somewhat amused and not a little annoyed at the interference of the old nurse, who was ever and anon throwing in a word of exhortation or rebuke to the little sinners before us.

"And now a few words in reference to the Savannah River Mission. From all I could hear, it is in a course of gradual and steady improvement. We have spent much labor on it in years gone by, but the planters seemed to take comparatively little interest in it for several years; and when the planter feels no interest, but barely permits the instruction of his people, the work gets on badly. The missionary should by all means be in communication with the planters, and have their confidence, nor should they treat him as though he were unworthy to be classed with gentlemen, else the overseers, who are very apt to take their cue from the proprietor, will find many opportunities for thwarting the benevolent efforts of the preacher. In this respect I think there is a decided improvement on this mission. Brothers Crook and Ogburn, who labor on this field, are receiving, to a large extent, the countenance of the planters, and the mission is constantly increasing in importance. It ought to be enlarged with a reinforcement of men."

*335 White Missionaries in 1860.*  Deems' Annals for 1855 gives the names of all Negro missions in Southern Methodism, together with the names of missionaries serving each field.  It is an amazing array,[43] showing the intense interest of the Church in this great work.  In 1860, the year in which the Civil War broke out, the Southern Methodist Church had 335 white missionaries at work in the field, and $125,044.36 was spent that year on the work. Between 1845 and 1860 this church alone spent $1,320,778.03 according to official reports on its Negro mission work.  Even in 1864, in the very heat of the struggle, when many white people were in desperate straits for the commonest necessities of life, the church spent $140,021.96 on its Negro missions.  The Negro members in 1860 were 207,000, and Bishop Haygood estimated that in all the churches in the South fully half a million Negroes were members.

*Presbyterian Evangelism.*  Constant reference to Negro evangelization is made throughout the minutes of the various Presbyterian Assemblies.  The minutes of the 1825 Assembly read:

"We notice with pleasure the enlightened attention which had been paid to the *religious instruction and evangelizing of the unhappy slaves and free people of color* of our country in some regions of our Church.  We would especially commend the prudence and zeal combined in this work of mercy by the Presbyteries of Charleston Union, Georgia, Concord, South Alabama, and Mississippi.  The millions of this unhappy people in our country, from their singular condition as brought to the gospel by a peculiar providence, constitute at home a mission field of infinite importance and of a most inviting character.  No more honored name can be conferred on a minister of Jesus Christ than that of *Apostle to the American slaves;* and no service can be more pleasing to the God of Heaven or more useful to our beloved country than that which this title designates." [44]

"In the winter of 1830 and the spring of 1831, two Associations of planters were formed in Georgia for the special object of affording religious instruction to the negroes by their own efforts and by missionaries employed for the purpose.  The first was formed by the Rev. Joseph Clay Stiles in McIntosh County, embracing the neighborhood of Harris's Neck, which continued in operation for some time, until by the withdrawment of Mr. Stile's labors from the neighborhood and the loss of some of the inhabitants by death and removals, it ceased.  The second was formed in Liberty County by the Midway Congregational Church and the Baptist Church under their respective pastors, the Rev.

[43] Deems: "Annals for 1855," pp. 218-225.
[44] Gillett: "History of the Presbyterian Church," p. 241 f.

Robert Quarterman and the Rev. Samuel Spry Law, which Association, with one suspension from the absence of a missionary, has continued its operations to the present time." [45]

*Planters Organize for Religious Work.* In 1837 there was organized in Liberty County, Georgia, an "Association for the Religious Instruction of the Negroes." Planters were the prime movers in this work. I have been able to find a few of the original printed reports of this Association, edited by the Rev. C. C. Jones. In the eleventh annual report running comments on work of the Presbyterians for 1845 show deep interest.[46] The Synod of Georgia reported, "the spiritual interests of the colored people have received increased attention." "The general rule in country churches is to devote half the Sabbath to them" (i.e., the Negroes.). The Synod of West Tennessee reports, "the attention of most of our churches has been specially directed to the religious instruction of our colored population." The Synod of Kentucky was planning for a missionary "whose duty it shall be to travel through the state and preach to the Negroes as he may have opportunity, and endeavor to arouse the churches and ministry to increased exertion upon this subject." The Synod of Alabama, which had for years been active in its work for Negroes, appointed a committee this year "to give the whole subject careful attention with a view to the production of some plan for the thorough and uniform instruction of the entire class of our colored population." The Synod of Mississippi boasted that it was leading all synods in its work for Negroes. One of its missionaries, supported independently by planters, wrote: "To no people do I find the same delight in preaching the Gospel. My Sabbath congregation is large and sometimes overflowing, the people attentive and orderly as any white congregation."

*Dr. John Adger.* About this time (1847) in Charleston, South Carolina, a rather remarkable movement was started by Dr. John B. Adger, a returned Presbyterian missionary from Armenia. He laid before the Charleston Presbytery a plea for organizing Negroes into a separate and independent church of which he should be pastor. The basis of his plea was that Negroes could not be accommodated in the space of the galleries allowed to them in white churches, that they did not attend the white churches, and that the white people had an obligation to give them the gospel.[47] There was at first much opposition lest the church might become a center of insurrection.

"The real ground of the opposition which I encountered on the

[45] Harrison: "Gospel Among the Slaves," p. 75.
[46] Annual Report of Liberty County, Georgia," 1846, p. 31 f. *passim.*
[47] Adger: "My Life and Times," p. 166.

part of many in the Charleston community, had a history which I have already given, and to which I must now again allude. Twenty-five years previously a plot had been discovered among the negroes for a murderous insurrection against the white people. Many negroes were arrested and tried, but most of them being found innocent, were released, yet some thirty-five or forty of them were executed. Of these, I myself, when a boy eleven years old, saw twenty-two hanged on one gallows. A very profound impression was made by these occurrences upon both the white the black population of the city. Unfortunately, whether justly or not, a separate colored church, which had existed some years, with a most excellent negro man for its minister, was accused of some complicity in the plot. The storm that arose wrecked the church." [48]

*Negro Church Buildings in Charleston.* Just three months after Dr. Adger made his proposal, the Diocesan Convention of the Episcopal Church in South Carolina met in St. Michaels Church in Charleston. This convention appointed Reverend Paul Trapier to establish an independent church for Negroes, of which he should be in charge.[49]

When the two church buildings—Presbyterian and Episcopal— were in process of erection, a mob gathered one night at the Episcopal edifice and were about to pull the walls down.

"Several influential citizens, jealous for the honor of their city, appeared in time to persuade the multitude to desist, promising that they would call a public meeting to test the sense of the community on the question. This meeting appointed a committee of fifty, of which Daniel Ravenel, Sr., was the chairman, to inquire into the matter. This committee corresponded with intelligent gentlemen all over the South, to collect information which should lead the city to a wise decision. Then another public meeting was called, and the City Hall was filled with an eager throng of leading men. The report of the committee of fifty as read, decidedly favoring the movement as both wise and good. The opposition was heard, first through their leader. I cannot recall his name, but my recollection is that he was no citizen of Charleston, a comparative stranger amongst us, and a man of not very good character. Then the Hon. Francis H. Elmore, who had been elected to fill out the unexpired term in the United States Senate, of the lamented Calhoun, moved the adoption of the report in a very eloquent speech. James L. Petigru, then, in many respects, the topmost citizen of Charleston, rose to second it. Mr. Elmore was a member of the congregation

[48] Adger: "My Life and Times," p. 165.
[49] *Ibid.*, p. 170.

of the Second Presbyterian church, and his wife was a professing member.  He had favored my project strongly from the very beginning, and I had supposed, of course, he would speak; but the speech of Mr. Petigru had not been counted on.  It was such a speech as is not often heard.  I wish I could recall and report it.  The assembly was thrilled as this great citizen poured forth his feelings.  But when he came to speak on the 'liberty of teaching' what was true and good to all men, his big heart swelled with emotion, and so did those of his hearers.  All I remember is 'the liberty of teaching! why, sirs, that was what brought many of our fathers here.'  Petigru was a Huguenot.  The assembly understood his allusion.  Not many words were required to be added.  The question was settled in Charleston for all time.  The nightmare, which had oppressed the mind and heart of the city for twenty-five years, vanished." [50]

*Dr. Girardeau's Ministry.*  Dr. Adger was succeeded as pastor of this Negro church by Dr. Girardeau, under whom the work prospered greatly.  "Starting with 36 members in 1854, there were in 1860 over 600 enrolled members, with a regular congregation of 1500 attendance." [51]  In 1857 Dr. Girardeau made an elaborate argument before the Synod in favor of the "Separate System," as it was styled. [52]  Dr. Girardeau was one of the greatest preachers of his time in the Presbyterian Church.  Colonel Robb, a prominent lawyer of Middle Tennessee, afterwards Colonel of the Forty-sixth Tennessee Regiment, C.S.A., a delegate to the National Democratic Convention held at Charleston in 1860, went with General Benjamin F. Butler of Massachusetts to hear Girardeau preach to his Negro congregation.  Colonel Robb described the occasion as follows:

"The prayer of the preacher was earnest, simple and humble as of a man pleading with God.  The singing was general, heartfelt and grand.  The sermon was tender and spiritual, and though profound, was plain, delivered with fire and unction.  After the preacher took his seat, deeply impressed, I was with closed eyes meditating on the wonderful sermon, when I heard some one sobbing.  Looking around I saw General Butler's face bathed in tears.  Just then the church officers came for the usual collection and at once General Butler drew from his pockets both hands full of silver coin (put there to tip the waiters), and cast it into the basket, with the audible remark, 'Well, I have never heard such a man and have never heard such a sermon.' " [53]

[50] Adger: "My Life and Times," p. 173.
[51] "Life Work of J. L. Girardeau," p. 32.
[52] *Ibid.,* p. 38 f.
[53] *Ibid.,* p. 58.

Thus the Presbyterian Church was giving of the finest flower of her ministry to bring the religious message to the Negroes.

*Work of the Episcopal Church.*  The Episcopal Church, while it never had as large a following among Negroes as some others, has a consistent and continuous history of endeavor on his behalf. In the Annual Report of the Association for the Religious Instruction of the Negroes in Liberty County, Georgia, for 1848, one may cull the following running excerpts concerning the work of this church: In the Diocese of Alabama twelve out of eighteen parishes reporting in full "contain notices of attention to the Negroes."  Bishop Otey of Tennessee and Mississippi writes: "The work in which you have been so long and so arduously engaged, is one which deeply interests me."  One planter in Mississippi offered $500 and board annually for the services of a clergyman on his plantation.  Bishop Elliott of Georgia claimed his greatest difficulty was not in getting a chance to work on the plantations, but to get "men to devote themselves to the work." "The *settled clergy* in the Diocese of South Carolina" were said "to include the servants in their regular services and hence their extended and extending labours and success in this field."  Bishop Whittingham of Maryland claimed that half his clergy "reported Negro baptisms, marriages and funerals."

*Baptist Work.*  During the Baptist revival between 1788 and 1792, many Negroes were converted and brought into this church. The first edifice for a separate colored Baptist Church was built in Charleston in 1792.  "Toward the close of this year the first colored Baptist Church in the city of Savannah began to build a place of worship.  The corporation of the city gave them a lot for that purpose.  The origin of this Church, the parent of several others, is briefly as follows: George Leile, sometimes called George Sharp, was born in Virginia about 1750.  His master sometime before the American war removed and settled in Burke County, Georgia.  Mr. Sharp was a Baptist and a deacon in a Baptist Church, of which Rev. Matthew Moore was pastor.  George was converted and baptized under Mr. Moore's ministry.  The Church gave him liberty to preach.  He began to labor with good success at different plantations.  Mr. Sharp gave him his freedom not long after he began to preach.  For about three years he preached at Brampton and Yamacraw, in the neighborhood of Savannah.  On the evacuation of the country in 1782 and 1783 he went to Jamaica.  Previous to his departure he came up from the vessel lying below the city in the river, and baptized an African woman by the name of Kate belonging to Mrs. Eunice Hogg, and Andrew, his wife Hannah, and Hagar, belonging to the venerable Mr. Jonathan Bryan.

"The Baptist cause among the negroes in Jamaica owes its origin to the indefatigable and pious labors of ' this worthy man, George Leile. It does not come within my design to introduce an account of his efforts in that island. I shall add only that in 1784 he commenced preaching at Kingston and formed a Church, and in 1791 had gathered a company of 450 communicants and commenced the erection of a commodious meeting-house. It finally cost, with steeple and bell, £4,000. He was alive in 1810 and about *sixty* years of age.

"About nine months after George Leile left Georgia, Andrew, surnamed Bryan, a man of good sense, great zeal, and some natural elocution, began to exhort his black brethren and friends. He and his followers were reprimanded and forbidden to engage further in religious exercises. He would, however, pray, sing, and encourage his fellow-worshipers to seek the Lord. Their evening assemblies were broken up and those found present were punished with stripes. . . .

"Not long after Andrew began his ministry he was visited by the Rev. Thomas Barton, who baptized eighteen of his followers on profession of their faith. The next visit was from the Rev. Abraham Marshall, of Kioka, who was accompanied by a young colored preacher by the name of Jesse Peter, from the vicinity of Augusta. On the 20th of January, 1788, Mr. Marshall ordained Andrew Bryan, baptized forty of his hearers, and constituted them with others, sixty-nine in number, a Church, of which Andrew was pastor. Such was the origin of the first colored Baptist Church in Savannah." [54]

*Growth of Negro Baptists.* Reports indicate there were eighteen or nineteen thousand Negro Baptists in 1795. In 1841 it was said: "There are more Negro communicants, and more churches regularly constituted, exclusively for Negroes, with their own regular houses of public worship, and with ordained Negro preachers, attached to the denomination in the United States." [55] It should be noted that the Baptists early began putting Negro preachers in charge of Negro churches, which may account for their rapid growth and disproportionate numbers. Many of the Baptist Associations, such as the Sunbury Association in Georgia, had white preachers who were missionaries to the Negroes within the bounds of the Association.

*Liberty County, Georgia.* Perhaps the most notable single piece of religious work undertaken for Negroes before the war was that in Liberty County, Georgia, to which reference has been made before. Reverend C. C Jones was secretary of this Asso-

[54] Harrison: "Gospel Among the Slaves," pp. 59, 60.
[55] *Ibid.*, pp. 90, 91.

ciation and published the reports over a series of years. In this county there were 5,493 slaves and Dr. Jones reports there were in all the churches seats for 2000 Negro worshipers. The sentiment of the planters was highly favorable. "Within my knowledge," he writes, 1845, "there is not a planter in our district of the county who interposes the least obstacle to the attendance of his people on public worship." [56] One could not better summarize the religious work for Negroes before the war than in the words of this same report:

"We behold the subject appearing in *the acts and doings of all our Ecclesiastical Meetings of all Denominations*: there is arising a holy emulation in the cause: the field affords ample space for all. We behold *individuals of the highest standing both in Church and State,* not only the open advocates, but most efficient laborers in the work. We behold *all the Religious Journals* in our country —especially those of most note and influence, in various ways calling the attention of the public to it. *Ministers* upon whom the labour devolves are acknowledging and acting more in fulfilment of their duties to their colored charges. *Theological Students* are giving serious consideration to the colored field, and leaving our seminaries with determination to devote themselves to it. Columbia has already sent forth Missionaries into the field: so has Princeton and more are to follow. Prince Edward will not be lacking. *The Secular Prints* appear in favour of our cause: the religious instruction of the negroes is alluded to in private and in public and is taking its place among *the important topics of conversation and thought* with the community at large. The public mind is becoming more tender: the impression that "more ought and must be done," is extending: *Owners* are awakening to their responsibilities: *wide doors of access* to the people, are thrown open. *The melioration of their condition* is perceptible: *the Negroes* themselves rise up and second the efforts for their good." [57]

*Negro Churches Desire Independence.* However valuable the religious instruction which the Negroes received in the white churches, or in churches of their own under the guidance of the white denominations, they early showed a restlessness and desire to be independent. Of course, in the South where most of the colored Christians were slaves, they were not free to withdraw from the white churches, but in the North it was different. There many of the colored Christians were free. The first group, therefore, to withdraw was the group of Negroes in the Methodist

[56] "Annual Report of Liberty County, Georgia," 1846, p. 17.
[57] *Ibid.,* p. 35.

THE NEGRO FROM AFRICA TO AMERICA

Episcopal Church. In 1796 a little congregation in New York City set up a separate organization known as Zion Church and organized the African Methodist Episcopal Zion Church. This organization was incorporated in 1801.[58] In 1816 two congregations, one in Philadelphia headed by Richard Allen, the first Negro ordained in the Methodist Church, and the other in Baltimore, withdrew from the Methodist Episcopal Church and organized the African Methodist Episcopal Church. Delegates to the number of sixteen assembled from Philadelphia, Baltimore, Wilmington, Attleborough, Pennsylvania, and Salem, New Jersey, and drew up the ecclesiastical compact which constituted the connection, and Richard Allen was elected the first bishop, Daniel Coker having refused the office.[59] These two churches had their main strength in the North, for independent congregations of Negroes were looked upon with considerable alarm in the South. The historian tells us that the A. M. E. church got a foothold in South Carolina but was completely suppressed after the Vesey plot in 1822.[60] The British Methodist Episcopal Church was formed in 1856 by the withdrawal of the Canadian colored churches from the A. M. E. church. The Colored Methodist Episcopal Church was organized in 1870, by the withdrawal of the Negro members of the Methodist Episcopal Church South. Including the colored members of the Methodist Episcopal Church itself, there are then at least five main branches of colored Methodism in America.

The first Negro Baptist church was organized at Silver Bluff, South Carolina, by eight slaves, sometime before 1778.[61]

We have already noted the organization of a separate Negro Baptist Church in Savannah in 1792. The Colored Baptist Church of Augusta was organized in 1790, one at Portsmouth, Virginia, 1841, one at Washington, D. C., 1832, one at Louisville, 1842, and a famous church in Richmond of which the President of Richmond College, Dr. Ryland, was pastor, organized in 1841. This church had 3822 additions by baptism between 1841 and 1865.[62]

*First Colored Baptist Association.* The first Colored Baptist Association was organized in Ohio in 1836, followed in 1838 by the Wood River Baptist Association in Illinois. Up to the time of the Civil War most of the Negro Baptists remained in white churches. After separation from these white churches, it was a long time before a real unity between the different Negro churches could be developed. The National Baptist Convention

[58] "One Hundred Years of the A. M. E. Zion Church," p. 56.
[59] Payne: "History of A. M. E. Church," p. 13.
[60] *Ibid.*, p. 45.
[61] Earnest: "Religious Development of the Negro in Virginia," p. 83.
[62] U. S. Census: Religious Bodies, 1916, Vol. I, p. 97.

,vas organized in 1895, although a preliminary organization had
taken place at St. Louis, 1886.[63]   The membership of this convention consisted of representatives of churches, Sunday schools,
Associations and State Conventions.   The convention acts through
four boards, namely: A Foreign Mission Board, a Home Mission
Board, an Educational Board, and a Baptist Young People's
Society Board.   The Home Mission Board handles a publishing
house.

*Cumberland Presbyterians.*   The Cumberland Presbyterian Church
(colored) was organized at Murfreesboro, Tennessee, in 1869.

*Presbyterian Church, U. S. A.*   The Presbyterian Church,
U. S. A., began work with the Negroes before the close of the
Civil War.   The General Assembly's committee on Freedmen has
carried forward an aggressive work, gathering into its various
churches some 25,000 members.   The colored churches are under
the general watch care of this committee.

*Presbyterian Church in the U. S.*   The Presbyterian Church in
the U. S. has fostered work among the Negroes which ultimately
developed into the Independent Presbyterian Synod.   The church
is not large but is doing rather thorough work.

*Other Churches.*   Besides these larger branches of the Negro
church there are a number of smaller ones, such as the Union
Methodist Episcopal Church, The National Convention of the
Colored Primitive Baptists, The Lott Carey Baptist Foreign Mission Convention, and the Congregational churches under the care of
the American Missionary Association.

All these church bodies have grown rapidly and now have a
large membership and large property holdings.   The total membership of all denominations (1916) was 4,602,805.   Total property
owned, $86,809,970.   Total indebtedness reported, $7,938,095,
and total current budget of expenses for the year, $18,529,827.[64]

*Negro Church Membership.*   The membership in the larger
denominations in 1916 was as follows: National Baptist Convention, 2,938,579; Colored Primitive Baptist, 15,144; Colored Free
Will Baptists, 13,362; Members of the Northern Baptist Convention, 53,842*; Colored Cumberland Presbyterian, 13,077; Members
of the Protestant Episcopal Church, 23,775*; Roman Catholic,
51,683*; Congregational, 13,205; Presbyterian, U. S. A., 31,951*;
Members of the Methodist Episcopal Church, 320,025*; African
M. E. Church, 548,355; African M. E. Zion Church, 257,169;
Colored M. E. Church, 247,749.[65]

* These are members of the parent white churches and have not separated
from them in ecclesiastical organization, though often having separate individual
churches.
[63] U. S. Census: Religious Bodies, Vol. II, p. 97.
[64] *Ibid.*, Vol. I, pp. 554-555.
[65] *Ibid.*

*Baptist Home Mission Committee.* The Negro Baptist Home Missionary Committee in 1916 reported 16 home missionaries, 750 churches aided and $17,408 contributed toward this work. The Foreign Board reported operations in South Africa, Central Africa, West Africa, South America, and the West Indies. This work employed 13 missionaries and 96 native helpers. The Educational Board reported 115 schools under its care, and $220,297 contributed toward their support. The property of these schools was valued at $1,872,620. The Woman's Auxiliary reported a training school for girls. The Young People's Band reported 12,550 societies with half a million members, and the Sunday School Board reported 1,181,270 scholars.[66]

*A. M. E. Church.* The African Methodist Episcopal Church reported in 1916 mission work in West Africa, Liberia, Sierra Leone, South Africa including the Transvaal, Orange Free State, Natal, Cape Town, the West Indies, and South America. This work employed 4 American missionaries and 156 native workers. On home mission or church extension $46,609 was spent in 1916. It maintains Wilberforce University, Payne and Turner Theological seminaries, the property of which is valued at one million dollars. The denomination has 6,302 churches, 1,867 parsonages, 311,051 Sunday school pupils.[67]

*A. M. E. Zion Church.* The African Methodist Episcopal Zion Church reports mission work in Liberia, the Gold Coast, Coast Colony, West Africa, and South America. It employs 4 American missionaries and 60 native helpers. It supports five colleges and academies, Livingstone College in Salisbury, North Carolina, being the chief one. The denomination has 2,495 churches, and 135,102 Sunday School scholars.[68]

*C. M. E. Church.* The Colored Methodist Episcopal Church reports 226 home missionaries, and 434 churches aided in 16 states. It has 5 colleges and 8 lower schools, properties of which are valued at $750,000. It had 895 Epworth Leagues with 61,253 members in 1916. There were 2,490 churches, and 167,880 Sunday school scholars.[69]

A number of smaller denominations are carrying forward an aggressive work.

In addition to the work carried forward by these Negro churches, there is a very large amount of home mission work carried on among the Negro people by white denominations. In 1920 the author made a careful compilation of such work, printed in a pamphlet, "Interracial Coöperation," from which we quote:

[66] U. S. Census: Religious Bodies, 1916, Vol. II, pp. 98-99.
[67] *Ibid.,* p. 495.
[68] *Ibid.,* p. 502.
[69] *Ibid.,* p. 514.

*"American Baptist Home Mission Society.* Established immediately following the civil war for the purpose of training Christian leaders and workers, and giving a general education to those who had no opportunity to secure one.  Its purpose is Christian training and education.  It works through schools, churches, and community houses.  The Southern states comprise its territory, including also the Northern states in religious and social work. Its income is derived from contributions from churches and some endowment.

"This Society maintains eight major colleges, with an average attendance of about 500 students each, including all departments. It also has twenty minor schools established and now managed and supported chiefly by the Negroes themselves, with an average attendance of about 400 students each.  Some of the colleges are: Virginia Union University, Richmond, Va.; Shaw University, Raleigh, N. C.; Benedict College, Columbia, S. C.; Morehouse College, Atlanta, Ga.; Bishop College, Marshall Texas.  Among the academies with some junior college work may be mentioned: Storer College, Harper's Ferry, W. Va.; State University, Louisville, Ky.; Roger Williams University, Nashville, Tenn.; Jackson College, Jackson, Miss.; Selma University, Selma, Ala.; Arkansas Baptist College, Little Rock, Ark.; and many others, a large part of which are now entirely supported and managed by the colored people.   Many Negro ministers have been educated at these schools, and many teachers, dentists, physicians and other leaders, and twenty-five or thirty missionaries.

*"Woman's American Baptist Home Mission Society.* Provides 91 matrons and teachers in 19 different colored Baptist schools throughout the South, and maintains 28 missionaries among Negroes in fifteen different states.

*"The American Church Institute for Negroes.* This Institution is a corporation chartered under the laws of the State of Virginia, in 1906, and has for its object the religious education of the Negro.  It comprises the following schools:

St. Augustine's School at Raleigh, North Carolina.
St. Paul's Industrial School at Lawrenceville, Virginia.
The Bishop Payne Divinity School at Petersburg, Virginia.
St. Athanasius' School at Brunswick, Georgia.
The Vicksburg School at Vicksburg, Mississippi.
St. Mark's School at Birmingham, Alabama.
St. Mary's School at Columbia, South Carolina.
Fort Valley School at Fort Valley, Georgia.

"These schools of the Institute either own or lease over two thousand acres of land, have plants worth considerably over $350,000 and are educating approximately twenty-six hundred pupils. Thus it will be seen that the Institute compares favorably in numbers with Hampton and Tuskegee, with this advantage, that as its schools are located in six different states, they are able to reach a large number of needy students who, on account of the long distance involved, are not able to avail themselves of the facilities at the larger schools. Fifteen industrial subjects are taught in these Institute schools, while St. Augustine's School at Raleigh has a well-equipped Hospital and a fine Training School for Nurses. Scholarships cost from $150 in the Bishop Payne Divinity School to $75 in one of the academic or normal schools, while an industrial scholarship costs only $50.

"*The American Missionary Association.* Organized in 1846 'For the propagation of the pure and free Christianity from which the sins of caste, polygamy, slave-holding and the like should be excluded.'

"The object is missionary and educational work among the less privileged races under the flag, Negroes, Indians, Orientals, Porto Ricans, Mexicans, white people of the Southern mountains and of Utah. The great aim is to promote higher education among these races, and *especially among the Negroes,* for the sake of leadership; that leaders may be raised up who shall at the same time be thoroughly educated and thoroughly Christian.

"The Hawaiian Islands, Porto Rico and the South are the special fields served. Contributions from churches, chiefly the Congregational, from individuals, legacies and endowment funds form the supporting income.

"A Negro agent is regularly employed. This agent is the only Negro on the Executive Committee of this Association. However, the Association has established among Negroes 154 churches, with a membership of 11,622, which are served by 97 home missionaries.

"This Association has been very active in establishing and supporting a series of the leading schools for Negroes throughout the whole South. Fisk University, of Nashville, Tennessee, and Atlanta University, Atlanta, Georgia, are two of the outstanding examples of the activities of this Board. It is a well known fact that the American Missionary Association has put several millions of dollars in education in the South, but their policy of having only a loose relationship to these schools, leaving their Board of Directors free and independent, means that this Board, though having contributed largely, controls comparatively few schools.

"*Freedman's Aid Society.* This Society of the Methodist Episcopal Church has 340,000 members, with twenty conferences; sixteen of these conferences and 300,000 members being located in the South. They have 3,500 preachers, and twenty schools, Gammon Theological Seminary, Atlanta, Georgia, for training their ministers, and Meharry Medical College, Nashville, Tennessee, for training a large percentage of all the Negro doctors for the South. The Board of Negro Education in this Church raises and spends $250,000 annually on its schools.

"In view of the Centenary fund, the following budget for helping Negroes in the South for the year 1920, was adopted by the Methodist Episcopal Church:

| | |
|---|---:|
| Educational endowment and buildings .............. | $460,000 |
| Other buildings, church, and otherwise ............. | 300,000 |
| Maintenance of teachers, ministers and others....... | 267,000 |
| Sunday School, Temperance and Epworth League Work ..................................... | 70,000 |
| Total .................................. | $1,097,000 |

"*Woman's Home, Mission Society, of the Methodist Episcopal Church.* This organization has Secretaries of Negro Work in a number of Southern states. This board maintains the following homes and schools for Negroes: Boylan Home Industrial Training School, Jacksonville, Fla.; The Kindergarten Thayer Home, Atlanta, Ga.; Haven Home, Savannah, Ga.; Elizabeth Rust Home, Holly Springs, Miss.; Browning Industrial Home and Mather Academy, Camden, S. C.; Allen Industrial Home and Lurandus Beach Industrial School, Asheville, N. C.; Eliza Dee King Industrial Home, Marshall, Texas; Adeline Smith Home, Little Rock, Ark.; Peck's School of Domestic Art and Science, New Orleans, La.; Faith Kindergarten, New Orleans, La.

"*Board of Missions, Methodist Episcopal Church, South.* The General Conference prior to 1920 levied an assessment on the Church of $55,250 per annum for Negro work. Of the Centenary funds, $993,000 will go to Negro work.

"The Woman's Department of the Board of Missions maintains an Annex to Paine College, Augusta, Ga., with organized departments for women. The College has an enrolment of 199, with a teaching force of eleven.

"Two Bethlehem Houses are also maintained by the Women's Board, one at Augusta, Ga., and the other at Nashville, Tenn. These Houses have ministered to some 6,000 Negroes through 858 homes; 121 colored children in kindergarten; 220 older children given instruction in industrial classes; 100 young women in Forward Quest Circles, 88 women in Mother's Clubs.

"The object is to relate the better type of educated Negro to the illiterate and purposeless class, and to bring the white church element into coöperation with these two groups.

"*Board of Church Extension of the M. E. Church, South.* Organized February, 1884. It gives aid by loans and donations to churches of the M. E. Church, South. Its business is conducted through a Board which meets annually, and also through an Executive Committee, which meets monthly. It serves the territory occupied by the M. E. Church, South, principally in the Southern states. This Board donated to the colored Methodist Church in 1920 $10,385.81, and coöperated with the Church Extension Board of the Colored Methodist Church. The work of these boards is to help in the building of churches by means of financial aid and expert advice as to location, architecture, etc. Plans are on foot to raise a permanent loan fund or not less than $15,000 for helping the Colored Methodist Extension Board.

*"Woman's Missionary Council, of the Methodist Episcopal Church, South.* This Board maintains Bethlehem Houses at Augusta, Ga., and Nashville, Tenn., as noted above. It also maintains the Paine Annex to Paine College, with an enrolment of two hundred students and eleven teachers. It has a Virginia Johnson Home for delinquent girls in Dallas, Texas, and a Door of Hope, in Macon, Georgia.

*"Executive Committee of Home Missions of the Southern Presbyterian Church.* Organized about 1890 by the General Assembly, and known as the Executive Committee of Colored Evangelization. In May, 1911 it was consolidated with the Extension Committee of Home Missions.

Its present object is the education of ministers and leaders for colored people, and the evangelization of the Negroes.

"It reaches the public by appeals and promotion in the religious press; also through the development of Negro churches, presbyteries, etc. Its paid agents are an evangelist, and the faculty of Stillman Institute, Tuscaloosa, Ala. Its field of work consists of the territory of the Presbyterian Church, U. S.

The Executive Committee of Home Missions has as one of its eight departments, Colored Evangelization. It promotes and maintains Snedecar Memorial Synod, consisting of four presbyteries with thirty-five ministers, serving sixty-two churches and missions, with 2,700 communicants. Missions schools for Negroes are maintained in Louisville, Ky., Atlanta, Ga., Richmond, Va., Abbeville, S. C., and Stillman Institute, Tuscaloosa, Ala. This last institute is for the education of the Negro ministry. Plans are being made to enlarge Stillman Institute by adding a department for girls, and erecting a dormitory, at a cost of $60,000.

*The Woman's Auxiliary of the Southern Presbyterian Church.* "The unique piece of work being done by the white women of the Southern Presbyterian Church is the Annual Conference for Colored Women held at Stillman Institute, Tuscaloosa, Ala. The object of these conferences is to bring modern methods of church and Sunday school work, of serving and cooking, and other useful industries, to the women who are too old for school. At the last meeting there were present 160 delegates from 59 towns in eleven states, representing eight denominations. The expenses of the majority of these delegates were borne by white women of the Southern Presbyterian Church.

"*The Board of Freedmen's Missions of the United Presbyterian Church, of North America.* Organized in 1864 to minister to the needs of Negroes, primarily in a spiritual sense, but incidentally physically and intellectually.

"Its purpose is to equip and maintain training schools and to train leaders most efficiently for the Negro population. It maintains thirteen mission schools in the South. Its field of work lies in sections of Tennessee, Alabama and the East. It is supported by gifts from the United Presbyterian Church.

"The total number of workers employed are one hundred and fifty-one. The Freedmen's Bureau maintains the following schools:

"Tennessee: Knoxville, Athens, Riceville.

"Alabama: Millers Ferry, Camden, Canton Bend, Prairie and Arlington (all in Wilcox County).

"Eastern Group: Henderson, Chase City, Norfolk, Townville, Blue Stone and Lakeville.

"Enrollment for 1919, thirty-two hundred students.

"Other schools maintained by the Board:

"Palatka Presbyterian School, Palatka, Fla.

"Laura Presbyterian School, Jacksonville, Fla.

"St. Augustine Presbyterian School, St. Augustine, Fla.

"*Board of Directors of the Women's General Missionary Society of the United Presbyterian Church of North America.* The purpose is to educate and Christianize in order to make good citizens and good Christians; also to supply leaders for the Negroes' own uplift. It establishes schools and churches in each of the twelve stations occupied by its Society. All its workers are paid. It serves Virginia, North Carolina, Tennessee, and Alabama. It is supported by contributions from Missionary Societies of the denomination.

"This work began very soon after the close of the war. It commenced with small community schools. The Women's Board and Freedmen's Board coöperate in each station. The women supply the domestic science and sewing teachers, and matrons of dormitories, and are responsible for the upkeep of the whole plants at Prairie, Alabama, and Miller's Ferry, Ala. The aim that better ideas of home and home-making be fostered has been accomplished. Ministers have been provided, as well as teachers, carpenters and painters. In fact, all professions and trades have been taught. The faculties at Knoxville College, the highest grade school of this Society, and Chase City, Va., are almost entirely composed of white teachers. All the other schools are manned by graduates of this denomination. The Board coöperates at Annie Manie, Prairie, Canton Bend, Miller's Ferry, Camden, Ala.; Athens, Riceville, Knoxville, Tenn.; Henderson, Townville, N. C.; and Chase City and Blue Stone, Va.

"*Board of Home Missions of the Reformed Church in the United States.* Organized in 1863 to coördinate Home Mission work in the Reformed Church in the United States.

"Its object is to establish the Kingdom of God in the life of America, to Americanize foreigners, to assist churches in erection of buildings, to carry forward work of evangelization and social service. Publicity is given through the "Outlook of Missions," lantern slides, lectures, pamphlets, etc., and through such local organizations as committees, conferences, etc. It employs a District Superintendent, and serves a territory including the United States and a portion of Canada. It receives its support through apportionment of churches, voluntary contributions by individuals, etc.

"This Board has 244 missions on roll; its income for the years 1917-1920 being $699,535, an increase of $140,000 over previous triennials. In all its work it attempts to serve Negroes as well as whites.

"*The Five Years Meeting of the Friends in America.* Maintains the following institutions for Negroes:

"1. Indianapolis Asylum for Friendless Colored Children, 21st St. and Boulevard Place, Indianapolis, Ind.

"2. New York Colored Missions, 225-227 West 30th St., New York City.

"3. Southland Institute, Southland, Ark. Transformed from an orphanage into a school, with enrollment of 350 colored students in 1919.

"4. High Point Normal and Industrial School, High Point, N. C. This school provides common and high school education and industrial training.

"Perhaps the most interesting of these schools is the Southland Institute.

"*Mission Board of the Christian Church.* Franklinton College, Franklinton, N. C., is the only institution this Church has for the Negroes. The College has a fine plant and is doing good work. The buildings are comparatively new, though the institution itself has been running for a number of years.

"*Christian Women's Board of Missions.* The Christian Woman's Board of Missions expended last year a little over $106,000 for Negro work divided into the following lines of activity:

"1. Social Settlement work—

"The Flanner House in Indianapolis, Ind., is presided over by Dr. Charles Lee, a white man. It has a nursery, tubercular work, and rescue work.

"2. Educational work—

"(a) The Southern Christian Institute, Edwards, Miss., eighteen white teachers and two colored. Enrollment, 250 from sixteen states and two foreign countries. 1,265 acres of land and a plant valued at $2,126,505.28. Total income, 35,128.97. Maintains primary school, the grades, academy and college.

"(b) The Jarvis Christian Institute, Hawkins, Texas, sixteen colored teachers. Enrollment, 148 from five states. 638 acres of land and a plant valued at $100,000.00. Total income, $26,-203.38. Maintains primary, the grades and academy.

"(c) The Piedmont Christian Institute, Martinsville, Va., eight colored teachers. Enrollment, 113, mostly local. 30 acres of land and a plant worth about $50,000. Total income, $7,951.80. Maintains from primary to 12th grade.

"(d) Alabama Christian Institute, Lum, Ala., seven colored teachers. Enrollment, 74, local. 60 acres and a plant worth $10,000. Total income, $3,717.73. Teaches first ten grades.

"(e) The Central Christian Institute, Louisville, Ky. Has just bought 136 acres of land and proposes to erect a junior college for theological training.

"3. Evangelistic work—

"The Board assists state evangelists in eight states and assists twelve local churches at strategic points. All evangelists colored.

"4. Organizing work—

"(a) Two Sunday school field workers are maintained for all their time to bring that work to a higher plane. Field workers colored.

"(b) One organizer for Woman's Missionary Societies. Organizer colored.

"5. General development work—

"(a) "The Gospel Plea," a weekly paper circulates in sixteen states and is accomplishing a most excellent work as it is being subscribed for by both colored and white.

"(b) General field work. The Superintendent visits most of the State conventions. Superintendent white.

"The colored churches raise from three to ten per cent of the maintenance money, by coöperating directly with the general work. We are aiming to carry them along on as nearly an equality as possible, always giving them a full share on the national programs.

"*American Christian Missionary Society.* The only work this Board is doing at present, 1920, among the Negroes, is through the Bible School Department, headed by P. H. Moss, located at Edwards, Miss. Other work is being done through the Christian Woman's Board at Indianapolis, Ind.

"*The Board of Missions for Freedmen of the Presbyterian Church in the U. S. A.* Organized in 1865. Emancipation led the General Assembly to organize a Committee on Freedmen, which was incorporated as a Board in 1882. The object was Christian education of the Negroes, especially in the South; the creation of a trained ministry; provision for higher education of those capable of receiving it, and so creating leaders. Provision is also made for needed teachers for colored schools; evangelization of all, and support of the needy churches in the North and South.

"Its work is conducted through the "New Era Magazine," church papers; study book, "The Negro, an American Asset"; leaflets, posters, articles in church publications and advertisements. It also works through such organizations as the General Assembly synodical and presbyterial societies, young people's societies, Sabbath Schools, and study classes. It employes four evangelists, and a Field Missionary. The North and South are the fields ministered to. Its support is received from churches, Sunday schools, women's societies, and individuals.

"In addition to the parent Board of this church, the Board of Publication and Sunday School Work, the Freedmen's Board of Home Missions, and the Women's Board for aid of Freedmen's Mission work, are organizations giving attention to the Negroes in the South.

"This Church has three synods in the South, composed of three presbyteries each. They have about 25,000 communicants, and in addition they are assisting financially the colored Cumberland Presbyterian Church, with some 25,000 more communicants.

"The Women's Board of Freedmen for Aid in the colored mission work is sustaining schools for Negro girls. They give industrial training, home economics, etc.

"This Church expended in 1918-19 $215,000 on Negro education in the South. It had two colleges, 25 secondary schools, 113 elementary schools. There were 150 collegiate students, three professional students, 1,610 secondary students, 16,316 elementary students, and a teaching staff of 434. Connected with the Sunday School Publishing Board there are thirteen Negro missionaries in the South.

"*Southern Baptist Convention.* Through the Home Mission Board the Southern Baptist Church has been covering a large field of work among the Negroes. The work has been directed chiefly to evangelism and religious instruction, and this effort has been richly rewarded by an unusually large membership among the Negroes in that denomination. Biblical and theological instruction has been given rather than along literary lines. The Baptist Mission Board is at present maintaining Bible instructors in a number of Negro Baptist schools with most gratifying results. It is the intention of the Board to enlarge the religious instruction for the Negroes in a measure commensurate with the needs and increased ability of Southern white Baptists to render this service.

"The Negro Baptists of the South have a number of denominational schools under their ownership and direction which have had the good will and moral support of white Baptists, and in some degree their financial support. It is the purpose of the Home Mission Board of the Baptist Church in the South to render such financial help as may be possible during the five-year period upon which they have entered. . . . For years a number of select, gifted and consecrated instructors have been maintained among the Negro Baptists. They are doing a work of abiding and far-reaching results in theological institutes, ministers' and deacons' meetings, and in teaching theological students in several of the schools that are being helped. . . .

"The Southern Baptist Convention has just undertaken to co-operate with the Negroes in establishing a theological seminary for training Negro ministers in Nashville, Tennessee. Two hundred thousand dollars is to be contributed, and as soon as the school is thoroughly launched, the direction of the same will be turned over to the Negro Baptists.

"*Home Missions Council Committee on Negro Work.* The Secretary of this Society works among the Northern Negroes. He was appointed to this special work when the multitude of Negroes migrated from the South. His task has been to assemble the leaders of both races, in city after city, and bring them face to face with questions relative to the adequacy of the program of the churches to meet the need of the Negroes, and to bring to the attention of the proper agencies the needs brought to light by these investigations. Conferences of this nature have been held in New York, Philadelphia, Newark, Cleveland and Pittsburgh. The object is to promote fellowship, conference and coöperation among Christian organizations doing missionary work among Negroes. The work is conducted to a great extent through conferences of leaders of all denominations. Donations from the Home Missions Council are made for carrying forward this work.

"The outstanding recent achievement of the Committee on Negro work was the conference called in 1919 of representatives of all the leading organizations for the welfare of Negroes, North and South. This conference of about one hundred white and colored men and women, presided over by a Bishop of the Church, formulated a pronouncement which was reported to the Federal

Council of Churches, and that body was asked to give it as wide circulation as possible. In that way this pronouncement, with its stirring appeal, has been scattered broadcast throughout the whole country, and has found its way into practically all religious and denominational papers and many secular periodicals, and has been published as a bulletin by the Home Missions Council under the caption of 'A Race Crisis.'

"*International Sunday School Association.* In the Department of Work Among Negroes, Sunday School Teacher Training Classes have been conducted in 190 educational institutions in twenty states, in the years 1918-1919. In eight years 17,619 students in these 190 institutions have specialized in Sunday school teacher training.

"*Colored Work Committee of the Young Women's Christian Association.* Present program planned in 1915 at meeting of both white and colored women in Louisville, Ky. Work grew out of desire of women of both races to face facts squarely together, and to work toward a solution of the problem.

"Its purpose is to make possible to a growing number of colored girls a richer life, using regular methods of the Young Women's Christian Association. Its channels of work lie through the regular Y. W. C. A. program, including boarding home, gymnasium, clubs among various groups of girls; educational classes, religious meetings, Bible classes, etc. The colored Association operates as an affiliated branch of the Central City Association, the General Secretary of the colored Association being a member of the Central City staff of secretaries. The United States is the field covered, with appropriations from National and field budgets, also contributions.

"The growth of the Y. W. C. A. has been phenomenal among the colored women. In 1920 there were fourteen headquarters' secretaries, a National Student Secretary, and ten industrial secretaries in as many centers. In twenty-two cities clubs of employed girls have been organized into a membership of 3,000, while approximately 7,000 others have been benefited through the club work, factory meetings and lectures. Much of the work of the Y. W. C. A. among colored women was made possible by the urgent need during the war, and a great many activities begun at that time have been continued. Conferences of various kinds are being held, viz.: Conference for training of both paid and volunteer workers, industrial conferences, and already six summer Student Conferences have been held. A great contribution is being made toward a better understanding between the races by conferences of both white and colored women, where together they face facts, and together plan a forward program. Colored secretaries have a sympathetic and cordial hearing at the large summer conferences, and what is more important, they are being invited to speak at smaller student gatherings, such as cabinet councils, where they have a chance to interpret the needs of the colored girl to the college women of this generation.

*"Colored Men's Department, International Committee of Young Men's Christian Associations.* This organization maintains 114 Associations in the colored colleges and schools of America, and 44 city industrial and other departments. It holds a Student Conference each year at King's Mountain, North Carolina, and a Summer School for training general secretaries at Harper's Ferry, West Virginia. Fifteen cities have buildings which cost more than $100,000, into each of which Mr. Julius Rosenwald has put $25,000. The work undertaken is of the same general type of that which is done for the white men."

*Types of Negro Religion.* Religion among Negroes has a wide variety. In some of the best city churches you will find as refined and orderly a congregation as you would find anywhere in the world. I have heard some of the very best sermons it has ever been my privilege to hear in Negro Churches. One of the most beautiful and deeply satisfying Sunday services I ever attended was a Negro service, in which no white person had any part. But in candor one must admit this is not true in the majority of churches. The religious experience of the majority of Negroes, like that of any other group of ignorant people, is crude, full of emotionalism and prone to be filled with superstitious elements. One could expect nothing else. Indeed, those Negro preachers who have been well trained find difficulty in living up to their ideals in many of their churches. Their congregations demand emotional appeals and feel grieved if they do not receive them. A Negro man who has worked for me for years, and is far more intelligent than the average, said his preacher was very smart, was a good lecturer, but couldn't preach much. When questioned closely about the difference between a good preacher and a good lecturer he said: "Well, you know he don't put on any gravy." His preacher did not put in the pathetic element, he didn't drop into the sing-song, he didn't shout and tell harrowing stories, so he couldn't preach much. Of course, one does not have to go to a Negro church to find the emotional type of religion, but it is to be regretted that it is still so prevalent among the Negroes.

*Emotionalism in Religion.* "Rev. W. H. Holloway, a graduate of Talladega College, a Congregational minister in charge of a colored church in Thomas County, Ga., in a study of the negro church in that county, wrote as follows:

"'The supreme element in the old system was emotionalism, and while we hate to confess it truth demands that we affirm it as the predominating element to-day. The church which does not have its shouting, the church which does not measure the ability of a preacher by the "rousement" of his sermons, and, indeed, which does not tacitly demand of its minister the shout-producing discourse, is an exception to the rule. This is true of the towns as well as the country. Of course, we all understand that it has always occupied first place in the worship of the Negro church; it is a heritage of the past. In the absence of clearly defined doctrines, the great shout, accompanied with weird cries and shrieks and contortions and followed by a multivaried "experience" which takes the candidate through the most heart-rending scenes—this to-day in Thomas County is accepted by the majority of the churches as unmistakable evidence of regeneration.' " [70]

*Church Centers Around Individuals.* Another weakness of the Negro church lies in the fact that it gathers itself too largely around individuals. If the preacher does not like the way some influential members act, he will withdraw, take half the congregation with him and set up a new church. Hence many Negro churches are family churches, and the churches of a community are not so organized or placed as to meet the needs of a whole community.

In a study I made some years ago of the Negro churches of Atlanta, I found seventeen out of fifty-four had less than one hundred members each, the average membership of these seventeen being thirty each. Only eight of the fifty-four at that time had more than two hundred members, and only four had more than three hundred members. Eleven out of the fifty-four churches were the outgrowth of church splits. At the same time an investigation of the churches of Nashville showed fifty-two, with an average membership of two hundred and seven, while the white churches of Nashville average three hundred and ninety. Seventeen of these Nashville Negro churches had less than one hundred members each. Small church membership often condemns the congregation to live in very poor church buildings.

*Poor Business Methods.* Another weakness of the Negro church is its lack of business methods. In a questionnaire sent out in 1903 by Atlanta University to 200 Negro laymen, the question was asked as to the morality of Negro preachers. It was rather amazing how many of these men charged ministers with being careless or even dishonest in handling money.[71] Perhaps it is not altogether the minister's fault. The financial program of the church may be such as to encourage carelessness. In fact, in many churches there is no policy. The books are never audited,

[70] Quoted from Weatherford: "Negro Life in the South," p. 131.
[71] "The Negro Church," p. 154 f.    Atlanta University Publications No. 8.

and criticism may come at any time.  This loose financial policy is the basis of many church quarrels and some church splits.

"Another condition which gives rise to our assertion that the church is not exercising its highest moral influence, is seen in its lax business methods.  Let us give one example, which we dare assert is true of nine-tenths of the churches in Thomas county and in the South: A contract is made with every incoming minister.  They promise him a stipulated sum for his year's service and when the year ends, he goes to conference with only about two-thirds of the pledge fulfilled.  If he is sent back to the same field, the second year finds the church still deeper on the debit side of the ledger.  If he is sent to another field the debt is considered settled, a new contract is made with the new preacher, and the same form is gone through.

"As far as I have been able to learn fully 75 per cent. of the churches in the county are in debt to their former preachers, and what is worse, there seems never to arise a question as to the honesty of the religious body." [72]

*Church too Inclusive.*  Another weakness of the Negro church lies in its all inclusive nature.  It has been literary society, debating club, social gathering, singing school, and place for spiritual admonition.  The semi-religious activities of the church have been greatly in danger of absorbing all the energy of the church.  If it can be the center of community life and not lose its message of spiritual life, then the church will be a mighty factor for good, but if it lose its message in the multiplicity of its activities, it will become impotent.

*Untrained Ministry.*  Perhaps the weakest point in the Negro church is its ministry.  In a questionnaire sent out by Dr. Earnest in preparing his Doctor's thesis at the University of Virginia, the fact came out that most white people have little faith in the Negro minister.  The surprising fact was that the Negro ministers themselves were extremely critical of the class.  Not more than forty per cent. of the ministers were efficient, according to the judgment of their own group.[73]  Reverend H. W. Halloway, in a study of the Negro church in Thomas County, Georgia, thinks that its weakest spot is in its ministry:

"We have been able to learn of about 120 preachers in the county.  Of this number fully seventy-five are either ordained or licensed.  The most of their names appear in the minutes of the various denominations.  Now this number may be almost doubled if we search for all those who call themselves preachers and fill the function of interpreters of the word of God.  This

[72] "The Negro Church," p. 60.
[73] Earnest: "Religious Development of the Negro in Virginia," pp. 170-171.

number molds as great a sentiment for or against the church as those who hold license.

"You will get some idea of the vast host who belong to this class when I tell you that the records of the last conference of the Southwest Georgia District of the African Methodist Episcopal Church show that there were forty-three applicants for admission to the conference. Note that this is only one of the four or five conferences of this church in the state. Be it said to the lasting credit of the conference that it in unmistakable terms put the stamp of condemnation upon the presumption of about thirty-five of them and sent them back to their homes disappointed men. And yet, while it sent them back home unadmitted, it did not make them less determined to preach, for in their several communities you will find them still exercising themselves in the holy calling.

"Now of this vast number, so far as I have been able to learn, only four of them hold diplomas from any institution giving record of previous fitness. Only about one per cent. of them can point to any considerable time spent in school.

"The course of study prescribed in the African Methodist Episcopal Church has helped some, but after all this, it can be truthfully said that for real fitness, fitness in the truest sense of the word, there is little to be found among the ministers of the county.

"Putting this another way is to say, that the majority of the ministers are unlearned or ignorant men, ignorant in the sense of fitness for leadership; for, learned or unlearned, the Negro preacher is to-day the leader of the race. If they are ignorant, then this ignorance manifests itself in any number of ways:

"1st. His home life as a general rule is on no higher level than that of his neighbor. In most cases he married before he began to preach and his wife is ignorant. Here, then, is no toning example for the community which he serves. I beg you to note that the pulpit is not the only place where the minister is to do powerful and eloquent preaching.

"2d. In morality he has much to learn. Morality as it affects: (1) Temperance; (2) debt paying and business honesty; (3) sexual morality." [74]

*A Gloomy Picture.* This is rather a gloomy picture of the Negro church, which is the institution most responsible for developing moral and religious life among ten millions of people. But there is another side.

*Hopeful Signs.* First of all, there is a growing company of Negro preachers who are well trained, quiet and effective. In a southern city recently I went in company with a leading minister

[74] "The Negro Church," pp. 61-62.

of the Southern Methodist Church to hear a Negro preacher.  His text was: "I am the way, the truth and the life."  His statement was clear and convincing.  He had fervor, but at the same time quiet dignity.  His service had a vital moral message.  When the service was over my preacher friend with whom I went remarked that the white church which we had visited in the morning would do very well indeed to exchange pastors with this colored church.  There is urgent need for more thoroughly educated ministers, but the company is growing, and no one needs despair.

*Influence of Negro Church.*  The all inclusive nature of the church is its greatest asset.  There is a decided tendency at present for the Negro to doubt the value of religion.  Whether we white people relish it or not, the majority of Negroes have decided questions in their minds about the transforming power of religion as it relates to the white man.  If you know them well enough they will tell you frankly that they cannot reconcile real religion with the unjust treatment they often receive.  If religion cannot transform a white man, what right have we to suppose it can change a Negro.  Doubtless the Negro argues in similar way.  I have often felt that the acid test of Christianity in the South is the question of race relations.  So many have failed to stand the test that the Negro is losing faith in religion and in the church, the teacher of religion.  But he still goes to the church in large numbers because it is his club as well as his church.  Secret societies are taking part of the club feature from the church, but still it may continue to be said it is his social club.  Because the church has this hold on him, there is a chance for it to grip him morally and religiously.

*Negro People Growing Morally.*  It cannot be made out that the Negro is worse now than during slavery.  We may hear more of his misdeeds, but a closer study reveals a growth of character which is a real achievement.  In this progress the Negro church has had a very large part.  The problem of the southern white man is to face facts squarely.  We know we live side by side with ten million Negroes.  We know their churches are poorly organized—but for that matter, so are ours.  We know their preachers are poorly trained—but who would claim perfection for our white ministers?  We know that better training and a more sympathetic attitude toward their religious life is the greatest need of the Negro to-day.  As statesmen of a new day we should see to it that the Negro church fulfills its high function of transforming the moral life of the Negro race.  There is every hope for the future —there is no basis for despair.

## CHAPTER XIII

## THE NEGRO AND THE LAW

*Prior to 1860.* We have noted in other chapters the legal status of the slave and of the freeman before 1860. Neither were allowed to assemble themselves freely; it was illegal in most of the states to teach them to read and to write, after the earliest years, they were not allowed a vote, freedom of movement from place to place was restricted, the type of occupation in which a free Negro could engage was strictly delimited, neither a free Negro nor a slave could testify against a white man in most of the states, and even the white master was strictly limited in his right to free his own slaves. The life of both free Negroes and slaves was thus thoroughly hedged about by the law. "Slaves are better protected as property," wrote Goodell in 1853, "than they are as sentient beings." [1] Careful inspection of these early laws makes clear that they were primarily drawn with the thought of protecting property and not with respect to protecting persons. Maryland's law said: "There must be a loss of service or at least the diminution of the faculty to labor, to warrant an action by the master," [2] against another who has molested a slave. The South Carolina law read: "If any negro or other slave who shall be employed in the lawful business of his master, owner, overseer, etc., shall be beaten, &c., by any person or persons not having sufficient cause or authority for so doing, and shall be *maimed,* or *disabled* by such beating from performing his or her work, such person or persons, *so offending,* shall forfeit and pay to the owner or owners of such slaves, the sum of *fifteen shillings* current money per diem, for every day of his *lost time,* and also the charge of the cure of such slave." [3] The Louisiana Statute said: "If the slave (*maimed,* &c.) be *forever rendered unable to work,* the offender shall be compelled to *pay the value of said slave,* according to the appraisement made by two freeholders, appointed by each of the parties; and the slave thus disabled shall for ever be maintained at the expense of the person who shall have thus disabled him, which person shall be compelled to maintain and

---

[1] Goodell: "The American Slave Code," p. 201.
[2] *Ibid.,* p. 202.
[3] *Idem.*

feed him, agreeably to the duties of masters and slaves, as ordered by this Act." [4]

*Law Protected Property More than Persons.* These quotations give the viewpoint of the law. It was as remarked above primarily for the protection of property, not for the protection of persons. "A slave can invoke neither Magna Charta nor common law. . . . In the very nature of things he is subject to despotism. Law to him is only a compact between his rulers, and the questions which concern him are matters agitated between them. The various acts concerning slaves contemplate throughout the subordination of the servile class to every free white person and enforce the stern policy which the relation of master and slave necessarily requires." [5]

*Injured Slaves Paid For.* This is more fully brought out in cases where slaves were injured by others than their masters. When this was the case the offender was usually forced by the courts to pay the master for the loss, and in case the slave were permanently disabled he must pay the price of the slave, in which case he—the offender—took possession of the slave and was required to care for him. This, of course, put the slave in the hands of one who was already ill-disposed toward him and who would all the more be ill-disposed because of losses imposed on him by the court. (Cf. Jourdan vs. Patten, Louisiana Courts 1818). [6] The court in this case, where a slave had been blinded by the mistreatment of Patten, was not unmindful of the fact that humanity was being injured by its decision, but held that it was bound to protect the master in his property: "The principle of *humanity,* which would lead us to suppose that the mistress, whom he had so long served, would treat her miserable blind slave with more kindness than the defendant, to whom the judgment ought to transfer him, *cannot be taken into consideration,* in deciding the case." [7] The rights of the slave to security were completely subservient to the rights of the master to his property.

*Courts Lenient With Slaves.* As noted, however, in the chapter on Plantation Life, southern courts were usually lenient to the slave and gave him every chance for presenting grievances. The master was made responsible for the protection of his slave. Judge O'Neall of South Carolina in the case of Tennent vs. Dendy, 1837, speaking for the Court of Appeals, said:

"They are human beings with passions and feelings like our own and with the same capability of right and wrong action. They,

[4] Goodell: "The American Slave Code," p. 203.
[5] Henry: "The Police Control of the Slave in S. C.," p. 11.
[6] Goodell: "American Slave Code," p. 205.
[7] *Ibid.,* p. 206.

if in a state of nature, would have the right of self-protection which is given by the great Creator to every human being. Their transfer from a state of nature to a state of slavery in society has not destroyed the right of personal protection; it has taken it from the slave and given it to the master. . . . In the relation of master and servant the dependence of the latter on the former alone for protection cannot be too much encouraged. The slave ought to be fully aware that his master is to him what the best administered government is to the good citizen, a perfect security from injury. When this is the case the relation of master and servant becomes little short of that of parent and child—it commences in the weakness of the one and ends in the strength of the other. Its benefits produce the corresponding consequences of deep and abiding grateful attachments from the slave to the master, and hence result (many) instances of devotion." [8]

*Slave Crimes.* Human nature being in large measure the same at all times, one would expect to find the slaves committing crimes as slaves, just as they do as freedmen; and such expectation proves true. Some have attempted to maintain that the slave was free from all crimes save insurrection. The author has heard it asserted frequently that there was no rape by slaves during the old régime. The records of crime are, of course, scant, for most crimes were punished by the master and never got to the courts for record. But that every type of crime was committed cannot be doubted. Murder, poisoning, arson, rape, stealing are among the crimes charged against slaves. Louisiana dealt with criminals in legal fashion: "The record stands, three slaves and one free negro legally executed for rape and two slaves legally executed for attempted rape. There are some instances reported of summary punishment, not death, being administered to negroes for inducing white girls to run away with them, or for living with white women." [9] The *Charleston Courier,* February 1826, reports a Negro convicted of attempting to set fire to a private kitchen to be punished as follows:

"Twenty lashes at Center-Market, on 10th inst,—twenty lashes on 3rd of March—twenty on 24th of March, and twenty on 14th of April. Or if he so choose he may leave the state after the first whipping." [10]

*The Rising Sun,* 1859, reports:

"Nathan, a slave was tried and convicted for stealing chickens from a Mr. ———, and sentenced to ninety-five lashes. Peter,

[8] Henry: "The Police Control of the Slave in S. C.," p. 13.
[9] Cutler: "Lynch Law," p. 126.
[10] Henry: "The Police Control of the Slave in S. C.," p. 54.

another slave, a witness in the case, being detected in several
falsehoods and being believed to have an interest in said chickens,
was sentenced to thirty lashes." [11]

*Cases of Crime.* From Phillips' Plantation and Frontier, Volume II, we quote several cases of crime:
From the Georgia *Gazette,* Savannah, December 1774:

"From St. Andrew's Parish we have the following melancholy
account, viz. That on Tuesday morning the 29th ult. six new
Negro fellows and four wenches, belonging to Capt. Morris, killed
the Overseer in the field, after which they went to the house,
murdered his wife, and dangerously wounded a carpenter named
Wright, also a boy who died next day; they then proceeded to the
house of Angus McIntosh, whom they likewise dangerously
wounded; and being there joined by a sensible fellow, the property of said McIntosh, they went to the house of Roderick M'Leod,
wounded him very much, and killed his son, who had fired upon
them on their coming up and broke the arm of the fellow who
had joined them. Their leader and McIntosh's negro have been
taken and burnt, and two of the wenches have returned to the
plantation." [12]

From the New Orleans *Bee,* March 6, 1845:

"MURDER. The Shreveport (Caddo) *Gazette* of the 26th
ult., says: A most shocking murder occurred in our parish on
Monday last at the mill of Mr. Cutliff. The superintendent of
the mill, a Mr. Scott, attempted to chastise, as we have learned, a
negro fellow belonging to Mr. Cutliff, when the negro seizing a
frower knocked him down, and repeated his blows, until he was
not only dead, but his skull completely shattered. The negro has
been brought to this place and safely lodged in jail to await his
trial. Instances of this kind are becoming quite frequent." [13]

*Louisiana Crimes.* From the Baton Rouge *Republic,* July 23,
1822:

"SHOCKING OCCURRENCE. Some negroes of the family
of Gen. G. L. Davidson, Iredell county, in this state, unwilling to
go to Alabama with the General and his family, who were about
to remove there, took the desperate resolution of destroying them
by poison, and shocking to relate, effected their purpose on two
of the General's daughters (Mrs. Simonton and Mrs. Falls,) while

[11] Henry: "The Police Control of the Slave in S. C.," p. 54.
[12] Phillips: "Plantation and Frontier," Vol. II, p. 118,
[13] *Ibid.,* p. 119.

their husbands were absent looking for suitable lands for settlement in a new state.

"The poison used, it is believed, was Hemlock, which was furnished by an old negro in the adjoining county of Cabbarus, and had been tried some months before the proper dose was given, to effect the horrid purpose. This has been since ascertained from the frequent sickness of the two ladies, which could not, at the time be accounted for. It is said a dose was ready for the General himself, the administering of which was prevented by the discovery of the horrid plot. Five negroes concerned in this affair, are at present in confinement in Iredell jail." [14]

*Crime in New Orleans.* From the New Orleans *Bee,* September 27, 1842:

"One of the most atrocious outrages we have ever heard of was committed a few weeks since in the parish of Rapides, by a negro on the person of a young orphan girl, 14 years old. She was seized by the miscreant while paying a visit to one of her relations, dragged into the woods, beaten most unmercifully, and then treated—in the most infamous manner. The poor creature was picked up, some time after, in a state of insensibility, but recovered sufficiently to relate the above facts. She died the next day after horrible suffering. The murderer has been apprehended." [15]

The following abstract of the court record of Baldwin County, Georgia, shows similar facts of crime:

"November 12, 1812: The State v. Major, a slave, the property of John Neeves, on the charge of rape. Verdict of guilty. Sentence of hanging.

"January 11, 1815: The State v. Fannie Micklejohn, a slave, the property of the heirs of William Micklejohn. Charged with murdering an infant. Verdict of not guilty.

.    .    .    .    .    .    .

"July 31, 1818: The State v. Aleck, a slave, the property of James Thomas, charged with assault with intent to murder. The prisoner pleaded guilty, and was sentenced to receive 50 lashes well laid on the bare back with a cow-skin whip three days in succession.

"February 17, 1819: The State v. Rodney, a slave, the property of Maj. John A. Jones, charged with arson. The prisoner was found guilty and sentenced to be hanged.

.    .,    .    .    .    .    .

[14] Phillips: "Plantation and Frontier," Vol. II, p. 120,
[15] *Ibid.,* p. 121,

"January 19, 1822: The State v. Davis, or Dave, a slave, the property of William Johns, charged with assault with intent to kill a white person. Verdict of guilty. Sentence not recorded.

"No date: The State v. John, a slave, the property of William Robertson, charged with burglary. Found guilty but recommended to mercy. Sentenced to be branded on the right cheek with the letter T, and to be given 39 lashes on three successive days.

"On the same day this same slave, John, was sentenced to be hanged for assaulting a white man with intent to kill.

. . . . . . .

"March 15, 1826: The State v. Elleck, a slave, the property of Andrew Elliott, charged with assault with intent to commit murder and rape. Verdict, guilty of assault with intent to kill. Sentence, hanging.

. . . . . .

May 21, 1832: The State v. Martin, a slave, the property of Farish Carter, charged with assault with intent murder. The prisoner pleaded guilty, and was sentenced to 39 lashes on three successive days." [16]

*State Prisoners.* The number of Negro prisoners in state prisons and penitentiaries in the slave states in 1850 was, according to Blake's "History of Slavery" 323, as against 988 native whites, and in the northern or non-slave holding states the corresponding figures were 565 and 2271.[17] Louisiana and Virginia kept more careful records than other states, and their criminal reports show great variety in crime. In Louisiana in 1860 there were 96 slave prisoners and 236 white prisoners; 11 free colored prisoners, and 83 of the slaves were serving life terms. "Classed by crimes, 12 of them had been sentenced for arson, 3 for burglary or housebreaking, 28 for murder, 4 for manslaughter, 4 for poisoning, 5 for attempts to poison, 7 for assault with intent to kill, 2 for stabbing, 3 for shooting, 20 for striking or wounding a white person, 1 for wounding a child, 4 for attempts to rape, and 3 for insurrection. This catalogue is notable for its omissions as well as for its content. While there were four white inmates of the prison who stood convicted of rape, there were no negroes who had accomplished that crime. Likewise as compared with 52 whites and 4 free negroes serving terms for larceny, there were no slave prisoners in that category. Doubtless on the one hand hand the negro rapists had been promptly put to death, and the slaves committing mere theft had been let off with whippings. Furthermore there were no slaves committed for counterfeiting

[16] Phillips: "Plantation and Frontier," Vol. II, pp. 123-125.
[17] Blake: "History of Slavery" (1860), pp. 837 and 838.

THE NEGRO FROM AFRICA TO AMERICA

or forgery, horse stealing, slave stealing or aiding slaves to escape." [18]

*Virginia's Record of Negro Crime.* The Virginia file of crime for 1780 to 1864 included 90 slaves convicted for arson, of whom 29 were women, 257 for burglary, 15 for highway robbery, 20 for stealing horses, 24 for other types of stealing, 346 for murder (including murder of masters, 56, mistresses 11, overseers 11, free Negroes 7, slaves 85, children 12, and others), for poisoning 56, for assault 111, for rape, 73, for attempted rape 32.[19] We have noted in another chapter the cases of insurrection (of The Problem of the Free Negro). Such a catalogue of crimes forever lays to rest the boast that there were no criminal slaves, and that the régime worked with such harmony and good will there was little friction between whites and blacks. One must not forget also that most of the minor offenses, and often the major offenses of one slave against another slave, never got to the courts at all. They were settled by the master, with the whip or with confinement sentence, occasionally by selling him further South.

*Situation at Close of Civil War.* At the close of the Civil War the southern white people found themselves facing a difficult situation. They had always feared the presence of the free colored people, but now they had between three and four millions of them. They knew that a few of these were criminally inclined, and now that the restraint of the master was removed, they looked for trouble. They were now in the same position as the northern states with reference to free Negroes, save as to the overwhelming numbers in the South. These southern states, therefore, followed suit in the laws of northern states governing free Negroes:

*Legal Restrictions in Northern States.* Delaware in 1851 "prohibited the emigration of free Negroes to (from) any state except Maryland." [20] Indiana in 1857 drew up a constitution which prohibited mulattoes and Negroes from coming into the state, and placed a fine of five hundred dollars on persons employing them.[21] Illinois, Iowa, Oregon, and New Mexico passed similar laws.[22] Ohio required Negroes living in the state to give bond for good behavior, excluded them from schools, denied them the right to testify against a white man in court,[23] and forced them to idleness by fining the white man who employed them.[24] Practically every northern state at some time before 1860 had some such law on its

Phillips: "American Negro Slavery," p. 457.
[19] *Ibid.*, pp. 457-458, *passim.*
[20] Wilson: "The Rise and Fall of the Slave Power in America," Vol. II, p 183.
[21] *Ibid.*, p. 185.
[22] *Ibid.*, p. 187.
[23] *Ibid.*, p. 170.
[24] Goodell: "American Slave Code," p. 259.

statute books.  If the northern states thus must protect themselves against a few free Negroes, how much more must the South—it was argued—protect itself against millions of free blacks.  The result of this logic was the black codes of 1865 to 1868.  Alabama provided that no Negro should keep a tavern or sell liquors, drugs or medicine.  South Carolina forbade a Negro to manufacture or sell liquor, or to enter the ranks of shopkeepers or artisans of any kind without a special license, for which license a liberal fee was charged.  In Mississippi the Negro was forbidden to rent or lease lands except in incorporated towns, and he must have a license for working in the towns.[25]  Florida and Mississippi made it a misdemeanor for any Negro to own, use, or keep a bowie-knife, dirk, sword, firearms or ammunition, unless he had a license for the same.  In Florida it was necessary to get certificates from two white citizens as to the peaceable character of the Negro before he could secure such license.  In South Carolina he could keep a shotgun for hunting, but could not keep a pistol.[26]  Many states made it an offense for a white man to sell whiskey to a Negro.  All these laws were precautions against uprisings on the part of the Negro.  There was general disorder and confusion at the close of the war, and fear lest there would be violence unless drastic measures were taken.

*Legal Restrictions on Labor Contracts.*  Labor contracts were made rigid because hundreds of Negroes in their new freedom were loafing about the towns refusing to work and when they did work, only staying at any job long enough to get a few dollars ahead.  This was most annoying to farmers, for just when the crops were to be gathered the planter would find himself without labor, and the work of the year would go for naught.  As a result of this situation most of the southern states passed laws requiring all contracts with Negroes to be put in writing, and attested by witnesses, often officers of the law.  These contracts must be read to the Negro in the presence of witnesses.  This was a real protection to the Negro against fraud or peonage.  But most of these laws had a second clause which easily gave itself to peonage in the hand of an unscrupulous employer.  This clause said that if a Negro quit his job before the expiration of his contract, he became a vagrant, he forfeited his salary for the whole year, he could be arrested and taken back to his place of work, and in case of necessity could be handled by the county court as a criminal.  While these laws were evidently meant to protect both white and colored, as a matter of fact they worked a great hardship on many Negroes.  Unscrupulous employers so drew their contracts as to hold ignorant and helpless Negroes on their farms without

[25] Stephenson: "Race Distinctions in American Law," pp. 42-43.
[26] *Ibid.*, pp. 43-44.

due compensation. The South Carolina laws were in particular detailed and burdensome. Hours of labor were regulated, hours for meals, time to begin and quit work specified, types of work that could be demanded, guilt for improper care in work, etc. The law stipulated the type of food a servant (Negro) might demand, it stipulated methods of adjusting lost time on the part of the servant, it described in detail how a servant might be discharged or might have the right to leave his master. It further prescribed the manners and social behavior of servants toward masters or employers. Mississippi had almost as detailed regulations.

*Laws of Apprenticeship.* Apprentice laws were placed on statute books in southern states and were also minute in detail. Negro children from two years and up might be apprenticed. When they had no parents or were illegitimate children, or when the parents were immoral, or unable to provide for the child, the courts might place the child in apprenticeship—if a boy, until twenty-one; if a girl, until eighteen. In most cases these laws did not refer to races, but they were everywhere meant primarily to deal with Negroes. In some states, like Kentucky, there was a difference made between white and Negro children. White children must be taught to read and write. In the case of colored children, if taught to read and write no money need be given them when the period of apprenticeship was ended.

*Vagrancy Laws.* Vagrancy laws were also drastic. All persons were required to prove they had fixed and permanent places of abode, that they had an honest and reputable livelihood, that they had license for business, and in some cases they must show license of marriage to prove they were not simply hangers on instead of real members of a family.[27] These stringent laws which seemed to the South justifiable in the light of conditions, were exceedingly distasteful to the North and had much to do with the inauguration of the reconstruction régime, which held the South in turmoil and poverty for a dozen years following the Civil War. The horror of that period has been too frequently written to need any word here. We only stop to say that it was a period of complete misunderstanding and bitter strife, engendering a disregard for law and order which was destined to bear much fruitage in crime as the years went by. The criminal record of the South cannot be clearly understood or evaluated without some knowledge of the reconstruction period and its influence on the attitude of ·the people toward constituted authority.

*Large Criminal Population.* It was but natural that the South should emerge from this period with a disproportionate criminal population. The white man had been forced for self-protection to do things which seemed lawless, and the Negro had been en-

[27] Cf. Laws of Mississippi, 1865.

couraged to believe that almost any acts were justifiable when directed against his former master. It would have been almost miraculous if crime had not multiplied under such conditions. It would naturally follow from the foregoing statements that punishment of the Negro following reconstruction would be rigid and severe. "The courts and jails became filled with the careless and ignorant, with those who sought to emphasize their new found freedom, and too often with innocent victims of oppression. The testimony of a Negro counted for little or nothing in court, while the accusation of white witnesses was usually decisive. The result of this was a sudden large increase in the apparent criminal population of the Southern states—an increase so large that there was no way for the state to house it or watch it even had the state wished to. And the state did not wish to. Throughout the South laws were immediately passed authorizing public officials to lease the labor of convicts to the highest bidder. The lessee then took charge of the convicts—worked them as he wished under the nominal control of the state. Thus a new slavery and slave-trade was established." [28]

*Cable's Indictment.* Writing in 1885, George W. Cable, a southern gentleman, said:

"We might almost assert beforehand that the popular sentiment and verdict would hustle the misbehaving, with shocking alacrity, into the State's prison under extravagant sentences or for trivial offenses, and sell their labor to the highest bidder who will use them in the construction of public works. The temptation gathers additional force through the popular ignorance of the condition and results of these penitentiaries, and the natural assumption that they are not so grossly mismanaged but that the convict will survive his sentence, and the fierce discipline of the convict camp 'teach him to behave himself.'

". . . A single glance at almost any of their reports startles the eye with the undue length of sentences and the infliction of penalties for mere misdemeanors that are proper only to crimes and felonies. In the Georgia penitentiary, 1880, in a total of nearly 1200 convicts, only 22 prisoners were serving as low a term as one year, only 52 others as low a term as two years, only 76 others as low a term as three years; while those who were under sentences of ten years and *over* numbered 538, although ten years, as the rolls show, is the *utmost* length of time that a convict can be expected to remain alive in a Georgia penitentiary. Six men were under sentence for simple assault and battery,—mere fisticuffing,—one of two years, two or five years, one of six years, one of seven, and one of eight. For larceny, three men were

[28] Atlanta University Publication No. 9: "Negro Crime in Ga."

serving under sentence of twenty years; five were sentenced each fifteen years; one, fourten years; six, twelve years; thirty-five, ten years; and one hundred and seventy-two, from one year up to nine years.  In other words, a large majority of all these had, for simple stealing, without breaking in or violence, been virtually condemned to be worked and misused to death.  One man was under a twenty years' sentence for 'hog stealing.'  Twelve men were sentenced to the South Carolina penitentiary, in 1881, on no other finding but a misdemeanor commonly atoned for by a fine of a few dollars, and which thousands of the State's inhabitants are constantly committing with impunity—the carrying of concealed weapons.  Fifteen others were sentenced for mere assault and assault and battery.  It is to be inferred—for we are left to our inferences—that such sentences were very short; but it is inferable, too, that they worked the customary loss of citizenship for life.  In Louisiana, a few days before the writing of this paper, a man was sentenced to the penitentiary for twelve months for stealing five dollars' worth of gunnysacks." [29]

*Present Harshness of Criminal Procedure.*  There thus comes into our modern penal system with reference to the Negro a severity which has had much to do with present comparative records of crime.

If we turn now to crime records in 1910, we find some rather alarming facts.  Although the Negroes of 1910 constituted 10.7 per cent of the total population, 30.6 per cent of the total criminal population were Negroes, and 21.9 per cent of all those committed to prison during that year were Negroes.  The Negro prisoners and juvenile delinquents January 1, 1910, were 424.6 per 100,000 population, while that of the whites was 114.8 per similar population.[30]  In the southern states 70 per cent of the prison population are Negroes, in the East about 12 per cent, and in the West about 6 per cent.[31]  In every case it is disproportionately high.  Commitments to prison are not so high in ratio as the prison population, but even here the ratio is alarming.  The ratio in cities is higher for Negroes than in rural sections, hence the North— where 77 per cent of all Negroes live in cities—show more Negro criminals in proportion to population than does the South.  Cable pointed out the long sentences of Negroes in 1885, and the situation has not materially changed since.  In 1910 62.6 per cent of all prisoners serving for life were Negroes, 54.8 of those serving ten years were Negroes, 46 per cent of those serving between five and ten years, 40.4 per cent of those serving between two and

[29] Cable: "The Silent South," pp. 152-153-154.
[30] U. S. Census: Negro Population in U. S., 1790-1915, p. 436.
[31] *Ibid.,* p. 437.

five years, 34.7 per cent of those serving one year, and 13.4 per cent of those serving less than one year were Negroes.[32] It will thus be seen that the sentence for Negroes is exorbitantly long, and thus the proportion of Negroes in criminal population would be greatly increased. In view of these facts the criminality of the Negro may be far less than his proportion of criminal population would indicate. The average length of sentence for Negroes and whites respectively in the South Atlantic States was 15.4 months and 9.6 months. The same figures for the East South Central States were 31.7 months and 16.2 months. It is thus seen that the sentence of the Negro averages almost twice as long as does that of the white man. This is partly due to difference of crimes, but more largely due to severity of judgment of the courts in dealing with the Negro. Judge William H. Sanford, of Montgomery, Alabama, speaking at the Southern Sociological Congress held in Nashville, Tennesee, 1912, said the Negro got justice and the white man far lighter sentences than justice in those southern communities where the Negro was in the majority. In those communities where the two races were almost equal, he thought the two races got fair justice. In those communities where the whites were in the majority he thought the white man got justice, but the Negro's punishment was much more severe than justice would demand.[33]

*Negro Gets Severe Sentences.* This statement needs to be modified. Where the case in question is between a Negro and a white man, the Negro always gets the severer sentence—if indeed the white man gets any sentence at all. In visiting certain county seats in the lower South I investigated the criminal records. I found very few white men convicted of murder, though not infrequent trials of the same. I remarked about this to the clerk of court in one county seat. Rather amazed he said to me, "You don't think you could convict a white man of murdering a Negro, do you?" It is a rare thing in these lower southern counties that a white man is convicted of an offense of any kind against a Negro.

*Negro Criminals Younger than Whites.* It is worthy of careful note that the age of Negro criminals is lower than that of whites. The Census of 1910 showed that of all the prisoners between 15 and 25, one-fourth were Negroes, the Negro being two and a half times more criminal in proportion to population during this age period. Between the ages of 25 and 35, one-eighth of the criminal population was colored, or one and a fourth times as criminal as the whites for this age group. Between the ages of 35 to 45, only one-twelfth of the criminal population was

[32] U. S. Census: Negro Population in U. S., 1790-1915, p. 442.
[33] "The Call of the New South," pp. 125-127.

colored, so that in this age group the whites are proportionately one-fifth more criminal. To put it another way, the ratio of criminality reaches its maximum among Negroes between the ages of 21 and 24, and among whites the maximum falls between the ages of 35 and 44. Also, the proportion of women criminals is higher among Negroes. 19.1 per cent of the Negro criminals committed in 1910 were women, and 7.2 per cent of the whites were women, or one out of every five Negro criminals was a female, one out of every thirteen whites was a female. The offenses charged against the white females are graver on the whole than those charged against Negro females, and the average sentence for white females is decidedly longer. The age of female criminals is lower than the age of male criminals among Negroes. Lesser homicide, assault and larceny are the most frequent offenses for Negro females. There are 33 times as many Negro women committed for assault as there are white women in proportion to population. But for prostitution, drunkenness and disorderly conduct the white women are much nearer the Negroes in proportion.[34] These are grave facts and call for some type of explanation. No conclusive theories may be defended, but there are certain patent facts which may help to throw light on the present situation.

*Economic Origin of Crime.* In the first place the larger proportion of Negro criminals may be in part economic in origin. Of this economic aspect of crime Dr. Parsons remarks:

"As the struggle for existence becomes more rigorous and wants and desires increase, the law of survival works with increasing rigor and cruelty. The mentally or physically strong, taking advantage of the increased opportunity for satisfaction of wants or gratification of desires, slowly but surely advance the standard of living. In the struggle to maintain their old standard or to keep pace with the new, the physically or mentally weak slowly but surely fall behind, or maintain the standard at the expense of vital wants and the exhaustion of nervous constitutions. As a result of this mal-nutrition and nervous exhaustion we soon have a large class born into the world much less fortunately equipped, either mentally or physically, than their parents to maintain their social position. A large number of these perish, falling an easy prey to disease; still another large portion of them become vagrants or dependents and fill our asylums, reformatories, and poor-houses; while the remainder either fall naturally into criminality or, filled with sullen anger at the society which exacts of them a standard of conduct which they are incapable of maintaining, turn upon their supposed oppressor and prey upon it.

[34] "Negro Population in U. S., 1790 to 1915." Census Report, pp. 445-7

This group, augmented by the degenerate offspring of the debauched superior class, constitutes our criminal population. Thus crime is, in a large measure, the result of the activity of the social wreckage which floats miserably along in the wake of progress." [35]

The Negro belongs to the lower economic group in America and would be expected to furnish a disproportionate number of criminals, just as the white people who live nearer the poverty line furnish a much larger proportion of white criminals than does the group which has a much larger income. It is not primarily a race problem but a class problem, in which the poverty class is the most fertile field for crime.

*Illiteracy and Crime.* Illiteracy among Negroes is four times as great as among whites, and this condition undoubtedly has an influence on crime. Not that being ignorant makes one a criminal, but the conditions which make for illiteracy also make for lack of ambition, idleness and crime. But it is objected that criminality has grown among Negroes. So has it grown among all the peoples of the world. We judge the criminality of a people by the number of persons committed for crime, and the number of persons committed is determined in part by the stringency of our laws. This is one reason why there are more juvenile delinquents among Negroes in the North than in the South, because they have much stricter laws than we have had in the South heretofore. It is a well known fact that the passage of compulsory education laws has increased the number of delinquents recorded. It has not actually increased crime, but it has increased the record of crimes. Every advance in civilization brings increased apprehension of crime.

*Social Advancement and Crime.* "Higher evolution means great and increasing complexity, specialization, interdependence, and consequent sensitiveness of the social life. The harm to one individual becomes more and more the injury to all. Society recognizes this, and the extension of the field of crime, the field of prohibited action, goes on apace. Nor does the criminal law stop, in modern times, with negative commands; it adds positive orders as well. Not only, thou shalt not kill, but, thou must have thy children educated. Not one of the great, progressive civilizations has been able to escape from the necessity of increasing, very largely and persistently, its criminal statutes during the nineteenth century. Naturally, the most crying evils are first made crimes. Afterwards, the lesser evils become more noticeable, and their increasing number and heinousness demand public attention and punishment. It becomes criminal for taskmasters to degrade women and children to the level of the brute for mere money

[35] Columbia University Studies, Vol. 34, Part 3, p. 16.

gain. Factory and mining legislation stamps out these great
abuses of the new industrialism. The horrors of train wrecking
cause intense public indignation and the enactment of ever heavier
penalties. Embezzlement is made a crime. Society begins to
punish fraudulent trustees, and those who seek to thrive by newly
discovered forms of fraud and forgery." [36]

While illiteracy has decreased and crime has increased, it still
remains true that a very much larger proportion of the illiterate
population is criminal than is true of the literate.

*Social Environment and Crime.* The social environment in
which great numbers of Negroes live is conducive to crime. It is
a well known fact that great numbers of Negroes live in the congested centers of the city,—near the railroad yards and shops,
near viaducts which have run the white people out, in the back
alleys and on the river banks. Filth and dirt break down pride
and are direct feeders to crime. Among white people living under
these conditions crime is much more prevalent than among well-
to-do whites. Any one who has carefully surveyed the Negro
quarter of a city and seen the terrible conditions under which
many Negroes live must have wondered that any of the poorer
ones come to maturity without falling into crime.

*Insanity and Feeble Mindedness.* Insanity and feeble mindedness add to the criminal record. Only seven per cent of the inmates of institutions for the feeble minded and insane are
Negroes, but this probably does not represent the true situation.
Any Southerner knows a number of feeble minded Negroes at
large, and, of course, a few feeble minded whites. It is this
group of the weak minded who are at large that helps to swell
the criminality of the Negro. There are almost no distinct institutions for Negroes, and their relatives are very apt to keep them
out of asylums, if possible. The female of this class is a most
dangerous element in society. She is taken advantage of by every
thug and then becomes the mother of thieves and murderers. On
the other hand the feeble minded white woman is much more
apt to be shielded at home, or sent to an institution. Economically
and for the good of society at large we are most stupid in not
giving more careful attention to the feeble minded Negro. Another factor which may explain somewhat the greater proportion
of whites in asylums lies in the city residence of the larger proportion of whites. Contrary to popular opinion, the proportion
of insanity is nearly twice as high for urban population as it is
for rural, both for white and colored people. The 'number in
insane asylums for 100,000 of urban and rural population respectively is, for colored 78 and 26.9 in 1910, and for whites 86.5
and 44. Since most of the Negroes in the North live in cities,

[36] Columbia University Studies, Vol. 15, p. 332.

this may be one reason why the northern Negro shows a very much larger percentage of insane, in some cases almost twice as large. In turn this larger percentage of insanity may have something to do with the higher criminal record of northern negroes. Among the feeble minded the statistics show ridiculously small figures for Negroes, and we are sure of the fact that few of this class of Negroes ever reach the institutions. Blindness among Negroes is one and one-half times as prevalent as among whites, due perhaps to less care of eyes, and more of venereal disease among Negro mothers.

*Poverty and Female Criminals.* Lastly, the lower age of Negro female criminals may be in part due to living conditions. Poverty means overcrowding, and that in turn means lack of privacy and loss of modesty. In a study of a section of Atlanta, Georgia, I found one house of two rooms and a "lean to," in which a man and his wife and three grown daughters lived, and they took in two men boarders. Under such conditions immorality must of necessity breed. All of these factors enter into the larger criminal record of the Negro.

*Unfair Trials.* In the trial of cases in which Negroes are involved, there has long been a feeling that race prejudice often overrode justice. The Civil Rights bill of 1875 declared: "That no citizen possessing all other qualifications which are or may be prescribed by law shall be disqualified for service as a grand or petit juror, in any court of the United States, or of any state, on account of race, color or previous condition of servitude, and any officer or other person charged with any duty in the selection or summoning of jurors who shall exclude or fail to summon any citizen for the cause aforesaid, shall upon conviction thereof be deemed guilty of a misdemeanor, and fined not more than five hundred dollars." In spite of this clause, not many Negroes have been allowed to serve on juries. Mr. Gilbert T. Stevenson made a careful investigation of this matter some years ago and found cases in Arkansas, Kentucky, Louisiana, Mississippi and South Carolina where Negroes occasionally served on juries.[37] But in most of the answers received by Mr. Stephenson it was clear that white men did not look with favor upon Negro jurors.

*What the Negro Wants—Jury Service.* John R. Hawkins, a Negro, reported to the Federal Council of Churches in 1918 fourteen things which the Negro in America wanted. Point thirteen declared they wanted: "Recognition of the Negro's right and fitness to sit on juries. The jury system is one of the fundamental principles of our government and the privilege of exercising this right should be extended to capable citizens without regard to race

[37] Stephenson: "Race Distinctions in American Law," pp. 254-267, *passim.*

relationships." [38]   It would seem that in the states where there is
the largest number of Negroes,—Mississippi and South Carolina
—the fairness of this demand has already been acknowledged in
certain counties at least.  This demand on the part of Negroes for
right of jury service when Negroes are involved arises out of the
feeling that injustice is frequently done where white men alone
sit on the jury.  There is a conviction that race prejudice enters
into jury decisions.  It would be difficult to show that such is not
the case.  If the Negro is not to have a place on the jury when
Negroes are on trial, then there must surely be a fair sense of
justice and less of race prejudice shown by white jurors.

*The Crime of Lynching.*  The twelfth article of Mr. Hawkins'
statement of the Negro's wants reads: "A fair and impartial trial
by jury instead of lynching.  No people are safe in a community
where mob violence is tolerated.  Violators of law should be
punished but by due process of law.  The lynching spirit has
become so strong in some sections that it borders on disregard for
all law, order and decency.  Innocent people are often the victims
of the mob; and peace and well being of the whole community
is seriously affected thereby." [39]   In 1890 there were 1392 persons
confined for rape, of whom 578 were Negroes.[40]   In 1910 there
were 1480 committed to jail for rape, of whom 380 were Negroes.[41]
In 1890 the Negroes sentenced for rape received an average sentence of 14.04 years and white men received an average of 12.72
years.  Most of these cases of rape among Negroes were upon
the women of their own race.  DuBois thinks that the number of
cases against white women is greatly exaggerated, many of them
being so reported on account of hysteria.  "But granting this and
making allowance for all exaggeration in attributing this crime to
Negroes, there still remains enough well authenticated cases of
brutal assault on women by black men in America to make every
Negro bow his head in shame.  Negroes must recognize their
responsibility for their own worst classes and never let resentment
against slander allow them even to seem to palliate an awful deed.
This crime must at all hazards stop.  Lynching is awful, and
injustice and caste are hard to bear; but if they are to be successfully attacked they must cease to have even this terrible
justification." [42]

*Lynching Widespread.*  Lynching is no new crime, nor is it
confined to the South.  The practice of summary justice rose
before the revolution.[43]   At first lynching did not mean killing,

[38] "The Negro Year Book, 1918-19," p. 122.
[39] *Ibid.*, 1922, p. 122.
[40] "Notes on Negro Crime" in Atlanta University Series No. 9, p. 16.
[41] "Negro Population in U. S., 1790-1815," p. 446.
[42] "Notes on Negro Crime," Atlanta University Publication No. 9, p. 56.
[43] Cutler: "Lynch Law," p. 33.

but whipping or other severe or summary punishment.[44] The "Regulators," as they were called in colonial times, were rather influential in maintaining peace and order. But what is permissible in a crude and primitive society will not necessarily be good for a better developed community. Lynching of a brutal type was known long before the Civil War. It was commonly practiced against slaves who plotted insurrection and against any who dared violate a white woman. Other heinous crimes were punished by lynching.

"In the month of May, 1835, two negroes were burned to death near Mobile, Alabama, for 'most barbarously murdering' two children. The murderers had their trial, the result of which is given in the following paragraph taken from a Mobile paper: 'As the Court pronounced the only sentence known to the law— the smothered flame broke forth. The laws of the country had never conceived that crimes could be perpetrated with such peculiar circumstances of barbarity, and had therefore provided no adequate punishment. Their lives were justly forfeited to the laws of the country, but the peculiar circumstances demanded that the ordinary punishment should be departed from—they were seized, taken to the place where they had perpetrated the act, and burned to death.' "[45]

*Lincoln on Lynching.* Speaking of the widespread disease of lynching, Abraham Lincoln said in 1837:

"Accounts of outrages committed by mobs form the every-day news of the times. They have pervaded the country from New England to Louisiana; they are neither peculiar to the eternal snows of the former nor the burning suns of the latter; they are not the creature of climate, neither are they confined to the slave-holding or the non-slaveholding States. Alike they spring up among the pleasure-hunting masters of Southern slaves, and the order-loving citizens of the land of steady habits. Whatever then their cause may be, it is common to the whole country.

"It would be tedious as well as useless to recount the horrors of all of them. Those happening in the State of Mississippi and at St. Louis are perhaps the most dangerous in example and revolting to humanity. In the Mississippi case they first commenced by hanging the regular gamblers—a set of men certainly not following for a livelihood a very useful or very honest occupation, but one which, so far from being forbidden by the laws, was actually licensed by an act of the legislature passed but a single year before. Next, negroes suspected of conspiring to raise an

[44] Cutler: "Lynch Law," pp. 166, 121, etc.
[45] *Ibid.*, p. 108.

insurrection were caught up and hanged in all parts of the State; then, white men supposed to be leagued with the negroes; and finally, strangers from neighboring States, going thither on business, were in many instances subjected to the same fate. Thus went on this process of hanging, from gamblers to negroes, from negroes to white citizens, and from these to strangers, till dead men were literally dangling from the boughs of trees by every roadside, and in numbers almost sufficient to rival the native Spanish moss of the country as a drapery of the forest.

"Turn then to that horror-striking scene at St. Louis. A single victim only was sacrificed there. This story is very short, and is perhaps the most highly tragic of anything of its length that has ever been witnessed in real life. A mulatto man by the name of McIntosh was seized in the street, dragged to the suburbs of the city, chained to a tree, and actually burned to death; and all within a single hour from the time he had been a freeman attending to his own business and at peace with the world.

"Such are the effects of mob law, and such are the scenes becoming more and more frequent in this land so lately famed for love of law and order, and the stories of which have been now grown too familiar to attract anything more than an idle remark." [46]

*Lynching Not Primarily to Defend Women.* Contrary to popular opinion, it is clear that lynching did not even originate out of a desire to defend womanhood and it never has been used primarily for that purpose. Cutler compiled from the files of the *New York Times* for the years 1871-1873 the following record of lynchings:

"Kentucky: 2 negroes hung for rape, 1 white hung for rape, 1 negro hung for murder, 3 negroes shot by masked men, 1 negro 'murdered' by Ku-Klux.

"Tennessee: 2 negroes hung for robbery and arson, 1 negro shot and hung for robbery and murder, 1 negro shot for attempted outrage, 1 negro hung and shot for murder, 1 white shot for murder of wife.

"Missouri: 5 horse thieves hung, 1 negro hung for outrage, 1 white hung for murder, 3 whites hung for murder and robbery, 3 whites shot for defending and being bondsmen of county officials accused of peculation.

"California: 2 whites hung for murder, 1 white hung and shot for murder, 1 Indian hung for murder, 1 Malay (steward of steamer) shot and thrown overboard near coast of California for ravishing sick girl, eleven years old.

⁴⁶ Cutler: "Lynch Law," p. 111,

"Montana: 2 whites hung for murder.
"Louisiana: 4 negroes hung for murder, 3 horse thieves hung.
"Virginia: 1 desperado, horse thief and murderer hung.
"Alabama: 1 white shot for murder.
"South Carolina: 2 whites shot for murder, 10 negroes shot and hung by Ku-Klux.
"Nevada: 1 desperado hung, 1 white hung for killing man in saloon row.
"Wisconsin: 1 white man hung for murder.
"Indiana: 3 negroes hung for murder, 1 white hung for murder.
"Nebraska: 1 negro and 1 white man 'killed' for robbery and shooting woman.
"Kansas: 2 whites hung for murder, 1 desperado and 1 horse thief 'killed in jail.'
"Colorado: 2 whites hung for keeping gambling outfit.
"Michigan: 2 whites died from beating which they received for killing a man in a German-Irish riot on the streets.
"Ohio: 2 whites hung for murder.
"Maryland: 1 negro hung for arson.
"Total: 41 whites, 32 negroes, 1 Malay, 1 Indian." [47]

The table of lynchings for 1889 to 1922, on the following page, gives a clear picture of the present situation.

Of the 3500 lynchings, 721 are known to be whites. Summarizing the crimes for which persons were lynched from 1889 to 1918, we find the following facts:

*Small Number Lynched for Rape.* "Among colored victims, 35.8 per cent were accused of murder; 28.4 per cent of rape and 'attacks upon women' (19 per cent of rape and 9.4 per cent of 'attacks upon women'); 17.8 per cent of crimes against the person (other than those already mentioned) and against property; 12 per cent were charged with miscellaneous crimes and in 5.6 per cent of cases no crime at all was charged. The 5.6 per cent. classified under 'Absence of Crime' does not include a number of cases in which crime was alleged but in which it was afterwards shown conclusively that no crime had been committed. Further, it may fairly be pointed out that in a number of cases where Negroes have been lynched for rape and 'attacks upon white women,' the alleged attacks rest upon no stronger evidence than 'entering the room of a woman' or brushing against her. In such cases as these latter the victims and their friends have often asserted that there was no intention on the part of the victim to

[47] Cutler: "Lynch Law," p. 151.

NUMBER OF WHITE AND COLORED PERSONS LYNCHED IN
UNITED STATES, 1889-1923

| Years | Total | White | Colored |
|---|---|---|---|
| 1889 | 175 | 80 | 95 |
| 1890 | 91 | 3 | 88 |
| 1891 | 194 | 67 | 127 |
| 1892 | 226 | 71 | 155 |
| 1893 | 153 | 39 | 114 |
| 1894 | 182 | 54 | 128 |
| 1895 | 178 | 68 | 110 |
| 1896 | 125 | 46 | 79 |
| 1897 | 162 | 38 | 124 |
| 1898 | 127 | 24 | 103 |
| 1899 | 109 | 22 | 87 |
| 1900 | 101 | 12 | 89 |
| 1901 | 135 | 27 | 108 |
| 1902 | 94 | 10 | 84 |
| 1903 | 104 | 17 | 87 |
| 1904 | 86 | 7 | 79 |
| 1905 | 65 | 5 | 60 |
| 1906 | 68 | 4 | 64 |
| 1907 | 62 | 3 | 59 |
| 1908 | 100 | 8 | 92 |
| 1909 | 89 | 14 | 75 |
| 1910 | 90 | 10 | 80 |
| 1911 | 71 | 8 | 63 |
| 1912 | 64 | 3 | 61 |
| 1913 | 48 | 1 | 47 |
| 1914 | 54 | 5 | 49 |
| 1915 | 96 | 43 | 53 |
| 1916 | 58 | 7 | 51 |
| 1917 | 50 | 2 | 48 |
| 1918 | 67 | 4 | 63 |
| 1919 | 83 | 5 | 78 |
| 1920 | 65 | 6 | 59 |
| 1921 | 64 | 8 | 56 |
| 1922 | 64 | 0 | 64 |
| Total | 3500 | 721 | 2779 [48] |

attack a white woman or to commit rape. In many cases, of
course, the evidence points to *bona fide* attacks upon women." [49]

[48] "Thirty Years of Lynching in the United States, 1889-1918," p. 29, and
supplementary material.
[49] *Ibid.*, p. 48.

*Lynchings Since 1919.* There were 83 lynchings in 1919, 27 of which were for murder, 14 for assault on women, 5 for attempted assault, 5 for insult, and the remainder for various causes. In 1920 there were 65 lynchings, 24 of which were for murder, 15 for assault on women, 1 for attempted assault, 3 for insult, and the remainder for less important causes. In 1921 there were 64 lynchings, 18 of which were for murder, 19 for assault on women, 1 for attempted assault, and the remainder for lesser causes. Of the 61 lynchings in 1922, we do not have the facts as to causes. Of the 212 lynchings in 1919, 1920, and 1921, 69 or 32 per cent were for murder, 48 or 22 per cent were for rape, 7 or 3 per cent for attempted rape, and 8 for insult to white women, while 80 or nearly 40 per cent were for minor crimes and in some cases no defined crime.

It will be seen from the foregoing statement that lynching did not arise out of a desire to protect women, nor has it been used primarily as a means of protecting women. It arose in lawless communities, to punish horse stealings and all manner of lawlessness, and was at first not a death penalty. It is continued at the present time in three out of four cases for crimes other than those against white women. Forty per cent of the lynchings are for crimes of varying degrees of heinousness.

*Arguments Made for Lynching.* The arguments for lynching have been made on every street corner often enough that they need only be mentioned here. It is necessary, it is claimed, because no legal punishment is severe enough to atone for the violation of white women. Those who make this argument, of course, do not know the history of lynching and they either neglect or do not know that three out of four persons lynched are not lynched for that crime. Again, it is argued that you cannot take a white woman into court to testify against a Negro who has attacked her. This, of course, is wide of the mark. It is not necessary for her to go to court. Her deposition may be taken, or the judge may clear the court room so as to give privacy to the hearing. Furthermore, the argument proceeds on the assumption that the woman is shielded from the public gaze by lynching the criminal rather than giving him a fair trial. This is a wholly gratuitous assumption. There could be no possible method devised better calculated to start every street loafer's imagination and tongue at work than that of a lynching. Every item of the hideous details is told and with gruesome additions, and the whole brutal story is heralded to the world at large when a lynching occurs. Instead of protecting women from the vulgar gaze, it turns the spot light on and blows a trumpet for the assembling of a vulgar and gaping crowd.

*Law and Order Conference Answers Arguments.* Speaking to

this point at the Law and Order Conference held at Blue Ridge, North Carolina in 1917, Mrs. Trawick said:

"Our next assumption is that lynching protects women from the ordeal of publicity. Nothing could be more fatuous than this statement. Under pretext of moral duty, and with no danger of later accountability, the mob finds an outlet for the exercise of deep seated race prejudice and hostility.

"We have already said that the spreading abroad of the details of cases of assault makes the crime worse through the power of suggestion. Mob violence increases by the workings of this same law of suggestion. Henry Bushnell Hart thinks that the worst enemies of the white women are the black brute, and the Buzzard Journalist who publishes name, place and gruesome details of the revolting crime.

"Where is the Southern chivalry and respect for womanhood, when we allow every item of the story to be given to a gloating public, and when we condemn the victim to life sentence of humiliation because she feels that she is known and branded?" [50]

*Lynching Does Not Deter Crime.* Again, it is argued that the crime is so terrible, punishment must be summary and terrible in order to deter further crimes of similar nature. But the facts do not bear out the argument. Instead of deterring crime, lynching has seemed to make crime epidemic, at least lynchings seem to go in waves, and tend to recur in the same or neighboring localities. Thus in Shelby County, Tennessee, there were three Negroes lynched in 1892, another Negro was lynched in the same county in 1893, and in 1894 there were six more lynched. In Lauderdale County, Tennessee, where there had never been a lynching before so far as I can ascertain, there occurred in Ripley a lynching in 1898. In 1900 there were four more lynchings, and in 1903 one, in 1904 one. The first record we have of lynching in Cooke County, Tennessee, is in 1900, when a Negro was lynched in Tiptonville; another Negro was lynched in the same town in 1901, another in the same county 1907, three more in the same town and county in 1908, and two more in the same town and county in 1910. The first record we have of lynching in Dyer County, Tennessee, was 1901, when one Negro was lynched; another lynching occurred in the same county in 1901, and then in 1913, 1916, and 1917 there was a lynching each year in this same county. In Lamar County, Texas, the first record of lynching was 1892, when four were killed. True to form, lynchings recurred again in the county in 1893, in 1895, in 1897, and in 1901. These lynchings for the five successive years all occurred

[50] "Lawlessness or Civilization, Which" pp. 59-60.

in the one town of Paris, showing still more conclusively the epidemic character of the disease. Grimes County, Texas, had lynchings in 1890, in 1892, and in 1893, in 1914 and 1917. Many other illustrations could be given. Any one who will take the records of lynchings for the last thirty years will see for himself just how epidemic it is. Of course, no one pretends to say that isolated lynchings do not occur.[51]

*Lynchings Tend to Become Epidemic.* The epidemic nature of lynching, which indicates that it incites both to disregard for law and to the committing of crime, is shown by the fact that most of the lynchings in individual states occur in restricted areas of contiguous counties. Davenport[52] pointed out in 1910 that one-sixth of all the lynchings in Kentucky had occurred in three counties, Logan, Todd, and Simpson, with a total population of less than one-fortieth of that of the State. An investigation of the Georgia Interracial Committee shows that three-fourths of all the lynchings in Georgia have occurred in thirty-five counties, fifty-eight other counties having very low records, and sixty-seven counties having never had a lynching. The Texas Interracial Committee has shown that two-thirds of all the lynchings in that State in the last twenty-two years have occurred in fifteen counties, and all those counties save one are located comparatively close to each other.[53] The facts are quite conclusive that lynching does not deter people from committing crime, and it evidently brutalizes the citizenship of a community. The two together explain the epidemic character of this form of punishment.

"It is universally conceded that lynching has no deterrent effect upon the class of crimes alleged to excite its vengeance. On the contrary, it probably has the opposite effect. The criminals and outlaws of the Negro race, who care nothing for life or death, may be thus hardened into resolves of revenge, and lie waiting to strike the hated race where the blow will be most keenly felt."[54]

*Slowness of Courts and Lynching.* Another argument made for lynching is that the courts are slow and often inefficient, so that the criminal, if he has money and influence, may ultimately go without punishment. There can be no doubt that court procedure in America is decidedly cumbersome. It is guided more by precedent than by principles of justice. Money will do much through shrewd lawyers who are willing to defend prisoners they know to be guilty. Tricks of the law and technicalities are too frequently resorted to, but it can hardly be shown that mobs are more capable of deciding questions of guilt than are even the most

---

[51] Cf. "Thirty Years of Lynching," Appendix II.
[52] Davenport: "Primitive Traits in Religious Revivals," p. 302 f.
[53] Mss. Copy of Interracial Studies.
[54] Miller: "Race Adjustment," p. 69.

faulty courts. Besides, mobs have not always acted because the court failed to act. Cases are on record where Negroes have been convicted immediately on apprehension, and before the law could take its course of execution, the criminal has been lynched. There can hardly be any doubt in the mind of any sane man that a Negro who had actually attacked a white woman would have any chance to escape punishment in a southern court. The thing is inconceivable.

If then punishment for this particular crime is inevitable, whether by the mob or by the court, why do Negroes continue to commit this crime of assault on white women? Kelly Miller thinks it may grow directly out of vengeance on the part of an oppressed race, which knows where a blow will be most keenly felt.[55] Mrs. Trawick says: "In the popular mind attacks upon women are attacks upon the integrity of the race, and are not only occasions of personal offense but of racial humiliation. This is frequently so meant by the criminal and so understood by the community."[56] I had a colored barber tell me once that he had heard one Negro plot to attack a white woman, because her brother or fiancé had despoiled some colored girl. Revenge and lust are perhaps equally responsible for the heinous crime.

*Constructive Measures.* In attempting to cope with the problem of lynching, as well as with the crime which is supposed to give rise to it, Judge Stephenson, of Winston-Salem, North Carolina, speaking at the Law and Order Conference at Blue Ridge, North Carolina in 1917, said:

"A change in criminal procedure that would do more than any other one thing to deter the mob would be for the trial judges habitually to charge the grand juries upon the laws about lynching and the duties of the grand jury to enforce them. At present the judge usually waits until the horse has been stolen before he locks the stable-door; that is, he waits until there has been a lynching in the county before he deems it necessary to charge the grand jury upon the subject. . . . The charge of the trial judge to the grand jury is the most weighty and impressive message the crowd that fills the courtroom during the call of the criminal docket ever hears. People who have a habit of attending criminal court seldom hear sermons or addresses on law and order, seldom read books or papers on law and order, and seldom hear the matter discussed in such a spirit as to encourage them to stand by the law. These people are the ones who usually have the most pronounced antipathy for the Negro, whose minds revel in the anger-provoking details of the crime, and who would excuse, rather

[55] Miller: "Race Adjustment," p. 69.
[56] "Lawlessness or Civilization, Which?" p. 59.

than condemn, those who take the law into their own hands. If the trial judge were to charge the jury vigorously and in plain English about lynching, he would arouse the jurors to make a real effort to discover lynchers, and he would make it easier for them to report lynchers, even though they were neighbors. When the impression got abroad that the grand jurors, whose deliberations are in secret, were taking seriously their duty to investigate and report lynchers, then would-be lynchers would be slow in doing anything to be reported for. The impression that such a charge would make upon the courtroom audience and, through references to it in the newspapers, upon the people at large would do much to create a compelling sentiment among the people to let the law take its course in the most provoking cases even. If every trial judge in the South for the space of one year would charge every grand jury that he faces plainly and vigorously about lynching, he would do more to put an end to mob violence than all of us laymen put together could do in a decade, this because he reached the people who do the lynching as nobody else does. I suggest that this conference, either by formal resolution or otherwise, bring to the attention of the trial judges of the South the unparalleled opportunity they have of promoting law and order by informing and arousing the grand juries." [57]

*Principles of the Georgia Interracial Commission.* The Georgia Interracial Committee has formulated four principles which it is thought will help to stop lynching:

"1. In order to secure convictions more frequently it is suggested that the Attorney General and Chief Justice of Georgia be given power to shift judges and solicitors for these special cases. This provision is in effective operation in several states, notably Alabama.

"2. In order that more lynchings may be prevented it is suggested that a state police force, similar to the Texas rangers, be added. This force would be very valuable in coping with any other cases where the criminals operate in several counties, such as cases of automobile theft and liquor running. Such a force is very effective in Tennessee, Pennsylvania, and Alabama.

"3. An immediate measure suggested is one which was originally asked for by Governor Northen in 1892, Governor Atkinson in 1896, and Governor Dorsey in 1919, and hinted for by Governors Hoke Smith, Candler and Slaton. This measure would provide for the removal of a sheriff who is proven derelict in his duty. South Carolina, Kentucky, and Florida have given the governor power to remove the sheriff. In Alabama the matter

---

[57] "Lawlessness or Civilization, Which?" p. 19.

is still further removed from politics by providing that the sheriff be tried before the Supreme Court.

"4. More vigorous local action in the counties is also suggested. Sheriffs and solicitors should be more strongly backed up. The action of the citizens of Athens and Clarke County in this respect was especially praised and recommended to other counties. In this place eight hundred citizens signed up to help the sheriff protect a prisoner if he thought it necessary. Because this was generally known, no mob formed."

*Constabulary Laws.* Constabulary laws have recently been passed by Kentucky and Tennessee, in accordance with which the governor may appoint a state constable in each county who shall be subject to the call of the governor. In case of trouble this constable is empowered to swear in as many citizens as he may deem necessary to preserve the peace. The men are one dollar per year workers save in cases of trouble, when regular salaries are paid. Thus a police force may be had on the grounds where any trouble may be reported to the governor as arising.

*Administration of Law Must Be Impartial.* The whole problem of the Negro and the law needs most careful consideration in every southern community. If the Negro's criminality is to be reduced he must somehow be brought to feel that the law is impartially administered and that he has an equal chance with the whites for justice. Cruel or unjust administration of law will never reduce crime but always increase it. Only when the honor of the law is upheld by all, when it is promptly and fairly administered, and when it deals with white and black alike can we expect to reduce the amount of crime perpetrated in our communities.

CHAPTER XIV

# THE NEGRO AND EDUCATION

*Early Elementary Training.* The early slave owners soon discovered that their slave laborers were too ignorant and stupid to be of much value as producers of wealth. Besides their religious scruples made them desirous of converting their slaves to Christianity, and this called for instruction. The two motives, therefore—economic efficiency and religious interest—soon led to elementary instruction of the slaves. We have already seen in the chapter on the religious life of the Negro how the Society for the Propagation of the Gospel sent its first missionaries to Goose Creek in South Carolina, where the first organized instruction to Negroes was given. Prior to this it is evident that many slaves had received instruction privately, but this seems to have been the first organized effort at training. The motive was distinctly religious. About the same time we noted that Elias Neau started a school in New York (1704) which was blamed for the insurrection of 1712. This school of Neau's was, however, exonerated and continued to run until the death of its founder in 1722. In 1741 two Negroes, Narry and Andrew, were bought by the Society for the Propagation of the Gospel, in order that they might be trained to teach their own people. A school building costing 308 pounds was erected in Charleston, South Carolina, and in 1744 these two Negroes opened a school.[1] It is not stated whether the pupils were slave or free Negroes, but it is likely they were free children.

*Free Negroes Taught.* From the earliest times there was no real opposition to instruction of free Negroes in Virginia.

"Throughout the period of the colony when the number of free negroes was comparatively small, and even in the nineteenth century before the time of the active propagation of antislavery doctrines, there existed little if any prejudice against the education of free colored persons. In the third quarter of the seventeenth century there was opposition to offering baptism to negro slaves until it was determined by law that the administration of the baptismal rite did not bestow freedom. This objection did not apply, however, to the religious instructions of free negroes or negro apprentices. Before the middle of the seventeenth century provision was made by certain white persons for guaranteeing

[1] Woodson: "The Education of the Negro Prior to 1861," p. 34.

religious instruction and education to negro servants who would eventually become free.   In 1654, when Richard Vaughan freed his negroes, he provided in his will that they should be taught to read and to make their own clothes, and that they should be brought up in the fear of God.

"In Colonial times the Anglican church did a great deal to provide for the religious instruction and baptism of the free colored class.   The reports made in 1724 to the English Bishop by the Virginia parish ministers are evidence that the few free negroes in the parishes were permitted to be baptized, and were received into the church when they had been taught the catechism. It had been a practice of the seventeenth century to stipulate in the indenture or contract by which a free negro was apprenticed to a master that the master, in return for the negro's services, must provide instruction in the Christian religion in addition to sufficient food, apparel, and lodging.

*Negro Wards of the Church.*   "In 1691 the church became the agency through which the laws of negro apprenticeship were carried out.   Free mulatto children born of white mothers and any free colored boy or girl without visible means of support were bound by the church wardens to serve white men for a certain term of years.   The custom of the churchwardens of requiring these masters to provide some degree of education for the colored apprentices remained in vogue throughout the colonial period, as is shown by numerous orders of the vestry meetings and orders of the county courts for binding out free colored children.   For example, in 1727 it was ordered that David James, a free negro boy, be bound to Mr. James Isdel, 'who is to teach him to read ye bible distinctly also ye trade of a gunsmith that he carry him to ye Clark's office & take Indenture to that purpose.'   By the Warwick County court it was 'ordered that Malacai, a mulatto boy, son of mulatto Betty be, by the church wardens of this Parish, bound to Thomas Hobday to learn the art of a planter according to law.' By the order of the Norfolk County court, about 1770, a free negro was bound out 'to learn the trade of a tanner.'   After 1785 the duty of binding out free colored children was placed upon the overseers of the poor, who required of the masters, according to the laws and the custom, an agreement to teach the apprentice reading, writing, and arithmetic." [2]

*Connecticut Law of 1650.*   As early as 1650 Connecticut passed a law that "all mothers of families doe, once a week at least cate-chise their children and servants in the grounds and principles of Religion." [3]   Maryland established a charity working school for

[2] Russell: "The Free Negro in Virginia, 1619-1865," pp. 137-139.
[3] Steiner: "History of Education in Connecticut," p. 17.

the education of orphans and other poor children and Negroes [4] in 1750. Reverend Thomas Bacon, who was a leader in this movement, in a printed sermon says: "Many poor white children have I found (I speak from sad experience) and many more undoubtedly there are, as ignorant as the children of the poor benighted Negroes. Yet even Negroes ought not to be neglected. They have souls to be saved as well as others, for the neglect of which let the consciences of their own masters answer, as they are accountable for it." [5]  The plan—so this sermon outlines—was to get teachers from England who "shall teach as many poor children as shall be determined by the trustees, and shall also instruct a certain number of Negroes, if so required." [6]  "It was also provided that such Negro children as shall be sent shall be taught to read and write, and instructed in the fear and the knowledge of the Lord gratis, but maintained at the expense of their respective owners." [7]

*S. P. G. Teaches Negroes.*  The Society for the Propagation of the Gospel had a missionary in Rhode Island in 1724, who taught Negroes as well as whites, and had baptized three Negroes, two Indians, and two mulattoes. [8]  In 1751 Reverend Hugh Neill undertook missionary work in Pennsylvania, a part of his task being the teaching of Negroes. [9]  In 1760 there were two schools for Negroes in Philadelphia. In 1773 the Quakers were working vigorously in Rhode Island. "Newport had a colored school maintained by a society of benevolent clergymen of the Church of England, with a handsome fund for a mistress to teach thirty children to read and write." [10]  The African Free School for Negroes was started in New York in 1787. In 1790 Cornelius Davis was the teacher with forty pupils. [11]

*Religious Instruction in North Carolina.*  In North Carolina we have seen that religious instruction was early given. As early as 1731 some of the more intelligent slaves were taught and some licensed to preach. [12]  Toward the close of the century schools for Negroes were organized in Richmond, Petersburg, and Norfolk. Robert Pleasants, a Quaker, emancipated his slaves at his death, 1801, and made provision for the establishment of a school for colored people. [13]  A glance through the records of any of the colonies reveals the fact that most of the white people were kindly

---

[4] Steiner: "History of Education in Maryland," p. 34.
[5] *Ibid.,* p. 35.
[6] *Idem.*
[7] *Idem.*
[8] Harrison: "Gospel Among the Slaves," p. 43.
[9] Woodson: "Education of the Negro Prior to 1861," p. 35.
[10] *Ibid.,* p. 95.
[11] *Ibid.,* p. 97.
[12] Cf. Bassett: "Slavery in the State of N. C.," p. 48.
[13] Woodson: "Education of the Negro Prior to 1861," p. 111.

disposed toward giving the Negro ability to read and write up to about 1800. After that time, because of the restlessness of the Negroes it begins to be discouraged. From 1790 to the close of the century San Domingo was in a state of turmoil and Haiti was in open revolt. News of the struggles of the colored people on these islands stirred the Negroes of America into a restless fever.

*Gabriel's Insurrection Retarded Training.* Gabriel's insurrection in Virginia in 1800 closed the door to real development of training for the slaves. The Vesey plot in Charleston in 1822 had a similar effect in South Carolina. South Carolina declared in 1800: "That assemblies of slaves, free negroes, mulattoes and mestizoes, whether composed of all or of any of such description of persons, or of all or any of the same, *and of a portion* of white persons met together *for the purpose of* MENTAL INSTRUCTION, in a confined or secret place, &c., &c., are declared to be an unlawful meeting; and magistrates, &c., &c., are hereby required, &c., to enter such confined places, &c., &c., and break doors, if resisted, and to disperse such slaves, free negroes, &c., &c.; and the officers dispersing such unlawful assemblage *may inflict such corporal punishment, not exceeding twenty lashes, upon such slaves, free negroes,* &c., as they may judge necessary for DETERRING THEM FROM SUCH UNLAWFUL ASSEMBLAGE IN FUTURE." "That it shall not be lawful for any number of slaves, free negroes, mulattoes, or mestizoes, *even in company with white persons,* to meet together *for the purpose of* MENTAL INSTRUCTION, either before the rising of the sun, or after the going down of the same." [14]

*Assemblage Forbidden.* Virginia passed a similar law in 1819, as follows: "That all meetings or assemblages of slaves, or free negroes or mulattoes mixing and associating with such slaves at any *meeting-house* or houses, &c., in the night; *or* at any SCHOOL OR SCHOOLS *for teaching them* READING OR WRITING, *either in the day or night,* under whatsoever pretext, shall be deemed and considered an UNLAWFUL ASSEMBLY; and any justice of a county, &c., wherein such assemblage shall be, either from his own knowledge or the information of others, of such unlawful assemblage, &c., may issue his warrant, directed to any sworn officer or officers, authorizing him or them to enter the house or houses where such unlawful assemblages, &c., may be, for the purpose of *apprehending or dispersing* such slaves, and *to inflict corporal punishment on the offender or offenders,* at the discretion of any justice of the peace, *not exceeding twenty lashes.*" [15]

*N. Carolina's Law Prohibiting Instruction for Negroes.* North

[14] Goodell: "American Slave Code," p. 319.
[15] *Ibid.,* p. 320.

Carolina in 1831 passed a law making it unlawful to teach a slave to read or write, or to sell him a book or pamphlet, since: "Teaching slaves to read and write tends to dissatisfaction in their minds, and to produce insurrection and rebellion." Georgia, 1829, made the teaching of a free Negro or slave to write an offense punishable by fine of $500 and imprisonment.[16] Delaware passed a restriction law in 1831, Florida and Alabama in 1832, Missouri forbade slaves to be taught in 1847. Tennessee and Kentucky did not pass laws forbidding the instruction of Negroes.

*Northern States Prohibit Training.* This reaction was not confined to the South. In Connecticut Prudence Crandall, a Quaker woman, had started a school in Canterbury. On admitting a Negro girl to the school, the white parents objected. Miss Crandall stood firm and her school was threatened with violence. All the white girls withdrew and Miss Crandall continued the school for colored girls. In order to destroy the school the legislature passed a law which forbade any school instructing colored children who were not inhabitants of the State, unless written permission should be granted by the authorities of the township where the school was located. Under this law Miss Crandall was arrested in 1833, condemned, but appealed, and the case was finally quashed. Miss Crandall finally abandoned the school on account of the bitter opposition. Fear of an increased Negro population caused many of the Northern states to oppose the training of Negroes.

In spite of all these reactionary laws, due to fear of insurrection, the masters and mistresses on southern plantations continued to teach their slaves to read, particularly that they might read the Bible. Furthermore, they felt the laws were primarily meant to stop indiscriminate teaching, which the owner could not control, and into which dangerous doctrines might be injected. "The education of the colored people as a public effort had been prohibited south of the border states," says Woodson, "but there was still some chance for Negroes of that section to acquire knowledge. Furthermore, the liberal white people of that section considered these enactments, as we have stated above, not applicable to southerners interested in the improvement of their slaves, but to mischievous abolitionists. The truth is that thereafter some citizens disregarded the laws of their states, and taught worthy slaves whom they desired to reward or use in business requiring an elementary education. As these prohibitions in slave states were not equally stringent, white and colored teachers of free blacks were not always disturbed. In fact, just before the middle of the nineteenth century there was so much winking at the violation of the reactionary laws that it looked as if some southern

[16] Goodell: "American Slave Code," p. 321.

states might recede from their radical position and let Negroes be educated as they had been in the eighteenth century.[17]

*How Negro Children Contrived to Learn.* Many a Negro, like Booker T. Washington, learned to read in all sorts of ways— such as asking the white children about advertisements, helping the younger children on the plantation, getting instruction clandestinely from other Negroes, etc. In many southern communities Negro schools were regularly taught in open defiance of the law, but in perfect accord with the sentiment of the people. Often these schools were under the patronage of the church, or were taught under the direction of the minister. The whole matter was that the slave owners did not desire to have their slaves taught by those whom they did not know or trust. In some cases, of course, masters were opposed to any instruction.

*Northern Army Schools.* When the Civil War opened the Negro was, of course, very eager to learn. He began flocking to the army camps where something must be done for him. The Atlanta University publication on Negro Common Schools says:

"During the war the first complication that confronted the armies was the continual arrival of fugitive slaves within the Union lines. At first the commands were rigid against receiving them. 'Hereafter,' wrote Halleck early in the war, 'no slaves shall be allowed to come within your lines at all.' Other generals however, thought differently. Some argued that the confiscating of slaves would weaken the South, others were imbued with abolition sentiment for right's sake. Twice attempts were made to free the slaves of certain localities by proclamation, but these orders were countermanded by the President. Still the fugitives poured into the lines and gradually were used as laborers and helpers. Immediately teaching began and gradually schools sprang up. When at last the Emancipation Proclamation was issued and Negro soldiers called for, it was necessary to provide more systematically for Negroes. Various systems and experiments grew up here and there. The freedmen were massed in large numbers at Fortress Monroe, Va., Washington, D. C., Beaufort and Port Royal, S. C., New Orleans, La., Vicksburg and Corinth, Miss., Columbus, Ky., Cairo, Ill., and elsewhere. In such places schools immediately sprang up under the army officers and chaplains. The most elaborate system, perhaps, was that under General Banks in Louisiana. It was established in 1863 and soon had a regular Board of Education, which laid and collected taxes and supported eventually nearly a hundred schools with ten thousand pupils under 162 teachers. At Port Royal, S. C., were gathered Edward L. Pierce's 'Ten Thousand Clients.' After the capture of Hilton

[17] Woodson: "The Education of the Negro Prior to 1861," p. 205.

Head in 1861 the Sea Islands were occupied and the Secretary of the Treasury designated this as a place to receive refugee Negroes. Mr. Pierce began the organization of relief societies in the North and established an economic system with schools. Eventually these passed under the oversight of General Rufus Saxton, who sold forfeited estates, leased plantations, received the camp-followers of Sherman's march to the sea and encouraged schools. In the West, General Grant appointed Colonel John Eaton, afterwards United States Commissioner of Education, to be Superintendent of Freedmen in 1862. He sought to consolidate and regulate the schools already established and succeeded in organizing a large system." [18]

*General Howard and the Freedman's Bureau.* At the close of the war General O. O. Howard was put in charge of these Freedman's Bureau Schools. He rapidly developed them into a real system and got support from Congress for the same. By 1870 there were 2677 schools, 3300 teachers and 149,581 pupils. The amount expended on these schools in 1870 was $1,536,853.20. In the six years from 1865 to 1870 a little more than five and a quarter million dollars was spent. [19]

*Development of the Public Schools.* The public school systems of the southern states were reëstablished following the Civil War. "In Mississippi the constitution of 1868 makes it the duty of the legislature to establish 'a uniform system of free public schools, by taxation or otherwise, for all children between the ages of 5 and 21 years.' Arkansas in 1868, Florida in 1869, Louisiana in 1868, North Carolina in 1869, South Carolina in 1868 and Virginia in 1870 established school systems. The constitution of 1868 in Louisiana required the General Assembly to establish 'at least one free public school in every parish,' and that these schools should make no 'distinction of race, color, or previous condition.' Georgia's system was not fully established until 1873." [20]

*Struggles of Early Schools.* These early public schools had a desperate struggle for existence. The vicissitudes of the Georgia system is a good illustration. In the Georgia Constitution of 1868 there was provision for a thorough system of "general education, to be forever free to all children of the State." [21] In October, 1870, the first public school law was enacted. Under this law General J. R. Lewis was made State School Commissioner and schools were opened. At the end of the year the State was in debt $300,000 for these schools. During the year 1872 there were no public schools in the state due to this heavy debt,

[18] "The Common School and the Negro American," p. 17.
[19] *Ibid.,* p. 20.
[20] *Ibid.,* p. 21.
[21] Jones: "Education in Georgia," p. 31.

but during that year special funds were raised, the debt was paid and schools reopened.[22]    The attendance of Georgia schools was in 1871 white 42,914, colored 6,664; for 1873 white 63,922, colored 19,755.[23]    Thus did the southern states in the midst of their poverty begin to provide for the training of the Negro now free.    Of course, the provision was inadequate, as indeed that for the white child was.    It was a struggle to maintain any type of school at all, as was indicated by Georgia's experience.    It is to the everlasting credit of the people of the South, both white and black, that they thus early set their faces like a flint in the direction of training for all the people.    When the reconstruction period was over there was fear in some quarters that Negro training would be set aside, but those who entertained such fears neither knew nor appreciated the real spirit of the old South.    If the Negro was to be efficient, he must be trained, and although there was much questioning as to what kind of training he needed, there was little doubt that he must have some type of training. A double system of schools was a heavy load on a poverty stricken section, but the load was at once taken up and has been carried forward without faltering to the present hour.    It is common knowledge, of course, that the Negro schools have never been given equal support with the whites.    In 1909 there was spent in South Carolina, to illustrate, $1,590,732.57 on white children, and $308,153.16 on colored, though the Negro children were in the majority.    The corresponding figures for Alabama were $2,143,662.15 for whites, $287,045.43 for colored; and for North Carolina, $1,857,376.57 for white and $366,724.38 for colored [24] Other states did about the same as those here mentioned.    Conditions are of course improving each year.

*Weaknesses—Small Funds.*    The weaknesses of the public schools for Negroes in the southern states may be summed up under the following heads:

First: lack of financial support.    The double system of education in the South is much more expensive than a single system would be, hence all the children must suffer, but it is evident from the facts that the colored children suffer much more than the whites.    Money spent per child in 1916 on the two types of children by states is shown in table on the opposite page.

These figures are most pitiable and yet they are very much better than in 1908 when I compiled the figures for expense of these schools.    There has been decided progress since these figures were compiled in 1916 by the United States Department of Education.    In some states the appropriations have been almost

[22] Jones: "Education in Georgia," p. 33.
[23] *Ibid.*, p. 35.
[24] "Common Schools for Negro Americans," p. 29.

| State | Whites | Colored |
|-------|--------|---------|
| Alabama ..................... | $9.41 | $1.78 |
| Arkansas .................... | 12.45 | 4.59 |
| Delaware .................... | 12.61 | 7.68 |
| Florida ...................... | 11.60 | 2.64 |
| Georgia ..................... | 9.58 | 1.76 |
| Kentucky .................... | 8.13 | 8.53 |
| Louisiana ................... | 13.73 | 1.13 |
| Maryland .................... | 13.74 | 6.38 |
| Mississippi .................. | 10.60 | 2.26 |
| North Carolina .............. | 5.27 | 2.02 |
| South Carolina .............. | 10.00 | 1.44 |
| Tennesse .................... | 8.27 | 4.83 |
| Texas ....................... | 10.08 | 5.74 |
| Virginia .................... | 9.64 | 2.74 |
| Oklahoma ................... | 14.21 | 9.96 |

doubled. Thus the amount spent for each child of school age in North Carolina for 1920 was $14.52 [25] as compared with the above.

*Short School Terms.* Length of school term is another item of great importance. According to Bulletin 90, for 1918, the reports available showed an average length of term throughout the South to be 111 days for colored and 148 days for the whites. "In the elementary schools of six Southern States the average term provided for colored children is 106 days, while the corresponding term for white children is 145 days. In the secondary schools of four Southern States the average term for colored children is 153 days, while the average term for white children is 165 days. It can be seen, therefore, that a greater difference exists between the length of term provided for white and colored children in the elementary schools than in the secondary schools." [26]

The variation in the several southern states in length of school term is:

"It is further found, as shown in the table and graph, that the average time attended by each colored pupil enrolled is only 70 days, while the corresponding average for white children is 100 days. It is shown, therefore, that the colored child gets only seven-tenths as much schooling as the white children in the Southern States. Part of this, however, is the fault of the colored child, since he loses on an average 37 per cent of the school term, while the white child loses only 32 per cent by irregular attendance. Stated in other terms, the colored pupils

[25] Cf. Biennial Report for 1919-1920.
[26] Bureau of Education Bulletin No. 90, p. 126.

"TABLE 17

SCHOOL TERM AND SCHOOL ATTENDANCE IN THE SOUTH, 1917-18

|  | Length of School Term | |
| State | In Colored Schools | In White Schools |
| Alabama | 102 | 133 |
| District of Columbia | 173 | 173 |
| Florida | 102 | 142 |
| Georgia | 101 | 159 |
| Kentucky | 119 | 152 |
| Louisiana | 94 | 156 |
| Maryland | 151 | 174 |
| North Carolina | 113 | 126 |
| Oklahoma | 145 | 157 |
| South Carolina | 78 | 150 |
| Texas | 132 | 149 |
| Virginia | 141 | 141 |
| Average | 111 | 148" [27] |

enrolled attend only 63 per cent of the school term, while the white children attend 68 per cent of the time." [28]

*Education Necessary for Democracy.* These figures are certainly disturbing for they do not indicate as great progress in Negro education as one would desire. If it be true that a democracy cannot live unless it make its people intelligent, then it is a most serious problem which the South faces. Of course, the Negro does not pay his full proportion of the school tax. It is very difficult to estimate just what proportion of the direct tax Negroes do pay. It is certain they do not pay their full proportion, and it is just as certain they are paying a rapidly increasing proportion. It must be said in all fairness, however, that payment of direct tax does not fairly represent the share the Negro contributes to the public expenses. All taxes are assessed on wealth of one form or another. Wealth is created from two sources and from two sources alone—natural resources and labor. Capital may consist of both natural resources and stored up labor, while labor may be both mental and physical. In the labor field it is clear the Negro furnishes a very large element of wealth producing power. As a wealth producer it is perfectly clear that he pays his due proportion of tax. It is furthermore clear that the business of the state is to provide for those who are least able to provide for themselves. Further-

[27] Bureau of Education Bulletin No. 90, p. 126.
[28] *Ibid.*, p. 128.

more, the more backward a group the more is the obligation of the state to see to it that this group is brought up to standard. In a democracy there is only one possible position to take, and that is to raise the standard of the whole population by giving equal advantages to all. The more backward a group the more careful the attention to be given. If these are sound principles of democracy, the South will need to give more careful attention to the training of the Negro.

*Inadequate School Equipment.* Another weakness of Negro training is that of poor school equipment. When the author prepared his statement in "Negro Life in the South" in 1910, North Carolina had still 195 log school houses. In 1920 there were only 94, and only 76 of these were used for Negro children. There were in this year 1,022 white schools and 1,020 colored schools which were still without modern desks. The Superintendent reports 56 districts without school houses for whites, and 126 districts without school houses for colored children.[29]

Commenting on the school equipment in rural sections of Kentucky, the State Educational Commission in 1921 said that nine out of ten were one-room houses, "box-like structures," "in all respects essentially alike," and "almost all bad." Half of these buildings they claim are unpainted, "the roofs leak," "the weatherboarding is off here and there, doors are broken, knobs gone, window panes out, walls stained, floor uneven and cracked, seats broken and out of place, and a pall of dust over all. These neglected schoolhouses teach eloquently the doctrine of shiftlessness, disorder and indifference. Their silent lessons will undoubtedly be reproduced in the home, on the farm, in the factory and the store."[30]

*Kentucky's School Condition—1921.* Due to poor heating facilities the "children are continuously on the move from one part of the room to another, either to get warm or to cool off amid indescribable confusion and disorder."[31] "Girls' toilets are usually clean, boys' toilets are filthy and offensive beyond belief."[32] "In many instances school sites have been chosen because the ground was worthless for other purposes."[33] "Rural school grounds are invariably small."[34] "In the rural section there is little difference between the buildings for white children and those for colored children, though the buildings for colored children are as a rule slightly inferior."[35]

[29] Cf. Biennial Report, N. C., 1919-20, p. 230.
[30] Report of Kentucky Educational Commission, 1921, pp. 72-3.
[31] *Ibid.*, p. 74.
[32] *Ibid.*, p. 75.
[33] *Idem.*
[34] *Idem.*
[35] *Ibid.*, p. 82.

This description from the Kentucky Educational Commission is fairly representative of the conditions all over the South. My own observation is that the colored schools are more poorly built and equipped, but are better and cleaner kept on the whole.

*Small Salaries for Teachers.* In line with these weaknesses of the Negro schools are the small salaries paid to most of their teachers. The salaries for white and colored alike are very meager. A good ditch digger can make as good wages as the average country school teacher. But the inadequacy of salaries is much more marked among the Negro teachers, most of whom are working in rural districts. Thus the average annual teachers' salaries for white and colored and for male and female in Alabama is as follows: White male $408, Negro male $186, white female $391, Negro female $157. In North Carolina in 1920 the total expenditure for teachers' salaries for rural schools was for white teachers $4,564,907.58, for Negro $819,372.03, or considerably less than one fifth for Negro teachers, although the white school population is only a little more than twice as large as the colored. In 1919 the average annual salary for white teachers in North Carolina was $296.80, that for colored was $157.15, the colored teacher receiving just a little more than half what the white teacher received. In Arkansas the salaries for teachers of the first grade for the year 1919 averaged $90 and $72 per month for male and female whites respectively, and $55 and $50 per month for male and female colored teachers. The total average of all teachers was $63 per month for white and $47 per month for colored. The colored school runs only 112 days in length and white schools 130 days in length, hence the average annual salary was for white $409.50 and for colored $263.20. These are fairly typical figures, and they show the poverty of both our white and colored rural teachers. If teaching in rural schools is ever to be made a profession and not simply a job, the salaries will have to be made adequate to maintain in decency the men and women who give their lives to this task.

*Inadequate Supervision.* Until recent years the Negro school has been almost wholly without supervision. Many superintendents did not visit Negro schools at all, and gave no attention to training Negro teachers. This weakness, as will be seen later, has been largely eliminated within the last ten years. Superintendents are giving most faithful and efficient attention to the Negro schools and the results can readily be seen.

*Maladjusted Curriculum.* Perhaps the weakest point in the Negro school is its maladjusted course of study. Most of the Negro children are located in the rural districts. These children, like the white rural children, are being taught from books made almost entirely by city teachers and adapted to city children. They talk about problems and situations arising in urban communities. The city is glorified and the country neglected. This has a tendency to make the usual child dissatisfied with the rural surrounding, and desirous of getting away to the city. I remember once going into a rural Negro school in Virginia and finding a third reader group spelling out the words of some court scene enacted in England. I would not have the rural child, either white or colored, shut off from any of the culture of the world, but if nine-tenths of the material in their readers and histories relate to things that do not concern their daily life, how can we expect their school work to give them any appreciation of their surroundings? We must remember that if the rural curriculum is unadapted to rural children, it is not the fault of rural teachers, either white or colored, for the course of study is outlined and the texts written almost entirely by those who have long been removed from the rural environment. We cannot blame the Negro teacher, therefore, if the school tends to urbanize the mind of the Negro child.

*Texts Needed for Negro Children.* There is great need that we have two sets of text books—one for rural children and one for urban children. Into the book of the urban child will go something of the best of rural life, and into the text of the rural child will go something of the best of city culture. But the body of the text of the rural child will deal with the materials at hand. It will teach him the beauty of nature, and it will help him observe the birds and bees, the flowers and plants and trees, it will help him see new beauty in the growing crops and the fallow fields. Who would dare say there was not as much real culture in studying the life about him as in studying the life offered by the city zoo. I am not sure that a country boy who knows all about a cow but has never seen a lion is not fully as cultured as a city boy who has seen numerous lions and knows about their native home but knows nothing about a cow and could not get a drop of milk from her even if he were starving. Culture and outlook on life are not determined by the kind of facts we have, half so much as by the interpretation we give to the facts we have. We may see the whole of life in a "flower in a crannied wall," or we may treat it as a noxious weed. What the rural child needs—and especially is this true of the Negro child—is a new ability to interpret the life that surrounds him. At Tuskegee the boys and girls are brought close to nature. In their arithmetic they learn how to measure not bushels, but bushels of corn or potatoes. They study chemistry not in the abstract, but the chemistry of making soap, or preparing specific foods.   And that is what every child needs—adaptation to his daily needs.

*Readers Should Give Stories of the Race.*   But there is another specialized need which should be met by the text for the Negro child.   Even the reader well adapted to the rural white child may not be well adapted to the rural colored child.   Into the reader for the colored child should go the material which will help him understand and appreciate his own people.   No race can ever become great which does not know and appreciate its own achievements.   The Negro child should be told of the achievements of Washington and Moton, Douglass, Coleridge-Taylor, Tanner, Dunbar, and a score of others.   Of course, I would not shut the Negro child up to the heroes of his own race. I would tell him of Washington, and Jefferson, Lincoln and Lee, Longfellow, and Lanier, Tennyson and Browning, just as I believe every white child should know of the heroes and achievements of other races including the Negro race.   If I were making a set of readers for the white children of the South I would not "Jim Crow" them into the life of the Anglo-Saxon race alone. I should want them to know of Mazzini of Italy, Tagore of India, Neesima of Japan, Confucius of China, Pushkin, the Russian Negro, Tanner, the painter of Negro blood, Booker T. Washington, the builder of a great race.   No child, white or colored, should be "segregated" in its mind to a special class or interest.   But that does not mean that I would not put emphasis on the achievements of the race to which a child belongs.   There is a growing race pride among the Negroes which should be fostered.   In the work of Reverend John Little in Louisville, Kentucky, a white lady said recently to a class of Negro boys in her Sunday school:   "Boys, let me tell you a story of a real boy!"   As quick as a flash one little black boy spoke up and said:   "Miss, if it's about a black boy, all right, but if it's about a white boy I don't want to hear it."   What he wanted was to hear something of the achievements of his own race.   The curriculum of our Negro schools must be so outlined as to fit the life of the Negro where he is, and create in him that pride and appreciation of his own race as will make him strive to lift it to higher levels.

*Adaptation of Curriculum.*   Another problem of the Negro public school is to adapt its curriculum to the peculiar mental responses of the average Negro child.   Recent careful scientific investigations prove conclusively that these responses are not the same for white and colored children, and they are not the same for all groups of colored children.   The most extensive data ever collected in mental responses of the Negro were gathered during the period of the war when all draft soldiers

were given careful mental tests.    (Cf. National Academy of
Sciences, Vol. XV, p. 705-f.)    These studies proved conclusively that Negroes who had had superior advantages,—i.e., those
in the North—possessed superior mental ability.  Grading from
A, equal to superior intelligence, down to D, equal to normal
intelligence for a ten-year-old child, the two groups of Negroes
graded according to the scale below.  Northern Negroes were
those from Illinois, Indiana, New York, New Jersey and
Pennsylvania.  Southern Negroes were from Alabama, Georgia,
Louisiana, and Mississippi.[36]

|  | Total No. | % Making D— | % Making D | % Making C— | % Making C | % Making C+ | % Making B | % Making A |
|---|---|---|---|---|---|---|---|---|
| Northern Negroes | 4705 | 14.4 | 31.2 | 25.8 | 18.0 | 7.2 | 2.7 | 0.7 |
| Southern Negroes | 6848 | 57.0 | 29.2 | 9.6 | 3.4 | 0.7 | 0.2 | 0.1 |

There were two types of tests given to all draft soldiers, Alpha
being perhaps more difficult,—at least calling for more intellectual
drill.  Beta was more largely in the realm of careful observation.
Where a soldier was illiterate he was of necessity forced to take
the Beta test.  Of the northern Negroes above examined, 58.2
per cent got their final rating in the Alpha test, while only 25.5
per cent of the southern Negroes got their rating in this test.[37]

Camp Sevier Measurements.  At Camp Sevier special comparisons were made of 188 Negroes with 188 whites of the same mental
age.  In these comparisons the Negroes excelled in picture completion tests,—i.e., observation, in association of ideas calling for
imagination, in use of language—forming sentences with given
words, in the handling of synonyms, and in designing from memory.  The whites excelled in arithmetic, number completion tests,
and in judgment tests.[38]  That is, the Negro mind excelled in concrete conceptions, the white mind excelled where the work was
abstract.  Ragsdale, who made a careful study of "The Psychology of the Negro," found that the Negro excelled in "memory
for concrete words."  "In quickness of reaction and in quickness
of perception and discrimination they also excelled."  Professor
Newbold, of the North Carolina Department of Education, has
made a careful summary of the studies of Negro psychology, and

[36] National Academy of Sciences, Vol. XV, p. 734.
[37] Ibid., passim.
[38] Cf. ibid., p. 738.

feels that the result should have influence in determining the type of curriculum of the public schools for Negro children.[39] Perhaps too little adaptation has been made to groups of varying advancement and capacity. We have treated all too much alike, trying to run all into the same mold.

These weaknesses of the Negro public school system are shared to some extent at least by the schools for the whites, but in almost every case they are decidedly more marked for colored than for white, and hence call for special study and attention. The facts of constructive work now going on in this field will show how much of careful thought has been put to these problems.

*Progress in Negro Schools—Rural Supervision.* The first and most marked item of progress in Negro rural schools was brought about largely through the Jeans Fund, of which Dr. James H. Dillard is the head. This fund was established in 1908 by a Quaker lady of Philadelphia. She left her entire fortune to be used for the upbuilding of the rural Negro school. At first it was difficult to know how best to use the fund. "After much consideration the decision was that we apply to country schools a plan already in use in certain cities, namely, to employ a teacher, trained in handicraft, to serve several schools. The idea of putting the schools more in touch with the immediate conditions of the life in the community around them was then just becoming a much-discussed problem. Cities had employed teachers of sewing and woodwork to go from school to school on certain days, and it was thought that such a plan might be worked in the rural districts." [39a] In pursuance of this plan extension teachers were appointed to work in five or six schools in a county. No work was undertaken without the express application of the county superintendent. Such coöperation was the policy of the Fund from the first.

About this time Mr. Jackson Davis, a Phi Beta Kappa graduate of old William and Mary College, a man of practical vision and insight, and one of the choicest spirits of the younger Virginia men, was County Superintendent of Henrico County in Virginia. He wanted to do something for his rural Negro schools which would make them more influential in building home ideals and increasing economic efficiency. "With this thought in mind, but feeling his way step by step, the superintendent of schools of Henrico County, Virginia, called into conference a little group of men, including Dr. H. B. Frissell, the late principal of Hampton, and Dr. S. C. Mitchell, a leader in the educational revival

[39] Newbold: Mss. Copy Term Paper prepared for Teacher's College, New York.
[39a] Dillard: "Fourteen Years of the Jeanes Fund."

in Virginia. Growing out of this conference, a plan was worked out to employ a supervising industrial teacher who would visit regularly the twenty-three colored schools in the whole county, organize the people for self-help in improving and equipping their schools, and help the teachers to introduce the simple industries of the home and farm. The teacher selected, Miss Virginia Randolph, had already shown her fitness for this pioneer work, having made her own school a center of helpfulness to the whole neighborhood.[40] The Jeanes Fund supplied her salary; Dr. James H. Dillard, the president, welcomed the idea of extending the plan to the whole county, and this plan was recommended wherever it could be put into operation.

*Results of Supervisors' Work.* I have visited myself numbers of schools where these rural supervising teachers have been at work and I have seen the marked results of their work. One school I visited in Henrico County is more or less typical of the results being achieved all over the South. We arrived at the school building—located eleven miles from the city—at about eleven thirty in the morning. The first thing we noticed was that the yard had been fenced—and we afterwards learned that the teacher and children had raised the money to do this. We noticed the grounds were very clean, no paper and no trash to be seen. We went to the well and found the dirt drawn up to the curb so the water which might be spilled would run away instead of seeping back into the well to contaminate the water. We examined the outhouses and found them white washed, screened, clean and sanitary. On entering the school room our eye was at once attracted to a row of nails driven into the wall, on each of which hung a tin cup, and above each of which was pasted the name of a pupil. "Individual drinking cups in a rural Negro school!" Somebody seemed to know about the danger of spreading disease through a common drinking cup. Some of us remember the time in our small town schools when the white boys did not even have a cup, but all drank out of the bucket at the well—allowing any water spilled to run back into the well. Two girls in this school room were preparing a dinner. They were twelve and thirteen years old. A little screen around the table, stove and cupboard made the kitchen in the corner private and kept it from disturbing the other children. The teacher asked us if we would not sample the cooking of these two girls. Fried chicken, hot chocolate, and delicious hot rolls, all prepared by these two girls, were served us along with butter, sweet potatoes, etc. It was a delicious meal and proved to us at least that the school training of these two girls was really effective. One of the weakest places in the rural Negro home

[40] Davis: "Building a Rural Civilization," p. 10.

is the poor food. Every girl who gets the kind of training these girls were getting will help to remedy this condition.

*Subjects Taught.* In these schools the boys are taught simple carpentering, shuck mat making, gardening, etc. The girls are taught sewing, cooking, gardening, canning, etc. The parents are usually very proud of the things made by the children. Many a Negro home I have visited is made more comfortable by the mats, or cabinets made by the boys, or are more attractive because of the scarfs, the curtains, or other things made by the girls. All this tends to give the children a greater confidence in their own ability to achieve, and gives parents and children alike a greater pride in the home, which is the first step in building a real civilization. This type of training has also had a marked effect on the interest in schools:

"In one county in Virginia, for example, the colored people built out of their own funds ten new schoolhouses, most of them of two rooms, with practically no assistance, but simply upon the assurance that the county would provide two teachers instead of one, and would maintain the schools for seven months instead of five, as had heretofore been the custom.

"This coöperation of public and private agencies has yielded the happiest results. Nothing has so impressed local school boards and inclined them to spend as much money upon Negro schools as their inadequate resources would permit, as the evidence of the sums raised by the colored people to build new houses, to extend terms, and to provide better equipment. On the other hand, the colored people, who have been furthest back, have received valuable discipline through self-help; and the success of their undertakings has revealed the resources of community effort with all the force of a new discovery. All this is a most valuable element in their own training for the duties and responsibilities of citizenship." [41]

These rural industrial supervisors are under the control of the county superintendent, and while they are at first paid altogether or in part by the Jeanes Fund, they are soon taken over by the county and paid out of public funds. In 1923, there were 269 counties having such teachers, $121,332 being expended from public funds, and $93,862 being supplied by the Jeanes Board.

*Slater Fund Trains Teachers.* Another fundamental step in the progress of Negro schools has been taken through the aid of the John F. Slater Fund, established in 1882. The largest usefulness of this fund has perhaps been achieved since Dr. James H. Dillard became its head. This fund, which has aided

[41] Davis: "Building a Rural Civilization," pp. 10-11.

many private institutions, is now primarily interested in developing a better teaching force for the public schools. With the coöperation of state and county superintendents it establishes and is fostering county training schools by making appropriations for the salaries of teachers on the following conditions:

"1. The school property shall belong to the state, county, or district, and the school shall be a part of the public school system.

"2. There shall be an appropriation for salaries of not less than $750 from public funds raised by state, county, or district taxation.

"3. The length of the term shall be at least eight months.

"4. The teaching shall extend through the eighth year, with the intention of adding at least two years as soon as it shall be possible to make such extension."

In 1922 the Fund was helping one hundred and fifty-six such county training schools, with 42,360 pupils enrolled and 3,782 students in the high school grades. Since most of the rural school teachers must be drawn from high school pupils, it is urgent that all high school pupils shall have available proper training in pedagogy, and this the Slater fund attempts to supply so far as the conditions will permit. State normals in various southern states are doing a great work in training teachers, as are all the colleges.

*General Education Board—State Supervision.* Still another advanced step in Negro training has been taken by the General Education Board under the leadership of Dr. Wallace Buttrick. Since state supervision is imperative if schools are to be kept up to standard, this board supplied the funds for a State Supervisor of Rural Negro Schools for Virginia in 1910. It was very fitting that Mr. Jackson Davis, who started the Jeanes work in Henrico County, should be chosen as the first one of these state workers. The board now maintains agents in Alabama, Arkansas, Georgia, Kentucky, Louisiana, Mississippi, North Carolina, South Carolina, Tennessee, Virginia, Florida, Oklahoma, and Texas. These agents are directly related to the State Departments of Education in their respective states. Mr. Jackson Davis has been appointed as the general agent of the General Education Board in connection with Negro Education. It is perhaps fair to say that this increase of supervision, supplementing that of the Jeanes teacher supervision, has done more than almost anything else to make the Negro schools efficient.

*Phelps Stokes Fund Special Studies.* During 1916 and 1917, the Phelps-Stokes Fund, with Dr. Thomas Jesse Jones as its expert worker, made a most careful study of all the "Private and Higher Schools for Colored People in the United States." The study was exhaustive and constructive. It pointed out the weaknesses and suggested remedies. It is an inexhaustible mine of information on these institutions. It not only helped those interested in giving money intelligently to Negro education, but it helped the schools themselves to strengthen their weak places and so become more worthy of the aid which they were seeking. The Phelps-Stokes fund has also helped the cause of Negro education in many other ways. It has established scholarships at the University of Georgia and the University of Virginia, where special studies in Negro life may be made by graduate students, and thus interest is aroused among students in these institutions. The fund has also supplied funds for libraries on race problems at George Peabody College for Teachers, at the Blue Ridge Association in North Carolina, and at Southern College of Young Men's Christian Associations. It has also coöperated in conferences on race relations at Blue Ridge, and has helped the Interracial Commission in its studies. It has founded and maintained the University Race Commission under the leadership of Dr. Dillard.

*Rosenwald School House Fund.* The school equipment has been greatly improved through the help and inspiration given by Mr. Julius Rosenwald of Chicago. In 1914 Mr. Rosenwald furnished a small fund to Dr. Booker T. Washington to aid in building a few Negro school buildings in Macon County, Alabama, the county in which Tuskegee Institute is located. The experiment worked so successfully that Mr. Rosenwald agreed to furnish further funds to coöperate with other communities in the state in building good houses, Mr. Rosenwald promising to give about one-third of the funds needed for any one building. Sixty-nine such buildings were erected the first year, costing seventy thousand dollars. Other states then applied for similar aid and a broader program of building was begun. At the present date (1923) there are 1,769 Rosenwald school buildings completed, costing $6,250,000, of which amount Mr. Rosenwald has contributed $1,250,000, or twenty per cent. The building program for the present year calls for two hundred and fifty more buildings at a cost of $750,000. Mr. S. L. Smith, who was formerly the State Supervisor of Rural Schools in Tennessee, is the General Field Agent for this fund, with offices in Nashville, Tennessee. The conditions for securing this aid and also aid on school homes have been most carefully worked out as follows:

"1. The Julius Rosenwald Fund will coöperate through the public school authorities in efforts to provide and equip better rural schoolhouses for the Negroes of the Southern States. Such equipment as desks, blackboards, heating apparatus, libraries and sanitary privies is deemed of equal importance with the schoolhouses themselves.

"2. The Fund will deposit with every coöperating State Department of Education a sum of money recommended by the General Field Agent to constitute working capital, from which the proper State official may make disbursements as required.

"3. The amount appropriated by The Fund shall not exceed $400 for a one-teacher school, $700 for a two-teacher school, $900 for a three-teacher school, $1,100 for a four-teacher school, $1,300 for a five-teacher school, $1,500 for a six-teacher school or larger, $900 for a teachers' home, and $200 for the addition of a classroom to a Rosenwald School already built.

.      .      .      .      .      .

"5. Aid will be granted toward the construction and equipment of only those schools where the term runs at least five consecutive months.

"6. It is a condition precedent to receiving the aid of The Fund that the people of the several communities shall secure, from other sources: to-wit—from public school funds, private contributions, etc., an amount equal to or greater than that provided by The Fund. Labor, land and material may be counted as cash at current market values. Money provided by The Fund will be available only when the amount otherwise raised, with that to be given by The Fund, is sufficient to complete and equip the building, including modern desks and two sanitary privies.

"7. The site and buildings of each school aided by The Fund shall be the property of the public school authorities.

"8. The school site must include ample space for playgrounds and for such agricultural work as is necessary for the best service of the community.

"9. Plans and specifications for every building shall be approved by the General Field Agent *before construction is begun.*

"10. In a limited number of selected localities, where the annual school term is eight months or more, The Fund will consider coöperation in the construction of Teachers' Homes, to be completed and furnished to correspond with the school building."

*South Greatly Benefited.* This school house building program for Negroes has been a wonderful blessing to the Negro schools of the South. Almost every county in the South has one or more of these buildings and in every case they are models for all other rural school buildings. The white as well as the colored schools have been greatly stimulated by this work. No white community is willing to allow the Negro children to have a better equipment than that furnished for the whites. Consequently when a Rosenwald school has been built for the Negroes it immediately brings pressure on the board of education to provide adequate equipment for the white children. Mr. Rosenwald has by his gifts called out the interest of the public school officials in the Negro schools, he has stimulated the Negroes to contribute liberally of their own means, he has set standards for schools, both white and black, and has given an impetus to rural education which is nothing short of remarkable.

*No Duplication by Educational Boards.* These five funds are thus coöperating with maximum efficiency without any duplication and without pauperizing the communities to which they minister. Furthermore, they are not putting over an outside organization, but are coöperating fully with, and working through the regular educational agencies of the state, county or local community. The Jeanes Fund is helping improve the supervision of the local schools and has made the instruction fit into life by furnishing trained industrial supervisors. The Slater Fund is helping to furnish better trained teachers through its county training schools and through encouraging normal training in the schools and colleges. The General Education Board is helping to furnish state supervision, and coöperating with the Jeanes Fund in county supervision. The Rosenwald Fund is encouraging better school equipment, and the Phelps-Stokes Fund is making special studies which are exceedingly helpful in planning a program for efficiency and progress. It is only fair to say that local, state and county officials and boards of education are aggressively carrying forward this work, and in most cases furnishing much more of money than any or all of these special agencies. The agencies have simply helped to stimulate interest and give initiative. The final task must be accomplished largely by public funds and coöperation. While much is to be accomplished, and our picture of difficulties seemed dark, there is every reason for real optimism. It is doubtful if any group of people anywhere in the world has made more rapid progress or had more constructive coöperation in that progress, than have the Negro people of the South during the last decade.

*Periods in Negro Education.* The first period of Negro training after the Civil War was that of the Freedmen's Aid; following that there arose the public school systems. With the founding of Hampton in 1868 and of Tuskegee Institute, 1881, there was ushered in a new era which might be called the era of industrial education. Both of these institutions are trying to fit the student to meet life problems. They teach all the industrial arts both for men and women and declare their belief that a student may—if rightly directed—get as much culture out of the study of the nature about him as he could get out of the study of Greek mythology or some other remote subject. Not that they desire to shut their students up to their present environment, but they put the prime emphasis on the present situation in which a student finds himself. In my many visits to both Hampton and Tuskegee I have come more and more to value their wonderful spirit, their unselfish nature, their earnestness of purpose, and their thoroughness of work. In Dr. Gregg at Hampton and Dr. Moton at Tuskegee we have worthy successors to the two great founders, General Armstrong and Dr. Washington.

*Influence of Hampton and Tuskegee.* The Hampton and Tuskegee idea is spreading throughout the South, and has greatly influenced the educational policies of both white and colored schools. Indeed these two institutions have a world-wide influence. Scarcely a day passes that some traveler from a foreign country does not visit one of these institutions to study its methods with the view to using such methods in their own countries.

*Advanced Education Needed.* The higher education of the Negro has not been neglected, but the facilities for training the leaders are not adequate. For many years there was much opposition to giving Negroes college training. Some thought they were incapable of receiving such training, others thought it made Negroes uppish and impudent, still others thought it unfitted them to live their lives in the communities to which they belonged. All these misconceptions have gradually been dissipated. Those who have studied the college trained Negro have come to see that there are not a few capable of taking the most advanced training. My observation of those who have been trained is that they are the most thoughtful and most modest of all the group. A little learning may be dangerous and give its possessor, white or black, the swell head, but sound scholarship has usually had the opposite effect with both white and black. Nor has it unfitted them to do their work among their own people. The faithful teachers, preachers and doctors who are serving their own race are ample answer to this objection. Nor can it be maintained that the race does not need college trained leaders. If a Negro doctor is to serve his race he must have the same preparation as the white doctor. A germ is no easier handled in a black skin than in a white skin. Disease knows no color line. In like manner if we are to have a pure Christianity taught we must have Negro ministers fully equipped. The hope of the Negro lies in a sound morality which can alone be maintained on a sound and rational religion. The teachers of such a religion must have thorough training. In like manner all educators recognize that the more ignorant a people, the more skillful and the better trained must the teacher be. The Negro colleges have not yet turned out even a small fraction of those needed to be the leaders of the race. In all the schools in the United States in 1917, there were only 2,641 Negro students of collegiate grade, according to the report of Dr. Jones.[42] Referring to the value of this education, Dr. Jones says:

"A number of the schools offering college courses have rendered a most valuable service. This is especially true of the institutions founded and supervised by the cultured men and women who went South to teach in schools for colored people. Though the curricula of these institutions may have frequently seemed to overemphasize the printed page in comparison with the application of knowledge to practical affairs, the daily conduct of teachers trained in the best traditions of American life gave to the colored people a more precious heritage than any type of curriculum could have given.

"Unfortunately, most of the schools with college courses are seriously handicapped, not only by inadequate funds, but also by the small number of pupils prepared to study college subjects. The facts presented in the chapter on college and professional education show that only three institutions have a student body, a teaching force and equipment, and an income sufficient to warrant the characterization of 'college.' Nearly half of the college students and practically all the professional students of college grade are in these three institutions. Fifteen other institutions are offering college courses which represent a wide variation of standards. Not more than 10 per cent of the pupils in these schools are in college classes. All of the fifteen institutions mentioned are rendering a valuable educational service and a few of them are really of college grade." [43] These figures were compiled some years ago and much progress has been made since their publication.

"The 15 institutions offering college subjects are schools of elementary and secondary grade whose teaching force make it possible to provide instruction in a few college subjects. They have neither the equipment nor the teachers to maintain college classes." [44]

*Numbers of College Students.* In 1917 there were only 400 medical students, 260 dental students, 132 pharmaceutical students, 441 theological students, 106 law students enrolled in Negro colleges fitted to offer such subjects.[45] The number of

[42] Jones: "Negro Education," Vol. I, U. S. Bulletin No. 38, p. 303.
[43] *Ibid.*, p. 11.
[44] *Ibid.*, p. 17.
[45] *Idem.*

Negro college graduates is pitiable when compared with the needs. In 1915 the "Negro Year Book" [46] reported 5,350 college graduates, and the total number at the present time could not be more than seven or eight thousand. What can so small a group do in furnishing trained leadership for a race of more than ten million?

There is desperate need for a real system of higher education, adequately endowed and carefully planned. There are ample funds in one or two southern cities, notably Atlanta, Nashville, and New Orleans, to make real institutions of higher education. But these funds are so divided as to be relatively useless. If all the institutions in Nashville could follow the example of Vanderbilt and Peabody, and locate their buildings in close proximity to each other, so that there might be real coöperation in class work, there could be built up here a great educational institution. The same could be true in Atlanta. If a series of five or six real educational institutions could be established at Howard in Washington, at Richmond, Nashville, Atlanta, New Orleans, Marshall, Texas, Charlotte, North Carolina, and Little Rock, Arkansas, they could probably meet the needs of the race at the present time. Each of these places should have a real Negro university, with collegiate department, and with well equipped departments for training teachers, preachers and doctors. There is also need for more nurse training institutions. The Negro woman has a real capacity for tending the sick, and with good training they could greatly change the present conditions among their own people.

*South Determined to Train the Negro.* The South long ago determined that the Negro should have training. However, lack of funds and fear of the results of training have made all efforts more or less half-hearted. But real training never has injured any one or made any man less valuable to society. The southern white man has within his own power the determining of the type of training the Negro has. If the present generation of southerners are to be as fair and courageous as our fathers of reconstruction days, we shall have to put heart and enthusiasm into giving the Negro child the same chance that we believe every citizen of a true democracy should have. To do less than this would delay the progress of the whole South, for no country is any stronger than its weakest citizens. In giving such training as this we not only will enrich the life of the Negro, but we will also enrich our own life.

[46] "Negro Year Book, 1916-17," p. 244.

## Chapter XV

# THE NEGRO AND SELF EXPRESSION

*Personality and Self-Expression.* Self-expression is of the very essence of personality. It is impossible to conceive of any person who does not desire to make himself known to other persons. Illingworth, in his rather remarkable volume on "Personality, Human and Divine," points out quite clearly that human desires move in two directions—acquisition and action. "We desire to incorporate and assimilate with ourselves the various contents of our material, moral, and intellectual environment, . . . and we also desire to project ourselves into and modify that environment, by exercising our wealth, or power, or skill, or mind upon it." [1] Now, this two-fold process of desire, acquisitive and active, irresistibly impels us into communion with other persons." [2] He goes on to say that a person cannot be satisfied with food or clothing, or material possessions of any kind. "We press on through it all till we have found persons like ourselves with whom to share it, and then we are at rest." [3] Self revelation is of the very nature of personality. Not only does my nature demand a chance to function through self revelation, but my nature cannot grow without such self expression. Functional psychology is now telling us that no thought is a completed thought until it has found expression, hence all growth is bound up with a process of self revelation. Human nature is older than any theory or treatise about it, and hence has been attempting to express itself through all the ages. Not only do individual persons attempt to express themselves, but races struggle for self expression. The Greeks uttered themselves in the highest forms of art, the Hebrews found expression in religion, the Romans expressed themselves in organization and government. It is evident, therefore, that self expression may take many forms according to the nature of the person or the peoples, but expression is a function of life which cannot be repressed.

*Self Expression in Africa.* The Negro, like every other race, has needed and found self expression. In the primeval African jungle he built up an elaborate system of folk lore which is rich

[1] Illingworth: "Personality Human and Divine," p. 36.
[2] *Ibid.*, p. 37.
[3] *Idem.*

in a simple philosophy of life. Every tribe had its story teller; and around the camp fire at night the hours were whiled away as each man vied with all others in the stories that went the round. There is no more charming volume of folk tales than those compiled from African bush life. The African Negro is quick in repartee and the riddle is one of the favorite forms of conversation.

Weeks has compiled for us a series of folk tales which would be wholesome reading for many a group of young people. Like Aesop's fables, they usually have a simple moral. Here is a story of patience which goes round the African camp fire:

## "WHY THE SMALL-ANT WAS THE WINNER"

*Folk Story of Patience.* "One day a fierce Driver-ant and a Small-ant had a long discussion as to which of them was the stronger. The Driver-ant boasted of his size, the strength of his mandibles, and the fierceness of his bite.

" 'Yes, all that may be true', quietly answered the Small-ant, 'and yet with all your size and strong jaws you cannot do what I can do.'

" 'What is that?' sneeringly asked the Driver-ant.

" 'You cannot cut a piece of skin off the back of that man's hand, and drop it down here,' replied the Small-ant.

" 'Can't I? All of you wait and see,' said the Driver-ant.

"Away he climbed up the man until he reached the back of his hand. At the first bite of the strong mandibles, the man started, and, looking down at his hand, saw the Driver-ant, picked it off, and dropped it dead at his feet right among the waiting crowd of ants.

"The Small-ant then climbed to the place, and gently, softly, with great patience he worked round a piece of skin until it was loose, and he was able to drop it to the ground. The waiting throng of ants proclaimed him the winner, for he had done by his gentleness and patience what the other had failed to do by his strength and fierceness." [4]

*Folk Story of Honesty.* Here is another African folk story which is a forerunner of Br'er Rabbit and the Tar Baby. It is a preachment for honesty. The Gazelle and the Leopard planted maize. When the crop was ripe, some one kept stealing the maize belonging to the Gazelle. "Friend Leopard," said the Gazelle, "who is stealing maize from my farm?"

" 'I don't know,' replied the Leopard. The Gazelle carved a wooden fetish called the *Nkondi,* and put it in his farm.

[4] Weeks: "Congo Life," p. 374.

"The next night the Leopard went and stole some more maize, and as he was leaving the farm the *Nkondi* said: 'Oh, you are the thief, are you?'

" 'If you talk like that,' growled the Leopard, 'I will hit you.'

" 'Hit me,' said the *Nkondi*. The Leopard hit him, and his paw stuck to the image.

" 'Let go,' cried the Leopard, 'or I will hit you with my other hand.'

" 'Hit me,' repeated the *Nkondi*. The Leopard hit him with the other hand, and that stuck also to the image.

" 'Let go,' angrily cried the Leopard, 'or I will kick and bite you.' Which he at once did, as the *Nkondi* would not let him go, and his feet and mouth stuck to the image; then both the Leopard and the *Nkondi* fell to the ground together.

"By and by the Gazelle arrived, and when he saw the Leopard sticking to the *Nkondi he said*: 'Oh, you are the thief,' and, having punished him, he cut some leaves and made a charm to set the Leopard free. After that the Leopard never again went stealing in the Gazelle's maize farm." [5]

*Folk Story of Truthfulness.* Here is another simple story of truthfulness and kindness:

"One day a Gazelle, being very hungry, went in search of food, and saw a fine bunch of palm-nuts hanging from a palm-tree; but having only hoofs he could not climb the tree. He therefore went in search of his friend the Palm-rat, and said to him: 'I know where there is a fine bunch of palm-nuts, and if you will promise to give me some I will show you where it is.'

"The Palm-rat readily promised to share the nuts. So together they went to the forest, and the Gazelle pointed out the nuts to his friend. With his strong, sharp claws the Palm-rat quickly mounted the palm-tree, and found there three bunches of palm-nuts; but instead of cutting them down, he sat on a palm-frond and began to eat them.

"After a time the Gazelle shouted out: 'Friend Palm-rat, throw me down some of the nuts according to your promise.'

" 'Oh,' cried the Palm-rat, 'when I am eating I am deaf, and cannot hear what is said to me.' And he continued to munch away at the nuts.

"The Gazelle waited a little, and again called out: 'Please throw me some of the palm-nuts, for I have hoofs, and cannot climb a tree like you.' But the Palm-rat ate greedily on, and took no notice of his friend's request, except to say that he was deaf when eating.

[5] Weeks: "Congo Life," p. 389.

"The Gazelle thereupon gathered some leaves, grass, twigs, and stubble, and made a large fire at the bottom of the palm-tree. In a short time the Palm-rat called out: 'Uncle Gazelle, put out your fire, the heat and smoke are choking me.'

" 'Oh,' replied the Gazelle, 'when I am warming myself by the fire I cannot hear what is said to me.' And he heaped more firewood and dried grass on the fire.

"The Palm-rat, choking with the smoke, lost his grip on the tree, and fell to the ground dead. The Gazelle returned to the town and took possession of all the goods belonging to the Palm-rat. If you make a promise, keep it; and if you want a kindness shown to you, you must do kind things to others." [6]

*Folk Lore an Index of Life.* Those who know the African best in his native heath find in these simple but effective stories a true index to the nature of the African people. There is no better way to know a people than to read their folk lore. Here we have revealed their inmost selves, for the stories that live are those that appeal to the hearts of the group. These African folk stories are the self revelation, or the self expression of a people. They reveal the native shrewdness, the suavity amounting almost to chicanery, but with all the reality and genuineness of the native heart.

*Folk Lore of the Slaves.* When the slaves came to America they brought with them their love of folk lore, and in particular the animal stories which had long been told around their camp fires. These stories were used by the slave "mammies" to charm the children of the big house. The African Gazelle with his craft and smooth manners was transferred into Br'er Rabbit, who usually wins by shrewdness what the stronger animals could not acquire through force. The rabbit was always the favorite animal of the slave, for he personified the Negro's method of life. The slave did not fight back. He won by his sense of humor, his smooth and suave manner. He rounded many a hard corner where a more stubborn race would have been broken. The African Leopard is transformed into a wolf or a fox in the slave stories, and Mr. Bear takes the place of the larger animals of the African jungle, such as the elephant. Joel Chandler Harris has gathered these animal stories into one of the most charming volumes of all folk tales. Every child of the old South has read these matchless stories. But we must remember that these stories were the self expression of the slave, long before they were gathered into a volume to entertain the white children. Through these stories the Negro found vent for his imagination, and also for his desire to preach. The old proverbs of the slave

* Weeks: "Congo Life," pp. 399-400.

days were also the crystallization of his simple philosophy of life. To take the smart Negro down, the slaves had a saying: "Ole man Know-All died las' year." For the Negro late at work he said: "Rails split 'fo bre'kfus' 'll season de dinner." For the self righteous Negro the slave philosophy hardened itself into the homely proverb: "Ef you wanter to see yo' own sins, clean up a new groun'." To the master who did not feed his slaves well they applied a proverb: "Hongry nigger won't w'ar his maul out." For the dandy they said: "Looks won't do ter split rails wid." Of the lazy Negro they made a bit of fun. "Nigger dat gits hurt wukkin' oughter show de skyars." To the Negro who tried to lie they said: 'You k'n hide de fire, but w'at you gwine do wid de smoke?" To the greedy Negro they said: "Hit's a mighty deaf nigger dat don't year de dinner-ho'n." To all those in trouble they brought consolation: "Troubles is seasoning'. Simmons ain't good twel dey 'er fros'-bit." "Watch out w'en you'er gittin' all you want. Fattenin' hogs ain't in luck." [7] In this simple but vital philosophy of life the slaves found expression.

*Folk Songs.* But the chief expression of the slaves took the form of song. These folk songs are intensely interesting and instructive because they come from the heart of the people. They are not the work of composers. No individual prepared them and sent them forth. They sprang out of the life experience of a whole people and hence are the vital record of that people's soul history. Krehbiel defines folksong as follows:

"Folksong is not popular song in the sense in which the word is most frequently used, but the song of the folk; not only the song admired of the people, but, in a strict sense, the song created by the people. It is a body of poetry and music which has come into existence without the influence of conscious art, as a spontaneous utterance, filled with characteristic expression of the feelings of a people. Such songs are marked by certain peculiarities of rhythm, form and melody which are traceable, more or less clearly, to racial (or national) temperament, modes of life, climatic and political conditions, geographical environment and language. Some of these elements, the spiritual, are elusive, but others can be determined and classified." [8]

*Folk Music True to Life.* Just because this music comes from the soul of the whole people, it is true to life and carries with it a record of traditions, beliefs, customs, and longings such as no individual literature could possibly possess. Krehbiel points out that while each of these songs may have been molded by succes-

[7] Harris: "Uncle Remus, His Songs and Sayings," p. 173 f.
[8] Krehbiel: "Afro-American Folksongs," p. 2.

sive individuals, they were molded in accordance with the group life and thought. Each individual's "idioms are taken off the tongue of the people; his subjects are the things which make for the joy or sorrow of the people, and once his song is gone out into the world his identity, as its creator, is swallowed up in that of the people." [9]

*They Represent the Deepest Impulses of the Soul.* The folk songs of any people which abide are, therefore, apt to represent the deepest passions and longings of the soul. They are more apt to preserve the record of their suffering and their struggles for life than they are to preserve the lighter moods of the group. Life runs deepest when it is trying to solve some great problem of existence, and since problems bring seriousness and usually involve birth pains of larger experience, the best folk music, and most of that which has lived in all countries has a note of seriousness and often a note of sadness. This note of suffering can be found in all folk music, because every people has had the long struggle of existence, with its physical suffering and its mental and spiritual growth.

*Prevailing Note is Serious.* However, it must not be forgotten that some of the old Negro folk songs are full of gaiety and joy. They express that light-heartedness for which the Negro was so remarkable. But since this mood does not bring out the deepest in life, fewer of such songs would survive. It must be further noted that the one common meeting place for the slaves was the church. Here alone he found a chance for united expression of his soul in song. The songs of the church would necessarily be the more serious ones, and due to their much more frequent use, would have a much better chance to survive. For this reason the great majority of the folk songs of the Negro preserved for us are those which deal with the serious side of life, and usually have a plaintive note of suffering in them. Slavery was a kind of imprisonment for them, and the one release from it was heaven—the hereafter. Krehbiel quotes a song of the old days which had this hope of the future in it:

1.  No more peck o' corn for me,
    No more, no more.
    No more peck o' corn for me,
    Many thousands go.

The other verses run: "No more driver's lash for me," "No more hundred lash for me," "No more mistress' call for me," "No more pint o' salt for me," with the refrain after each line. Perhaps this song would not have been allowed save as a religious expression of longing for future life. Sung under other condi-

[9] Krehbiel: "Afro-American Folksongs," p. 4.

tions, it might have sounded like insurrection and so been repressed. The cloak of religion, therefore, was thrown around the longing for freedom and made possible the expression of that deepest passion of the Negro's soul, which it is certain could not have otherwise been expressed. What could express more vividly the weariness of the slave than this song given by Higginson in his Army Life of a Black Regiment:

> "I know moon rise, I know star rise,
>     Lay dis body down,
> I'll walk in de graveyard,
>     To lay dis body down.
> "I'll lie in de grave and stretch out my arms,
>     Lay dis body down,
> I'll go to de Judgment in de evenin' of de day,
>     When I lay dis body down.
> And my soul and your soul will meet in de day,
>     When I lay dis body down." [10]

*Songs Reveal the Negroes' Life.* "Nothing," says Dr. Washington, "tells more truly what the Negro's life in slavery was, than the songs in which he succeeded, sometimes, in expressing his deepest thoughts and feelings. What, for example, could express more eloquently the feelings of despair which sometimes overtook the slave than these simple and expressive words:

> O Lord, O my Lord! O my good Lord!
>     Keep me from sinking down."

*Plaintive Air of Folk Music.* It has been often remarked that all folk music has a plaintive minor note which has been attributed to the fact of suffering in the life of the people. This is the almost universal popular interpretation of the peculiar strain of the primitive music. Tylor points out that this modal characteristic of primitive music arises out of a pentatonic or five-toned scale instead of our seven-toned scale, which lends to this music its plaintive air. [11]  Krehbiel made a careful analysis of 527 Negro folk songs, gathered by three different compilers, and found only 62 written in the minor key, 111 written in pentatonic style, while 331 were in major key. [12]  Perhaps it is the emotional color plus what the musicians call "timbre" of the Negro voice, as well as in the voice of all primitive peoples, that gives the impression of sadness or suffering. Certain it is that Negro melodies sung by white people lose most of that peculiar

[10] Quoted from Washington's "History of the Negro," Vol. II, p. 263.
[11] Tyler: "Anthropology," p. 292.
[12] Krehbiel: "Afro-American Folksongs," p. 5.

quality which makes them so compelling when sung by Negroes of the older type. The peculiar note of sadness, and the weird air of Negro music is certainly not always due to the minor key.

*Folk Music Long Unappreciated.* The value and meaning of this folk music have been too little appreciated both by the colored people and by the whites. The Negroes for a long time after the Civil War would not sing these songs because they recalled slavery days. The white people often take them as comic performances. I have often seen the smile on the faces of white people as the students at Fisk, Tuskegee or Hampton sang these wonderful records of the soul struggles of a race. It grates on one's nerves to hear applause after the singing of some of these most beautiful spirituals. It is like cheering a great sermon, or clapping after the organ has finished playing the Messiah. James Weldon Johnson, himself a Negro, has caught something of the significance of this primitive music in his "O Black and Unknown Bards." [13]

> O black and unknown bards of long ago,
> How came your lips to touch the sacred fire?
> How, in your darkness, did you come to know
> The power and beauty of the minstrel's lyre?
> Who first from midst his bonds lifted his eyes?
> Who first from out the still watch, lone and long,
> Feeling the ancient faith of prophets rise
> Within his dark-kept soul, burst into song?
>
> Heart of what slave poured out such melody
> As "Steal away to Jesus"? On its strains
> His spirit must have nightly floated free,
> Though still about his hands he felt his chains.
> Who heard great "Jordan roll"? Whose starward eye
> Saw chariot "swing low"? And who was he
> That breathed that comforting, melodic sigh,
> "Nobody knows de trouble I see"?
>
> What merely living clod, what captive thing,
> Could up toward God through all its darkness grope,
> And find within its deadened heart to sing
> These songs of sorrow, love and faith, and hope?
> How did it catch that subtle undertone,
> That note in music heard not with the ears?
> How sound the elusive reed so seldom blown,
> Which stirs the soul or melts the heart to tears.

[13] Johnson: "The Book of American Negro Poetry," p. 73.

Not that great German master in his dream
Of harmonies that thundered amongst the stars
At the creation, ever heard a theme
Nobler than "Go down, Moses."  Mark its bars
How like a mighty trumpet-call they stir
The blood.  Such are the notes that men have sung
Going to valorous deeds; such tones they were
That helped make history when Time was young.

There is a wide, wide wonder in it all,
That from degraded rest and servile toil
The fiery spirit of the seer should call
These simple children of the sun and soil.
O black slave singers, gone, forgot, unfamed,
You—you alone, of all the long, long line
Of those who've sung untaught, unknown, unnamed,
Have stretched out upward, seeking the divine.

You sang not deeds of heroes or of kings;
No chant of bloody war, no exulting pean
Of arms-won triumphs; but your humble strings
You touched in chord with music empyrean.
You sang far better than you knew; the songs
That for your listener's hungry hearts sufficed
Still live,—but more than this to you belongs:
You sang a race from wood and stone to Christ.

*Folk Music Must Not Be Lost.*  It will be a great loss to
whites and blacks alike if ever these songs are neglected.  They
do not, of course, represent the Negro to-day, but they have so
much of the past in them, they show so much of the Negro's
capacity for aspiration, they are so full of the atmosphere of
old plantation days, that the South will be much poorer for the
loss of them.  Indeed music itself will be impoverished if they
are lost.  They are the one original contribution to music which
America has made, thinks Krehbiel: "Nowhere save on the
plantations of the South could the emotional life which is essential to the development of true folksong be developed; nowhere
else was there the necessary meeting of the spiritual cause and
the simple agent and vehicle.  The white inhabitants of the continent have never been in the state of cultural ingenuousness which
prompts spontaneous emotional utterance in music.  Civilization
atrophies the faculty which creates this phenomenon as it does
the creation of myth and legend.  Sometimes the faculty is gal-
vanized into life by vast calamities or crises which shake all the

fibres of social and national existence; and then we see its fruits in the composition of popular musicians." [14]

*Early Poetry.* The animal stories and the folk songs were not the only forms of the Negro's self-expression. Early in slavery days expression of his longing were found in poetic verse. Forerunner of all these spokesmen for the race was Phillis Wheatley. Born in Africa in the Senegal, brought to Boston Harbor in 1761 and sold on the public block in Boston as a slave, she fell into the hands of a kindly woman who gave her instruction and started her on her career of study and writing. She became a classical scholar of some attainments and wrote a clear, beautiful English. One of her little poems which breathes the spirit of her life is "On Being Brought From Africa to America": [15]

> 'Twas mercy brought me from my pagan land,
> Taught my benighted soul to understand
> That there's a God—that there's a Saviour too;
> Once I redemption neither sought nor knew.
> Some view our sable race with scornful eye . . .
> "Their color is a diabolic dye."
> Remember, Christians, Negroes black as Cain
> May be refined, and join th' angelic train.

*Phillis Wheatley in England.* In 1773 Phillis Wheatley went to England where she was received by the Countess of Huntingdon and many of the ladies of the court. She read her poems before royalty and received every attention. There is in the library of Harvard University an engrossed copy of the folio edition of "Paradise Lost," presented to Phillis Wheatley during this visit by Brook Watson, Lord Mayor of London.

Perhaps the best poem of Phillis Wheatley was "On Imagination": [16]

> Imagination! Who can sing thy force?
> Or who describe the swiftness of thy course?
> Soaring through air to find the bright abode,
> Th' empyreal palace of the thundering God,
> We on thy pinions can surpass the wind,
> And leave the rolling universe behind:
> From star to star the mental optics rove,
> Measure the skies, and range the realms above;
> There in one view we grasp the mighty whole,
> Or with new worlds amaze th' unbounded soul.

[14] Krehbiel: "Afro-American Folksongs," pp. 22-23.
[15] Brawley: "The Negro in Literature and Art," p. 14.
[16] *Ibid.*, p. 31.

Wheatley was not a great poet, but one cannot help but admire her energy, and appreciate her attempts at expressing her soul. Born in a pagan land, reared a slave, she did well and we cannot withhold from her a meed of praise.

*George Moses Horton.* George Moses Horton, a slave in North Carolina, was born in 1797. He published in 1829, with the help of white friends, a little volume of poems called "The Hope of Liberty." His desire was to sell these and secure enough money to buy his freedom; but his master was unwilling to sell him. Bitterly disappointed, he ceased writing and spent the remainder of his life working around the University of North Carolina, at Chapel Hill.

In 1854 there appeared a little volume of "Poems on Miscellaneous Subjects," by Frances Ellen Watkins, which had some literary merit. One of her poems runs:

Make me a grave where'er you will,
In a lowly plain or a lofty hill;
Make it among earth's humblest graves,
But not in a land where men are slaves. [17]

Another one of her poems celebrates the Emancipation Proclamation:

It shall flash through coming ages,
It shall light the distant years;
And eyes now dim with sorrow
Shall be brighter through their tears. [18]

Just following emancipation a company of Negro writers came forward. What they wrote has no permanent value, but was an outburst of the soul and a people happy and exultant in its new freedom.

*Paul Laurence Dunbar.* The first real poet of the American Negro was Paul Laurence Dunbar. Born in Dayton, Ohio, 1872, from parents who had been slaves, he was a pure blood Negro, and entered in deepest sympathy into their strivings. He went to high school in Dayton, where he was editor of the monthly student publication, the *High School Times;* he wrote the song of his senior class, and was recognized as the student of outstanding literary ability. "Oak and Ivy" appeared in 1893, and other poems followed. These attracted the attention of no less a literary critic than William Dean Howells, who wrote a review of them for *Harper's Weekly.* In 1896 *"Lyrics of Lowly Life"*

[17] Quoted from "The Negro in Literature and Art," p. 76.
[18] *Ibid.,* p. 76.

appeared with an introduction by Mr. Howells.  In this introduction Howells said:

*Howells' Estimate of Dunbar.*  "What struck me in reading Mr. Dunbar's poetry was what had already struck his friends in Ohio and Indiana, in Kentucky and Illinois.  They had felt, as I felt, that however gifted his race had proven itself in music, in oratory, in several of the other arts, here was the first instance of an American negro who had evinced innate distinction in literature.  In my criticism of his book I had alleged Dumas in France, and I had forgetfully failed to allege the far greater Pushkin in Russia; but these were both mulattoes, who might have been supposed to derive their qualities from white blood vastly more artistic than ours, and who were the creatures of an environment more favorable to their literary development.  So far as I could remember, Paul Dunbar was the only man of pure African blood and of American civilization to feel the negro life aesthetically and express it lyrically.  It seemed to me that this had come to its most modern consciousness in him, and that his brilliant and unique achievement was to have studied the American negro objectively, and to have represented him as he found him to be, with humor, with sympathy, and yet with what the reader must instinctively feel to be entire truthfulness.  I said that a race which had come to this effect in any member of it, had attained civilization in him, and I permitted myself the imaginative prophecy that the hostilities and the prejudices which had so long constrained his race were destined to vanish in the arts; that these were to be the final proof that God had made of one blood all nations of men.  I thought his merits positive and not comparative; and I held that if his black poems had been written by a white man, I should not have found them less admirable.  I accepted them as an evidence of the essential unity of the human race, which does not think or feel black in one and white in another, but humanly in all." [19]

*Human Element in Dunbar's Poems.*  One of the elements of Dunbar's poetry is its humanness.  He takes the little every-day affairs of life and makes them live.  Here is a little poem inspired by the singing of Dunbar's Negro mother, in which he tells the white people that they have not the musical sensibility of his own race:

### "WHEN MALINDY SINGS

G'way an' quit dat noise, Miss Lucy—
     Put dat music book away;
What's de use to keep on tryin'?
     Ef you practise twell you're gray,

[19] Introduction to "Complete Poems of Paul Laurence Dunbar," pp. viii-ix.

You cain't sta't no notes a'flyin'
　　Lak de ones dat rants and rings
F'om de kitchen to de big woods
　　When Malindy sings.

You ain't got no nachel o'gans
　　Fu' to make de soun' come right,
You ain't got de tu'ns an' twistin's
　　Fu' to make it sweet an' light.
Tell you one thing now, Miss Lucy,
　　An' I'm tellin' you fu' true,
When hit comes to raal right singin',
　　'T ain't no easy thing to do.

Easy 'nough fu' folks to hollah,
　　Lookin' at de lines an' dots,
When dey ain't no one kin sence it,
　　An' de chune comes in, in spots;
But fu' real melojous music,
　　Dat jes' strikes yo' hea't and clings,
Jes' you stan' an' listen wif me
　　When Malindy sings.

Ain't you nevah hyeahd Malindy?
　　Blessed soul, tek up de cross!
Look hyeah, ain't you jokin', honey?
　　Well, you don't know whut you los'.
Y' ought to hyeah dat gal a-wa'blin',
　　Robins, la'ks, and all dem things,
Heish dey moufs an' hides dey faces
　　When Malindy sings.

Fiddlin' man jes' stop his fiddlin',
　　Lay his fiddle on de she'f;
Mockin'-bird quit tryin' to whistle,
　　'Cause he jes' so shamed hisse'f.
Folks a-playin' on de banjo
　　Draps dey fingahs on de strings—
Bless yo' soul—fu'gits to move em,
　　When Malindy sings.

She jes' spreads huh mouf and hollahs,
　　"Come to Jesus," twell you hyeah
Sinnahs' tremblin' steps and voices,
　　Timid-lak a-drawin' neah;

Den she tu'ns to "Rock of Ages,"
    Simply to de cross she clings,
An' you fin' yo' teahs a-drappin'
    When Malindy sings.

Who dat says dat humble praises
    Wif de Master nevah counts?
Heish yo' mouf, I hyeah dat music,
    Ez hit rises up an' mounts—
Floatin' by de hills an' valleys,
    Way above dis buryin' sod,
Ez hit makes its way in glory
    To de very gates of God!

Oh, hit's sweetah dan de music
    Of an edicated band;
An' hit's dearah dan de battle's
    Song o' triumph in de lan'.
It seems holier dan evenin'
    When de solemn chu'ch bell rings,
Ez I sit an' ca'mly listen
    While Malindy sings.

Towsah, stop dat ba'kin', hyeah me!
    Mandy, mek dat chile keep still;
Don't you hyeah de echoes callin'
    F'om de valley to de hill?
Let me listen, I can hyeah it,
    Th'oo de bresh of angels' wings,
Sof' an' sweet, "Swing Low, Sweet Chariot,"
    Ez Malindy sings.[20]

*Love of Children.* Dunbar's love of children was expressed in "Little Brown Baby," "Lullaby," "The Plantation Child's Lullaby," "Chrismus is a-Comin'" "Two Little Boots," and others. His sense of humor is displayed in "Accountability," "Breaking the Charm," "The Turning of the Babies in the Bed," and a score of other poems.

*Appreciation of the Old South.* The remarkable thing about Dunbar's poetry is its real appreciation of the old South. He never lived on a plantation, nor did he ever live in the South, yet his insight into the spirit of the life of the old South is most remarkable. "Chris-mus on the Plantation" is as fine a tribute both to the old master and to the loyalty of the Negro as could be

[20] "Complete Poems of Paul Laurence Dunbar," p. 82.

written—and it was true to life.  Many a master struggled to protect his former slaves and give them a chance to live on the old place, and not a few ex-slaves proved their abiding love for those who had protected them.  "The Deserted Plantation" is so true to the best spirit of the freed Negroes that one cannot forego quoting it:

Oh, de grubbin'-hoe's a-rustin' in de co'nah,
    An' de plow's a-tumblin' down in de fiel',
While de whippo-will's a'wailin' lak a mou'nah
    When his stubbo'n hea't is tryin' ha'd to yiel'.

In de furrers whah de co'n was allus wavin',
    Now de weeds is growin' green an' rank an' tall;
An' de swallers roun' de whole place is a-bravin'
    Lek dey thought deir folks had allus owned it all.

An' de big house stan's all quiet lak' an' solemn,
    Not a blessed soul in pa'lor, po'ch, er lawn;
Not a guest, ner not a cai'age lef' to haul 'em,
    Fu' de ones dat tu'ned de latch-string out air gone.

An' de banjo's voice is silent in de qua'ters,
    D' ain't a hymn ner co'n-song ringin' in de air;
But de murmur of a branch's passin' waters
    Is de only soun' dat breks de stillness dere.

Wha's de da'kies, dem dat used to be a-dancin'
    Ev'ry night befo' de ole cabin do'?
Wha's de chillun, dem dat used to be a-prancin'
    Er a-rollin' in de san' er on de flo'?

Whah's ole Uncle Mordecai an' Uncle Aaron?
    What's Aunt Doshy, Sam, an' Kit, an' all de res'?
Whah's ole Tom de da'ky fiddlah, how's he farin'?
    Whah's de gals dat used to sing an' dance de bes'?

Gone! not one o' dem is lef' to tell de story;
    Dey have lef' de deah ole place to fall away.
Couldn't one o' dem dat seed it in its glory
    Stay to watch it in de hour of decay?

Dey have lef' de ole plantation to de swallers,
    But it hol's in me a lover till de las';
Fu' I fin' hyeah in de memory dat follers
    All dat loved me an' dat I loved in de pas'.

So I'll stay an' watch de deah ole place an' tend it
   Ez I used to in de happy days gone by.
'Twell de othah Mastah thinks it's time to end it,
   An' calls me to my qua'ters in de sky.[21]

*No Bitterness in Dunbar.* I once visited the little home in
Dayton where Dunbar lived and wrote. His old ex-slave mother
still lives there and shows you his room with great pride. I told
her she must have been remarkable in her good spirit, for in
nothing her son wrote was there one note of bitterness. She
looked at me sharply and said: "You must think I'm an angel to
have been a slave seventeen years and yet have no bitter memories." But it is true that Dunbar has no bitterness. Whatever
may have been in his heart, it certainly cannot be found in his
writings. Only occasionally are we made to feel his deep lone-
liness and his desire to have a larger field of service, which is
denied him by his color.

## Sympathy

I know what the caged bird feels, alas!
   When the sun is bright on the upland slopes;
When the wind stirs soft through the springing grass,
And the river flows like a stream of glass;
   When the first bird sings and the first bud opes,
And the faint perfume from its chalice steals—
I know what the caged bird feels!

I know why the caged bird beats his wing
   Till its blood is red on the cruel bars;
For he must fly back to his perch and cling
When he fain would be on the bough a-swing;
   And a pain still throbs in the old, old scars
And they pulse again with a keener sting—
I know why he beats his wing!

I know why the caged bird sings, ah me,
   When his wing is bruised and his bosom sore,—
When he beats his bars and he would be free;
It is not a carol of joy or glee,
   But a prayer that he sends from his heart's deep core,
But a plea, that upward to Heaven he flings—
I know why the caged bird sings! [22]

[21] "Complete Poems," p. 67.
[22] *Ibid.,* p. 102.

*Dunbar's Stories.* Dunbar not only wrote poetry but he has several volumes of stories which portray the old plantation life. In all of these he has made the old South live again, he has shown the best of the white master, without in any sense compromising the value and worth of his own race.

*Chestnutt's Work.* The best novelist of the Negro race is Charles W. Chestnutt. He has written three novels, "The House Behind the Cedars," appearing 1900, "The Marrow of Tradition" in 1901, and "The Colonel's Dreams" in 1905. The first of these is perhaps his masterpiece. The motif of the story centers around a mulatto girl, and her desire to move forward and achieve. The injustice of her position as a half-cast, the limitations of her ambitions, the sin of the white man who brings mulatto children into the world and then leaves them with aspirations but without hope, are all presented with power and dramatic skill. The novel is written with a purpose—the portrayal of the injustice of the present situation. It carries one's sympathies, and one lays the book down feeling as the author feels that much injustice has been done. Chesnutt has several volumes of short stories, all of which revolve about the same central theme.

*Later Writers Set Aside Dialect.* During the last few years there has arisen a school of Negro writers who have moved away from the dialect in which Dunbar won his fame. They are writing of all the aspirations of a human soul. Speaking of the place of dialect in Negro literature, Johnson says:

"It may be surprising to many to see how little of the poetry being written by Negro poets today is being written in Negro dialect. The newer Negro poets show a tendency to discard dialect; much of the subject-matter which went into the making of traditional dialect poetry, 'possum, watermelons, etc., they have discarded altogether, at least, as poetic material. This tendency will, no doubt, be regretted by the majority of white readers; and, indeed, it would be a distinct loss if the American Negro poets threw away this quaint and musical folk-speech as a medium of expression. And yet, after all, these poets are working through a problem not realized by the reader, and, perhaps, by many of these poets themselves not realized consciously. They are trying to break away from, not Negro dialect itself, but the limitations on Negro dialect imposed by the fixing effects of long convention.

"The Negro in the United States has achieved or been placed in a certain artistic niche. When he is thought of artistically, it is as a happy-go-lucky, singing, shuffling, banjo-picking being or as a more or less pathetic figure. The picture of him is in a log cabin amid fields of cotton or along the levees. Negro dialect is naturally and by long association the exact instrument for voicing this phase of Negro life; and by that very exactness it is an instrument with but two full stops, humor and pathos. So even when he confines himself to purely racial themes, the Afro-American poet realized that there are phases of Negro life in the United States which cannot be treated in the dialect either adequately or artistically. Take for example the phases rising out of life in Harlem, that most wonderful Negro city in the world. I do not deny that a Negro in a log cabin is more picturesque than a Negro in a Harlem flat, but the Negro in the Harlem flat is here, and he is but part of a group growing everywhere in the country, a group whose ideals are becoming increasingly more vital than those of the traditionally artistic group, even if its members are less picturesque.

"What the colored poet in the United States needs to do is something like what Synge did for the Irish; he needs to find a form that will express the racial spirit by symbols from within rather than by symbols from without, such as the mere mutilation of English spelling and pronunciation. He needs a form that is freer and larger than dialect, but which will still hold the racial flavor; a form expressing the imagery, the idioms, the peculiar turns of thought, and the distinctive humor and pathos, too, of the Negro, but which will also be capable of voicing the deepest and highest emotions and aspirations, and allow of the widest range of subjects and the widest scope of treatment.

*Dialect Inadequate to Express Present Life.* "Negro dialect is at present a medium that is not capable of giving expression to the varied conditions of Negro life in America, and much less is it capable of giving the fullest interpretation of Negro character and psychology. This is no indictment against the dialect as dialect, but against the mould of convention in which Negro dialect in the United States has been set. In time these conventions may become lost, and the colored poet in the United may sit down to write in dialect without feeling that his first line will put the general reader in a frame of mind which demands that the poem be humorous or pathetic. In the meantime, there is no reason why these poets should not continue to do the beautiful things that can be done, and done best, in the dialect." [23]

*James Weldon Johnson.* James Weldon Johnson, whose poem, "O Black and Unknown Bards," we have quoted above, is one of these new writers. He has a constructive message of hope and prophecy. One of his most striking poems is a plea that the

[23] Johnson: "The Book of American Negro Poetry," Introduction, pp. xxxix-xli.

South—the land of his birth, shall cease to live in the past and meet the issues of the present hour:

## O SOUTHLAND!

O Southland! O Southland!
　Have you not heard the call,
The trumpet blown, the word made known
　To the nations, one and all?
The watchword, the hope-word,
　Salvation's present plan?
A gospel new, for all—for you!
　Man shall be saved by man.

O Southland! O Southland!
　Do you not hear today
The mighty beat of onward feet,
　And know you not their way?
'Tis forward, 'tis upward,
　On to the fair white arch
Of Freedom's dome, and there is room
　For each man who would march.

O Southland, fair Southland!
　Then why do you still cling
To an idle age and a musty page,
　To a dead and useless thing?
'Tis springtime! 'Tis work-time!
　The world is young again!
And God's above, and God is love,
　And men are only men.

O Southland, my Southland!
　O birthland! do not shirk
The toilsome task, nor respite ask,
　But gird you for the work.
Remember, remember
　That weakness stalks in pride;
That he is strong who helps along
　The faint one at his side.[24]

*Braithwaite, McKay, and Others.* Perhaps the three most worth-while poets of the day are William Stanley Braithwaite, Claude McKay and Georgia Douglas Johnson. Fenton Johnson, Joseph S. Cotter, Jr. (now dead), Daniel Webster Davis, and a

[24] Johnson: "The Book of American Negro Poetry," p. 84.

score of others are doing creditable work.   It is a pity that the
white people do not hear these voices.   Space permits us to say
only a word about two of the above.   "Mrs. Georgia Douglas
Johnson is a poet neither afraid nor ashamed of her emotions." [25]
She writes with passion and with power.   She has that intensity
of emotion which is characteristice of all true poetry.   Through
all her poems one can see the subdued longing for a fuller chance
at life.   There is a deep dread written in it all that makes one
shudder.   Listen to the disappointment and sorrow in "The Heart
of a Woman":

> The heart of a woman goes forth with the dawn,
> As a lone bird, soft winging, so restlessly on,
> Afar o'er life's turrets and vales does it roam
> In the wake of those echoes the heart calls home.
>
> The heart of a woman falls back with the night,
> And enters some alien cage in its plight,
> And tries to forget it has dreamed of the stars
> While it breaks, breaks, breaks on the sheltering bars. [26]

The mute agony of her soul comes out in her poem on
"Contemplation":

> We stand mute!
> No words can paint such fragile imagery,
> Those prismic gossamers that roll
> Beyond the sky-line of the soul;
> We stand mute! [27]

Even in her poem "Peace" the same pathos can be traced:

> I rest me deep within the wood,
>     Drawn by its silent call,
> Far from the throbbing crowd of men
>     On nature's breast I fall.
>
> My couch is sweet with blossoms fair,
>     A bed of fragrant dreams,
> And soft upon my ear there falls
>     The lullaby of streams,
>
> The tumult of my heart is stilled,
>     Within this sheltered spot,
> Deep in the bosom of the wood,
>     Forgetting, and—forgot! [28]

[25] Johnson: "The Book of American Negro Poetry," Introduction, p. xliv.
[26] Johnson: "The Heart of a Woman," p. 1.
[27] *Ibid.*, p. 5.
[28] *Ibid.*, p. 9.

Or read her disappointment in "Illusions";

Who hath not built his castles in the free and open air?
Who hath not dreamed his rosy dreams, more fair than all the
    fair?
Who hath not seen his castles fall, all scattered to the ground?
Who bears his dream unshattered, from the dreamland where
    they're found? [29]

The mother heart flashes forth in "Love's Tendril":

> Sweeter far than lyric rune
> Is my baby's cooing tune;
> Brighter than the butterflies
> Are the gleams within her eyes;
> Firmer than an iron band
> Serves the zephyr of her hand;
> Deeper than the ocean's roll
> Sounds her heart-beat in my soul.[30]

Who would not be glad to have written that swinging verse
on "Joy":

> There's a soft rosy gloe o'er the whole world today,
> There's a freshness and fragrance that trembles in May,
> There's a lilt in the music that vibrates and thrills
> From the uttermost glades to the tops of the hills.
>
> Oh! I am so happy, my heart is so light,
> The shades and the shadows have vanished from sight,
> This wild pulsing gladness throbs like a sweet pain—
> O soul of me, drink, ere night falleth again! [31]

James Weldon Johnson says of this writer: "In her ingenu-
ously wrought verses, through sheer simplicity and spontaneous-
ness, Mrs. Johnson often sounds a note of pathos or passion that
will not fail to waken a response." [32]

*Claude McKay.* Perhaps the most powerful voice of Negro
poetry is that of Claude McKay, a full blood Negro of Jamaica
who came to America to live in 1912. Although at present a
very young man, he has shown real genius. I quote four of his
poems from a volume recently published: [33]

Johnson: "The Heart of a Woman," p. 50.
[20] *Ibid.*, p. 61.
[31] *Ibid.*, p. 25.
[32] Johnson: "The Book of American Negro Poetry," Introduction, p. xliv.
[33] McKay: "Harlem Shadows," pp. 22, 23, 52, and 53.

## HARLEM SHADOWS

I hear the halting footsteps of a lass
      In Negro Harlem when the night lets fall
Its veil.  I see the shapes of girls who pass
      To bend and barter at desire's call.
Ah, little dark girls who in slippered feet
Go prowling through the night from street to street!

Through the long night until the silver break
      Of day the little gray feet know no rest;
Through the lone night until the last snow-flake
      Has dropped from heaven upon the earth's white breast,
The dusky, half-clad girls of tired feet
Are trudging, thinly shod, from street to street.

Ah, stern harsh world, that in the wretched way
      Of poverty, dishonor and disgrace,
Has pushed the timid little feet of clay,
      The sacred brown feet of my fallen race!
Ah, heart of me, the weary, weary feet
In Harlem wandering from street to street.

## THE WHITE CITY

I will not toy with it nor bend an inch.
Deep in the secret chambers of my heart
I muse my life-long hate, and without flinch
I bear it nobly as I live my part.
My being would be a skeleton, a shell
If this dark Passion that fills my every mood,
And makes my heaven in the white world's hell,
Did not forever feed me vital blood.
I see the mighty city through a mist—
The strident trains that speed the goaded mass,
The poles and spires and towers vapor-kissed,
The fortressed port through which the great ships pass,
The tides, the wharves, the dens I contemplate,
Are sweet like wanton loves because I hate.

## BAPTISM

      Into the furnace let me go alone;
Stay you without in terror of the heat.
I will go naked in—for thus 'tis sweet—
Into the weird depths of the hottest zone.

I will not quiver in the frailest bone,
You will not note a flicker of defeat;
My heart shall tremble not its fate to meet,
My mouth give utterance to any moan.
The yawning oven spits forth fiery spears;
Red aspish tongues shout wordlessly my name.
Desire destroys, consumes my mortal fears,
Transforming me into a shape of flame.
I will come out, back to your world of tears,
A stronger soul within a finer frame.

## IF WE MUST DIE

If we must die, let it not be like hogs
Hunted and penned in an inglorious spot,
While round us bark the mad and hungry dogs,
Making their mock at our accursed lot.
If we must die, O let us nobly die,
So that our precious blood may not be shed
In vain; then even the monsters we defy
Shall be constrained to honor us though dead!
O kinsmen! we must meet the common foe!
Though far outnumbered let us show us brave,
And for their thousand blows deal one death-blow!
What though before us lies the open grave?
Like men we'll face the murderous, cowardly pack,
Pressed to the wall, dying, but fighting back!

*Estimate of McKay.* These poems show something of the passion of McKay's soul. He loves his own people and there is a bitterness towards those who have oppressed them. Max Eastman, one of our ablest literary critics, wrote the introduction to this volume of poems, in which he said:

"These poems have a special interest for all the races of man because they are sung by a pure-blooded Negro. They are the first significant expression of that race in poetry. We tried faithfully to give a position in our literature to Paul Laurence Dunbar. We have excessively welcomed other black poets of minor talent, seeking in their music some distinctive quality other than the fact that they wrote it. But here for the first time we find our literature vividly enriched by a voice from this most alien race among us. And it should be illuminating to observe that while these poems are characteristic of that race as we most admire it—they are gentle, simple, candid, brave and friendly, quick of laughter and of tears—yet they are still more characteristic of what is deep and universal in mankind. There is no special or exotic kind of merit in them, no quality that demands a transmutation of our own natures to perceive. Just as the sculptures and wood and ivory carvings of the vast forgotten African Empires of Ifé and Benin, although so wistful in their tranquillity, are tranquil in the possession of the qualities of all classic and great art, so these poems, the purest of them, move with a sovereignty that is never new to the lovers of the high music of human utterance. . . .

"The quality is here in them all—the pure, clear, arrow-like transference of his emotion into our breast, without any but the inevitable words—the quality that reminds us of Burns and Villon and Catullus, and all the poets that we call lyric because we love them so much. It is the quality that Keats sought to cherish, when he said that 'Poetry should be great and unobtrusive, a thing which enters into the soul, and does not startle or amaze with itself but with its subject.' Poetry with this quality is not for those whose interest is mainly in the manufacture of poems. It will come rather to those whose interest is in the life of things. It is the poetry of life, and not of the poet's chamber. It is the poetry that looks upon a thing, and sings. It is possessed by a feeling and sings. May it find its way a little quietly and softly, in this age of roar and advertising, to the hearts that love a true and unaffected song." [34]

*Poetry and Negro Growth.* The poetry of the Negro is an indication of life and growth. No people is decadent, which is producing a poetry of emotion and passion. The Negro has by nature a poetic gift. He has long been recognized as capable in the field of oratory. Douglass, Washington, Moton, cannot be surpassed in their ability to move people to action. Negro preachers like C. T. Walker and John Jasper of Richmond have moved masses of people with their eloquence. The same vividness of imagination, the same fervor of emotion, the same power of word picture which has made these orators powerful, is destined to speak through their poetry. Already their voice is beginning to be heard, and it would not take a prophet to see that advancing culture and larger opportunities for expression will bring from the Negro race in future years some of our most striking poetry.

*Negro Music.* Closely akin to Negro poetry is Negro music. As we have seen in the first of this chapter, the Negro has a musical nature, which in Africa expressed itself in bush songs, and around the camp fire, and during slavery in America expressed itself in the spirituals which are the supreme expression of slave aspiration. Most white people do not know of the larger reaches of Negro music. The power of Negro music was per-

[34] Introduction, "Harlem Shadows," pp. ix and xvii.

haps first made generally known to America through the famous
Fisk Jubilee Singers, who started out from Fisk University in
1871, and traveled through the United States, England, Scotland,
Ireland, Holland, Switzerland, and Germany.   They sang before
great musical societies, before royalty, and many of the world's
greatest persons.   Out of the proceeds of this tour they built
Jubilee Hall, one of the most substantial buildings on the Fisk
Campus in Nashville, a building which would to-day cost three
hundred thousand dollars.

*Coleridge-Taylor.*   The first Negro composer to really win
world recognition was Samuel Coleridge-Taylor, whose father
was a native of Sierra Leone, Africa.   He graduated from the
Royal College of Music in London, 1893, and immediately became prominent as a performer.   His "Hiawatha's Wedding
Feast," produced at the Royal College in 1898, gave him world
fame.   It was followed by "The Death of Minnehaha" and
"Hiawatha's Departure," forming a trilogy that any great musi-
cian might be proud to have written.   I once heard the Atlanta
University musical organization render the first of this trilogy
at a commencement occasion, and the weirdness of the music
together with the power of performance by those Negro students
made an impression on me which I will never forget.

*Burleigh.*   The leading composer among the Negroes of
America is Harry T. Burleigh, the famous baritone singer of
St. George's Episcopal Church in New York.   He has written
many wonderful songs, among the best known of which are
"Jean," "Deep River," and "The Young Warrior."

*Roland Hayes.*   During recent months Roland Hayes has made
a tour through America and has charmed white and black alike
with his wonderful singing.   I have never heard a tenor voice with
more of sweetness and with finer control.

*The Negro Press.*   The most recent and perhaps the most
influential expression of the Negro is his press.   The first Negro
paper published in America was *Freedom's Journal,* edited and
managed by Samuel Cornish and John B. Russwurm.   "The in-
ception of this Journal," says Penn, "was the result of a meeting
of Messrs. Russwurm, Cornish, and others at the home of Mr.
Boston Crummell in New York, called to consider the attacks" [35]
of a local paper on the Afro-Americans of New York City.   The
paper had a short and stormy career.   Its name was changed to
*Rights of All,* and its career was ended in 1830.

The first Negro magazine appeared in 1841, published by the
A. M. E. Church, and edited by George Hogarth.[36]

*Early Papers.*   Detweiler reports twenty-four periodicals pub-

[35] "The Afro-American Press and Its Editors," p. 27.
[36] "Social Betterment Among Negro Americans," p. 109.

lished by Negroes at various times before the Civil War. Among these were the *Mirror of Liberty, The Elevator, The Clarion, The Genius of Freedom,* the *Alienated American,* the *Colored American.*[37] One of the most famous of all these pre-war newspapers was the *North Star,* published by Frederick Douglas, an ex-slave, whose freedom had been bought by Quaker friends in England. These same friends furnished twenty-five hundred dollars with which Douglass started his paper. It was published in Rochester, New York, until 1863, the name meanwhile being changed to *Frederick Douglass Paper.*[38]

Douglass tells us in his autobiography what his main purpose was in establishing this paper. He thought slavery persisted because white men did not believe the Negro had capacity. "In my judgment, a tolerably well-conducted press in the hands of persons of the despised race would, by calling out and making them acquainted with their own latent powers, by enkindling their hope of a future and developing their moral force, prove a most powerful means of removing prejudice, and awakening an interest in them."[39] He first thought of publishing his paper in Boston, but opposition of his friends, and fear lest he might have conflicts with those who had been his supporters caused him to go to Rochester. He, like other editors, had a hard financial struggle. He pays tribute to Mrs. Julia Griffiths Crafts, who came to his relief when his funds were exhausted, and enabled him to increase the circulation of his paper from 2000 to 4000.[40] Others "held festivals and fairs to raise money, and assisted me in every possible way to keep my paper in circulation."[41]

*Opposition to Negro Press.* There was much opposition to all Negro papers and particularly to the *North Star,* one of the most vigorous of all. "The *New York Herald,* true to the spirit of the times, counselled the people of the place to throw my printing press into Lake Ontario and to banish me to Canada."[42] But Douglass managed to keep afloat until the slaves were actually freed.

The first colored paper started in the South was the *Colored American* at Augusta, Georgia, 1865, and its purpose was to keep before the colored race the duties and responsibilities of freedom.[43] The Atlanta University conference in 1909 published a list of 185 papers which were then in circulation, and claimed it was not exhaustive.[44] Detweiler claims there were 492 Negro

[37] Detweiler: "The Negro Press," p. 39.
[38] "Life and Times of Frederick Douglass," p. 315 f.
[39] *Ibid.,* p. 317.
[40] *Ibid.,* p. 324.
[41] *Ibid.,* p. 325.
[42] *Ibid.,* p. 326.
[43] "The Afro-American Press and Its Editors," p. 101 f.
[44] "Efforts for Social Betterment among Negro Americans," p. 114.

papers in existence in the summer of 1921.[45]   There are thirty-
one magazines, eighty-two school periodicals, two college frater-
nity magazines, a number of official organs of fraternal orders,
several business journals, five music magazines, and a magazine
for children.[46]   One of the most ambitious, if not the very most
ambitious publishing operations of the day is the *Journal of Negro
History*, published by Carter Woodson in Washington.   Six volumes of this magazine have already appeared.   It is a serious
attempt to study the history and progress of the Negro race, and
to publish such records.   It is readily seen, therefore, that the
Negro press is no small item of the present life of the race.   Most
white people are not aware of the great number of Negro papers
and their broad influence on the Negro people.   *The Crisis*, which
has the largest circulation of any Negro magazine, has between
sixty and seventy thousand circulation each month, and the
*Chicago Defender* reports a circulation of 150,000, while the
total circulation of Negro papers reaches over one million.[47]   It
is fair to say that practically every Negro in America is directly
influenced by the Negro press for if he is not able to read he at
least is able to get the race news from his neighbor.   It is amazing how well informed even the most ignorant Negro is on matters that affect the race.

*Negro Papers in Cities.*   New York City has a full list of
papers, including *The Crisis, The New York Age, The New
York News, The Messenger, The Crusader, The Negro World*,
and others; Chicago publishes *The Defender, The Whip, The Enterprise, The Broad Ax*, and at least six fraternal organs.   Philadelphia is said to have more than a dozen publications, and
Indianapolis has five.   Nashville, Charlotte, Richmond, Memphis, Birmingham, and Atlanta have from two to five papers
each published by the colored people.   Referring evidently to
the *Chicago Defender*, Mr. Leavell in his report on Negro Migration says:

"The Chicago Negro weekly referred to may be an extreme
illustration of the attitude and policy of the northern Negro press
as it circulates in the South.   Certainly the single copies I have
seen of Negro papers in New York, Washington, and Indianapolis have been more self-contained.   The significant point, however, is that this extreme Chicago paper is the one that circulates
most largely among the Negro masses in Mississippi.   Its popu-
larity is evinced by the fact that in an important town of that
State one little Negro boy formerly had trouble in disposing of
ten copies a week, so that he was often late at Sunday school.

[45] Detweiler: "The Negro Press," p. 1.
[46] *Ibid.*, p. 126 f.
[47] *Ibid.*, p. 6.

Now, since the exodus has begun, he has had no trouble in selling his papers in time to get to Sunday School; and many other small boys are doing a lively business selling additional copies." [48]

*Wide Circulation of Negro Papers.* It is evident from this quotation that Negroes in the South are not dependent on their own local papers, but are subscribers to and readers of the papers from all parts of the country.

*Content of These Papers.* What, then, do these papers contain? In 1920 I subscribed to and reviewed and clipped a large number of Negro papers, in order that I might know what the press was saying. Some of these papers gave a fair amount of world news, but most of them did not justify their names as newspapers. Local news was, of course, given, but very little of world events or current events of any kind was given. Most of these papers specialized on race news. Whenever a Negro had achieved a great success these papers rightly played it up big. Where a Negro had been mistreated or injured by a white man this also was played up strong with big headlines. Occasionally an article told of some white man doing a real service to the race. On the whole they are a bit grudging of their praise for white men, in most cases doubting his motives even though he has gone out of his way to do the race a service. We could hardly hold this against these papers, for our own white papers have had exactly the same policy toward the Negro for many decades.

*Protests.* Here is a typical illustration of protest against discrimination taken from the *New York Age,* December 6, 1919. This is in answer to a statement by the *New York Tribune* saying the Negroes wanted to eat with the whites in the Congressional Library Café.

"On the complaint of certain colored citizens of Washington that colored people were being discriminated against in the restaurant of the Congressional Library by the newly appointed superintendent, the National Advancement Association took the matter up with the chairman of both the House Committee and the Senate Committee on Library . . .

"Up to a recent time colored people could go across from the Capitol to the Congressional Library and be served there. This continued to be so while the Superintendent of the Library was a man from Boston. Now a new superintendent has been appointed; we don't know how a man from Boston has held the position so long. We don't know where this new superintendent is from, but we are willing to wager he is an impecunious, red-necked rebel from somewhere in Dixie. Since he has been in

[48] "Negro Migration in 1916-17."

charge of the Library he has put into execution the policy against which the Advancement Association is protesting.

"Why does the *Tribune,* which is supposed to be a Republican newspaper—although being a Republican newspaper doesn't mean much for the Negro in this day and time—why does it as a great metropolitan daily descend to twisting this legitimate protest on the part of colored people into a demand for the 'right to eat with white folks'? *For the information of the 'Tribune,' if it does not already know it, we will say that in this matter the colored people of Washington and the rest of the country do not care a single solitary damn whether any white people ever eat in the restaurant of the Congressional Library or not.* What they are protesting against is this gross and open practice of injustice in a building owned by the nation and supported by common taxation, and against the humiliation and inconvenience to which they are subjected."

*Protest Against Lynching.* Here is a bitter protest against lynching, copied by Kerlin from the *Galveston New Era,* October 1919:

## "GEORGIA'S BLOOD-CURDLING DEED

"Was there ever a more shocking, disgraceful scene upon this American continent—this land of the free and the home of the brave—than that which occurred in old blood-stained heathen Georgia last week, when sixty-five 'good white men,' proud, civilized, and intelligent white men, lynched Eugene Hamilton, already convicted of assault and attempt to murder? This blood-curdling dastardly savage deed is almost too brutal to print.

          .    .    .    .    .

"If white America really stands for liberty (and this is what our President and Government have preached and still preach) it must hold out to every citizen, regardless of color, creed or previous condition of servitude, the scepter of true democracy, backed by the law of this government. If liberty is sacred (and this is what the white people preached to the world, to justify America's entrance into the war against Germany) law is also sacred. The Constitution of these United States provides for but one king in America, and that is the law, and no republic or government can continue to stand upon such constant and increasing disregard of its only king.

"White men make the law, white men execute the law, white men keep all of the jails, then, why should there ever be any need of them lynching a Negro if guilty of any sort of crime? This Negro boy had been arrested, tried and convicted in the courts of Georgia, by Georgia white men and was still in the hands of Georgia white men for safe keeping—why should other Georgia white men lynch him, except to vent that savage bloodthirsty nature which seems to be a part of the white race?

"American white men, governors, senators, representatives, judges, statesmen and political leaders are braying like thirsty jack-asses, frothing at the mouth and railing upon Mexico for her reported atrocities against American citizens, and wanting this government to order an intervention to stop what these white American proselytes of rebel democracy call 'savagery.' But, can white America successfully do this, without first 'clearing her own conscience?'

"We can't bring ourselves to believe that the soil of Russia, China, or Mexico, has ever been marked with such barbarous crimes as these perpetrated in old hell-charged heathen Georgia and half-civilized America." [49]

*Note of Defiance.* There is a note of retaliation sounded by some of the papers. In fact, a few of the papers published by Negroes would be called strongly radical. Here is one editorial taken from the *Wisconsin Weekly Blade:*

## "RADICALISM

"We used to think that certain of our leading men who continually harped upon and protested against discrimination and injustice were entirely 'too radical'; that they ought to go quietly and modestly about their own personal affairs and by the acquisition of property and education make themselves worthy of better treatment; that if they were denied the right to occupy property owned by them in a desirable neighborhood, they purchase property elsewhere and by their own acts improve that neighborhood. And there are lots of Colored people who think that now.

"But we have long since changed our views upon the subject. We think differently now. We really doubt if it is possible to be too radical in one's opposition to race hatred, discrimination and injustice.

"Radicalism does things. Be sure your cause is just and be as radical as you can. You cannot be too radical in a righteous cause." [50]

Here is a fiery editorial from the pen of Reverend William A. Byrd in the *Cleveland Gazette:*

". . . It is plain to the most casual observer that colored people are not rioting but are defending themselves against the hordes

[49] Kerlin: "The Voice of the Negro," p. 115.
[50] *Ibid.,* p. 9.

of white desperadoes. There is no propaganda afoot to dissuade white demons from perpetuating their riots but sychophant black men, some in high places, are calling upon colored men to desist from rioting. These dastardly cowards are better dead than alive! Colored men are simply defending their lives and homes. We say to them—continue defending them until the last man falls and then let the women take up the fight! The Knoxville riot it simply one of many that are coming in the South. Southern 'crackers' were at the foundation of the riots in Washington and Chicago. They failed to overawe the colored men in those cities and now the attempt is to take it into the south where they hope to be more successful. In this they are sadly mistaken. Colored men in no portion of this country will run, unless it is some of the cringers in high places who are living off the life-blood of the colored men who are giving standing and backbone to the race. Those Negro bishops and other sychophants that called upon colored men to be quiet while white villains were destroying their homes, brutalizing their women, robbing them of manhood and reducing the entire race to serfdom; we repeat, those bishops should be driven out of the country. They are unworthy of respect. Ireland in its fight for liberty has its clergy in front leading! American Negroes in their fight for life and liberty, have their clergy skulking and cringing, making appeals to them to continue as slaves. Such a clergy does not deserve the respect of savages. We believe in order and law. We desire all men to live up to this standard. But we demand of the colored race to protect themselves at all hazards! Gentlemen, you are not rioting, but are doing your duty. It is the duty of municipalities where rioting is, to force white men to respect the law. What a contrast! White ministers are not rushing into print advising their people to be law-abiding and orderly. Judges and officers of the law are not appealing to white men to desist from mobbing colored people. The militia is sent for when they see colored men 'mopping up the white trash.' But Negroes of every shade are giving advice to colored men 'to stop.' Don't heed the infamous cowards! Protect your homes. Don't start anything but when something is started make it hot for them and finish it!" [51]

*Much of Bitterness.* Having scanned a great many Negro papers I have come to the conclusion that there is much more of bitterness over injustices and lynching than most white people know. We have so long thought of the Negro as a docile person it is hard for most men to understand that he really and truly means to fight.

[51] Quoted from Kerlin: "The Voice of the Negro," pp. 16-17.

*The Challenge of* New York (October, 1921) says:

"Every day we are told to keep quiet.
"Only a fool will keep quiet if he is being robbed of his birth-right. Only a coward will lie down and whine under the lash if he, too, can give back the lash.
"There is little pity from the strong for the one that is weak. There is no altruistic religion in the soul of the strong for dispensation among the weak. The only pity obtained is that obtained by superior strength.
"America hates, lynches, enslaves us not because we are black, but because we are weak. A strong, united Negro race will not be mistreated any more than a strong united Japanese race. It is always strength over weakness, might over right.
"But with education comes thought, with thought comes action; with action comes freedom.
"Read! Read! Read! Then when the mob comes, whether with torch or with gun, let us stand at Armageddon and battle for the Lord." [52]

One paper, the *New York Age* (November, 1919) advocates boycott of work in any community which does not give the Negroes justice:

"What should be the method of meeting the present reign of terror and all the other forces against the race? *A combination of forces on the part of the Negro.*
"Suppose the Negroes of the United States had in one efficiently conducted organization for the protection of their rights a million members—and a million is not more than they ought to have in such an organization—individual colored men who were threatened would not need to stand in their own puny strength, they could stand in the strength of organization.
*Method of a Boycott.* "See how such an organization could be made to work now. Take the situation in Jacksonville, Florida, where it is reported that several prominent colored men have been warned to leave the city. Suppose the organization we suggest existed, and had, say, ten thousand members in Jacksonville —that is not too many for a city with more than sixty thousand colored people. The Jacksonville branch of the organization could say to the white people of the city, *'We hold you responsible for the safety of these men, and we intend to see that they are protected.'*
"The declaration to protect the men who might be threatened need not necessarily be backed up by any show of physical force;

[52] Quoted from Kerlin: "The Voice of the Negro," p. 19

and *an organization of such proportions could bring enough industrial pressure to make good its declaration.*   Suppose they should
say, *'If these men are harmed or forced to leave the city, not a
meal will be cooked, not a garment will be washed, not a team
will be hitched, not a brick or a piece of timber will be moved,
not a nail will be driven by any Negro until justice is done.'*

"That would be a general strike, and an organization such as
we have been discussing would have the power to call it.   We
know of nothing that would be more effective.   *A threat by the
Negroes in any Southern city to make the white people do their
own work would carry greater terror than a brandishing of shot-
guns."*

*Against Lynching.*   The whole question of lynching arouses
the bitter resentment of the Negro press.   Their bitterness is all
the more intense because they have no protection against the
aggression of white men among their own women.   *The Chicago
Defender* (November, 1919) quotes an editorial from *The Hawkeye,* a Negro paper of Savannah, Georgia:

"The Savannah, Ga., Hawkeye, in printing the story of the
death of a wealthy and influential citizen, but brings to light
one of the thousands of similar cases.   It says: 'Dying as he
had lived, with the Colored woman next to his heart, Mr. F. H.
Chaplin, the wealthy Savannahian, left his entire estate to Bessie
Lee, the Negro woman that had lived with him as his wife for
thirty-seven years.   A son thirty-five years old, with a bunch of
children, also survives Chaplin.   His children pass as Colored in
the community.   Bessie Lee, his Colored wife—as she was—is
made the administratrix without bond, and she will take charge
of his estate and proceed to enjoy the fruits of her life with the
man who couldn't be her legal husband because she was a
Colored woman and he a white man.   That hundreds of other
cases exist here is the belief of the old-timers, who know what
the habits of certain rich men are.   In the old days to have a
Negro wife was considered the first cut of a gentleman.'

"Here is a confession in a southern newspaper with a sting
to it for many a soul below the Mason and Dixon line, but
it is true, nevertheless.   What an upheaval there would be if the
masks could be ruthlessly torn from pretenders.   Men occupying
the highest positions in the gift of man on down the scale to the
loathsome 'cracker.'   Wouldn't it be fun to sit in the gallery
where this motley mass gathered and list to them devising ways
and means for making black the standard color and erasing the
stigma they themselves helped to put on this shade.   If the
prejudiced white man knew what we really think about him and

how little we care for his threats he wouldn't be puffed up and be the bag of wind he is. He grows big today because he thinks he is riding on the wave of popular sentiment. But right must eventually prevail, and when it does, where is he?"

*Negro Press Loyal.* The *Baltimore Daily Herald* (November 1919) declares that the Negro editors are not radicals, but are as loyal as any American citizen:

"The report of the Bureau of Investigation is going to be used as the basis for a new propaganda against Negroes and charges of radicalism, Bolshevism, and I. W. W. affiliations will be substituted for the overworked and worn charge of criminal 'assault' and 'rape' and will furnish new and sympathetic grounds for immunity for lynchers; therefore it ought to be promptly challenged by a united array of Negro editors and publishers."

*Attempting to Provoke Thought.* The Negro press is determined to make the Negro people think, observe, and then act. It believes that continual protestation against wrongs and injustices will ultimately bring redress. It believes that the whole Negro race must stand together—if need be it must die together fighting for liberty. If fighting for liberty is radical then the whole Negro press is radical. If fighting for justice and an opportunity to develop is patriotism, then the Negro press is aflame with patriotism. These papers as I have said are not primarily newspapers, they are race papers. They are a call to race consciousness. They are a spur to race achievement. They are even a call to race militarism. These papers may be a great blessing or they may be a great curse. It seems the white people are the ones in position to decide which. If real justice shall be done, if the Negro shall be given a square deal, the ground will be cut from under any who may be radical, but if lynchings and injustices continue to occur, we may count on it this will be fertile soil from which the rankest crop of radicalism will spring.

As never before in his history the Negro is finding self expression. In music, poetry, art, in books and in the press he is saying what he thinks. He is no longer the silent, suffering, cringing person we once knew. He is boldly speaking his mind, and it behooves the American people to give earnest heed to his voice. The Negro race has come to its own in self expression, and in so doing has proven that it is not a dying race but one filled with the strength of an advancing civilization.

CHAPTER XVI

## NEGRO LEADERSHIP AND SELF DETERMINATION

*Africa Lacks Leaders.* One reason why Africa has remained almost stagnant during the passing centuries lies in the fact that superstition has systematically killed off all her leaders. No sooner does a man make a step forward in an African tribe than people begin to suspect him of using witchcraft to accomplish his extraordinary feats. He is soon put to the poison test and eliminated. No nation or people can make progress which has such a perfect machine for eliminating leadership.

*Hero Worship.* Hero worship is instinctive to all men. We speak of the boy "passing through" the period of hero worship— but the truth is he never emerges on the other side. All men worship at the shrine of their heroes. Without leadership with vision the people perish. The greatest single gift to any group is a real leader. Life is born from within and not from without. We cannot superimpose a program of life on any people, but such life must spring up from within and be sponsored by its own leadership. Every race has produced leaders, and indeed it would be impossible for any large group to maintain a solidarity of life without the influence of leadership.

*Negro Capacity for Leadership.* The Negro race in America early showed its capacity to produce leaders. Richard Allen, the first ordained Negro bishop of America, was a man of real power. Nat Turner and Vesey, the leaders of insurrections, were clear proof that the Negro had ability to lead. We have referred to Bishop Capers' estimate of Henry Evans as a preacher of rare power.

*Leaders of Power.* Edward Pollard, of Virginia, published in 1859 a volume called "Black Diamonds," in which he sets forth the real worth and true leadership of many slave Negroes. Toussaint L'Ouverture, of the Island of Haiti, has often been called the Napoleon of the West, and indeed a careful study of his life and his struggles to liberate his people shows him to have been a man of genuine leadership. Under the conditions of slavery there were few opportunities for developing initiative or leadership, yet the head man on scores of plantations was a Negro who because of native ability and worth of character had won a position of trust and influence. Certainly the achievements of the slave would lead us to expect capacity for leadership in the Negro race.

*Condition of Growth of Leadership.* The prime condition for the growth of leadership is pride of race, and consciousness of kind. No group can work together that does not believe in itself. Nor will any group follow the lead of one of their own number so long as they believe all the race is of inferior mold. The Negro must become conscious of himself and his own race before he can grow into a group of power. We will, therefore, look with interest to see if the Negro is developing a consciousness of his own race solidarity. We do not mean by this a narrow egotism or exclusiveness. As I said in an earlier volume:

*Race Pride Not Race Separation.* "Race pride, race consciousness, and race coöperation do not mean race segregation. The fact that one is an Anglo-Saxon does not cut him off from interest in and sympathy with the whole world. It simply gives a vantage ground from which the characteristics of other races may be serenely reviewed. A man is more of a world citizen because he is a good American, and likewise a man is more thoroughly sympathetic with humanity because he belongs to, works for, and is a genuine part of, one group of the human family.

"Therefore, when we talk about the growth of race pride and race consciousness on the part of the American Negro, we do not mean that he will be less an American, but more a Negro. He is more a Negro that he may be more an American. He is not less interested in humanity because he finds himself interested in his own race, but the very fact of his race appreciation gives him a new consciousness of the dignity of all human kind. Thus it seems clear that if the Negro is ever to become efficient, it must be because he shall come to realize the value and worth of his own race. We cannot hope to make a people worthy so long as they expect to be nothing and do not believe in themselves." [1]

*Signs of Race Pride.* There are many signs of a growing race consciousness. Dr. Washington tells us that as a young man he heard so many hard things said about the Negro that he almost despaired and thought once of running away from the whole matter by leaving America. Later he concluded "that the world must come to respect the Negro for just those virtues for which some people say he is despised, namely because of his patience, his kindliness, and his lack of resentment toward those who do him wrong and injustice." [2] The very fact that his people were

---

[1] The author's "Present Forces in Negro Progress," p. 37.
[2] Washington: "The Story of the Negro," Vol. I, p. 12.

criticized and often suffered injustice finally drove Washington to the determination to throw in his lot with his own people, and to work for them with a tireless energy and growing enthusiasm until the day of his death. Speaking of his love for his people he said:

"What I have said here of my own feelings in regard to my race is representative of the feelings of thousands of others of the black people of this country. Adverse criticism has driven them to think deeper than they otherwise would about the problems which confront them as a race, to cling closer than they otherwise would have done to their own people, to value more highly than they once did, the songs and the records of their past life in slavery. The effect has been to give them, in short, that sort of race pride and race consciousness which, it seems to me, they need to bring out and develop the best that is in them.

"Perhaps it will not be out of place for me to say here, at the beginning of this book, that the more I have studied the masses of the race to which I belong, the more I have learned not only to sympathise but to respect them. I am proud and happy to be identified with their struggle for a higher and better life." [3]

*Moton Proud of His Race.* Dr. R. R. Moton, who succeeded Washington as principal at Tuskegee, tells us in his autobiography of his trip abroad and his observations. He was, of course, keenly aware of the injustice in America, particularly of lynching, and saw that it was scarcely practiced in any other part of the civilized world. However, when he returned to America he says:

"At the end of this trip I landed on American shores with a feeling that whatever may be the disadvantages and inconveniences of my race in America I would rather be a Negro in the United States than anybody else in any other country in the world. My subsequent experiences abroad have confirmed me in this conviction." [4]

It is a most significant fact that the best trained Negroes are those who are most intensely interested in their own people. If you wish to find yourself the subject of scornful denunciation, suggest to a group of trained and self-respecting Negroes that they desire so-called "social equality." I saw a governor of the South who was a real friend of the Negro place himself in that most embarrassing position once by reminding a group of Negro leaders that he did not believe in intermingling of the races. The severe rebuke they gave him sent him away, I think, with a new sense of the Negro's "pride of race."

[3] Washington: "The Story of the Negro," Vol. I, pp. 13, 15.
[4] Moton: "Finding a Way Out," p. 152.

*Negro Folk Music.* The fact of this growth of racial conscious-ness is well illustrated in the attitude of Negro leaders toward the Negro folk music. There was a time following the Civil War when the Negro would not sing the songs of his people because they revived memories of the unhappy past. But that time is gone. Professor Work of Fisk University, who has done so much to preserve these songs, says that the southern white people who loved this old music kept insisting that it be sung, until the Negroes came to realize its true value. He thinks there is now no danger of the Negro losing this heritage. At Hampton, Tuskegee, Fisk, and at many other institutions these old melodies are now studied and sung by all students. The growth in appreciation of this distinctive Negro music is an indication of a growing pride in the achievements of the race.

*Pride in Negro History.* The Negro is also coming to have a new interest in the history of the Negro peoples. My graduate class in applied anthropology recently visited Tuskegee Institute. Perhaps the most interesting class we saw while there was one on the history of the Negro. Every student in the room—perhaps one hundred—was keenly alert and interested. Pride for the achievement of the Negro people was clearly marked in everything that was said and done. In a number of Negro colleges such courses are now being given, and I am informed by teachers that they prove most popular. The most ambitious attempt to bring into prominence the history of the Negro is that of the "Journal of Negro History," edited by Carter Woodson. It publishes facts about Negro leadership, and is an attempt to give the Negro his proper place in American life.

*Negro Dolls and Race Pride.* There are other indications of growing race pride. Some years ago Dr. R. H. Boyd, of the National Baptist Publishing House in Nashville, undertook a venture of selling real Negro dolls. In order to get Negro dolls made which would represent the Negro people he made a personal visit to Germany to confer with the manufacturers. At first they refused to manufacture such dolls, saying there was no sale for them. But Dr. Boyd persisted, and insisted on real likenesses. He told me he sent scores of pictures of real Negroes to Germany in order that he might get composite likenesses. The venture was most successful. Thousands of dolls were sold each Christmas for a number of years. These Negro dolls were more expensive than the regulation white dolls because made specially to order, but the entire supply of many thousands was sold to Negroes each holiday season, up to the time of the European war, when, of course, the supply was cut off. Fifty years ago this would have been impossible. Negroes wanted white dolls for their children because white carried with it the idea of privilege and advance-

ment.  It is significant that this is now changed, and that the
Negro doll carries with it the sense of race pride and race achievement.

*Negro Turns to His Own Leaders.*  It is also significant that
the Negro people are turning more and more to their own leaders.
Any one visiting Tuskegee will be struck at the present time not
only by the simplicity, beauty, and dignity of the Washington
monument built by a grateful people to their great leader, but as
one visits various class rooms and buildings one is struck by the
fact that every society hall, every class room, has a picture of the
great founder.  Many of these pictures have been placed by
students who honor the memory and achievements of Washington.
They are a clear indication of a growing race pride.  Almost
every country Negro school has a picture of Booker T. Washington.  It appears far more frequently than the picture of George
Washington appears in the white rural school.  Frederick Douglass is also in evidence in every Negro school.  The literature of the
day is filled with references to these characters.  The most marked
case of hero worship is that of Garvey, who planned to build a
Negro World Empire so to speak.  While he was opposed by
many Negro leaders, he had a very large following, and undoubtedly acquired a considerable amount of property for his scheme.
One would hesitate to say whether there is anything worth while
in his scheme or not.

*Negro Biography.*  The number of volumes appearing recently
as studies of Negro biography and Negro achievement is most
remarkable.  "Unsung Heroes," by Elizabeth Ross Haynes, "The
Negro in Literature and Art," by Brawley, "The Negro in
American History," by Cromwell, "A Short History of the
American Negro," by Brawley, "The New Negro," by Pickens,
are among the number of recent volumes.  Dr. DuBois and
Kelly Miller have written extensively of the achievements of the
race.  Dr. C. V. Roman of Nashville, a most brilliant Negro, has
written a volume on "American Civilization and the Negro,"
which is full of appreciation of what the Negro people can and
have done.  One would go a long way to find a more compelling
little volume than one written by Brawley, called "Women of
Achievement," telling just what some of these heroic Negro
women have done and are doing.  Meta Warrick Fuller and Mary
McLeod Bethune are women who should be known to every
American girl, white and black.  Of course, Dr. Washington's
books telling of the achievements of the Negro people are widely
used.  All of these are clear proof that the Negro is awakening
to the sense of his own race growth.[5]

---

[5] For further illustrations of Negro leaders, see the author's "Present Forces
in Negro Progress," Chapter II.

*A New Type of Negro.* There is a New Negro, says Pickens. He is not the old time cringing "darky" who did not believe in himself, but he is a self-respecting man who believes he can really achieve.

"The new Negro is a sober, sensible creature, conscious of his environment, knowing that not all is right, but trying hard to become adjusted to this civilization in which he finds himself by no will or choice of his own. He is not the shallow, vain, showy creature which he is sometimes advertised to be. He still hopes that the unreasonable opposition to his forward and upward progress will relent. But, at any rate, he is resolved to fight, and live or die, on the side of God and the Eternal Verities." [6]

*The Negro and the New Democracy.* The Negro has entered into and absorbed, he perhaps has helped create, the new sense of democracy which is sweeping over the world. We are no longer living in an age of aristocracy. A handful of men might govern a medieval state, but no small group can now long hope to dominate any state, or even any large institution. Democracy is the desire of all to have some share in working out their own destiny. A few years ago Dr. Albion Small wrote a brilliant book called "Between Eras, from Capitalism to Democracy." It was a plea for the right of the laboring man to have some voice in the management of the business in which he was a worker. Since that time scores of big industries have tried this out. It works. It not only produces more goods and better goods, but it does it without loss of time or energy, and with the maximum peace of mind for both owners and workers. It does not take a prophet to see that it is only a question of a few years when every great business in America will be on a democratic basis, in which all men share responsibility.

*Industrial Democracy and Service.* But the real benefit of this industrial democracy lies not in the fact that it produces goods, but that it produces men. Dr. Small contends that industry is not primarily for profit but for service, and that no industry can ultimately prosper which does not get this conception. One of the largest services an industry can render is to develop character in its workers. A business must ultimately be judged not by the dividends it declares, but by the kind of characters it develops. If dividends were the final standard, a saloon would be better than a grocery store, and far better than a private school. But we know that dividends are not the final standard.

There cannot be any doubt that the business of the state is to develop its citizenship. The purpose of the state is not alone to protect its people, and to help them to accumulate wealth. These

[6] Pickens: "The New Negro," p. 239.

are two functions without which a state would be helpless, but they do not include the whole responsibility of the state. Indeed, these two functions are not ends in themselves but means to an end—and that end is development of persons.

In the industrial field there can be little doubt left that those industries develop the best personalities which give all the workers the largest possible share in the management of the business. Fair play, unity of spirit, loyalty alone will develop largest dividends and largest persons.

This same principle of participation in order to develop character is practiced regularly in our best schools and colleges. No real school would think of running now on the old basis of force and compulsion. Teachers and professors no longer attempt to play the rôle of detectives and policemen. We have a system of coöperation in government by which students and faculty work together in carrying out the principles of self-determination. No spy system can handle the discipline of the modern school, first because the students in large measure can outwit it, and secondly because it defeats the program of development of persons which is the sole purpose of a school or college. In the development of a school every teacher knows that school spirit is all important, and that means the students must share in responsibility.

*Democracy and Race Development.* Surely there can be no doubt that this same principle holds in developing a race. There must be participation in responsibility, if we are to get loyalty, coöperation, and character development. England's success as a great colonizer has undoubtedly arisen from this policy of participation. More than any other nation her political sagacity has told her that no people can be well governed which does not find itself in accord with the government. The consent of the governed must become the coöperation of the governed. England has always hunted out the best leaders of each native people and has made them copartners with her in her rule. In so far as she has failed to do this she has failed to rule well, and it is just because she has done this more systematically and more thoroughly than any other European nation that she has been the most successful colonizer.

The lessons from every field are "writ large" for us if we can only read and interpret. If we desire to develop the Negro people into a self-respecting, wealth-producing, law-abiding citizenship, we must as fast as they are able to assume it give them a share in working out their own destiny. No white man or group of white men can work out the destiny of another race. They must, so to speak, lift themselves by their own boot straps. The most the white man can do is to give them a chance for self-development.

This is all the Negro asks, this is the least we should demand he have.

*What the Negro Wants.* What, then, does the Negro want? Or, a better way to put it is, what do we want for him? For it must be evident that no sane southerner can want anything which will keep the Negro from developing his best self. The Negro and the white man live side by side in the South. The retardation of one means the retardation of the other. We cannot keep the Negro down without staying down with him, as Washington so well said. We must for our own development and protection desire to see the Negro grow into self-respect and self-conscious-ness. Edgar Gardner Murphy long ago pointed out that repression would hurt the white man more than it would hurt the Negro:

"An attitude of unreasoning and permanent repression is to us more intolerable than to the Negro. We are too busy, too much interested in other things, too eager for large enterprises and freer minds, to be consumingly engaged in the business of keeping some one down. The thing, moreover, is impossible. Not only is the Negro daily growing stronger, but the whole world will daily add to his strength in direct proportion to the repression which he suffers. The universe—like the peacemaker in the streets—cannot hear our quarrel till the strong man let the weak go. The South will never have its hearing till the fury goes out of certain eyes and the noise of certain of our public men is stilled. As the world takes the Negro's part, as the Negro gains in strength, as the South wearies of its more morbid preoccupations, as the cruder policies of repression begin to tremble in the rigid framework of their terms, the representatives of our reactionary leadership—in the honest but pitiful hysteria of their fears—would seek the remedy in more repression, and would attempt by the shrieking rancor of their appeals to galvanize into further life the old terrors, and to banish into still fainter distances the better angels of our age." [7]

Murphy made an earnest plea for a dual civilization. Two races living side by side, each helping the other and neither begrudging the other any real advancement.

This does not mean social intermingling, for neither Negro nor white man wants this. But it does mean social justice. It is only by giving social justice that we can build up the Negro to where he finds full satisfaction in his own life. In 1910 I wrote a paragraph which I have seen no reason to change:

*Negro Must Be Self-sufficient.* "If we are to have perfect dis-tinctness of life in this section, we must make the Negro sufficient

[7] Edgar Gardner Murphy: "The Basis of Ascendency," p. 47.

unto himself. So long as all honor lies in being associated with the white man, the Negro will want social intermingling. So long as there are none of his own race that can meet him on a high plane and can satisfy the longings of his soul, just so long will he be driven to seek fellowship with white men. But build him up, make him sufficient in himself, give him within his own race life that which will satisfy, and the social question will be solved. The cultivated Negro is less and less inclined to lose himself and his race in the sea of another race. As he develops, he is finding a new race consciousness, he is building a new race pride. He no longer objects to being called a Negro—it is becoming the badge of his race and the mark of his self-sufficiency. We have nothing, therefore, to fear from giving him a chance. With every new chance he becomes more satisfied to live his life within the pale of his own race. If ever the Negro is to become an efficient workman and a real economic factor, it will be because he has so far been elevated in his desires and needs that only constant labor can satisfy his wants. We shall increase his efficiency by increasing his wants. If ever he is to become a good citizen, it will be because he has been so elevated as to desire decency and honor, and not because he fears the law if he lives otherwise. If he is to be kept as a separate and distinct race, without any desire to mingle in social life with the white race, it will be by making his race so self-sufficient that he can find his desires, his ambitions, his social longings satisfied within his own ranks. This must come through the elevation of the whole race." [8]

*We Desire Full Expression of Self for the Negro.* We want for the Negro a chance for the fullest expression of himself, and we want him to share to the fullest in his own self control. We want this because no outside repression can possibly make him what he really is not, and because no outside force can develop in him his latent capacities. Perhaps the reason for the failure of the Negro to coöperate more fully than he has in the administration of the law of the land could be found in the fact that he has no share or voice in it. No college boy will coöperate fully with the faculty in carrying out superimposed rules, and one wonders whether the Negro should be expected to coöperate to the full in carrying out laws about which he has not even been consulted, and about which he is sometimes told he never will be consulted. No faculty, however benevolent or however paternal in its attitude, can secure the following of a student body when that body has no voice, and when it does not even have the right of making its mind known. The whole labor union movement is just an attempt—of course, sometimes a crude attempt, but nevertheless

[8] "Negro Life in the South," pp. 173-4.

an attempt—to express the mind of the laborer on questions of production and distribution. If the present labor unions, because of selfishness, should die, other organizations will spring up to take their places. Labor will never again be left without a voice. Precisely this same thing is taking place among the Negro people. The demand for a share in their self-control will never end until they have reached this goal. Already some such share is being given. In a number of southern cities (notably Knoxville, Tennessee) Negro police have been appointed for the distinctly Negro sections of the city. According to the testimony of the best white men the experiment has worked admirably. Not only do these police know how to follow down and detect crime among their own people better than a white man would know, but they are also getting a coöperation from the Negroes which no white man could ever get. Human nature being what it is, we could not expect any other result. Wherever the experiment has been tried, it seems to be a success so far as I have been able to get the facts.

Not only can the Negro not grow until he has some chance of self-determination, but the white man by his side cannot grow so long as we withhold that power. The two races are inextricably tied together. Edgar Gardner Murphy saw that twenty years ago when he wrote:

*We Need a Strong Negro Race.* "A policy of fixed political humiliation toward any class of our population comports even less with our instincts than with our interests and our laws. There is no place in our American system for a helot class. Our country is a democracy; and whether we will or no we are the inheritors of a Constitution. This is the second irreducible factor of our problem. Not only is the Negro a Negro, and not only is that fact among the realities, but it is also among the realities that the re-creation of our institutions and the transformation of the political and social assumptions of our age are not among our privileges. Nor are such enterprises among our conjectures or desires. We want no fixed and permanent populations of 'the inferior.' We may in every personal or social sense desire separation—that is an issue of personal reserve. It trenches upon no legal or social right. It inflicts no degradation of personal, industrial or political status. It is a dogma, not of repression, but of self-protection and self-development. But to legislate the permanent and indiscriminate political proscription of a whole population is to attempt the refounding of a country which is not exclusively our own, and the revival and reconstitution of an epoch of class autocracy which Jefferson, Washington and Marshall had themselves surpassed. Indeed, our own greater preference is our greater country. The men of the South—whatever may be their political expedients of the moment—have seriously no more interest in the rĕactionary philosophies of caste than in the political conceptions of Nicholas II. If the conscious and deliberate acceptance of such a status by the weaker group be the only condition of 'peace,' then we had better have something less than peace, for it would indicate an absence of manhood in the weaker population far more serious than an inadequate or belated political capacity, and an absence of moral sagacity in the stronger far more costly than any of the conceivable consequences of racial or political disturbance. To rear the population of a stronger race surrounded by an environment of the lowly and the menial is difficult enough, but to rear such a population—virile in spirit and sensitive to the finer instinct of self-dependence— thronged by the *deliberately* menial, by those who are not only inferior, but who have made a compact to be so, by those whose lot is an accepted subordination and a consenting subserviency, would be more difficult by far. The stronger group within the South, as I have already tried to illustrate, has suffered inde- scribably from being pressed upon, from either side, by a weaker racial life; yet this 'fate of the strong' has been light compared to the fate involving that higher racial group which through long periods of time should be subjected to the personal, domestic and industrial contact of a race of men and women wearing the self- accepted and self-approving status of general proscription. It would involve a peril to everything in our life that is self-resource- ful, wholesomely self-respecting and soundly strong. For the member of a weaker race to accept the plain personal fact, in this instance or that, that his race is inferior, that it has incapacities or weaknesses, is one thing; for a whole race deliberately to accept a fixed legal and collective inequality of status in a democracy is quite another thing; a thing as injurious to a stronger group as to a weaker; a thing, moreover, which there is a Constitution to prevent, and (should the Constitution sleep) the quick instinct of the South itself to weigh and to reject." [9]

*The Ballot.* One form of self-determination is the ballot. In the earliest years of slavery, many free Negroes were permitted to vote, but in the early decades of the nineteenth century practically all the states passed laws eliminating that right. Alabama, Arkan- sas, California, Colorado, Florida, Georgia, Illinois, Indiana, Iowa, Louisiana, Michigan, Minnesota, Mississippi, Missouri, Nevada, Ohio, Oregon, South Carolina, West Virginia, Kansas, Kentucky and Texas, North Carolina, and Tenessee had restrictions on Negro voting.[10]

[9] Murphy: "The Basis of Ascendancy," *passim.*
[10] Stephenson: "Race Distinctions in American Law," p. 284 f.

Following 1865 Negroes voted in most of the states, though New York State did restrict his suffrage in 1868, and a number of northern states,—Minnesota, Wisconsin, Iowa, and others were slow about extending the suffrage to Negroes. There were fifteen northern states which restricted Negro suffrage at the time of the ratification of the Fifteenth Amendment.[11] After the passage of this amendment some cases of intimidation of Negro voters are reported in northern states and later on it was practiced on a large scale by the Ku Klux throughout the entire South. It is scarcely necessary to treat the problems of reconstruction in this volume, since any good history of the United States gives the full account of the constitutional amendments and the struggle that grew out of them, and the reconstruction story has been told many times. It is only necessary here to remark that the giving of the franchise to Negroes just out of slavery, illiterate and innocent of all knowledge of governmental affairs, was a colossal blunder. It aroused bitter prejudices which have never been overcome. It was the most cruel thing that could have been done to or for the Negro. It thrust upon him responsibilities for which he had no particle of preparation, and in which, of course, he could be used as the tool of wicked politicians. The situation was all the more critical, and detrimental to the position of the Negro, because most of the white men were at the time disfranchised. This tended to embitter the whites, and the good feeling which existed before the war has never been fully regained. To be sure, the southern white man should have recognized that the Negro was in no sense responsible for the situation. Any race would have acted just as they did in eagerly seizing the chance to express themselves, and any race just out of slavery would likely have been led astray just as easily. Yet we can readily understand how it came about that the southern masters felt rebellious as they saw their former slaves under 'carpet bag' leadership squandering what little cash and credit the southern states had left and administering affairs in a completely inefficient and biased manner. Nor can we condemn the northern man wholly for his blunder. The conditions of the times were not conducive to sober judgment and dispassionate thinking. The North felt sure that the South meant to keep the Negroes in virtual slavery, and giving the Negro the ballot seemed to be the way to prevent this. The South felt that the North was foisting Negro control on it purely as a means of humiliation, and the Negro was the football between the two. All three parties made great mistakes in impugning the motives of the others.

*The Grandfather Clauses.* Out of this bitterness and ill feeling there arose a definite determination on the part of the whites in

[11] Stephenson: "Race Distinctions in American Law," p. 288.

the South that Negroes should not vote, and this ultimately gave basis for the struggle which ended in complete dominance of the white man. In order to carry this dominance to its logical conclusion it seemed necessary legally to eliminate the Negro entirely from politics, and so the famous—or perhaps infamous—"grandfather clauses" came into being.

For a number of years prior to 1890 Negroes were not allowed to vote in southern states, not because it was illegal but because it was not "healthy for them to do so," as one old man put it. They were simply intimidated and did not vote. In 1890 Mississippi adopted a new constitution which did not violate the Federal Constitution by discriminating against the Negro because of color or previous condition of servitude. This document and all others like it, while raising literacy and property qualification standards which eliminated Negroes, provided for white voters, without so naming them, by allowing all who were able to vote before 1860 to continue to vote, or all who were grandsons of veterans of the Revolution, or those who bore arms in defense of their state in the Civil War, or some other such subterfuge. It is readily seen that such clauses would admit all whites and exclude all Negroes. South Carolina thus amended its constitution so as to eliminate Negroes from the vote in 1895; Louisiana in 1898; North Carolina in 1900; Alabama and Virginia in 1901; Georgia in 1908. These famous "grandfather clauses" have stood the test of the supreme court and are considered legal. While they are technically legal, they are unjust to the whole South. They are not unjust to the Negro, for if he has no property and is illiterate he should not vote. They are unjust to the white man because they allow him to vote without proper qualification, and hence remove the incentive which he should have to qualify. They are unjust to the whole section because it condemns us to the rule of demagogues who can play on the prejudice of ignorant people. Cole Blease, Vardeman, and all the other Negro haters who have ridden into office on race prejudice, find their greatest allies in these ignorant and unqualified voters. Perhaps the most harmful effect of the plan is in the sense of injustice created in the mind of the Negro. No people can be happy and prosperous which does not deal fairly and equally with all its individual members. The sense of injustice in the hearts of parts of the people will eat away all unity of life and all common endeavor.

*Negroes Now Voting.* At the present time large numbers of Negroes are acquiring both the property and the educational qualifications to vote, and they are voting. I asked Dr. Booker T. Washington what proportion of the Negroes voted, and he replied he did not know any really qualified Negroes who could not vote. Of course, he added that he knew a good many unqualified white men who voted, also. When Dr. Moton first went to Tuskegee to succeed Dr. Washington, he tells me the judge urged him to register and vote, and Dr. Moton tells me quite a number of both colored men and colored women in Macon County do vote regularly. This power to vote and thus have a share in self-control is much more widespread now than ever before, but, of course, is not universal or anywhere near universal. It is one of the sorest points with the Negro. He is willing that the standards shall be put as high as any one desires, but he feels that when they are set they should apply to whites and blacks alike. In other words, he does not object to exclusion of Negroes because they are illiterate, but he does object to inclusion of whites when they are equally illiterate. Until this sense of injustice is removed there can be no harmony or unity in the South.

*Constructive Suggestion.* Sober judgment seems to dictate that we should raise both our property qualification and our intellectual qualifications. It would seem wise to require four or five times as much property ownership as the states now require, and it would be well to require proof that the voter has completed a certain number of grades in the school. This would at once eliminate a great majority of the Negroes and, of course, many of the whites. This is only right. A popular government is safe only in the hands of an intelligent people. And it is safe in the hands of intelligent people who have character. If such a qualification should be made, then it would be incumbent on those who could vote and control to see that our public schools were so administered as to give not only intelligence but character. When, therefore, the younger generation of Negroes and whites came to the age when they could vote, we would have such a qualified group that no one need really fear the results. The exact plan for such a procedure must, of course, be worked out state by state, in accordance with the conditions maintaining in those states.

*Louisiana Reaction.* Recently in Louisiana Mr. R. G. Pleasants has proposed an amendment to the constitution which he claims stands for "intellectuality as the basis for suffrage." He would allow all to vote "whose ancestors, as shown by historical and anthropological evidence, inhabited any portion of the earth north of the twentieth degree of North latitude, immediately previous to the discovery of America." [12] This is a clear attempt to read the Negro out of politics, not on the basis of illiteracy, but on the basis of race inheritance. Mr. Pleasants seems to think that no peoples south of the said twentieth degree North latitude have ever made much intellectual progress and so he would eliminate the Negro because his ancestor was ignorant, perhaps he would

[12] Cf. Pamphlet: "Intellectuality as the Basis for Suffrage," p. 3.

say incapable.  Of course, he would maintain that the Negro in Africa was ignorant solely on the basis of inferiority and hence his descendant, being inferior, could never attain to true intellectuality.  This seems to be just another phase of the "grandfather clauses," and deserves no more credit than those which have long been in use.  Its pseudo anthropological basis can hardly be justified, even with the support of Mr. Stoddard and Putnam Weale.

*Evils of Disfranchisement.*  Archibald Grimke, himself a Negro, makes a strong plea for the Negro to have a share in his own control.  He first claims this right of at least partial self-control is necessary to take the sense of injustice out of the heart of the Negro.

"No party, no State, no section, can, therefore, deprive him of those rights without leaving in his mind a sense of bitter wrong, of being cheated of what belongs to him, cheated in defiance of law, of the supreme law of the land, and in spite of his just claim to fairer treatment at the hands of his fellow-countrymen. . . .

". . . Does any one think that he will ever cease to strive for the restoration of his rights as an American citizen, and all of his rights, if he rise in character, property and intelligence?  To think the contrary is to think an absurdity.  But if he fall in the human scale in consequence of the wrong done him, he will surely drag the South down with him." [13]

Second, he claims disfranchisement is bad for the South because it degrades labor.  We boast of a good laboring class:

"But to get the best and most out of labor, it must also be free —free to rise or sink in the social scale.  It must have a voice in making the laws under which it lives.  Otherwise, those laws will operate to hinder, not to help it to make the best fight of which it is capable for possession of home and foreign markets.  Without this voice the laws will become more and more unequal and oppressive.  A labor class deprived of freedom, of a voice in government, cannot maintain the advantage which mere intelligence and skill may have gained for it in the struggle for existence.  As it loses freedom, a voice in government, it will lose ultimately its skill, its intelligence as an industrial factor." [14]

*Repression Not Successful.*  It would be hard for a right thinking man to deny these statements.  One reason why the Negro laborer is leaving the South in such large numbers is that he has no voice in his own self-control.  Let me say again that this cannot be brought about hurriedly, and it must be worked out in the light

[13] Grimke: "Why Disfranchisement is Bad," pp. 1, 2.
[14] *Ibid.,* p. 3.

NEGRO LEADERSHIP AND SELF DETERMINATION 439

of local conditions, but it is just as impossible to stem the rising tide of democracy as it is to sweep the tides back with a broom. Either we will give the Negro a larger share in his own control, or we will drive him from the South. If he goes from the South, we must either perish economically or get a new labor supply. What would that labor supply be! Quite probably it would be South European, a group with different language, with a different religion or no religion, with radical conceptions of government or perhaps even worse, and with ideals entirely different from our own. It would seem a bad exchange. Most of us would prefer the Negro who speaks our own language, who believes in our own religion, though like us he practices it rather poorly, who was never known to be anarchistic, who has always been loyal, and whose one real fault, to some, lies in the fact that he is man enough to want to have some share in his own affairs. The choice is clear cut and most of us would prefer the Negro.

*Other Things Wanted.* But there are other ways in which the Negro wants a share in self-government. I have before me as I write five different platforms prepared by five different persons or groups of persons for the Negro people. They are all at one in the urgent plea for fair play to the Negro. They call for a fairer distribution of school facilities; they ask for equal accommodations for equal money in travel; they ask justice in the courts; they ask for destruction of lynching; they want a share in the juries that try Negroes; they want a chance to express themselves in favor of or against the officers who do not give them a square deal. They ask for parks and libraries and claim they help pay for them. They call attention to poor street lighting in the Negro districts, and usually no paving at all. They ask for respect and consideration, and in particular for respect and protection of their women. These demands at first seem large to the white man who has supposed the Negro was satisfied. Not a few white men shut their eyes and declare everything is all right,— there is no unrest. But beneath the surface there is great heart-burning and anguish of soul. Writing in the *Intercollegian,* Dr. Isaac Fisher, of Fisk University, has said:

*New Negro and New Desires.* "The thought that under the beneficent reign of democracy, he (the Negro) will come into possession of privileges long withheld from him has stirred the American Negro to the depths. He has followed the words of the President as he defined, again and again, the objects for which the Allies were fighting; and this same Negro went willingly across the seas to help bring full manhood rights to all nations. Back from war-torn Europe he has sent to his friends in America some notions of the new vision of brotherhood which he has caught in the Valley and Shadow of Death 'over there.' He will never be the same Negro again; and whether we wish it or not, he will have his visions of a kinder, fairer world, day after day, when he lays down the warrior's sword. Whatever else they do not do, I hope that our white people in Dixie who live so close to the colored people here will never again, as they did but yesterday, permit them to dream dreams, to cherish resentments, all alone. Mistakenly, in my weak judgment, the Negro who was willing to say what the Negro wanted was set aside as an undesirable citizen; and the man who said, "All is well with the Negro" was taken to be the good citizen. One day our South awoke, not only those who do not care for us, but those who have carried us in their hearts as well, all awoke to find that *all was not well with the Negro;* and that in a steady stream which has not yet ceased to flow he was severing the ties of a lifetime, turning his back upon the place and people of his birth, and going a stranger into a strange clime to live with a people whom he knew not, simply because all was not well and there had been no ear into which he could pour out his complaints.

*The South Will Meet the Issue.* "I say, not in threat but in prophecy, that soon or late all the things which the Negro wants to say for and about himself will be said. They will be said freely and frankly right here in the South by the Negroes who love this part of the Union and feel kindly toward their white friends with whom they have lived all their lives; or they will be said elsewhere by colored men whose hearts overflow and whose voices choke with bitterness against the Land of the Magnolias. I believe that it will be better to have these words said—the Negro's case pleaded—right here by colored people whom we know; and we can make no greater mistake than to penalize into sullen silence, by applying reproachful terms to them, those who wish to talk frankly to our white neighbors of the planks in the Negro's platform." [15]

*Has the White Man all Political Wisdom?* After all, why should the white man be so sure that he alone has political wisdom? Why should he suppose that no other race has any contribution to make to civilization? Mr. Philip Ainsworth Means has made a plea for openmindedness in his "Racial Factors in Democracy." He claims that we will never have a true democracy until we are willing to get the best that the whole world has to offer, and weave it into a consistent whole for ourselves. But this at once takes for granted that all races and groups do have something to contribute. We have been prone to suppose the Negro had no contribution to make. But that may be simply our egotistical assumptions. Perhaps he has not made much contribution because we have not given him a chance. If given more of an opportunity he might

[15] Isaac Fisher: "Christian Justice and the Negro."

add as much to our civic and business life as he has added to our music.  At least he should have the chance to try.

*Negro Has Shown Political Leadership.*  It is not true, as was shown in an earlier chapter, that the Negro has never developed any governmental life.  Wherever conditions of intercommunication have been favorable he has built up strong and enduring governments.  Perhaps we have jumped to our conclusions about his inability to govern, largely on the basis of our own desire to govern.  The wish has been father to the thought.  We hear the oft-repeated statement that this is a white man's country.  Not so by any inheritance—but only by virtue of his using it to bless all humanity.  This is not the white man's country.  It is the country of all those who by character and loyal endeavor help to make it the land of happiness, plenty, and freedom.  Any man who can contribute to that end has a rightful share in this country.  We took it from the Indian because he was using it poorly; we should share it with all who are willing to help make it all that it is capable of becoming.

*All the People Needed.*  To develop the South all the people will be needed.  We will need the loyal endeavor of blacks as well as whites.  To get the best from all, we must share the best with all.  In such a sharing the white man need have no fear.  He is twice as numerous as the blacks, he has thousands of years the start in the race.  He surely can hold his own.  But there is a deeper basis for believing that only good will come from trusting all the people and that reason is the fundamental belief we have in the essential worth of all peoples.  "Everything I know about history," said Woodrow Wilson, "every bit of experience and observation that has contributed to my thought, has confirmed me in the conviction that the real wisdom of human life is compounded out of the experiences of ordinary men." [16]  Again he says: "I am one of those who absolutely reject the trustee theory, the guardianship theory.  I have never found a man who knew how to take care of me, and reasoning from that point out, I conjecture that there isn't any man who knows how to take care of the people of the United States." [17]  No one can take care of the people of the United States for the simple reason that any people which is taken care of, which does not take care of itself, soon falls into decadence.  No man can grow who does not have forced upon him the responsibility of his own life.  If we of the South want the Negroes to develop into industrial and economic usefulness, if we want them to become a law-abiding and liberty-loving people, if we want them to become a people within whose bounds they find life and satisfaction, then we must give them increasingly a chance to express themselves, for in so doing alone can they be expected to grow into larger life.

[16] Wilson: "The New Freedom," p. 79.
[17] *Ibid.,* p. 61.

Chapter XVII

## CONSTRUCTIVE MOVEMENTS

*No Patent Solution.* "What is your solution to the race question?" is frequently hurled at those who are interested in inter-racial understanding, as if any great human question had any patent solution. I always frankly admit that I have no final solution, and that I doubt the sanity of any man who claims he has one. No problem involving the interrelation of human beings can ever be solved once for all, for the very obvious reason that persons will not stay "put." No sooner do we think we have it all worked out than a new element arises, such as a change in social sentiment or a variable of psychic response which we had not taken into account. But when we say there cannot be a final solution put into formulas it does not mean we cannot see clearly the path we must travel if we are to approach a more harmonious relationship. Every real student of human society discerns clearly, it seems to me, some general laws which must govern us if we are to approach the goal of our search. No quick or patent method may be found, but principles of procedure may be dis-covered. We would naturally look for these principles to be evolved out of the experimentations of earnest workers who, with open minds and earnest hearts, have been launching on the great adventure of bringing about a mutual helpfulness and good will among the races.

*Light Through Experience.* As in every other great question, most light has come through the process of doing the next thing. Dr. Wallace Buttrick, of the General Education Board, in summing up the five most characteristic factors in the achievement of Dr. Booker T. Washington, states this as one: "He early learned that one contributes best to the progress of human civilization by 'doing the next thing.' " [1] This is not opportunism, as Dr. Buttrick well points out, it is the method of experimentation on which all science, indeed all progress, is built. We cannot know all the factors of life and hence cannot lay down a full philosophy which will be once for all complete. If we can do the thing which now seems to us to be right—the truth and the way will gradually emerge. It has been in this spirit that each forward step has been taken, and the way is slowly becoming clearer.

[1] *The Southern Workman,* December, 1922.

*Conference for Education in the South.* One of the first experimentations in good will for the Negro was that of the Conference for Education in the South, organized by Dr. J. L. M. Curry and Dr. Hollis B. Frissell. These men who were interested in all the children of the South, white and black alike, felt that the whole people should be aroused to the ignorance which maintained, and which was holding back the section from its rightful influence in the nation. Mr. Robert C. Ogden, the untiring supporter and leader in this movement, at the Fourteenth Conference held in Jacksonville, Florida, in 1911, declared:

"It is a loose-jointed organization—too loose-jointed—having no written constitution, no by-laws, no dues, no conditions of membership. Its object is to develop interest in public education, especially in rural districts, to create such intelligent public opinion as will improve the laws, uplift the standard of the schools, augment taxation and appropriation for education, and thus push forward the chances for the training in intelligence and morals of every child throughout the Southland, thus bringing each child of every race, whether American or foreign born, into its birthright of a good English education." [2]

*Influence of this Conference.* This conference, during its twenty years of existence, powerfully influenced public sentiment in favor of popular education, and this, of course, included the Negro child. While the organization had no money to give away, it influenced the raising of millions of dollars through public taxation and through private donations. Through it a renaissance of education in the South was begun. More than many people know, this conference influenced the various boards, such as the Jeanes Board, the Slater Board, and the General Education Board, in finding a wise procedure for helping the Negro in his forward struggle. The work of these boards has already been discussed under the head of Negro Training. In this connection we cannot omit a reference to a whole group of schools which—while, of course, educational—are doing a far-reaching work in bringing about better relations between white and colored people in the South. Such a school is that of Mrs. Bethune, at Daytona, Florida, known as the Daytona Normal and Industrial Institute. This school has been literally "prayed up, sung up, and talked up." By its cleanliness, its emphasis on efficiency, and by its ideals it has helped colored people to believe in themselves and, of course, the result has been a new belief in them on the part of the white people. Another such remarkable institution is Penn School on St. Helena Island, South Carolina, under the leadership

[2] Proceedings of the Fourteenth Conference for Education in the South, p. 61.

of two remarkably cultured and efficient white women, Miss Rossa B. Cooley and Miss Grace Bigelow House. To see the way they have influenced the whole Island for better living, not only gives one confidence in the school, but gives a new faith in the people for whom the school works. These are typical of scores of other schools which have done more than almost any other single influence to convince the white people that the Negro can become efficient and useful, and hence is worthy of a place in American life. In this sense these institutions are potent social forces making for a better understanding between the races.

*Mr. Little's Work—Louisville, Ky.* A peculiarly interesting work has been carried on in Louisville, Kentucky, under the very able leadership of Reverend John Little. While this work is local in extent, it is far reaching in its influence as demonstrating how good feeling may be worked out between the races. Mr. Little is an Alabama man, the son of former slaveholders, a graduate of the University of Alabama, and of the Presbyterian Theological Seminary in Louisville. While a student in the seminary he undertook a piece of Sunday school work for Negro children, in one of the neglected sections of the city. The work grew rapidly, so that it had taken on considerable proportions by the time Mr. Little was ready to graduate. The Negro people were eager that he should continue his work and offered to coöperate in every way possible. Mr. Little decided to stay, and has now been at work there for more than twenty years. He now has three mission stations with large attendance at each, he is carrying forward industrial training for hundreds of boys and girls, he has established baths for the Negroes of those congested districts, he has helped raise funds for Negro libraries, and is in every way the friend and advisor of the Negroes of the city. If every city in the South had a man like Mr. Little at work in its midst, there would be very little real friction between the races. This work is chiefly significant in that it shows how mutual understanding and good will grow out of mutual helpfulness and not out of philosophizing about the relationship.

*The Southern Sociological Congress.* Another agency which had much to do with a better understanding between the races was the Southern Sociological Congress, organized in Nashville, Tennessee, under the patronage of Mrs. E. W. Cole and Governor Ben Hooper, with Mr. J. E. McCulloch as its executive officer. It at once offered the broadest platform which had ever been offered in the South for whites and blacks to meet face to face and talk out their difficulties. Successful annual meetings were held at Atlanta, Memphis, Houston, Birmingham, New Orleans, Washington, and other places. The full published reports of these congress meetings formed a nucleus of vital literature on the subject of race relations which was a real stimulus to study and friendly action. It is to be regretted that the organization lost its original vision and got switched to other subjects perhaps not so vital. It, however, did a great work and set the cause of mutual understanding forward many steps.

*The University Race Commission.* The University Race Commission, organized by Dr. James H. Dillard, under the patronage of the Phelps-Stokes Fund, has brought together for a number of years official representatives of all the southern state universities. The purpose is to study the conditions of the Negro and, if possible, to help bring about among university students a better understanding of the white man's obligation to the Negro of to-day. The Commission has issued a number of open letters on questions of lynching, Negro education, Negro migration, and similar topics. It attempts to bring about larger interest on the part of university faculty men. It is coöperating in encouraging the study of race relations in the departments of sociology, economics, or history. At the present time members of the Commission are working on a source book of information which will supplement various text books to be used in curriculum studies.

*The Southern Publicity Committee.* Some years ago the Southern Publicity Committee was organized with Mrs. John D. Hammond as secretary. The Phelps-Stokes Fund furnished money for carrying forward this work. The purpose was to gather news about Negro achievements and release this in prepared form to magazines, newspapers, and other periodicals. This was an attempt to overcome the handicap under which the Negro labors due to unfair publicity. The Negro feels that his achievements are rarely mentioned in the white press, but his misdeeds are given great prominence. This not infrequently happens. It was felt that many papers would print stories of achievement if provided with them. This proved to be the case, and hundreds of southern papers did carry these news stories. This is significant in that it shows how little the whites and blacks know of the life of each other. The average newspaper has no method of finding out what the colored people are doing. No reporters follow their lives, and most white newspapers do not have the colored papers on their exchange tables. The service rendered was, therefore, a vital one.

*Other Publicity Agencies.* This same service is now being carried forward by the Interracial Commission, under the special direction of Mr. Robert B. Eleazer, a man of high social vision and insight. Two other organizations which were working in the field of publicity were the Tennessee Law and Order League, under the leadership of Dr. Edwin Mims of Vanderbilt University, and the Mississippi Welfare League directed by Mr. J. C.

Wilson, Mr. Alfred Stone, and Senator Percy. These organizations in the respective states attempted for a few years to meet the need of giving more publicity to the evils of lynching, and to bring to bear on the public the influence of a constructive statesmanship for right attitudes.

*Negro Movements.* Among the Negro peoples themselves many organizations have sprung up. First we have those which are attempting to develop a race unity by showing what the Negro has done in the past. Notable among these are the Negro Society for Historical Research, The American Negro Academy, and the Association for the Study of Negro Life and History. Other societies for bringing about coöperation among Negroes are: The National Negro Press Association, The International Uplift League, The National Association of Colored Women, The National Association for the Advancement of Colored People, The National Urban League, The National Association of Negro Musicians, The National Negro Business League, The National Negro Bankers Association, The National Negro Medical Association, The National Association of Colored Graduate Nurses, The National Home Finding Society, The National Funeral Directors Association. The Interstate Association of Negro Trainmen of America, and a score of state organizations like the Negro Organization Society of Virginia, and State Anti-Tubercular Associations. Such a list as this is clear proof that the Negro is feeling out for a solidarity and unity of life, and that he is learning to work coöperatively.[3]

*The Churches' Contribution.* Almost every church in America is doing something for the Negro through its various boards. The greatest weakness in this work is the scattered nature, its lack of integration into the life of the South, and the fact that it is often *for* the Negro instead of *with* the Negro. But a great volume of splendid work has been done, for which all must be profoundly grateful. Among others, the following boards and societies are actively at work:

1. American Baptist Home Missionary Society.
2. Woman's American Baptist Home Mission Society.
3. American Church Institute for Negroes (Episcopalian).
4. American Missionary Association (Congregationalist).
5. Freedmen's Aid Society (Methodist Episcopal).
6. Woman's Home Missionary Society, M. E. Church.
7. Board of Missions, Methodist Episcopal Church, South.
8. Board of Church Extension of the M. E. Church, South.
9. Women's Home Missionary Council, M. E. Church, South.

For description of the work of each ot these organizations see the author's pamphlet on "Interracial Coöperation," published by the Interracial Commission.

10. Executive Committee of Home Missions of the Southern Presbyterian Church.
11. The Woman's Auxiliary of the Southern Presbyterian Church.
12. Board of Freedmen's Missions of the United Presbyterian Church of North America.
13. Board of Directors of the Women's General Missionary Society of the United Presbyterian Church of North America.
14. Board of Home Missions of the Reformed Church in the United States.
15. Five Years Meeting of the Friends of America.
16. Board of Colored Missions of the Synodical Conference of North America.
17. Mission Board of the Christian Church.
18. Christian Women's Board of Missions.
19. American Christian Missionary Society.
20. Board of Missions for Freedmen of the Presbyterian Church in the United States of America.
21. Southern Baptist Convention, Home Mission Board.
22. Home Mission Council Committee on Negro Work.
23. International Sunday School Association.
24. Catholic Boards.
25. Colored Work Committee of the Y. W. C. A.
26. Colored Men's Department, International Committee Y. M. C. A.[4]

*Training Social Workers.* One of the most significant developments of recent years has been that of training social and religious workers. The Presbyterians have Stillman Institute at Tuscaloosa, Alabama; the Southern Methodist Church has Paine College in Augusta, Georgia; the Southern Baptists are just now establishing a theological seminary in Nashville, Tennessee, for Negroes.

The Atlanta School of Social Service, for training social workers among Negroes was organized in 1920. The impulse for this school came from the National Conference of Social Workers meeting in New Orleans that year. The first year there were fourteen students and the school bids fair to make a real contribution. Courses are offered in economics, social problems, home economics, social research, social case work, medical social problems, and kindred topics.

*Libraries, Parks and Playgrounds, Etc.* The movement for public libraries, parks and playgrounds open to Negroes is making real

[4] For description of the work of each of these, see the author's "Interracial Coöperation."

headway.  Twelve years ago when I made a careful investigation of twenty southern cities, there were few libraries, fewer parks and playgrounds.[5]    Now almost every southern city of any size has made such provision for its Negro population.

*Movement for Industrial Betterment.*  Perhaps even more significant than any of these is the development in industry of plans for caring for Negro industrial workers.  These workers are growing more and more numerous and they live in congested cities.  Without proper environment they may become a great menace, but with proper attention they may be molded into a great force for righteousness.  The very fact that they live close together makes them a potent influence either for good or for evil.  Perhaps as good an illustration of this kind of work as any other is that done at the American Cast Iron Pipe Company of Birmingham, Alabama.  Here the Company built a large Young Men's Christian Association plant, part of which was turned over to the colored men's department with a secretary in charge, paid by the Company.  In this building there are shower baths for the men when they come from work, there are sleeping quarters where night workers may get a clean bed during the day for ten or fifteen cents, there are rooms for club meetings, recreation rooms, and quarters for religious work.  In addition to this, the Company has coöperated in organizing a boy's band for the Negro boys, it has provided a ball park, and every facility for recreational life is at hand.  There are medical and dental offices manned by competent physicians to look after the health of Negroes as well as white people.  The Company has built a number of model houses with flower yards and gardens attached, and competent instruction is furnished in flower growing and gardening.  There is a plan of profit sharing by which all workers are encouraged to buy stock and share in the benefits of production.  With such a scheme as this it is no wonder that this plant has suffered much less from the northern migration of Negro labor than has many another plant where much less thought is given to the workers.  Many other plants throughout the South are undertaking similar helpful movements.

*Study Classes of Y. M. C. A.*  A most encouraging sign of progress is the new interest in the study of race relations.  In 1910 there appeared a little book meant for a text to be studied by college students in the voluntary groups of the college Young Men's Christian Associations.[6]  It was published with much doubt as to whether students would be interested.  Such a thing had never been tried, and no one knew how it would be received.  Contrary to all expectations, it was eagerly accepted and the first

[5] Cf. the author's "Present Forces in Negro Progress," Ch. VII.
[6] See the author's "Negro Life in the South."

year four thousand students were enrolled in the study of this book. The following year nearly six thousand enrolled in these small groups, and the college women began taking up the study. Since this book and its companion volume [7] were published perhaps thirty thousand white college men and women have studied one or the other of them. It has made a tremendous change in college sentiment. Hundreds of students have undertaken definite service tasks with Negroes during these years. Negro Boys' clubs have been organized, night classes taught, civic discussion groups conducted, and in one university a Negro club house was undertaken.[8] This has brought about a much better understanding between the college students and the Negroes of the community. It is a rare thing now to find any race friction in a university town in the South. The interest in knowing the facts has gone further.

*The Phelps-Stokes Fellowships.* The Phelps-Stokes Foundation has established two scholarships, one at the University of Georgia and one at the University of Virginia, where a graduate student each year works out some special study along racial lines for a Master's degree. Mr. Hill, of the State Department of Education in Georgia, and Mr. Woofter, of the Interracial Committee, were two of the earlier holders of these scholarships.

*Graduate Courses in Race Relations.* When Southern College of Young Men's Christian Associations was chartered in 1919, working in Nashville, Tennessee in coöperation with Vanderbilt and Peabody, one of the first graduate courses established was that of Applied Anthropology, which deals with the question of racial contacts, giving special attention to race relations in the South. The work is graduate in grade and is taken by graduate students in Vanderbilt University as well as students from Vanderbilt School of Religion and Southern College. A number of Master's theses have been inspired by this work, including a careful study of the "Economic Conditions of Negroes in Nashville," "The Negro Boy Problem of Nashville, Tennessee," "Race Psychology as a Factor in Religious Education," "Interracial Coöperation Between the Southern Baptists and the Negro," "The Housing of the Negro in Nashville," and others.[8a]

George Peabody College introduced a chair of race studies in 1921, and a number of students each year do special work under the direction of this professor. Most notable among such students have been Mr. Leo Favrot, now of the General Education Board, New York, and Mr. S. L. Smith, who heads the Rosenwald Rural School Building Fund.

[7] The author's "Present Forces in Negro Progress."
[8] University of North Carolina.
[8a] Bound Mss. in Southern College Library.

*Summer Conferences.* For a number of years there has been held each summer in connection with the Southern Student Conferences of the Y. M. C. A. at Blue Ridge, N. C., and at Hollister, Mo., a professor's conference for the study of racial questions. In all the conferences at Blue Ridge each summer this theme bulks large, so that several thousand people gathering there each year go away with a new sense of responsibility. Special arrangements have been made so that it is possible for a Negro speaker to appear from time to time at Blue Ridge to present the cause of his own race. Dr. Moton of Tuskegee, Dr. Isaac Fisher of Fisk, and numerous others of the best representatives of the race have thus been able to lay their messages on the hearts of some of the South's most influential people.

*Southern Interracial Commission.* The most ambitious movement for better understanding between the races is the Interracial Commission. This Commission sprang out of the needs for readjustment following the war, and due to strained relations between white and colored people—particularly returned soldiers of both races. The Commission is composed of white and colored men, and women, including business men, professional men, college presidents and professors, and representatives of the leading denominations.

*Origin of the Commission.* The first conception of this Commission was to help the colored ex-soldier readapt himself to his surroundings. This of necessity involved bringing about a proper relationship of white and black in the local communities.

Immediately after the armistice a series of ten-day schools was held to study community readjustments and the proper care of the returning soldier. The schools for white representatives were held at Blue Ridge, North Carolina, under the leadership of W. D. Weatherford, where eight hundred and twenty-four men were trained in eight separate schools. The schools for colored leaders were held at Gammon Theological Seminary, in Atlanta, Georgia, under the leadership of W. W. Alexander, where 509 colored men were trained in five separate groups. The funds for these schools were furnished by the War Work Council of the Young Men's Christian Associations.

About half of these men were ministers of the various denominations and a careful program for the follow-up of soldiers through the churches was planned. Using these men thus, trained, the Interracial Commission conceived the plan of organizing in every county of the South a county committee, usually composed of both white and colored men, though at times there were two committees, one of each race, which held occasional joint meetings.

*Work of the County Committees.* These county committees are undertaking to study the specific needs of our communities and so far as possible meet these needs.   They are functioning in specific matters, such as justice before the law, adequate educational facilities, justice in public conveyances, economic justice, and handling any acute situation which arises between the races.

There is a county committee now organized in each of six hundred or more counties where the greatest number of Negroes are concentrated.   There is a State Committee in each state with a chairman and at least part of the time of a paid secretary.   The Commission holds annual meetings where experiences are exchanged and plans of further coöperation are developed.   The executive secretary, Mr. W. W. Alexander, and the publicity secretary, Mr. R. B. Eleazer, together with the representative of the churches, Dr. Haynes, and the woman's secretary, Mrs. Luke Johnson, are in constant communication with the various fields, giving counsel and aid.

*Notable Achievements.*  Many notable achievements have been worked out by the local, state, and the general commission.   Only a few can be listed to show the method of operation.   In Georgia where lynchings have been most serious and frequent for years the Commission determined to follow down and see that prosecutions were carried through.   In the famous Williams Farm Case the Commission was very active in gathering the data and seeing that the prosecution was pushed vigorously.

*Some Results in Georgia.*   "On September 20, 1922, the grand jury of Liberty County returned a bill against the deputy sheriff of Wayne County, the city marshal of Jesup, the city marshal's brother, and the two citizens of Liberty County, indicting them for murder in connection with the lynching of two Negroes whose execution had been stayed for thirty days by Governor Hardwick.

"In the thirty-seven years from 1885 to 1922 there had been, so far as the records show, only one indictment in 437 cases in Georgia.   These indictments returned in Liberty County make a record for 1922 as follows:

Lynching cases.............................    8
Number of cases in which indictments were returned    4
Total number of people indicted...............   22
Total number sent to penitentiary.............    4
Total number to be tried.....................   15

It is significant that the majority of these indictments, as in the case of Liberty County, are for murder.   Hitherto the efforts have been to convict them for riotous assemblage.

"In addition to these cases of actual lynching, there have been several cases in which the mob was unsuccessful.   In two of these cases damage suits have been instituted against members of the mob by the victims and eight men have been indicted." [9]

*Work in Tennessee.* In Tennessee due to an economy campaign the legislature was about to sell a State Industrial School for Negro girls which was just being completed. The State Interracial Committee took the matter up with the Governor, with leading representatives and senators, and had members of the Commission all over the State to write their representatives. After a long hard fight the school was retained. Had there been no organization to stand for the colored people, there is no doubt the school would have been abolished.

*Coöperation With Other Agencies.* In almost every state the county commissions have coöperated fully with the State Board of Health in putting on Health Week. Institutes have been held, special addresses given in churches and Sunday schools, and healthmobiles have toured the counties.

The general Commission has sent speakers to the leading church conferences to present the cause of interracial coöperation. Many communities have been induced to provide better play grounds for Negro children, swimming pools have been provided in certain cities, parks have been opened, and help has been rendered in securing school buildings.

*Woman's Department Organized.* In 1920 a group of southern white women and a few Negro women met in Memphis, Tennessee, under the auspices of the Interracial Commission. The result of this conference was the organization of the woman's department of the Commission. Naturally the women have specialized on the school, the home, the treatment of children, the treatment of women workers, and the care of children. The women's clubs of the South have been interested and great changes of sentiment will surely come from this new force. The Negroes themselves have hailed this movement as the most hopeful sign since the Civil War. Dr. Isaac Fisher, of Fisk University, one of the most brilliant of the Negro leaders of the South, says: "In the history of the South this was the first agency ever set up to give the Negroes and whites a chance to see into each other's hearts on a large scale." While the Young Men's Christian Association were most largely instrumental in organizing this work, and are still giving it large financial support, churches and other agencies have coöperated so as to make it a south-wide movement.

*Other Movements.* There are many other movements on a small scale arising throughout the South, and all testifying to a new interest. The significant fact about all these movements is not primarily the things they have done but the spirit they exhibit. First of all they show that Negroes and whites have once again

[9] Special Report of the Publicity Director.

come to know more of each other. It has often been assumed that the southern white man knows the Negro, but this is far from true. Most white people know only the servant Negro. They know the industrial Negro, but they do not know the teacher, the preacher, the business man, the doctor or the dentist. Long ago Edgar Gardner Murphy realized that it was difficult for the leaders of the two races to know each other. The very conditions of life made this true:

"The white man, North as well as South," says Murphy, "feels —and feels wisely—that the social barrier should remain. So long, however, as it remains it shuts out not only the negro from the white man but the white man from the negro. Seeing the negro loafer on the streets, the negro man or woman in domestic service, the negro laborer in the fields, is not seeing the negro. It is seeing the negro on one side. It is seeing the negro before achievement begins, often before achievement—the achievement which the world esteems—is possible. Knowing the white man only under those conditions would not be knowing the white man. Yet this side of the negro is usually the only side of which the white community has direct and accurate knowledge. It is the knowledge of industrial contact, and of industrial contact upon its lower plane. It is not the knowledge of reciprocal obligations, of social revelation. And at the point where this lower contact ceases, at the point where the negro's real efficiency begins, and he passes out of domestic service or unskilled employment into a larger world, the white community loses its personal and definite information; the negro passes into the unknown. As the negro attains progress, he, by the very fact of progress, removes the tangible evidence of progress from the immediate observation of the white community. Thus the composite idea, the social conception of the negro which is beginning to obtain among us, is determined more largely by the evidence of negro retrogression or negro stagnation than by the evidence, the real and increasing evidence, of negro advancement." [10]

*Need to Bring Races Together.* This being the situation, it is urgently important that opportunities be given for the best elements of the two races to come face to face with each other. All of these movements are just so many attempts of the leaders of the two races to come to understand each other, and this is decidedly wholesome.

*A New Respect Between the Races.* These movements also point to a new respect arising between the races. If you do not respect a man you will not spend much time discussing his

[10] Murphy: "The Present South," p. 167.

difficulties with him, or helping him meet those difficulties.  We
have evidently come to the place where the white man of the
South does not fear to respect the Negro.  Considering him a man,
or giving him a man's title, it was once thought, would lead
directly to "social equality."    That seems silly enough to us
now.   But it has not always been so simple.   Men have been
afraid to recognize the Negro as a man lest he might get out of
his so called "place."   But the best South has come to the conclusion that we cannot elevate ourselves by pushing the Negro down.
We have come to the conclusion that if it is right to help the
Negro up we will do it and let the future take care of itself.
Doing right now is not apt to bring evil after awhile.   At least
we cannot hedge the universe about with our restrictions.   We
cannot look forward and determine what shall be a hundred years
from now.   Our sons and grandsons will do that according to
their own way of thinking, whether we like it or not.   "If you
educate the Negro," says one, "will he not want social equality?"
Well, if you mean a man's chance to live, I think he will ; but if
you mean he will prefer white company to black company, I would
say no.   He has a pride in his own race just as I have in mine.
He sees no reason why black is not as honorable as white.   God
never proclaimed white as the only good color ; it was the white
man who did that.   Anyhow, training alone can secure safety in
a democracy.   Only the intelligent can live side by side without
crime.   It is my duty to do the next thing as I see it, and trust
those who come after to have as much wisdom, as much Christian
spirit, and as much sense of justice as I have.   They will in all
probability have more and hence can deal with the questions of
the next century better than I can.   I must do my duty now and
trust the results to God and future humanity.   This is the clear
message of these movements toward understanding.

*Humanity of the Negro.*   Yet again these attempts at service
to another race are an indication that we have come to believe the
Negro is worthy to be served.   We no longer think of him as a
beast of burden.   The better South recognizes him as a human
being with all the aspirations of soul that a white man has.   He is
human—just plain human.   I am interested in the Negro not
because he is a Negro, but because he is a man.   He has a personality just as I have and is capable of becoming a growing and
progressing person.   All men are not born equal.   Indeed, no two
men are ever exactly equal.   Equality is a matter of character
and not of birth.   The fact that any being has personality means
that he may grow in character.   I have known some Negroes
whose character was above reproach.   Every southern white man
has known at least one such Negro.   It is this which these forward
movements represent.   They mean that we are no longer going

to quibble over straw men, we are not going to waste our time on impossible situations of social mingling, but we are eager to put our hands to constructive tasks.

*Growing Confidence.* Lastly, these movements mean, it would seem, a growing of confidence on the part of each race in the other. This confidence we say is growing. It could not fail to grow when two people come to know each other. There is enough of good in all people that a real knowledge of them makes for confidence. It was almost pathetic, the confidence expressed in the will of an ex-slave who died recently:

*A Notable Will.* "James McAllister, aged 94, one time a slave in the Fuller family of North Carolina, died recently, leaving his humble estate by will to W. W. Fuller, of New York, one of his 'white folks.' 'I do this,' read the will, 'for the reason that Mr. Willie Fuller has always helped me when I needed it and has been my nearest and best friend. My wife, now deceased, belonged to his father and mother. It was my pleasure to be near the family during and after the war, and the intimacy that sprang up between me and Mr. Willie, then a small boy, has been continued through life. When I was in trouble and needed either help or advice I knew where to turn, and Mr. Willie never failed me.' " [11]

*Conclusions.* To those who can discern the meaning of things it is clear that a new light is dawning. Men are coming to desire a larger knowledge of all other men. Wise men realize that each group has a contribution to make to the world's civilization, and the sooner all groups can be brought to efficiency the sooner will the whole world be blessed with such contributions. Neither individuals nor races work out their destinies alone, but in coöperation. Dr. Bliss, of Beirut College, once said, "All the world needs all the rest of the world." Working together for the good of all each race may have its individual life and yet live in peace and harmony—yes, in helpfulness to the other races, which lives by its side. It behooves every true lover of his land to strive to know better all its peoples, to help each and all in the struggle upward, envying no man his success, hating none, blessing and blessed by all.

[11] Quoted from "Good Will," published by the Commission on Interracial Coöperation.

CHAPTER XVIII

REVIEW OF SOURCES

ON THE DEVELOPMENT OF MAN

FOLKWAYS—Sumner, *Ginn & Co.*
This is a very full and careful study of the customs and modes of life of primitive peoples. It throws light on the way in which customs arise and the degree to which they affect the life of a race.

THE MIND OF PRIMITIVE MAN—Boas, *Macmillan Company*
"Proud of his wonderful achievements, civilized man looks down upon the humbler members of mankind. He has conquered the forces of Nature and compelled them to serve him." "With pity he looks down upon those members of the human race who have not succeeded in subduing Nature. What wonder if civilized man considers himself a being of higher order as compared with primitive man, if he claims that the white race represents a type higher than all others."

But is it true? The assumption is based on two lines of reasoning: first, that achievement is due to faculty or aptitude; second, that variation from the white standard indicates inferiority. These two assumptions Boas views from a number of angles. First, all races seem to be capable of great progress where environmental conditions are right, and hence, we dare not conclude that because a race is now primitive or belated that it will always be so, or that it is lacking in aptitude.

Further, it is questionable whether in the history of races, the mingling of different races has lowered the standard of humanity. It is admitted that according to Mendel's Law, the offspring of two different stocks will usually follow one or other of the stocks, and rarely be a median of the two; but it is not clear to Boas that the lower forms will predominate, even though he admits there is danger they may.

Under "Traits of Primitive Culture," he claims that we judge unfairly when we say primitive races do not have initiative or

456

self-control, etc. They do have these qualities, and exercise them in certain fields of interest. To illustrate: we consider the African Negro lazy and lacking in self-control. He has not enough self-mastery to make him work in order that he may have plenty laid by. But he may not need to lay by a store, and yet have self-control in a field where he thinks it important. It is well known that he will literally starve to death rather than touch a bite of food which is taboo.

This book is a thoroughly scientific study of the basis of advanced and retarded civilization, and will help very much to give one a clear perspective for the study of Race Problems. Boas does not have the Negro primarily in mind, but his book is the best background I have found for an unbiased study of the problems of Race.

THE CONFLICT OF COLOR—Weale, *Macmillan Company*

The subject of this book is world politics and world movements as affected by the fact of color. It is the contention of the author that there is a growing consciousness of power on the part of the colored world, and that the white world has failed to adjust itself to this new consciousness, or what is worse, has failed to realize that there is such a consciousness. Speaking of England, he says, "It may be said that practically every one of the political arrangements entered into of recent years by England, savor of mere politicians' devices for warding off evil rather than statesmanlike attempts to go to the root of troubles and determine, once for all, what should be done during a long term of years." He further rightly calls attention to the blindness of the white world, superinduced by its vaunted egotism and feeling of superiority.

We cannot agree with Mr. Weale in his advocacy of a scheme of balance of power among the colored races, nor in his advocacy of preparedness for war as a schooling for all real growth and power, nor in his slighting attitude toward religion as the real solvent for race problems, but we believe his book rightly points out certain weaknesses in our relation to colored races which will be helpful to all real students.

THE RISING TIDE OF COLOR—Stoddard, *Charles Scribner's Sons*

One of the most thoughtful books is this one, the main thesis of which is "the basic factor in human affairs is not politics but race."

A full and detailed chapter is given to each of the great racial divisions: the yellow race, or races of the far East, numbering 500,000,000; the brown races of Southern Asia and the near East, numbering 150,000,000; the black peoples of Africa and America, numbering 150,000,000; and the red people of the Americas, numbering 40,000,000.

The author maintains that each of these races have a new self-consciousness, and that all of them combined have a distinct race consciousness as over against the white race which has up to this time assumed a rather lordly air toward all colored races. The book calls attention to the fact that the Russo-Japanese war was the first great war between a white and a colored people, and that all the colored races have looked on this present great war between groups of the white race as the passing of the supremacy of the white man.

Mr. Stoddard thinks that white lordship over the colored sections of the world is destined to pass. India, Africa, and even the near East must ultimately become self-governing. This he does not look upon with alarm. But the shifting of colored populations, such as Japanese into South America or the Arabs into Africa, he fears may bring great complications to world affairs in the decades not far distant.

It is further pointed out that two large races living in close juxtaposition nearly always means friction. It is claimed that our whole problem of immigration should be restudied, both with reference to the Orientals and the South Europeans.

Some anthropologists may not agree with Mr. Stoddard and Madison Grant that the bringing of a great mass of South Europeans tends to break down the ethnic stability of America, but they defend their thesis well. Quoting from Humphrey, the biologist, Mr. Stoddard says: "Our melting pot would not give us in a thousand years what enthusiasts expect of it—a fusing of all our various racial elements into a new type which shall be the true American. It will give us for many generations a perplexing diversity of ancestry, and since our successors must reach back into their ancestry for characteristics, this diversity will increase the uncertainty of their inheritance. They will inherit no stable blended character, because there is no such thing. The immigrant tide must at all costs be stopped and America given a chance to stabilize her ethnic being."

The book is a challenge to real thought, and a basis for action. Whether we agree with its findings, we cannot fail to heed its earnest warnings of danger ahead.

EARLY CIVILIZATION—Goldenweiser, *Alfred A. Knopf*

A study of early civilizations, including industry, art, religion, and social relationships. He throws light on the way in which civilization has grown.

# MEN OF THE OLD STONE AGE—Osborn, *Charles Scribner's Sons*

A study of the origin of man, his early cultures and the development of human characteristics. One of the clearest and fullest discussions of the origin and migrations of the human race, with a full statement of the influence of these early races on modern European civilizations.

# ANTHROPOLOGY—Tyler, *D. Appleton & Company*

A recent reprint of one of the older books which studies the development of the races of mankind, their language, writings, arts and primitive science.

### THE AFRICAN BACKGROUND OF THE NEGRO

# FETISHISM IN WEST AFRICA—Nassau, *Charles Scribner's Sons*

The African Negro is essentially and universally religious. His whole life is cast in the religious mold. He is not like many of the white Americans, who are religious only on Sunday. The Negro does nothing without seeing in it some religious significance. He is constantly and consciously in the presence of the spirit world, so that most of his fears are associated with the evil spirits and most of his joys come from the favor of the kindly spirits.

If one live constantly in the presence of innumerable spirits, it is but natural that one shall try to find a means of placating the evil ones. Hence will arise a practice of life which is known as fetishism. A fetish is any rag, string, tooth, bit of hair, shell, or what not, into which a witch doctor has persuaded a spirit to take up its abode. This spirit is carried by the believer as a defense against all evil. It will readily be seen, therefore, that every piece of work, every hunt, every battle, must be preceded by the proper religious ceremony. No one can really understand the life and customs of the Negro who has not come to know the heart of their religion.

Dr. Nassau was forty years a missionary in Western Africa and writes from fullest knowledge. What is more, he writes sympathetically of the life of the Negro. The volume is invaluable.

# CONGO LIFE AND FOLKLORE—Weeks, *Religious Tract Society, London*

In this volume of 462 pages the author gives us a clear picture of village life, the funeral orgy, the witch doctor, and his trial of suspected persons by the ordeal, some of the games and pastimes of the people; the hunting customs, the modes of native warfare, marriage customs and festivals; in fact, the whole round of life among the Congo peoples.

Mr. Weeks was for many years a worker under the Baptist Missionary Society in the Congo region of Africa and speaks from first hand knowledge.

To me the most interesting part of this volume is the last third, which relates a number of the old folk tales. In no way can one come to know the inner life of a people so well as by reading their folk tales. There the soul of the people is laid bare; there the imagination runs riot and there the people speak without dissembling. One can see at a glance the revealing character of folklore when he remembers that the hero animal of the African is the gazelle (in America it is the rabbit) which is a mild and defenseless animal, but always shrewd and winning by cleverness, while the hero animal of the Indian is the buffalo, or some other fighting animal who wins by force. Is this not true to the two peoples? The Negro—mild, docile, suave, shrewd, winning by cleverness; the Indian—fierce, warlike, stubborn, winning or losing by brute force. The folk tales in this volume throw a flood of light on the Negro character.

## THE NEGRO RACES—VOLS. I AND II—Dowd, *Neale Publishing Company*

Mr. Dowd, of the University of Oklahoma, undertook some years ago a rather ambitious study of the Negro races. His first volume published by Macmillan, contained studies of the Negritos of Central and South Africa, the Negritians of the Sudan, and the Fellatahs of the Central Sudan. Unfortunately, this first volume is already out of print. The second volume contains the study of the other two great divisions of African peoples, the Gallas of East Africa, including the peoples from Lake Victoria as far north as Abyssinia, and the Bantus, which occupy the whole of Central Africa; beginning on the East Coast parallel with Lake Victoria, sweeping southward and toward the west around Lake Tanganyika, thence west to the coast and north as far as Old Calabar, including the whole Congo basin.

While the slaves in America come from almost every section of Africa, the overwhelming majority of them were brought from the west coast. The Gold Coast, the Slave Coast, the Bight of Renin, and Bight of Biafre, down as far as the mouth of the Congo was the scene of the most of the slave raiding.

Professor Dowd gives a clear picture of the economic, social, religious, and political life of the tribes from which these slaves were brought.

## THINKING BLACK—Crawford, *George H. Doran Company*

Angola is a vast wilderness lying south of the Congo River, inhabited by the Bantu Negroes. Many slaves from this section were sold in Charleston during the early slave trading days. They were reputed as good slaves, though they were somewhat noted as runaways. Mr. Crawford, a fellow of the Royal Geographical Society, landed at Benguella on the Angola coast, some five hundred miles south of the mouth of the Congo in the year 1889, and thence "bored" himself into the interior for more than a thousand miles. Here on Lake Mweru he lived and worked for twenty-three years, so identifying himself with the natives that he actually "thinks black."

The book is written in a rather enigmatic English style, but careful reading reveals a full knowledge of the black people which few other travelers have attained. It is a bit slow and tedious reading, but withal, entertaining and amply rewarding to those who would know this section of the Bantu peoples.

## RELATION OF THE ADVANCED AND THE BACKWARD RACES OF MANKIND—James Bryce, *Henry Frowde*.

A clear and dispassionate statement of observed relationships that will be helpful to all readers.

## DAWN IN DARKEST AFRICA—Harris, *Smith, Elder & Co., London*

The first half of this volume is a clear, attractive and most readable account of the customs and life of the natives of Central West Africa. The customs of cicatrization, hair-dressing, weddings, births, deaths, etc., are discussed.

In Part Two, the living conditions as to climate, health, government, of various European nations is rather carefully studied. Much light is thrown on the colonial policies of the various European countries.

In Part Three, the economic situation is studied, labor, slavery and the future of the Congo-Belg, is discussed.

In Part Four there is a study of the native resources of West Central Africa.

## AFRICA, SLAVE AND FREE—Harris, *Student Christian Movement, London*

This little volume is a plea for the natural worth and dignity of the African people. Speaking of the white man's accustomed superior attitude, Mr. Harris tells of how he misinterpreted one of the native customs to the discredit of the African people. But on more careful investigation he realized that he was wrong and they were right. "In a flash the wisdom of the native custom was revealed; abashed and ashamed, the author renewed a forgotten vow never to condemn a native custom without first making exhaustive inquiry."

To those who desire to know the problems of modern Africa, particularly with reference to her political, economic, and labor problems, this little volume will amply repay the time of its reading.

## THE JUNGLE FOLK OF AFRICA—Milligan, *Fleming H. Revell Company*

This is a study of bush life, including talks about the camp-fire, customs of the bush people, and something of the work of missionaries in the African field. It gives a most sympathetic view of the Negro's life and customs, and is helpful in showing the capacity of the Negro peoples.

## IMPRESSIONS OF SOUTH AFRICA—James Bryce, *The Century Co.*

A most thorough study of the physical features, health conditions, animal and vegetable life, and a story of the South African peoples; written in a thorough, scholarly fashion by one of Europe's greatest statesmen.

## TRAVELS IN WEST AFRICA—Kingsley, *Macmillan Company*

Miss Kingsley is a most entertaining and instructive writer. She sees things with a keen eye and puts them in most readable form. Her observations have on the whole been among the most reliable. Anyone who desires to know fully the native customs of African life can find much help here.

## NEGRO CULTURE IN WEST AFRICA—Ellis, *Neale Publishing Co.*

A book which has been much referred to. It is somewhat disappointing in that it is too general, but does have the mark of first hand information.

## TRAVELS OF MUNGO PARK, VOLUMES I AND II— John Murray, *London*

Mungo Park was the first explorer sent out by London Society for the explortion of Africa. His first journey was undertaken in 1796 and a second journey in 1805. His attempt was to find the source of the Niger River. He gives very realistic pictures of some of the early slave caravans. It is one of the best volumes for getting the real background of the African Negro.

## THE NEW MAP OF AFRICA—Gibbon, *The Century Co.*

Setting forth the changes in geographical and political relationship that have arisen in Africa in recent years.

## THE GOLDEN AGE OF PRINCE HENRY, THE NAVIGATOR—Martins, *Dutton & Co.*
Telling in full the story of Prince Henry, who brought the first African slaves to Portugal and thus started the vicious practice of enslaving black men by the white men. Told in most fascinating manner and showing the thorough sanction of religion for the enslaving process.

THE SLAVE TRADE

## THE AFRICAN SLAVE TRADE—Buxton, *John Murray, London*
A rather careful study of the process of capture, transportation and sale of the early slaves, giving full details of mortality, cruelty and other conditions of the trade.

## HISTORY OF THE SLAVE TRADE, VOLS. I AND II—Clarkson, *Longmans, Green & Co.*
Giving a study of the rise, progress and accomplishment and the abolition movement of the slave trade by the British Parliament. It deals fully with the long process of freeing the seas of the slave trade.

## EVIDENCE OF THE SLAVE TRADE—*American Tract Society*
An abstract of the evidence delivered before a select committee of the House of Commons in the years 1790 and 1791, and the part of the petitioners for the abolition of the slave trade. This little volume, which was reprinted by the American Tract and Book Society in 1859, is filled with the details of the method of capture, transportation and sale of slaves. It is at all times harrowing, but has the value of giving original facts.

SLAVERY IN THE WEST INDIES

## THE NEGRO IN THE NEW WORLD—Sir Harry H. Johnson, *Macmillan Company*
A very full and on the whole unbiased statement of slavery in South America and the West Indies, together with full chapters on slavery in the Southern states.

## THE WEST INDIES—Fisk, *G. P. Putnam's Sons*
A readable story of the discovery and early development of these islands, with special chapters throwing light on the Negro as a slave.

## HAITI, HER HISTORY AND HER DETRACTORS—
Leger, *Neale Publishing Co.*

Leger was Envoy Extraordinary of Haiti to the United States. He writes with a passion for his own people, and shows the terrible struggle through which Haiti was forced to pass in winning freedom.

## THE FRENCH REVOLUTION IN SAN DOMINGO—
Lathrop, Stoddard, *Houghton Miffln Co.*

Rather a full statement of the native population and government of the island. There are special chapters given to the mulatto, the slave, and the great revolutionary movement of San Domingo. The book is particularly instructive in throwing light on the Negro insurrections and uprising in America.

## THE DANISH WEST INDIES—Westergard, *Macmillan Company*

A study of the early occupation of the white man of the West India Islands, the slave trade, the growth of the plantation system, the economic vicissitudes of the planter, together with studies of the government of the island and the conditions of the slaves.

STUDIES IN AMERICAN SLAVERY

## THE RISE AND FALL OF THE SLAVE POWER IN AMERICA, VOLS. I, II, III—Henry Wilson, *Osgood & Company,* 1875

An elaborate and detailed account of all the political and social vicissitudes of the slave system, giving full quotations from government documents, debates in the halls of Congress and local enactments.

## SLAVERY AND COLOR—Chambers, *London,* 1857

Being the record of the observations of William Chambers in a tour through the Southern states. On the whole it is openminded, unbiased, giving the reaction of a keen observer who was far enough away from the problem to bring light and not heat.

## HISTORY OF NEGRO EDUCATION PRIOR TO 1861—
Woodson, *Association for the Study of Negro Life and History.*
Well done.

## SEABOARD SLAVE STATES—Olmsted, *Mason*

A running account of an extended journey through the seaboard states by a prosperous farmer from the North. His report of observations is one of the best storehouses of information on the general customs and conditions of slavery before the war.

## A JOURNEY IN THE BACK COUNTRY—Olmsted, *Mason,* 1863

## A JOURNEY THROUGH TEXAS—Olmsted, *Mason,* 1857

These two volumes, like the Seaboard Slave States, are the report of journeys made in order to study conditions in the South. They are a mine of information on Southern conditions. On the whole, fair-minded.

## A SOUTHERN PLANTER—Smedes, *James Pott & Co.*

Being the reminiscence of Mrs. Smedes, the daughter of Thomas Dabney, one of the large slave owners in the state of Mississippi in the closing years before the war. It gives a good picture of the best relationships between master and slave.

## SOUTHSIDE VIEW OF SLAVERY—Adams, *T. R. Marvin,* 1854

Being the reactions of a Northern abolitionist who came South for health purposes, who was greatly surprised at the kindly relations existing between the slaves and master class. Somewhat biased but interesting and suggestive.

## SLAVERY AND FINANCES—Walker, *Ridgway, London,* 1864

Mr. Walker was a member of the United States Senate from Mississippi from 1836 to 1845. Was a member of President Polk's Cabinet and was in position to be acquainted with the facts of life in the South. This statement is a compilation of figures showing the retardation of Southern industry and economic progress due to the handicap of slavery.

## COTTON IS KING; pro-slavery argument—Elliott, *Augusta, Ga.,* 1860

A most voluminous statement of various aspects of the slavery question, including the study of the economic relations of slavery, the justification of slavery from the culture basis, and the social life and relations of slavery and an argument for slavery in the light of political science. Interesting enough, it also has a full statement of slavery in the light of ethnology. There is a very extended statement of the decisions of the Supreme Court with reference to slavery included in this volume.

## A JOURNAL OF A RESIDENT ON A GEORGIA PLAN-TATION—Kemble, *London,* 1863

Fanny Kemble was an English actress who married a Mr. Butler, who was the owner of a large plantation and many slaves in the coast section of Georgia. Fanny Kemble spent a year on these plantations under considerable protest, and her letters and journals reveal the conditions she found there. Mr. Butler was evidently a ne'er-do-well, and evidently did not keep his plantations in good condition, and consequently, made a very unenviable impression on his actress wife. It is helpful in that it gives a close-up view of conditions that might have existed during the slave period.

## PLANTATION LIFE BEFORE EMANCIPATION—Mallard, *Whettett & Shepperson, Richmond*

A close-up view of slavery in the lower South. Written from an unfavorable viewpoint, but also having the spirit of kindliness and deep interest.

## THE LIFE AND TIMES OF BISHOP KAVANAUGH—Redford, *Nashville, Tenn.,* 1884

Having interesting side lights on the relation of the Southern Methodist Church to the Negro.

## SUPPRESSION OF THE SLAVE TRADE—Du Bois, *Harvard University Press*

One of the most thorough and careful studies of the fight against slavery that has been published, giving carefully compiled data.

## THE LIFE OF BISHOP CAPERS—Wightman, *Nashville, Tenn.,* 1858

Giving full accounts of Capers' work for the Negroes and the early development of interest on the part of the Southern Methodist Church in Negro missions.

## MY LIFE AND TIMES—John B. Adger, *Presbyterian Committee of Publications, Richmond, Va.*

Giving a study of the early developments of the independent churches in Charleston, S. C., of which Dr. Adger was pastor.

## GIRARDEAU'S LIFE WORK—Compiled by George A. Blackburn. Published by the *State Company,* Columbia, S. C.

Dr. Girardeau was pastor of Negro congregations in South Carolina and one of the most brilliant preachers that the Southern Presbyterian Church has ever produced. It throws much light on the Presbyterian Church and its part in the religious life of the Negro.

## ANNALS OF SOUTHERN METHODISM—Deems, *Nashville, Tenn.*

These are the annual reports of the conferences of the Southern Methodist Church. Each volume contains a chapter on the work of the Southern Methodist Church in connection with the Negro. Some of the volumes give complete lists of white pastors appointed to these Negro churches. In these lists the names of some of the best known ministers of the Southern Methodist Church occur.

## THE RELIGIOUS DEVELOPMENT OF THE NEGRO IN VIRGINIA—J. B. Earnest

This is a thesis offered to the faculty of the University of Virginia for the Doctor of Philosophy degree. It has been rather carefully done and gives detailed information about the growth of the religious life of the Negro during slavery and following.

## JOHN HOPKINS UNIVERSITY STUDIES IN HISTORICAL AND POLITICAL SCIENCE: *Baltimore*

A most thorough and illuminating series.

1. Government of the Colony of South Carolina, E. L. Whitney,
2. The Study of Slavery in New Jersey, S. H. Cooley,
3. Slavery and Servitude in the Colony of North Carolina, J. S. Bassett,
4. Slavery in the state of North Carolina, J. S. Bassett,
5. The Negro in the District of Columbia, Edward Ingle,
6. The Religious Development of the Province of North Carolina, S. B. Weeks,
7. The History of Slavery in Virginia, J. C. Ballagh,
8. A note on the Progress of the Colored People of Maryland Since the War, J. R. Brackett,
9. The Early Period of Reconstruction in South Carolina, J. P. Hollis,
10. Local Government in the South and Southwest, E. W. Bemis,
11. The History of Suffrage in Virginia, J. A. C. Chandler,
12. The Transition of North Carolina from Colony to Commonwealth, E. W. Sykes,
13. The Early Relation Between Maryland and Virginia, John H. Lapane,
14. Slavery in Missouri 1804 to 1865, H. R. Trexler,
15. Anti-Slavery Leaders of North Carolina, J. S. Bassett,
16. The Political History of Virginia During the Reconstruction, H. J. Eckenrode,
17. The International Beginning of the Congo Free State, J. S. Reeves,

18. Justice in Colonial Virginia, O. P. Chitwood,
19. State Rights and Political Parties in North Carolina, H. G. Wagstaff,
20. White Servitude in Maryland, E. I. McCormac,
21. History of Reconstruction in Louisiana, J. R. Ficklen,
22. A History of the Tobacco Industry in Virginia 1860 to 1894, W. B. Arnold,
23. White Servitude in the Colony of Virginia, J. C. Ballagh.

ATLANTA UNIVERSITY SERIES—*Atlanta University Press*, 1896-1906

No.
1. Mortality among Negroes in Cities, 1896,
   Mortality among Negroes in Cities, 1903,
2. Social and Physical Conditions of Negroes in Cities, 1897,
3. Some Efforts of Negroes for Social Betterment, 1898,
4. The Negro in Business, 1899,
5. The College Bred Negro, 1900 (two editions),
6. The Negro Common School, 1901,
7. The Negro Artizan, 1902,
8. The Negro Church, 1903,
9. Notes on Negro Crime, 1904,
10. A Select Bibliography of the Negro American, 1905,
11. Health and Physique of the Negro American, 1906.

AMERICAN NEGRO SLAVERY—Phillips, D. *Appleton & Co.*

American Negro Slavery is a very full and carefully prepared volume of five hundred pages, giving a survey of the beginning and growth of the African Slave trade, a study of the types of Negroes brought to the New World, and the conditions attendant upon this slave trade. Space is devoted to the shifting of slave population in America together with the causes for the same:

Plantation life and practices, not only in America but in Jamaica and other islands, are fully set forth so that the old regime lives again.

The whole question of the slave as an economic asset or liability is discussed, and figures set forth in telling array. It is perhaps the most carefully prepared volume that has appeared on the race question in the last decade.

DOCUMENTARY HISTORY OF THE UNITED STATES, VOLS. I AND II—Phillips, *Arthur H. Clark Co.*

Dr. Phillips is professor of American History in the University of Michigan, and has made more than one splendid contribution to the study of race problems. His Documentary History of

American Industrial Society, Volumes I and II, was published while Dr. Phillips was yet professor of History and Political Science at Tulane University. In this volume he brings together a rare list of manuscripts on the economic and social conditions of the Southern plantation days.

## THE GOSPEL AMONG THE SLAVES—Harrison and Barnes, *Methodist Publishing House, Nashville,* 1893

This is a rare old volume now out of print, but still obtainable in some of the old second hand book shops. It gives more original and source material about the moral and religious conditions of the Negro during the slave regime than any other volume I know. It is well worth securing for any library on race problems.

## OLD VIRGINIA AND HER NEIGHBORS, VOLS. I AND II —John Fiske, *Houghton Mifflin Co.*

Old Virginia comprised the territory extending from and including Maryland down to Florida Keys, and stretched back as far as there were any known settlements. From it was carved Maryland, West Virginia, North Carolina, South Carolina and Florida. Its early settlement was epoch making in American history. Naturally, the growth of servitude—first the indentured whites and then the Negro slaves—forms a large chapter in the social and economic life of this colony. Fiske has given the facts of this slave system in close and succinct form.

## VIRGINIA'S ATTITUDE TOWARD SLAVERY AND SECESSION—Munford, *Longmans, Green & Co.*

This book is a study of the growing sentiment in the South against slavery as shown in the manumission of hundreds of slaves by men like Robert E. Lee, John Randolph, Sanders, Herndon, and others. The large numbers of men who thus desired to free their slaves in the early decades of the nineteenth century, were prevented from so doing, often because to leave them in the community where others were slaves caused civic disturbance, and to settle them in non-slave states was very expensive and often illegal.

A study of the attitude of these leading men, together with the reaction following the abolition movement is most instructive. It is another clear instance that the radical reformer often delays rather than helps forward progress.

## THE FACTS OF RECONSTRUCTION—Lynch, *Neale Publishing Co.*

John R. Lynch was a member of Congress from Mississippi and a former fourth Auditor of the United States Treasury, in the

Reconstruction days.  He is a Negro man who by intelligence and ability held a place in Mississippi politics.

His book is a statement from the Negro point of view, of the effect of Negro enfranchisement at the close of the war.

So much has been written and said about the reconstruction period—most of it from the Southern White man's point of view —that it is refreshing to read the other side from a Negro who writes clearly and lucidly, even if he often fails to convince.

## THE AFTERMATH OF THE CIVIL WAR IN ARKANSAS
   —Clayton, *Neale Publishing Co.*

Being a study of the reconstruction and operation of the Ku Klux Klan, the martial law and facts of social progress during the reconstruction days.

## THE   AFTERMATH   OF   SLAVERY—Sinclair, *Small-Maynard Co.*

Including a study of reconstruction, the black code, war on the Negro suffrage, the Negro in Politics, and the achievements of the Negro race.

### THE PRESENT SITUATION

The books of Dr. Booker T. Washington throw light on the growth of the Negro after the war and the progress during the last few decades.  Among these volumes of Dr. Washington's are:

## UP FROM SLAVERY—Washington, *Doubleday, Page & Co.*

If I had a group of people who were prejudiced against the Negro, who thought the Negro useless and unimprovable, who believed that he had no heroism and was inferior, I would rather put "Up from Slavery" into their hands, and its message into their hearts than any other single volume I know.

First of all, it is a story of real achievement.  Perhaps few men have actually achieved more, and none have battled against greater odds.  Secondly, it is so full of human interest and sympathy; and thirdly, it is so free from all passion, all malice, all criticism.  There are few of us who could have passed through the battles which this man fought and come out with as sweet a spirit and as brave a soul as had Washington.

I could wish that every boy and girl in America could read this inspiring biography.

## THE  STORY  OF  THE  NEGRO, VOLS.  I  AND  II—
   Washington, *Doubleday, Page & Co.*

Anything from the pen of Dr. Washington has a clear, forceful style, is simple and straightforward, and is sure to be entertainingly written. These books have the advantage of being among those on which Dr. Washington put a great deal of thought and study. He was eager to know the background of his race and to use that to show how far the Negro in America had traveled.

The first volume deals quite extensively with the African background of the Negro, showing his West Coast home. The second half of this volume deals with conditions of slavery.

Volume Two is a most hopeful and far seeing volume, dealing with facts of progress of the Negro race.

Other books by Booker T. Washington:
MY LARGER EDUCATION
THE MAN FARTHEST DOWN
WORKING WITH THE HANDS
TUSKEGEE AND ITS PEOPLE
CHARACTER BUILDING

*Doubleday, Page & Co.*

HALF A MAN—Ovington, *Longmans, Green & Co.*

Miss Ovington has made a careful study of the New York Negro, his housing conditions, his children, his means of earning a living, his womankind, and his relation to the community. She set out to find whether the Negro had an equal and fair chance in New York City. Her conclusion is that a Negro has only half a man's chance even in New York. His treatment by the police, the courts, the public utilities, is quite amazing. She believes that discrimination against the Negro in New York is increasing.

Her word about our standards for the Negro is well said. We set up our own personal standards and all who do not conform to them are judged inferior. This is truly American, but it is surely unfair.

This book will help us to see how the Negro lives in the North and will lead us to a more sympathetic understanding of his problems of self-respect and citizenship.

THE NEGRO FACES AMERICA—Seligman, *Harper & Brothers*

This is a most scathing volume filled with ugly and unpalatable facts, but facts which it will do us all good to ponder. The Chicago, Washington, Omaha and Arkansas race riots are fully and frankly discussed. Like Miss Ovington in "Half a Man," Seligman claims that color prejudice makes it well-nigh impossible for a white man to fairly judge a Negro. His chapter on the "South's Color Psychosis" is scorching. He claims that it is practically impossible to argue the case with the mass of South-

ern white men.  They have a dogma which admits of no questioning.  It is high heresy, more, it is treason, to question the
superiority of the white race, or to deny that this is a white
man's country, and the Negro has no rights which we need respect.

As a Southern man, I must admit with shame that most of his
facts are correct, but the spirit in which he presents them is bad.
The book gives the facts, but misses the truth, for facts can often
be stated in such manner as to miss the whole truth of a situation.

The book will be most helpful to those who will read with an
open and tolerant mind.  It will decidedly anger those who are
less open to the facts.

IN WHITE AND BLACK—Hammond, *Fleming H. Revell
Company*

Mrs. Hammond has made a powerful plea for fair play in this
volume.  The chapter titled, "In Terms of Humanity," sets forth
the fact that men must be judged in the broader human aspects
and not by some petty failure or shortcoming.  The chapter on
"The Basis of Adjustment" faces squarely and fearlessly the
injustice of the courts, the inequality of traveling accommodations, and the injustice we do the Negro in allowing him to do
less than his best.  There is a chapter devoted to "Houses and
Homes," one to "Human Wreckage," and one to "Coöperation,"
and two to the forward look.

Mrs. Hammond is a Southern woman of broad culture, deep
sympathy, judicial outlook, and her book bears the mark of much
thought and study.

PRESENT FORCES IN NEGRO PROGRESS—W. D.
Weatherford, *Association Press.*

A summary of those forces which are making for progress
among Negroes.  There are chapters on "Race Pride and the
Growth of Race Consciousness," "The Population and Distribution of Negroes in America," "The New Type of Negro Farmer,"
"Progress in Negro Training," what is being done by various
agencies at work on this problem, etc.  Perhaps one of the most
helpful sections of the book is that on Negro leadership.  This,
also, has been used as a text book in college study classes.

NEGRO LIFE IN THE SOUTH—W. D. Weatherford, *Association Press*

An attempt to state in concise form some of the fundamental
principles underlying race relations.  It has been used as a text
book by some thirty thousand students in the voluntary study
classes of the Young Men's Christian Associations.  Dr. Booker
T. Washington said of it: "It will be of mutual help to both races,

showing the Negro what the better class of white people think of him, and thereby encouraging him to further advance, and showing that the Negro is a real economic, educational and moral factor in the South, and therefore deserving of more serious study and consideration." (From *The Outlook*).

## THE VOICE OF THE NEGRO—Kerlin, *E. P. Dutton & Co.*

Realizing that the present relation between the races is strained, and that few white men know the mood of the Negro, Dr. Robert T. Kerlin, professor of English Literature at Virginia Military Institute, undertook to read and clip more than fifty Negro papers, and has brought together this material in a little volume called, "The Voice of the Negro." His material is grouped under ten headings: The Colored Press, The New Era, The Negro's Reaction to the World War, The Negro's Grievance and Demands, Riots, Lynching, The South and the Negro, The Negro and Labor Unionism and Bolshevism, Negro Progress, and the Lyric Cry.

Only the briefest possible comment is thrown into heading paragraphs to set forth the purpose of the articles quoted. It is my deliberate judgment that not one white person out of each thousand really knows what the Negro is thinking. It is also very doubtful if many Negroes understand the white man, for the difference of environment and mental background of the two races make understanding of each other very difficult. However, the Negro has the great advantage of the white man, for he reads our papers, and we do not so much as know that he has a daily and weekly press.

For a number of years I have had coming to my office a dozen or more Negro papers, and during the past year I have scanned and clipped more than twenty such sheets from every part of America. I have been doing this that I might get some inside knowledge of what the Negro really thinks and feels. Surely no one can have any adequate idea of another race who does not superficially, at least, know their literature and their daily press. In this book the Negro press has been allowed to tell its own story.

The total impression of the book is most alarming. It shows the horrible injustices which the Negro must suffer and his attitude toward them. It shows a race no longer cringing and fawning, but a race at bay, long-suffering, more than patient, but growing sullen and vindictive. It shows a people becoming conscious of its own power, proud of its own achievement, and justly demanding fair treatment and respect.

It is a most challenging statement, which every American citizen should read. No white man, we believe, will agree with all that is quoted, just as we would not agree with all in a similar set of quotations from white papers, but no white man dare neglect the fact that such things are being said, and that they are molding the opinions, the mood and spirit of the Negro race.   The stage is surely set for great difficulties in the future, unless those who have both leadership and Christianity give heed to this timely warning.

THE NEGRO PRESS IN THE UNITED STATES—Det-
    weiler, *University of Chicago Press*
    A rather careful study of the five hundred or more newspapers and magazines of the Negro race at the present time, setting forth their message, their make-up, and their contribution to the Negro people.

THE NEW NEGRO—Pickens, *Neale Publishing Co.*
    An attempt to set forth the progress of the Negro since emancipation and describing the Negro as he is today.

THE TREND OF THE RACES—George E. Haynes, *Missionary Education Movement*
    A study of sixty years of progress in the Negro race.   His present achievement and his outlook for the future.

THE VANGUARD OF THE RACE—L. H. Hammond, *Missionary Education Movement.*
    Being a biographic study of some of the leading characters of the race, including a study of Dr. Chas. V. Roman, Miss Nannie H. Burrows, Mrs. Maggie L. Walker and Harry P. Burleigh.

UNSUNG HEROES—Haynes, *DuBois and Dill*
    A study of seventeen leaders of the Negro race.

WOMEN OF ACHIEVEMENT—Brawley, *Woman's American Baptist Mission Society*
    Being a brief biography of five Negro women who are leaders of their race.

THE NEGRO IN CHICAGO—The Chicago Commission on Race Relations, *The University of Chicago Press*
    After the riots in Chicago in 1919, Governor Frank O. Lowden appointed a special commission to study fully the conditions of the Negro in Chicago.   More than two years were occupied in the study of this problem and full reports were submitted in 1922. This is the most complete statement of the conditions of the Negro in the North that has yet been published.

THE NEGRO YEAR BOOK—Being an annual publication of Monroe N. Work, of Tuskegee, Ala. It is a store house of general information and statistical facts. Invaluable to anyone who is undertaking to evaluate the present conditions of the Negro.

BLACK AND WHITE IN THE SOUTHERN STATES—
Evans, *Longmans-Green & Company*
Mr. Evans was a member of Parliament in the South African Union and came to America as a special commissioner to study the conditions of the Negro in the South. He brings to bear upon the problem a rich experience from South Africa, which is useful in interpreting the facts as present in this section.

THE SOUTHERN SOUTH—Hart, *D. Appleton & Co.*
A study of the development of the lower South before and following the Civil War.

SLAVERY AND ABOLITION—Hart, *Harper & Brothers.*
Being a study of the conditions which led to the abolition of slavery.

FOLLOWING THE COLOR LINE—Ray Stannard Baker, *Doubleday, Page & Co.*
A clear, fair statement of race conditions, as seen by a Northern man on an extended tour through the South; perhaps the sanest book on the topic by a Northern man.

RACE TRAITS AND TENDENCIES OF THE AMERICAN NEGRO—Hoffman, American Economic Association, *Macmillan & Company,* 1896
The most scholarly and exhaustive study yet made of population, vital statistics, anthropometry, and race amalgamation. Somewhat biased.

RACE ADJUSTMENTS—Kelley Miller, *The Neale Publishing Co.*
Strictly reliable as to facts, showing deep insight into the life of the race; a little critical of the white man.

THE NEGRO AND THE NATION—George S. Miriam, *Young People's Missionary Movement*
An historical statement of the political questions arising out of slavery.

THE NEGRO, THE SOUTHERNER'S PROBLEM—Thomas Nelson Page, *Charles Scribner's Sons*
Characterized by thorough familiarity with the "old-time" Negro, with less accurate knowledge of the present conditions.

Prone to magnify all the virtues of the slave, and all the vices of the present Negro.

**RACIAL INTEGRITY**—A. H. Shannon, *Smith & Lamar*
   A study of race amalgamation and other topics.

**THE COLOR LINE**—W. B. Smith, *McClure, Phillips & Co.*
   Brilliant in its statements, but bitter in its sarcasm.  It is doubtful if the conclusions reached as to the future decay of the Negro will prove true.

**THE AMERICAN NEGRO**—W. H. Thomas, *Macmillan Company*
   The harshest arraignment of the race by one of its own members.  While showing clear insight into Negro character, it is certainly unfair.

**THE LOWER SOUTH IN AMERICAN HISTORY**—William Garratt Brown, *Macmillan Company.*
   A true picture of the rise of the Old South and its early influence; just a little pessimistic in tone.

**LYNCH LAW**—James Elbert Cutler, Longmans-Green & Co.
   A careful compilation of the facts of lynching and a statement of the causes and effects.  It should be read by every Southern man.

**SOCIOLOGY AND MODERN SOCIAL PROBLEMS**—Chas. A Ellwood, *American Book Co.*
   Contains a very illuminating chapter on the "Negro Problem."

**THE WHITE MAN'S BURDEN**—B. F. Riley, *Published by the Author, Birmingham, Ala.*
   A very sane and sympathetic discussion of the Negro question from a Southern man's standpoint.

**RACE DISTINCTIONS IN AMERICAN LAW**—Gilbert T. Stephenson, *D. Appleton & Co.*
   A clear, unbiased and helpful statement of just the distinction— and at times discriminations—made throughout the United States in the laws governing race relationships.

**A CENTURY OF NEGRO MIGRATION**—Woodson, *The Association for Study of Negro Life and History*

## NEGRO MIGRATION—Woofter, *W. D. Gray, New York*

A study of the conditions that led up to the migration of the Negro from Southern farms. A careful study.

## NEGRO MIGRATION DURING THE WAR—Scott, *Oxford University Press*

Being a study of the conditions in the South which encouraged Negro migration during the great war.

## NEGRO EDUCATION—Thomas Jesse Jones, *U. S. Department of Education*

A careful study of higher educational institutions for the Negro in America, giving a full statement after personal investigation of the equipment, resources, management and educational values of these institutions. Invaluable to anyone desiring to have the full facts about these institutions.

### BIOGRAPHY AND LITERATURE

## THE LIFE AND TIMES OF BOOKER T. WASHINGTON—Riley, *Fleming H. Revell Company.*

A careful and helpful statement by a Southern white man.

## BOOKER T. WASHINGTON, BUILDER OF CIVILIZATION—Scott and Stowe, *Doubleday, Page & Co.*

A most appreciative life of a really great leader.

## THE NEGRO IN LITERATURE AND ART—Brawley, *Macmillan Company*

Being a biographical study of some of the Negroes who have achieved in the last half century.

## A SHORT HISTORY OF THE AMERICAN NEGRO—Brawley

Rather too brief to fulfill its title, but well worth while.

## THE NEGRO IN AMERICAN HISTORY—Cromwell

Not very full. Inadequately done.

## FINDING A WAY OUT—Moton, *Doubleday, Page & Co.*

An autobiography.

### LITERATURE

## THE MARROW OF TRADITION,

## THE WIFE OF HIS YOUTH,

THE HOUSE BEHIND THE CEDARS,
Three novels by Chas. N. Chestnutt, *Houghton, Mifflin Co.*
These three novels center around the idea of the Mulatto Negro.

THE CONJURE WOMAN—Chestnutt, *Houghton, Mifflin Co.*
A series of stories depicting Negro life.

GRANNY MAUMEE AND OTHER DRAMAS, by Torrence,
*Macmillan Company*
Written with real power and centering around the problem of
lynching.

THE HEART OF A WOMAN—Johnson.   Gems of real verse.

POEMS BY PAUL LAURENCE DUNBAR—*Doubleday,
Page & Co.*
Some of the best of the Negroes' efforts.

WEH DOWN SOUF—Davis, *Hillman-Taylor Co.*

LYRICS OF LIFE AND LOVE—Braithwaite, *Turner & Co.*

THE JOURNAL OF NEGRO HISTORY, VOLS. I TO VI—
*Washington, D. C.*

### UNIVERSITY STUDIES IN NEGRO LIFE

THE NEGRO BOY PROBLEM IN NASHVILLE, TEN-
NESSEE—Beaty.   Bound manuscript, *Library Southern College of Young Men's Christian Associations.*

INTERRACIAL    COOPERATION    BETWEEN    THE
SOUTHERN BAPTIST AND THE NEGRO—Haygood,
Bound manuscript.   Vanderbilt University.

RACE PSYCHOLOGY AS FEATURED IN RELIGIOUS
EDUCATION—Reynolds.   Manuscript.   Vanderbilt University Library.

ECONOMIC CONDITIONS OF THE NEGRO IN NASH-
VILLE—Hardwick.   Bound manuscript.   Southern College
of Young Men's Christian Associations Library.

PHELPS-STOKES STUDIES—UNIVERSITY OF GEORGIA

1. THE NEGROES OF ATHENS, GEORGIA,

2. RURAL SURVEY OF CLARKE COUNTY, GEORGIA,

3. SCHOOL CONDITIONS IN CLARKE COUNTY, GEORGIA,

4. THE NEGROES OF CLARKE COUNTY, GEORGIA, DURING THE GREAT WAR,

5. THE NEGRO WOMEN OF GAINESVILLE, GEORGIA —Reed

THE NEGRO AN ECONOMIC FACTOR IN ALABAMA —Henry, *Nashville, Tenn.*

# INDEX

481